Greek to GCSE: Part 2

Greek to GCSE

PART 2

John Taylor

Bristol Classical Press

This impression 2006
Corrected edition 2005
First published in 2003 by
Bristol Classical Press
an imprint of
Gerald Duckworth & Co. Ltd.
90-93 Cowcross Street, London EC1M 6BF
Tel: 020 7490 7300
Fax: 020 7490 0080
inquiries@duckworth-publishers.co.uk
www.ducknet.co.uk

A catalogue record for this book is available
from the British Library

ISBN 1 85399 660 2
EAN 9781853996603

Typeset by John Taylor
Printed and bound in Great Britain by
Biddles Ltd, King's Lynn, Norfolk

Contents

Chapter 9

Chapter 10

Chapter 11

Chapter 12

Practice passages

Revision sentences

Vocabulary

Abbreviations

acc	accusative
adj	adjective
adv	adverb
aor	aorist
dat	dative
f	feminine
foll	following
fut	future
gen	genitive
imperf	imperfect
indic	indicative
inf	infinitive
irreg	irregular
lit	literally
m	masculine
n	neuter
nom	nominative
opt	optative
pass	passive
perf	perfect
pl	plural
prep	preposition
pres	present
sg	singular
subj	subjunctive
usu	usually
voc	vocative

Vocabulary and glossing

As in Part 1, the vocabulary checklists at the end of each chapter should be learned thoroughly. The sum of these throughout the course equates to the vocabulary at the back of the book (and to the combined GCSE prescriptions). Additional words required for translation passages are glossed as they occur. Underlining is not repeated within a passage when a word occurs again on the same page. Where a passage extends to a new page, glossing (except of proper names) is usually repeated. This inevitably means that words are sometimes glossed twice in quick succession.

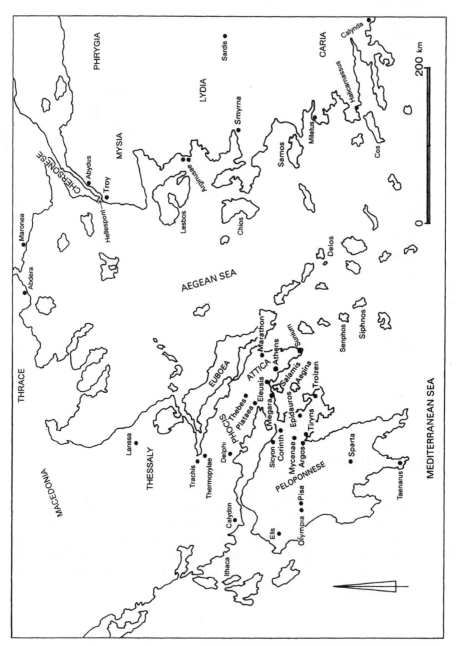

Map: Greece and the Aegean

Chapter 7

Passive voice

Consider the following sentences:

> The soldiers guard the village.
> The village is guarded by the soldiers.

Both describe the same process, but in the second the grammatical subject is having the action done to it and has a *passive verb*.

• This distinction in the use of the verb is referred to as *voice*. The Greek verb forms you have met so far have all been in the *active* voice (the subject doing the action). The *passive* voice gets its name from the Latin stem *pass-* = suffer (compare the related Greek verb πάσχω: both refer not necessarily to suffering something bad or painful, but simply experiencing or being on the receiving end of an action done by someone else).

present passive:

παύ-ομαι	I am stopped
παύ-η*	you (*sg*) are stopped
παύ-εται	he/she/it is stopped
παυ-όμεθα	we are stopped
παύ-εσθε	you (*pl*) are stopped
παύ-ονται	they are stopped

* the spelling παύ-ει is also possible, but in this book παύ-η will be used to avoid confusion with the third person singular of the active (in texts using the ambiguous form, the context usually allows you to deduce which it is)

• The translation *I am <u>being</u> stopped* (suggesting *at this moment*) is also possible for the present passive, and indeed often preferable.

Exercise 7.1

Translate into Greek:
1   We are being chased.
2   You (*sg*) are being guarded.
3   They are sent.
4   He is being taught.
5   I am persuaded.

Agent and Instrument

• As we saw, in a sentence with a passive verb the person or thing having the action done to them is the grammatical subject and therefore of course is nominative.

• The *person by whom* the action is done is called the *agent*. This is usually expressed in Greek by the preposition ὑπό with the genitive*:

ἡ κώμη ὑπὸ τῶν στρατιωτῶν φυλάσσεται.
The village is (being) guarded by the soldiers.

Note that, compared with the original active sentence - *The soldiers guard the village* - what was in the active version the object has become the subject, and what was the subject has become the agent. (*In Chapter 6 you met ὑπό with the *dative*, meaning *under*.)

• It is also possible (alternatively or additionally) to state *the thing with which* the action is done. This is called the *instrument*, and is expressed in Greek by the dative without a preposition:

ἡ κώμη τοῖς ὅπλοις φυλάσσεται.
The village is (being) guarded with the weapons.

ἡ κώμη ὑπὸ τῶν στρατιωτῶν τοῖς ὅπλοις φυλάσσεται.
The village is (being) guarded by the soldiers with the weapons.

• Contrast this with Latin: there too the agent has a preposition (*a* or *ab* = by) and the instrument does not, but *both* are expressed by the ablative. As elsewhere, Greek divides the ablative jobs between genitive and dative (often in the process making more - or clearer - distinctions).

• Not every sentence with a passive verb will necessarily have either agent or instrument: we may just be being told the action is done, by person and means unspecified.

• Especially when a sentence has both agent and instrument, the translation *with* is often clearer for the instrument (keeping *by* for the agent). But *by* is also possible for the instrument in English, and in some sentences sounds better.

Exercise 7.2

Translate into English:
1   οἱ λόγοι ὑπὸ τῶν παίδων μανθάνονται.
2   τὸ πλοῖον ἐν τῷ λιμένι λείπεται.
3   αἱ βοαὶ ὑπὸ τῆς παιδὸς ἀκούονται.
4   ἀγόμεθα ὑπὸ τοῦ στρατηγοῦ τοῦ ἀνδρείου.
5   ἡ μάχη τῇ νυκτὶ παύεται.
6   ἆρα διώκεσθε, ὦ σύμμαχοι;
7   ὁ στρατὸς τῷ ποταμῷ κωλύεται.
8   οἱ ἵπποι ὑπὸ τοῦ δούλου λύονται.

9   ὑπὸ τοῦ τῆς νήσου ἄρχοντος πέμπομαι.
10   διδάσκῃ ὑπὸ τοῦ γέροντος.

Exercise 7.3

Translate into Greek:
1   The slaves are being chased by the young man.
2   The victory is announced in the agora by the messenger with a shout.
3   The army is being drawn up by the general.
4   The horse is left in the road.
5   We are all being taught by the same teacher.

Exercise 7.4

Thales and the Well

Thales (about 600 BC) was the first Greek philosopher. His wide interests included astronomy. He is said to have predicted accurately an eclipse of the sun in 585 BC. This story (recorded 200 years later by Plato, the most famous Greek philosopher) shows him as an absent-minded eccentric.

ὁ <u>Πλάτων</u> λέγει <u>ὅτι</u> <u>Θαλῆς</u> ὁ <u>φιλόσοφος</u> <u>ἀστρονομῶν</u> καὶ <u>ἄνω</u> <u>βλέπων</u> εἰς <u>φρέαρ</u> ἔπεσεν. <u>θεράπαινα</u> δέ τις ἰδοῦσα <u>ἔσκωψεν</u> αὐτόν· "σὺ ὑπὸ πάντων θαυμάζῃ ὡς φιλόσοφος <u>κλεινὸς</u> ὤν. <u>ἀληθῶς</u> μέντοι μωρὸς εἶ. τὰ μὲν γὰρ ἐν οὐρανῷ ἐθέλεις γιγνώσκειν, τὰ δὲ <u>πρὸ</u> τῶν ποδῶν οὐ γιγνώσκεις". λέγει
5 δὲ καὶ ὁ Πλάτων ὅτι πάντες οἱ φιλόσοφοι πάσχουσι τὸ αὐτό, <u>ὥσπερ</u> ὁ Θαλῆς. περὶ γὰρ τῶν ἀπόντων <u>σπεύδουσι</u>, τῶν δὲ παρόντων <u>ἀμελοῦσιν</u>. πολλάκις οὖν ὑπὸ τῶν πολιτῶν σκώπτονται.

	Πλάτων -ωνος ὁ	Plato
	ὅτι	that
	Θαλῆς ὁ	Thales
	φιλόσοφος -ου ὁ	philosopher
	ἀστρονομέω	I study astronomy
	ἄνω	upwards
	βλέπω	I look
	φρέαρ -ατος τό	well
	θεράπαινα -ης ἡ	maidservant
	σκώπτω ἔσκωψα	I mock, I make fun of
	κλεινός -ή -όν	famous
	ἀληθῶς	truly, really
	πρό	in front of (+ *gen*)
5	ὥσπερ	just as, like
	σπεύδω	I am enthusiastic
	ἀμελέω	I do not care about, I ignore (+ *gen*)

3

Present passive participle

• This is extremely simple in form: the verb stem has -ομεν- added, then 2-1-2 endings exactly like σοφος

		masculine	feminine	neuter	
sg	nom	παυόμεν-ος	παυομέν-η	παυόμεν-ον	being stopped
	acc	παυόμεν-ον	παυομέν-ην	παυόμεν-ον	
	gen	παυομέν-ου	παυομέν-ης	παυομέν-ου	
	dat	παυομέν-ῳ	παυομέν-ῃ	παυομέν-ῳ	
pl	nom	παυόμεν-οι	παυόμεν-αι	παυόμεν-α	
	acc	παυομέν-ους	παυομέν-ας	παυόμεν-α	
	gen	παυομέν-ων	παυομέν-ων	παυομέν-ων	
	dat	παυομέν-οις	παυομέν-αις	παυομέν-οις	

• The passive participle behaves like a passive verb in being able to have an agent and/or instrument, and like any other participle in its usage (i.e. circumstantial or attributive; with or without the article; having its tense in relation to that of the main verb, etc).

Exercise 7.5

Give the Greek for:
1   Being admired (*masculine nominative singular*)
2   Being drawn up (*masculine accusative plural*)
3   Being led (*feminine genitive singular*)
4   Being stolen (*neuter nominative plural*)
5   Being written (*masculine dative singular*)

Exercise 7.6

Translate into English:
1   οἱ στρατιῶται, ὑπὸ τῶν πολεμίων διωκόμενοι, πρὸς τὴν
         θάλασσαν ἔφυγον.
2   οἱ λόγοι οἱ νῦν μανθανόμενοι οὔκ εἰσι χαλεποί.
3   τίνες εἰσὶν οἱ τῷ ποταμῷ κωλυόμενοι;
4   ἐθέλω ἀκούειν τὰ ὑπὸ τοῦ ξένου ἀγγελλόμενα.
5   ὁ δοῦλος ὁ ὑπὸ τοῦ γίγαντος διωκόμενος οὐκ ἔφυγεν.
6   ἆρα αἱ εἰς τὴν κώμην ἀγόμεναι τὴν μάχην εἶδον;
7   οἱ ὑπὸ τοῦ ποιητοῦ πειθόμενοι μῶροί εἰσιν.
8   τίνος ἐστὶν ἡ βίβλος ἡ εἰς τὸ πῦρ βαλλομένη;
9   οἱ στρατιῶται, ὑπὸ τοῦ σοφοῦ στρατηγοῦ ἀγόμενοι, οὐδένα
         φόβον εἶχον.
10   τὸ δεῖπνον τὸ ὑπὸ τῶν παίδων νῦν ἐσθιόμενον κακόν ἐστιν.

Exercise 7.7

Translate into Greek:
1   The slave, while being chased by the boys, fell into the river.
2   The horse that is being released by the slave is mine.
3   The enemy captured the village which was being guarded by our soldiers.
4   The letter now being written is long.
5   Who is the man who is being sent to the harbour?

Passive infinitive

• This is formed by adding -εσθαι to the present stem (instead of the -ειν of the active infinitive). The meaning is *to be ~ed*, e.g. παύεσθαι = *to be stopped*. (Distinguish the infinitive ending carefully from the second person plural ending -εσθε.)

• Like the passive finite verb, the participle and infinitive can have an agent and/or instrument.

Exercise 7.8

Give the Greek for:
1   To be announced
2   To be carried
3   To be harmed
4   To be guarded
5   To be heard

Exercise 7.9

Translate into Greek:
1   The lion wants to be admired.
2   The slave is ready to be released.
3   I ordered the messenger to be sent away.
4   We do not want to be chased by the boys.
5   The horse is not able to be eaten.

Exercise 7.10

Socrates and the Philosophers

A visiting foreigner and an Athenian discuss the famous Athenian philosopher who was Plato's teacher and inspiration.

Ξένος	ἀλλὰ ὁ <u>φιλόσοφος</u>, <u>ποῖός</u> τίς ἐστιν;
Ἀθηναῖος	<u>δῆλόν</u> ἐστιν <u>ὅτι</u> φίλος ἐστὶ τῆς σοφίας. ἐθέλουσι γὰρ οἱ φιλόσοφοι τὴν σοφίαν εὑρίσκειν τε καὶ γιγνώσκειν.
Ξεν	καὶ διδάσκειν;
5 Ἀθ	ἐθέλουσι <u>καὶ</u> διδάσκειν.
Ξεν	καὶ θαυμάζεσθαι;
Ἀθ	δῆλόν ἐστιν ὅτι οἱ μὲν αὐτῶν ἐθέλουσι καὶ θαυμάζεσθαι ...
Ξεν	ἀλλὰ ποία ἐστὶν ἡ σοφία ἡ ὑπὸ τῶν φιλοσόφων διδασκομένη;
Ἀθ	πολλοὶ φιλόσοφοί εἰσι, καὶ πολλαὶ <u>γνῶμαι</u>. οἱ μὲν γὰρ λέγουσιν
10	ὅτι πάντα ἐστὶ γῆ, οἱ δὲ ὅτι ἐστὶν <u>ἀήρ</u>, <u>ἢ</u> πῦρ, ἢ ὕδωρ ...
Ξεν	καὶ ἄλλοι ὅτι ἡ <u>σελήνη</u> οὐκ ἔστι θεά, ἀλλὰ γῆς <u>βῶλός</u> τις ...
Ἀθ	<u>Σωκράτης</u> μέντοι οὐ περὶ τῆς τε γῆς καὶ τοῦ οὐρανοῦ λέγει, ἀλλὰ περὶ τοῦ τῶν ἀνθρώπων βίου. λέγει γὰρ ὅτι ἡ φιλοσοφία <u>πρὸς</u> τὴν <u>ἀμαθίαν</u> ἐστὶν <u>ὥσπερ</u> ὁ βίος πρὸς τὸν θάνατον. πάντα
15	γὰρ ὑπὸ τοῦ φιλοσόφου <u>ἐξετάζεται·</u> ὁ γὰρ <u>ἀνεξέταστος</u> βίος οὐ <u>βιωτὸς</u> ἀνθρώπῳ.
Ξεν	ἀλλὰ τίς βίος <u>ἄριστός</u> ἐστιν; ἆρα ὁ τοῦ <u>τυράννου</u>, ἢ τοῦ <u>ῥήτορος</u>, ἢ τοῦ στρατηγοῦ ... ;
Ἀθ	περὶ τῶν βίων καὶ τῆς ἑκάστου <u>ἀρετῆς</u> λέγει τε καὶ <u>φροντίζει</u>.
20	ἐν γὰρ τῇ ἀγορᾷ καὶ ἐν ταῖς ὁδοῖς ἀεὶ λέγει, "τί ἐστιν ἡ

	φιλόσοφος -ου ὁ	philosopher
	ποῖος -α -ον	what sort of ... ? what ... like?
	δῆλος -η -ον	clear
	ὅτι	that
5	καί	(*here*) also
	γνώμη -ης ἡ	idea
10	ἀήρ ἀέρος ὁ	air
	ἤ	or
	σελήνη -ης ἡ	moon
	βῶλος -ου ἡ	clod
	Σωκράτης ὁ	Socrates
	πρός	(+ *acc*) (*here*) in relation to, compared to
	ἀμαθία -ας ἡ	ignorance
	ὥσπερ	just as, like
15	ἐξετάζω	I examine
	ἀνεξέταστος	unexamined
	βιωτός -όν	worth living
	ἄριστος -η -ον	best
	τύραννος -ου ὁ	tyrant
	ῥήτωρ -ορος ὁ	politician, public speaker
	ἀρετή -ῆς ἡ	excellence, virtue
	φροντίζω	I think, I consider

δικαιοσύνη;" καί, "τί ἐστιν ἡ <u>ἀνδρεία</u>;" καὶ ἴσως λέγει τις τῶν
παρόντων περὶ τῆς ἀνδρείας, "<u>εἴ</u> τις εἰς οἰκίαν <u>καιομένην</u>
εἰστρέχει ὡς <u>παιδίον</u> τι <u>σώσων</u>". ἀλλὰ ὁ Σωκράτης λέγει, "οὐ
περὶ τῆς ἀνδρείας λέγεις· παρέχεις γὰρ <u>παράδειγμά</u> τι μόνον τῆς

25   ἀνδρείας. τί μέντοι ἐστὶν ἡ ἀνδρεία αὐτή;" καὶ οἱ παρόντες οὐχ
οἷοί τ' εἰσὶ λέγειν. καὶ δι' ὀργὴν ἀποβαίνουσιν.

Ξεν   <u>εἰκότως</u> <u>δή</u>. οὐδέν ἐστιν ἄλλο ὁ Σωκράτης <u>ἢ</u> <u>πολυπράγμων</u> καὶ
<u>ὀχληρός</u>.

Ἀθ   <u>ἐκ προνοίας</u> ἐστίν. λέγει γὰρ <u>ὅτι</u> <u>οἶστρός</u> ἐστιν. ἀεὶ <u>βομβεῖ</u> ὁ
30   οἶστρος· τοὺς ἵππους <u>ταράσσει</u>, καὶ κωλύει* <u>καθεύδειν</u>. ὁ οὖν
Σωκράτης <u>ὁμοίως</u> τοὺς πολίτας ταράσσει, <u>ὥστε</u> <u>ἀναγκάζονται</u>
πάντα <u>ἐξετάζειν</u>. καὶ <u>θαυμάσια</u> λέγει, ὅτι οὐδεὶς <u>ἑκὼν</u> <u>ἁμαρτάνει</u>·
εἰ γὰρ κακὰ <u>πράσσομεν</u>, <u>δῆλόν</u> ἐστιν ὅτι τὸ ἀγαθὸν οὐ
γιγνώσκομεν. καὶ εἴ τις λέγει ὅτι κακὰ πράσσει καίπερ τὸ
35   ἀγαθὸν γιγνώσκων, ὁ Σωκράτης λέγει ὅτι οὐ <u>παντελῶς</u>
γιγνώσκει ὁ ἄνθρωπος· οὐδεὶς γὰρ ἐθέλει κακὰ πράσσειν, οὐδεὶς
κακὰ πάσχειν· καὶ εἴ τις κακὰ πράσσει, τὴν <u>ψυχὴν</u> βλάπτει·
καὶ <u>ἄμεινόν</u> ἐστι κακὰ πάσχειν ἢ κακὰ πράσσειν ...

* an infinitive after κωλύω needs to be translated '(prevent) from (doing X)'

20	ἀνδρεία -ας ἡ	courage
	ἴσως	perhaps
	εἰ	if
	καιόμενος -η -ον	burning, on fire
	παιδίον -ου τό	small child
	σῴζω *fut* σώσω	I save
	παράδειγμα -ατος τό	example
25	εἰκότως	reasonably
	δή	indeed
	ἤ	(*here and in line 38*) than
	πολυπράγμων	interfering
	ὀχληρός -ά -όν	troublesome
	ἐκ προνοίας	deliberately
	ὅτι	that
	οἶστρος -ου ὁ	gadfly
	βομβέω	I buzz
30	ταράσσω	I annoy
	καθεύδω	I sleep
	ὁμοίως	similarly
	ὥστε	with the result that
	ἀναγκάζω	I force, I compel
	ἐξετάζω	I examine
	θαυμάσιος -α -ον	remarkable
	ἑκών -οῦσα -όν (ἑκοντ-)	willing(ly)
	ἁμαρτάνω	I err, I make a mistake, I sin
	πράσσω	I do
	δῆλος -η -ον	clear
35	παντελῶς	completely
	ψυχή -ῆς ἡ	soul
	ἄμεινον	better

Ξεν	περὶ ἀνθρώπου τινὸς λέγεις, ἢ περὶ θεοῦ;
40 Ἀθ	περὶ ἀνθρώπου <u>δή</u>. ὁ γὰρ Σωκράτης οἷός τ' ἐστὶν οἶνον πίνειν ὡς οὐδεὶς ἄλλος, καίπερ <u>οὔποτε μεθύων</u>. καὶ στρατιώτης ὢν τοὺς φίλους <u>ἔσωσεν</u>. καὶ εἴδομεν αὐτὸν ἐν <u>χειμῶνι</u> πᾶσαν τὴν νύκτα <u>στάντα</u> καὶ <u>φροντίζοντα</u>, <u>ἱμάτιον</u> μόνον καὶ <u>πέδιλα</u> ἔχοντα.
Ξεν	ἆρα <u>γενναῖός</u> τίς ἐστιν ὁ Σωκράτης;
45 Ἀθ	<u>οὐδαμῶς</u>. ἡ μὲν γὰρ μήτηρ <u>μαῖα</u> ἦν, ὁ πατὴρ <u>ἀγαλματοποιός</u>. καὶ λέγει ὁ Σωκράτης ὅτι τὰ αὐτὰ πράσσει· μαῖα γάρ τίς ἐστι τῶν <u>γνωμῶν</u>· οἱ γὰρ <u>μαθηταὶ</u> αὐτοῦ γνωμὰς <u>τίκτουσιν</u>. καὶ <u>ὥσπερ</u> ὁ ἀγαλματοποιὸς τὸ <u>ἄγαλμα</u> ἐν τῷ λίθῳ <u>ἐκκαλύπτων</u>, ὁ Σωκράτης <u>ὁμοίως</u> τὰς γνώμας ἐκκαλύπτει.

	ἤ	(*here*) or
40	δή	indeed
	οὔποτε	never
	μεθύω	I am drunk
	σῴζω ἔσωσα	I save
	χειμών -ῶνος ὁ	winter
	στάς στᾶσα στάν	
	(stem σταντ-)	standing (*irreg aor participle*)
	φροντίζω	I think
	ἱμάτιον -ου τό	cloak
	πέδιλα -ων τά	sandals
	γενναῖος -α -ον	noble, of noble birth
45	οὐδαμῶς	not at all
	μαῖα -ας ἡ	midwife
	ἀγαλματοποιός -οῦ ὁ	sculptor
	γνώμη -ης ἡ	idea
	μαθητής -οῦ ὁ	student
	τίκτω	I give birth to
	ὥσπερ	just as, just like
	ἄγαλμα -ατος τό	statue
	ἐκκαλύπτω	I uncover, I reveal
	ὁμοίως	in the same way

NB: from the vocabulary for this passage, note three important words and various features of them:

ῥήτωρ -ορος   means *public speaker* and therefore *politician* (persuading large audiences was the route to political success in Athens). Note that words starting with rho always have a rough breathing. (Rho seems to have been regarded as in some ways like a vowel: compare how it is first declension nouns whose stem ends in a vowel <u>or rho</u> that add singular endings with alpha rather than eta.) English words starting *rh-* come from Greek (though it would be more logical to transliterate as *hr-*).

ἤ   means *or* or *than*, according to context (*or* when giving alternatives, *than* in a comparison)

ἑκών -οῦσα -όν means *willing(ly), (being) willing* - an adjective (though often better translated as an adverb) which declines like a present active participle

• Note also that (as we have seen in this passage) καί is very commonly used when it is not needed in its normal sense as a connective *and*. In these contexts *also* or *even* is normally an appropriate translation. (In Latin *et* has a similar range of uses and meanings.)

Background: Socrates (1)

Socrates (469-399 BC) was Plato's teacher and hero, but himself wrote nothing. In the works of Plato and of his other disciples, he is often the mouthpiece for the author's own views. This makes it difficult to get back to the real Socrates.

Socrates was of fairly humble origin, the son of a stonemason/sculptor and a midwife. He became a stonemason himself. He later drew metaphors from both skills: the notion of a finished statue having been somehow 'already there' in a block of stone illustrates the process of understanding; and by discussion ideas can be (as it were) helped to birth. Socrates lived and died in Athens, travelling elsewhere only on military service (where his courage and endurance but also his eccentricity attracted notice).

Earlier philosophers like Thales were interested mainly in natural science - how the world is made. Socrates in his youth shared these interests, but in maturity changed the focus of enquiry to *moral* philosophy (how we should live) and *epistemology* (how we know anything). The significance of this change is signalled by the fact that we call the earlier thinkers 'Pre-Socratics'. Socrates was especially interested in the meaning of abstract qualities such as courage, justice, equality: how we can recognise them, and whether they have an existence above and beyond particular acts and examples in which they are shown.

Socrates was not paid for teaching. He talked in public places in Athens to anyone who would listen. He thought truth would be arrived at by relentless questioning and shared discussion. His paradoxes were famous: *Virtue is knowledge, No-one errs willingly, It is better to suffer wrong than to do it* (the last more startling in a pre-Christian world). They express his central concerns (if we *truly* knew what was right, we would inevitably do it: our obvious and frequent failures are really failures of *knowledge*), but they also illustrate his delight in being provocative, in acting (as he put it) like a gadfly to the sluggish horse represented by his Athenian contemporaries.

This and That

Words for *this* and *that* (and others we shall meet later such as *so many*) are called *demonstratives* because they point out or demonstrate (*this one here, that one there*, etc).

The normal Greek word for *this* is οὗτος. It has normal 2-1-2 endings (though, because it can be a pronoun, with -ο rather than -ον in the neuter nominative and accusative singular), and its stem undergoes some variation:

		masculine	*feminine*	*neuter*	
sg	*nom*	οὗτ-ος	αὗτ-η	τοῦτ-ο	this
	acc	τοῦτ-ον	ταύτ-ην	τοῦτ-ο	
	gen	τούτ-ου	ταύτ-ης	τούτ-ου	
	dat	τούτ-ῳ	ταύτ-ῃ	τούτ-ῳ	
pl	*nom*	οὗτ-οι	αὗτ-αι	ταῦτ-α	these
	acc	τούτ-ους	ταύτ-ας	ταῦτ-α	
	gen	τούτ-ων	τούτ-ων	τούτ-ων	
	dat	τούτ-οις	ταύτ-αις	τούτ-οις	

• The basic stem is τουτ-. The tau is replaced by a rough breathing in exactly the same places as it is in the definite article: masculine and feminine, nominative singular and plural (underlined). The -ου- in the stem is replaced by -αυ- in the feminine (except the genitive plural, which just follows the masculine and neuter), and in the neuter nominative and accusative plural.

• Despite looking similar, no part of this word is identical to any part of αὐτός (the feminine nominative, singular and plural, is closest - but the breathing and accent are different).

• It can be used either as a *pronoun* (according to gender and number: *this woman, these things* etc), or as an *adjective*.

• When used as an adjective, it has *the article as well* (not translated), but is *not sandwiched*:
οὗτος ὁ δοῦλος   this slave
ταῦτα τὰ δῶρα   these gifts

• As a pronoun *in the nominative*, it is commonly used just for *he* (as well as *this man*), because αὐτός cannot be used in this way in the nominative (it can in the other cases, for *him* etc).

Exercise 7.11

Give the Greek for:
1   These horses (*nominative*)
2   For this old man
3   Of these goddesses
4   This poet (*accusative*)
5   These prizes (*nominative*)

Exercise 7.12

Translate into English:
1   οὗτοι οἱ ναῦται ἀνδρεῖοί εἰσιν.
2   τίς ἐστιν αὕτη ἡ παῖς;
3   ὁ τῶν συμμάχων ἄγγελος ταῦτα ἤγγειλεν.
4   αὕτη ἡ θεὰ δῶρα κάλλιστα παρέχει.
5   οὗτοι τὰ αὐτὰ λέγουσιν.
6   ἡ κώμη αὕτη* ὑπὸ τῶν γερόντων φυλάσσεται.
7   τίς ἐστιν οὗτος; ἆρα ὁ σὸς φίλος;
8   ταῦτα ἔπαυσε τὴν μάχην.
9   ἐγὼ ἵππον οὐκ ἔχω, ἀλλὰ οὗτος ἔχει.
10   οὗτοι οἱ δοῦλοι, οἱ ὑπὸ τῶν πολεμίων διωκόμενοι, οὐκ ἤκουσαν
         τοὺς τοῦ ἀγγέλου λόγους.

* this word order is also possible for the adjective use of οὗτος, though less common: the crucial point is that it does not sandwich

Exercise 7.13

Translate into Greek:
1   This girl has a fine horse.
2   Who announced these things?
3   This man is not a sailor but a magistrate.
4   These women admire the laws of the country.
5   Were you carrying this book, slave?

An alternative (rather less common) word for *this* is ὅδε. It does not involve any new learning, as it is simply the definite article with -δε on the end:

		masculine	*feminine*	*neuter*	
sg	*nom*	ὁ-δε	ἡ-δε	τό-δε	this
	acc	τόν-δε	τήν-δε	τό-δε	
	gen	τοῦ-δε	τῆσ-δε	τοῦ-δε	
	dat	τῷ-δε	τῇ-δε	τῷ-δε	
pl	*nom*	οἵ-δε	αἵ-δε	τά-δε	these
	acc	τούσ-δε	τάσ-δε	τά-δε	
	gen	τῶν-δε	τῶν-δε	τῶν-δε	
	dat	τοῖσ-δε	ταῖσ-δε	τοῖσ-δε	

• The use of ὅδε both as a pronoun and as an adjective (with untranslated definite article, and not sandwiched) is similar to that of οὗτος. And often there is no difference of meaning. There is however a preference for ὅδε when the implication is *this one actually present*, to *point* to what is described.

• Often parts of οὗτος refer backwards to something already mentioned, parts of ὅδε forwards to something about to be mentioned. This is especially common in the neuter:
    ἤγγειλε ταῦτα.
    He announced these things *(already quoted).*

    ἤγγειλε τάδε.
    He announced these things *(about to be quoted).*
  or He announced the following.

Exercise 7.14

Translate into English:
1   ὅδε ὁ δοῦλος νῦν πάρεστιν.
2   ἆρα ἔγραψας τήνδε τὴν ἐπιστολήν;
3   τίνες εἰσὶν αἵδε αἱ ὑπὸ τοῦ παιδὸς διωκόμεναι;
4   τάδε τὰ ὅπλα οὐκ ἔστιν ἐμά.
5   ἐφυλάσσομεν τούς τε ἡμετέρους ἵππους καὶ τούσδε.

11

The word for *that* is ἐκεῖνος (compare ἐκεῖ: literally the one *over there*, further away than something referred to as *this*). It has normal 2-1-2 endings (though again, because it can be a pronoun, with -o rather than -ov in the neuter nominative and accusative singular).

		masculine	feminine	neuter	
sg	nom	ἐκεῖν-ος	ἐκείν-η	ἐκεῖν-ο	that
	acc	ἐκεῖν-ον	ἐκείν-ην	ἐκεῖν-ο	
	gen	ἐκεῖν-ου	ἐκείν-ης	ἐκείν-ου	
	dat	ἐκείν-ῳ	ἐκείν-ῃ	ἐκείν-ῳ	
pl	nom	ἐκεῖν-οι	ἐκεῖν-αι	ἐκεῖν-α	those
	acc	ἐκεῖν-ους	ἐκείν-ας	ἐκεῖν-α	
	gen	ἐκείν-ων	ἐκείν-ων	ἐκείν-ων	
	dat	ἐκείν-οις	ἐκείν-αις	ἐκείν-οις	

• The use of ἐκεῖνος both as a pronoun and as an adjective (with untranslated definite article, and not sandwiched) is again similar to that of οὗτος.

• As a pronoun in the nominative, ἐκεῖνος can (like οὗτος) be used just for *he* (as well as *that man*).

Exercise 7.15

Give the Greek for:
1   That boy (*accusative*)
2   Of those letters
3   For that teacher
4   Those villages (*nominative*)
5   That giant (*nominative*)

Exercise 7.16

Translate into English:
1   ἐκεῖνοι οἱ στρατιῶται ξένοι εἰσίν.
2   αὗται ἔμειναν, ἀλλὰ ἐκεῖναι ἔφυγον.
3   τίς ἐστιν ἐκεῖνος, ὁ ἐν τῇ νήσῳ;
4   ἆρα ἀπέβαλες ἐκείνας τὰς βίβλους;
5   δεῖπνον παρέσχομεν ἐκείνοις.

Exercise 7.17 (Assorted demonstratives)

Translate into Greek:
1   Is this slave here guarding the house?
2   These girls are being taught by a wise old man.
3   We were chasing those horses towards the river.
4   This village has new gates.
5   Those weapons will not harm you, friends.

Background: Socrates (2)

The only surviving account of Socrates written during his lifetime is a send-up in a play by the comic playwright Aristophanes. Comedy exaggerates and distorts to get laughs. Also, Aristophanes seems to make Socrates into the typical eccentric philosopher or mad scientist (compare the story about Thales and the well). He is shown in the play doing experiments in physical science (such as astronomy), but this - as we saw - was an interest only of his youth (as it had been of earlier philosophers, such as Thales). He is also shown running a school (called a *Phrontisterion*, an invented word meaning *Think-tank*), whereas the real Socrates seems to have taught only by informal discussion in public places (the agora, the gymnasium) or private houses. His distinctive appearance (unheroic, pot-bellied, with bulging eyes, a broad nose and a bull-like expression) made him well-known in Athens, and explains why Aristophanes chose him as the object of satire. Socrates was a good target because he was local and familiar. The real Socrates is said to have been in the audience at the first performance of *Clouds*, and to have stood up at the end (as if to say 'Look how unlike that ridiculous caricature I am!'). The true target of the play seems to have been a group called the *Sophists*. They were travelling teachers, drawn to Athens by the demand in the newly flourishing democracy for skills in public speaking: young men hoped to make their way in the city by persuasiveness in the assembly or lawcourt. Sophists ranged from charlatans out to make a quick profit to serious and original philosophers. Many of them (in contrast to Socrates) charged high fees, and many were associated with a doctrine of *relativism*, implying that there are no fixed or divinely inspired values. Such ideas were widely seen as a recipe for social unrest. Similarly, the public-speaking exercise of learning to argue both sides of a case with equal conviction was regarded as dangerous, in putting aside the question of right and wrong. Plato emphasises how far removed Socrates was from all this; but the fact that Aristophanes could choose him as a symbol of the new ideas suggests that many people would be more struck by similarities than differences. The truth no doubt lies somewhere in the middle.

Comedies (like other plays) were put on in Athens at two big public festivals during the early spring of each year. Aristophanes (about 445-385 BC) specialised in political and social satire, making fun of people and issues in the public eye. His play *Clouds* (named after its chorus, whom philosophers supposedly worship instead of the traditional gods) was first staged in 423 BC, though re-written some years later. At the time of the play Athens and her empire were engaged in a long war (the *Peloponnesian War*, 431-404 BC) with Sparta and her allies, who included Corinth (mentioned in the following passage).

Exercise 7.18

Socrates in Comedy (1)

The main character of the play, Strepsiades (his name means Twister), *is an elderly and dishonest Athenian farmer who has been financially ruined by his son's taste for the aristocratic hobby of horses and chariot-racing. He has heard that Socrates can 'make the worse cause appear the better' (arguing either side of a case), and sees this as a way of arguing the family out of debt. His son refuses to go to the Phrontisterion, so Strepsiades goes himself. In the first passage he has just seen some of the students and various pieces of scientific equipment in the school.*

Στρεψιάδης	νὴ τοὺς θεούς, τίνα ταῦτα τὰ θηρία;
Μαθητής	τίς ἡ βοή; διὰ τί θαυμάζεις· ἡμεῖς γὰρ μαθηταί ἐσμεν.
Στρ	ἀλλὰ τί πράσσει ὁ εἰς τὴν γῆν βλέπων;
Μαθ	τὰ ὑπὸ τῇ γῇ ἐθέλει εὑρίσκειν.

5 Στρ   ἐθέλει οὖν βολβοὺς ἐσθίειν. μὴ φρόντιζε, ὦ φίλε μαθητά.
       καλοὶ γὰρ βολβοὶ ἐν τοῖς ἐμοῖς ἀγροῖς εἰσιν. ἀλλὰ τίνες αὗται αἱ
       μηχαναί;
  Μαθ αὗται εἰς ἀστρονομίαν. πρὸς τὸν οὐρανὸν αὐταῖς βλέπομεν.
  Στρ καὶ ἐκεῖναι;
10 Μαθ εἰς γεωμετρίαν. αὕτη δ᾽ ἐστὶ γῆς περίοδος· καὶ ἐνθάδε αἱ ᾽Αθῆναι.
  Στρ τί λέγεις; οὐ πιστεύω, διότι δικαστήριον οὐ πάρεστιν. ποῦ δ᾽
       ἐστὶν ἡ ἐμὴ οἰκία;
  Μαθ ἐνθάδε ἐστίν.
  Στρ ἀλλὰ ποῦ ἐστιν ἡ Λακεδαίμων;
15 Μαθ αὕτη ἐστίν.
  Στρ οἴμοι. ὡς ἐγγὺς ἡμῶν ἡ Λακεδαίμων. ὡς ἐγγὺς τῆς ἐμῆς οἰκίας οἱ
       πολέμιοι. ἢ ἄπαγε αὐτοὺς ἀφ᾽ ἡμῶν ἢ ἀπόβαλλε τὴν περίοδον.
  Μαθ οὐχ οἷός τ᾽ εἰμί.

(*Socrates swings into view on the crane used in serious plays for the appearance of gods*)

  Στρ ἀλλὰ λέγε μοι, τίς οὗτος ὁ ἐν τῇ κρεμάθρᾳ ὤν;
20 Μαθ αὐτός.
  Στρ τίς αὐτός;
  Μαθ ὁ Σωκράτης.

	Στρεψιάδης ὁ	Strepsiades
	νή	by ... ! (+ *acc*)
	θηρίον -ου τό	wild beast
	μαθητής -οῦ ὁ	student
	πράσσω	I do
	βλέπω	I look
5	βολβός -οῦ ὁ	truffle (*edible fungus growing underground*)
	μή	(*with imperative*) don't ... !
	φροντίζω	(*here*) I worry
	μηχανή -ῆς ἡ	device, piece of equipment
	εἰς	(*here*) for (the purpose of)
	ἀστρονομία -ας ἡ	astronomy
10	γεωμετρία -ας ἡ	earth-measuring
	περίοδος -ου ἡ	map (*literally* circuit)
	δικαστήριον -ου τό	lawcourt (*Athenians were notorious for their love of sitting on juries*)
	Λακεδαίμων -ονος ἡ	Sparta, Spartan territory
15	οἴμοι	oh no!
	ὡς	(*here*) how ... !
	ἢ ... ἢ	either ... or
	κρεμάθρα -ας ἡ	hanging basket

Imperfect passive

This has the augment like the active past tenses, and endings which are similar to (or recognisable variants of) those of the present passive.

imperfect passive:

ἐ-παυ-όμην	I was being stopped
ἐ-παύ-ου	you (*sg*) were being stopped
ἐ-παύ-ετο	he/she/it was being stopped
ἐ-παυ-όμεθα	we were being stopped
ἐ-παύ-εσθε	you (*pl*) were being stopped
ἐ-παύ-οντο	they were being stopped

• You have now met two sets of endings which (by the typical economy of Greek grammar) are used for other jobs as well as the present and imperfect passive, so it is important to learn them thoroughly. (Compare how we have already seen in the active tenses the same endings used for present and future, and the same ones for imperfect and second [strong] aorist.) The endings we have seen on the present passive are (like the -ω -εις -ει active ones) called *primary,* and the ones we have seen on the imperfect passive are (like the -ον -ες -ε active ones) called *historic*.

• Here are the primary and historic Greek endings, active and passive, side by side:

active:			*primary*	*historic*
	sg	*1*	-ω	-ον
		2	-εις	-ες
		3	-ει	-ε(ν)
	pl	*1*	-ομεν	-ομεν
		2	-ετε	-ετε
		3	-ουσι(ν)	-ον

passive:			*primary*	*historic*
	sg	*1*	-ομαι	-ομην
		2	-η (*or* -ει)	-ου
		3	-εται	-ετο
	pl	*1*	-ομεθα	-ομεθα
		2	-εσθε	-εσθε
		3	-ονται	-οντο

• Notice in both active and passive that the first and second persons plural for primary and historic are identical. Only the augment here indicates a past (historic) tense.

Exercise 7.19

Translate into Greek:
1   You (*pl*) were being sent.
2   I was being harmed.
3   We were being taught.
4   He was being carried.
5   They were being drawn up.

Exercise 7.20

Translate into English:
1   οἱ πολέμιοι ὑπὸ τῶν συμμάχων ἐδιώκοντο.
2   ἡ πύλη ὑπὸ τῶν παίδων ἐφυλάσσετο.
3   ἐκεῖνοι οἱ νεκροὶ ὑπὸ τῶν ξένων ἐθάπτοντο.
4   οἱ στρατιῶται τοῖς τῶν γιγάντων ὅπλοις ἐβάλλοντο*.
5   τὸ ἱερὸν ὑπὸ τοῦ στρατηγοῦ θαυμάζεται.
6   ἐφερόμεθα ὑπὸ τούτων τῶν δούλων.
7   ἆρα ἐβλάπτου τῷ δένδρῳ, ὦ ἄγγελε;
8   ἡ βοὴ ὑπὸ τῆς κόρης ἠκούετο.
9   οἱ λόγοι ὑπὸ πάντων τῶν παίδων ἐμανθάνοντο.
10   ὁ δῆμος τοῖς τοῦ ἀγγέλου λόγοις ἐπείθετο.

    * note that the alternative meaning *I pelt, I hit* (rather than *I throw*) is appropriate for βάλλω here

Exercise 7.21

Translate into Greek:
1   The letter was being carried by the slave.
2   You (*pl*) were being persuaded by the stranger.
3   We are being chased by the giant.
4   The soldiers were being drawn up by the general.
5   The harbour was being guarded by the fleet.

Revision checkpoint:

Make sure you know:
• present passive
• imperfect passive
• primary and historic endings, active and passive
• present passive participle
• the words for *this* (two different ones) and *that*, and their declensions

Socrates in Comedy (2)

Στρεψιάδης   ὦ Σώκρατες, ὦ <u>Σωκρατίδιον</u>, ἆρα <u>ἀληθῶς</u> πάρει;
Σωκράτης   τίς ἡ βοή; τίς <u>βίᾳ εἰσῆλθεν</u> εἰς τὸ τῶν σοφῶν <u>φροντιστήριον</u>;
    Στρ   ἐγώ, ὁ Στρεψιάδης. ἀλλὰ οὐ βίᾳ εἰσῆλθον.
    Σωκ   διὰ τί πάρει, ὦ <u>ἐφήμερε</u>; διὰ τί εἰσῆλθες;
5   Στρ   ἐθέλω <u>παρὰ</u> σοῦ μανθάνειν. ἤκουσα γὰρ περὶ σοῦ ὡς σοφοῦ
           ὄντος. καὶ ὁ <u>μαθητὴς</u> πολλὰ εἶπε περὶ τῆς <u>ἀστρονομίας</u>, τῆς
           <u>γεωμετρίας</u>, τῶν <u>βολβῶν</u>, τῆς ἐμῆς οἰκίας, τῶν <u>Λακεδαιμονίων</u>
           ἐγγὺς ὄντων ...
    Σωκ   μωρὸς εἶ σὺ καὶ <u>ἄγροικος</u>.
10   Στρ   <u>κάτεχε</u> τὴν ὀργήν, ὦ Σώκρατες. ἀλλὰ τί πράσσεις ἐν τῇδε τῇ
           <u>κρεμάθρᾳ</u> ὤν;
    Σωκ   <u>ἀεροβάτης</u> ὢν περὶ τοῦ <u>ἡλίου</u> <u>φροντίζω</u>.
    Στρ   διὰ τί ἀπὸ κρεμάθρας, ἀλλ᾽ οὐκ ἀπὸ τῆς γῆς; τί εὑρίσκεις, ἢ τί
           μανθάνεις, ἐν τῇ κρεμάθρᾳ ὤν; πῶς τοῦτο χρήσιμόν ἐστιν;
15   Σωκ   οὐδὲν οἷός τ᾽ εἰμὶ μανθάνειν ἢ εὑρίσκειν <u>κάτω</u> φροντίζων.
           κωλύει γὰρ ἡ γῆ τὴν <u>φροντίδα</u>.
    Στρ   ἀλλ᾽, ὦ Σώκρατες, διὰ τί οὐ καταβαίνεις; ἐγὼ γὰρ εἰς τὸ
           φροντιστήριον ἦλθον διότι ὑπὸ τῶν <u>χρηστῶν</u> ἐδιωκόμην,
           <u>ὑπόχρεως</u> ὢν καὶ πολλὰ χρήματα <u>ὀφείλων</u>.
20   Σωκ   ἀλλὰ πῶς τοῦτο πάσχεις;
    Στρ   ὁ μὲν <u>υἱὸς</u> <u>ἱππομανής</u> ἐστιν, ἐγὼ δὲ ὑπόχρεως. οἱ γὰρ ἵπποι τὰ

Σωκρατίδιον	dear little Socrates (*diminutive, expressing affection*)
ἀληθῶς	truly, really
βία -ας ἡ	force
εἰσῆλθον	I came in (*irreg aor*)
φροντιστήριον -ου τό	Think-tank
ἐφήμερος -ον	creature of a day, short-lived
5 παρά	(+ *gen*) from (a person)
μαθητής -οῦ ὁ	student
ἀστρονομία -ας ἡ	astronomy
γεωμετρία -ας ἡ	earth measuring
βολβός -οῦ ὁ	truffle
Λακεδαιμόνιοι -ων οἱ	Spartans
ἄγροικος -ου ὁ	ignoramus, boor
10 κατέχω	I restrain
κρεμάθρα -ας ἡ	hanging basket
ἀεροβάτης -ου ὁ	walker on air
ἥλιος -ου ὁ	sun
φροντίζω	I think
15 κάτω	down below
φροντίς -ίδος ἡ	thought process
χρήστης -ου ὁ	creditor (*person owed money*)
ὑπόχρεως	in debt
ὀφείλω	I owe
υἱός -οῦ ὁ	son
20 ἱππομανής	horse-mad

χρήματα ἐσθίουσιν. ἀεὶ δὲ ὑπὸ τῶν <u>χρηστῶν</u> διώκομαι. ἀλλὰ
διδασκέ με ἐκεῖνον τὸν <u>λόγον</u> τὸν <u>θαυμάσιον</u>. πολλὰ γὰρ περὶ
τοῦ λόγου ἤκουσα.

25 Σωκ τίς ἐστιν οὗτος ὁ λόγος;

Στρ διδασκέ με τὸν <u>ἄδικον</u> λόγον, τὸν τὰ <u>χρέα</u> παύοντα. τοῦτον γὰρ
τὸν λόγον μαθὼν τοὺς χρήστας πείσω λέγων <u>ὅτι</u> οὐδὲν <u>ὀφείλω</u>.

Σωκ πρῶτον μὲν ἐπὶ τῆς <u>κλίνης</u> <u>καθίζων</u> περὶ τοῦ βίου, τοῦ <u>υἱοῦ</u>, τῶν
χρέων <u>φρόντιζε</u>. <u>πόρον</u> οὖν <u>ἴσως</u> αὐτὸς εὑρήσεις ... *(pause)* ἆρα

30 <u>γνώμην</u> τινὰ ἔχεις;

Στρ τόδε μόνον, ὅτι οἱ ἐν τῇ κλίνῃ <u>κόρεις</u> ἐμὲ δεινῶς <u>δάκνουσιν</u>,
ὥσπερ οἱ <u>Κορίνθιοι</u> τοὺς Ἀθηναίους.

Σωκ <u>οὐδὲν λέγεις</u>, ὦ γέρον.

Στρ ἀλλὰ γνώμην τινὰ νῦν ἔχω.

35 Σωκ τὴν γνώμην λέγε.

Στρ τὴν <u>σελήνην</u> κλέψω.

Σωκ τί λέγεις; ἆρα τὴν σελήνην κλέψεις; πῶς τοῦτο χρήσιμον;

Στρ ἄκουε. οἱ γὰρ χρῆσται τὰ χρήματα συλλέγουσιν τῇ <u>νουμηνίᾳ</u>.
ἐγὼ οὖν τὴν σελήνην κλέψω. <u>ἔσται</u> οὖν οὐδεμία νουμηνία, καὶ

40 οἱ χρῆσται τὰ χρήματα οὐ συλλέξουσιν. καὶ ἐγὼ καλῶς <u>πράξω</u>,
οὐκέτι ὑπ' αὐτῶν διωκόμενος.

Σωκ <u>εἰς κόρακας</u>. μῶρος γὰρ εἶ καὶ <u>ἄγροικος</u>. οὐκέτι οὖν διδάξω σε,
<u>οὕτω</u> μῶρον ὄντα.

	χρήστης -ου ὁ	creditor
	λόγος -ου ὁ	(*here*) argument
	θαυμάσιος -α -ον	miraculous
25	ἄδικος -ον	unjust
	χρέα -ων τά	debt
	ὅτι	(*here*) that
	ὀφείλω	I owe
	κλίνη -ης ἡ	couch
	καθίζω	I sit
	υἱός -οῦ ὁ	son
	φροντίζω	I think
	πόρος -ου ὁ	way out, solution
	ἴσως	perhaps
30	γνώμη -ης ἡ	idea
	κόρεις -εων οἱ	bugs
	δάκνω	I bite
	Κορίνθιοι -ων οἱ	Corinthians (*enemies of the Athenians; the word also provides a pun on* κόρεις)
	οὐδὲν λέγω	I talk rubbish
35	σελήνη -ης ἡ	moon
	νουμηνία -ας ἡ	(day of) new moon
	ἔσται	there will be
40	πράσσω *fut* πράξω	I do, I fare
	εἰς κόρακας	to the crows! (*i.e.* go to hell!)
	ἄγροικος -ου ὁ	ignoramus, boor
	οὕτω	so

Comparison of adjectives

An ordinary adjective (e.g. σοφός = wise) is called the *positive*: it simply states that the person or thing has that quality, but is not commenting on the extent. To make a comparison with others, we use the *comparative* (English *-er*, or *more* ~), often followed by *than*. To state that the quality exists in a very high degree, we use the *superlative* (English *very* ~ or *[the] ~est*). As in English, the definite article with the superlative implies <u>the</u> ~ *est*, and is naturally followed by a genitive *of (the group)*.

• In Greek the basic *comparative* form for regular adjectives ends in -τερος.

• And the basic *superlative* form ends in -τατος.

• These are normally put onto the stem after either *omicron* or *omega*:
e.g.   δειν-ό-τερος   δειν-ό-τατος
         σοφ-ώ-τερος   σοφ-ώ-τατος

• This works on a compensation principle. If the last or only syllable of the adjective stem is *long* (usually meaning it contains a long vowel or diphthong), it adds the *short* omicron. If the last or only syllable of the adjective stem is *short* (containing a short vowel, alone or followed by only one consonant) it adds the *long* omega: δειν- is long and so adds omicron, σοφ- is short and so adds omega.

• The comparative and superlative decline like ordinary adjectives. The comparative goes (in the nominative singular, across the genders) -ος -α -ον (like φίλιος), the superlative goes -ος -η -ον (like σοφός itself). This is because the comparative stem (i.e. after adding -οτερ- or -ωτερ-, but before the ending itself) ends in rho (regarded as equivalent to a vowel, as in the noun χώρα) whilst the superlative stem ends in the consonant tau. Hence:

comparatives
δεινότερος -α -ον
σοφώτερος -α -ον

superlatives
δεινότατος -η -ον
σοφώτατος -η -ον

• To express *than* after a comparative, the usual method is to use ἤ (= *than*), with the noun after it in the same case as the noun with which it is being compared.

e.g.   ὁ παῖς σοφώτερός ἐστιν ἢ ὁ γέρων.
        The boy is wiser than the old man.
        (*both nouns nominative, because the verb could be supplied again with the old man as subject:* The boy is wiser than the old man <u>is</u>.)

οὐδένα φίλον ἔχομεν σοφώτερον ἢ τὸν κριτήν.
We have no friend wiser than the judge.
(*both nouns accusative, because the verb could be supplied again with the judge as object:* We have no friend wiser than we have the judge [as a friend].)

• However it is also possible, in simple comparisons, to miss out the word for *than* and put the second noun into the gentitive. This is called the *genitive of comparison* (like the Latin ablative of comparison; whilst the use of ἤ corresponds to Latin *quam*).

e.g.   ὁ παῖς σοφώτερός ἐστι τοῦ γέροντος.
The boy is wiser than the old man.

(*no difference of meaning from the other version, but literally:* The boy is wiser - *or* rather wise (*another meaning of the comparative*) - [by the standard] of the old man.)

Exercise 7.23

Give the comparative (masculine nominative singular) of:
1   ἀνδρεῖος
2   μακρός*
3   φίλιος
4   μῶρος
5   χαλεπός

* even though the alpha is short, the two following consonants here make the syllable of the stem long

Exercise 7.24

Give the superlative (masculine nominative singular) of:
1   μῶρος
2   ἐλεύθερος
3   νέος
4   ἑτοῖμος
5   ἀνδρεῖος

Exercise 7.25

Translate into English:
1   ὁ στρατηγὸς μωρότερός ἐστιν ἢ ὁ δοῦλος.
2   οὐδεὶς κίνδυνος δεινότερός ἐστι τῆς θαλάσσης.
3   ἆρα ἡ κόρη σοφωτέρα ἐστὶν ἢ ὁ παῖς;
4   οἱ πολῖται ἀνδρειότατοι ἦσαν.
5   αὕτη ἡ βίβλος νεωτάτη ἐστίν.
6   ὁ ἀνδρειότατος τῶν πολιτῶν ὑπὸ πάντων ἐθαυμάζετο.
7   τὸ ναυτικὸν ἑτοιμότερον ἦν τοῦ στρατοῦ.
8   ὁ σοφώτατος κριτὴς πρὸς τὴν νῆσον ἐπέμπετο.
9   ἥδε ἡ θεὰ φιλιωτέρα ἢ ἐκείνη.
10   οὗτος ἀνδρειότατός ἐστι τῶν νῦν.

Exercise 7.26
The Wisdom of Socrates

In 399 BC, at the age of 70, Socrates was put on trial, accused of corrupting the young men of Athens with dangerous (mainly political) ideas, and of not believing in the gods of the city. We shall return to his trial and death in Chapter 8 (by then you may have formed an opinion about how justified the charges were). Here Socrates, while defending himself in court, looks back to the early days when he began to ask philosophical questions of himself and others. The oracle at Delphi in central Greece was the most famous in the ancient world, consulted by both states and individuals on important questions. The replies of the god Apollo were mediated though an old woman called the Pythia, whose ecstatic utterances were put into intelligible form by priests.

ὁ δὲ Σωκράτης, καίπερ σοφώτατός τε καὶ <u>δικαιότατος</u> ὤν, <u>ἠναγκάζετο</u>
<u>ἀπολογίαν</u> περὶ τοῦ βίου ἐν τῷ <u>δικαστηρίῳ</u> λέγειν· καὶ <u>ἤδη</u> γέρων ἦν.
<u>ἐδικάζετο</u> γὰρ ὡς τούς τε νεανίας <u>διαφθείρων</u> καὶ τοὺς θεοὺς οὐ
<u>νομίζων</u>. "ὦ Ἀθηναῖοι," <u>ἔφη</u>, "τὸν <u>θόρυβον</u> <u>κατέχετε</u>. οὐ γὰρ <u>μέγα λέγω</u>.
5   περὶ δὲ τῆς ἐμῆς σοφίας, εἴ τινα ἔχω, <u>μάρτυς</u> ἐστὶν ὁ ἐν <u>Δελφοῖς</u> θεός.
περὶ δὲ τοῦ <u>Χαιρεφῶντος</u> ἠκούσατε πάντες. οὗτος γὰρ ὁ ἐμὸς φίλος <u>ἐκ</u>
<u>νέου</u> ἦν. ὁ δὲ Χαιρεφῶν εἰς Δελφοὺς <u>ποτε</u> ἦλθεν. γιγνώσκειν γὰρ ἤθελε
εἴ τίς ἐστι σοφώτερος ἢ ὁ Σωκράτης. ἡ δὲ <u>Πυθία</u> 'οὐδείς,' ἔφη, 'σοφώτερός
ἐστιν'. ὁ δὲ Χαιρεφῶν <u>ὕστερον</u> ἀπέθανεν, ἀλλὰ ὁ ἐμὸς <u>ἀδελφὸς</u> μάρτυς
10   ἐστὶ τούτων. ἐγὼ δὲ τοὺς τοῦ Ἀπόλλωνος λόγους ἀκούσας ἐθαύμασα·
τί οὖν λέγει ὁ θεός; ἆρα <u>αἴνιγμά</u> ἐστιν; ἐγὼ γὰρ <u>οὐδαμῶς</u> σοφός εἰμι.
διὰ τί λέγει ὁ Ἀπόλλων ὅτι σοφώτατός εἰμι; οὐ γὰρ <u>ψευδομάρτυς</u> ἐστὶν

	δίκαιος -α -ον	just
	ἀναγκάζω	I force, I compel
	ἀπολογία -ας ἡ	defence, speech in defence
	δικαστήριον -ου τό	lawcourt
	ἤδη	now, already
	δικάζω	I try (*in court*), I put on trial
	διαφθείρω	*lit* I destroy, (*here*) I corrupt
	νομίζω	(*here*) I believe in
	ἔφη	he said (*usually interrupting direct quote*)
	θόρυβος -ου ὁ	commotion
	κατέχω	I restrain
	μέγα λέγω	I boast (*lit* talk big)
5	μάρτυς -υρος ὁ	witness
	Δελφοί -ῶν οἱ	Delphi
	Χαιρεφῶν -ῶντος ὁ	Chaerephon
	ἐκ νέου	from youth
	ποτε	(*not in a question*) once
	Πυθία -ας ἡ	Pythia (*priestess of Apollo at Delphi*)
	ὕστερον	later
	ἀδελφός -οῦ ὁ	brother
10	Ἀπόλλων -ωνος ὁ	Apollo
	αἴνιγμα -ατος τό	riddle
	οὐδαμῶς	in no way
	ψευδομάρτυς -υρος ὁ	false witness

21

ὁ θεός. τέλος δὲ τὴν <u>ἀλήθειαν</u> ἔμαθον. πολλοὶ μὲν γὰρ λέγουσιν <u>ὅτι</u>
σοφοί εἰσιν, οὐκ ὄντες· ἐγὼ δὲ <u>οἶδα</u> ὅτι οὐδὲν οἶδα. τούτῳ οὖν σοφώτερός
15 εἰμι τῶν ἄλλων πολιτῶν."

ἀλήθεια -ας ἡ	truth
ὅτι	that
οἶδα	I know

NB: from the vocabulary for this passage, note the important word ἔφη = *he/she said*, usually placed a few
words inside, and interrupting, quotation of the speaker's actual words. In translation it is often better moved
to the beginning or end of the quoted words.

Comparison of adverbs

As we saw in Chapter 3, most ordinary adjectives can be made into adverbs by changing the
-ων of the genitive plural to -ως:

σοφός	wise
σοφῶς	wisely

• The comparative adverb is the same as the *neuter <u>singular</u>* of the comparative adjective:

σοφώτερον	more wisely

• The superlative adverb is the same as the *neuter plural* of the superlative adjective:

σοφώτατα	very wisely, most wisely

• It is easy to see how these formations have come about:

σοφώτατα εἶπεν.	*literally* He said very wise things.
is of course equivalent to	He spoke very wisely.

• Adverbs do not change their endings. An adverb usually goes just in front of the verb.

Exercise 7.27

Give the Greek for:
1   More strangely
2   Very dangerously
3   Most bravely
4   More stupidly
5   Very usefully

Exercise 7.28

Translate into English:
1   ὁ παῖς σοφώτερον εἶπεν ἢ ὁ γέρων.
2   οἱ ἐν τῇ κώμῃ τὰς πύλας ἀνδρειότατα ἐφύλασσον.
3   ἐκεῖνος ὁ δοῦλος μωρότερός ἐστι τῶν ἄλλων, καὶ μωρότερον λέγει.

4	τίς τῶν λεόντων φιλιώτατα προσβαίνει;
5	ὁ τοῦ κριτοῦ δοῦλος σοφώτατα γράφει.
6	ὁ ἄγγελος χρησιμώτερον εἶπεν ἢ ὁ στρατηγός.
7	οἱ ἡμέτεροι σύμμαχοι ἐν τῷ πολέμῳ δεινότατα ἔπαθον.
8	τὰ τῶν πολεμίων ὑπὸ τῶν πολιτῶν ἀνδρείως ἐκλέπτετο.
9	οὗτοι οἱ παῖδες μωρότερον ἔγραψαν ἢ ἐκεῖνοι.
10	οἱ στρατιῶται πρὸ τῶν πυλῶν ἀνδρειότατα ἔμειναν.

Exercise 7.29

Translate into Greek:
1 The messenger spoke very wisely.
2 The sailors suffered more terribly than the soldiers.
3 This slave teaches in a very useful way.
4 The general very stupidly trusted the letter.
5 The gates are being more bravely guarded by us than by the allies.

Ten more adjectives:
1	ἄθλιος -α -ον	miserable, wretched
2	ἄξιος -α -ον	worthy, deserving (of, + *gen*)
3	ἀρχαῖος -α -ον	old, ancient
4	δῆλος -η -ον	clear
5	δίκαιος -α -ον	just, right
6	ἱερός -ά -όν	holy, sacred
7	ἰσχυρός -ά -όν*	strong
8	πιστός -ή -όν †	trustworthy, faithful
9	πλούσιος -α -ον	rich, wealthy
10	ὑψηλός -ή -όν	high

* Here it is not easily deducible whether the upsilon, and hence the last syllable of the stem, is long or short: in fact it is long, so the comparative and superlative are -οτερος, -οτατος (not -ωτερος, -ωτατος). Problematic instances like this are rare.

† Here, although the iota is short, the syllable is made long by the two following consonants, so the comparative and superlative are -οτερος, -οτατος. (We saw that the same is true of the alpha in μακρός.)

Exercise 7.30

Translate into English:
1	ὁ ξένος ἀξιώτερός ἐστι τῆς τιμῆς ἢ πάντες οἱ στρατιῶται.
2	ὁ τῶν συμμάχων ἄγγελος δίκαιος ὢν δικαίως λέγει.
3	πᾶσαι αἱ ἐν τῇ κώμῃ ἀθλιώτατα ἔπασχον.
4	αὕτη ἐστὶν ἀρχαιοτάτη τῶν βίβλων.
5	οἱ παῖδες ὑπὸ τοῦ διδασκάλου δήλως καὶ σοφῶς ἐδιδάσκοντο.
6	ἡ τῆς θεᾶς οἰκία ἱερωτάτη ἐστίν.
7	οἱ ἰσχυρότατα φυλασσόμενοι οὐδὲν ἤκουσαν.
8	ὅδε ὁ ἄγγελος πιστότερον εἶπεν ἢ ἐκεῖνος.

9   ὁ ἄρχων πλουσιώτερός ἐστι τῶν ἄλλων πολιτῶν.
10   αἱ τοῦ στρατοπέδου πύλαι ὑψηλόταταί εἰσιν.

Exercise 7.31

Translate into Greek:
1   The faithful slave spoke very clearly.
2   The giant is stronger than all the soldiers.
3   The laws are worthy of honour.
4   The boy very foolishly ran away.
5   The village being guarded very bravely by the soldiers is ancient.

Relative clauses

Consider the following sentences:
     (a) The slave <u>who</u> was running away fell into the river.
     (b) Who are the strangers <u>whom</u> the soldiers are guarding?
     (c) The girl <u>whose</u> book I have is not here.
     (d) The old man <u>for whom</u> I provided dinner is very wise.

As we saw in Chapter 5, sentence (a) would naturally be translated with a participle for the *who ...* :
     ὁ δοῦλος ὁ φεύγων εἰς τὸν ποταμὸν ἔπεσεν.

Sentence (b) could also be translated with a participle, but only by recasting in the passive:
     Who are the strangers (who are) being guarded by the soldiers?
     τίνες εἰσὶν οἱ ξένοι οἱ ὑπὸ τῶν στρατιωτῶν φυλασσόμενοι;

Sentences (c) and (d) however could not easily be translated with a participle. For them a relative clause must be used; for (a) and (b) a relative clause could be used as an alternative to the participle construction. A relative clause is introduced by the relative pronoun (equivalent to Latin *qui, quae, quod*). The form of this is very straightforward:

relative pronoun:

	m	*f*	*n*	
sg	ὅς	ἥ	ὅ	who, which
	ὅν	ἥν	ὅ	
	οὗ	ἧς	οὗ	
	ᾧ	ᾗ	ᾧ	
pl	<u>οἵ</u>	<u>αἵ</u>	ἅ	
	οὕς	ἅς	ἅ	
	ὧν	ὧν	ὧν	
	οἷς	αἷς	οἷς	

• This is essentially just the endings for a 2-1-2 adjective like σοφός (or the nouns λόγος, τιμή, δῶρον) with a rough breathing, except that (as usual for pronouns) the neuter nominative and accusative singular is -ο rather than -ον.

• The three bits underlined are spelled in the same way as the equivalent parts of the definite article, and the neuter nominative/accusative singular in the same way as a different part of the article, namely the masculine nominative singular. Ambiguity is avoided by context, and by the fact that <u>the relative pronoun always has an accent</u> (whilst corresponding parts of the article normally do not).

• A relative clause has a finite verb (i.e. a verb with a tense and a person ending). As in Latin, the relative pronoun agrees with the *antecedent* (the noun in the main clause it refers to) in *number* and *gender*, but not necessarily in *case*. This is because the relative clause has its own grammar, equivalent to a separate sentence:

This is the slave whom I saw

equates to

This is the slave (*nominative*)

plus

I saw him (*accusative*)

hence

οὗτός ἐστιν ὁ δοῦλος <u>ὃν</u> εἶδον.

• Going back to our example sentences:

(a) The slave who was running away fell into the river.

This is straightforward because the slave is the subject both in the main clause and in the relative clause, hence:

ὁ δοῦλος ὃς ἔφευγεν εἰς τὸν ποταμὸν ἔπεσεν.

(b) Who are the strangers whom the soldiers are guarding?

This has the strangers as the subject in the main clause, but the object in the relative clause (the soldiers are guarding *them*), hence:

τίνες εἰσὶν οἱ ξένοι οὓς οἱ σρατιῶται φυλάσσουσιν;

(c) The girl whose book I have is not here.

This has the girl as the subject in the main clause, but in the genitive in the relative clause (I have *the girl's* book), hence:

ἡ κόρη ἧς τὴν βίβλον ἔχω οὐ πάρεστιν.

(d) The old man <u>for whom</u> I provided dinner is very wise.

This has the old man as subject in the main clause, but in the dative in the relative clause (I provided dinner *for him*), hence:

ὁ γέρων ᾧ δεῖπνον παρέσχον σοφώτατός ἐστιν.

• Although both the use of the relative pronoun and (for some bits) the form of it put it very close to the article + participle construction, it is important to understand how the grammar differs:

25

(a) οἱ δοῦλοι οἳ φεύγουσι μῶροι εἰσίν. (*relative clause*)

(b) οἱ δοῦλοι οἱ φεύγοντες μῶροι εἰσίν. (*article + participle*)

These seem and are very similar as translations of:

The slaves who are running away are stupid.

However the differences are more apparent if we translate by both methods the sentence:

We saw the slaves who were running away.

(i) εἴδομεν τοὺς δούλους οἳ ἔφευγον. (*relative clause*)

(ii) εἴδομεν τοὺς δούλους τοὺς φεύγοντας. (*article + participle*)

(i) Here the relative clause has followed the rule about agreement: number and gender the same as the antecedent δούλους (which is the object in the main clause), but with the relative pronoun in the nominative because it is the subject in its own clause, equivalent to *they*. The finite verb *were running away* is in the imperfect tense as the meaning requires.

(ii) Here the participle is still accusative, agreeing with its noun in number, gender *and case*: as usual with participles, it is behaving as an adjective (*the running-away slaves* is grammatically equivalent to e.g. *the foolish slaves*). And its tense is present because the tense of the participle is in relation to the tense of the main verb: it was present *at the time* when the main action (in the aorist) happened. (This explains, incidentally, why there is no imperfect participle: if a sentence seems to call for one, the *present* participle is required.)

• The relative pronoun *who, which* (ὅς ἥ ὅ) must of course be distinguished from the interrogative pronoun *who? which? what?* (τίς; τί; *gen* τίνος;).

• The use of *whom* in English for cases of *who* other than the nominative is one of the few surviving examples of inflection. But it is dropping out of use: in the sentence

The woman *whom I saw* is not here

the relative clause would commonly be expressed by (the strictly ungrammatical)

The woman *who I saw* ...

or   The woman *that I saw* ...

or just   The woman *I saw* ... (leaving out the pronoun altogether)

• A relative clause (ὁ δοῦλος ὃς ἔφευγεν ἔπεσεν) is commonly equivalent to the *attributive* use of the participle (ὁ δοῦλος ὁ φεύγων ἔπεσεν = *The slave who was running away fell*, with repeated article, often implying e.g. *as opposed to others who were not running away*). But it can also replace the *circumstantial* use: ὁ δοῦλος φεύγων ἔπεσεν = *The slave, who was running away (at the time), fell* (equivalent to *when he was ...*): here only the commas in English make the distinction between the two slightly different uses of *who*.

• The version of the article + participle which has no noun (οἱ φεύγοντες = *those running away*) could in theory be expressed, using the relative construction, by e.g. ἐκεῖνοι οἳ (relative) φεύγουσιν. But the participle version (where the insertion of ἐκεῖνοι would be wrong) is much preferred for this idiom.

26

Ten more nouns like λόγος (all masculine):

1	ἀγρός	field
2	ἀδελφός	brother
3	αἰχμάλωτος	prisoner (of war)
4	ἄνεμος	wind
5	ἔνοικος	inhabitant
6	ἰατρός	doctor
7	λίθος	stone
8	σῖτος	food
9	σκότος	darkness
10	χρυσός	gold

Exercise 7.32

Translate into English:

1 οἱ αἰχμάλωτοι οὓς ἐκεῖ ἐλάβομεν ἀνδρεῖοί εἰσιν.
2 ὁ δοῦλος ἔκλεψε τὸν χρυσὸν ὃν ὁ στρατιώτης ἐφύλασσεν.
3 ὁ παῖς ᾧ τὸ δῶρον παρέσχομεν οὐ πάρεστιν.
4 οὗτός ἐστιν ὁ ἰατρὸς οὗ τοῖς λόγοις ἀεὶ πιστεύω.
5 ποῦ εὗρες τὸν λίθον ᾧ* τὸν γίγαντα ἀπέκτεινας;
6 ὁ σῖτος ὃν ἐν ἐκείνῃ τῇ οἰκίᾳ ἐφάγετε κακὸς ἦν.
7 ἆρα οἱ ἄγγελοι ὧν τοὺς λόγους ἠκούσαμεν πιστοί εἰσιν;
8 τὸν χρυσὸν ὃν ἐν τῷ ἀγρῷ ἔλιπες οὐχ οἷοί τ' ἦμεν ἐν τῷ σκότῳ εὑρίσκειν.
9 ὁ ποιητὴς οὗ τοὺς λόγους ἐθαύμαζες ὁ ἐμὸς ἀδελφός ἐστιν.
10 ἆρα ἡ νῆσος ἣν εἴδομεν ἐνοίκους ἔχει;

*note that the instrumental use of the dative is found not only with passive verbs

Exercise 7.33

Translate into Greek (using relative clauses):

1 The prisoners who are in the prison are very miserable.
2 Did you (*sg*) see the doctor who sent the letter?
3 The boy whom you sent is very stupid.
4 The giant who eats men is not in the field now.
5 The stones which were being thrown by the boys were very big.

Ten more nouns like τιμή (all feminine):

1	Ἀθῆναι (*plural*)	Athens (*singular* Ἀθήνη = *the goddess Athene*)
2	ἀνάγκη	necessity, compulsion
3	ἀρετή	excellence, courage, virtue*
4	ἀρχή	rule, empire; *also* beginning **
5	δίκη	right, lawsuit, penalty
6	κεφαλή	head
7	σιγή	silence

27

8	Σπάρτη	(the city of) Sparta †
9	τέχνη	skill
10	ὕλη	wood, forest

* these meanings are linked by the idea of *efficiency in fulfilling a role*
** these meanings are linked by the idea of being *first* or *in leading position*
† Λακεδαίμων -ονος ἡ (Lacedaemon) is used for Spartan territory as a whole

Background: Protagoras

Protagoras (born about 485 BC) was the first and most famous of the Sophists. Born in Abdera (in the far north of Greece) he gravitated like many others to Athens. The wealth, democratic government, and rich cultural life of the city offered unrivalled scope. Protagoras professed to teach ἀρετή (*excellence*, but better translated in some contexts as *success* or *virtue*). He interpreted this as mainly practical and material success in life, through the efficient management of public and private affairs. He appears as the opponent of Socrates in a famous dialogue by Plato named after him. Plato's dialogues are written almost like the text of a play: the conversations they supposedly record often took place years before they were written, so they should be taken as literary works blending fact and fiction, with the characters expressing views with which they were generally associated, rather than their actual words on any one occasion.

Protagoras is especially associated with the sophistic doctrine of relativism, summed up by his slogan 'Man is the measure of all things'. According to this view, there is no absolute and universal truth, valid for all times and places: we must simply accept that something is true for an individual if he takes it to be so. The experience of travel and the observation of cultural diversity (some societies bury their dead, some burn them, some even eat them) made such an outlook seem compelling in this period. It was often accompanied, as in Protagoras' case, by an agnostic attitude towards the gods. Socrates had definite (if individual) religious views. He interpreted ἀρετή in a different, more strictly moral way, and did not think it was necessarily teachable. He (and even more strongly Plato, whose mouthpiece he is) believed in absolute values, seeing relativism as dangerous. Nonetheless Protagoras is treated with considerable respect for his personal and intellectual integrity.

Exercise 7.34

Protagoras comes to town

Socrates relates how Hippocrates came to tell him Protagoras had arrived in Athens. He makes a comparison with the young student's namesake Hippocrates of Cos, the most famous Greek doctor.

τῆς δὲ παρελθούσης νυκτὸς Ἱπποκράτης ὁ τοῦ Ἀπολλοδώρου υἱὸς τὴν ἐμὴν θύραν βακτηρίᾳ σφόδρα ἔκοψεν. ἐπεὶ δὲ ὁ δοῦλος ἤνοιξε τὴν θύραν εἰστρέχων εἶπεν, "ὦ Σώκρατες, ἔτι καθεύδεις;" καὶ ἐγὼ τὴν φωνὴν αὐτοῦ ἀκούων εἶπον, "οὗτός ἐστιν Ἱπποκράτης. ἆρα νέον τι ἀγγέλλεις, ὦ φίλε;"

παρῆλθον	(*irreg aor*) I passed, I went by
Ἱπποκράτης ὁ	Hippocrates
Ἀπολλόδωρος -ου ὁ	Apollodorus
υἱός -οῦ ὁ	son
βακτηρία -ας ἡ	stick
σφόδρα	violently
κόπτω ἔκοψα	I knock (on)
ἤνοιξα	(*irreg aor*) I opened
καθεύδω	I sleep

28

"ἀγαθὰ <u>δή</u>."
"τί οὖν ἐστιν;"
"<u>Πρωταγόρας</u> ἐν Ἀθήναις πάρεστιν."
"<u>ἤδη</u> γιγνώσκω· ἀλλὰ τί σοι τοῦτο; ἆρα ὁ Πρωταγόρας ἔβλαψέ σε;"
"<u>νὴ</u> τοὺς θεούς," ἔφη ὁ Ἱπποκράτης, "διότι οὗτος μόνος ἐστὶ σοφός, ἐγὼ
10   δὲ τῆς σοφίας αὐτοῦ οὐ <u>μετέχω</u>."
ἐγὼ δ' εἶπον, "ἀλλὰ <u>εἴ</u> τις <u>ἱκανὰ</u> χρήματα παρέχων πείθει αὐτόν, ὁ
Πρωταγόρας ἐθέλει διδάσκειν τε καὶ τῆς σοφίας <u>μοῖράν</u> τινα παρέχειν."
"παρέξω οὖν," ἔφη ὁ Ἱπποκράτης, "οὐ μόνον τὰ ἐμὰ χρήματα, ἀλλὰ καὶ
τὰ τῶν φίλων. πάντες γὰρ λέγουσιν <u>ὅτι</u> ὁ Πρωταγόρας σοφώτατός ἐστιν."
15   "ἀλλὰ διὰ τί ἐθέλεις <u>μαθητὴς</u> τοῦ Πρωταγόρου εἶναι, χρήματα παρέχων;
ὁ γὰρ ἄλλος Ἱπποκράτης, ὃς τοῦ σοῦ ὀνόματος μετέχει, ἰατρὸς <u>κλεινός</u>
ἐστιν· οἱ οὖν μαθηταὶ αὐτοῦ τὴν <u>ἰατρικὴν</u> μανθάνουσι, καὶ ἐθέλουσι
ταύτης τῆς τέχνης μετέχειν. καὶ εἴ τις λέγει αὐτοῖς 'χρήματα τούτῳ
παρέχετε ὡς τίνι ὄντι;' οἱ μαθηταὶ ἀεὶ λέγουσιν 'ὡς ἰατρῷ ὄντι'. τὰ γὰρ
20   χρήματα παρέχουσιν αὐτῷ, καὶ <u>δι' ὀλίγου</u> οἱ μαθηταὶ αὐτοὶ ἰατροί εἰσιν.
ἀλλὰ τί περὶ τοῦ Πρωταγόρου λέξομεν; ὡς τίνι ὄντι ἐθέλεις αὐτῷ τά τε
χρήματα παρέχειν καὶ τὴν <u>ψυχὴν</u> <u>ἐπιτρέπειν;</u>"
"<u>σοφιστὴς</u> ἐστιν," ἔφη ὁ <u>νεανίας</u>.
"χρήματα οὖν παρέξεις αὐτῷ ὡς σοφιστῇ ὄντι;"
25   "<u>ναί</u>."
"καὶ ἐθέλεις αὐτὸς σοφιστὴς εἶναι;"
ὁ Ἱπποκράτης οὐδὲν εἶπεν. ἐγὼ δὲ εἶπον, "δῆλόν ἐστιν ὅτι <u>ἐρυθραίνω</u> σε.
ἆρα οὖν <u>αἰσχρόν</u> ἐστι τοῦτο;"
"οὐκ ἐθέλω σοφιστὴς εἶναι."
30   "τί οὖν;"
"ἐθέλω τὴν σοφίαν μανθάνειν."
"ἀλλὰ περὶ τίνος σοφός ἐστιν ὁ σοφιστής;"

5	δή	indeed
	Πρωταγόρας -ου ὁ	Protagoras
	ἤδη	already
	νή	yes, by ... ! (+ *acc*)
10	μετέχω	I share, I have a share of (+ *gen*)
	εἰ	if
	ἱκανός -ή -όν	enough, sufficient
	μοῖρα -ας ἡ	part, share
	ὅτι	that
15	μαθητής -οῦ ὁ	student
	κλεινός -ή -όν	famous
	ἰατρική -ῆς ἡ	(the art of) medicine
20	δι' ὀλίγου	soon
	ψυχή -ῆς ἡ	soul
	ἐπιτρέπω	I entrust (X *acc* to Y *dat*)
	σοφιστής -οῦ ὁ	Sophist
25	ναί	yes
	ἐρυθραίνω	I make (someone) blush
	αἰσχρός -ά -όν	shameful

"οἱ <u>μαθηταὶ</u> αὐτοῦ οἷοί τ' εἰσὶ σοφώτατα λέγειν."
"ἀλλὰ περὶ τίνος; οἱ γὰρ τοῦ ἰατροῦ μαθηταὶ οἷοί τ' εἰσὶ περὶ τῆς
35 <u>ἰατρικῆς</u> σοφώτατα λέγειν. ἀλλὰ τί διδάσκει ὁ σοφιστής;"
"τοῦτο, ὦ Σώκρατες," ἔφη ὁ Ἱπποκράτης, "οὐχ οἷός τ' εἰμὶ λέγειν."
"δῆλον οὖν ἐστιν ὅτι εἰς κίνδυνον εἰσβαίνεις, οὐ γιγνώσκων τὰ ὑπὸ τοῦ
Πρωταγόρου διδάσκομενα. <u>ἐπιτρέπεις</u> γὰρ τὴν <u>ψυχὴν</u> αὐτῷ οὐχ οἷός
τ' ὢν λέγειν <u>πότερον</u> ἀγαθός ἐστιν ὁ διδάσκαλος ἢ κακός."
40 "ἀλλὰ τίς ταῦτα <u>κρίνει</u>;"
"δῆλόν ἐστιν ὅτι ἤδη μαθητής τις εἶ ἄξιος τοῦ Πρωταγόρου."

30	μαθητής -οῦ ὁ	student
35	ἰατρική -ῆς ἡ	(the art of) medicine
	ἐπιτρέπω	I entrust (X *acc* to Y *dat*)
	ψυχή -ῆς ἡ	soul
	πότερον ... ἤ	whether ... or
40	κρίνω	I judge

Exercise 7.35 (Revision)

Translate into English:
1 ὁ τοῦ ἰατροῦ ἀδελφὸς ἐν τῇ ἐκκλησίᾳ σοφώτατα εἶπεν.
2 οἱ τὸν σῖτον ἐσθίοντες ξένοι εἰσίν.
3 τίς ἐστιν ὁ νέος ἔνοικος;
4 ἐκείνη ἡ οἰκία ἀρχαιοτάτη ἐστίν.
5 ὁ ἄνεμος τά τε δένδρα καὶ τὰς οἰκίας δεινότατα ἔβλαψεν.
6 τὰ πλοῖα τῷ ἀνέμῳ ἠλαύνετο.
7 ὁ γέρων λίθους ἰσχυρότερον βάλλει ἢ ὁ παῖς.
8 οἱ αἰχμάλωτοι, ὑπὸ τῶν ἐνοίκων διωκόμενοι, εἰς τὸν ποταμὸν
      εἰσέδραμον.
9 αἱ τὴν κώμην πέντε ὥρας φυλάξασαι ἄξιαί εἰσι τῆς μεγίστης τιμῆς.
10 τὸ πλοῖον ἐν ᾧ πρὸς τὴν νῆσον προσήλθομεν οὐκ ἔστιν ἐν τῷ λιμένι.

Exercise 7.36

Translate into English:
1 ἡ Ἀθήνη ἐκ τῆς τοῦ Διὸς κεφαλῆς ἐξῆλθεν.
2 ἆρα θαυμάζεις τὴν ἐκείνου τοῦ ποιητοῦ τέχνην;
3 οἱ αἰχμάλωτοι τὸν χρυσὸν ἐν τῇ ὕλῃ ἔκρυψαν.
4 ἡ ἀρετὴ ἣν ἐν τῇ μάχῃ εἴδομεν οὐ πολλάκις νῦν εὑρίσκεται.
5 οὐκ ἐθέλομεν τούτοις τοῖς λόγοις πιστεύειν, ἀλλὰ τῇ ἀνάγκῃ
      ἐλαυνόμεθα.
6 ἡ τοῦ ποιητοῦ τέχνη ὑπὸ πάντων ἐθαυμάζετο.
7 αἱ Ἀθῆναι ἐθαυμάζοντο ὡς ἀρχὴν μεγίστην λαβοῦσαι.
8 ἐν τῇ Σπάρτῃ οἱ νόμοι ὑπὸ πάντων ἰσχυρότατα φυλάσσονται.
9 πᾶσαι αἱ παροῦσαι τὰς οἰκίας σιγῇ* ἐφύλασσον.
10 οἱ πλουσιώτατοι οὐκ ἀεὶ τῆς τιμῆς ἀξιώτατοί εἰσιν.
      * the dative of σιγή is often used like an adverb: *in silence, silently*

Exercise 7.37

Translate into Greek:
1 The forest which I saw was very big.
2 The head of the giant is higher than the tree.
3 The disease is found by the skill of the doctor.
4 All the people present admired that courage.
5 I sent the boy whom I trusted to the village.

Ten more verbs, all with first (weak) aorists:

		aorist	aorist stem	
1	ἀναγκάζω	ἠνάγκασα	ἀναγκασ-	I force, I compel
2	ἁρπάζω	ἥρπασα	ἁρπασ-	I seize, I snatch
3	διαφθείρω	διέφθειρα	διαφθειρ-	I destroy, I corrupt
4	καθίζω	ἐκάθισα*	καθισ-	I sit
5	κολάζω	ἐκόλασα	κολασ-	I punish
6	κρύπτω	ἔκρυψα	κρυψ-	I hide
7	πράσσω	ἔπραξα	πραξ-	I do, I fare (well/badly etc)
8	σῴζω	ἔσωσα	σωσ-	I save
9	τρέπω	ἔτρεψα	τρεψ-	I turn
10	τύπτω	ἔτυψα	τυψ-	I hit, I strike

* although this is strictly a κατα- compound (with the prefix elided), in practice this has been forgotten, so the augment comes before rather than after the prefix

Exercise 7.38

Protagoras and his Teaching

A young man and an old man discuss the famous Sophist.

Νεανίας διὰ τί αἰσχρόν ἐστι τὸ τοῦ σοφιστοῦ ὄνομα; οὐδὲν γὰρ ἄλλο
ἐστὶν ὁ σοφιστὴς ἢ σοφός τις.
Γέρων ἀλλὰ οἱ νεανίαι πολλὰ χρήματα τοῖς σοφισταῖς παρέχουσιν
διδασκόμενοι.
5 Νε εἰκότως δή. οἱ γὰρ σοφισταὶ τήν τε σοφίαν καὶ τὴν ἀρετὴν
διδάσκουσιν.
Γε ἀλλὰ τί ἐστι τοῦτο τὸ χρῆμα, ᾧ τὸ ὄνομα 'ἀρετή' ἐστιν; ἆρα
διδακτόν τί ἐστιν; καὶ εἰ μή, τί διδάσκουσιν οἱ σοφισταί;

	αἰσχρός -ά -όν	shameful
	σοφιστής -οῦ ὁ	Sophist
5	εἰκότως	reasonably
	δή	indeed
	χρῆμα -ατος τό	thing
	διδακτός -ή -όν	teachable
	εἰ μή	if not

31

Νε περὶ τούτου οὐχ οἷός τ᾿ εἰμὶ λέγειν. οἱ μέντοι νεανίαι ταύτας τὰς

10 τέχνας μαθόντες τοὺς ἀκούοντας ἀεὶ πείθουσιν, καὶ τὰ <u>πολιτικὰ</u>
    σοφῶς πράσσουσιν.

Γε ἐγὼ δὲ περὶ τοῦ Πρωταγόρου κακὰ ἀκούω, ὅτι τοὺς νεανίας
    <u>παροχετεύει</u> δεινὰ λέγων.

Νε τίνα ταῦτα;

15 Γε λέγει ὁ Πρωταγόρας ὅτι πάντων <u>χρημάτων</u> <u>μέτρον</u> ἄνθρωπός
    ἐστιν.

Νε καὶ τὴν <u>ἀλήθειαν</u> λέγει. οὐ γὰρ οἷοί τ᾿ ἐσμὲν περὶ ὕδατος
    ἐν <u>ἀγγείῳ</u> λέγειν <u>πότερον</u> <u>θερμὸν</u> ἢ <u>ψυχρόν</u> ἐστι· τοῦτο ἕκαστος
    <u>διακρίνει</u>. <u>εἰ</u> τις <u>χειμῶνος</u> εἰς τὴν οἰκίαν εἰσβαίνει καὶ τὴν <u>χεῖρα</u>

20 εἰς τὸ ἀγγεῖον εἰσβάλλει, λέγει ὅτι τὸ ὕδωρ θερμόν ἐστιν. εἰ δέ
    τις ἐγγὺς τοῦ πυρὸς καθίζων τὰ αὐτὰ πράσσει, λέγει οὗτος
    ὅτι τὸ ὕδωρ ψυχρόν ἐστιν. καὶ <u>ἀμφότεροι</u> τὴν ἀλήθειαν
    λέγουσιν.

Γε ταῦτα <u>ἴσως</u> καλά. οὐ μέντοι περὶ ὕδατος ἀλλὰ περὶ τῆς τε

25 δικαιοσύνης καὶ τῆς ἀρετῆς λέγομεν.

Νε καὶ περὶ τούτων ἕκαστος διακρίνει.

Γε ἀλλὰ ταῦτα <u>ἀνομίαν</u> ἐν ταῖς Ἀθήναις παρέχει. καὶ λέγουσιν οἱ
    <u>σοφισταὶ</u> ὅτι οὐδέν ἐστιν ἡ δικαιοσύνη <u>εἰ μὴ</u> <u>ἐξουσία</u> τις τοῖς
    <u>κρατεροῖς</u> πράσσειν ὡς ἐθέλουσιν.

30 Νε οἱ μὲν τῶν σοφιστῶν ἴσως ταῦτα λέγουσιν, ὁ δὲ Πρωταγόρας
    διδάσκει τοὺς νεανίας τοὺς νόμους φυλάσσειν.

Γε ἀλλὰ καὶ εἰ ὁ Πρωταγόρας αὐτὸς ἀγαθός τις καὶ δίκαιός ἐστιν,
    τοὺς <u>μαθητὰς</u> εἰς κίνδυνον εἰσάγει οὐχ <u>ἑκών</u>. καὶ περὶ τῶν θεῶν
    τάδε τὰ δεινὰ λέγει· "περὶ τῶν θεῶν οὐχ οἷός τ᾿ εἰμὶ γιγνώσκειν

10	πολιτικά -ῶν τά	politics
	παροχετεύω	I lead astray
15	χρήματα -ων τά	(here) things
	μέτρον -ου τό	measure
	ἀλήθεια -ας ἡ	truth
	ἀγγεῖον -ου τό	bucket
	πότερον ... ἤ	whether ... or
	θερμός -ή -όν	warm, hot
	ψυχρος -α -ον	cold
	διακρίνω	I determine, I judge
	εἰ	if
	χειμών -ῶνος ὁ	winter
	χείρ χειρός ἡ	hand
20	ἀμφότεροι -αι -α	both
	ἴσως	perhaps
25	ἀνομία -ας ἡ	lawlessness
	σοφιστής -οῦ ὁ	Sophist
	εἰ μή	except
	ἐξουσία -ας ἡ	possibility, power
	κρατερός -ά -όν	strong
30	μαθητής -οῦ ὁ	student
	ἑκών -οῦσα -όν	willing(ly)

35	Νε	πότερόν εἰσιν ἢ μή, οὐδὲ <u>ὁποῖοί</u> εἰσιν. πολλὰ γὰρ κωλύει τὴν <u>ἐπιστήμην</u>· τὸ γὰρ <u>πρᾶγμα</u> χαλεπόν ἐστιν, καὶ ὁ τοῦ ἀνθρώπου βίος οὐ μακρός."

35   πότερόν εἰσιν ἢ μή, οὐδὲ <u>ὁποῖοί</u> εἰσιν. πολλὰ γὰρ κωλύει τὴν
     <u>ἐπιστήμην</u>· τὸ γὰρ <u>πρᾶγμα</u> χαλεπόν ἐστιν, καὶ ὁ τοῦ ἀνθρώπου
     βίος οὐ μακρός."

Νε   καὶ περὶ τούτων τὴν ἀλήθειαν λέγει. ἡμεῖς μὲν τοὺς ἡμετέρους
     θεοὺς <u>θεραπεύομεν</u>, οἱ δὲ ξένοι ἄλλους. καὶ οἱ μὲν τῶν
40   ἀνθρώπων τοὺς νεκροὺς θάπτουσιν, οἱ δὲ <u>καίουσιν</u> ἢ ἐσθίουσιν.

Γε   ἀλλὰ ταῦτα λέγοντες οἱ <u>σοφισταὶ</u> τὰ <u>πάτρια</u> διαφθείρουσιν. τοῖς
     γὰρ νεανίαις οἱ ἄριστοι διδάσκαλοι οὐχ οἱ σοφισταὶ ἀλλὰ οἱ
     ποιηταί εἰσιν.

Νε   ἀλλὰ τί λέγουσιν οἱ ποιηταὶ περὶ τῶν θεῶν; οὐχ ὅτι <u>ψεύδουσι</u>
45   καὶ κλέπτουσι καὶ <u>μοιχεύουσιν</u>;

Γε   οὐ πάντες οἱ ποιηταὶ ταῦτα λέγουσιν. οἱ γὰρ ποιηταὶ καὶ οἱ
     <u>πρόγονοι</u> πολλὰ καὶ κάλλιστα <u>παραδείγματα</u> παρέχουσιν, ἀφ᾽ ὧν*
     οἱ νεανίαι οἷοί τ᾽ εἰσὶ μανθάνειν. ταῦτα καὶ νῦν καὶ ἀεὶ λέξω.

Νε   σὺ μὲν ταῦτα λέγεις, ἄλλοι ἄλλα. τοῦτο δὲ <u>οὔπω</u> γιγνώσκομεν,
50   τίς τὴν ἀλήθειαν λέγει.

* as noted in Chapter 5, if elision leaves pi before a rough breathing, it changes to phi, the aspiration spreading from vowel to preceding consonant (compare the use of οὐχ before a rough breathing)

35	ἢ μή	or not
	ὁποῖος -α -ον	of what sort, what ... like
	ἐπιστήμη -ης ἡ	knowledge
	πρᾶγμα -ατος τό	matter
	θεραπεύω	I worship
40	καίω	I burn
	σοφιστής -οῦ ὁ	Sophist
	πάτρια -ων τά	ancestral customs, traditions
	ψεύδω	I tell lies
45	μοιχεύω	I commit adultery
	πρόγονος -ου ὁ	ancestor
	παράδειγμα -ατος τό	example
	οὔπω	not yet

Exercise 7.39

Translate into English:

1   οἱ αἰχμάλωτοι ὑπὸ τῶν στρατιωτῶν ἁρπάζονται.
2   οἱ ἐκ τοῦ δεσμωτηρίου φυγόντες ὑπὸ τῶν τῆς κώμης ἐνοίκων
    πολλάκις ἐσῴζοντο.
3   πῶς ἠνάγκασας τοὺς δούλους ταῦτα πράσσειν, ὦ στρατηγέ;
4   πάντες οἱ παρόντες πρὸς τὸν ποιητὴν τὰς κεφαλὰς ἔτρεψαν.
5   οἵδε οἱ σύμμαχοι ἐν τῷ πολέμῳ καλῶς ἔπραξαν.
6   οἱ ναῦται, τὸν γίγαντα τύψαντες, ἔλιπον τὴν νῆσον.
7   ὁ ἄνεμος διέφθειρεν ἐννέα δένδρα.
8   οἱ γέροντες πρὸ τοῦ ἱεροῦ σιγῇ ἐκάθιζον.
9   ποῦ ἔκρυψατε τὸν χρυσόν, ὦ παῖδες;
10 ἐθέλομεν κολάζειν τὸν ταῦτα πράξαντα.

Exercise 7.40

Give one English derivative from:
1   ἄνεμος
2   ἀρχαῖος
3   ἰατρός
4   κρύπτω
5   λίθος

Revision checkpoint

Make sure you know:
• comparison of adjectives, with rules about adding -οτερος, -οτατος or -ωτερος, -ωτατος
• comparison of adverbs
• relative pronoun
• relative clauses, with rules for agreement of relative pronoun with antecedent, and relation to article + participle construction

Exercise 7.41

Plato's Parable of the Cave (1)

Plato believed that there are two levels of reality: the ordinary everyday world we experience with the senses, and an eternal world lying beyond. He saw Socrates as pointing people towards this, and he saw an answer to the relativism of the Sophists in the 'Theory of Forms': the idea that there is an ideal model of every object and quality (a perfect chair, perfect courage) in the eternal world. One of his most famous dialogues The Republic *begins as a typical Socratic search for a definition, in this case of justice. In order to see the problem more clearly, Socrates proposes to talk about justice as it appears in a city-state before going on to justice as it appears in an individual. This provides the cue for Plato to describe his ideal society. During the course of the dialogue Socrates tells a parable to explain why the true structure of reality is not obvious to everyone. Plato also intends it as a comment on Socrates' own fate.*

ὁ Σωκράτης εἶπεν, "<u>εἰ</u> ἐθέλεις περὶ τοῦ ἡμετέρου βίου μανθάνειν, τόδε τὸ <u>εἴδωλον</u> παρέχω. οἱ ἄνθρωποί εἰσιν <u>ὥσπερ</u> ἐν <u>ἄντρῳ</u> τινὶ ὑπὸ τῇ γῇ καθίζοντες. καὶ ἐκεῖ <u>ἐκ παίδων</u> ἀναγκάζονται μένειν. τά τε <u>ἄρθρα</u> καὶ αἱ κεφαλαὶ αὐτῶν ἐν <u>δεσμοῖς</u> ἔχονται. τὰς οὖν κεφαλὰς οὐχ οἷοί τ᾽ εἰσὶ
5   τρέπειν, γιγνώσκοντες οὐδὲν ἄλλο ἢ τὰ <u>πρὸ</u> αὐτῶν. καὶ <u>οὕτως</u> ἀεὶ

	εἰ	if
	εἴδωλον -ου τό	image
	ὥσπερ	as if, just like (*here* people ...)
	ἄντρον -ου τό	cave
	ἐκ παίδων	from childhood
	ἄρθρον -ου τό	limb
	δεσμός -οῦ ὁ	chain
5	πρό	in front of (+ *gen*)
	οὕτως	in this way

34

μένουσιν. ἔστι μέντοι ἐν τῷ <u>ἄντρῳ</u>, <u>ὄπισθε</u> τῶν ἐκεῖ καθιζόντων, πῦρ μέγιστον, ὃ παρέχει <u>φῶς</u> αὐτοῖς. καὶ <u>μεταξὺ</u> τοῦ πυρὸς καὶ τῶν ἀνθρώπων ἐστὶν ὁδός, καὶ <u>παρὰ</u> ταύτην <u>τειχίον</u>. ὄπισθε τοῦ τειχίου βαίνουσί τινες <u>ἀνδριάντας</u> φέροντες καὶ ζῷα λίθου καὶ ἄλλα <u>παντοῖα</u>. πάντα ταῦτα, τοῦ
10 τειχίου <u>ὑπερέχοντα</u>, <u>σκιὰς</u> βάλλει (οὕτως καὶ οἱ <u>θαυματοποιοὶ</u> πολλάκις πράσσουσιν). οἱ ἐν τῷ ἄντρῳ καθίζοντες οὐδὲν ἄλλο γιγνώσκουσιν ἢ τὰς σκιὰς ἃς τὸ πῦρ βάλλει. ἰδόντες μέντοι τὰς σκιάς, πιστεύουσιν αὐταῖς. τὸ γὰρ τῶν σκιῶν <u>εἴδωλον</u> τοῖς ἐν τῷ ἄντρῳ ἐστὶν ὁ <u>κόσμος</u>."

	ἄντρον -ου τό	cave
	ὄπισθε	behind (+ gen)
	φῶς φωτός τό	light
	μεταξύ	between (+ gen)
	παρά	(+ acc) alongside
	τειχίον -ου τό	wall
	ἀνδριάς -άντος ὁ	statue (of a person)
	παντοῖος -α -ον	of all kinds
10	ὑπερέχω	I project above (+ gen)
	σκιά -ᾶς ἡ	shadow
	θαυματοποιός -οῦ ὁ	puppeteer (operating with shadows behind translucent screen)
	εἴδωλον -ου τό	image
	κόσμος -ου ὁ	world, universe

Irregular third declension nouns (1)

As we saw in Chapter 5, the endings for the vast majority of third declension nouns can be worked out easily if you know the genitive stem. But a handful of common nouns have irregularities of various kinds and to various extents:

(1) πατήρ (father), μήτηρ (mother) and θυγάτηρ (daughter) basically shorten the -ηρ of the nominative to -ερ- for the stem (compare the similar shortening in e.g. λιμήν, -ένος). But (no doubt reflecting pronunciation in practice) the epsilon of the stem is then dropped in the genitive and dative singular and the dative plural. Hence:

		father (m)	mother (f)	daughter (f)
sg	nom	πατήρ*	μήτηρ*	θυγάτηρ*
	acc	πατέρα	μητέρα	θυγατέρα
	gen	πατρός	μητρός	θυγατρός
	dat	πατρί	μητρί	θυγατρί
pl	nom	πατέρες	μητέρες	θυγατέρες
	acc	πατέρας	μητέρας	θυγατέρας
	gen	πατέρων	μητέρων	θυγατέρων
	dat	πατράσι(ν)	μητράσι(ν)	θυγατράσι(ν)

*vocatives πάτερ, μῆτερ, θύγατερ (note the vowel shortening: compare γέρον)

(2) ἀνήρ, ἀνδρός (*man*) is basically predictable but resembles the -ηρ words above in having vocative -ερ and dative plural -ασι (ἄνδρσι would be unpronounceable: here the dative plural is *expanded* to enable it to be pronounced, rather than telescoped like that of more typical third declension nouns). Also mainly predictable is γυνή, γυναικός (*woman*): the oddity is simply that the nominative singular looks like a first declension word of the τιμή type, and seems rather remote from the stem γυναικ- (for which a nominative such as γυναιξ might have been inferred).

		man (*m*)	woman (*f*)
sg	nom	ἀνήρ*	γυνή*
	acc	ἄνδρα	γυναῖκα
	gen	ἀνδρός	γυναικός
	dat	ἀνδρί	γυναικί
pl	nom	ἄνδρες	γυναῖκες
	acc	ἄνδρας	γυναῖκας
	gen	ἀνδρῶν	γυναικῶν
	dat	ἀνδράσι(ν)	γυναιξί(ν)

*vocatives ἄνερ, γύναι

ἀνήρ is *man* = male, like Latin *vir*; ἄνθρωπος is *man* = human being, like Latin *homo*
ἀνήρ is also used for *husband*, and similarly γυνή for *wife*

(3) Ζεύς (Zeus, *m*) changes to a completely different stem (Δι-) after the nominative:

nom	Ζεύς*
acc	Δία
gen	Διός
dat	Διί

*vocative Ζεῦ

Zeus has of course no plural; for the change of stem, compare Latin *Juppiter*, genitive *Iovis*

Root aorists

As well as the first (weak) and second (strong) aorists we have seen already (Chapter 4), there is a third type of aorist used for a handful a verbs: this is the *root aorist*, so called because person endings are just added to the *root* (basic stem) of the verb. Two important examples are βαίνω (root -βη-) and γιγνώσκω (root -γνω-):

ἔ-βη-ν	I went
ἔ-βη-ς	you (*sg*) went
ἔ-βη	he/she/it went

ἔ-βη-μεν	we went
ἔ-βη-τε	you (*pl*) went
ἔ-βη-σαν	they went

aorist participle: βάς, βᾶσα, βάν (βαντ-): i.e. 3-1-3 declensions, with stem βαντ- for masculine and neuter - this example is just like a first (weak) aorist participle such as παύσας

ἔ-γνω-ν	I got to know
ἔ-γνω-ς	you (*sg*) got to know
ἔ-γνω	he/she/it got to know
ἔ-γνω-μεν	we got to know
ἔ-γνω-τε	you (*pl*) got to know
ἔ-γνω-σαν	they got to know

aorist participle: γνούς, γνοῦσα, γνόν (γνοντ-): i.e. 3-1-3 declensions, with stem γνοντ- for masculine and neuter - this differs only in the masculine nominative singular from the endings of a normal present or second (strong) aorist active participle:

		masculine	
sg	*nom*	γνούς	having got to know
	acc	γνόντ-α	
	gen	γνόντ-ος	
	dat	γνόντ-ι	
pl	*nom*	γνόντ-ες	
	acc	γνόντ-ας	
	gen	γνόντ-ων	
	dat	γνοῦσι(ν)*	

*for γνοντσι(ν): notice yet again how the shortened dative plural resembles the nominative singular

• Note that βαίνω is far more commonly found in compounds than in its simple form: hence e.g. ἐκβαίνω = *I go out*, εἰσβαίνω = *I go in*.

Exercise 7.42

Translate into English:
1 ὁ τῆς παιδὸς πατὴρ πλουσιώτερός ἐστιν ἢ ὁ ἐμός.
2 οἱ δοῦλοι, ὑπὸ τοῦ στρατιώτου διωκόμενοι, πρὸς τοὺς ἀγροὺς προσέβησαν.
3 διὰ τὸν σκότον ἀναγκαζόμεθα παύειν τὴν μάχην.
4 ταύτῃ τῇ γυναικὶ δύο θυγατέρες εἰσίν.
5 οὐδεὶς τὸ τοῦ Διὸς ἱερὸν πιστότερον φυλάσσει ἢ ὅδε ὁ ἀνήρ.
6 οὗτοι οἱ αἰχμάλωτοι ὑπὸ τῶν παίδων λίθοις ἐτύπτοντο.

7   ἐκεῖνοι οἱ νεανίαι, τάς τε ὁδοὺς καὶ τὴν χώραν γνόντες, ἡμῖν
        χρησιμώτατοι ἦσαν.

8   οἱ αἰχμάλωτοι, τὸν ποταμὸν τὸν χαλεπώτατον διαβάντες, οὐκ ἄξιοί
        εἰσι κολάζεσθαι.

9   ἆρα ὁ σὸς ἀδελφός, ᾧ ἀεὶ ἐπίστευες, ταῦτα τῇ μητρὶ εἶπεν;

10   ὁ ἰατρὸς τὸ τῆς νόσου ὄνομα ἔγνω.

Exercise 7.43

Translate into Greek:

1   The inhabitants of the village are forced to run away.
2   We got to know those words.
3   Did you hide the gold in the field, boys?
4   The slave who was being chased by the soldier went into the temple.
5   The women* to whom I reported these things were sitting in the marketplace.

* note that as the antecedent of a relative pronoun, the noun 'women' needs to be put in here (you cannot use just the feminine article, as in a participle construction or with a preposition phrase)

Exercise 7.44

Plato's Parable of the Cave (2)

ὁ μὲν οὖν Σωκράτης ταῦτα περὶ τῶν ἐν τῷ <u>ἄντρῳ</u> εἶπεν. ὁ δὲ <u>Γλαύκων</u>
πάντα ἀκούσας, "δεινόν ἐστι τὸ <u>εἴδωλον</u>, καὶ δεινοὶ οἱ ἄνθρωποι περὶ ὧν
λέγεις." "εἰσὶν <u>ὥσπερ</u> ἡμεῖς," εἶπεν ὁ Σωκράτης, "τί γὰρ ἄλλο
γιγνώσκουσιν ἢ τὰς <u>σκιὰς</u> ἃς τὸ πῦρ βάλλει;" "δῆλόν ἐστιν ὅτι οὐδὲν
5 ἄλλο γιγνώσκουσιν, εἰ ἀναγκάζονται τά τ' <u>ἄρθρα</u> καὶ τὰς κεφαλὰς ἀεὶ ἐν
<u>δεσμοῖς</u> ἔχειν."

καὶ ὁ Σωκράτης εἶπεν, "οὗτοι νῦν πρὸς σκιὰς <u>βλέπουσιν</u> καὶ οὐδὲν ἄλλο.
<u>ὑπολάμβανε</u> δὲ τόδε· λύεταί τις τῶν ἐκεῖ καθιζόντων ἀπὸ τῶν δεσμῶν,
καὶ τὴν κεφαλὴν τρέψας προσβαίνει πρὸς τὸ πῦρ· τί <u>τότε</u> πράξει; καίπερ
10 πρῶτον <u>τυφλὸς</u> ὢν διὰ τὸ τοῦ πυρὸς <u>φῶς</u>, μετὰ ὀλίγον χρόνον τὴν περὶ

	ἄντρον -ου τό	cave
	Γλαύκων -ωνος ὁ	Glaucon (*friend taking part in dialogue with Socrates*)
	εἴδωλον -ου τό	image
	ὥσπερ	just as, just like
	σκιά -ᾶς ἡ	shadow
5	ἄρθρον -ου τό	limb
	δεσμός -οῦ ὁ	chain
	βλέπω	look (at: πρός + *acc*)
	ὑπολαμβάνω	I imagine
	τότε	then, at that time
10	τυφλός -ή -όν	blind
	φῶς φωτός τό	light

τοῦ πυρὸς καὶ τῶν <u>σκιῶν</u> <u>ἀλήθειαν</u> <u>εὑρήσει</u>. καὶ πάντα ταῦτα αὐτῷ νῦν
μῶρα ἐστίν. καὶ ἐκ τοῦ <u>ἄντρου</u> ἐξελθών, πρῶτον μὲν αὖθις <u>τυφλὸς</u> ὢν
διὰ τὸ τοῦ ἡλίου <u>φῶς</u>, μετὰ ὀλίγον χρόνον πρὸς τοὺς ἀνθρώπους καὶ τὰ
τῆς γῆς καὶ τὰ τοῦ οὐρανοῦ <u>βλέψει</u>. ἔπειτα δέ, τὴν <u>ἀληθινὴν</u> οἰκίαν
15 γνοὺς καὶ εἰς τὸ ἄντρον αὖθις εἰσελθών, λέξει τοῖς ἄλλοις περὶ τοῦ
<u>κόσμου</u> καὶ περὶ τοῦ ἀληθινοῦ φωτός. καὶ <u>ἐθελήσει</u> τοὺς <u>δεσμοὺς</u> αὐτῶν
λύειν, καὶ κελεύσει πάντας ἐκ τοῦ ἄντρου εἰς τὸν κόσμον φεύγειν· οἱ δὲ
<u>οὐδαμῶς</u> τοῦτο πράξουσιν. <u>μᾶλλον</u> γὰρ ἐθέλουσι πρὸς σκιὰς βλέπειν· καὶ
πάντα τὰ λεγόμενα αὐτοῖς μῶρα ἐστίν. καὶ τέλος τὸν ἄγγελον διώξουσιν
20 ὡς ἄξιον ὄντα θανάτῳ κολάζεσθαι."

σκιά -ᾶς ἡ	shadow
ἀλήθεια -ας ἡ	truth
εὑρήσω	*future of* εὑρίσκω
ἄντρον -ου τό	cave
τυφλός -ή -όν	blind
φῶς φωτός τό	light
βλέπω	look (at: πρός + *acc*)
ἀληθινος -η -ον	true
15 κοσμος -ου ὁ	world
ἐθελήσω	*future of* ἐθέλω
δεσμός -οῦ ὁ	chain
οὐδαμῶς	in no way
μᾶλλον	more, rather

Result clauses

He is <u>so</u> clever <u>that</u> he always learns everything.
The women guarded the village <u>so</u> bravely <u>that</u> the enemy ran away.
The danger was <u>so great</u> that we stayed in the camp.

• These sentences can usually be identified easily in English by a signpost word (*so* etc) in
the first half, which is picked up by a word for *that* at the start of the second half which
expresses the *result* or outcome. Because the clause expressing the result follows on in such
an integral way, result clauses are also sometimes known as *consecutive* clauses.

• The normal word for *so* in the first half of the sentence is οὕτω (οὕτως before a vowel),
usually followed by an adjective or adverb. The word for *that* at the start of the second half
(the result clause proper) is ὥστε. Because Greek uses other words to translate the (quite
different) uses of the English *that* in other contexts (e.g. ἐκεῖνος for *that one there*), <u>the
occurrence of ὥστε is a cast-iron guarantee that you are dealing with a result clause</u>.

• As in Latin, there are special words for *so great/so many/(of) such (a sort)*, which are used
instead of οὕτω(ς) with an ordinary adjective:

τοσοῦτος, τοσαύτη, τοσοῦτο	so great, so big
τοιοῦτος, τοιαύτη, τοιοῦτο	such, of such a sort

As should be clear from the masculine, feminine, and neuter nominatives quoted here, these decline in the same way as οὗτος, αὕτη, τοῦτο = *this*; but instead of the variable beginning of *this* (rough breathing in the masculine and feminine nominatives, tau elsewhere), the words for *so great* and *such* have their distinctive prefix throughout: τος- indicating *size/quantity*, τοι- indicating *type/quality*.

They correspond respectively to Latin *tantus* and *talis*. But whereas in Latin the plural of *tantus* means *such big (plural things)* and there is a separate word for *so many* (the indeclinable *tot*), in Greek the plural parts of τοσοῦτος normally mean *so many*. (They could, far less commonly, also mean *such big* ... ; this would have to be deduced from the context.)

• In straightforward sentences indicating a result that actually occurs, the verb in the result clause is indicative, in the same tense as the equivalent English. (As we shall see later, there is an alternative construction for potential, rather than actual, results: *He is foolish enough to do this* [= He is so foolish that he *might* do this], using an infinitive as in English.)

The sentences given above would therefore be translated:

He is so clever that he always learns everything.
οὕτω σοφός ἐστιν ὥστε ἀεὶ πάντα μανθάνει.

The women guarded the village so bravely that the enemy ran away.
αἱ γυναῖκες οὕτως ἀνδρείως τὴν κώμην ἐφύλασσον ὥστε οἱ πολέμιοι ἔφυγον.

The danger was so great that we stayed in the camp.
τοσοῦτος ἦν ὁ κίνδυνος ὥστε ἐν τῷ στρατοπέδῳ ἐμένομεν.

• Occasionally ὥστε starts a new sentence (or comes after a colon), when there is no signpost word in what has preceded. In this case ὥστε should be translated *as a result*:
σοφώτατός ἐστιν. ὥστε πάντες θαυμάζουσιν αὐτόν.
He is very wise. As a result, everyone admires him.
The thought behind this is equivalent to: *He is so wise that everyone admires him.*

• οὕτω(ς) is the adverb formed from οὗτος (*literally* 'this-ly'. i.e. *thus, in this way, so*). It is used in many different contexts.

Exercise 7.45

Translate into English:
1   ὁ ῥήτωρ οὕτω σοφός ἐστιν ὥστε πείθει τοὺς πολίτας.
2   οὗτος ὁ δοῦλος οὕτω μώρως πράσσει ὥστε ἀναγκαζόμεθα κολάζειν αὐτόν.
3   ὁ σῖτος τοιοῦτός ἐστιν ὥστε πάντες ἐθέλουσιν ἔχειν.
4   οἱ τοῦ διδασκάλου λόγοι οὕτω δῆλοι ἦσαν ὥστε πάντες οἱ παῖδες εὖ ἐμάνθανον.

5	ὁ γέρων τὸν χρυσὸν οὕτω σοφῶς ἔκρυψεν ὥστε οὐδεὶς οἷός τ' ἦν εὑρίσκειν αὐτόν.
6	οὗτος ὁ ἵππος οὕτω καλός ἐστιν ὥστε τοῦ ἡμετέρου στρατηγοῦ ἄξιός ἐστιν.
7	τοσοῦτοι τῶν ἀνδρῶν ἐν τῷ στρατῷ εἰσιν ὥστε αἱ γυναῖκες ἄθλιαί εἰσιν.
8	ἐκεῖνοι οἱ ναῦται οὕτως ἀνδρεῖοί εἰσιν ὥστε ἐν πάσαις ταῖς ναυμαχίαις τὴν νίκην ἔχουσιν.
9	ὁ τῆς παιδὸς πατὴρ οὕτω πλούσιός ἐστιν ὥστε κάλλιστα δῶρα ἀεὶ παρέχει.
10	ὁ δεσπότης νῦν ἄπεστιν. ὥστε οἱ δοῦλοι πάντα τὸν οἶνον πίνουσιν.

εὖ	well
δεσπότης -ου ὁ	master

Exercise 7.46

Translate into Greek:
1 These women are so wise that all the generals trust them.
2 The soldiers were so brave that they chased the enemy into the river.
3 The boy was so stupid that he learned nothing.
4 The enemy were so many that the citizens did not stay in the village.
5 Socrates always speaks very wisely. As a result, we admire him.

Exercise 7.47

The Myth of Er

At the end of the ten books of The Republic, *Socrates (acting as usual as Plato's mouthpiece) rounds off the discussion of the nature of justice in man and society by telling this story about a back-from-the-dead experience.*

τοῖς οὖν δικαίοις ἆθλα καὶ δῶρα καὶ χρήματα ὑπὸ τῶν τε θεῶν καὶ τῶν ἀνθρώπων παρέχεται. ἀλλὰ πάντα ταῦτα οὐδέν ἐστι πρὸς ἐκεῖνα τὰ ἀγαθὰ ἃ ἀποθανόντα ἕκαστον περιμένει. μῦθον γὰρ ἄκουε ὃν νῦν λέξω περὶ ἀνδρείου τινός, Ἦρος τοῦ Ἀρμενίου. οὗτος δὲ ὁ στρατιώτης ἐν
5 πολέμῳ ἀπέθανεν. τῇ δὲ δεκάτῃ ἡμέρᾳ μετὰ τὴν μάχην, ἐπεὶ οἱ φίλοι παρῆσαν ὡς θάψοντες αὐτόν, τοὺς μὲν ἄλλους νεκροὺς εὗρον σαθροὺς ὄντας, τὸν δὲ αὐτοῦ ἔτι ἀγαθόν. οἱ οὖν φίλοι ἐθαύμασαν, ἀλλὰ τὸν

πρός	(+ *acc*) (*here*) compared to
περιμένω	I lie in wait for
Ἦρ Ἦρός ὁ	Er
Ἀρμένιος -ου ὁ	Armenian (*from Armenia, territory straddling modern border of Turkey and Russia*)
5 σαθρός -ά -όν	rotten, decayed

41

νεκρὸν <u>οἴκαδε</u> ἔφερον. ἐπεὶ δ'<u>ἐπὶ</u> τῇ <u>πυρᾷ</u> ἦν, ὁ νεκρὸς <u>ἀναβιῶν</u> εἶπεν,
"ἡ ἐμὴ <u>ψυχή</u>, ἐκ τοῦ σώματος φυγοῦσα, μετ' ἄλλων κατῆλθεν εἰς τόπον
10 τινὰ δεινόν. ἐκεῖ ἦν δύο <u>χάσματα</u> ἐν τῇ γῇ καὶ δύο ἐν τῷ οὐρανῷ.
οἱ δὲ τῶν ἀποθανόντων κριταὶ <u>μεταξὺ</u> τῶν χασμάτων ἐκάθιζον καὶ εἰς τὰ
πρῶτα χάσματα ἔπεμψαν τοὺς προσβαίνοντας. τοὺς μὲν γὰρ δικαίους
ἐκέλευσαν εἰς τὴν <u>δεξιὰν</u> καὶ διὰ τοῦ οὐρανοῦ <u>βαδίζειν</u>, τοὺς δὲ <u>ἀδίκους</u>
εἰς τὴν <u>ἀριστερὰν</u> καὶ <u>κάτω</u>. καὶ εἶχον <u>ἑκάτεροι</u> <u>σήματα</u> τῶν ἐν τῷ βίῳ
15 <u>πραγμάτων</u>. ἐμοὶ δὲ προσβαίνοντι εἶπον οἱ κριταὶ 'πέμψομέν σε τοῖς
ἀνθρώποις ὡς ἄγγελον περὶ τῶν ἐνθάδε. ἄκουε οὖν καὶ μάνθανε πάντα τὰ
ἐν τῷδε τῷ τόπῳ.' καὶ ἐκέλευσάν με πάντα ἀγγέλλειν τοῖς ἐμοῖς φίλοις
καὶ πολίταις.

"τούτους οὖν τοὺς λόγους ἀκούσας, ἐγὼ τάδε τὰ <u>θαυμάσια</u> εἶδον· διὰ γὰρ
20 τῶν πρώτων χασμάτων ἀπῆλθον αἱ ψυχαὶ ἐπεὶ οἱ κριταὶ <u>κατεδίκασαν</u>, ἡ
μὲν <u>ἄνω</u>, ἡ δὲ κάτω. ἐκ δὲ τῶν ἄλλων χασμάτων <u>ὡσαύτως</u> εἶδον ἄλλας
ψυχὰς ἐκβαινούσας, τὰς μὲν ἐκ τῆς γῆς <u>αὐχμοῦ</u> <u>μεστάς</u>, τὰς δὲ ἐκ τοῦ
οὐρανοῦ <u>καθαράς</u>. πᾶσαι δὲ αἱ ψυχαὶ ὥσπερ ἐκ μακρᾶς <u>πορείας</u> ἦλθον
<u>χαίροντες</u> εἰς <u>λειμῶνά</u> τινα. αἱ δὲ ἐκ τῆς γῆς ἐλθοῦσαι ἤκουσαν περὶ τῶν
25 ἐν τῷ οὐρανῷ, καὶ αἱ ἐκ τοῦ οὐρανοῦ ὡσαύτως περὶ τῶν ὑπὸ τῇ γῇ.
καὶ αἱ μὲν <u>ἐδάκρυον</u> λέγουσαι περὶ πάντων ἃ ἔπαθον καὶ εἶδον ἐν τῇ

	οἴκαδε	home, homewards
	ἐπί	(+ *dat*) on
	πυρά -ᾶς ἡ	funeral pyre (for cremation)
	ἀναβιόω	I come back to life
	ψυχή -ῆς ἡ	soul
10	χάσμα -ατος τό	chasm
	μεταξύ	between (+ *gen*)
	δεξιά -ᾶς ἡ	right (hand side)
	βαδίζω	I walk
	ἄδικος -ον	unjust
	ἀριστερά -ᾶς ἡ	left (hand side)
	κάτω	down, downwards
	ἑκάτερος -α -ον	each of two
	σῆμα -ατος τό	sign, mark
15	πρᾶγμα -ατος τό	(*here*) deed
	θαυμάσιος -α -ον	wonderful, miraculous
20	καταδικάζω κατεδίκασα	I pass judgement
	ἄνω	upwards
	ὡσαύτως	likewise, in the same way
	αὐχμός -οῦ ὁ	dirt, filth
	μεστός -ή -όν	full
	καθαρός -ά -όν	clean
	πορεία -ας ἡ	journey
	χαίρω	I rejoice, I am happy
	λειμών -ῶνος ὁ	meadow
25	δακρύω ἐδάκρυσα	I weep, I cry

πορείᾳ (ἡ δὲ πορεία ἐστὶ χιλιέτης), αἱ δὲ ἔχαιρον περὶ τῶν ἐν οὐρανῷ καλῶν. μισθὸς γὰρ δεκάκις παρέχεται ἑκάστῳ τῶν ἐν τῷ βίῳ.

πάντες οὖν οἱ δίκαιοι ἆθλα κάλλιστα ἔχουσιν. τῆς μέντοι πρὸς θεοὺς καὶ
30 πατέρας ἀσεβείας μεγίστη ἐστὶν ἡ τιμωρία. ἤκουσα γὰρ τόνδε τὸν
διάλογον· εἶπε δέ τις, 'ποῦ ἐστιν Ἀρδιαῖος ὁ μέγας;' (οὗτος δὲ τόν τε
γέροντα πατέρα ἀπέκτεινε καὶ τὸν ἀδελφόν). καὶ ἄλλος τις 'οὐ πάρεστιν·'
ἔφη, 'ἐπεὶ γὰρ ἐγγὺς τοῦ στομίου ἦμεν, ἐκεῖνόν τε καὶ ἄλλους εἴδομεν, ὧν
πολλοὶ ἦσαν τύραννοι· τούτους οὖν οὐκ ἔλαβε τὸ στόμιον, ἀλλὰ ψόφος
35 δεινότατος ἦν. εἰ γάρ τις ἱκανὴν δίκην οὐκ ἔτισε, τῷ στομίῳ οὕτως
κωλύεται. καὶ ἄνδρες τινὲς ἄγριοι εὐθὺς παρῆσαν, τὸν δ' Ἀρδιαῖον καὶ
τοὺς ἄλλους συμποδίσαντες καὶ ἐκδείραντες παρὰ τὴν ὁδὸν εἵλκυσαν,
φαίνοντες τοῖς παροῦσιν τὴν τῆς τιμωρίας αἰτίαν, καὶ τέλος εἰς τὸν
Τάρταρον εἰσέβαλον. ὥστε ἡμεῖς αὐτοὶ πρὸς τὸ στόμιον προσβαίνοντες
40 φόβον μέγιστον τοῦδε τοῦ ψόφου εἴχομεν, καὶ διὰ τὴν σιγὴν ἐχαίρομεν.'
ταῦτα οὖν περὶ τῶν χασμάτων ἤκουσα καὶ εἶδον," ἔφη ὁ τοῦ στρατιώτου
νεκρός, "ἀλλὰ ἐπεὶ ἐμείναμεν ἑπτὰ ἡμέρας ἐν τῷ λειμῶνι, τοῦτον τὸν
τόπον τῇ ὀγδόῃ ἐλίπομεν. καὶ μετὰ τέσσαρας ἡμέρας ἤλθομεν ὅθεν εἶδον

	πορεία -ας ἡ	journey
	χιλιέτης	1000 years long
	χαίρω	I rejoice, I am happy
	μισθός -οῦ ὁ	pay, reward/punishment
	δεκάκις	ten times (over)
30	ἀσέβεια -ας ἡ	impiety, disrespect
	τιμωρία -ας ἡ	punishment
	διάλογος -ου ὁ	dialogue, conversation
	Ἀρδιαῖος -ου ὁ	Ardiaeus
	στόμιον -ου τό	mouth, opening
	τύραννος -ου ὁ	tyrant
	ψόφος -ου ὁ	noise
35	εἰ	if
	ἱκανός -ή -όν	sufficient
	δίκη -ης ἡ	(here) penalty
	τίνω ἔτισα	I pay
	ἄγριος -α -ον	cruel, savage
	συμποδίζω συνεπόδισα	I bind together
	ἐκδέρω ἐξέδειρα	I flay, I strip the skin off
	παρά	(+ acc) along
	ἕλκω εἵλκυσα	I drag
	αἰτία -ας ἡ	cause, reason
	Τάρταρος -ου ὁ	Tartarus
40	χάσμα -ατος τό	chasm
	λειμών -ῶνος ὁ	meadow
	ὅθεν	from where

ἄνωθεν <u>φῶς</u> <u>ὀρθόν</u> τε καὶ μέγιστον, ὥσπερ <u>κίονα</u>. καὶ τοῦτο τὸ φῶς τῇ
45 <u>Ἴριδι</u> <u>ὅμοιον</u> ἦν, ἀλλὰ <u>λαμπρότερον</u>, καὶ διὰ πάντος τοῦ οὐρανοῦ καὶ τῆς
γῆς <u>διατεῖνον</u>. ἐνθάδε ἦσαν τρεῖς <u>Μοῖραι</u>, <u>στέμματα</u> ἐπὶ ταῖς κεφαλαῖς
ἔχουσαι, <u>Λάχεσίς</u> τε καὶ <u>Κλωθὼ</u> καὶ ᾽Ατροπος. ἡ μὲν Λάχεσις <u>ᾄδει</u> τὰ
<u>πρίν</u>, ἡ δὲ Κλωθὼ τὰ <u>νῦν</u> ὄντα, ἡ δὲ ᾽Ατροπος τὰ <u>μέλλοντα</u>. καὶ
<u>προφήτης</u> τις τὰς <u>ψυχὰς</u> πρὸς τὴν Λάχεσιν ἤγαγεν. ἔπειτα δὲ ἔλαβεν ἐκ
50 τῶν <u>γονάτων</u> αὐτῆς <u>κλήρους</u> τε καὶ βίων <u>παραδείγματα</u>, καὶ ἀπὸ <u>βήματος</u>
εἶπεν, ''Ανάγκης θυγάτηρ Λάχεσις λέγει τάδε· ὦ ψυχαὶ <u>ἐφήμεροι</u>, πάρεστιν
<u>ἀρχὴ</u> ἄλλης <u>περιόδου</u> τοῖς <u>θνητοῖς</u>. οὐχ ὑμᾶς <u>ἐκλέξει</u> <u>δαίμων</u>, ἀλλὰ ὑμεῖς
δαίμονα. ὁ πρῶτος <u>λαχὼν</u> πρῶτος ἐκλέξει. ἡ <u>ἀρετὴ</u> δεσπότην οὐκ ἔχει· ὁ
μὲν τὴν ἀρετὴν πράξας ἀρετὴν ἕξει, ὁ δὲ <u>ἀτιμάζων</u> οὐκ. <u>αἰτία</u> ἐστὶ τῷ
55 ἐκλέγοντι· θεὸς <u>ἀναίτιος</u>'.

	ἄνωθεν	(here coming) from above
	φῶς φωτός τό	light
	ὀρθός -ή -όν	straight, in a straight line
	κίων -ονος ὁ	column, pillar
45	ἶρις -ιδος ἡ	rainbow
	ὅμοιος -α -ον	like (+ dat)
	λαμπρός -ά -όν	bright
	διατείνω	I extend
	Μοῖραι -ῶν αἱ	Fates, goddesses of destiny
	στέμμα -ατος τό	wreath, garland
	Λάχεσις ἡ	Lachesis (literally Spinner, i.e. she spun the thread of Destiny)
	Κλωθώ ἡ	Clotho (literally Apportioner: she drew off the thread)
	᾽Ατροπος ἡ	Atropos (literally Inflexible: she cut the thread)
	ᾄδω	I sing
	πρίν	before, in the past
	μέλλω	I am about to (be)
	προφήτης -ου ὁ	interpreter
	ψυχή -ῆς ἡ	soul
50	γόνυ -ατος τό	knee
	κλῆρος -ου ὁ	lot, portion
	παράδειγμα -ατος τό	example
	βῆμα -ατος τό	platform
	᾽Ανάγκη -ης	(here as proper name) Necessity (as a goddess)
	ἐφήμερος -ον	ephemeral, of a day
	ἀρχή -ῆς ἡ	(here) beginning
	περίοδος -ου ἡ	cycle
	θνητός -ή -όν	mortal
	ἐκλέγω ἐξέλεξα	I choose
	δαίμων -ονος ὁ	divine spirit, deity
	λαγχάνω ἔλαχον	I obtain by lot, I get a turn
	ἀρετή -ῆς ἡ	virtue
	ἀτιμάζω	I dishonour
	αἰτία -ας ἡ	blame
55	ἀναίτιος -ον	not to blame

ταῦτα εἰπὼν ὁ προφήτης ἔβαλε τοὺς κλήρους, καὶ ἕκαστος τὸν ἐγγὺς
πεσόντα ἀνέλαβεν. καὶ δῆλον ἦν ὁπόστος ἔλαχεν. μετὰ δὲ ταῦτα τὰ τῶν
βίων παραδείγματα ἔθηκεν ἐπὶ τὴν γῆν, πλεῖστά τε καὶ παντοδαπὰ ὄντα,
ὥστε ἕκαστος οἷός τ' ἦν οὐ χαλεπῶς ἐκλέγειν. ζῴων γὰρ πάντων ἦσαν
βίοι, ἐν οἷς καὶ ἀνθρώπινοι πάντες. ὁ δὲ πρῶτος λαχὼν ἐξέλεξεν εὐθὺς
τὴν μεγίστην τυραννίδα, οὐκ ἐπιμελῶς φροντίζων. ἔπειτα δὲ κατὰ σχολὴν
ἐξετάζων εὗρε τῶν ἑαυτοῦ παίδων ἐδωδὴν καὶ ἄλλα κακά. ταῦτα οὖν
μαθὼν ἐδάκρυσε, τοῖς τοῦ προφήτου λόγοις οὐκ ἐμμένων ἀλλὰ τὸν θεὸν
ἐν αἰτίᾳ ἔχων. οἱ δὲ πολλοὶ ἐξέλεξαν κατὰ τὴν τοῦ προτέρου βίου
συνήθειαν. ἡ γὰρ τοῦ Ὀρφέως ψυχὴ ἐξέλεξε κύκνου βίον, τὴν δὲ τοῦ
γελωτοποιοῦ Θερσίτου πιθήκου βίον εἶδον ἐκλέγουσαν. τέλος δὲ ἡ
Ὀδυσσέως ψυχὴ προσῆλθε, καὶ μνήμῃ τῶν προτέρων πόνων πλεῖστον
χρόνον περιέβαινεν· ἤθελε γὰρ βίον ἀνδρὸς ἰδιώτου ἀπράγμονος ἔχειν,

	προφήτης -ου ὁ	interpreter
	κλῆρος -ου ὁ	lot, portion
	ἀναλαμβάνω ἀνέλαβον	I pick up
	ὁπόστος -η -ον	where in the order, in what numerical place
	λαγχάνω ἔλαχον	I obtain by lot, I get a turn
	παράδειγμα -ατος τό	example
	ἔθηκα	(irreg aor) I placed
	πλεῖστοι -αι -α	very many
	παντοδαπός -ή -όν	of every kind
	ἐκλέγω ἐξέλεξα	I choose
60	ἀνθρώπινος -η -ον	human
	τυραννίς -ίδος ἡ	tyranny
	ἐπιμελῶς	carefully
	φροντίζω	I consider
	κατὰ σχολήν	at leisure
	ἐξετάζω	I examine
	ἑαυτοῦ	his own
	ἐδωδή -ῆς ἡ	eating
	δακρύω ἐδάκρυσα	I cry, I weep
	ἐμμένω	I abide by, I keep to (+ dat)
	ἐν αἰτίᾳ	to blame
	κατά	(+ acc) according to
65	συνήθεια -ας ἡ	habit, custom
	Ὀρφεύς -έως ὁ	Orpheus (legendary poet and musician)
	ψυχή -ῆς ἡ	soul
	κύκνος -ου ὁ	swan
	γελωτοποιός -οῦ ὁ	buffoon, clown
	Θερσίτης -ου ὁ	Thersites (rebellious common soldier in Homer's Iliad)
	πίθηκος -ου ὁ	monkey
	Ὀδυσσεύς -έως ὁ	Odysseus
	μνήμη -ης ἡ	memory
	πόνος -ου ὁ	toil, trouble
	ἰδιώτης -ου ὁ	private citizen, ordinary person
	ἀπράγμων gen -ονος	free from trouble

καὶ <u>μόλις</u> εὗρεν (οἱ γὰρ ἄλλοι <u>ἠτίμαζον</u> τοῦτον τὸν βίον), καὶ <u>χαίρων</u>
70 <u>ἐξέλεξεν</u>. ἐπειδὴ οὖν πᾶσαι αἱ <u>ψυχαὶ</u> τοὺς βίους εἶχον, προσῆλθον πρὸς
τὴν <u>Λάχεσιν</u>· <u>ἡ δὲ</u> συνέπεμψεν ἑκάστῃ <u>δαίμονα</u> ὃν ἐξέλεξεν ὡς φύλακα
τοῦ βίου. ἔπειτα δὲ πᾶσαι <u>ὑπὸ</u> τὸν τῆς Ἀνάγκης <u>θρόνον</u> ἦλθον, καὶ δι'
ἐκείνου εἰς τὸ τῆς <u>Λήθης</u> <u>πεδίον</u>, καὶ <u>ὑπὸ νύκτα</u> πρὸς τὸν ποταμόν. καὶ
ἕκαστος ἠναγκάζετο <u>μέτρον</u> τοῦ ὕδατος πίνειν· ὁ γὰρ πιὼν πάντων
75 <u>ἀμνημονεύει</u>. τότε δὲ <u>βροντή</u> τε καὶ <u>σεισμὸς</u> ἦν, καὶ αἱ ψυχαὶ πρὸς τοὺς
βίους ἐφέροντο. ἐγὼ δέ, κωλυόμενος πίνειν, εἰς τὸ σῶμα αὖθις ἦλθον,
καὶ <u>ἐξαίφνης</u> εἶδον <u>ἐμαυτὸν</u> ἐπὶ τῇ <u>πυρᾷ</u>.

	μόλις	with difficulty
	ἀτιμάζω	I dishonour
	χαίρω	I am happy, I rejoice
70	ἐκλέγω ἐξέλεξα	I choose
	ψυχή -ῆς ἡ	soul
	Λάχεσις ἡ	Lachesis
	ἡ δὲ	and she
	δαίμων -ονος ὁ	divine spirit, deity
	ὑπό	(+ acc) under
	θρόνος -ου ὁ	seat
	Λήθη -ης ἡ	Lethe (*Underworld plain and river of forgetting*)
	πεδίον -ου τό	plain
	ὑπὸ νύκτα	just before nightfall
	μέτρον -ου τό	measure
75	ἀμνημονεύω	I forget (+ *gen*)
	βροντή -ῆς ἡ	thunder
	σεισμός -οῦ ὁ	earthquake
	ἐξαίφνης	suddenly
	ἐμαυτόν	myself
	πυρά -ᾶς ἡ	funeral pyre

Revision checkpoint

Make sure you know:
• irregular third declension nouns πατήρ, μήτηρ, θυγάτηρ, ἀνήρ, γυνή, Ζεύς
• root aorists ἔβην, ἔγνων
• result clauses

Vocabulary checklist for Chapter 7

ἀδελφός -οῦ ὁ	brother
᾿Αθῆναι -ων αἱ	Athens
᾿Αθήνη -ης ἡ	Athene (*goddess*)
ἄθλιος -α -ον	miserable, wretched
αἰχμάλωτος -ου ὁ	prisoner (of war)
ἀναγκάζω ἠνάγκασα	I force, I compel
ἀνάγκη -ης ἡ	necessity, compulsion
ἀνήρ ἀνδρός ὁ	man, male, husband
ἄξιος -α -ον	worthy, deserving (of, + *gen*)
ἀρετή -ῆς ἡ	excellence, courage, virtue
ἁρπάζω ἥρπασα	I seize, I snatch
ἀρχαῖος -α -ον	old, ancient
ἀρχή -ῆς ἡ	rule, empire; beginning
γυνή γυναικός ἡ	woman, wife
δακρύω ἐδάκρυσα	I cry, I weep
δεσμός -οῦ ὁ	chain
δεσπότης -ου ὁ	master
δῆλος -η -ον	clear
διαφθείρω διέφθειρα	I destroy, I corrupt
δίκαιος -α -ον	just, right
δίκη -ης ἡ	right (*abstract noun*), lawsuit, penalty
εἰ	if
ἐκεῖνος -η -ο	that
ἑκών -οῦσα -όν (ἑκοντ-)	willing(ly)
ἔνοικος -ου ὁ	inhabitant
εὖ	well
ἔφη	he/she said
ἤ	or; than
ἥλιος -ου ὁ	sun
θυγάτηρ -τρος ἡ	daughter
ἰατρός -οῦ ὁ	doctor
ἱερός -ά -όν	holy, sacred
ἰσχυρός -ά -όν	strong
καθίζω ἐκάθισα	I sit
καίω ἔκαυσα	I burn
κεφαλή -ῆς ἡ	head
κολάζω ἐκόλασα	I punish
κρύπτω ἔκρυψα	I hide
Λακεδαιμόνιοι -ων οἱ	Spartans
μᾶλλον	more, rather (*adv*)
μήτηρ -τρός ἡ	mother
ὅδε, ἥδε, τόδε	this (*implying* here present, near me); the following
ὅς ἥ ὅ	who, which

οὗτος, αὕτη, τοῦτο	this
οὕτω(ς)	so, to such an extent, thus, in this way
πατήρ -τρός ὁ	father
πιστός -ή -όν	trustworthy, faithful
πλούσιος -α -ον	rich, wealthy
πράσσω ἔπραξα	I do, I fare (well/badly *etc*)
ῥήτωρ -ορος ὁ	orator, public speaker, politician
σιγή -ῆς ἡ	silence
σῖτος -ου ὁ	food
σκότος -ου ὁ	darkness
Σπάρτη -ης ἡ	Sparta
σῴζω ἔσωσα	I save
τέχνη -ης ἡ	skill
τοιοῦτος -αύτη -οῦτο	such, of such a kind
τοσοῦτοι -αῦται -αῦτα	so many
τοσοῦτος -αύτη -οῦτο	so great, so big
τότε	then, at that time
τρέπω ἔτρεψα	I turn
τύπτω ἔτυψα	I hit, I strike
ὕλη -ης ἡ	wood, forest
ὑπό	(+ *gen*) by (*agent with passive verb*)
ὑψηλός -ή -όν	high
χρυσός -οῦ ὁ	gold
ὥσπερ	as if; just as, just like
ὥστε	(with the result) that

(68 words)

Chapter 8

Middle voice and deponent verbs

• In Chapter 7 we met the passive voice, and saw how active sentences are made passive:

The boy teaches the slave.
ὁ παῖς τὸν δοῦλον διδάσκει.

The slave is taught by the boy.
ὁ δοῦλος ὑπὸ τοῦ παιδὸς διδάσκεται.

• The *middle* voice is so called because it is midway between active and passive. It is at first sight difficult to see how this would work, how there could be a halfway point between teaching and being taught. But consider the sentence *The boy gets the slave taught*: here the boy (actively) causes the slave to be taught (passively, and implying by a third party). This is one important use of the middle in Greek. In the present tense, and the imperfect, the middle and passive are identical in form, hence:

The boy gets the slave taught.
ὁ παῖς τὸν δοῦλον διδάσκεται.

The context allows the middle to be distinguished from the passive: what we have here is an apparently active sentence with an apparently passive verb. This is sometimes called the *causative* use of the middle: what the subject (actively) causes to be done (passively).

• Words such as *cause* or *get* need not necessarily occur in the English. Consider the sentences:
Winston Churchill built garden walls.
and
Cardinal Wolsey built Hampton Court.

The first tells us that the wartime prime minister literally engaged in bricklaying as a hobby, but the second hardly suggests the same about the Tudor prelate: it means he *had it built* (another possible translation), and in Greek the verb would be middle.

• Another very common use of the middle is where a verb that would normally be transitive (i.e. have a direct object) is used intransitively or *reflexively*. *I washed the floor* is active and transitive; *I washed before going to bed* is intransitive/reflexive, implying I washed *myself*, and would in Greek be middle. Significantly the translation *I got washed* is also possible (at least colloquially) for this use of the middle (though this time without implying by a third party). Hence:

The boy hides the gold.   *active and transitive*
ὁ παῖς τὸν χρυσὸν κρύπτει.

The boy hides in the forest.   *middle and intransitive/reflexive*
ὁ παῖς ἐν τῇ ὕλῃ κρύπτεται.

In Latin the intransitive version would have to put in the reflexive pronoun: *puer in silva se celat*. Greek achieves the same effect by making the verb middle. In the *reflexive* use of the middle, the sense of being halfway between active and passive (or simultaneously both active and passive) is conveyed by the fact that the same person is both doing the action (active) and having it done to them (passive).

• With some verbs the insertion of a reflexive pronoun in English is natural (*he washes himself*), with others it is intelligible but less likely (*he hides himself*). Especially when the subject is not a person (*the battle stops*), this use is really just intransitive rather than reflexive. But in all these examples the verb would be middle. Hence:

The general stops the battle.   *active and transitive*
ὁ στρατηγὸς τὴν μάχην παύει.

The battle stops (*or* ceases).   *middle and intransitive*
ἡ μάχη παύεται.

Exercise 8.1

Translate into English:
1   οἱ γέροντες τοὺς νεανίας ἐδιδάσκοντο.
2   ἡ ναυμαχία αὖθις παύεται.
3   ὁ ναύτης ἐν τῷ λιμένι ἐκρύπτετο.
4   ἡ κόρη τὸν χρυσὸν ἐν τῇ γῇ ἔκρυψεν.
5   ἡ ἐν τῇ νήσῳ νόσος οὐ παύεται.

Exercise 8.2

Translate into Greek:
1   The soldiers are hiding under the trees.
2   The boy hid the books.
3   The long sea-battle stops.
4   The judge was getting the boys taught.
5   The slave is being taught by the old man.

• Some verbs have a special idiomatic meaning in the middle voice:

| ἄρχω | I rule (+ *gen*) | ἄρχομαι | I begin |
| λύω | I release | λύομαι | I ransom |

πείθω	I persuade	πείθομαι	I obey (+ *dat*)
φαίνω	I show	φαίνομαι	I appear ... ; I clearly am ...
φέρω	I carry	φέρομαι	I win (a prize *etc*)

In each case the explanation is slightly different. ἄρχω and ἄρχομαι are linked by the idea *be first* (in power or sequence: compare the two senses of the noun ἀρχή, which we saw in Chapter 7); λύομαι is a specific sense of the causative middle: *I get someone released* (by paying money etc); πείθομαι and φαίνομαι are reflexive middles - *I persuade myself* (to do what someone else wants) and *I show myself* (as being X); φέρομαι means *I carry off for myself*.

• Note an important distinction in the use of φαίνομαι: it is commonly followed by an infinitive, as in English

> φαίνεται μῶρος εἶναι.
> He appears to be stupid (*often implying* but may not be really).

But if followed by a participle

> φαίνεται μῶρος ὤν
> the meaning is (literally)
> He appears (before us) as being stupid.
> i.e. He clearly is stupid.

Exercise 8.3

Translate into English:

1   ὁ νεανίας τὸν δοῦλον λύεται.
2   οὗτος ὁ παῖς φαίνεται μῶρος εἶναι.
3   πάντες οἱ πολῖται τοῖς νόμοις πείθονται.
4   ποῦ ἐστιν ἡ χώρα ἧς ἄρχεις;
5   οἱ μὲν λόγοι παύονται, ὁ δὲ πόλεμος ἄρχεται.
6   ἐκείνη ἡ παῖς πολλὰ ἄθλα ἀεὶ φέρεται.
7   ἆρ' ἐφύγετε τῷ ῥήτορι πειθόμενοι, ὦ πολῖται;
8   οἱ ἵπποι ὑπὸ τῶν νεανιῶν ἐλύοντο.
9   αἱ γυναῖκες οὐκ ἐθέλουσιν ἐκείνῳ τῷ ἀνδρὶ πείθεσθαι.
10 ὅδε ὁ γέρων φαίνεται σοφώτατος ὤν.

• Some verbs are only ever found (or are normally found) in the middle form. These behave as if they were active. They correspond to Latin deponent verbs. Twelve common deponent verbs are:

1	αἰσθάνομαι	I perceive
2	ἀποκρίνομαι	I answer, I reply
3	βούλομαι*	I want, I wish
4	γίγνομαι	I become, I happen
5	δέχομαι	I receive
6	ἕπομαι	I follow (+ *dat*)

7	ἔρχομαι †	I come, I go
8	μάχομαι	I fight
9	ὀργίζομαι	I get angry
10	πορεύομαι	I march
11	πυνθάνομαι	I enquire; I find out (by enquiry)
12	στρατοπεδεύομαι	I set up camp, I encamp

* βούλομαι is stronger in meaning than ἐθέλω, which often means only *be willing* rather than positively *want*

† ἔρχομαι is used as the present tense of the verb for which we have already met the irregular second (strong) aorist active ἦλθον

(In a few of these cases, an active form exists but is less common: e.g. ὀργίζω = *I anger*. With some others an active form probably once existed, but has become obsolete. Where an active form does lie behind a deponent verb in this way, the deponent may be better explained as passive rather than middle. But in practice the distinction usually does not matter.)

• The present infinitive and participle (like the present and imperfect tenses) have exactly the same form in the middle and the passive voice: infinitive -εσθαι, participle -ομενος -η -ον.

• There is also an imperative:
  sg παύου   cease!
  pl παύεσθε
This too can also be passive, but is much more commonly found as middle/deponent.

Exercise 8.4

Translate into English:

1   ὁ γίγας τοὺς ἄνδρας αἰσθανόμενος ὀργίζεται.
2   ἆρα βούλεσθε ἀκούειν τοὺς τοῦ ποιητοῦ λόγους;
3   αἱ γυναῖκες τῷ στρατῷ ἕπονται.
4   οἱ πολέμιοι πρὸς τὴν ἡμετέραν χώραν νῦν πορεύονται.
5   ὁ γέρων αἰσθάνεται τὸν δοῦλον φεύγοντα.
6   θαυμάζομεν τοὺς σοφώτατα ἀποκρινομένους.
7   ὁ διδάσκαλος τὰ γιγνόμενα ἀεὶ πυνθάνεται.
8   οἱ ἐν τῷ ἀγῶνι δραμόντες ἆθλα δέχονται.
9   οἱ στρατιῶται ἐν τῇ ὕλῃ ἐστρατοπεδεύοντο.
10 οἱ σύμμαχοι ἀνδρείως μάχονται, ἀλλὰ μετὰ δέκα ὥρας ἡ μάχη
       παύεται.

Exercise 8.5

Translate into Greek:
1   The boy becomes* a man.
2   The armies were fighting for ten hours.
3   All the soldiers want to set up camp in this field.
4   That old man is now getting angry.
5   The allies are following our general.

* *become* (like *be*) takes not a direct object but a *complement* (another nominative)

Background: Socrates (3)

As well as Plato, other followers and admirers of Socrates recorded his life and teaching, and wrote dialogues showing him in conversation on philosophical topics. Plato, as we have seen, makes Socrates the mouthpiece of his own views, including elaborate theories about a world beyond the ordinary one we perceive. In contrast Xenophon (from whom the following passage is adapted) shows a more down-to-earth Socrates, offering practical and often homely wisdom. Both authors doubtless to some extent depict Socrates in their own image (Xenophon was a soldier, gentleman farmer and historian, not a philosopher) but they also show different sides of the historical Socrates. And there are large areas of overlap between their portraits. Both show a Socrates interested in the definition of words in ordinary use (particularly terms of moral evaluation), and in ascertaining what constitutes a good life. Both show him in dialogue with Sophists.

Hippias of Elis (a city in southern Greece) was a Sophist famous for his encyclopaedic knowledge (of grammar, poetry, mathematics, astronomy) and for his feats of memory. He made a cult of self-sufficiency, liking to point out as he lectured that he had made all the clothes he was wearing. He compiled a list of all victors in the history of the Olympic Games (whose four-yearly cycle formed the basis of the Greek calendar).

Exercise 8.6

Socrates on Not Doing Wrong

ὁ Σωκράτης ἐν παντὶ τῷ βίῳ ἐφαίνετο τὴν δικαιοσύνην πράσσων.
πολλάκις δὲ <u>διελέγετο</u> περὶ τοῦ δικαίου τοῖς τε ἄλλοις φίλοις καὶ* Ἱππίᾳ
τῷ Ἠλείῳ.

	Ἱππ	ἔτι γὰρ σύ, ὦ Σώκρατες, ἐκεῖνα τὰ αὐτὰ λέγεις ἃ ἐγὼ πάλαι σου
5		ἤκουσα;
	Σωκ	ἆρα <u>σκώπτεις</u>, ὦ Ἱππία; ἐγὼ γὰρ οὐ μόνον ἀεὶ τὰ αὐτὰ λέγω,
		ἀλλά (ὃ τούτου δεινότερόν ἐστι) περὶ τῶν αὐτῶν· σὺ δ' <u>ἴσως</u>,
		<u>πολυμαθὴς</u> ὤν, περὶ τῶν αὐτῶν <u>οὔποτε</u> τὰ αὐτὰ λέγεις.
	Ἱππ	<u>ναί·</u> βούλομαι γὰρ ἀεὶ νέον τι λέγειν. καὶ νῦν περὶ τοῦ δικαίου
10		<u>γνώμην</u> ἔχω πρὸς ἣν <u>οὔτε</u> σὺ <u>οὔτ'</u> ἄλλος οὐδεὶς† οἷός τ' εἶ
		<u>ἀντιλέγειν.</u>
	Σωκ	<u>νὴ</u> τοὺς θεούς, μέγιστον ἀγαθὸν λέγεις, διότι οἱ ἄνθρωποι νῦν
		<u>οὐδαμῶς</u> οἷοί τ' εἰσιν τὰ αὐτὰ περὶ τοῦ δικαίου λέγειν. πολέμους
		γὰρ μάχονται, δίκας <u>δικάζουσι,</u> τοὺς τῶν ῥητόρων λόγους ἐν τῇ
15		ἐκκλησίᾳ <u>προθύμως</u> ἀκούουσιν. ἆρα σὺ παύσεις πάντα ταῦτα;
	Ἱππ	νὴ τὸν Δία, νῦν σκώπτεις καὶ σύ· ἀεὶ γὰρ καὶ ἐμὲ καὶ ἄλλους
		<u>ἐλέγχεις,</u> τὴν δὲ σὴν γνώμην οὔποτε <u>ἀποφαίνεις</u> περὶ οὐδενός†.
	Σωκ	ἀλλ' οὔποτε παύομαι ἀποφαίνων ἃ περὶ τοῦ δικαίου <u>νομίζω.</u>

*Greek says *both others and (especially) X*, where English says *X among others*

† Greek often uses this 'reinforcing' negative (strictly redundant, but giving emphasis), saying e.g.
nor <u>no-one</u> else with the sense *nor <u>anyone</u> else*

	διαλέγομαι	I converse, I engage in dialogue
	Ἱππίας -ου ὁ	Hippias
	Ἠλεῖος	of Elis (city in southern Greece)
5	σκώπτω	I joke
	ἴσως	perhaps
	πολυμαθής	polymath, knowledgeable on many subjects
	οὔποτε	never
	ναί	yes
10	γνώμη -ης ἡ	opinion, idea
	οὔτε ... οὔτε	neither ... nor
	ἀντιλέγω	I speak against, I gainsay
	νή	by ... ! (+ acc)
	οὐδαμῶς	in no way, not at all
	δικάζω	I try, I judge
15	προθύμως	eagerly
	ἐλέγχω	I interrogate
	ἀποφαίνω	I reveal
	νομίζω	I think

	Ἱππ	ἆρ' ἐθέλεις λόγον περὶ τούτου παρέχειν;
20	Σωκ	οὐ λόγῳ ἀλλ' ἔργῳ τοῦτο ἀποφαίνω. ἆρα γάρ εἰμι ψευδομάρτυς; ἢ συκοφάντης; ἢ κλέπτης; ἢ προδότης; ἆρα τοὺς φίλους εἰς κίνδυνον ἄγω;
	Ἱππ	οὐδαμῶς.
	Σωκ	ἆρ' οὐ τοῦτό ἐστι τὸ δίκαιον, τῆς ἀδικίας ἀπέχειν;
25	Ἱππ	ἀλλὰ φαίνῃ, ὦ Σώκρατες, οὐκ ἐθέλων λέγειν τὴν σὴν γνώμην περὶ τοῦδε· "τί ἐστι τὸ δίκαιον;" οὐ γὰρ ἃ πράσσουσιν οἱ δίκαιοι, ἀλλ' ἀφ' ὧν ἀπέχουσι, ταῦτα ἀεὶ λέγεις.
	Σωκ	τοῦτό μοι ἱκανόν ἐστι τῆς δικαιοσύνης ἐπίδειγμα, τῆς ἀδικίας ἀπέχειν. εἰ δέ σοι τοῦτο οὐχ ἱκανόν ἐστι, τόδε ἄκουε· λέγω ὅτι
30		τὸ νόμιμον δίκαιόν ἐστιν.
	Ἱππ	ἆρα τὸ αὐτὸ λέγεις, ὦ Σώκρατες, νόμιμόν τε καὶ δίκαιον;
	Σωκ	ναί· τίνες γὰρ εἰσιν οἱ τῶν Ἀθηνῶν νόμοι;
	Ἱππ	οὓς οἱ πολῖται ἐγράφοντο, βουλόμενοι τοὺς ἐνθάδε τὰ μὲν πράσσειν, τῶν δὲ ἀπέχειν.
35	Σωκ	ἆρ' οὐ νόμιμος ὁ κατὰ τοὺς νόμους πράσσων, ἄνομος ὁ παραβαίνων;
	Ἱππ	πῶς γὰρ οὔ;
	Σωκ	οὕτως οὖν δίκαια πράσσει ὁ τούτοις πειθόμενος, ἄδικα ὁ οὐ πειθόμενος;
40	Ἱππ	καλῶς λέγεις.

	λόγος -ου ὁ	(here) account
20	ἀποφαίνω	I reveal
	ψευδομάρτυς -υρος ὁ	false witness
	συκοφάντης -ου ὁ	blackmailer
	κλέπτης -ου ὁ	thief
	προδότης -ου ὁ	traitor
	οὐδαμῶς	in no way, not at all
	ἆρ'(=ἆρα) οὐ	surely?
	ἀδικία -ας ἡ	injustice
	ἀπέχω	refrain from, avoid (+ gen)
25	γνώμη -ης ἡ	idea
	ἱκανός -ή -όν	sufficient
	ἐπίδειγμα -ατος τό	demonstration
30	νόμιμος -η -ον	lawful
	ναί	yes
	γράφομαι	I frame, I make
35	κατά	(+ acc) in accordance with
	ἄνομος -ον	lawless
	παραβαίνω	I contravene, I go against
	πῶς γὰρ οὔ;	certainly (lit for how not?)
	ἄδικος -ον	unjust

Σωκ	οἱ μὲν οὖν τὰ δίκαια πράσσοντες δίκαιοί εἰσιν, οἱ δὲ τὰ <u>ἄδικα</u> ἄδικοι;
Ἱππ	<u>ναί</u>.
Σωκ	οὕτως ὁ μὲν <u>νόμιμος</u> δίκαιός ἐστιν, ὁ δ' <u>ἄνομος</u> ἄδικος. καὶ διὰ

45 ταῦτα τῶν ἀρχόντων οὗτοι <u>ἄριστοί</u> εἰσιν, οἳ τοὺς πολίτας
πείθουσι τοῖς νόμοις πείθεσθαι. καὶ αὕτη ἡ <u>πόλις</u> καὶ ἐν εἰρήνῃ
καὶ ἐν πολέμῳ ἰσχυροτάτη ἐστίν, ἐν ᾗ οἱ πολῖται τοῖς νόμοις
πείθονται. τίνι δε <u>μᾶλλον</u> πιστεύει ἡ πόλις ἢ τῷ δικαίῳ, καὶ τίνι
οἱ σύμμαχοι; τίνι μᾶλλον πάντες βούλονται φίλοι γενέσθαι; ἐκ δὲ

50 τούτων τὸ αὐτὸ νόμιμόν τε καὶ δίκαιον λέγω. εἰ δ' ἄλλην
<u>γνώμην</u> ἔχεις, δίδασκε.

Ἱππ	οὐκ <u>ἄλλως</u> λέγω.
Σωκ	<u>τί δέ</u>; <u>ἀγράφους</u> τινὰς νόμους γιγνώσκεις, ὦ Ἱππία;
Ἱππ	γιγνώσκω.

55
Σωκ	τίνες οὖν οἱ τούτων <u>νομοθέται</u>;
Ἱππ	οἱ θεοί, ὡς <u>ἔγωγε</u> <u>νομίζω</u>.
Σωκ	ἆρα κολάζονται οἱ τούτους τοὺς λόγους <u>παραβαίνοντες</u>; ἆρα <u>ἔρημοι</u> φίλων γίγνονται;
Ἱππ	πῶς γὰρ οὔ;

60
Σωκ	οἱ οὖν <u>ἐμμένοντες</u> τούτοις τοῖς ἀγράφοις νόμοις εὖ πράσσουσιν. καὶ ἐκ τούτου πάντες οἷοί τ' εἰσιν γιγνώσκειν ὅτι καὶ οἱ θεοὶ τὸ αὐτὸ νόμιμόν τε καὶ δικαιὸν λέγουσιν.

	ἄδικος -ον	unjust
	ναί	yes
	νόμιμος -η -ον	lawful
	ἄνομος -ον	lawless
45	ἄριστος -η -ον	best
	πόλις ἡ	city
	μᾶλλον	more, rather
50	γνώμη -ης ἡ	opinion, idea
	ἄλλως	otherwise
	τί δε;	what, then? (*introducing a new point*)
	ἄγραφος -ον	unwritten
55	νομοθέτης -ου ὁ	lawgiver
	ἔγωγε	I at least, I for my part
	νομίζω	I think
	παραβαίνω	I contravene, I go against
	ἔρημος -η -ον	(*here*) lacking (+ *gen*)
60	ἐμμένω	I abide by (+ *dat*)

Aorist middle

• In the aorist (unlike the present and imperfect) there are separate forms for the middle, distinct from the passive.

• Within the aorist middle (as with the aorist active) there are separate forms for first (weak) and second (strong) aorist.

• Despite this apparent complexity, the amount of new material to be learned is very limited, and the tenses are formed by the usual building-block method.

• The first (weak) aorist middle (corresponding to the active ἔπαυσα) is predictably formed by   - augment
   - aorist stem (normally = present stem + sigma)
   - endings that mostly include alpha (like the corresponding active), and are variants of the usual historic middle/passive ones (-αμην etc rather than -ομην etc). Hence:

first (weak) aorist middle:

ἐπαυσ-άμην	I ceased (stopped myself, got something stopped, etc)
ἐπαύσ-ω*	you (*sg*) ceased
ἐπαύσ-ατο	he/she/it ceased
ἐπαυσ-άμεθα	we ceased
ἐπαύσ-ασθε	you (*pl*) ceased
ἐπαύσ-αντο	they ceased

* because -ω represents an earlier form -ασο (the sigma has dropped out, and the two vowels have combined), this ending too includes alpha, but in concealed form. This -ω ending must of course be carefully distinguished from the first person singular ending of some active tenses. (The -ου of the equivalent part of the imperfect middle/passive likewise represents an earlier form -εσο.)

participle   παυσάμενος -η -ον   having ceased

• The second (strong) aorist middle (corresponding to the active ἔλαβον) is even more straightforward, and is predictably formed by
   - augment
   - (second [strong]) aorist stem
   - historic middle/passive endings. Hence:

second (strong) aorist middle:

ἐλαβ-όμην	I took for myself*
ἐλάβ-ου	you (*sg*) took for yourself
ἐλάβ-ετο	he/she/it took for himself/herself/itself
ἐλαβ-όμεθα	we took for ourselves
ἐλάβ-εσθε	you (*pl*) took for yourselves
ἐλάβ-οντο	they took for themselves

* other idiomatic meanings of the middle of λαμβάνω are *take hold of, grasp, get possession of*, all normally followed by the genitive

participle λαβόμενος -η -ον   having taken for oneself

• Each type of aorist middle has, for any given verb, the same stem as the equivalent aorist active: hence e.g.

active	*middle*
ἔπεμψα	ἐπεμψάμην
ἔμαθον	ἐμαθόμην

• Just as, in the active, the second (strong) aorist ἔλαβον needs to be distinguished carefully from the imperfect ἐλάμβανον (the two tenses having the same endings but different stems), so too the aorist ἐλαβόμην needs to be distinguished from the imperfect ἐλαμβανόμην. But whereas ἐλαμβανόμην can be middle or passive, ἐλαβόμην is used only for the middle.

• Many of the middle verbs (i.e. deponents, and those with a special sense in the middle) form their aorists in an entirely predictable way. The following have first (weak) aorists that are either completely regular or (in the case of some of the verbs that can have an active form) make the same slight adjustment to the stem (to accommodate the added sigma) as the future and the aorist active:

present	*aorist*	*aorist stem*	
ἄρχομαι	ἠρξάμην	ἀρξ-	I began
δέχομαι	ἐδεξάμην	δεξ-	I received
λύομαι	ἐλυσάμην	λυσ-	I ransomed
στρατοπεδεύομαι	ἐστρατοπεδευσάμην		I set up camp
		στρατοπεδευσ-	

A few deponent verbs have a first (weak) aorist with slight irregularity:

ἀποκρίνομαι	ἀπεκρινάμην	ἀποκριν-	I answered, I replied
μάχομαι	ἐμαχεσάμην	μαχεσ-	I fought

(ἀπεκρινάμην has no sigma before the ending because the stem ends in nu - compare e.g. the active μένω, aorist ἔμεινα; ἐμαχεσάμην adds -εσ- to the stem; the respective aorist participles are ἀποκρινάμενος -η -ον, μαχεσάμενος -η -ον)

• Other deponent verbs have a second (strong) aorist, with (as usual) telescoping or alteration of the stem:

present	aorist	aorist stem	
αἰσθάνομαι	ᾐσθόμην	αἰσθ-	I perceived
γίγνομαι	ἐγενόμην	γεν-	I became, I happened
ἕπομαι	ἑσπόμην	ἑσπ-	I followed
πυνθάνομαι	ἐπυθόμην	πυθ-	I enquired; I found out

(the respective aorist participles are: αἰσθόμενος, γενόμενος, [none in common use for ἕπομαι], πυθόμενος)

• Note a peculiarity in the formation of πείθομαι. The active πείθω has a first (weak) aorist ἔπεισα, but the middle has a second (strong) aorist ἐπιθόμην.

Exercise 8.7

Translate into Greek:
1   They perceived.
2   You (*sg*) received.
3   We became.
4   You (*pl*) obeyed.
5   He fought.

Exercise 8.8

Translate into English:
1   ἐλυσάμεθα ἐκεῖνον τὸν αἰχμάλωτον ὡς φίλον γενόμενον.
2   πάντες οἱ στρατιῶται τῷ στρατηγῷ τῷ ἀνδρείῳ ἐπίθοντο.
3   ἡ ναυμαχία καίπερ μακρὰ οὖσα τέλος ἐπαύσατο.
4   ὁ παῖς ὁ εὖ δραμὼν ἐδέξατο τὸ ἆθλον.
5   ποῦ ἐστρατοπεδεύσασθε, ὦ ἄνδρες;
6   ὁ περὶ τοῦ πολέμου πυθόμενος σοφός ἐστιν.
7   δέκα ὥρας ἐν τῇ νήσῳ ἐμαχεσάμεθα.
8   τίς εἶδε τὴν τὸν χρυσὸν δεξαμένην;
9   ἡ ἐν τῷ λιμένι μάχη τότε ἤρξατο.
10   οἱ τοῦ γέροντος δοῦλοι ἐλάβοντο τοῦ σίτου.

Exercise 8.9

Translate into Greek:
1   I ransomed all those prisoners of war.
2   The girls finally received a fine prize.
3   After three days the sea-battle ceased.
4   The sailors fought bravely near the river.
5   The soldiers, having set up camp in the field, took hold of the horses.

Exercise 8.10

The Magic Ring

Would people be just if they could be unjust and sure of getting away with it? While exploring this question in Plato's Republic, *Socrates' companion Glaucon (Plato's brother) tells the following story, to illustrate his view that justice is simply a matter of expediency.*

ἦν δε ποτε ποιμήν τις Γύγης ὀνόματι, δοῦλος ὤν· ὁ δὲ δεσπότης αὐτοῦ βασιλεὺς τῆς Λυδίας ἦν. καὶ ἐν ἐκείνη τῆ χώρα σεισμὸς ἦν. διὰ ταῦτα χάσμα ἐν τῆ γῆ ἐγένετο ἐγγὺς τοῦ ἀγροῦ ἐν ᾧ ὁ Γύγης τὰ πρόβατα ἐφύλασσεν. θαυμάσας δὲ ὁ ποιμὴν εἰς τὸ χάσμα κατέβη, καὶ ἐκεῖ εἶδεν
5 ἵππον ξύλινον κοῖλον, ἐν ᾧ ἦν νεκρὸς μέγιστος. οὗτος δὲ γυμνὸς ἦν, οὔτε ἱμάτιον ἔχων οὔτ' ἄλλο οὐδὲν πλὴν δακτυλίου. ὁ δὲ ποιμὴν λαβὼν τὸν δακτύλιον ἐξῆλθεν αὖθις ἐκ τοῦ χάσματος, καὶ πρὸς τὸ ἔργον ἐτρέπετο. καὶ οὐ διὰ πολλοῦ πρὸς τοὺς φίλους ἐλθών, ηὗρεν αὐτοὺς περὶ ἑαυτοῦ διαλεγομένους· οὐ γὰρ εἶδον αὐτόν, διὰ τὸν θαυμάσιον δακτύλιον. ὁ δὲ
10 Γύγης, "διὰ τί," ἔφη, "διαλέγεσθε περὶ ἐμοῦ, ὥσπερ ἀπόντος; πάρειμι γὰρ αὐτός, καὶ πολλὰ καὶ θαυμάσια ὑμῖν λέξω". οἱ δὲ ἑταῖροι θαυμάσαντες εἶπον, "ποῦ εἶ; τὴν γὰρ φωνὴν ἀκούομεν, ἰδεῖν δ' οὐχ οἷοί τ' ἐσμέν". ὁ δὲ ποιμὴν (συνετὸς γὰρ ἦν) οὐδὲν ἀπεκρίνατο, ἀλλὰ σιγῆ ἀπῆλθεν· ὥστε οἱ ἄλλοι, ἐπεὶ οὐδὲν ἔτι ἤκουον, εἶπον, "οὐδεὶς πάρεστιν· ἀπάτη οὖν ἦν". ὁ
15 δὲ Γύγης, τοσαύτην τέχνην εὑρών (ἀφανὴς γὰρ ἐγένετο τὸν δακτύλιον

	ποτε	once
	ποιμήν -ένος ὁ	shepherd
	Γύγης -ου ὁ	Gyges
	βασιλεύς ὁ	king
	Λυδία -ας ἡ	Lydia
	σεισμός -οῦ ὁ	earthquake
	χάσμα -ατος τό	chasm, gaping hole
	πρόβατα -ων τά	sheep
5	ξύλινος -η -ον	made of wood
	κοῖλος -η -ον	hollow
	γυμνός -ή -όν	naked
	ἱμάτιον -ου τό	cloak
	πλήν	except (+ gen)
	δακτύλιος -ου ὁ	ring
	τρέπομαι	I turn my attention to
	οὐ διὰ πολλοῦ	not long afterwards
	ἑαυτοῦ	himself (gen)
	διαλέγομαι	I have a conversation
	θαυμάσιος -α -ον	miraculous
10	ἑταῖρος -ου ὁ	comrade, companion
	ἰδεῖν	(irreg infinitive) to see
	συνετός -ή -όν	clever
	ἀπάτη -ης ἡ	trick, illusion
15	ἀφανής	invisible

περὶ τοῦ <u>δακτύλου</u> ἔχων), εἰς τὴν οἰκίαν τὴν πολίτου τινός πλουσίου
<u>λάθρᾳ</u> εἰσῆλθεν. χρυσὸν οὖν καὶ πολλὰ ἄλλα ἔκλεψεν. οὐδεὶς γὰρ
ἐκώλυσεν. καὶ τοιαῦτα πολλάκις ἔπρασσεν, ὥστε πλουσιώτατος ἐγένετο.
τέλος δ᾽ εἰς τὰ <u>βασίλεια</u> εἰσῆλθεν. <u>οὔτε</u> γὰρ οἱ φύλακες εἶδον αὐτὸν <u>οὔτε</u>
20 ὁ <u>βασιλεύς</u>. τοῦτον οὖν ἀποκτείνας καὶ τὴν γυναῖκα αὐτοῦ <u>ὑβρίσας</u> τὴν
ἀρχὴν αὐτὸς ἔλαβεν. οὕτως οὖν πάντων ἀνθρώπων <u>κάκιστος</u> ἐγένετο. τί
οὖν, ὦ Σώκρατες, ἀπὸ τούτου τοῦ μύθου μανθάνομεν; <u>ἀρ᾽ οὐχ</u> ὁ δίκαιος,
περὶ οὗ ἀεὶ λέγεις, τοῦτον τὸν <u>δακτύλιον</u> ἔχων τοιαῦτα πράξει καὶ
αὐτός;

	δάκτυλος -ου ὁ	finger
	λάθρᾳ	secretly
	βασίλεια -ων τά	palace
	οὔτε ... οὔτε	neither ... nor
20	βασιλεύς ὁ	king
	ὑβρίζω ὕβρισα	(here) I rape
	κάκιστος -η -ον	worst
	ἀρ᾽ (= ἄρα) οὐ	surely?
	δακτύλιος -ου ὁ	ring

Seven more third declension neuter nouns:

1	αἷμα -ατος τό	blood
2	ἅρμα -ατος τό	chariot
3	κτῆμα -ατος τό	possession
4	πρᾶγμα -ατος τό	matter, affair, business
5	στόμα -ατος τό	mouth
6	τείχισμα -ατος τό	fortification
7	τραῦμα -ατος τό	wound

Exercise 8.11

Translate into English:
1 οἱ ἀνδρείως μαχεσάμενοι πολλὰ τραύματα ἔχουσιν.
2 τί ἐπύθετο ὁ ἄγγελος περὶ τῶν ἐκεῖ πραγμάτων;
3 οἱ τοῦ αἰχμαλώτου ὀφθαλμοὶ αἵματι ἐκρύπτοντο.
4 ὁ παῖς οὐκ ἀπεκρίνατο ὡς σῖτον ἐν τῷ στόματι ἔχων.
5 ἡ γυνή, πολλὰ κτήματα δεξαμένη, πλουσιωτάτη ἐγένετο.
6 τοσοῦτο ὕδωρ ἐν τῷ τειχίσματι ἦν ὥστ᾽ οἱ φυλάσσοντες δέκα
   ἡμέρας ἔμενον.
7 πολλοὶ τῶν συμμάχων ἐκείνῳ τῷ στρατηγῷ ἕσποντο.
8 ὁ στρατιώτης ἐκ τοῦ ἅρματος πεσὼν τραῦμα δεινὸν ἔλαβεν.
9 τίνες εἰσιν αἱ γυναῖκες αἷς ἐπίθου, ὦ δοῦλε;
10 ὁ τοῦ τειχίσματος φύλαξ οὐδὲν ᾔσθετο.

Aorist passive

• As we saw, in the aorist there are separate forms for middle and for passive.

• The distinction between first (weak) and second (strong) aorist - which is so important in the active and middle - does not really apply to the passive: all aorist passives have the same endings.

• The aorist passive normally has a stem ending in theta: this theta is the mark of a distinctively passive tense. Some verbs with a first (weak) aorist insert a sigma before the theta: hence the aorist passive stem of παύω is παυσθ-.

• In one important respect the aorist passive is unusual and anomalous. Although its meaning is passive, its form resembles that of an active tense: its endings are identical to those of the root aorist active ἔβην. Hence:

aorist passive:

ἐπαύσθ-ην	I was stopped
ἐπαύσθ-ης	you (*sg*) were stopped
ἐπαύσθ-η	he/she/it was stopped
ἐπαύσθ-ημεν	we were stopped
ἐπαύσθ-ητε	you (*pl*) were stopped
ἐπαύσθ-ησαν	they were stopped

• However very many verbs do not insert the sigma before the theta: so for example the aorist passive of λύω is ἐλύθην. This is the one respect in which παύω is not a completely typical and regular verb. But the sigma issue is not a major problem: as always, common examples will quickly become familiar (and there are even a few verbs where Greek authors themselves vary in whether or not they put in the sigma). Details can easily be checked in the full list of verbs in the Reference Grammar, as can the (often slightly irregular) aorist passives of verbs which have a second (strong) aorist active: e.g. λαμβάνω, aorist passive ἐλήφθην.

Exercise 8.12

Translate into Greek:
1   I was saved.
2   It was thrown.
3   We were seized.
4   You (*sg*) were left.
5   They were persuaded.

• The resemblance (in form, not meaning) of the aorist passive to an active tense applies also to its participle. Other middle and passive participles are 2-1-2 in declension (e.g. παυόμενος -η -ον). But the aorist passive participle is 3-1-3, like an active participle (e.g.

παύων -ουσα -ον, with masculine/neuter stem παυοντ-). Hence:

aorist passive participle: (basic aorist passive stem παυσθ- ; masculine/neuter genitive
                                    stem of participle παυσθεντ-)

        having been stopped

		masculine	feminine	neuter
sg	nom	παυσθείς	παυσθεῖσ-α	παυσθέν
	acc	παυσθέντ-α	παυσθεῖσ-αν	παυσθέν
	gen	παυσθέντ-ος	παυσθείσ-ης	παυσθέντ-ος
	dat	παυσθέντ-ι	παυσθείσ-η	παυσθέντ-ι
pl	nom	παυσθέντ-ες	παυσθεῖσ-αι	παυσθέντ-α
	acc	παυσθέντ-ας	παυσθείσ-ας	παυσθέντ-α
	gen	παυσθέντ-ων	παυσθεισ-ῶν	παυσθέντ-ων
	dat	παυσθεῖσι(ν)	παυσθείσ-αις	παυσθεῖσι(ν)

• There is very little new learning here, if you compare this to an active participle such as παύων or παύσας. Given the nominative singulars and genitive stem, it is easy to work out the other bits. The masculine is normal third declension, with usual adjustment to the dative plural (here for παυσθεντσι). The feminine is first declension, adding - compare present active παύουσα, first (weak) aorist active παύσασα - a syllable ending in sigma (here -εισ-)*, then endings like θάλασσα. The neuter is a predictable neuter variant of the masculine, with nominative/accusative singular a shortened form of the stem: compare present active παύον, first (weak) aorist active παύσαν.

* The dative plural of the masculine provides a clue to the vowel(s) before the sigma in the feminine: hence παύουσι(ν) gives παύουσα, παύσασι(ν) gives παύσασα, and παυσθεῖσι(ν) gives παυσθεῖσα.

• Whatever form the stem for the tense has (extra sigma or not, or other irregularities), the participle follows suit. Hence from ἐλύθην the participle is λυθείς -εῖσα -έν (basic aorist passive stem λυθ-; masculine/neuter genitive stem of participle λυθεντ-), and from ἐλήφθην the participle is ληφθείς -εῖσα -έν (basic aorist stem ληφθ-; masculine/neuter genitive stem of participle ληφθεντ-).

• A few verbs do not have the theta on the aorist passive stem, but the tense and participle endings are added as usual:

		aorist passive	aor pass stem	participle
θάπτω	I bury	ἐτάφην	ταφ-	ταφείς -εῖσα -έν (ταφεντ-)
κλέπτω	I steal	ἐκλάπην	κλαπ-	κλαπείς -εῖσα -έν (κλαπεντ-)
κόπτω	I cut	ἐκόπην	κοπ-	κοπείς -εῖσα -έν (κοπεντ-)

Exercise 8.13

Give the Greek for:
1   Having been hindered (*m nom pl*)
2   Having been heard (*f acc sg*)
3   Having been announced (*n nom pl*)
4   Having been forced (*m acc sg*)

5   Having been saved (*f nom pl*)

Exercise 8.14

Translate into English:
1   ἡ ἐκκλησία τῷ σκότῳ ἐπαύσθη.
2   ὁ ἵππος, ὑπὸ τῆς παιδὸς λυθείς, ἐκ τοῦ ἀγροῦ ἐξέδραμεν.
3   ὁ χρυσὸς ὑπὸ τῶν πολεμίων ἐλήφθη.
4   ὁ στρατός, τῷ ποταμῷ κωλυθείς, ἐν τῷ στρατοπέδῳ ἔμενεν.
5   ὁ ἄγγελος ὁ πρὸς τὴν κώμην πεμφθεὶς νῦν πάρεστιν.
6   τίνες εἰσὶν οἱ ὑπὸ τοῦ στρατηγοῦ ληφθέντες;
7   οἱ ἐν τῷ δεσμωτηρίῳ ἐλύθησαν πάντες.
8   πᾶσαι αἱ ὑπὸ τῶν πολεμίων ληφθεῖσαι μετὰ δύο ἡμέρας ἐλύθησαν.
9   αἱ ἐπιστολαί οὕτω σοφῶς ἐκρύφθησαν ὥστε οὐδεὶς ηὗρεν.
10   οἱ ὑπὸ τοῦ γίγαντος διωχθέντες ἀπὸ τῆς νήσου ἔφυγον.

Exercise 8.15

Translate into Greek:
1   The battle was stopped by the allies' general.
2   The lion, when it had been released by the slave, ran towards the village.
3   Those soldiers were not hindered by the sea.
4   The boy who had received a wound was sent to the doctor's house.
5   All the women who had been chased out of their houses fled into the fortification.

Future middle and passive

• In the present tense, the active παύω has the corresponding form παύομαι, which can be either middle or passive (decided by context). In the future tense, the active παύσω likewise has a corresponding form παύσομαι, but this is used *for the middle only*.

future middle:
   παύσ-ομαι   I shall cease (stop myself, get something stopped, etc)
   παύσ-ῃ   you (*sg*) will cease
   παύσ-εται   he/she/it will cease

   παυσ-όμεθα   we shall cease
   παύσ-εσθε   you (*pl*) will cease
   παύσ-ονται   they will cease

   participle: παυσόμενος -η -ον   about to cease

• The future passive is formed from the the aorist passive stem (which as we saw normally ends in theta, with or without preceding sigma). It then adds -ησ- (introducing a further sigma) before the normal middle/passive primary endings:

future passive:

παυσθήσ-ομαι	I shall be stopped
παυσθήσ-η	you (*sg*) will be stopped
παυσθήσ-εται	he/she/it will be stopped
παυσθησ-όμεθα	we shall be stopped
παυσθήσ-εσθε	you (*pl*) will be stopped
παυσθήσ-ονται	they will be stopped

participle: παυσθησόμενος -η -ον   about to be stopped

• Correspondingly for a verb which does not insert sigma before theta, the future passive λυθήσομαι is formed from the aorist passive ἐλύθην; and for an irregular verb the future passive ληφθήσομαι is formed from the aorist passive ἐλήφθην. (Again, forms such as this can easily be looked up in the Reference Grammar: the commoner ones will quickly become familiar.)

• These tenses are formed by the familiar building-block method. With the vast majority of verbs the theta is there as a marker of the distinctively passive forms of the aorist and future. Sometimes slight adjustment to the stem is needed to accommodate the theta: so for example the future passive of διώκω is διωχθήσομαι (the aspiration spreads from the theta to convert kappa into chi: this is standard when a consonant which has an aspirated equivalent available comes before another already aspirated).

• Deponent verbs (and verbs with a special idiomatic meaning in the middle) usually have as their future the middle form. This is normally easy to work out (either completely regular, or with the slight adjustment to the stem - to accommodate the added sigma - which is already familiar from the future and first aorist active). Hence:

present	*future*	
ἄρχομαι	ἄρξομαι	I shall begin
δέχομαι	δέξομαι	I shall receive
ἕπομαι	ἕψομαι	I shall follow
λύομαι	λύσομαι	I shall ransom
πείθομαι	πείσομαι	I shall obey
πορεύομαι	πορεύσομαι	I shall march
στρατοπεδεύομαι	στρατοπεδεύσομαι	I shall set up camp

A few verbs, whilst still adding the usual future middle endings, make greater changes to the stem:

αἰσθάνομαι	αἰσθήσομαι	I shall perceive
γίγνομαι	γενήσομαι	I shall become, I shall happen
πυνθάνομαι	πεύσομαι	I shall enquire

Exercise 8.16

Translate into Greek:
1   We shall be hindered.
2   You (*sg*) will begin.
3   He will perceive.
4   They will be chased.
5   You (*pl*) will follow.

Exercise 8.17

Translate into English:
1   ἆρα στρατοπεδευσόμεθα ἐν ἐκείνῳ τῷ ἀγρῷ;
2   οἱ ἵπποι ὑπὸ τοῦ παιδὸς λυθήσονται.
3   τί νῦν γενήσεται, ὦ στρατηγέ;
4   ἡ μάχη τῷ σκότῳ παυσθήσεται.
5   οἱ ἄρχοντες οὐ δέξονται ταῦτα τὰ δῶρα.
6   ποῦ εἰσιν οἱ στρατιῶται οἱ ἡμῖν ἑψόμενοι;
7   οὕτω σοφός ἐστιν ὁ παῖς ὥστε διδάσκαλος γενήσεται.
8   οὗτοι οἱ ἄνδρες τῷ ποταμῷ οὐ κωλυθήσονται.
9   πάντες οἱ πολῖται ἐκείνῳ τῷ ῥήτορι πείσονται.
10   τίνες εἰσὶν οἱ αἰχμάλωτοι οἱ νῦν λυθησόμενοι;

Exercise 8.18

Translate into Greek:
1   When will the war cease?
2   This horse will not be released.
3   The soldiers will march towards the sea.
4   The men who are running away will be stopped by the giant.
5   Those women will receive prizes.

Revision checkpoint

Make sure you know:
• the middle voice (with the various jobs it does) and deponent verbs
• the distinction between the tenses where the middle and passive forms are the same
(present and imperfect), and those where there are separate forms for each (future and aorist)
• the two types of aorist middle: first (weak) and second (strong)
• aorist passive (theta as marker, quite often preceded by sigma; resemblance in form to an
active tense)
• future middle and passive
• the building-block method by which the tenses are constructed

Exercise 8.19

Antigone

The theme of unwritten or natural laws (rules and obligations above and beyond the laws of any particular society), which came up in Socrates' conversation with Hippias, is central to Antigone, *a famous tragic drama by Sophocles. The story forms part of a cycle of myths about the royal family of Thebes (a city in central Greece) in the distant past. Oedipus, son of the royal house, was abandoned in infancy because of a dreadful prophecy from the gods, but survived and unknowingly killed his own father Laius and married his own mother Jocasta. Problems continued in the next generation, with Oedipus' children (also of course his half-brothers and half-sisters). His daughter Antigone defies the law of the state because of the obligation to her brother Polyneices dictated by the unwritten laws of the gods.*

μετὰ δὲ τὸν τοῦ <u>Οἰδίποδος</u> θάνατον, οἱ <u>υἱοὶ</u> δύο ὄντες, ὁ μὲν Ἐτεοκλῆς
ὁ δὲ <u>Πολυνείκης</u> ὀνόματι, πρῶτον μὲν τῆς ἀρχῆς <u>μετέσχον</u> ἐν ταῖς
<u>Θήβαις</u>. ἔπειτα δὲ ἦν ἀγὼν δεινός. ὁ μὲν γὰρ Ἐτεοκλῆς οὐκέτι ἐθέλων τῆς
ἀρχῆς μετέχειν <u>ἐξήλασε</u> τὸν ἀδελφόν. ὁ δ' οὖν Πολυνείκης συμμάχους
5   ηὗρε τοὺς <u>Ἀργείους</u>, καὶ στρατὸν πρὸς τὰς Θήβας ἤγαγεν. ἦν δὲ τότε
πόλεμος, ἐν ᾧ οἱ ἀδελφοὶ <u>ἡγεμόνες</u> τε καὶ στρατηγοὶ ἦσαν, ὁ μὲν
Ἐτεοκλῆς τῶν <u>Θηβαίων</u>, ὁ δὲ Πολυνείκης τῶν Ἀργείων. ἦσαν δὲ ταῖς
Θήβαις ἑπτὰ πύλαι, καὶ ἑκάστη φύλαξ. ὁ δὲ τῆς ἑβδόμης πύλης φύλαξ ὁ
Ἐτεοκλῆς ἦν, καὶ ταύτῃ <u>προσέβαλεν</u> ὁ Πολυνείκης. τῇ δὲ <u>τελευταίᾳ</u> τοῦ
10 πολέμου μάχῃ οἱ μὲν Θηβαῖοι ἀνδρείως ἐμαχέσαντο, οἱ δὲ Ἀργεῖοι
ἔφυγον. οἱ μέντοι ἀδελφοὶ ἀπέκτειναν <u>ἀλλήλους</u>.

μετὰ δὲ ταῦτα ὁ μὲν Ἐτεοκλῆς <u>τάφον</u> τε καὶ τιμὴν ἐδέξατο. ὁ δὲ τοῦ
ἀδελφοῦ νεκρὸς ἐν τῷ <u>πεδίῳ</u> ἔμενεν. ὁ γὰρ <u>Κρέων</u>, ὁ τῆς <u>Ἰοκάστης</u>
ἀδελφὸς ἐν ταῖς Θήβαις νῦν ἄρχων, εἶπε τάδε· "οὗτος κάκιστός ἐστι τῶν
15 πολεμίων ὃς τῇ <u>πατρίδι</u> προσβάλλει, βουλόμενος τοὺς φίλους ἀποκτείνειν.

	Οἰδίπους -οδος ὁ	Oedipus
	υἱός -οῦ ὁ	son
	Ἐτεοκλῆς ὁ	Eteocles
	Πολυνείκης ὁ	Polyneices
	μετέχω μετέσχον	I share (+ *gen*)
	Θῆβαι -ων αἱ	Thebes
	ἐξελαύνω ἐξήλασα	I drive out
5	Ἀργεῖοι -ων οἱ	Argives, men of Argos (*city in southern Greece*)
	ἡγεμών -όνος ὁ	leader
	Θηβαῖοι -ων οἱ	Thebans, men of Thebes
	προσβάλλω προσέβαλον	I attack (+ *dat*)
	τελευταῖος -α -ον	final
10	ἀλλήλους	each other
	τάφος -ου ὁ	tomb
	πεδίον -ου τό	plain, open ground
	Κρέων -οντος ὁ	Creon
	Ἰοκάστη -ης ἡ	Jocasta (*mother and wife of Oedipus*)
15	πατρίς -ίδος ἡ	fatherland, native city

τοὺς οὖν Θηβαίους κελεύω τοῦτον <u>ἄνευ</u> <u>τάφου</u> λείπειν. θανάτῳ δὲ κολασθήσεται ὁ τὸν νεκρὸν θάψας."

ταῦτα δὲ τοῖς Θηβαίοις ἐφαίνετο <u>ἀδίκως</u> λεχθῆναι. σιγῇ μέντοι τοὺς λόγους διὰ φόβον ἐδέξαντο. ἡ δ' <u>Ἀντιγόνη</u>, ἡ τῶν ἀποθανόντων <u>ἀδελφή</u>,
20 μαθοῦσα τὴν τοῦ ἀδελφοῦ <u>ἀτιμίαν</u>, οὐκ ἤθελε τῷ <u>τυράννῳ</u> πείθεσθαι. πάντα οὖν παρασκευάσασα <u>ἔωθεν</u> ἐξῆλθεν ὡς τὸν νεκρὸν θάψουσα. ἐλήφθη μέντοι ὑπὸ τῶν τοῦ Κρέοντος στρατιώτων τὸν νεκρὸν θάψασα, καὶ <u>παρὰ</u> τὸν τύραννον ἤχθη. ὁ μὲν οὖν Κρέων, "διὰ τί," ἔφη, "ἐμοὶ οὐ πείθῃ;" ἡ δ' Ἀντιγόνη ἀπεκρίνατο, "οἱ μὲν σοὶ νόμοι <u>ἐφήμεροί</u> εἰσιν, οἱ δὲ
25 τῶν θεῶν ἀεί μένουσιν. οὐδεὶς δὲ οἷός τ' ἐστὶ γιγνώσκειν <u>ὁπόθεν</u> ἦλθον, <u>ὁπότε</u> ἤρξαντο. τούτοις μέντοι τοῖς νόμοις καὶ νῦν καὶ ἀεὶ πείσομαι, τοῖς <u>ἀγράφοις</u>."

	ἄνευ	without (+ *gen*)
	τάφος -ου ὁ	tomb
	ἀδίκως	unjustly
	Ἀντιγόνη -ης ἡ	Antigone
	ἀδελφή -ῆς ἡ	sister
20	ἀτιμία -ας ἡ	dishonourable treatment
	τύραννος -ου ὁ	tyrant, ruler
	ἔωθεν	at dawn
	παρά	(+ *acc*) before, into the presence of
	ἐφήμερος -ον	of the day, temporary
25	ὁπόθεν	where from
	ὁπότε	when
	ἄγραφος -ον	unwritten

Overview of participles

Summary table (showing masculine nominative singular of each):

	active	*middle*	*passive*
present	παύων	παυόμενος	
future	παύσων	παυσόμενος	παυσθησόμενος
first (weak) aorist	παύσας	παυσάμενος	παυσθείς
second (strong) aorist	λαβών	λαβόμενος	ληφθείς

Full grammar detail and meanings of the participles shown above:

present
 active
   παύων -ουσα -ον (3-1-3 decl; m/n gen stem παυοντ-)
   stopping
   (indicative: παύω *I stop*)

 middle/passive
   παυόμενος -η -ον (2-1-2 decl)
   ceasing, stopping oneself (middle); *being stopped* (passive)
   (indicative: παύομαι *I cease, I stop myself; I am stopped*)

future
 active
   παύσων -ουσα -ον (3-1-3 decl; m/n gen stem παυσοντ-)
   about to stop
   (indicative: παύσω *I shall stop*)

 middle
   παυσόμενος -η -ον (2-1-2 decl)
   about to cease, about to stop oneself
   (indicative: παύσομαι I shall cease, I shall stop myself)

 passive
   παυσθησόμενος -η -ον (2-1-2 decl)
   about to be stopped
   (indicative: παυσθήσομαι I shall be stopped)

aorist
 first (weak) active
   παύσας -ασα -αν (3-1-3 decl; m/n gen stem παυσαντ-)
   having stopped
   (indicative: ἔπαυσα I stopped)

 first (weak) middle
   παυσάμενος -η -ον (2-1-2 decl)
   having ceased, having stopped oneself
   (indicative: ἐπαυσάμην I ceased, I stopped myself)

 second (strong) active
   λαβών -οῦσα, -όν (3-1-3 decl; m/n gen stem λαβοντ-)
   having taken
   (indicative: ἔλαβον I took)

 second (strong) middle
   λαβόμενος -η -ον (2-1-2 decl)
   having taken for oneself
   (indicative: ἐλαβόμην I took for myself)

 passive
   παυσθείς -εῖσα -έν (3-1-3 decl; m/n gen stem παυσθεντ-)
   having been stopped
   (indicative: ἐπαύσθην I was stopped)

• You have now met all the participles in common use. Participles are one of the most characteristic features of Greek, giving the language immense flexibility. The two-stage process of understanding what each participle literally means, then thinking of appropriate English in the context, is crucial to translating successfully.

Exercise 8.20

For each of the following participles, state the tense, voice (active, middle or passive), gender, case, and number (singular or plural):
e.g. παυσάσαις = aorist active, feminine dative plural
(sometimes more than one answer is possible, e.g. a form could be masculine or neuter)

1   παύοντες
2   παυούσης
3   παυσθεῖσαν
4   παυσαμένους
5   παύσοντας
6   παυσάντων (*two answers*)
7   παύοντι (*two answers*)
8   παυσομένου (*two answers*)
9   παυσθησομένων (*three answers*)
10 παυόμενον (*six answers*)

Ten more adverbs:
1   δεῦρο   (to) here
2   ἤδη   already
3   λάθρα   secretly
4   μάτην   in vain
5   μόλις   with difficulty, scarcely
6   πάλιν   again, back again
7   πανταχοῦ   everywhere
8   σχεδόν   nearly, almost
9   τότε   then, at that time
10 ὕστερον   later

Exercise 8.21 (Revision of participles)

Translate into English:
1   οἱ ξένοι, ἑπτὰ ὥρας ἤδη μαχεσάμενοι, οὐκέτι τοῖς στρατηγοῖς
        ἐπείθοντο.
2   ὁ ταῦτα μαθὼν σοφώτερός ἐστι τῶν ἄλλων.
3   οἱ σύμμαχοι δεῦρο πορευόμενοι τῷ ποταμῷ ἐκωλύθησαν.
4   οὕτως ἀνδρεῖός ἐστιν ὁ τὰς γυναῖκας λάθρα λύσας ὥστε πανταχοῦ
        θαυμάζεται.
5   οἱ πολέμιοι εἰς τὴν θάλασσαν διωχθέντες σχεδὸν πάντες ἀπέθανον.
6   ὁ νεανίας, καίπερ πολλὰ ἆθλα ἤδη δεξάμενος, ἔτι ἐβούλετο νίκην
        ἔχειν.

7   αἱ παῖδες τὰς βοὰς πάλιν ἀκούσασαι εἰς τὸ τείχισμα πάλιν
     εἰσῆλθον.
8   οἱ τὴν τιμὴν οὐκ ἔχοντες τά τε κτήματα καὶ τὸν χρυσὸν μάτην
     διώξουσιν.
9   οὗτος ὁ παῖς, τὴν βίβλον μόλις εὑρών, ὕστερον ἀπέβαλεν.
10   ἆρα οἱ τότε ῥήτορες γενόμενοι δικαιότεροι ἦσαν ἢ οἱ νῦν;

Exercise 8.22

Translate into Greek:
1   The people who were chasing the horse caught it with difficulty.
2   The poet, after writing many books, became a soldier again.
3   The man who had ransomed the allies was admired by all.
4   The boys ran away when they were about to be stopped by the old man.
5   The woman who had guarded the village with difficulty received a very big prize.

Genitive absolute

• Participle phrases can exist in any grammatical case, the case being determined as usual by
the job being done in the sentence:

οἱ δοῦλοι φεύγοντες τῷ ποταμῷ ἐκωλύθησαν.
The slaves while running away were hindered by the river.
(*noun + circumstantial participle, in the nominative as subject*)

ἆρ᾽ εἶδες τοὺς στρατιώτας τοὺς μαχομένους;
Did you see the soldiers who were fighting?
(*noun + defining/attributive participle, in the accusative as object*)

οὐδὲν ἤκουσα περὶ τοῦ παιδὸς τοῦ δεῦρο πεμφθέντος.
I heard nothing about the boy who had been sent here.
(*noun + defining/attributive participle, in the genitive governed by* περί)

πάντες βουλόμεθα δῶρα παρέχειν τοῖς γέρουσιν τοῖς ἐνθάδε μένουσιν.
We all want to provide gifts for the old men who are staying here.
(*noun + defining/attributive participle, in the dative as indirect object*)

But if a participle phrase is unconnected grammatically with the rest of the sentence (merely
denoting an 'attendant circumstance', i.e. telling us about something else that was true or
applicable at the time) it goes into the genitive: this is called the *genitive absolute*, from the
original Latin meaning of 'absolute' as *set free* or *independent* (rather than the modern
English meaning *complete* or *utter*). Hence:

τῶν δούλων φευγόντων, οἱ πολῖται οὐδὲν ἤκουσαν.
While the slaves were running away, the citizens heard nothing.

τῶν συμμάχων ἀποπεμφθέντων, οὐκ ἠθέλομεν μάχεσθαι.
Because the allies had been sent away, we did not want to fight.

ταῦτα ἐγένετο τοῦ γέροντος παρόντος.
These things happened with the old man present.

• The genitive absolute corresponds to the ablative absolute in Latin: this is another example of the Greek genitive doing one of the ablative jobs.

• The Greek genitive absolute is however less common than the Latin equivalent. In Latin many examples of the ablative absolute are necessitated by the limited number of participles available, in particular the lack (for all except deponent verbs) of a past (perfect, but mostly corresponding to the Greek aorist) active participle. So *Having done these things, he left* must in Latin be turned round into *With these things having been done, he left* (making the participle passive, and the phrase ablative absolute). In Greek, with the flexibility afforded by a full set of participles, there is no need to do this.

Exercise 8.23

Translate into English:
1 τῶν πολεμίων φευγόντων, οὐκέτι ἐν κινδύνῳ ἐσμέν.
2 ταύτης τῆς ὁδοῦ χαλεπῆς οὔσης, ἀναγκαζόμεθα ἄλλην εὑρίσκειν.
3 ὀλίγων στρατιωτῶν παρόντων, ἄγγελον πρὸς τὸ στρατόπεδον
      πέμψομεν.
4 τοῦ ὕδατος δεινοῦ ὄντος, ἡ κώμη οὐδενὸς ἀξία ἐστίν.
5 τῆς γυναικὸς ἀποθανούσης, ὁ γέρων ἄθλιος ἦν.
6 οἱ σύμμαχοι πρὸς τὸ τείχισμα λάθρα προσῆλθον, οὐδενὸς κωλύοντος.
7 τὸ ναυτικὸν ἐκ τοῦ λιμένος ἐξεπέμφθη, τοῦ στρατηγοῦ κελεύσαντος.
8 τοῦ ποταμοῦ χαλεποῦ ὄντος, ἐγγὺς τῆς κώμης ἐστρατοπεδευσάμεθα.
9 τοῦ διδασκάλου ὀργιζομένου, οἱ παῖδες ἀπέδραμον.
10 τῶν δεσμῶν λυθέντων, ὁ αἰχμάλωτος εὐθὺς ἔφυγεν.

Exercise 8.24

Translate into Greek:
1 Because the allies are few, we no longer hear about victories.
2 When the women had learned the words, the men took away the books.
3 Because the sea was hindering the army, the men in the assembly did not want to
      fight.
4 While the girls were running away, the teacher heard a shout.
5 When the general had ransomed the slaves, we all went away.

Future tense of *to be*

The future of εἰμί, though active in meaning (*to be* can have no middle or passive sense), resembles a middle in form:

ἔσομαι	I shall be
ἔσῃ	you (*sg*) will be
ἔσται*	he/she/it will be
ἐσόμεθα	we shall be
ἔσεσθε	you (*pl*) will be
ἔσονται	they will be

* this has been shortened to aid pronunciation from ἔσεται, the form that might have been predicted

participle: ἐσόμενος -η -ον   about to be

Active verbs with middle-form futures

• Some ordinary verbs use a middle form for their future (with active sense):

present	*future*	
ἀκούω	ἀκούσομαι	I shall hear
βαίνω	βήσομαι	I shall go
γιγνώσκω	γνώσομαι	I shall get to know
διώκω	διώξομαι*	I shall chase, I shall pursue
λαμβάνω	λήψομαι	I shall take
μανθάνω	μαθήσομαι	I shall learn
πάσχω	πείσομαι†	I shall suffer
φεύγω	φεύξομαι	I shall run away, I shall flee

* however the active διώξω is also sometimes used

† note that this is identical to the future of πείθομαι (*I shall obey*), but the context should make clear which it is

• There is no obvious explanation for this: βαίνω and γιγνώσκω are also unusual in having a root aorist active (ἔβην and ἔγνων respectively), but ἀκούω has a perfectly normal first (weak) aorist ἤκουσα (stem ἀκουσ-), and there seems no reason why the future could not be ἀκούσω. Minor peculiarities such as this have to be accepted as part of a language with a rich history: they can be irritating at first, but they can easily be checked in the Reference Grammar. And because it is very often the commonest words that have irregular features (because they have been bashed about with use), they quickly become familiar. It is also worth noting here that we have already seen one verb with middle form in the present, active in the aorist: ἔρχομαι, aorist ἦλθον. This phenomenon of mixed middle/deponent and active forms is broadly comparable to semi-deponent verbs in Latin, e.g. *gaudeo, gaudere, gavisus sum* (active present tense and infinitive, deponent - i.e. passive form - perfect).

73

Deponent verbs with passive-form aorists

• As we saw, deponent verbs are middle in form, and therefore normally use the middle versions of the future and aorist forms. But a few of them prefer the passive form for the aorist. Hence:

present	aorist
ὀργίζομαι	ὠργίσθην
πορεύομαι	ἐπορεύθην

• With ὀργίζομαι it is fairly easy to explain this: ὠργίσθην is in origin a genuine passive of the underlying (but rarer) active and transitive verb ὀργίζω = *I anger* (someone); hence *I was angered* (by someone/something) for *I got angry*. Not quite so obvious is πορεύομαι: though it is worth noting here that Greek authors themselves vary, sometimes writing ἐπορεύσαντο rather than ἐπορεύθησαν for *they marched*.

Exercise 8.25

Translate into Greek:
1   We shall hear.
2   They got angry.
3   He will go.
4   You (*pl*) marched.
5   You (*sg*) will learn.

Revision checkpoint

Make sure you know:
• all participles (what they mean and how they decline)
• how the genitive absolute works
• future of *to be*
• active verbs with middle-form futures
• deponent verbs with passive-form aorists

Exercise 8.26

Read the following passage then answer the questions below:

Socrates refuses to join in an illegal trial

Socrates generally avoided public life, but he also believed in the duty of citizens to serve their city when required. He served in the army as a hoplite (heavy-armed infantryman), and was distinguished by his courage, physical resilience, and concern for his comrades. When he became briefly involved in political affairs, his behaviour matched up to his principles. Athenian democracy meant that any adult male citizen might serve his turn as chairman for a day of the Assembly (ecclesia). Socrates happened to be chairman when a controversial matter came before the meeting. In 406 BC (in the closing stages of the Peloponnesian War: see the next background section) Athens won a naval victory over Sparta and her allies at Arginusae (islands off modern Turkey). But this was tainted by criticism of the behaviour of the Athenian commanders after the battle. Eight generals (out of ten annually elected to command both land and sea forces) were tried by the Assembly: Socrates alone stood up against a tide of popular indignation and objected to the proposed method of doing this.

ὁ δὲ Σωκράτης ἦν σοφώτατός τε καὶ <u>ἄριστος</u> τῶν τότε ᾿Αθηναίων.
καὶ <u>ἐπιστάτης</u> τῆς ἐκκλησίας <u>ποτε</u> ὤν, οὐκ ἠθέλησε τῷ δήμῳ πείθεσθαι,
ὡς βουλομένῳ ὀκτὼ στρατηγοὺς μιᾷ <u>ψήφῳ</u> <u>παρὰ</u> τοὺς νόμους ἀποκτείνειν.
ἦν δὲ τοῖς ᾿Αθηναίοις νίκη ἐν ναυμαχίᾳ τινὶ πρότερον· οὗτοι μέντοι οἱ
5 στρατηγοὶ οὐχ οἷοί τ᾿ ἦσαν, μεγάλου <u>χειμῶνος</u> γενομένου, τοὺς
᾿Αθηναίους <u>ναυαγοὺς</u> σῴζειν. διὰ δὲ τοῦτο ἐβούλετο ὁ δῆμος πάντας
<u>ὁμοίως</u> κολάζειν. καὶ οἱ μὲν πολῖται μάλιστα ὠργίσθησαν διότι ὁ
Σωκράτης οὕτως ἐκώλυεν, καὶ ἐκέλευσαν αὐτὸν <u>ἑαυτοῖς</u> πείθεσθαι.
ὁ δὲ Σωκράτης, "ἀκούετέ μου," ἔφη, "ὦ ἄνδρες ᾿Αθηναῖοι. τοῦτο γὰρ
10 πράξαντες, <u>ἀδικίας</u> μεγίστης <u>αἴτιοι</u> ἔσεσθε, ὅτι οὐ δίκαιόν ἐστι τῶν ὀκτὼ
πάντων μιᾷ ψήφῳ θάνατον <u>καταγιγνώσκειν</u>. ἐν γὰρ ταῖς ᾿Αθήναις πᾶς ὁ
<u>φεύγων</u> <u>χωρὶς</u> <u>δικάζεται</u>." ἐπεὶ μέντοι ὁ Σωκράτης οὐκ ἔπεισε τὴν
ἐκκλησίαν, οἱ στρατηγοὶ μετὰ ὀλίγας ἡμέρας ἀπέθανον.

	ἄριστος -η -ον	best
	ἐπιστάτης -ου ὁ	leader, chairman
	ποτε	(*not in a question*) once
	ψῆφος -ου ἡ	vote
	παρά	(+ *acc*) contrary to
5	χειμών -ῶνος ὁ	storm
	ναυαγός -οῦ ὁ	shipwrecked man
	ὁμοίως	in the same way
	ἑαυτούς -άς	themselves (*reflexive pronoun; no nominative in use*)
10	ἀδικία -ας ἡ	injustice
	αἴτιος -α -ον	responsible for, the cause of (+ *gen*)
	καταγιγνώσκω	I condemn (someone *gen*) to (a penalty *acc*)
	φεύγων -οντος ὁ	defendant, person on trial
	χωρίς	separately
	δικάζω	I try, I judge

(1) How is Socrates described in line 1? (3)
(2) Why is τῷ δήμῳ (line 2) dative? (1)
(3) What did the Assembly want to do (lines 2-3)? (3)
(4) What had the generals been unable to do, and why (lines 4-6)? (4)
(5) What does Socrates say about the proposed course of action
      (lines 9-11)? (3)
(6) What principle of normal Athenian justice does Socrates
      appeal to (lines 11-12)? (2)
(7) What was the outcome (lines 12-13)? (4)

_____

20 marks

The 'other εἶμι': *I shall go*

As well as the very common εἰμί = *I am*, there is another εἶμι (also irregular, but different in conjugation) used as the future of ἔρχομαι (the 'ordinary εἰμί ' is shown alongside for comparison:

εἶμι	I shall go	εἰμί	I am
εἶ	you (*sg*) will go	εἶ	you (*sg*) are
εἶσι(*ν*)	he/she/it will go	ἐστί(*ν*)	he/she/it is
ἴμεν	we shall go	ἐσμέν	we are
ἴτε	you (*pl*) will go	ἐστέ	you (*pl*) are
ἴασι(*ν*)	they will go	εἰσί(*ν*)	they are

• Accents distinguish otherwise identical forms: the two first person singulars; and the third person singular *he will go* as against the third person plural *they are*. In the second person singular however the accents too are identical, hence no help in differentiating, but context almost always avoids ambiguity.

• The iota characteristic of the plural forms *we shall go* etc is related to the Latin *imus* etc (from *eo, ire*); the two Greek verbs are often referred to by tagging on their Latin equivalents - 'εἰμί *sum*' (I am) and 'εἶμι *ibo*' (I shall go).

• There is a participle from εἶμι *ibo* in common use. This however normally has a present sense (*going*, rather than *about to go*):

ἰών, ἰοῦσα, ἰόν (*genitive stem for masculine/neuter* ἰοντ-)   going

This is formed by putting normal present active participle endings onto the stem ἰ-: this one-letter stem distinguishes it from the participle of εἰμί *sum*:

ὤν, οὖσα, ὄν (*genitive stem for masculine/neuter* ὀντ-)   being

• Similarly εἶμι *ibo* has an infinitive ἰέναι, again normally with present sense; compare εἶναι from εἰμί *sum*.

• Both εἰμί *sum* and εἶμι *ibo* can form compounds. But whereas εἰμί *sum* is compounded with a limited range of prefixes implying staying somewhere (hence e.g. πάρειμι *I am here*, ἄπειμι *I am away*), εἶμι *ibo* can (like ἔρχομαι itself) take a whole range of prefixes denoting motion. Hence for example:

ἔξιμεν	we shall go out
προσίοντες	going towards (*masculine nominative plural*)

76

Ten more nouns:
first declension feminine
1   βία -ας ἡ   force, violence
2   γλῶσσα -ης ἡ   tongue; language
3   γνώμη -ης ἡ   opinion, belief
4   στρατιά -ᾶς ἡ   army (*synonym of* στρατός)
5   συμφορά -ᾶς ἡ   disaster
second declension masculine
6   πεζοί -ῶν οἱ   infantry, footsoldiers
7   υἱός -οῦ ὁ   son
8   χαλκός -οῦ ὁ   bronze
second declension neuter
9   δάκρυον -ου τό   tear, teardrop
10 πεδίον -ου τό   plain, open country

Exercise 8.27

Translate into English:
1   ὁ φύλαξ μόλις ἀκούσεται ἐκείνους τοὺς λόγους.
2   ἡ πρὸς τὴν θάλασσαν ὁδός, χαλεπὴ ἐσομένη, κωλύσει τοὺς πεζούς.
3   ἆρα πάντες οἱ ὑμέτεροι σύμμαχοι ἄπεισιν, ὦ πολῖται;
4   μετὰ ὀλίγον χρόνον ὁ ἄγγελος πρὸς τὴν ἀγορὰν προσεῖσιν.
5   ὁ τοῦ δεσπότου υἱὸς βίᾳ ἐκώλυσεν* τοὺς δούλους φεύγειν.
6   ἆρα τόδε τὸ ἆθλον χαλκοῦ ἐστιν, ὦ νεανία;
7   τὴν τοῦ κριτοῦ γνώμην νῦν μαθησόμεθα.
8   ἡ τοῦ ξένου γλῶσσα οὐκ ἐνθάδε διδάσκεται.
9   ἐπεὶ τὰ τοῦ γέροντος δάκρυα εἶδεν, ὁ ἄγγελος ἐπαύσατο περὶ τῆς
      συμφορᾶς λέγων.
10 ἡ ἡμέτερα στρατιὰ πρὸς τὸ πεδίον ἐπορεύθη.

* as previously noted, κωλύω + infinitive means *prevent (someone) from (doing)*

Exercise 8.28

Translate into Greek:
1   After the assembly, we shall go to the harbour.
2   This disaster, which is going to be terrible, will stop the war.
3   The women who are going to learn these things are very clever.
4   Those who are fighting will receive* many wounds.
5   These slaves will be useful for our master.

* use λαμβάνω

Reflexive pronouns

• These are very straightforward, adding relevant parts of αὐτός after the appropriate personal pronoun, in the singulars (and third person plural) compressed into one word:

first person

		masculine	feminine	
sg	acc	ἐμαυτόν	ἐμαυτήν	myself*
	gen	ἐμαυτοῦ	ἐμαυτῆς	
	dat	ἐμαυτῷ	ἐμαυτῇ	

pl	acc	ἡμᾶς αὐτούς	ἡμᾶς αὐτάς	ourselves*
	gen	ἡμῶν αὐτῶν	ἡμῶν αὐτῶν	
	dat	ἡμῖν αὐτοῖς	ἡμῖν αὐταῖς	

literally me-self, us-selves

second person

		masculine	feminine	
sg	acc	σεαυτόν	σεαυτήν	yourself*
	gen	σεαυτοῦ	σεαυτῆς	
	dat	σεαυτῷ	σεαυτῇ	

pl	acc	ὑμᾶς αὐτούς	ὑμᾶς αὐτάς	yourselves*
	gen	ὑμῶν αὐτῶν	ὑμῶν αὐτῶν	
	dat	ὑμῖν αὐτοῖς	ὑμῖν αὐταῖς	

literally you-self, you-selves

third person

		masculine	feminine	neuter	
sg	acc	ἑαυτόν	ἑαυτήν	ἑαυτό	himself, herself, itself
	gen	ἑαυτοῦ	ἑαυτῆς	ἑαυτοῦ	
	dat	ἑαυτῷ	ἑαυτῇ	ἑαυτῷ	

pl	acc	ἑαυτούς	ἑαυτάς	ἑαυτά	themselves
	gen	ἑαυτῶν	ἑαυτῶν	ἑαυτῶν	
	dat	ἑαυτοῖς	ἑαυταῖς	ἑαυτοῖς	

An alternative plural for third person masculine and feminine exists, following the two-word pattern:

σφᾶς* αὐτούς	σφᾶς αὐτάς	themselves
σφῶν αὐτῶν	σφῶν αὐτῶν	
σφίσιν αὐτοῖς	σφίσιν αὐταῖς	

* parts of σφᾶς alone are sometimes used in a non-reflexive sense (equivalent to αὐτούς etc)

• These pronouns, in their nature as reflexives (denoting that the action is *reflected back* onto the subject), cannot have nominative forms. *The general blamed himself* is reflexive; *The general himself fled* is not, and in Greek would of course be ὁ στρατηγὸς αὐτὸς ἔφυγεν.

• Reflexive pronouns are less common in Greek than in Latin. One main reason for this is that where Latin insists on inserting a reflexive accusative in intransitive/reflexive expressions like *he washed (himself)*, *he hid (himself)*, Greek (as we saw) just makes the verb middle. The active with the reflexive pronoun would often amount to the same as the middle, but is normally only used to give extra emphasis, or in unusual expressions where the sense of the middle would not be obvious.

Third person possessives

As we saw in Chapters 5 and 6, the first and second person pronouns have associated adjectives:

pronoun	*adjective*	
ἐγώ, ἐμέ etc	ἐμός -ή -όν	my
σύ	σός, σή, σόν	your (of you *sg*)
ἡμεῖς	ἡμέτερος -α -ον	our
ὑμεῖς	ὑμέτερος -α -ον	your (of you *pl*)

When used with a noun, these need the article as well, and they sandwich:

ἡ ἡμέτερα οἰκία

our house

Though often the article alone is enough, if the context makes the possessive sense obvious:

ὁ Οἰδίπους τὸν πατέρα ἀπέκτεινεν.

Oedipus killed his father.

• It would be possible in theory to use the genitive of the pronoun instead of the possessive adjective: *the house of me*. This is intelligible, but unnatural - just as in English. If an adjective is available, it should be used.

• In the third person however there is no Greek adjective meaning *his, her, their* etc in common use, and so (if the article alone is not enough to convey the meaning) you do have to say *the house of him*.

• There is a crucial distinction here between *his/of him(self)* referring back reflexively to the subject, and *his/of him* referring to someone else.

• For the reflexive possessive the appropriate genitive part of ἑαυτον etc is used, and <u>needs to be sandwiched</u> with the article:

ὁ διδάσκαλος ἔπεμψε τὴν ἑαυτοῦ βίβλον.

The teacher sent his own book.

οἱ ναῦται τὸν ἑαυτῶν σῖτον ἔφαγον.
The sailors ate their own food.

• For the non-reflexive possessive the appropriate genitive part of αὐτός is used, and needs the article but <u>must not be sandwiched</u>:

πᾶσαι αἱ γυναῖκες θαυμάζουσι τὴν ἀρετὴν αὐτοῦ.
All the women admire his courage.

οἱ στρατιῶται ἔλαβον τὴν κόρην καὶ τὰ χρήματα αὐτῆς.
The soldiers captured the girl and her money.

• In Latin there is an adjective for the reflexive third person possessive (*suus -a -um*), but not for the non-reflexive (where the genitive of a pronoun must be used, e.g. *eius*, genitive of *is, ea, id*). In Greek the pronoun method has to be used for both versions.

• Because (as we saw) other uses of the Greek reflexive pronouns are relatively uncommon, the third person possessive genitive is likely to be the form most frequently met. As with the first and second person possessive adjectives, the third person possessive genitive pronouns are frequently used for emphasis or to express a contrast (where the article alone would not be enough).

Exercise 8.29

Translate into English:
1   οἱ ναῦται οὐκέτι τὸν ἑαυτῶν σῖτον ἤσθιον ἀλλὰ τὸν τοῦ
        αἰχμαλώτου.
2   ὁ στρατηγὸς τὴν ἑαυτοῦ θυγατέρα ἀπέκτεινεν.
3   οἱ σοφοὶ οὐ θαυμάζουσιν ἑαυτούς.
4   ἆρα βούλῃ σῴζειν σεαυτόν, ὦ γέρον;
5   ὁ κριτὴς αὐτὸς τὴν ἐπιστολὴν ἔγραψεν.
6   πιστεύω τῷ τε παιδὶ καὶ τῇ μητρὶ αὐτοῦ.
7   ὁ στρατιώτης, ταῦτα μαθών, ἀπέκτεινεν ἑαυτόν.
8   τί λέξομεν περὶ ἡμῶν αὐτῶν, ὦ πολῖται;
9   τὴν ἐμὴν βίβλον ἔχει ἐκεῖνος, οὐ τὴν ἑαυτοῦ.
10   τὰς γνώμας αὐτῶν πρότερον γνωσόμεθα ἢ τὰς ἡμετέρας.

Exercise 8.30

Translate into Greek:
1   The woman now wants to save herself.
2   The old man sent his own money to the temple.
3   I heard a story about myself.
4   The girl chases the boy and his horse.
5   Having suffered such a disaster, we do not admire ourselves.

Background: Socrates (4)

As we saw in Chapter 7, Socrates at the end of his life was put on trial, accused of corrupting the young men of the city (apparently taken to mean with dangerous political ideas), and of not believing in the gods the city believed in but introducing new gods of his own. Whether or not the charges were justified, we may wonder why his accusers waited until he was 70, since Socrates as a self-styled 'gadfly' had all his life set out to be provocative.

The answer is that Athens had changed. The confident, relaxed city he had grown up in (with its democratic government and rich cultural life, financed by a firmly controlled empire) had fought and eventually lost the crippling twenty-seven-year Peloponnesian War (431-404 BC) against Sparta and her allies, the other big power block in the Greek world, which had become alarmed at the ambition of Athens. Criticism, mockery and radical religious ideas could now less easily be tolerated. The democratic constitution was twice overthrown, to be replaced (temporarily but painfully) by harsh right-wing regimes. Friends and disciples of Socrates (for example Critias, Plato's uncle) were known to be involved. Socrates would certainly have distanced himself from their violent methods, and from the belief (associated with some of the Sophists) that 'justice is (simply) the right of the stronger' or 'might is right'. But it could be argued that the right-wing opponents of democracy were in some respects putting into practice an elitist strain in Socrates' thought, as he often stressed that experts should be trusted: since you clearly would want surgery performed not by someone chosen at random from the street but by a skilled doctor, why was government any different?

Plato and Xenophon both wrote versions of the *Apology* (= speech in self-defence, not 'apologetic' in our sense) which Socrates delivered in court, recounting and justifying his life. These written accounts amplify but probably do not misrepresent Socrates' actual words. He explains that he is neither a Sophist nor a 'natural philosopher ' (i.e. scientist). As we saw in Chapter 7, he insists that his only wisdom consists in knowing that he knows nothing. Though he hears a divine voice which deters him from wrongdoing (described in terms perhaps unfamiliar to many of his audience), this does not make him neglect normal religious observance.

It is unlikely that Socrates' accusers expected or wanted the death penalty to be inflicted. Voluntary exile would have been possible before the verdict. At the point after it where both sides proposed a penalty, he could have suggested a moderate fine. In fact (believing unconditionally in his innocence) he provoked the jury by suggesting that, so far from being punished, he should be given free dinners for life in the public hall in Athens (a privilege normally accorded to Olympic victors and others who brought glory on the city). This so annoyed the jurors that on a second vote more of them voted for the death penalty than had voted him guilty in the first place. Execution was postponed for a month while the Athenian state ship was engaged on a sacred mission (because it would have been ill-omened to carry out the death penalty during this period). Meanwhile Socrates was held in prison, and was visited by his friends, whose conversations are recorded in Plato's dialogues *Crito* and *Phaedo*. The latter ends with a moving description of how Socrates calmly accepted the cup of hemlock by which the death penalty was carried out in Athens.

Exercise 8.31

Socrates on Trial

Socrates begins his speech in court, after the prosecution have put the case against him:

"καλοῖς μὲν λόγοις, ὦ ἄνδρες Ἀθηναῖοι, οὐχ οἷός τ᾽ εἰμι λέγειν, ἀληθείᾳ
δ᾽ ἴσως. τοῖς μέντοι ὑπὸ τῶν κατηγόρων λεχθεῖσιν οὐδαμῶς πιστεύω.
ἀλλ᾽ οὐ μόνον πρὸς τοὺς νῦν κατηγόρους λέξω, ἀλλὰ καὶ πρὸς τοὺς
πρότερον. πολλοὶ γὰρ ἦσαν καὶ δεινοί, οἱ περὶ ἐμοῦ πολλὰ μὲν λέγοντες,
5 οὐδὲν δὲ δίκαιον. ἠκούσατε γὰρ ἐκ παίδων πάντες ὑμεῖς ὡς Σωκράτης τίς
ἐστι, τά τε ἐν τῷ οὐρανῷ καὶ τὰ ὑπὸ τῇ γῇ ἀεὶ διώκων, καὶ λέγων ὅτι ὁ
ἄδικος λόγος δίκαιός ἐστι, καὶ ἄλλους διδάσκων τὰ αὐτὰ ταῦτα. καὶ οἱ
πολῖται τοιαῦτα ἀκούσαντες λέγουσιν ὅτι τοὺς θεοὺς οὐ νομίζω. τὰ δὲ
τῶν ἄλλων κατηγόρων ὀνόματα οὐχ οἷός τ᾽ εἰμι λέγειν, πλὴν ἑνός. οὗτος
10 δὲ κωμῳδοποιός ἐστιν. πολλοὶ γὰρ ὑμῶν ἐν τῷ θεάτρῳ παρῆτε. ἔστι δ᾽ ἐν
τῇ κωμῳδίᾳ Σωκράτης τις περιφερόμενος, ἀεροβάτης ὢν καὶ περὶ πολλῶν
οὐδὲν λέγων. ἀλλὰ ὑμεις μάρτυρές ἐστε· τίς γὰρ ἤκουσέ μου περὶ
τοιούτων λέγοντος; χρήματα δ᾽ οὔποτε ἐδεξάμην διδάσκων, ὥσπερ
Πρωταγόρας καὶ Ἱππίας καὶ οἱ ἄλλοι σοφισταί. οὗτοι γὰρ διδάσκουσι καὶ
15 χρήματα δέχονται, σοφοὶ ὄντες. ἐγὼ δ᾽ οὐδαμῶς σοφός.

"καὶ λέγουσιν οἱ κατήγοροι ὅτι, οὐ νομίζων τοὺς θεοὺς οὓς ἡ πόλις
νομίζει, δαιμόνια εἰσφέρω ἄλλα καὶ νέα· καὶ ὅτι τοὺς νεανίας τοὺς
Ἀθηναίους διαφθείρω. τοιαῦτα γὰρ πολλάκις ἠκούετε· "ὁ Σωκράτης λέγει

	ἀλήθεια -ας ἡ	truth
	ἴσως	perhaps
	κατήγορος -ου ὁ	accuser
	οὐδαμῶς	in no way, not at all
	πρός	(*here*) in response to
5	ἐκ παίδων	from childhood
	ὡς	(*here*) that, how
	ὅτι	that
	ἄδικος -ον	unjust
	νομίζω	(*here*) I believe in
	πλήν	except (+ *gen*)
10	κωμῳδοποιός -οῦ ὁ	writer of comedy (*Socrates refers to Aristophanes and his play* Clouds)
	θέατρον -ου τό	theatre
	κωμῳδία -ας ἡ	comedy
	ἀεροβάτης -ου ὁ	walker on air
	οὐδὲν λέγω	I talk rubbish
	μάρτυς -υρος ὁ	witness
	οὔποτε	never
	Πρωταγόρας ὁ	Protagoras
	Ἱππίας ὁ	Hippias
	σοφιστής -οῦ ὁ	Sophist
15	δαιμόνιον -ου τό	divine being
	διαφθείρω	(*here*) I corrupt

ὅτι ὁ ἥλιος λίθος ἐστίν, οὐ θεός, καὶ ἡ <u>σελήνη</u> γῆ." οὐ μέντοι ἐγὼ ἀλλ᾿
20 ὁ ᾿Αναξαγόρας ταῦτα πάλαι ἔγραψεν· τὴν δὲ βίβλον οἷοί τ᾿ ἐστὲ μιᾶς
<u>δραχμῆς</u> ἐν τῇ ἀγορᾷ <u>ἀγορεύειν</u>. ἐγὼ δ᾿ <u>οὐδαμῶς</u> ταῦτα λέγω. θεούς τε
γὰρ καὶ <u>δαιμόνια νομίζω</u>. ἔστι δὲ καὶ δαιμόνιον, ὥσπερ φωνή τις
λέγουσα, ὃ ἀεὶ κωλύει με τῆς <u>ἀδικίας</u>.

"οὐδὲ φόβος ἔχει με πρὸς θάνατον ἰόντα. ὁ γὰρ θάνατος ἢ ὥσπερ ὕπνος
25 <u>ἀτάρακτός</u> ἐστιν, ἢ ὥσπερ ὁδός τις <u>ἐνθένδε</u> εἰς ἄλλον τόπον. καὶ ἐκεῖ
οἷός τ᾿ ἔσομαι τοῖς τε ἄλλοις <u>διαλέγεσθαι</u> καὶ τῷ ῾Ομήρῳ. στρατιώτης
γὰρ ὢν <u>οὔποτε</u> ἔφυγον ἐγὼ ἀλλ᾿ ἔμεινα ὑπὸ τῶν ᾿Αθηναίων στρατηγῶν
ταχθείς· οὐδὲ <u>φιλόσοφος</u> ὢν ἔφυγον ἀλλ᾿ ἔμεινα ὑπὸ τῶν θεῶν ταχθείς,
τούς τε ἄλλους καὶ ἐμαυτὸν <u>ἐξετάζων</u>· οὐδὲ νῦν φεύξομαι."

	ὅτι	that
	σελήνη -ης ἡ	moon
20	᾿Αναξαγόρας ὁ	Anaxagoras (*philosopher a generation before Socrates, who speculated about the physical make-up of the universe*)
	δραχμή -ῆς ἡ	drachma (*Athenian unit of currency; here 'genitive of price' - translate* for ~)
	ἀγορεύω	I buy
	οὐδαμῶς	in no way, not at all
	δαιμόνιον -ου τό	divine being
	νομίζω	(*here*) I believe in
	ἀδικία -ας ἡ	injustice
	ἤ ... ἤ	either ... or
25	ἀτάρακτος -ον	undisturbed
	ἐνθένδε	from here
	διαλέγομαι	I have a conversation (with, + *dat*)
	῞Ομηρος -ου ὁ	Homer
	οὔποτε	never
	φιλόσοφος -ου ὁ	philosopher
	ἐξετάζω	I examine

Future infinitives

The ordinary infinitives (active παύειν = *to stop*, middle/passive παύεσθαι = *to cease/to be stopped*) are present tense. Greek also has infinitives in other tenses. Here are the future ones (entirely predictable in formation):

active   παύσειν   (compare future indicative παύσω)
literally   to be going to stop, to be about to stop

middle   παύσεσθαι   (compare future indicative παύσομαι)
literally   to be going to cease, to be about to cease

passive   παυσθήσεσθαι   (compare future indicative παυσθήσομαι)
literally   to be going to be stopped, to be about to be stopped

The literal translations of course sound absurdly clumsy and are rarely appropriate. Future infinitives have a number of jobs (we shall see some more in Chapter 9), but note here their use with the verb

μέλλω = I intend to, I am about to

Here the future infinitive just reinforces the sense of the verb, and is translated like the present:

μέλλω τοὺς πολεμίους διώξειν.

I intend to chase the enemy.

(not a sort of doubly-future *I intend to be about to* ...)

The future infinitive of εἰμί *sum* is ἔσεσθαι (compare future indicative ἔσομαι).

ὁ Σωκράτης μέλλει ἀεὶ δίκαιος ἔσεσθαι.

Socrates intends always to be just.

Compound negatives (1)

• As well as the simple negative οὐ (οὐκ, οὐχ), there are several compounds. You have seen most of them already, but they are listed here:

οὐδαμῶς	in no way, not at all
οὐδέ	and not, not even
οὐδείς οὐδεμία οὐδέν (stem οὐδεν-)	no-one, nothing, no (not any)*
οὐδέποτε	never†
οὐκέτι	no longer
οὔποτε	never†
οὔτε ... οὔτε	neither ... nor

* used as both pronoun (οὐδείς = no-one) and adjective (οὐδεὶς δοῦλος = no slave)

† the two words for *never* are interchangeable, but οὐδέποτε tends to be used with the present and future tenses, οὔποτε with past tenses

• The usual position, especially for the simple negative, is immediately before a verb. If a negative comes elsewhere, the usual principle is that it refers to (or 'negatives') the word immediately following.

Revision checkpoint

Make sure you know:
• εἶμι = *I shall go*
• reflexive pronouns
• third person possessives (using genitive pronouns)
• future infinitives
• compound negatives

Exercise 8.32

Socrates' Final Day

Two friends of Socrates discuss his final day. Echecrates discovers that Phaedo was with him, and is given a detailed account.

Ἐχεκράτης   ἆρα αὐτός, ὦ <u>Φαίδων</u>, παρῆσθα ἐκείνῃ τῇ ἡμέρᾳ, ᾗ ὁ Σωκράτης
     τὸ <u>φάρμακον</u> ἔπιεν ἐν τῷ δεσμωτηρίῳ, ἢ <u>παρ</u>᾽ ἄλλου τινὸς τὰ
     γενόμενα ἐπύθου;
Φαίδων   αὐτὸς παρῆν, ὦ Ἐχέκρατες.
5   Ἐχε   λέγε μοι, εἰ βούλῃ· πῶς ἀπέθανεν ὁ ἀνήρ; οὐδεὶς γὰρ τῶν
     ἐνθάδε πολιτῶν οἷός τ᾽ ἦν ἡμῖν τὰ γενόμενα λέγειν. τόδε μόνον
     ἠκούσαμεν, <u>ὅτι</u> φάρμακον πιὼν ἀπέθανεν.
   Φαι   οὐδὲ τὰ περὶ τῆς δίκης ἐπύθεσθε, τίνι <u>τρόπῳ</u> ταῦτα ἐγένετο;
   Ἐχε   <u>ναί</u>, ταῦτα μὲν ἐπυθόμεθα, καὶ ἐθαυμάζομεν ὅτι πάλαι γενομένης
10   τῆς δίκης πολλῷ ὕστερον (ὥς <u>γε</u> φαίνεται) ἀπέθανεν ὁ Σωκράτης.
     διὰ τί οὖν οὕτως ἐγένετο;
   Φαι   <u>τύχη</u> τις αὐτῷ ἐγένετο, ὦ φίλε. <u>τῇ</u> γὰρ <u>προτεραίᾳ</u> τῆς δίκης τὸ
     πλοῖον, ὃ εἰς <u>Δῆλον</u> οἱ Ἀθηναῖοι πέμπουσιν, ἔμελλεν <u>ἀνάξεσθαι</u>.
   Ἐχε   τοῦτο δὲ τί ἐστιν;
15   Φαι   τοῦτό ἐστι τὸ πλοῖον, ὥς γε οἱ Ἀθηναῖοι λέγουσιν, ἐν ᾧ <u>Θησεύς</u>
     ποτε εἰς <u>Κρήτην</u> τοὺς <u>δὶς</u> ἑπτὰ (νεανίας τε καὶ κόρας) ἤγαγεν.
     πάντας δὲ τούτους σώσας, καὶ τὸν <u>Μινώταυρον</u> κτείνας, ὁ
     Θησεὺς <u>πιστόν</u> τε καὶ δῶρον τοῖς θεοῖς παρέχειν ἐβούλετο. οἱ
     οὖν Ἀθηναῖοι ἔτι καὶ νῦν <u>κατ</u>᾽ ἔτος πλοῖον εἰς Δῆλον
20   πέμπουσιν. καὶ ἐν ταῖς Ἀθήναις οὐδεὶς θανάτῳ κολάζεται τοῦ

	Ἐχεκράτης ὁ	Echecrates
	Φαίδων ὁ	Phaedo
	φάρμακον -ου τό	poison
	παρά	(+ *gen*) from
5	ὅτι	that
	τρόπος -ου ὁ	way
	ναί	yes
10	γε	at least
	τύχη -ης ἡ	good luck
	τῇ προτεραίᾳ	on the day before, on the day prior to (+ *gen*)
	Δῆλος -ου ἡ	Delos (*sacred island with important annual festival*)
	ἀνάγομαι	I put to sea
15	Θησεύς ὁ	Theseus
	Κρήτη -ης ἡ	Crete
	δίς	twice (*the archaic phrase 'twice seven' was traditional in the story for 'fourteen'*)
	Μινώταυρος -ου ὁ	Minotaur
	πιστόν -οῦ τό	pledge
	κατ᾽ ἔτος	each year

πλοίου ἀπόντος. νόμος γάρ τις τοῦτο κωλύει ὡς <u>δύσφημον</u> ὄν. καὶ <u>ἐνίοτε</u> μακρὸν χρόνον τὸ πλοῖον ἄπεστι, τῶν ἀνέμων <u>κατεχόντων</u>. διὰ ταῦτα ὁ Σωκράτης ἐν τῷ δεσμωτηρίῳ ἔμενεν.

Ἐχε   τί δ' <u>ἔχεις</u> λέγειν περὶ τοῦ θανάτου τοῦ ἀνδρός; καὶ τί εἶπεν ὁ
25   Σωκράτης <u>πρὸ</u> τοῦ θανάτου; ἆρα παρῆσαν ἄλλοι τινές;

Φαι   παρῆσαν ὁ <u>Ἀπολλόδωρος</u> καὶ <u>Κρίτων</u> καὶ <u>Κριτόβουλος</u> καὶ πολλοὶ ἄλλοι φίλοι· ὁ δὲ <u>Πλάτων</u> διὰ νόσον τινὰ οὐ παρῆν.

Ἐχε   τίνες οὖν ἦσαν οἱ λόγοι; βούλομαι γὰρ πάντα ἀκούειν, εἰ <u>σχολή</u> σοί ἐστιν.

30 **Φαι**   <u>ναί</u>, <u>προθύμως</u> ἐθέλω ἐξ ἀρχῆς πάντα λέγειν, ἐπεὶ ἀκούειν βούλῃ. ἀεὶ γὰρ καὶ τὰς <u>πρόσθεν</u> ἡμέρας <u>συνελεγόμεθα</u> <u>ἕωθεν</u> εἰς τὸ <u>δικαστήριον</u>, ἐν ᾧ ἐκείνη ἡ δίκη ἡ οὐκ ἀξία ἐγένετο· ἦν γὰρ ἐγγὺς τοῦ δεσμωτηρίου. ἐκεῖ οὖν ἐμένομεν <u>ἐκάστοτε</u>, <u>ἕως</u> ὁ <u>θυρωρὸς</u> ἡμᾶς εἰσῆγεν, καὶ <u>τὰ πολλὰ</u> <u>διετρίβομεν</u> πᾶσαν τὴν
35   ἡμέραν <u>διαλεγόμενοι</u> τῷ ἀνδρί. ἐκείνη δὲ τῇ ἡμέρᾳ καὶ <u>πρῳαίτερον</u> παρῆμεν· <u>τῇ</u> γὰρ <u>προτεραίᾳ</u>, ἐπεὶ ἐξήλθομεν ἐκ τοῦ δεσμωτηρίου ἑσπέρας, εἰπέ τις ἡμῖν, "τὸ πλοῖον ἐκ Δήλου πάρεστιν". αὕτη οὖν ἡ ἡμέρα ἐφαίνετο <u>τελευταία</u> ἐσομένη. ἡμᾶς οὖν ἕωθεν παρόντας ὁ θυρωρὸς ἐκέλευσε <u>περιμένειν</u>· "λύουσι

	δύσφημος -ον	ill-omened
	ἐνίοτε	sometimes
	κατέχω	I hold back
	ἔχω	(+ *inf*) I am able
25	πρό	before (+ *gen*)
	Ἀπολλόδωρος -ου ὁ	Apollodorus (*friend of Socrates, like the next two named*)
	Κρίτων -ωνος ὁ	Crito
	Κριτόβουλος -ου ὁ	Critobulus
	Πλάτων -ωνος ὁ	Plato (*another friend, and author of the account*)
	σχολή -ῆς ἡ	leisure
30	ναί	yes
	προθύμως	eagerly
	πρόσθεν	previous, preceeding
	συλλέγομαι	
	imperfect συνελεγόμην	I meet, I assemble
	ἕωθεν	at dawn
	δικαστήριον -ου τό	lawcourt
	ἑκάστοτε	every time
	ἕως	until
	θυρωρός -οῦ ὁ	jailer (*lit* door-keeper)
	τὰ πολλά	usually
	διατρίβω	I spend (time)
35	διαλέγομαι	I have a conversation
	πρῳαίτερον	earlier
	τῇ προτεραίᾳ	on the day before, on the previous day
	τελευταῖος -α -ον	final
	περιμένω	I wait

40 γάρ," ἔφη, "οἱ ἕνδεκα αὐτὸν καὶ παραγγέλλουσι τὸν θάνατον".
μετὰ δ' ὀλίγον χρόνον ἐκελεύσθημεν ἕπεσθαι αὐτῷ. ἑσπόμεθα οὖν
καὶ κατελάβομεν τὸν μὲν ἄνδρα ἄνευ δεσμῶν, τὴν δὲ Ξανθίππην
(γιγνώσκεις γὰρ αὐτήν) ἔχουσάν τε τὸ παιδίον καὶ δυσθύμως
καθιζούσαν. καὶ ὁ μὲν Σωκράτης αὐτὸς ἀτάρακτος ἦν, ἡ δὲ γυνὴ

45 ἐπεὶ εἶδεν ἡμᾶς δακρύουσα τῷ ἀνδρὶ εἶπεν, "νῦν ὕστατον οἷός
τ' ἔσῃ τοῖς φίλοις διαλέγεσθαι, καὶ ἐκεῖνοί σοι". καὶ ὁ Σωκράτης
τῷ Κρίτωνι, "αἰσθάνῃ," ἔφη, "ἃ πάσχει· βούλομαι οὖν τινα
οἴκαδε αὐτὴν ἀπάγειν." καὶ ἐκείνην μὲν ἀπήγαγόν τινες
δακρύουσαν. ὁ δὲ Σωκράτης πολλὰ τοῖς παροῦσιν ἀνδράσι

50 διελέγετο. καὶ ἔγωγε θαυμάσια ἔπαθον· οὐ γὰρ οἶκτος εἰσῆλθέ με
καίπερ παρόντα ἀνδρὶ φίλῳ· εὐδαίμων γὰρ ὁ ἀνὴρ ἐφαίνετο. καὶ
πάντες οἱ παρόντες τὸ αὐτὸ ἔπαθον ἀκούοντες τοὺς ἐκείνου
λόγους, οἷς ἐδίδασκε περὶ τοῦ θανάτου· οὐ γὰρ κακόν τί ἐστιν
ἐπεὶ ἡ ψυχὴ οὔτ' ἀποθνῄσκει οὔτε διαλύεται.

40	οἱ ἕνδεκα	the Eleven (*board of magistrates responsible for law and order in Athens*)
	παραγγέλλω	I give the order for (*the prisoner was released from chains for his final hours*)
	καταλαμβάνω κατέλαβον	I come upon, I find
	ἄνευ	without (+ *gen*)
	Ξανθίππη -ης ἡ	Xanthippe (*wife of Socrates*)
	παιδίον -ου τό	small child
	δυσθύμως	despondently
	ἀτάρακτος -ον	undisturbed, calm
45	δακρύω	I cry
	ὕστατον	for the last time
	διαλέγομαι	I have a conversation
	οἴκαδε	home, homewards
50	ἔγωγε	I at least, I for my part
	θαυμάσιος -α -ον	wonderful
	πάσχω ἔπαθον	(*here*) I experience
	οἶκτος -ου ὁ	pity
	εὐδαίμων	happy
	ψυχή -ῆς ἡ	soul
	διαλύω	I dissolve

Exercise 8.33

The Death of Socrates

καὶ ἦν ἤδη ἐγγὺς ἡλίου <u>δυσμῶν</u>· μετὰ δὲ τὸ <u>λουτρὸν</u> ὁ Σωκράτης
ἐκάθιζε, μετὰ τῶν φίλων λέγων. καὶ ὁ τῶν <u>ἕνδεκα</u> <u>ὑπηρέτης</u> εἰσελθὼν
εἶπεν, "ὦ Σώκρατες, οὐ <u>καταγνώσομαί</u> σου ὥσπερ τῶν ἄλλων
καταγιγνώσκω, διότι ὀργίζονται ἐπεὶ <u>παραγγέλλω</u> αὐτοῖς πίνειν τὸ
5 <u>φάρμακον</u>, τῶν ἀρχόντων ἀναγκαζόντων. σὺ δὲ <u>γενναιότατός</u> τε καὶ
<u>ἄριστος</u> εἶ πάντων τῶν δεῦρο ἐλθόντων. καὶ οὐκ ἐμοὶ <u>χαλεπαίνεις</u>, ἀλλὰ
τοῖς <u>αἰτίοις</u>. νῦν δὲ <u>χαῖρε</u>, καὶ ἀνδρείως πρᾶσσε τὰ <u>ἀναγκαῖα</u>." ὁ δὲ
Σωκράτης, "καὶ σύ," ἔφη, "χαῖρε· ἐγὼ δὲ ταῦτα πράξω." καὶ ὁ ὑπηρέτης
<u>δακρύων</u> ἐξῆλθεν. καὶ ὁ Σωκράτης τοῖς φίλοις, "<u>ὡς</u> <u>ἀστεῖος</u>," ἔφη, "ὁ
10 ἄνθρωπος. ἀλλ', ὦ Κρίτων, πείσομαι αὐτῷ. κέλευε οὖν τινα τὸ φάρμακον
φέρειν, εἰ ἕτοιμόν ἐστιν." ὁ δὲ Κρίτων, "πολλοί," ἔφη, "τοὺς τοῦ ὑπηρέτου
λόγους ἀκούσαντες μετὰ τῶν φίλων ἐσθίουσί τε καὶ πίνουσι· <u>μὴ</u> οὖν
<u>σπεῦδε</u>." ὁ δὲ Σωκράτης ἀπεκρίνατο τάδε· "οὗτοι μὲν δικαίως πράσσουσιν·
ἐγὼ δ' οὐκ ἐθέλω σῴζειν τὸν ἐμὸν βίον."

15 ὁ δὲ Κρίτων ἐκέλευσε παῖδά τινα παρόντα· καὶ ὁ παῖς <u>ἐπανῆλθεν</u> ἄγων
τὸν τὸ φάρμακον ἔχοντα, ἐν <u>κύλικι</u> φερόμενον. ὁ δὲ Σωκράτης, ἐπεὶ εἶδε
τὸν ἄνθρωπον, "ὦ ἀγαθέ," ἔφη, "πῶς πράξω τὰ κελευσθέντα; σὺ γὰρ
<u>ἔμπειρος</u> εἶ." "πιὼν <u>περιβάδιζε</u>· τῶν δ' <u>ἄρθρων</u> <u>βαρυνομένων</u>, <u>κατακλίνου</u>."

δυσμαί -ῶν αἱ	setting
λουτρόν -οῦ τό	bath
οἱ ἕνδεκα	the Eleven
ὑπηρέτης -ου ὁ	servant
καταγιγνώσκω	
fut καταγνώσομαι	I condemn (+ gen)
παραγγέλλω	I give the order
5 φάρμακον -ου τό	poison
γενναῖος -α -ον	noble
ἄριστος -η -ον	best
χαλεπαίνω	I am angry with (+ dat)
αἴτιος -α -ον	responsible, to blame
χαῖρε	farewell!
ἀναγκαῖος -α -ον	necessary, unavoidable
δακρύω	I cry
ὡς	(here) how ... !
ἀστεῖος -α -ον	civilised
10 μή	(with imperative) do not ... !
σπεύδω	I hurry
15 ἐπανέρχομαι ἐπανῆλθον	I return
κύλιξ -ικος ἡ	cup
ἔμπειρος -ον	experienced
περιβαδίζω	I walk around
ἄρθρον -ου τό	limb
βαρύνομαι	I become heavy
κατακλίνομαι	I lie down

88

καὶ τὴν <u>κύλικα</u> παρέσχεν· ὁ δὲ Σωκράτης οὐδαμῶς φοβούμενος ἐδέξατο.
20 "ἆρα <u>ἔξεστιν</u>," ἔφη, "τοῖς θεοῖς ἐκ τῆς κύλικος <u>σπένδειν</u>;" ὁ δ' ἄνθρωπος
ἀπεκρίνατο, "ὦ Σώκρατες, οὐ <u>περίεστι</u>· <u>φάρμακον</u> γὰρ παρασκευάζομεν
ὁ <u>ἱκανόν</u> ἐστι πίνειν." "μανθάνω," ἔφη, "ἀλλὰ τοῖς θεοῖς <u>εὔχομαι</u> ὁδὸν
ἀγαθὴν ἀπὸ τῆς γῆς <u>ἐκεῖσε</u> ἔχειν." ταῦτα δ' εἰπὼν <u>ἐξέπιε</u> τὸ φάρμακον.

καὶ οἱ πολλοὶ ἡμῶν οὐκέτι οἷοί τ' ἦσαν τὰ δάκρυα <u>κατέχειν</u>. ὁ δὲ
25 Σωκράτης ἐκέλευσεν ἡμᾶς <u>ἡσυχάζειν</u>. "διὰ ταῦτα γάρ, ὦ φίλοι," ἔφη, "τὴν
γυναῖκα πρότερον ἀπέπεμψα. ἀλλ' ἀνδρεῖοι ὄντες ἡσυχάζετε." καὶ ἡμεῖς
μὲν ἀκούσαντες <u>αἰσχύνην</u> ἐπάθομεν· <u>ὁ δὲ</u> <u>περιβαδίζων</u>, ἐπεὶ <u>ἐβαρύνετο</u>
τὰ <u>ἄρθρα</u>, <u>ὕπτιος</u> <u>κατεκλίνετο</u>. καὶ ὁ ἄνθρωπος πρῶτον μὲν τοὺς πόδας,
ἔπειτα δὲ τὰς <u>κνήμας</u> <u>ἐπίεσεν</u>. ὁ μέντοι Σωκράτης οὐδὲν ἔπαθεν· εἶπε δὲ
30 τοὺς <u>τελευταίους</u> λόγους. "ὦ Κρίτων," ἔφη, "τῷ <u>Ἀσκληπιῷ</u> <u>ὀφείλομεν</u>
<u>ἀλεκτρυόνα</u>· <u>θύε</u> μοι τοῦτον." "ταῦτα ἔσται·" ἔφη ὁ Κρίτων, "ἆρα ἐθέλεις
ἄλλο τι λέγειν;" ὁ δὲ Σωκράτης οὐδὲν ἄλλο ἀπεκρίνατο. καὶ ὁ Κρίτων
<u>συνέλαβε</u> τό τε στόμα καὶ τοὺς ὀφθαλμούς. ἥδε ἡ <u>τελευτή</u>, ὦ Ἐχέκρατες,
τοῦ ἡμετέρου φίλου ἐγένετο, ἀνδρὸς ἐκ πάντων <u>ἀρίστου</u> καὶ σοφωτάτου
35 καὶ δικαιοτάτου.

	κύλιξ -ικος ἡ	cup
20	ἔξεστι(ν)	it is possible
	σπένδω	I pour a libation
	περίεστι	there is a surplus
	φάρμακον -ου τό	poison
	ἱκανός -ή -όν	sufficient
	εὔχομαι	I pray
	ἐκεῖσε	to there, to that place (*here implying* the next world)
	ἐκπίνω ἐξέπιον	I drink up, I drink all of
	κατέχω	I restrain
25	ἡσυχάζω	I am quiet
	αἰσχύνη -ης ἡ	shame
	ὁ δέ	but he
	περιβαδίζω	I walk around
	βαρύνομαι	I become heavy
	ἄρθρον -ου τό	limb
	ὕπτιος -α -ον	on one's back
	κατακλίνομαι	I lie down
	κνήμη -ης ἡ	shin
	πιέζω ἐπίεσα	I press
30	τελευταῖος -α -ον	final
	Ἀσκληπιός -οῦ ὁ	Asclepius (*god of medicine and healing: whilst showing his conventional religious observance, Socrates also implies that for him death is a cure for the ills of life*)
	ὀφείλω	I owe
	ἀλεκτρυών -όνος ὁ	cock, cockerel
	θύω	I sacrifice
	συλλαμβάνω συνέλαβον	I close
	τελευτή -ῆς ἡ	end
	ἄριστος -η -ον	best

Vocabulary checklist for Chapter 8

αἷμα -ατος τό	blood
αἰσθάνομαι ᾐσθόμην	I perceive
ἀλλήλους -ας	each other
ἀποκρίνομαι ἀπεκρινάμην	I answer, I reply
ἆρ' (= ἆρα) οὐ	surely .. ?
ἄριστος -η -ον	best, very good
ἅρμα -ατος τό	chariot
ἄρχομαι ἠρξάμην	I begin
ἄρχω ἦρξα	I rule (+ *gen*)
βία -ας ἡ	force, violence
βούλομαι *imperfect* ἐβουλόμην	I wish, I want
γίγνομαι ἐγενόμην	I become, I happen
γλῶσσα -ης ἡ	tongue; language
γνώμη -ης ἡ	opinion, belief
δάκρυον -ου τό	tear, teardrop
δεῦρο	(to) here
δέχομαι ἐδεξάμην	I receive
ἑαυτόν ἑαυτήν ἑαυτό	himself, herself, itself (*reflexive*)
ἑαυτούς ἑαυτάς ἑαυτά	themselves (*reflexive*)
εἶμι *infinitive* ἰέναι	I shall go
ἐμαυτόν ἐμαυτήν	myself
ἕπομαι ἑσπόμην	I follow (+ *dat*)
ἔρχομαι ἦλθον	I come, I go
ἤ ... ἤ	either ... or
ἡγεμών -όνος ὁ	leader
ἤδη	already
ἡμᾶς αὐτούς, ἡμᾶς αὐτάς	ourselves (*reflexive*)
κάκιστος -η -ον	worst, very bad
κόπτω ἔκοψα	I cut; I knock
κτῆμα -ατος τό	possession
λάθρα	secretly
λαμβάνομαι ἐλαβόμην	I take for myself, I grasp hold of (+ *gen*)
λύομαι ἐλυσάμην	I ransom
μάτην	in vain
μάχομαι ἐμαχεσάμην	I fight
μέλλω	I am about to, I intend to (+ *fut inf*)
μόλις	with difficulty, scarcely
ὀργίζομαι ὠργίσθην	I get angry
ὅτι	that
οὐ μόνον ... ἀλλὰ καί	not only ... but also
οὐδαμῶς	in no way, not at all
οὐδέ	not even
οὐδέποτε	never
οὔποτε	never

οὔτε ... οὔτε	neither ... nor
πάλιν	again, back again
πανταχοῦ	everywhere
πατρίς -ίδος ἡ	native land, fatherland
παύομαι ἐπαυσάμην	I cease, I stop myself
πεδίον -ου τό	plain, open country
πεζοί -ῶν οἱ	infantry, footsoldiers
πείθομαι ἐπιθόμην	I obey (+ *dat*)
πορεύομαι ἐπορεύθην	I march
πρᾶγμα -ατος τό	matter, affair, business
προσβάλλω προσέβαλον	I attack (+ *dat*)
πυνθάνομαι ἐπυθόμην	I enquire; I learn by enquiry
σεαυτόν σεαυτήν	yourself (*reflexive*)
στόμα -ατος τό	mouth
στρατιά -ᾶς ἡ	army
στρατοπεδεύομαι ἐστρατοπεδευσάμην	I set up camp, I encamp
συμφορά -ᾶς ἡ	disaster
σφᾶς *gen* σφῶν	them
σφᾶς αὐτούς, σφᾶς αὐτάς	themselves (*reflexive*)
σφόδρα	very much, strongly
σχεδόν	nearly, almost
τείχισμα -ατος τό	fort, fortification
τραῦμα -ατος τό	wound
υἱός -οῦ ὁ	son
ὑμᾶς αὐτούς, ὑμᾶς αὐτάς	yourselves (*reflexive*)
ὕστερον	later
φαίνομαι *imperf* ἐφαινόμην	I appear
φέρομαι ἠνεγκάμην	I win (prizes etc)
χαλκός -οῦ ὁ	bronze
(73 words)	

Chapter 9

Irregular third declension nouns (2)

Third declension nouns ending in sigma in the nominative singular usually have accusative singular in nu rather than alpha. (This is of course in line with first and second declension nouns e.g. τιμήν, λόγον. And we saw in Chapter 5 that the normal third declension accusative e.g. φύλακα probably arose as a substitute for an unpronounceable φυλακ-ν.) The simplest example of this (other nouns in this category making further small changes, as we shall see) is:

ἰχθύς -ύος ὁ = fish (stem ἰχθυ-)

sg	nom	ἰχθύς
	acc	ἰχθύ-ν
	gen	ἰχθύ-ος
	dat	ἰχθύ-ι

pl	nom	ἰχθύ-ες
	acc	ἰχθύ-ας
	gen	ἰχθύ-ων
	dat	ἰχθύ-σι(ν)

Third declension (3-1-3) adjectives

A common type of third declension adjective declines in a way related to this. 'Third declension' is here shorthand for 3-1-3: most third declension adjectives have a separate feminine, which is (as usual) first declension. In this they are comparable to 3-1-3 participles e.g. παύων -ουσα -ον, παύσας -ασα -αν, παυσθείς -εῖσα -έν. (You have already met in Chapter 6 one common 3-1-3 adjective: πᾶς πᾶσα πᾶν = all.) They differ therefore from third declension adjectives in Latin, almost all of which are 3-3 (i.e. without a separate feminine).

• These adjectives also differ slightly from ἰχθύς, because although the basic stem ends in upsilon, after the accusative they behave in effect as if it were epsilon.

• As with the 3-1-3 participles, the feminine adds an extra syllable, in this case -ει-.

3-1-3 declensions
βαρύς = heavy

		masculine	*feminine*	*neuter*
sg	nom	βαρύς	βαρεῖα	βαρύ
	acc	βαρύν	βαρεῖαν	βαρύ
	gen	βαρέος	βαρείας	βαρέος
	dat	βαρεῖ	βαρείᾳ	βαρεῖ
pl	nom	βαρεῖς*	βαρεῖαι	βαρέα
	acc	βαρεῖς	βαρείας	βαρέα
	gen	βαρέων	βαρειῶν	βαρέων
	dat	βαρέσι(ν)	βαρείαις	βαρέσι(ν)

* this is a *contraction* of ε + ες (more on this below), and the accusative simply follows suit (compare how in Latin third declension plurals nominative and accusative are always the same)

Six common adjectives like βαρύς:

1	βαθύς	deep
2	βραδύς	slow
3	εὐρύς	broad, wide
4	ἡδύς	sweet, pleasant
5	ὀξύς	sharp
6	ταχύς	quick, swift

• The adverbs formed from these end in -εως (notice the epsilon again), hence e.g.

βαρέως	heavily (*also often* seriously, grievously*)
ταχέως	quickly

*especially in the idiom βαρέως φέρω = *I take (something) badly*

• The comparative and superlative of most of these end respectively -υτερος -α -ον, -υτατος -η -ον, hence e.g.

βαρύτερος -α -ον	heavier
βαρύτατος -η -ον	heaviest, very heavy

However ἡδύς and ταχύς form their comparative and superlative in a different way, as we shall see in Chapter 10.

• As with any comparative and superlative, the adverb versions use respectively the neuter singular and neuter plural of the equivalent adjective, hence:

βαρύτερον	more heavily
βαρύτατα	most heavily, very heavily

• βαθύς, βαρύς and βραδύς are classic examples of *easily confusable words*. A list including these and many others will be found in Appendix 1 at the back of this book. Knowledge of English derivatives can also help avoid confusion.

Exercise 9.1

Translate into English:

1   καλοὶ ἰχθύες εὑρίσκονται ἐν ἐκείνῳ τῷ ποταμῷ, βαθυτάτῳ ὄντι.
2   ὅδε ὁ ἵππος οὐδέποτε ταχὺς ἔσται.
3   οἱ πεζοὶ βραδύτερον ἐπορεύοντο τοῦ ἡγεμόνος οὐ παρόντος.
4   τοὺς αἰχμαλώτους μόλις ἐλυσάμεθα τῇ τρίτῃ ἡμέρᾳ.
5   τὸ πεδίον τὸ ἐγγὺς τῆς θαλάσσης οὐκ εὐρύ ἐστιν.
6   οἱ σύμμαχοι λίθοις ὀξέσι τραύματα ἔπαθον.
7   τοῦτο τὸ ἅρμα βαρύτερόν ἐστι τοῦ ἡμετέρου.
8   ὁ ῥήτωρ βαρέως ἔφερεν τὰ τῶν Ἀθηνῶν πράγματα.
9   πᾶσαι αἱ γυναῖκες τὰ δῶρα ἡδέως ἐδέξαντο.
10 οἱ πολέμιοι ὑμῖν ταχέως μὲν λάθρᾳ δὲ ἕπονται.

Exercise 9.2

Translate into Greek:
1   Is that wine sweet?
2   Did you catch a fish in the wide river, slave?
3   We saw very heavy chains in the prison.
4   The doctor's daughter does not eat that sort of food.
5   The master is slowly getting angry.

   that sort of = τοιοῦτος

Mixed declension adjectives

Two extremely common adjectives start as if they were 3-1-3, but switch to 2-1-2 (like σοφός) after the accusative singular:

μέγας = great, big   (stem for 2-1-2 parts μεγαλ-)

		masculine	*feminine*	*neuter*
sg	nom	μέγας	μεγάλ-η	μέγα
	acc	μέγαν	μεγάλ-ην	μέγα
	gen	μεγάλ-ου	μεγάλ-ης	μεγάλ-ου
	dat	μεγάλ-ῳ	μεγάλ-ῃ	μεγάλ-ῳ
pl	nom	μεγάλ-οι	μεγάλ-αι	μεγάλ-α
	acc	μεγάλ-ους	μεγάλ-ας	μεγάλ-α
	gen	μεγάλ-ων	μεγάλ-ων	μεγάλ-ων
	dat	μεγάλ-οις	μεγάλ-αις	μεγάλ-οις

This mostly behaves as if it had started μεγάλος, and indeed the masculine vocative is μεγάλε.

Similarly:

πολύς = much, *pl* many   (stem for 2-1-2 parts πολλ-)

		masculine	*feminine*	*neuter*
sg	nom	πολύς	πολλ-ή	πολύ
	acc	πολύν	πολλ-ήν	πολύ
	gen	πολλ-οῦ	πολλ-ῆς	πολλ-οῦ
	dat	πολλ-ῷ	πολλ-ῇ	πολλ-ῷ
pl	nom	πολλ-οί	πολλ-αί	πολλ-ά
	acc	πολλ-ούς	πολλ-άς	πολλ-ά
	gen	πολλ-ῶν	πολλ-ῶν	πολλ-ῶν
	dat	πολλ-οῖς	πολλ-αῖς	πολλ-οῖς

Here you can see clearly that the masculine could have continued like βαρύς, or like ἰχθύς, whereas in fact it mostly behaves as if it had started πολλός, πολλόν (forms which are actually found in some early authors and in some Greek dialects). Note that the initial third declension parts of the masculine and neuter have single lambda, the 2-1-2 parts double.

Exercise 9.3

Translate into English:
1   πολλοὶ τούτων τῶν ἰχθύων οὐ μεγάλοι εἰσίν.
2   πολὺν χρόνον ἐμένομεν, τῆς ὁδοῦ βραδείας οὔσης.
3   τραύματα πολλὰ καὶ αἷμα πολὺ ἐν τῇ μάχῃ εἴδομεν.
4   οἱ ἐν τῇ ἐκκλησίᾳ πολλοῖς λόγοις τέλος ἐπείσθησαν.
5   ἆρα τὸ ἐκεῖ τείχισμα μέγα ἦν;

Exercise 9.4

Translate into Greek:
1   A big chariot and many boys were in the road.
2   The judge's wife sent many books to the prisoners.
3   Many horses are heavier than that one.
4   I released the chain with a sharp stone.
5   The swift messenger marched towards the plain.

Revision checkpoint

Make sure you know:
• irregular third declension noun ἰχθύς
• third declension (3-1-3) adjectives like βαρύς
• mixed declension adjectives μέγας, πολύς

Verbs with epsilon contraction

We saw in Chapter 1 that there is just one main conjugation in Greek. However if the stem ends in a vowel, that vowel coalesces with the vowel of the ending. The commonest verbs of this type end in -εω = *I love, I like*. (They bear some resemblance to second conjugation verbs in Latin, e.g. *moneo*.) We have already seen occasional examples of contraction - this process whereby adjacent vowels blend - e.g. βαρεῖς for βαρε-ες as the masculine nominative plural of βαρύς. It is important to memorise the rules for such contractions and apply them (rather than laboriously learning every instance). For contraction with epsilon the rules are:

> ε followed by ε becomes ει
> ε followed by ο becomes ου
> ε followed by a long vowel or diphthong disappears

Hence:

φιλέω = I love, I like

		present active:		*present middle/passive:*	
sg	1	φιλῶ	[φιλε-ω]	φιλοῦμαι	[φιλε-ομαι]
	2	φιλεῖς	[φιλε-εις]	φιλῇ (*or* -εῖ)	[φιλε-η (*or* -ει)]
	3	φιλεῖ	[φιλε-ει]	φιλεῖται	[φιλε-εται]
pl	1	φιλοῦμεν	[φιλε-ομεν]	φιλούμεθα	[φιλε-ομεθα]
	2	φιλεῖτε	[φιλε-ετε]	φιλεῖσθε	[φιλε-εσθε]
	3	φιλοῦσι(*ν*)	[φιλε-ουσι(*ν*)]	φιλοῦνται	[φιλε-ονται]

participle:	*participle:*
φιλῶν -οῦσα -οῦν (stem φιλουντ-)	φιλούμενος -η -ον
[φιλε-ων -ουσα -ον (φιλε-οντ-)]	[φιλε-ομενος -η -ον]

infinitive:	*infinitive:*
φιλεῖν	φιλεῖσθαι
[φιλε-ειν]	[φιλε-εσθαι]

		imperfect active:		*imperfect middle/passive:*	
sg	1	ἐφίλουν	[ἐφιλε-ον]	ἐφιλούμην	[ἐφιλε-ομην]
	2	ἐφίλεις	[ἐφιλε-ες]	ἐφιλοῦ	[ἐφιλε-ου]
	3	ἐφίλει	[ἐφιλε-ε]	ἐφιλεῖτο	[ἐφιλε-ετο]
pl	1	ἐφιλοῦμεν	[ἐφιλε-ομεν]	ἐφιλούμεθα	[ἐφιλε-ομεθα]
	2	ἐφιλεῖτε	[ἐφιλε-ετε]	ἐφιλεῖσθε	[ἐφιλε-εσθε]
	3	ἐφίλουν	[ἐφιλε-ον]	ἐφιλοῦντο	[ἐφιλε-οντο]

For the (first/weak) aorist and future of these verbs, the epsilon is lengthened to eta before adding the sigma, but the endings after the sigma are normal (as it has inserted a barrier, so contraction does not take place). Hence:

aorist active ἐφίλησα
aorist middle ἐφιλησάμην
aorist passive ἐφιλήθην

future active φιλήσω
future middle φιλήσομαι
future passive φιληθήσομαι

• Note that the singular imperative is φίλει (φιλε-ε), distinguished by the accent from the third person singular φιλεῖ (φιλε-ει): this is an important example of accent affecting meaning. The plural imperative is φιλεῖτε (like the ordinary second person plural, as with non-contracted verbs).

• It is conventional to quote these verbs in uncontracted form in a wordlist or dictionary (to make the formation clear), but to write them with the contraction in a sentence or passage.

Sixteen verbs with epsilon contraction:

1	ἀδικέω	I act unjustly (towards)
2	ἀθυμέω	I am despondent
3	αἰτέω	I ask for*
4	ἀναχωρέω	I retreat
5	ἀπορέω	I am at a loss
6	βοηθέω**	I help, I run to help (+ *dat*)
7	ζητέω	I seek, I search for
8	κρατέω	I control, I rule (+ *gen*)
9	μισέω	I hate
10	ναυμαχέω	I fight a sea-battle
11	οἰκέω	I live
12	ὁμολογέω	I agree
13	ποιέω	I make, I do
14	πολιορκέω	I besiege
15	προχωρέω†	I advance
16	ὠφελέω	I help, I am of service to

* *often with double accusative:* ask someone (*acc*) for something (*acc*)

** *literally* I rush (θέω) in response to a shout (βοή)

† this is a compound with the prefix προ- (= *in front* or *forwards*), hence the augment for past tenses comes as usual after the prefix; however (unlike e.g. ἀπο-) προ- does not drop its omicron but contracts it with the augment to -ου-, this unusual feature being usually shown by retaining the breathing: hence aorist προὐχώρησα (in contrast to e.g. ἀπέβαλον)

The augment and verbs beginning with a vowel

We have seen numerous examples already of what happens when the augment is added to a verb beginning with a vowel (e.g. ἀγγέλλω, imperfect ἤγγελλον). This seems similar to contraction, but is really a lengthening of the existing vowel. It should be noted however that:

- alpha lengthens to eta, rather than to long alpha (as in the example above)
- epsilon normally also lengthens to eta (e.g. ἐθέλω, imperfect ἤθελον), but in a few cases *does* follow the epsilon contraction rule, producing ει (e.g. ἔχω, imperfect εἶχον)

This list shows the effect of adding the augment to verbs starting with vowels/diphthongs:

original vowel	result after augment
α	η
ᾳ, αι, ει	ῃ
αυ, ευ	ηυ
ε	η, or sometimes ει
ι	ι (long)
ο	ω
οι	ῳ
υ	υ (long)

Exercise 9.5

Translate into English:
1   ὁ Σωκράτης οὔποτε ἠδίκησε τοὺς πολίτας.
2   οἱ αἰχμαλώτοι ᾔτησαν τὸν στρατηγὸν σῖτόν τε καὶ ὕδωρ.
3   τίνες εἰσὶν οἱ τοῦτο τὸ τείχισμα ποιήσαντες;
4   οἱ πολέμιοι οὐδέποτε κρατήσουσι τῆς ἡμετέρας χώρας.
5   αἱ ἐν τῇ κώμῃ ὠφελήσουσι τὸν τὴν ὁδὸν ζητοῦντα.
6   τοῦ στρατηγοῦ ἀθυμοῦντος, οἱ στρατιῶται αὐτοὶ προὐχώρησαν.
7   οἱ Ἀθηναῖοι πολὺν χρόνον τὸν τῶν πολεμίων λιμένα ἐπολιόρκουν.
8   φίλει τοὺς τὴν δικαιοσύνην ζητοῦντας, ὦ παῖ.
9   καίπερ πολλὰς ὥρας ἀπορήσαντες, οἱ ἄρχοντες τέλος ὡμολόγησαν.
10 οἱ ἐγγὺς τῆς νήσου μαχόμενοι πολλὰ κακὰ πείσονται.

Exercise 9.6

Translate into Greek:
1   The doctor was at a loss for many days.
2   The girls, after helping the old man, ran to the village.
3   Those who control this island are very wealthy.
4   The slave is being treated unjustly by his master.
5   Were you retreating after the battle, allies?

Background: Greek Myth (1)

The story of Socrates' imprisonment in Chapter 8 (where the mission of the Athenian sacred ship to Delos commemorated the triumph of Theseus) showed that traditional myths were highly influential in fifth-century Athens: religious ceremonies, festivals, and customs constantly alluded to events believed to have taken place in the Heroic Age - in historical terms, the Bronze Age (roughly 1000 years before the lifetime of Socrates). Greeks were familiar with their myths from childhood. As the story of Antigone showed, myth formed the normal subject matter for serious drama or 'tragedy' (though not every play necessarily had an unhappy ending). Because audiences would know the story, at least in outline, originality for a dramatist consisted of subtle variation on a familiar theme. Suspense was a matter not of surprise about the turn of events, but of waiting to see just how and when the inevitable would happen. The sense of events as 'fated' was no doubt helped by the simple fact of the audience already knowing how the story 'had to end'. Myths became traditional, achieved their status as myths, because they possessed some universal significance or enduring quality: they spoke across time, dealing with recurrent human dilemmas. Through myth, tragedy was able to confront issues highly relevant to the city (like the nature of justice, the tug of duties between public and private life), but in a distanced, generalised way. (Comedy in contrast - as we saw in Chapter 7 with the treatment of Socrates by Aristophanes in *Clouds* - was normally set in the present, and used a made-up story, though often involving real people.)

Some myths are undoubtedly romanticised versions of historical events. Most though not all historians would put the stories of the Trojan War in this category. Other myths are better explained as completely fictitious, but 'true' in the sense that they fulfil wishes, or confront fears, which we all recognize. They may be folk tales (simple adventure stories, with elements of ingenious trickery and magic: much of the *Odyssey* comes under this heading), or darker psychological parables (like the story of Antigone's father Oedipus). These categories however are fluid. Whatever their origin, Greek myths have recurrent elements: the interaction of men and gods (in a time when this was possible, when men were of a nobler stamp than subsequently), and recurrent story patterns - in particular that of the Quest (for a treasure, a bride, a homecoming, knowledge). Long and difficult journeys have to be undertaken, monsters killed, and the tricks of enemies thwarted: only then can the hero win his reward. In this chapter we shall read several stories in which you can identify these elements. So influential were the story patterns of myth that, as we shall see in Chapter 10, Greek authors such as the historian Herodotus applied them also to more recent events; and Plato (as we saw in the stories of the Cave, the Magic Ring, and the adventures of Er) in effect made up his own myths as a powerful means of getting his philosophical message across.

We look first at the story of Theseus. This seems to reflect a time even earlier than that of most myths, when the island of Crete was the dominant force in the Greek world (a period archaeologists call Minoan, after the mythical king Minos). Somewhere around 1500 BC power passed from Crete to the Greek mainland city of Mycenae, which in due course became the context for the Trojan War stories.

Exercise 9.7

Theseus and the Minotaur (1)

Aegeus (king of Athens) becomes the enemy of Minos (king of Crete) with dire consequences, but later meets the girl who will bear him a son. Theseus is born, and a challenge laid down.

ὁ <u>Αἰγεὺς</u> <u>βασιλεὺς</u> τῶν ᾿Αθήνων πάλαι ἦν· <u>ἅμα</u> δ᾿ἐκράτει τῆς <u>Κρήτης</u> ὁ
<u>Μίνως</u>, μεγίστην ἀρχὴν τῶν τότε ἔχων. ἐπεὶ δὲ ὁ Αἰγεὺς <u>δόλῳ</u> ἀπέκτεινεν
ἕνα τῶν Μίνωος υἱῶν, ὁ τῆς Κρήτης βασιλεὺς τοὺς ᾿Αθηναίους δίκην
ᾔτησεν. <u>οἱ δὲ</u> πρῶτον μὲν οὐκ ἤθελον, ὕστερον δὲ (τοῦ Μίνωος αὐτῶν
5   πολέμῳ κρατήσαντος) ἕτοιμοι ἦσαν τὰ κελευσθέντα ποιεῖν. ὁ δὲ Μίνως
ἐκέλευσεν αὐτοὺς <u>κατ᾿ ἔτος</u> πέμπειν τῷ <u>Μινωταύρῳ</u> ἑπτά τε νεανίας καὶ
ἑπτὰ κόρας.

ὁ δὲ Μινώταυρος <u>θηρίον</u> δεινότατον ἦν, τὸ μὲν <u>ἥμισυ</u> ἄνθρωπος, τὸ δὲ
ἥμισυ <u>ταῦρος</u>. ἡ γὰρ τοῦ Μίνωος γυνή, <u>Πασιφάη</u> ὀνόματι, δεινὸν <u>ἔρωτα</u>
10   ταύρου τινὸς εἶχεν. καὶ τὸν ταῦρον φιλήσασα τὸν Μινώταυρον <u>ἔτεκεν</u>. ὁ
δὲ Μίνως δικαίως ὀργισθεὶς ἐβούλετο κρύπτειν τὸ θηρίον. ὁ οὖν
<u>Δαίδαλος</u>, <u>δημιουργὸς</u> σοφώτατος ὤν, τὸν <u>λαβύρινθον</u> ἐποίησεν, ἐν ᾧ ὁ
Μινώταυρος ᾤκει, τοὺς εἰσελθόντας ἐσθίων.

ὁ δ᾿ Αἰγεὺς πολὺν μὲν χρόνον ἠθύμει διότι οὐκ ἦν υἱὸς αὐτῷ. ἔπειτα δ᾿
15   <u>ἀποδημῶν</u> πρὸς τὴν <u>Τροιζῆνά</u> ποτε προσῆλθεν· καὶ ἐκεῖ ὁ <u>Πιτθεὺς</u>
βασιλεὺς ἦν. ὁ δ᾿ Αἰγεὺς ἐφίλησε τὴν θυγατέρα αὐτοῦ, <u>Αἴθραν</u> ὀνόματι·

	Αἰγεύς ὁ	Aegeus
	βασιλεύς ὁ	king
	ἅμα	at the same time
	Κρήτη -ης ἡ	Crete
	Μίνως -ωος ὁ	Minos
	δόλος -ου ὁ	trick
	οἱ δέ	but they (*see note at the end of this passage*)
5	κατ᾿ (= κατὰ) ἔτος	each year
	Μινώταυρος -ου ὁ	Minotaur
	θηρίον -ου τό	beast, monster
	ἥμισυ	half
	ταῦρος -ου ὁ	bull
	Πασιφάη -ης ἡ	Pasiphae
	ἔρως -ωτος ὁ	passion, lust (for, + *gen*)
10	τίκτω ἔτεκον	I give birth to
	Δαίδαλος -ου ὁ	Daedalus
	δημιουργός -οῦ ὁ	inventor, craftsman
	λαβύρινθος -ου ὁ	labyrinth
15	ἀποδημέω	I travel, I am away from home
	Τροιζήν -ῆνος ἡ	Troezen (*city in southern Greece*)
	Πιτθεύς ὁ	Pittheus
	Αἴθρα -ας ἡ	Aethra

100

καὶ αὕτη παῖδα <u>ἔτεκεν</u>. ὁ μέντοι Αἰγεύς, διότι ἐχθροὶ αὐτῷ <u>πανταχοῦ</u> ἦσαν, οὐκέτι ἤθελεν ἐν τῇ Τροιζῆνι μένειν. ὁ μὲν οὖν παῖς, <u>Θησεὺς</u> ὀνόματι, μετὰ τῆς τε μητρὸς καὶ τοῦ <u>πάππου</u> ἐκεῖ ἐλείφθη. ὁ δ' Αἰγεὺς
20 <u>ξίφος</u> τε καὶ <u>πέδιλα</u> ὑπὸ <u>πέτρῳ</u> ἔκρυψεν. "ἐπεὶ ὁ Θησεύς," ἔφη, "οἷός τ' ἔσται τὸν λίθον <u>κινήσας</u> ταῦτα λαμβάνειν, γνώσεται τὸ τοῦ πατρὸς ὄνομα." ἔπειτα δὲ πρὸς τὰς Ἀθήνας <u>ἐπανῆλθεν</u> ὁ Αἰγεύς.

	τίκτω ἔτεκον	I give birth to
	πανταχοῦ	everywhere
	Θησεύς ὁ	Theseus
	πάππος -ου ὁ	grandfather
20	ξίφος -ους τό*	sword
	πέδιλα -ων τά	sandals
	πέτρος -ου ὁ	rock
	κινέω ἐκίνησα	I move
	ἐπανέρχομαι ἐπανῆλθον	I return

*this type of neuter third declension noun with epsilon contraction is explained below

Article marking change of subject

From the passage above note the important idiom whereby the nominative definite article followed by δέ starts a new sentence, marking a change of subject to someone who was in the previous sentence (or clause before semi-colon) in a different case:

ὁ τῆς Κρήτης βασιλεὺς τοὺς Ἀθηναίους δίκην ᾔτησεν. <u>οἱ δὲ</u> πρῶτον μὲν οὐκ ἤθελον ...
The king of Crete asked the Athenians for justice. <u>But they</u> at first were unwilling ...

We saw an example in the *Myth of Er* in Chapter 7:

αἱ ψυχαὶ ... προσῆλθον πρὸς τὴν Λάχεσιν· <u>ἡ δὲ</u> συνέπεμψεν ἑκάστῃ δαίμονα ...
The souls ... came to Lachesis; <u>and she</u> sent to each a divine spirit ...

The article is translated *he, she, they* - and δέ *and* or *but* - as appropriate. This idiom is a survival of the use of the article as a pronoun which was common in earlier Greek. (You need, as usual, to *look ahead* to distinguish this idiom from the article simply with a new noun.)

Adjectives with epsilon contraction

Contraction resulting from an epsilon stem joining an ending whose first letter is a vowel affects some nouns and adjectives, as well as verbs. Contracted third declension adjectives such as ἀληθής = *true* are fairly common (but unusual in being 3-3 rather than 3-1-3, i.e. having no separate feminine - unlike the βαρύς type, but like third declension adjectives in Latin).

ἀληθής = true

		masculine/feminine		*neuter*	
sg	nom	ἀληθής		ἀληθές	
	acc	ἀληθῆ	[ε-α]	ἀληθές	
	gen	ἀληθοῦς	[ε-ος]	ἀληθοῦς	[ε-ος]
	dat	ἀληθεῖ	[ε-ι]	ἀληθεῖ	[ε-ι]
pl	nom	ἀληθεῖς	[ε-ες]	ἀληθῆ	[ε-α]
	acc	ἀληθεῖς	[ε-ας*]	ἀληθῆ	[ε-α]
	gen	ἀληθῶν	[ε-ων]	ἀληθῶν	[ε-ων]
	dat	ἀληθέσι(ν)		ἀληθέσι(ν)	

* but again the accusative plural just follows the nominative instead of producing its own contraction

Four common adjectives with epsilon contraction:
1 ἀσθενής   weak
2 ἀσφαλής   safe
3 δυστυχής   . unlucky, unfortunate
4 εὐτυχής   lucky, fortunate

• The adverbs formed from these end as usual in -ῶς (the accent showing the contraction), hence e.g.
   ἀληθῶς truly

• The comparative and superlative of most of these end respectively -εστερος -α -ον, -εστατος -η -ον, hence e.g.
   ἀληθέστερος -α -ον   truer
   ἀληθέστατος -η -ον   truest, very true

Compound adjectives and privative alpha

• A few second declension adjectives are 2-2 rather than 2-1-2, i.e. without a separate feminine. These are normally compounds (i.e. the stem has a prefix, or has more than one element: compare compound *verbs* such as ἀποβάλλω). Examples are:

   ἄδικος -ον   unjust
   βάρβαρος -ον   barbarian, foreign

βάρβαρος is in origin an onomatopoeic coinage to represent the sound of unintelligible foreign languages: people who go around saying *bar-bar* instead of speaking Greek (compare our use of *rhubarb, rhubarb* for the noise of a crowd on stage). The alpha in ἄδικος means *not* or *-un* and is called *privative* (it *deprives* the word it is prefixed to of its normal meaning: compare δίκη, δίκαιος, δικαιοσύνη). The 3-3 adjectives with epsilon contraction we have just met are also compounds: ἀσθενής and ἀληθής mean in origin *not strong* and *not deceptive*, whilst δυστυχής and εὐτυχής mean respectively *badly* and *well* supplied with luck, τύχη.

• The privative alpha also occurs as a verb prefix. We have just met three examples:
ἀδικέω (like the adjective), ἀθυμέω (lack θυμός = *spirit*) and ἀπορέω (lack πόρος = *resource*).

Nouns with epsilon contraction

There is a group of common third declension neuter nouns with epsilon contraction such as
γένος = *race, nation, type, kind*. These need particular care to avoid confusion with second
declension nouns like λόγος (compare how in Latin nouns such as *corpus*, *genus* - the same
word as in Greek - and *opus* are third declension neuter, not second declension masculine
like *servus*).

γένος -ους τό = race, family, kind

sg	nom	γένος	
	acc	γένος	
	gen	γένους	[ε-ος]
	dat	γένει	[ει]
pl	nom	γένη	[ε-α]
	acc	γένη	[ε-α]
	gen	γενῶν	[ε-ων]
	dat	γένεσι(ν)	

The nominative and accusative plural of these nouns must of course also be distinguished
from first declension nominative singulars like τιμή. As always, the definite article serves as
a useful marker.

Six common nouns like γένος:

1	ἔθνος	tribe, nation
2	ἔτος	year
3	ξίφος	sword
4	ὄρος	mountain
5	πλῆθος	crowd
6	τεῖχος	wall

There are also a few masculine and feminine third declension nouns with epsilon
contraction:
τριήρης -ους ἡ = trireme, warship (with three banks of oars)

sg	nom	τριήρης	
	acc	τριήρη	[ε-α]
	gen	τριήρους	[ε-ος]
	dat	τριήρει	[ε-ι]

pl	nom	τριήρεις	[ε-ες]
	acc	τριήρεις	[ε-ας]
	gen	τριήρων	[ε-ων]
	dat	τριήρεσι(ν)	

And some proper names:

sg	nom	Σωκράτης*	
	acc	Σωκράτη	[ε-α]
	gen	Σωκράτους	[ε-ος]
	dat	Σωκράτει	[ε-ι]

*vocative Σώκρατες

These must be distinguished from first declension masculine nouns like κριτής -οῦ (a few proper names - e.g. Ξέρξης [the Persian king Xerxes] - *do* go like κριτής rather than like Σωκράτης).

Exercise 9.8

Translate into English:
1   ἆρα οἱ τοῦ Σωκράτους λόγοι ἀεὶ ἀληθεῖς ἦσαν;
2   τί ἔθνος ἐκείνου τοῦ πεδίου κρατεῖ;
3   ὁ παῖς τὸν ἵππον ξίφει ὀξεῖ ἔλυσεν.
4   τῶν τειχῶν ἰσχυρῶν ὄντων, ἀσφαλεῖς ἐκεῖ ἐσόμεθα.
5   οἱ Ἀθηναῖοι πολλαῖς τριήρεσιν εὐτυχῶς ἐναυμάχησαν.
6   οὐδεμία οἰκία ἐστὶ τῷ δυστυχεῖ γέροντι.
7   αἱ ἐν τῷ πλήθει τὸν λέγοντα ἐμίσουν.
8   ὁ παῖς καίπερ ἀσθενὴς ὢν μόνος ἐφύλασσε τὸ τείχισμα.
9   πολλὰ ὄρη τοὺς προχωροῦντας κωλύσει.
10   ἆρα ἡ τῶν βαρβάρων γλῶσσα ἡδεῖά ἐστιν;

Exercise 9.9

Translate into Greek:
1   We saw the trireme near the island.
2   The race of the giants no longer exists*.
3   We admired both the sea and the mountains.
4   The unjust do not seek peace.
5   Did you run to help the unfortunate slave, Socrates?

* *just* is

Revision checkpoint

Make sure you know:
• verbs with epsilon contraction (φιλέω)
• adjectives with epsilon contraction (ἀληθής)
• compound adjectives (2-2 ἄδικος) and privative alpha
• nouns with epsilon contraction (γένος, τριήρης, Σωκράτης)

Exercise 9.10

Theseus and the Minotaur (2)

τῷ δὲ <u>ἕκτῳ καὶ δεκάτῳ</u> ἔτει ἡ <u>Αἴθρα</u> τὸν <u>Θησέα</u>, νεανίαν ἰσχυρὸν ἤδη
γενόμενον, πρὸς τὸν <u>πέτρον</u> ἤγαγεν. ὁ δέ, τοῦτον <u>κίνησας</u> καὶ τὰ περὶ τοῦ
πατρὸς μαθών, ἐκ τῆς <u>Τροιζῆνος</u> ἐξῆλθεν, οὐδὲν ἄλλο ἔχων ἢ ξίφος ὀξὺ
καὶ <u>ἱμάτιον</u>. ἡ δὲ διὰ τῶν ὀρῶν ὁδὸς μακρὰ ἦν καὶ χαλεπωτάτη. οἱ γὰρ
5 ἐκεῖ οἰκοῦντες πολλὰ ἔτη <u>κακῶς ἐποίουν</u> τούς τε <u>ποιμένας</u> καὶ τοὺς
<u>ὁδοιπόρους</u>. ὁ μέντοι Θησεὺς πολλούς τε <u>κλέπτας</u> καὶ πολλὰ <u>θηρία</u>
ἀποκτείνας πρὸς τὰς Ἀθήνας ἀσφαλῶς προσῆλθεν. πολλὰ οὖν περὶ
τούτου τοῦ νεανίου ἠγγέλθη ὡς τὰ θηρία ἀποκτείναντος. ὁ δὲ Θησεὺς τὸ
ὄνομα ἑαυτοῦ ἔκρυψεν· ἐβούλετο γὰρ πρῶτον τὰ ἐκεῖ πράγματα
10 γιγνώσκειν. ὁ οὖν <u>Αἰγεὺς</u> (τὸν υἱὸν οὐ γιγνώσκων) ἐφοβεῖτο αὐτὸν ὥσπερ
ἐχθρὸν ὄντα. καὶ ἐκάλεσεν αὐτὸν <u>ἐπὶ</u> δεῖπνον, βουλόμενος <u>φαρμάκῳ</u>
ἀποκτείνειν. τοῦ δὲ παιδὸς τὸ ξίφος <u>ἑλκύσαντος</u> (τὰ γὰρ <u>κρέα</u> ἤθελε
<u>τέμνειν</u>), ὁ Αἰγεὺς <u>ἀναγνωρίζων</u> αὐτὸν <u>ἀπελάκτισε</u> τὴν <u>κύλικα</u> τὴν τὸ
φάρμακον ἔχουσαν. καὶ ἡδέως ἐδέξατο τὸν υἱόν.

	ἕκτος καὶ δέκατος	sixteenth
	Αἴθρα -ας ἡ	Aethra
	Θησεύς -έως ἡ	Theseus
	πέτρος -ου ὁ	rock
	κινέω ἐκίνησα	I move
	Τροιζήν -ῆνος ἡ	Troezen
	ἱμάτιον -ου τό	cloak
5	κακῶς ποιέω	I treat badly
	ποιμήν -ένος ὁ	shepherd
	ὁδοιπόρος -ου ὁ	traveller
	κλέπτης -ου ὁ	robber
	θηρίον -ου τό	wild beast
10	Αἰγεύς -έως ὁ	Aegeus
	ἐπί	(+ *acc*) to
	φάρμακον -ου τό	poison
	ἕλκω εἵλκυσα	(*here*) I draw (sword *etc*)
	κρέα -ῶν τά	meat
	τέμνω	I cut
	ἀναγνωρίζω	I recognise
	ἀπολακτίζω ἀπελάκτισα	I kick away
	κύλιξ -ικος ἡ	cup

15 οὗτος οὖν, τῶν τε νεανιῶν καὶ τῶν κορῶν ἤδη ἐννέα ἔτη τῷ Μινωταύρῳ
πεμφθέντων, ἔπεισε τὸν πατέρα ἑαυτὸν ἐν τοῖς νεανίαις πέμπειν· "τὸν γὰρ
Μινώταυρον ἀποκτείνας," ἔφη, "σώσω ἐμαυτόν τε καὶ τοὺς ἄλλους". ὁ
οὖν Αἰγεὺς ὡμολόγησεν. ἡ τῶν Ἀθηναίων ναῦς ἱστία μέλανα εἶχεν πρὸς
τὴν Κρήτην πλέουσα, ὥσπερ πρὸς θάνατον. ὁ δ' Αἰγεὺς ἐκέλευσε τὸν υἱὸν
20 τὴν μὲν νίκην λευκοῖς ἱστίοις φαίνειν, τὴν δὲ συμφορὰν τὰ μέλανα ἔτι
ἔχοντα.

ἐπεὶ δ' εἰς τὴν Κρήτην ἀφίκοντο, ὅ τε Θησεὺς καὶ οἱ ἄλλοι πρὸς
δεσμωτήριον ἤχθησαν. καὶ ἐκεῖ ἰσχυρῶς ἐφυλάσσοντο. ἡ μέντοι Ἀριάδνη,
ἡ τοῦ Μίνωος θυγάτηρ, ἔπει εἶδε τὸν Θησέα ἐφίλει αὐτὸν καὶ ἐβούλετο
25 σῴζειν. πρὸς οὖν τὸ δεσμωτήριον τῆς νυκτὸς προσελθοῦσα τὸν Θησέα
ἐκάλεσεν· "ὦ Θησεῦ, Ἀριάδνη πάρειμι· βουλόμενη σῴζειν, παρέχω
σοι τοῦτο τὸ ξίφος καὶ τοῦτο τὸ λίνον. ταῦτα γὰρ ἔχων οἷός τ' ἔσῃ τὸν
Μινώταυρον ἀποκτείνας ἐκ τοῦ λαβυρίνθου ἀσφαλῶς φεύγειν". ὁ δὲ
Θησεὺς μάλιστα θαυμάζων τό τε ξίφος καὶ τὸ λίνον ἐδέξατο.

30 ἡμέρας δὲ γενομένης οἱ τοῦ Μίνωος δοῦλοι ἤγαγον τοὺς Ἀθηναίους πρὸς
τὸν λαβύρινθον. ὅ τε Θησεὺς καὶ οἱ ἑταῖροι ἠναγκάσθησαν εἰσελθεῖν.
οἱ μὲν οὖν ἄλλοι μάλιστα ἐφοβοῦντο, ὁ δὲ Θησεὺς ἀνδρείως
προὐχώρησεν ὡς τὰ τῆς Ἀριάδνης δῶρα ἔχων. τῷ μὲν γὰρ λίνῳ τὴν ὁδὸν
ἐγίγνωσκε, καίπερ τοῦ λαβυρίνθου ποικίλου ὄντος· τῷ δὲ ξίφει τὸν
35 Μινώταυρον ἀπέκτεινεν. ὁ οὖν Θησεὺς καὶ οἱ ἄλλοι οὕτω σωθέντες ἀπὸ
τῆς Κρήτης ἔφυγον. τοὺς μέντοι τοῦ πατρὸς λόγους ἀμελῶν ὁ Θησεὺς τὰ
μέλανα ἱστία μετὰ τὴν νίκην οὐκ ἤλλαξεν. ὁ οὖν Αἰγεύς, ὥσπερ τοῦ υἱοῦ
ἀποθανόντος, ἔρριψεν ἑαυτὸν εἰς τὴν θάλασσαν (ἡ μετὰ ταῦτα τὸ ὄνομα
αὐτοῦ ἔχει).

15	Μινώταυρος -ου ὁ	Minotaur
	ἱστία -ων τά	sails
	μέλας -αινα -αν	black
	Κρήτη -ης ἡ	Crete
20	λευκός -ή -όν	white
	Ἀριάδνη -ης ἡ	Ariadne
	Μίνως -ωος ὁ	Minos
25	λίνον -ου τό	thread
	λαβύρινθος -ου ὁ	labyrinth
30	ποικίλος -η -ον	intricate, complex
35	ἀμελέω	I forget about, I disregard
	ἀλλάσσω ἤλλαξα	I change
	ῥίπτω ἔρριψα	I hurl

Irregular epsilon verbs

• As always, you should not worry too much about minor irregularities: these and other forms can easily be checked in the list of verbs in the Reference Grammar. It is much more important to understand and be able to apply the basic principle of contraction.

Epsilon verbs involving various forms of irregularity:

1	αἱρέω*	I take	(middle αἱρέομαι = I choose)
2	ἀφικνέομαι	I arrive	
3	δοκέω	I seem	
4	ἐπαινέω	I praise	
5	καθαιρέω	I take down, I demolish	
6	καλέω	I call, I invite	
7	παραινέω	I advise (+ *dat*)	
8	πλέω	I sail	
9	σκοπέω	I look at, I consider	
10	ὑπισχνέομαι	I promise (+ *fut inf*)	

* in many contexts synonymous with λαμβάνω, but αἱρέω tends to be more emphatic (meaning in origin something like *seize*, whereas λαμβάνω may imply only something like *get*)

• As we saw, most verbs with stems ending in epsilon lengthen this vowel to eta before adding the sigma for the future and first (weak) aorist: φιλέω, φιλήσω, ἐφίλησα. But a few keep the epsilon:

present		*future*	*weak (first) aorist*
ἐπαινέω	I praise	ἐπαινέσω	ἐπήνεσα
παραινέω	I advise	παραινέσω	παρήνεσα

These are compounds of a basic verb αἰνέω = *I approve*. In the aorist the augment has (as usual with compounds) been added after the prefix.

• The extremely common verb καλέω = *I call* also basically keeps the epsilon (hence aorist ἐκάλεσα), but in Attic normally has future καλῶ (i.e. exactly like the contracted present, and distinguishable only by context) instead of the expected καλέσω.

• Another very common verb δοκέω = *I seem* forms its future and aorist by in effect removing the epsilon from the stem: hence δόξω, ἔδοξα (compare διώξω, ἐδίωξα from διώκω).

• Most verbs with stems ending in epsilon have a first (weak) aorist. A few however have a second (strong) aorist. As with any second aorists, the aorist stem can be: telescoped from the present stem; changed a bit more; or completely unrelated. The aorist does not involve any contraction. Hence:

present	aorist	aorist stem
	telescoped from present:	
ἀφικνέομαι	ἀφικόμην	ἀφικ-
	changed a bit more:	
ὑπισχνέομαι	ὑπεσχόμην	ὑποσχ-
	completely unrelated:	
αἱρέω	εἷλον	ἑλ-
αἱρέομαι	εἱλόμην	

Like many highly irregular forms, the aorist of αἱρέω quickly becomes familiar because it is very common (the compound καθαιρέω has a predictable aorist καθεῖλον).

• σκοπέω forms its future and aorist as if from σκέπτομαι: hence σκέψομαι, ἐσκεψάμην.

• Finally, when a stem with epsilon is only one syllable long, the verb contacts only when the added ending begins with epsilon. Hence:

πλέω		I sail
πλεῖς	[ε-εις]	you (sg) sail
πλεῖ	[ε-ει]	he/she/it sails
πλέομεν		we sail
πλεῖτε	[ε-ετε]	you (pl) sail
πλέουσι(ν)		they sail

infinitive	πλεῖν
participle	πλέων -ουσα -ον (stem πλεοντ-)
aorist	ἔπλευσα

• Here are the ten slightly irregular epsilon verbs again, each with its aorist to illustrate the type of irregularity involved, and aorist stem (as seen e.g. in the participle):

	present		aorist	(aorist stem)
1	αἱρέω	I take	εἷλον	(ἑλ-)
	αἱρέομαι	I choose	εἱλόμην	(ἑλ-)
2	ἀφικνέομαι	I arrive	ἀφικόμην	(ἀφικ-)
3	δοκέω	I seem	ἔδοξα	(δοξ-)
4	ἐπαινέω	I praise	ἐπήνεσα	(ἐπαινεσ-)
5	καθαιρέω	I take down, I demolish	καθεῖλον	(καθελ-)
6	καλέω	I call, I invite	ἐκάλεσα	(καλεσ-)
7	παραινέω	I advise (+ dat)	παρήνεσα	(παραινεσ-)
8	πλέω	I sail	ἔπλευσα	(πλευσ-)
9	σκοπέω	I look at, I consider	ἐσκεψάμην	(σκεψ-)
10	ὑπισχνέομαι	I promise (+ fut inf)	ὑπεσχόμην	(ὑποσχ-)

Futures with epsilon contraction

• Most verbs of course form their future by adding sigma to the present stem, then using the primary active endings. We saw in Chapter 8 one sort of variant: verbs that become middle/deponent in the future (with no distinction of meaning), e.g. ἀκούω, ἀκούσομαι.

• Another variant is seen in a group of verbs which, though they do not have an epsilon on the present stem, form their future like the present of an epsilon verb (and without the sigma of a normal future: thus in effect they add epsilon instead of sigma). These verbs include some deponents. Common examples (here showing the future in the contracted form in which it would occur in a sentence or passage) are:

present	future
ἀγγέλλω	ἀγγελῶ (accent shows contraction; similarly with the other forms in this list)
ἀποθνήσκω	ἀποθανοῦμαι*
ἀποκρίνομαι	ἀποκρινοῦμαι
ἀποκτείνω	ἀποκτενῶ
βάλλω	βαλῶ
διαφθείρω	διαφθερῶ
μάχομαι	μαχοῦμαι
μένω	μενῶ
ὀργίζομαι	ὀργιοῦμαι
πίπτω	πεσοῦμαι*
τρέχω	δραμοῦμαι*
φαίνω	φανῶ

* these futures are doubly unusual: they change to a middle/deponent form *and* use an contracted-epsilon form

Background: Greek Myth (2)

Myths often deal with thought patterns or anxieties which are deeply rooted in human beings, but which in modern societies may be cloaked by the veneer of civilisation or argued away by a rationalist scientific outlook keen to avoid the taint of superstition. A good example is 'sympathetic magic': a mysterious connection between two apparently quite separate things, in particular the idea that a person's wellbeing is bound up with some object or action. This is most familiar to us in Voodoo (where you make a wax model of your enemy, stick pins in it, and wait for the results). Similarly, primitive people are often unwilling to be photographed: the photograph might fall into the wrong hands, be accidentally or maliciously destroyed, and the subject therefore (so runs this train of thought) be destroyed too. This principle underlies the following story, about the hero Meleager.

Exercise 9.11

Meleager

ὁ <u>Οἰνεὺς</u> τῆς <u>Καλυδῶνος</u> <u>ἐβασίλευεν</u>. καὶ ἡ γυνὴ αὐτοῦ, Ἀλθαία ὀνόματι,
υἱὸν <u>ἔτεκεν</u>, ὃν ἐκάλεσαν <u>Μελέαγρον</u>. τούτου δὲ γενομένου, μεθ᾽ ἑπτὰ
ἡμέρας οἱ ἐν τῇ οἰκίᾳ <u>ἑορτὴν</u> καὶ δεῖπνον παρεσκεύαζον. <u>ἐπὶ</u> δὲ τὴν
ἑορτὴν ἦλθον ἄλλοι τε πολλοὶ καὶ αὐταὶ αἱ <u>Μοῖραι</u>. αὗται δὲ περὶ τοῦ
5   παιδὸς εἶπον τάδε· "σκοπεῖτε τοῦτο τὸ <u>ξύλον</u> <u>ἐπὶ</u> τῆς <u>ἑστίας</u>· τοῦ ξύλου
<u>κατακαυθέντος</u>, ὁ Μελέαγρος ἀποθανεῖται". ἐπεὶ δὲ ἡ μήτηρ ταῦτα
ἤκουσε, τὸ ξύλον ἐκ τοῦ πυρὸς ταχέως λαβοῦσα ἐν <u>θήκῃ</u> ἔκρυψε, καὶ
<u>ἐπιμελῶς</u> ἐφύλασσεν.

μετὰ δὲ πολλὰ ἔτη ὁ Οἰνεὺς, ὃς ἐπεὶ <u>καρπὸν</u> ἐκ τῆς γῆς ἔλαβεν <u>ἀπαρχὰς</u>
10   πᾶσι τοῖς θεοῖς ἀεὶ <u>ἔθυε</u>, τὴν Ἀρτεμίδα <u>ἅπαξ</u> <u>ἐξέλιπεν</u>. ὀργισθεῖσα οὖν
ἡ θεὰ <u>κάπρον</u> <u>ἄγριον</u> ἔπεμψεν ὡς τὴν γῆν καὶ τοὺς ἀνθρώπους
διαφθεροῦντα. μαθὼν δὲ ὁ Οἰνεὺς τὰ ὑπὸ τοῦ κάπρου ποιούμενα,
<u>συνεκάλεσε</u> τοὺς ἀρίστους ἐκ πάσης τῆς χώρας ὡς τὸ <u>θηρίον</u>
ἀποκτενοῦντας. καὶ <u>συνῆλθον</u> <u>εἴκοσιν</u> ἀνδρεῖοι ἐπὶ τὴν <u>ἄγραν</u>, μεθ᾽ ὧν

Οἰνεύς ὁ	Oeneus
Καλυδών -ῶνος ἡ	Calydon (*town in central Greece*)
βασιλεύω	I am king
Ἀλθαία -ας ἡ	Althaea
τίκτω ἔτεκον	I give birth to
Μελέαγρος -ου ὁ	Meleager
ἑορτή -ῆς ἡ	feast
ἐπί	(+ *acc*) to
Μοῖραι -ῶν αἱ	Fates (*goddesses of destiny*)
5 ξύλον -ου τό	log
ἐπί	(+ *gen*) on
ἑστία -ας ἡ	hearth
κατακαίω	
aor pass κατεκαύθην	I burn completely, I burn away
θήκη -ης ἡ	chest, box
ἐπιμελῶς	carefully
καρπός -οῦ ὁ	crop, harvest
ἀπαρχαί -ῶν αἱ	first-fruits, offerings
10 θύω	I sacrifice
Ἄρτεμις -ίδος ἡ	Artemis (*virgin goddess of hunting*)
ἅπαξ	once, a single time
ἐκλείπω ἐξέλιπον	I leave out
κάπρος -ου ὁ	boar
ἄγριος -α -ον	wild
συγκαλέω συνεκάλεσα	I call together
θηρίον -ου τό	wild beast
συνέρχομαι συνῆλθον	I come together, I meet
εἴκοσι(ν)	twenty
ἄγρα -ας ἡ	hunt

110

15 ἦσαν ἀδελφοὶ δύο τῆς Ἀλθαίας, καὶ ἡ <u>Ἀταλάντη</u> ἡ ἐξ <u>Ἀρκαδίας</u>,
<u>παρθένος</u> οὖσα περὶ τῆς <u>ἄγρας</u> <u>ἐμπειροτάτη</u>. καὶ τούτων τινὲς εἶπον,
"οὐδαμῶς ἄξιόν ἐστιν εἰ ἡμεῖς ἄνδρες ὄντες ἀναγκασθησόμεθα μετὰ
γυναικὸς <u>θηρεύειν</u>." τοῦτο δ' ἀκούσας ὁ Μελέαγρος, νεανίας νῦν
γενόμενος, ὠργίσθη διότι ἐφίλει τὴν Ἀταλάντην, καὶ ἐβούλετο πάντας
20 ἐπαινεῖν αὐτήν. τέλος μέντοι πάντες ὁμολογήσαντες ἐπὶ τὴν ἄγραν
ἐξῆλθον. καὶ πρώτη ἡ Ἀταλάντη τὸν <u>κάπρον</u> <u>ἐτόξευσε</u> τὸ <u>νῶτον</u>. τοῦ δὲ
<u>θηρίου</u> διὰ ταῦτα ὀργιζομένου ἡ Ἀταλάντη ἐν μεγίστῳ κινδύνῳ ἦν. ὁ
μέντοι Μελέαγρος εὐθὺς προσδραμὼν τὸν κάπρον τῷ ξίφει ἀπέκτεινεν.

ἀποθανόντος τε τοῦ κάπρου, τὸ <u>δέρμα</u> <u>ἔδωκεν</u> ὁ Μελέαγρος τῇ
25 Ἀταλάντῃ, ὡς πρώτη τοξευσάσῃ. οἱ δὲ τῆς Ἀλθαίας ἀδελφοί, ὀργισθέντες
διότι παρθένος ἀνδρῶν παρόντων τὸ τοῦ δέρματος δῶρον ἔλαβεν, εἶπον,
"εἰ μὲν Μελέαγρος ὁ τὸ θηρίον ἀποκτείνας βούλεται τὸ δέρμα λαβεῖν,
καλόν ἐστιν· <u>εἰ δὲ μή</u>, ἡμεῖς ληψόμεθα ὡς <u>συγγενεῖς</u> ὄντες". ὁ δὲ
Μελέαγρος <u>μάλιστα</u> ὀργισθεὶς τὸ ξίφος αὖθις λαβὼν <u>ἀμφοτέρους</u>
30 ἀπέκτεινεν. ἡ δ' <u>ἀδελφὴ</u> αὐτῶν Ἀλθαία, τοὺς θανάτους βαρέως φέρουσα,
τὸ <u>ξύλον</u> ὃ ἐφύλασσεν ἐκ τῆς <u>θήκης</u> ἐξελοῦσα εἰς τὸ πῦρ κατέβαλεν·
<u>κατακαυθέντος</u> δὲ τοῦ ξύλου εὐθὺς ἀπέθανεν ὁ Μελέαγρος.

15	Ἀταλάντη -ης ἡ	Atalanta
	Ἀρκαδία -ας ἡ	Arcadia (*wild and mountainous region of southern Greece*)
	παρθένος -ου ἡ	virgin
	ἄγρα -ας ἡ	hunt
	ἔμπειρος -ον	experienced
	θηρεύω	I hunt
20	κάπρος -ου ὁ	boar
	τοξεύω ἐτόξευσα	I shoot (with a bow)
	νῶτον -ου τό	back (*here 'accusative of part affected': in the ~*)
	θηρίον -ου τό	wild beast
	δέρμα -ατος τό	skin, hide
	ἔδωκα	(*irreg aor*) I gave
25	εἰ δὲ μή	but if not, otherwise
	συγγενής -ές	related
	μάλιστα	very much
	ἀμφότεροι -αι -α	both
30	ἀδελφή -ῆς ἡ	sister
	ξύλον -ου τό	log
	θήκη -ης ἡ	chest, box
	κατακαίω	
	aor pass κατεκαύθην	I burn completely, I burn away

Irregular third declension nouns (3)

Finally (these are the last noun forms you need to learn), there are a few third declension nouns involving various irregularities, but linked by having genitive singular ending in -εως (lengthening the normal omicron) and genitive plural ending in -εων:

111

πόλις -εως ἡ = city, city-state   ναῦς, νεώς ἡ = ship

sg	nom	πόλις	ναῦς
	acc	πόλιν	ναῦν
	gen	πόλεως	νεώς
	dat	πόλει	νηί

pl	nom	πόλεις	νῆες
	acc	πόλεις	ναῦς
	gen	πόλεων	νεῶν
	dat	πόλεσι(ν)	ναυσί(ν)

βασιλεύς -έως ὁ = king   ἄστυ -εως τό = city, town **

sg	nom	βασιλεύς*	ἄστυ
	acc	βασιλέα	ἄστυ
	gen	βασιλέως	ἄστεως
	dat	βασιλεῖ	ἄστει
		*vocative βασιλεῦ	

pl	nom	βασιλῆς or -εῖς†	ἄστη
	acc	βασιλέας	ἄστη
	gen	βασιλέων	ἄστεων
	dat	βασιλεῦσι(ν)	ἄστεσι(ν)

** ἄστυ is often used for *town* as opposed to countryside

† βασιλεῖς is a later form; but with ἱππεύς = *horseman* the plural ἱππεῖς = *cavalry* is the norm

Exercise 9.12

Translate into English:
1   ἆρα εἶδες τοὺς εἰς τὴν πόλιν ἀφικνουμένους;
2   ὁ στρατηγὸς τοὺς ναύτας ἐπαινέσας ἐκ τοῦ λιμένος ἐξέπλευσεν.
3   οἱ ἐν τῇ πόλει ἀσφαλεῖς ἦσαν, καίπερ τῶν τειχῶν καθαιρουμένων.
4   αἱ τὸν γίγαντα ἀποκτενοῦσαι ἑτοῖμαί εἰσιν.
5   ὁ βασιλεὺς τοῖς φυλάσσουσιν οὐδὲν ἀποκρινεῖται.
6   οἱ ἱππεῖς ἐκ τῶν ἀγρῶν εἰς τὸ ἄστυ ἀφίκοντο.
7   ἡ τοῖς παισὶ παραινέσασα σοφωτάτη ἐστίν.
8   τὸ τείχισμα ἑλόντες, οἱ πεζοὶ πρὸς τὴν θάλασσαν δραμοῦνται.
9   οἱ σύμμαχοι τὴν βουλὴν σκεψάμενοι οὐδέποτε μαχοῦνται.
10   ἐν τῇδε τῇ νηὶ πάντες μενοῦμεν.

Exercise 9.13

Translate into Greek:
1   Will the allies run out of the city?
2   Having praised the girls, the teacher looked at the letter.
3   I saw three ships sailing into the harbour.
4   The woman promised to reply.
5   Why did you choose that book, boy?

Exercise 9.14

Perseus (1)

This is one of the most famous of all Greek myths. It is an adventure story, a quest containing many of the classic folk-tale elements. It is also, like many myths, a meditation on the nature of death and man's confronting of it: Perseus' feats make him in many ways master of death, yet he remains mortal. The long story begins and ends with his grandfather Acrisius. Here too is a recurrent story pattern: the very steps taken to try to prevent a dire prophecy from coming true serve only to hasten it.

ὁ ᾿Ακρίσιος βασιλεὺς τοῦ <u>῎Αργους</u> <u>ποτὲ</u> ἐγένετο. ἦν δ᾿ αὐτῷ θυγάτηρ καλλίστη, <u>Δανάη</u> ὀνόματι. βουλόμενος δὲ υἱὸν ἔχειν, ἀγγέλους πρὸς <u>Δελφοὺς</u> ἔπεμψεν ὡς ἀπὸ τοῦ θεοῦ πευσομένους διὰ τί υἱὸς οὐκ ἐστὶν αὐτῷ. ὁ δ᾿ ᾿Απόλλων οὐδὲν περὶ τούτου ἀπεκρίνατο, ἀλλ᾿ εἶπεν, "ὦ
5   βασιλεῦ, ἔσται τῇ σῇ θυγατρὶ υἱὸς ὃς ἀποκτενεῖ σε". ὁ οὖν ᾿Ακρίσιος τὴν Δανάην ἐν <u>οἰκήματι</u> χαλκοῦ ὑπὸ τῇ γῇ κρύψας ἰσχυρῶς ἐφύλασσεν.

ὁ δὲ Ζεὺς ἐν <u>ὑετῷ</u> χρυσοῦ <u>ὡς</u> τὴν Δανάην ἐλθὼν προσεῖπεν αὐτῇ ἐκ τῆς <u>ὁμίχλης</u>. μετὰ δ᾿ ἐννέα <u>μῆνας</u> ἡ Δανάη υἱὸν <u>ἔτεκε</u>, καὶ οὗτος ὁ παῖς <u>Περσεὺς</u> ἐκλήθη. ἐπεὶ δὲ ὁ ᾿Ακρίσιος περὶ τοῦ Περσέως ἤκουσε, <u>μάλιστα</u>
10   ὠργίσθη. καὶ τῷ περὶ τοῦ Διὸς λόγῳ οὐδαμῶς πιστεύων, <u>ἐμέμφετο</u> τὸν

	᾿Ακρίσιος -ου ὁ	Acrisius
	῎Αργος -ους τό	Argos (*city in southern Greece*)
	ποτέ	once
	Δανάη -ης ἡ	Danae
	Δελφοί -ῶν οἱ	Delphi
	᾿Απόλλων -ωνος ὁ	Apollo
5	οἴκημα -ατος τό	room, chamber
	ὑετός -οῦ ὁ	shower
	ὡς	(+ *acc*) to (a person)
	ὁμίχλη -ης ἡ	mist
	μήν μηνός ὁ	month
	τίκτω ἔτεκον	I give birth to
	Περσεύς -έως ἡ	Perseus
	μάλιστα	very much
10	μέμφομαι	I blame

<u>Πρωτέα</u> τὸν ἑαυτοῦ ἀδελφὸν ὃν <u>μάλιστα</u> ἐμίσει, λέγων ὅτι τὴν τοῦ <u>οἰκήματος</u> <u>κλῆδα</u> κλέψας λάθρα εἰσῆλθεν.

ἔπειτα δὲ ὁ Ἀκρίσιος μεγάλην <u>θήκην</u> <u>ξυλίνην</u> ἐποιήσατο. οὐ γὰρ ἤθελε τὴν θυγατέρα καὶ τὸν υἱὸν αὐτῆς ἀποκτείνειν, τὴν τῶν θεῶν ὀργὴν
15 φοβούμενος· εἶπε δὲ πρὸς ἑαυτόν, "ἡ θήκη <u>ἴσως</u> <u>καταδύσει</u>, ἀλλ᾽ οὐκ <u>αἴτιος</u> ἐγώ". ἐν δὲ τῇ θήκῃ ἥ τε Δανάη καὶ τὸ <u>βρέφος</u> διὰ τῆς θαλάσσης πᾶσαν τὴν νύκτα ἐφέροντο. καὶ ἡ Δανάη ᾔτησε τὸν Δία σῴζειν αὐτούς.

ἡμέρας δὲ γενομένης, ἡ θήκη πρὸς νῆσον τινὰ ἐφέρετο. καὶ <u>ἁλιεύς</u> τις, <u>Δίκτυς</u> ὀνόματι, τήν τε Δανάην καὶ τὸν παῖδα εὑρὼν πρὸς τὴν οἰκίαν
20 ἤγαγεν. ἐκεῖ οὖν πολὺν χρόνον ᾤκουν, ἐν ᾧ ὁ Περσεὺς νεανίας ἀνδρεῖός τε καὶ σοφὸς ἐγένετο. καὶ ὁ <u>Πολυδέκτης</u>, ὅ τε τῆς <u>Σερίφου</u> βασιλεὺς καὶ ὁ τοῦ Δίκτυος ἀδελφὸς ὤν, περὶ αὐτῶν τέλος ἀκούσας ἐβούλετο <u>γαμεῖν</u> τὴν Δανάην, ἣ καλλίστη ἔτι ἦν, καὶ νῦν τῆς Ἀθήνης <u>ἱέρεια</u>. ἡ δὲ Δανάη ἐμίσει αὐτὸν ὡς <u>ἀγριώτατον</u> ὄντα. ὁ οὖν βασιλεὺς ἐβούλετο βίᾳ
25 λαμβάνειν τὴν Δανάην· ἀλλὰ τοῦτο χαλεπὸν ἦν, διότι ὁ Περσεὺς ἀεὶ παρῆν ὡς τὴν μητέρα φυλάξων.

ὁ οὖν Πολυδέκτης, <u>μηχανὴν</u> ζητῶν ὡς τὸν Περσέα <u>ἀφαιρήσων</u>, πάντας τοὺς τῆς νήσου νεανίας πρὸς <u>ἑορτὴν</u> μεγάλην ἐκάλεσεν· ἐν δὲ τούτοις ἦν ὁ Περσεύς. ἐκελεύσθησαν δὲ πάντες δῶρον <u>ὀνομάζειν</u> τοῦ βασιλέως
30 ἄξιον. τοῖς μὲν οὖν ἄλλοις ἵππος ἔδοξε δῶρον ἄξιον εἶναι· ὁ δὲ Περσεὺς

Πρωτεύς -έως ὁ	Proteus
μάλιστα	very much
οἴκημα -ατος τό	room, chamber
κλῆς κλῆδος ἡ	key
θήκη -ης ἡ	chest, box
ξύλινος -η -ον	wooden
15 ἴσως	perhaps
καταδύνω *future* καταδύσω	I sink
αἴτιος -α -ον	to blame, responsible
βρέφος -ους τό	baby
ἁλιεύς -έως ὁ	fisherman
Δίκτυς -υος ὁ	Dictys
20 Πολυδέκτης -ου ὁ	Polydectes
Σέριφος -ου ἡ	Seriphos (*small Greek island*)
γαμέω	I marry
ἱέρεια -ας ἡ	priestess
ἄγριος -α -ον	(*here*) cruel
25 μηχανή -ῆς ἡ	means, device
ἀφαιρέω *future* ἀφαιρήσω	I get rid of
ἑορτή -ῆς ἡ	feast
ὀνομάζω	I name

114

εἵλετο τὴν τῆς <u>Γοργόνος</u> τῆς <u>Μεδούσης</u> κεφαλήν. τοῦτο δ' εἶπε τῆς
'Αθήνης πειθούσης· ἡ γὰρ θεά, ὀργισθεῖσα διότι ἡ <u>ἱέρεια</u> ἡ Δανάη <u>κακῶς</u>
<u>ἐποιήθη</u>, ἐβούλετο τὸν Πολυδέκτην κολάζειν. <u>τῇ</u> οὖν <u>ὑστεραίᾳ</u> οἱ νεανίαι
αὖθις παρῆσαν. ἕκαστος δὲ τῶν ἄλλων ἵππον καλὸν ἦγεν· ὁ δὲ Περσεὺς
35   οὐδὲν δῶρον εἶχεν. ὁ οὖν Πολυδέκτης ὀργισθεὶς ἐκέλευσεν αὐτὸν τὴν τῆς
Μεδούσης κεφαλὴν <u>κομίζειν</u>· "<u>εἰ δὲ μή</u>, τὴν σὴν μητέρα βίᾳ λήψομαι".
καὶ ὁ Περσεὺς ὑπέσχετο, "ἢ τοῦτο ποιήσω ἢ ἀποθανοῦμαι".

	Γοργών -όνος ἡ	Gorgon (*female monster with serpents in its hair, and glaring eyes*)
	Μέδουσα -ης ἡ	Medusa
	ἱέρεια -ας ἡ	priestess
	κακῶς ποιέω	I treat badly
	τῇ ὑστεραίᾳ	on the next day
35	κομίζω	I fetch
	εἰ δὲ μή	otherwise

Tense and aspect (1): Aorist imperative

• *Tense* refers to the *time* an action happens (present, future, or past). *Aspect* refers to the *type of time*, the way of looking at it (e.g. single action, long or continuous process, etc).

• In its normal (i.e. *indicative*) form, the aorist refers to *a single action* that is *in the past*:
ἐκελεύσαμεν   we ordered
ἔμαθες   you (*sg*) learned

• In other parts of the verb the aorist can denote just *a single action*, not necessarily one in the past. In this case the aorist is being used *by aspect*.

• This is most clearly illustrated by the aorist imperative, the active forms of which are:
first (weak) aorist
sg   παῦσον   stop (something)! (stressing *now, on this one occasion*)
pl   παύσατε

second (strong) aorist
sg   λαβέ   take (something)! (stressing *now, on this one occasion*)
pl   λάβετε
The imperative is clear-cut because it is hard to see how an imperative could refer to the past (insofar it has a tense at all, any imperative is in effect a sort of future, because the thing being commanded has not happened yet).

• The distinction between the present and aorist imperative is not always hard and fast, but the present is normally used for a command that is generalised or that envisages the action being repeated, the aorist to stress that the command applies to a single occasion. Surrounding words often help:

τοὺς λόγους ἀεὶ μάνθανε.
Always learn the words!　　　　　(*present imperative*)

τούτους τοὺς λόγους εὐθὺς μαθέ.
Learn these words immediately!　　(*aorist imperative*)

• The forms of the aorist imperative are partly predictable. The singular of the first (weak) aorist imperative παῦσον is slightly unexpected (and is like the neuter of the future participle). Its plural παύσατε is however just the second person plural of the aorist indicative without the augment (which only the indicative ever has). The second (strong) aorist is easier: it is simply the present imperative endings (-ε, -ετε) added to the aorist stem, hence e.g. present imperative λάμβανε, aorist imperative λαβέ. (Compare how the second [strong] aorist participle likewise uses the present endings on the aorist stem: the second [strong] aorist borrows its *indicative* endings from the imperfect, but all its *other* endings from the present.)

More imperatives

• We saw the middle/deponent present imperative in Chapter 8:
present
sg　παύου　　　　　　cease! (*generally*)
pl　παύεσθε

Middle/deponent aorist imperatives (used in the way described above) are also in common use:
first (weak) aorist
sg　παῦσαι　　　　　　cease! (*once*)
pl　παύσασθε

second (strong) aorist
sg　λαβοῦ　　　　　　take for yourself! (*once*)
pl　λάβεσθε

Notice again the relation *of the plurals* to the equivalent indicative: the present is identical, the aorists simply remove the augment.

• Passive imperatives also exist, but are less common in practice and it is not a high priority to learn them. For the present, they are identical to the middle. For the aorist, they use the aorist passive stem, hence:
sg　παύσθητι　　　　　be stopped!
pl　παύσθητε

sg　λήφθητι　　　　　be taken!
pl　λήφητε

Notice yet again how the plurals are like the equivalent indicative without the augment.

Summary table of imperatives in common use:

		active	middle
present			
	sg	παῦε	παύου
	pl	παύετε	παύεσθε

first (weak) aorist			
	sg	παῦσον	παῦσαι
	pl	παύσατε	παύσασθε

second (strong) aorist			
	sg	λαβέ	λαβοῦ
	pl	λάβετε	λάβεσθε

Exercise 9.15

Translate into English:

1 παῦσαι εἰς τὴν οἰκίαν σκοπῶν, ὦ παῖ.
2 τὴν δικαιοσύνην ἀεὶ ἐπαίνει, ὦ κριτά.
3 τόδε τὸ ξίφος ἅρπασον.
4 μηκέτι ταῦτα τὰ κακὰ ἔργα φιλεῖτε, ὦ πολῖται.
5 ἐν πάσαις ταῖς μάχαις ἀνδρείως μάχου, ὦ στρατιῶτα.

Revision checkpoint

Make sure you know:
• irregular epsilon verbs
• futures with epsilon contraction
• irregular third declension nouns πόλις, ναῦς, βασιλεύς, ἄστυ
• the distinction between tense and aspect, and the use of the aorist imperative by aspect
• all imperatives in common use

Use of μή: Compound negatives (2)

• The negative used with the indicative (and normally with participles, and other parts of the verb and constructions expressing facts) is οὐ, which (as we saw in Chapter 8) comes with a whole set of compound versions (οὐδαμῶς, οὐδέποτε, etc).

• We have also however seen several examples of μή. This is used with parts of the verb and constructions expressing possibilities or ideas. Predictably therefore (since a command may not in fact be carried out) μή is always used with imperatives. (However negative commands referring to a single occasion are normally expressed not - as might be expected - by μή with the aorist imperative, but by a different construction explained in Chapter 11).

- There is a corresponding set of compound versions of μή, entirely predictable in form:

οὐ version	μή version	meaning
οὐδαμῶς	μηδαμῶς	in no way, not at all
οὐδέ	μηδέ	and not, not even
οὐδείς οὐδεμία οὐδέν	μηδείς μηδεμία μηδέν	no-one, nothing, no (not any)
οὐδέποτε	μηδέποτε	never
οὐκέτι	μηκέτι	no longer
οὔποτε	μήποτε	never
οὔτε ... οὔτε	μήτε ... μήτε	neither ... nor

- The use of οὐ and μή roughly corresponds to the use of *non* and *ne* in Latin.

Exercise 9.16

Perseus (2)

ἀπὸ δὲ τῶν <u>βασιλείων</u> πρὸς τὴν θάλασσαν ἀποδραμών, ὁ Περσεὺς πολὺν χρόνον ἠπόρει. οἱ μέντοι θεοὶ εἶδον αὐτὸν οὕτως ἀθυμοῦντα, καὶ εὐθὺς παρῆσαν ἥ τ' Ἀθήνη καὶ ὁ Ἑρμῆς. ὁ οὖν τῶν θεῶν ἄγγελος, "ὦ Περσεῦ," ἔφη, "μὴ ἀθύμει· πάρεσμεν γὰρ ὡς παντὶ <u>τρόπῳ</u> σε ὠφελήσοντες.
5 λαβὲ οὖν τήνδε τὴν <u>ἅρπην</u> <u>ἀδαμάντινον</u>, ᾗ ὁ <u>Κρόνος</u> τὸν <u>Οὐρανὸν</u> <u>ἐξέτεμεν</u>. οὐδὲν γὰρ ὀξύτερόν ἐστι τῆς ἅρπης, ἣ μόνη οἵα τ' ἐστὶ τὴν τῆς <u>Γοργόνος</u> κεφαλὴν <u>ἀποτεμεῖν</u>." καὶ ἡ Ἀθήνη, "<u>πρὸς</u> δὲ τούτοις," ἔφη, "λαβὲ τήνδε τὴν <u>ἀσπίδα</u> τὴν <u>λαμπροτάτην</u>. εἰ γὰρ ἄνθρωπός τις πρὸς τὴν Μέδουσαν σκοπεῖ, εἰς λίθον εὐθὺς διὰ φόβον τρέπεται. τὴν μέντοι <u>εἰκόνα</u>
10 αὐτῆς ἐν τῇ ἀσπίδι σκοπῶν ἐν οὐδενὶ κινδύνῳ ἔσῃ." καὶ ὁ Ἑρμῆς, "<u>νῦν</u>

βασίλεια -ων τά	palace
Ἑρμῆς -οῦ ὁ	Hermes
τρόπος -ου ὁ	way
5 ἅρπη -ης ἡ	sickle
ἀδαμάντινος -ον	of adamant (*fabulously hard steel*)
Κρόνος -ου ὁ	Cronos (*father of Zeus*)
Οὐρανός -οῦ ὁ	Uranus (*father of Cronos*)
ἐκτέμνω ἐξέτεμον	*lit* I cut out, *here* I castrate
Γοργών -όνος ἡ	Gorgon (*female monster with snakes in its hair, and glaring eyes*)
ἀποτέμνω ἀπέτεμον	I cut off
πρός	(+ *dat*) in addition to
ἀσπίς -ίδος ἡ	shield
λαμπρός -ά -όν	shining, bright
εἰκών -όνος ἡ	image, reflection

ἄπελθε· ἡ γὰρ μήτηρ ὑπὸ τοῦ <u>Δίκτυος</u> φυλαχθήσεται. ἔσται δέ σοι ὁδὸς μακροτάτη. πρῶτον μὲν <u>ὡς</u> τὰς <u>Γραίας</u> ἐλθών, <u>παρὰ</u> τούτων μάθε <u>ὅπου</u> εὑρήσεις τὰς <u>νύμφας</u> τὰς <u>ὄπισθε</u> τοῦ <u>Βορέου</u> οἰκούσας. αὗται δὲ χρήσιμά τέ τινα παρέξουσι καὶ τὰ περὶ τῶν Γοργονων <u>ἐξηγήσονται</u>."

15 ἔστιν <u>ἄντρον</u> <u>ἐρῆμον</u>, ἐν ᾧ αἱ Γραῖαι οἰκοῦσιν· εἰσὶ δὲ τρεῖς. αὗται αἱ <u>ἀδελφαὶ</u> οὔποτε νέαι ἦσαν, ἀλλ᾽ ἀεὶ <u>γρᾶες</u>. ἔστι δ᾽ αὐταῖς εἷς ὀφθαλμός, εἷς <u>ὀδούς</u>· τούτων γὰρ <u>μετέχουσιν</u>. ὁ οὖν Περσεὺς οὐκέτι ἀθυμῶν εἰς τὸ ἄντρον σιγῇ εἰσῆλθεν. καὶ τῆς μὲν τῶν Γραιῶν τὸν ὀφθαλμὸν ἀδελφῇ <u>προτεινούσης</u>, ὁ νεανίας λάθρα ἔλαβεν. "ὦ Γραῖαι, τὸν ὑμέτερον
20 ὀφθαλμὸν ἔχω. ἀληθῶς οὖν ἀποκρίνασθε. <u>εἰ δὲ μή</u>, ἐν σκότῳ ἀεὶ ἔσεσθε." αἱ δὲ ὡμολόγησαν, ὥσθ᾽ ὁ Περσεὺς περὶ τῶν <u>νύμφων</u> ἔμαθεν. ταύτας οὖν ὄπισθε τοῦ Βορέου ηὗρεν· καὶ φιλίως ἐδέξαντο αὐτόν. ὁ οὖν Περσεὺς μετὰ τῶν νυμφῶν <u>τέως</u> ἔμενεν. τέλος δ᾽ εἶπεν, "ὦ καλαὶ νύμφαι, νῦν ἄπειμι ὡς τὴν <u>Μέδουσαν</u> ἀποκτενῶν. εἴπετέ μοι, ποῦ οἰκοῦσιν αἱ
25 Γοργόνες; καὶ πῶς ἀποκτενῶ τὴν Μέδουσαν;" "πρῶτον μὲν <u>πέδιλα</u> <u>πτερυγωτὰ</u> παρέξομεν, οἷς τὰς τῆς Μεδούσης ἀδελφὰς φεύξῃ· ἔπειτα δὲ τήνδε τὴν <u>κίβισιν</u>, ἐν ᾗ τὴν κεφαλὴν φέρειν οἷός τ᾽ ἔσῃ· τέλος δὲ τὴν τοῦ ῞Αιδου <u>κυνῆν</u>. ὁ γὰρ ταύτην <u>φορῶν</u> <u>ἀφανὴς</u> γίγνεται." ταῦτα οὖν πάντα

	Δίκτυς -υος ὁ	Dictys
	ὡς	(+ acc) to (a person)
	Γραῖαι -ῶν αἱ	Graeae (personifications of old age, and sisters of the Gorgons)
	παρά	(+ gen) from
	ὅπου	where
	νύμφη -ης ἡ	nymph
	ὄπισθε	behind (+ gen)
	Βορέας -ου ὁ	North Wind
	ἐξηγέομαι	I explain
15	ἄντρον -ου τό	cave
	ἐρῆμος -η -ον	lonely
	ἀδελφή -ῆς ἡ	sister
	γραῦς γραός ἡ	old woman
	ὀδούς -όντος ὁ	tooth
	μετέχω	I share (+ gen)
	προτείνω	I hold out
20	εἰ δὲ μή	otherwise
	νύμφη -ης ἡ	nymph
	τέως	for a while
	Μέδουσα -ης ἡ	Medusa
25	πέδιλα -ων τά	sandals
	πτερυγωτός -ή -όν	winged
	κίβισις -εως ἡ	bag
	Ἀΐδης -ου ὁ	Hades (lit the invisible one)
	κυνῆ -ῆς ἡ	cap
	φορέω	I wear
	ἀφανής -ές	invisible

δεξάμενος, καὶ τὴν ὁδὸν μαθών, ὁ Περσεὺς αὖθις ἐπορεύθη, τὰς <u>νύμφας</u>
30 <u>χαίρειν κελεύσας</u>.

ἐπεὶ δ' ἐγγὺς τῆς τῶν Γοργόνων χώρας ἦν, πολλοὺς ἀνθρώπους <u>λιθίνους</u>
εἶδε, καὶ πολλὰ <u>θηρία</u> τὸ αὐτὸ παθόντα. πάντες γὰρ λίθινοι ἐποιήθησαν
διότι τὰς Γοργόνας ἐσκέψαντο. ἔπειτα δ' εἶδε τὰς <u>ἀδελφὰς</u> αὐτάς, <u>ὑπὸ</u> τῷ
ἡλίῳ <u>καθευδούσας</u>. αἱ δὲ Γοργόνες <u>ὀδόντας</u> μεγάλους εἶχον, ὥσπερ <u>ὗες</u>,
35 καὶ <u>χεῖρας</u> χαλκοῦ· ἦσαν δὲ καὶ τῇ Μεδούσῃ <u>δράκοντες</u> περὶ τὴν
κεφαλὴν <u>ἀντὶ κόμης</u>. καὶ ἡ μὲν Μέδουσα <u>θνητὴ</u> ἦν, αἱ δ' ἀδελφαὶ
<u>ἀθάνατοι</u>. ὁ δὲ Περσεύς, τὴν τοῦ Ἅιδου <u>κυνῆν φορῶν</u>, λάθρα προσῆλθεν,
οὐδὲν ἄλλο σκοπῶν ἢ τὴν <u>εἰκόνα</u> τὴν ἐν τῇ <u>λαμπρᾷ ἀσπίδι</u>. ἔπειτα δέ,
καίπερ <u>μάλιστα</u> φοβούμενος, καὶ τὴν εἰκόνα μόνην ἔτι καὶ νῦν σκοπῶν,
40 τὴν <u>ἄρπην εἵλκυσεν</u>· καὶ μιᾷ <u>πληγῇ</u> τὴν κεφαλὴν τὴν δεινοτάτην
<u>ἀποτεμὼν</u> εἰς τὴν <u>κίβισιν</u> εἰσέβαλεν.

	νύμφη -ης ἡ	nymph
30	χαίρειν κελεύω	I say farewell to (*literally* I order to rejoice)
	λίθινος -η -ον	made of stone
	θηρίον -ου τό	wild animal
	ἀδελφή -ῆς ἡ	sister
	ὑπό	(+ *dat*) (*here*) in (*literally* under)
	καθεύδω	I sleep
	ὀδούς -όντος ὁ	tooth
	ὗς ὑός ὁ	pig
35	χείρ χειρός ἡ	hand
	δράκων -οντος ὁ	snake
	ἀντί	instead of (+ *gen*)
	κόμη -ης ἡ	hair
	θνητός -ή -όν	mortal
	ἀθάνατος -ον	immortal
	Ἀΐδης -ου ὁ	Hades
	κυνῆ -ῆς ἡ	cap
	φορέω	I wear
	εἰκών -όνος ἡ	image, reflection
	λαμπρός -ά -όν	bright, shining
	ἀσπίς -ίδος ἡ	shield
	μάλιστα	very much
40	ἄρπη -ης ἡ	sickle
	ἕλκω εἵλκυσα	(*here*) I draw (weapon)
	πληγή -ῆς ἡ	blow, stroke
	ἀποτέμνω ἀπέτεμον	I cut off
	κίβισις -εως ἡ	bag

Tense and aspect (2): Aorist infinitive

• In the indicative the aorist is unambiguously used as a tense, or 'by tense' (single action in the past), and in the imperative it is unambiguously used as an aspect, or 'by aspect'.

• Notice however that 'by tense' is here shorthand for 'by tense *as well as* aspect' (because the 'single action' idea still applies, distinguishing the aorist from the imperfect), whereas 'by aspect' implies 'by aspect *only*'.

• The aorist *participle* is almost always* used by tense, like the indicative:

> οἱ στρατιῶται εἰς τὴν κώμην ἀφικόμενοι ἐστρατοπεδεύσαντο.
> The soldiers, having arrived at the village, set up camp.
> *or*   The soldiers, when they had arrived at the village, set up camp.

i.e. they first arrived (single action), then set up camp. As we have seen frequently, the aorist participle normally refers to something that happened *before* the action referred to by the main verb of the sentence (whilst the present participle refers to something happening at the same time).   * Some exceptions are shown in Chapter 12.

• In some parts of the verb however the aorist form can be used *either* by tense *or* by aspect, depending on context. This is most clearly illustrated by the aorist infinitive, whose active forms are:

weak (first) aorist	παῦσαι	to stop (once) *or* to have stopped
strong (second) aorist	λαβεῖν	to take (once) *or* to have taken

• Of the two possible meanings, the use by aspect is commoner (but we shall see an important example of the use by tense in Chapter 10).

• The form of the first (weak) aorist infinitive needs to be learned, though it has the predictable sigma and alpha (and is coincidentally the same as the singular first [weak] aorist middle imperative). The form of the second (strong) aorist infinitive is entirely predictable, adding the present infinitive ending to the aorist stem (just as the corresponding participle and imperative add the equivalent present endings).

Indirect command

• A clear example of the use of the aorist infinitive by aspect is in an indirect (or 'reported') command:

> *direct*   λαβὲ τὰ χρήματα.
> Take the money!

> *indirect*   ἐκελεύσαμεν αὐτὸν λαβεῖν τὰ χρήματα.
> We ordered him to take the money.

Because the aorist imperative in the original direct speech was used by aspect, the infinitive follows suit: it *behaves like what it is replacing*. The aorist infinitive in the indirect command represents an aorist imperative in the direct command.

• Similarly a present infinitive is used in an indirect command to represent a present imperative (for a generalised order) in the original direct speech:

direct   τὰ τῆς πόλεως τείχη ἀεὶ φυλάσσετε.
          Always guard the walls of the city!

indirect ἐκέλευσα τοὺς πολίτας τὰ τῆς πόλεως τείχη ἀεὶ φυλάσσειν.
          I ordered the citizens always to guard the walls of the city.

• Greek always uses the infinitive for an indirect command.
This is unlike Latin, where the infinitive is used only after certain verbs (*iubeo, veto*), others requiring a more complex construction with *ut* and the subjunctive.
Indirect commands in Greek are very straightforward, and we have in fact seen several examples already: they translate naturally into English.

• As with direct commands, and all constructions referring to possibilities rather than actual facts (because a command may not actually be carried out), the negative in an indirect command is μή.

More infinitives

• We met παύεσθαι in Chapter 8 as the present middle infinitive (meaning *to cease*), and in Chapter 7 as the present passive infinitive (meaning *to be stopped*).

• We met the future active, middle, and passive infinitives in Chapter 8:
active   παύσειν   (compare indicative παύσω)
middle   παύσεσθαι   (compare indicative παύσομαι)
passive παυσθήσεσθαι   (compare indicative παυσθήσομαι)

• As with participles, Greek has a full set of infinitives. Most of them are predictable.

• Aorist middle and passive infinitives (respectively *to cease* (once)/*to have ceased* etc; *to be stopped* (once)/*to have been stopped* etc) are:
           first (weak) aorist
middle   παύσασθαι   (compare indicative ἐπαυσάμην)
passive παυσθῆναι   (compare indicative ἐπαύσθην)

           second (strong) aorist
middle   λαβέσθαι   (compare indicative ἐλαβόμην)
passive ληφθῆναι   (compare indicative ἐλήφθην)

Revision overview of infinitives

	active	middle	passive
present	παύειν	παύεσθαι	
future	παύσειν	παύσεσθαι	παυσθήσεσθαι
first (weak) aorist	παῦσαι	παύσασθαι	παυσθῆναι
second (strong) aorist	λαβεῖν	λαβέσθαι	ληφθῆναι

Table showing correlation of indicative/imperative/infinitive/participle

		indicative (1 sg)	imperative (sg)	infinitive	participle (m nom sg)
present	active	παύω	παῦε	παύειν	παύων
	middle	παύομαι	παύου	παύεσθαι	παυόμενος
	passive	(all same as middle)			
future	active	παύσω	-	παύσειν	παύσων
	middle	παύσομαι	-	παύσεσθαι	παυσόμενος
	passive	παυσθήσομαι	-	παυσθήσεσθαι	παυσθησόμενος
imperfect	active	ἔπαυον	-	-	-
	middle	ἐπαυόμην	-	-	-
	passive	(same as middle)			
1st (weak) aorist	active	ἔπαυσα	παῦσον	παῦσαι	παύσας
	middle	ἐπαυσάμην	παῦσαι	παύσασθαι	παυσάμενος
	passive	ἐπαύσθην	(παύσθητι)	παυσθῆναι	παυσθείς
2nd (strong) aorist	active	ἔλαβον	λαβέ	λαβεῖν	λαβών
	middle	ἐλαβόμην	λαβοῦ	λαβέσθαι	λαβόμενος
	passive	ἐλήφθην	(λήφθητι)	ληφθῆναι	ληφθείς

Exercise 9.17

Translate into English:

1 διῶξον τὸν δοῦλον τὸν φεύγοντα, ὦ φίλε.
2 ὁ στρατηγὸς ἐκέλευσε τοὺς στρατιώτας λίθους βαλεῖν.
3 οὐ κελεύσω τούτους τοὺς συμμάχους ἐνθάδε μαχέσασθαι.
4 τὴν δικαιοσύνην ἀεὶ ζήτει τε καὶ φίλει, ὦ παῖ.
5 ἆρα βούλῃ τὴν πόλιν ληφθῆναι;
6 ξίφος ἑλόμενος μάχεσαι, ὦ μῶρε.
7 κάλεσον τὸν τὸ ἅρμα ἐλαύνοντα, ὦ γύναι.
8 οὐ φοβοῦμαι τὴν μάχην τὴν παυσθησομένην.
9 εἰς τὸν λιμένα νῦν πλεύσατε, ὦ νεανίαι.
10 οἱ πεζοὶ ἐκελεύσθησαν σκέψασθαι τὴν ὁδὸν τὴν διὰ τῶν ὀρῶν.

Exercise 9.18

Translate into Greek:
1   Take the money, girls!
2   The master ordered the slave to throw a sharp stone.
3   Always obey the teacher, boy!
4   Shall we fall into the deep river?
5   The general was ordered by the politicians to capture the city.

Revision checkpoint

Make sure you know:
• use of μή in simple form and compounds
• indirect commands and the use of the aorist infinitive by aspect
• all infinitives in common use
• the correlation of indicative, imperative, infinitive, and participle

Exercise 9.19

Perseus (3)

οἱ δὲ δράκοντες συρίζοντες τὰς τῆς Μεδούσης ἀδελφὰς ἐξ ὕπνου
ἐκίνησαν. αὗται οὖν ὡς τὸν τῆς ἀδελφῆς θάνατον τιμωρήσουσαι
προσέδραμον, τὸν πράξαντα ζητοῦσαι. ὁ μέντοι Περσεὺς τοῖς πεδίλοις
τοῖς πτερυγωτοῖς διὰ τοῦ οὐρανοῦ ἀπέφυγεν. μετὰ δὲ πολὺν χρόνον εἶδε
5   κόρης καλλίστης ἀνδριάντα ἐν τη ἀκτῇ, πέτρῳ γλυπτόν. ἐγγύτερον μέντοι
προσελθών, εἶδε κόρην (οὐκ ἀνδριάντα) τῷ πέτρῳ δεθεῖσαν. "ὦ κορὴ
καλλίστη," ἔφη, "ὡς οἰκτείρω σε, οὐκ ἄξια πάσχουσαν". "τίς εἶ σύ, τὴν
᾽Ανδρομέδην οὕτως οἰκτείρων; καὶ πόθεν καλεῖς;" ὁ μὲν οὖν Περσεύς, τὴν

	δράκων -οντος ὁ	snake
	συρίζω	I hiss
	Μέδουσα -ης ἡ	Medusa
	ἀδελφή -ῆς ἡ	sister
	κινέω ἐκίνησα	I move, I set in motion
	τιμωρέω ἐτιμώρησα	I avenge
	πεδίλα -ων τά	sandals
	πτερυγωτός -ή -όν	winged
5	ἀνδριάς -άντος ὁ	statue
	ἀκτή -ῆς ἡ	shore
	πέτρος -ου ὁ	rock
	γλυπτός -ή -όν	carved
	ἐγγύτερον	nearer
	δέω *aorist passive* ἐδέθην	I bind, I fasten
	ὡς	how ... !
	οἰκτείρω	I pity
	᾽Ανδρομέδη -ης ἡ	Andromeda

τοῦ Ἅιδου κυνῆν ἀφελών, περὶ ἑαυτοῦ ἔλεξεν· ἡ δ᾽ Ἀνδρομέδη τὸν τῶν
10 δεσμῶν λόγον ἐξηγήσατο.

ἡ γὰρ Κασσιόπεια, ἡ τῆς Ἀνδρομέδης μήτηρ, περὶ ἑαυτῆς κάλλους μέγα
ἔλεγεν ὡς καλλίστη οὖσα. αἱ οὖν ἄλλαι Νηρηίδες, διὰ ταῦτα μάλιστα
ὀργισθεῖσαι, τὸν Ποσειδῶνα ᾔτησαν κολάζειν αὐτήν. ὁ οὖν Ποσειδῶν
θηρίον δεινότατον ἔπεμψεν, ὃ διέφθειρεν πᾶσαν τὴν χώραν ἧς ὁ Κεφεύς,
15 ὁ τῆς Ἀνδρομέδης πατήρ, βασιλεὺς ἦν.

ἠγγέλθη δὲ τότε τὸ μαντεῖον τόδε· ὁ βασιλεὺς οἷός τ᾽ ἐστὶ τὴν τοῦ θηρίου
ὀργὴν παῦσαι εἰ ἐθέλει τὴν θυγατέρα τοῖς πέτροις δῆσαι. καὶ ὁ Κεφεὺς
ὑπὸ τῶν πολιτῶν ἠναγκάσθη τὴν θυγατέρα οὕτως ἀδικῆσαι. ὁ δὲ
Περσεύς, τὴν Ἀνδρομέδην ἤδη φιλῶν, τὴν θάλασσαν ἐσκέψατο. τοῦ δὲ
20 θηρίου αὖθις προσιόντος, τὴν τῆς Γοργόνος κεφαλὴν ἐκ τῆς κιβίσεως
ἑλὼν καὶ πρὸ τῶν τοῦ θηρίου ὀφθαλμῶν τῶν δεινοτάτων προτείνων, ὁ
Περσεὺς τοῦ θηρίου ἐκράτησεν. σιγῇ οὖν ἔμενε τὸ θηρίον, ψυχρόν τε
καὶ ἀκίνητον· λίθος γὰρ ἐγένετο. οὕτως οὖν ὁ Περσεύς, τῇ ἅρπῃ τῇ
ἀδαμαντίνῃ τοὺς δεσμοὺς λύσας, τὴν Ἀνδρομέδην ἔσωσεν.

25 πάντες οὖν νῦν ἔχαιρον. ὁ δὲ Περσεὺς ἐβούλετο τὴν Ἀνδρομέδην τὴν
ἑαυτοῦ γυναῖκα γενέσθαι. τοῦ δὲ πατρὸς ὁμολογήσαντος, ὁ γάμος
ἐποιήθη, καὶ ἑορτὴ μεγάλη. πάντων μέντοι ἡδέως πινόντων τε καὶ
ἐσθιόντων, εἰσῆλθεν ἄνθρωπός τις ἄγριός τε καὶ μέγιστος, ξίφος ἔχων.

	Ἅιδης -ου ὁ	Hades
	κυνῆ -ῆς ἡ	cap
	ἀφαιρέω ἀφεῖλον	I remove, I take off
10	ἐξηγέομαι ἐξηγησάμην	I explain
	Κασσιόπεια -ας ἡ	Cassiopia
	κάλλος -ους τό	beauty
	μέγα λέγω	I boast
	Νηρηίδες -ων αἱ	Nereids
	μάλιστα	very much
	Ποσειδῶν -ῶνος ὁ	Poseidon
	θηρίον -ου τό	(here) monster
	Κεφεύς -έως ὁ	Cepheus
15	μαντεῖον -ου τό	oracle
	πέτρος -ου ὁ	rock
	δέω ἔδησα	I bind, I fasten
20	κίβισις -εως ἡ	bag
	προτείνω	I hold out
	ψυχρός -ά -όν	cold
	ἀκίνητος -ον	motionless
	ἅρπη -ης ἡ	sickle
	ἀδαμάντινος -η -ον	of adamant
25	χαίρω	I rejoice, I am happy
	γάμος -ου ὁ	marriage
	ἑορτή -ῆς ἡ	feast
	ἄγριος -α -ον	wild, savage

125

οὗτος θεῖος κακὸς τῆς Ἀνδρομέδης ἦν, Φινεὺς ὀνόματι, τὴν τοῦ ἀδελφοῦ
30 θυγατέρα ἀνοσίως φιλῶν. "ἢ πάρεχε τὴν κόρην μοι, ἢ τοὺς ἄνδρας
ἀποκτενῶ, τὰς γυναῖκας λήψομαι, τὴν πόλιν κατακαύσω." τοῦ μέντοι
Περσέως τὴν τῆς Μεδούσης κεφαλὴν αὖθις προτείνοντος, ὁ Φινεὺς λίθος
ἐγένετο.

μετὰ δὲ ταῦτα οὐ πολλῷ ὅ τε Περσεὺς καὶ ἡ Ἀνδρομέδη ἀποπλεύσαντες
35 πρὸς τὴν Σέριφον ἀφίκοντο. τὰ μέντοι ἐκεῖ πράγματα οὐδαμῶς εὐτυχῆ ἦν.
ἥ τε γὰρ Δανάη ὑπὸ τοῦ Πολυδέκτου δούλη ἐποιήθη, ὁ δὲ Δίκτυς ἐν
δεσμωτηρίῳ ἐδέθη. τὴν οὖν Ἀνδρομέδην ἐν τῇ νηὶ λιπών, ὁ Περσεὺς
πρὸς τὰ βασίλεια προσῆλθεν.

τὸν δὲ βασιλέα ηὗρε μετὰ τῶν φίλων ἐσθίοντα. ὁ δὲ εἶπεν, "ἆρα δῶρόν
40 μοι φέρεις, ὦ Περσεῦ;" "ναί, ὥσπερ καὶ ὑπεσχόμην." "μὴ φλυάρει·
οὐδαμῶς γὰρ φοβοῦμαι." ἔπειτα δὲ ὁ Περσεὺς τὴν τῆς Γοργόνος κεφαλὴν
αὖθις ἐξεῖλεν. ἔτι καὶ νῦν οἱ λίθοι ἐν τῇ νήσῳ εἰσίν.

τοῦ δὲ Πολυδέκτου καὶ τῶν φίλων λιθίνων ποιηθέντων, ὁ Δίκτυς τῆς
Σερίφου βασιλεὺς ἐγένετο· καὶ τὴν Δανάην ἔγημεν. ὁ δὲ Περσεὺς καὶ ἡ
45 Ἀνδρομέδη αὖθις ἀπέπλευσαν, ὡς ἐν τῷ Ἄργει οἰκήσοντες. ἐν δὲ τῇ ὁδῷ
πρὸς τὴν Λάρισαν ἀφίκοντο. ἐκεῖ δ' ἀγῶνες ἤγοντο, ἐν οἷς ὁ Περσεὺς
πολλὰ ἆθλα ἐφέρετο. δίσκον μέντοι οὕτως ἰσχυρῶς ἔβαλεν ὥστε γέροντά
τινα ἐν τοῖς θεαταῖς εὐθὺς ἀπέκτεινεν· καὶ οὗτος Ἀκρίσιος ἦν, ὃς τὸ
Ἄργος ἔλιπε διότι ἐφοβεῖτο τοὺς τοῦ θεοῦ λόγους.

	θεῖος -ου ὁ	uncle
	Φινεύς -έως ὁ	Phineus
30	ἀνοσίως	wickedly, unholily
	κατακαίω *fut* κατακαύσω	I burn down
	προτείνω	I hold out
35	Σέριφος -ου ἡ	Seriphos
	Δανάη -ης ἡ	Danae
	Πολυδέκτης -ου ὁ	Polydectes
	δούλη -ης ἡ	(female) slave
	Δίκτυς -υος ὁ	Dictys
	δέω *aorist passive* ἐδέθην	I tie up
	βασίλεια -ων τά	palace
40	ναί	yes
	φλυαρέω	I talk rubbish
	λίθινος -η -ον	(made of) stone
	γαμέω ἔγημα	I marry
45	Ἄργος -ους τό	Argos
	Λάρισα -ης ἡ	Larissa (*town in central Greece*)
	ἄγω	(*here*) I hold, I celebrate
	δίσκος -ου ὁ	discus
	θεατής -οῦ ὁ	spectator
	Ἀκρίσιος -ου ὁ	Acrisius

Vocabulary checklist for Chapter 9

ἄγαν	too much, excessively
ἀδικέω ἠδίκησα	I do wrong (to), I act unjustly (towards)
ἄδικος -ον	unjust
ἀθυμέω ἠθύμησα	I am despondent
αἱρέομαι εἱλόμην	I choose
αἱρέω εἷλον	I take
αἰτέω ᾔτησα	I ask for, I beg
ἀληθής -ές	true
ἀναχωρέω ἀνεχώρησα	I withdraw, I retreat
ἀπορέω ἠπόρησα	I am at a loss
ἀσθενής -ές	weak
ἀσπίς -ίδος ἡ	shield
ἄστυ -εως τό	city, town
ἀσφαλής -ές	safe
ἀφικνέομαι ἀφικόμην	I arrive
βαθύς -εῖα -ύ	deep
βάρβαρος -ον	barbarian, foreign, non-Greek
βαρέως φέρω	I take (something) badly
βαρύς -εῖα -ύ	heavy
βασιλεύς -έως ὁ	king
βοηθέω ἐβοήθησα	I help, I run to help (+ *dat*)
βραδύς -εῖα -ύ	slow
γένος -ους τό	race, kind, type
δοκέω ἔδοξα	I seem; I think
δυστυχής -ές	unlucky, unfortunate
ἔθνος -ους τό	nation, tribe
ἐπαινέω ἐπῄνησα	I praise
ἔρως -ωτος ὁ	love, sexual passion
ἔτος -ους τό	year
εὐρύς -εῖα -ύ	broad, wide
εὐτυχής -ές	lucky, fortunate
ζητέω ἐζήτησα	I seek, I search for
ἡδέως	sweetly; gladly
ἡδύς -εῖα -ύ	sweet, pleasant
ἱππεύς -έως ὁ	horseman, *pl* cavalry
ἰχθύς -ύος ὁ	fish
καθαιρέω καθεῖλον	I take down, I demolish
καλέω ἐκάλεσα	I call, I invite
κρατέω ἐκράτησα	I rule, I control (+ *gen*)
μέγας μεγάλη μέγα (μεγαλ-)	great, big
μή	not (*in contexts other than statements of fact*)
μηδαμῶς	in no way, not at all
μηδέ	not even
μηδείς, μηδεμία, μηδέν (μηδεν-)	no-one, nothing, (*as adj*) no (not any)

μηδέποτε	never
μηκέτι	no longer
μήποτε	never
μήτε ... μήτε	neither ... nor
μισέω ἐμίσησα	I hate
ναυμαχέω ἐναυμάχησα	I fight a sea-battle
ναῦς νεώς ἡ	ship
ξίφος -ους τό	sword
οἰκέω ᾤκησα	I live (in)
ὁμολογέω ὡμολόγησα	I agree
ὀξύς -εῖα -ύ	sharp
ὄρος -ους τό	mountain
παραινέω παρήνεσα	I advise (+ *dat*)
πλέω ἔπλευσα	I sail
πλῆθος -ους τό	crowd
ποιέω ἐποίησα	I make, I do, (+ *adv and acc*) I treat
πολιορκέω ἐπολιόρκησα	I besiege
πολίς -εως ἡ	city
πολύς πολλή πολύ (πολλ-)	much, *pl* many
προχωρέω προὐχώρησα	I advance, I go forward
σαφής -ές	clear
σκοπέω ἐσκεψάμην	I look at, I examine
ταχύς -εῖα -ύ	quick, swift
τεῖχος -ους τό	wall
τέλος -ους τό	end, outcome
τοξεύω ἐτόξευσα	I shoot (fire an arrow)
τριήρης -ους ἡ	trireme, warship
ὑπισχνέομαι ὑπεσχόμην	I promise
φιλέω ἐφίλησα	I love, I like
φοβέομαι ἐφοβήθην	I fear, I am afraid (of)
ὠφελέω ὠφέλησα	I help
(75 words)	

Chapter 10

Indirect statement: Introduction

A *direct* statement quotes the speaker's actual words:

"The old man is very wise" says Socrates.

If this is put into *indirect* speech (i.e. if it is *reported* by someone else) it naturally turns into:

Socrates says <u>that</u> the old man is very wise.

The words do not have to be spoken aloud:
"The old man is very wise" thinks Socrates (to himself)
similarly becomes
Socrates thinks <u>that</u> the old man is very wise.

• An indirect statement comes after a verb in which the voice, mind, or one of the senses is used: *say, think, hear, find, know*.

A *that* clause is the most common way of expressing this in English. But we have three methods altogether:

Socrates says <u>that</u> the old man is very wise.	('that' clause)
Socrates believes the old man <u>to be</u> very wise.	(infinitive construction)
Socrates regards the old man <u>as being</u> very wise.	(participle construction)

Greek similarly has all three constructions. As in English, particular verbs or types of verb prefer one or the other. (Latin in contrast has only the infinitive construction.)

Indirect statement (1): with 'that' clause

• This is the normal method with verbs of *saying*, especially λέγω with its aorists ἔλεξα and the commoner εἶπον (and with some verbs that *imply* saying, e.g. ἀποκρίνομαι = *reply, answer*; ἀγγέλλω = *report, announce*). The word for *that* is ὅτι, or (less commonly) ὡς.

• The *that* clause behaves like an independent sentence, with its subject in the nominative, οὐ as the negative, and the verb usually indicative*. Hence the direct statement
    "ὁ γέρων σοφώτατός ἐστιν"
becomes the indirect
    ὁ Σωκράτης λέγει ὅτι ὁ γέρων σοφώτατός ἐστιν.

• The verb in the indirect statement *retains the tense of the original direct statement*, regardless of the introductory verb:

ὁ Σωκράτης εἶπεν ὅτι ὁ γέρων σοφώτατός ἐστιν.
English however changes the tense in the indirect statement if the introductory verb is past, so this sentence must be translated:

Socrates said that the old man was very wise (*rather than the literal translation* is).

On this principle, an original *present* tense (i.e. present tense in the direct statement, and in Greek retained as such in the indirect statement) comes out as an *imperfect* in English; an original *past* tense comes out as a *pluperfect* (*had* ...): notice in both these cases how we move back a tense. An original future comes out as a *would* or *was/were going to* (the so-called 'future in the past').

This principle of retaining the *tense of the original* applies to all three indirect statement constructions in Greek (as it does to the infinitive construction in Latin). It is more straightforward than it may seem: just take account of what was said or thought at the time, then express the reported form of this in natural English.

When translating into Greek, likewise think about and reproduce what was said or thought at the time (i.e. unscramble the change English has made).

* If the introductory verb is past tense, the verb in the indirect statement can be put into a form called the *optative*: see Chapter 12. The indicative (i.e. one of the normal tenses, used to express facts) is however commonly used to evoke in a strongly vivid way - as the rule about its tense also does - the original direct speech lying behind the reported version.

Exercise 10.1

Translate into English:

1   ὁ ἄγγελος λέγει ὅτι οἱ σύμμαχοι προσέρχονται.
2   ὁ στρατηγὸς εἶπεν ὅτι οἱ πολέμιοι φεύγουσιν.
3   αἱ γυναῖκες ἔλεξαν ὅτι πολλὰς βόας ἤκουσαν.
4   ὁ ναύτης λέγει ὅτι ἡ ναυμαχία παύσεται.
5   ἡ παῖς εἶπεν ὅτι ἔλυσε τὸν ἵππον.
6   οἱ γέροντες ἔλεξαν ὅτι βούλονται ἐν τῇ πόλει μένειν.
7   ὁ παῖς ἀπεκρίνατο ὅτι ἔμαθε πάντας τοὺς λόγους.
8   ὁ βασιλεὺς ἤγγειλεν ὡς ἡ πόλις τέλος ἐλήφθη.
9   οἱ ἄρχοντες εἶπον ὅτι πάντες οἱ φυγόντες διωχθήσονται.
10   οἱ δοῦλοι λέγουσιν ὅτι οὐδαμῶς ἀδικοῦσιν.

Exercise 10.2

Translate into Greek:

1   Socrates says that the boy is stupid.
2   The soldiers said that they had seen nothing.
3   The people on the island said that they were in danger.
4   The women said that they would send letters.
5   Did you say that the battle had ceased, messenger?

Indirect statement (2): with infinitive

This version is particularly used with verbs of *thinking*, e.g. νομίζω. Here the *subject* of the original direct statement (assuming it is different from the subject of the introductory verb) is put in the accusative, and the verb is put in the infinitive. Hence:

direct   ὁ γέρων σοφώτατός ἐστιν.
indirect   ὁ Σωκράτης νομίζει <u>τὸν γέροντα</u> σοφώτατον <u>εἶναι</u>.
literally   Socrates thinks the old man to be very wise.
or, in better English,
           Socrates thinks that the old man is very wise.

Notice again that, though the literal translation sounds odd when introduced by *thinks*, the infinitive version can more easily be retained in English after *believes* or *considers*.

• Just as with the 'that' clause construction, the infinitive *keeps the tense of the original*, where English makes the adjustment described above if the introductory verb is past:

          ὁ Σωκράτης ἐνόμιζε τὸν γέροντα σοφώτατον εἶναι.
          Socrates thought that the old man *was* very wise.

• An *aorist infinitive* therefore here represents an original *aorist indicative*, for a *statement*: the aorist infinitive is used *by tense*, meaning *to have done X* (rather than *by aspect*, meaning *to do X [once]*).

This follows the principle explained in Chapter 9: the aorist infinitive in indirect speech *behaves like what it is replacing*. In an indirect *statement* it replaces the *tense* of the aorist indicative in the direct statement (*did X*), whereas in an indirect *command* it replaces the *aspect* of the aorist imperative in the direct command (*do X [once]!*).

• The use of the aorist infinitive in indirect statement roughly corresponds to the use of the perfect infinitive in Latin:

          ὁ διδάσκαλος ἐνόμιζε τὴν παῖδα εὖ ἀποκρίνασθαι.
literally   The teacher thought the girl to have answered well.
or, in better English,
          The teacher thought that the girl had answered well.

• The use of the various infinitives can be summarised as follows.

	literally	*normal English*
present introductory verb with:		
present inf	he thinks X to be ...	he thinks that X is ...
aorist inf	he thinks X to have ...	he thinks that X (has) ... -ed
future inf	he thinks X to be going to ...	he thinks that X will ...
past introductory verb with:		
present inf	he thought X to be ...	he thought that X was ...
aorist inf	he thought X to have ...	he thought that X had ...
future inf	he thought X to be going to ...	he thought that X would ...

• The infinitive construction is similar to the Latin accusative and infinitive. It may seem puzzling that a *subject* should be accusative. But notice how a sentence such as *Socrates considers the old man to be ...* could be cut short as *Socrates considers the old man.* Clearly *the old man* cannot here be nominative. A sentence can only introduce a *new* nominative (after the main subject slot has been occupied, as here by Socrates) if there is a new *finite* verb (i.e. verb with a person ending): by definition the *infinitive* does not qualify (whereas the indicative of a 'that' clause of course does). Hence the natural case for *subject of an infinitive* (used, as we shall see, in other constructions as well as indirect statement) is *accusative*.

• If the infinitive in the indirect statement itself has an object, that too will be accusative. You can tell which is which by word order (as well as context) - the *subject* accusative almost invariably comes first:

ὁ στρατηγὸς ἐνόμιζε τοὺς συμμάχους πολλοὺς αἰχμαλώτους λαβεῖν.
The general thought that the allies had captured many prisoners.

• The point about not being able to introduce a *new* nominative leads on to an important further feature (and difference from Latin). In Greek, if the subject of the infinitive is *the same as* the subject of the introductory verb, it is normally just left out:

ὁ νεανίας ἐνόμιζεν ἀνδρείως μαχέσασθαι.
The young man thought that he had fought bravely.

But if it *is* put in (for emphasis), or is shown by an adjective or complement, it is *nominative*:

ὁ νεανίας ἐνόμιζεν αὐτὸς ἀνδρείως μαχέσασθαι.
The young man thought that he himself (*perhaps implying* as distinct from others) had fought bravely.

ἡ παῖς νομίζει οἵά τ᾽ εἶναι τοῦ ἵππου κρατῆσαι.
The girl thinks that she can control the horse.

ὁ Σωκράτης ἐνόμιζεν εἶναι κριτής.
Socrates thought that he was judge.

We usually call this version of the infinitive construction *nominative and infinitive* even though the nominative is often not actually there but just understood.

• This contrasts with Latin, where the indirect statement construction is invariably *accusative* and infinitive. If the subject of the indirect statement is the same as that of the introductory verb, it must be put in as a reflexive accusative:
    iuvenis se fortiter pugnavisse putabat.
    The young man thought that he (*himself*) had fought bravely.
The choice of pronoun distinguishes the reflexive from the non-reflexive accusative:
    iuvenis eum fortiter pugnavisse putabat.
    The young man thought that he (*someone else*) had fought bravely.

• The use of the nominative and infinitive, along with the use of the middle as a reflexive, explains why the reflexive pronouns ἑαυτόν etc are much less common than their Latin equivalents.

• After an 'understood' nominative, there may of course still be an accusative as *object* of the infinitive (the sense and context normally avoiding ambiguity):

ὁ παῖς ἐνόμιζε τοὺς λόγους μαθεῖν.
The boy thought that he had learned the words.

• The contrast between the nominative (for same subject, and for emphasis) and the accusative in the infinitive construction provides a good illustration of different uses of αὐτός:

ὁ γέρων νομίζει αὐτὸς σοφὸς εἶναι.
The old man thinks that he himself (*emphatic*) is wise.

ὁ γέρων νομίζει αὐτὸν σοφὸν εἶναι.
The old man thinks that he (*someone else*) is wise.

• The infinitive version of indirect statement (as we see from its use with *think*) carries the idea of *expressing an opinion*, where the 'that' clause states a fact. This difference in shade of meaning explains why there is a separate word for *say* used with the infinitive: φημί, implying *assert, express the opinion*. (You have already met the idiomatic use of part of this: ἔφη = *he/she said* with <u>direct</u> speech, usually - like Latin *inquit* - interrupting the quotation.) This is another example of an irregular verb which is also very common.

present	say (assert, express the opinion)
φημί	I say
φής	you (*sg*) say
φησί(ν)	he/she/it says
φαμέν	we say
φατέ	you (*pl*) say
φασί(ν)	they say

*imperfect (but normally used as simple past tense)**	
ἔφην	I said
ἔφησθα	you (*sg*) said
ἔφη	he/she/it said
ἔφαμεν	we said
ἔφατε	you (*pl*) said
ἔφασαν	they said

* there is also (less commonly found) a regular first (weak) aorist ἔφησα

infinitive	φάναι
participle	*sg* φάσκων -ουσα -ον (stem φασκοντ-) †
	pl φάντες, φᾶσαι, φάντα (stem φαντ-)
imperative	*sg* φαθί, *pl* φάτε

† borrowed from φάσκω, a less common present tense with similar meaning

• In an indirect statement using the infinitive construction, the negative is οὐ (as with a 'that' clause):

ὁ στρατηγὸς ἐνόμιζε τοὺς συμμάχους οὐκ ἀφίκεσθαι.

The general thought that the allies had not arrived.

But if the introductory verb used is φημί, that is negatived instead of the infinitive:

ὁ διδάσκαλος οὐκ ἔφη τὴν βίβλον χρησίμην εἶναι.

literally The teacher denied that the book was useful.

or, in better English,

The teacher said that the book was not useful.

The normal translation of οὐ φημί therefore is *say that ... not* (this corresponds to the use of *nego* in Latin). This idiom is linked to the idea of φημί being used to express an opinion.

Contrast with it:

ὁ διδάσκαλος οὐκ εἶπεν ὅτι ἡ βίβλος χρησίμη ἐστίν.

The teacher did not say that the book was useful.

(*i.e. he did not make a statement at all*)

Exercise 10.3

Translate into English:

1   οἱ ἐν τῷ στρατοπέδῳ ἐνόμιζον τὸν ποταμὸν ἔτι χαλεπώτατον εἶναι.
2   ἆρα νομίζετε τοὺς δούλους φυγεῖν;
3   ὁ κριτὴς ἔφη δικαιότατος εἶναι.
4   ἐνομίζομεν τὴν πόλιν ὀλίγων ἡμερῶν ληφθήσεσθαι.
5   αἱ γυναῖκες οὐκ ἔφασαν τοὺς τοῦ ἀγγέλου λόγους ἀληθεῖς εἶναι.
6   ὁ στρατηγὸς νομίζει τὰς παῖδας ἀνδρείως τὰ τείχη φυλάξαι.
7   ὁ ῥήτωρ οὐκ ἔφη αὐτὸς τὸν δῆμον ἀδικῆσαι.
8   ἆρα νομίζεις τοὺς συμμάχους ἀφίξεσθαι;
9   αὐτὴ πάρεστι φάσκουσα τὸν ἀδελφὸν ἀπελθεῖν.
10 ὁ παῖς οὐκ ἔφη αὐτὸς ἀλλὰ τήν μητέρα φοβεῖσθαι.

Exercise 10.4

Translate into Greek (using the infinitive construction):
1   The slave thought that his master had gone out.
2   The girl's father says that the wine is good.
3   Who thinks that that old man is wiser than Socrates?
4   The boy thought that he had not acted unjustly.
5   Did you say that you were going to send a letter, father?

Indirect statement (3): with participle

This version is used with verbs of *perceiving* (hear, see, know, realise, find out), e.g.

αἰσθάνομαι τὸν γέροντα σοφώτατον ὄντα.
literally   I perceive the old man as being very wise.
or, in better English,
               I perceive that the old man is very wise.

Exactly the same rule about retaining the tense of the original (actual or implied: what was heard, or what someone thought) which we saw with the 'that' clause and infinitive constructions applies here too:

ὁ στρατηγὸς ἔγνω τοὺς πολεμίους προσβαίνοντας.
literally   The general got to know the enemy (as) approaching.
or, in better English,
               The general got to know that the enemy were approaching.

Exactly the same rule about the subject in the indirect statement being accusative if it is different from the subject of the introductory verb, but nominative if it is the same, applies here as with the infinitive. Because however the participle necessarily has a case ending, the nominative here is always shown rather than being left to be understood:

ὁ δοῦλος γιγνώσκει διωκόμενος.
The slave realises that he is being chased.

A pronoun can still be put in for extra emphasis:

ἡ παῖς ἔγνω αὐτὴ τὸν διδάσκαλον πείσασα.
The girl realised that she herself had persuaded the teacher.

You have already met several verbs which take the participle contruction:
αἰσθάνομαι   I perceive
ἀκούω   I hear
γιγνώσκω   I get to know, I realise

μανθάνω	I learn
πυνθάνομαι	I learn by enquiry, I find out

Also the irregular aorist:

εἶδον	I saw (*the present tense* I see *occurs later in this chapter*)

In addition there is the very common but highly irregular verb οἶδα = I know:

present*

οἶδα	I know
οἶσθα	you (*sg*) know
οἶδε(ν)	he/she/it knows
ἴσμεν	we know
ἴστε	you (*pl*) know
ἴσασι(ν)	they know

past*

ᾔδη	I knew
ᾔδησθα	you (*sg*) knew
ᾔδει(ν)	he/she/it knew
ᾖσμεν	we knew
ᾖστε	you (*pl*) knew
ᾖσαν *or* ᾔδεσαν	they knew

infinitive	εἰδέναι
participle	εἰδώς -υῖα -ός (stem εἰδοτ-)*
imperative	*sg* ἴσθι, *pl* ἴστε

* the 'present' here is strictly a perfect tense (see Chapter 11) *I have come to see* (from the same root as εἶδον), and the 'past' strictly a pluperfect (see Chapter 12). The participle has the form of a perfect participle (again see Chapter 11, or Reference Grammar; but its 3-1-3 forms are predictable).

• Note that οἶδα is also sometimes used with a 'that' clause (to emphasise knowledge of a *fact*).

Exercise 10.5

Translate into English:

1   ἀκούω τὸν τῶν συμμάχων ἄγγελον ἤδη παρόντα.
2   ὁ στρατηγὸς ἔγνω τοὺς ἐν τῇ νήσῳ ἀθυμοῦντας.
3   ἆρ᾽ οὐκ εἴδετε τὰ τείχη καθαιρέθεντα;
4   ἡ γυνὴ οἶδεν οἵα τ᾽ οὖσα τὸν στρατηγὸν πείθειν.
5   ὁ παῖς οὐκ ᾔδει τὸν ποταμὸν βαθύν τε καὶ χαλεπὸν ὄντα.
6   ὁ βασιλεὺς ἐπύθετο τοὺς στρατιώτας εὖ μαχεσαμένους.

7	οἱ παῖδες μανθάνουσι τὸ ἔργον χαλεπὸν ὄν.
8	ᾐσθόμεθα τέλος κρατοῦντες τῶν πολεμίων.
9	οἱ τὴν πόλιν πολιορκοῦντες ᾔδεσαν ὅτι ὁ στρατηγὸς ἀπέθανεν.
10	οἱ Ἀθηναῖοι οὐκ ἔγνωσαν τὴν νόσον γενησομένην.

Exercise 10.6

Translate into Greek:
1	The king hears that all the citizens are amazed.
2	We heard that the enemy were at a loss.
3	The girl realises that she is getting angry.
4	Do you (*sg*) know that the slave has run away?
5	The old man did not know that the boy had helped him.

Indirect Statement: Summary

• For all three constructions ('that' clause, infinitive, participle) the indirect statement *retains the tense of the original*. English adjusts this if the introductory verb is past tense.

• For all three constructions the negative is οὐ.

• Each construction is associated with a particular type of verb:

'that' clause	verbs of saying, especially λέγω/εἶπον
infinitive version	verbs of thinking (plus φημί, and verbs that do not come into either of the other two categories)
participle version	verbs of perception

• With the infinitive and participle versions, a new subject in the indirect statement is *accusative*. If the subject is the same as that of the introductory verb, it is *nominative* or left out.

Exercise 10.7

Helen in Egypt

The ten-year Trojan War was fought to recover Helen, wife of Menelaus, who had been kidnapped by the Trojan prince Paris (after Aphrodite, inducing him to declare her winner in a beauty contest with the other goddesses Hera and Athene, promised him the most beautiful woman in the world). The reaction of Menelaus and the other Greeks when they finally found Helen again was a subject of considerable dramatic potential, of which there are various accounts (Homer's authoritative Iliad *stopping before this point). A more radical retelling of the story (undercutting the whole purpose of the war) denied that Helen had ever been in Troy at all. This version of it is told by the fifth-century historian Herodotus.*

οἱ ἐν τῇ Αἰγύπτῳ ἱερεῖς τάδε τὰ θαυμάσια περὶ τῆς Ἑλένης λέγουσιν.
ἐγὼ δὲ νομίζω καὶ τὸν Ὅμηρον τοῦτον τὸν μῦθον ἀκοῦσαι, οὐ μέντοι
διηγήσασθαι ὡς οὐκ εὐπρεπῆ τῇ Ἰλιάδι ὄντα. ἐπεὶ δὲ τοὺς ἱερέας
ἠρόμην εἰ οἱ Ἕλληνες ἀληθῶς λέγουσι τὰ περὶ τῆς Τροίας, εἶπον τάδε·
5   τῆς δὲ Ἑλένης ἁρπασθείσης, ἦλθεν εἰς τὴν Τροίαν στρατιὰ πολλὴ τῶν
Ἑλλήνων τῷ Μενελάῳ βοηθοῦσα. ἐκβάντες δ' εἰς γῆν, ἔπεμψαν εἰς τὸ
Ἴλιον ἀγγέλους. οἱ δέ, ἐπεὶ εἰσῆλθον εἰς τὴν πόλιν, ἀπῄτουν τήν τε
Ἑλένην καὶ τὰ χρήματα ἃ ἔκλεψεν ὁ Πάρις. οἱ δὲ Τρῶες ἀεὶ τὸν αὐτὸν
λόγον ἔλεγον, ὅτι ἔχουσιν οὔτε τὴν Ἑλένην οὔτε τὰ χρήματα· πάντων δὲ
10   τούτων ἐν τῇ Αἰγύπτῳ ὄντων, αὐτοὶ οὐκ ἄξιοί εἰσι κολάζεσθαι. οἱ δὲ
Ἕλληνες νομίζοντες ἐπισκώπτεσθαι ὑπ' αὐτῶν ἐπολιόρκουν τὴν πόλιν. τὴν
μέντοι Τροίαν μετὰ δέκα ἔτη ἑλόντες οὐχ εὗρον ἐκεῖ τὴν Ἑλένην, ἀλλὰ
τὸν αὐτὸν λόγον ἔτι καὶ νῦν ἤκουσαν. οὕτως οὖν τὸν Μενέλαον αὐτὸν
πρὸς τὴν Αἴγυπτον ἀπέπεμψαν. ὁ δὲ ἐκεῖσε ἀφικόμενος εὗρε τὴν Ἑλένην,
15   καὶ ἀπαθῆ ἀπέλαβεν.

	Αἴγυπτος -ου ἡ	Egypt
	ἱερεύς -έως ὁ	priest
	θαυμάσιος -α -ον	remarkable
	Ἑλένη -ης ἡ	Helen
	Ὅμηρος -ου ὁ	Homer
	διηγέομαι διηγησάμην	I relate, I tell
	εὐπρεπής -ές	fitting
	Ἰλιάς -άδος ἡ	the *Iliad*
	ἠρόμην	(*irreg aor*) I asked
	Ἕλλην -ηνος ὁ	Greek
	Τροία -ας ἡ	Troy
5	ἁρπάζω *aor pass* ἡρπάσθην	I seize, I snatch
	Μενέλαος -ου ὁ	Menelaus
	Ἴλιον -ου τό	(the city of) Troy
	ἀπαιτέω *imperfect* ἀπῄτουν	I demand back
	Πάρις -ιδος ὁ	Paris
	Τρῶες -ων οἱ	Trojans
10	ἐπισκώπτω	I make fun of
	ἐκεῖσε	there, to that place
15	ἀπαθής -ές	unharmed

Impersonal verbs

An impersonal verb is one which has *it* rather than as a person as the subject. Its form is third person singular. It is followed by an infinitive. You have already seen an example: ἔξεστι(ν) = *it is possible.*

Other common ones are:

δεῖ	it is necessary (*implying compulsion*)
χρή	it is necessary (*implying moral obligation*)

The infinitive which follows will be present or aorist determined *by aspect* (aorist to stress something which is to happen just once). This use by aspect (*to do X [once]*) is the 'default mode' for the aorist infinitive (in contrast to its use in indirect statement to reproduce the *tense* of the original):

> δεῖ φυγεῖν.
> It is necessary to run away (*now, on this occasion*).

If a subject is put in with δεῖ or χρή, it is accusative:

> δεῖ σὲ φυγεῖν.
> It is necessary for you to run away.
> *or* It is necessary that you (should) run away.

This is another example of the subject of an infinitive naturally being accusative (because the nominative slot has already been used up by 'it').

However ἔξεστι(ν) and other impersonal verbs are followed by a dative (as impersonal verbs normally are in English):

> ἔξεστι σοὶ φυγεῖν.
> It is possible for you to run away.

• Some impersonals are forms of verbs which can also be used with a personal subject: ἔξεστι is a compound of εἰμί (hence its imperfect is ἐξῆν) and δεῖ is in origin part of δέω = *I bind*). An important example of this is δοκεῖ. The ordinary verb δοκέω usually means *I seem*. The impersonal use (again with the dative) implies *it seems a good idea to X* i.e. *X decides*:

> δοκεῖ μοι φυγεῖν.
> It seems a good idea to me to run away.
> *i.e.* I decide to run away.

• δοκεῖ is often found in the aorist (because it implies a single crisp action):

> ἔδοξέ μοι μαχέσασθαι.
> I decided to fight.

• δεῖ is often found in the imperfect form ἔδει. There is also an aorist ἐδέησε(ν).

• χρή is often found in an imperfect form: ἐχρῆν or, frequently, an unaugmented form χρῆν. Because it implies moral obligation, *ought* is often an appropriate translation for χρή. Greek however (unlike English) can say *I oughted (at the time) to do X*. This must be recast as *I ought to have done X* (making the infinitive rather than the impersonal verb past tense):

> χρῆν με τὸν γέροντα ὠφελεῖν.
> *literally* I oughted to help the old man.
> *i.e. in correct English,*
>> I ought to have helped the old man.

• It is also possible to form impersonal verbs from a neuter adjective plus ἐστί (again followed by a dative):
>> ἀγαθόν ἐστιν ἐλπίζειν.
>> It is good to hope.

This can also be explained (and translated) by taking the adjective with the infinitive, which is then regarded as a neuter noun:
>> To hope is (a) good (thing).

• An impersonal passive (a third person singular passive verb, with 'it' understood as the subject) is also often found, for example introducing an indirect statement:

>> ἐνομίζετο πολλοὺς τῶν αἰχμαλώτων λυθῆναι.
>> It was thought that many of the prisoners had been released.

Infinitive after verbs

• The infinitive following naturally after another verb is technically called *prolative* ('carried forward'), but operates naturally, as in English. As well as impersonal verbs, it follows verbs meaning *want (to)*, *be able (to)*, *begin (to)* etc. As we saw above, an aorist infinitive in such contexts is used *by aspect* (to stress something which is to happen just once).

• We also saw in Chapters 8 and 9 that some verbs are followed by a future infintive. Common examples are:

ἐλπίζω	I hope (to)
μέλλω	I am about to, I intend (to)
ὑπισχνέομαι	I promise (to)

Here the future infinitive simply reinforces the sense of the verb, and so e.g. ἐλπίζω ἀφίξεσθαι is translated *I hope to arrive* (not *I hope to be going to arrive*).

Exercise 10.8

Translate into English:

1   ἆρ' ἔξεστι τῇ ἐκκλησίᾳ τὰ περὶ τῆς ναυμαχίας μαθεῖν;
2   δεῖ πάντας τοὺς παρόντας εὐθὺς φυγεῖν.
3   ἔδοξε τοῖς στρατηγοῖς τὴν τῶν πολεμίων πόλιν πολιορκῆσαι.
4   ἐχρῆν ἡμᾶς τοῖς αἰχμαλώτοις βοηθεῖν.
5   οἱ παῖδες ἔμελλον τὸν πατέρα χρήματα αἰτήσειν.
6   χαλεπόν ἐστι τοὺς φυγόντας ἐν τῇ ὕλῃ εὑρίσκειν.
7   οἱ δοῦλοι ὑπέσχοντο τὰ κελευσθέντα πράξειν.
8   αὕτη ἡ κόρη ἐλπίζει τοὺς λόγους ταχέως γνώσεσθαι.
9   ἔδει τοὺς αἱρέθεντας πολὺν χρόνον ἐκεῖ μένειν.
10   ἔδοξε τῷ κριτῇ τὴν βίβλον δέξασθαι.

Exercise 10.9

Translate into Greek:

1   It is necessary for the allies to suffer bad things.
2   It was possible for the women to hear all the words.
3   The teacher decided to send another letter.
4   Did the girl promise to examine the books?
5   It is good to receive such gifts.

Background: Herodotus (1)

Herodotus (about 490-425 BC) was the first Greek historian, and is one of the world's great storytellers. Stories from Herodotus occupy most of the rest of this book. His *Histories* in nine books have as their climax the wars between Greece and Persia which were taking place in his early childhood. Herodotus was born and grew up in Halicarnassus, a Greek city on the edge of Persian territory (in modern western Turkey). He writes in the Ionic dialect of Greek (though the stories in this book are adapted into Attic). Because he sees the conflict between Greece and Persia as the expression of a fundamental cultural divide betwen east and west, more than half his work (forming a vast introduction) explores the Mediterranean and near eastern world in the century or so before his time. The account is loosely organized around the theme of the build-up of Persian power. Herodotus however has great interest in foreign cultures and customs for their own sake, and is happy to digress (most spectacularly with a whole book devoted to Egypt, which becomes relevant at the point when the Persians conquer it).

His colourful (and frankly often tall) stories ensured that 'the Father of History' came also to be called 'the Father of Lies'. But in fact Herodotus often distances himself from the stories he tells, and does not commit himself to their truth. And stories that may not be literally true often still have some symbolic point, or illustrate a wider theme.

Early in his work Herodotus makes a distinct change of gear from myth (stories like the seizing of Helen) to ascertainable history, which he takes from about 600 BC (150-175 years before he is writing). Yet his stories about characters from relatively recent history often have the characteristics of myth. Traditional epic poetry was going out of fashion. Herodotus wrote instead a prose epic, to show that recent wars had a

141

heroic grandeur comparable to the wars of the mythic past.

The Greek world was changing rapidly during the period Herodotus covers. For about a hundred years (mid-seventh to mid-sixth century BC) many Greek city-states went through a stage of political evolution known as *tyranny*. It is important to stress that Greek tyrants were not necessarily (as the word now implies) cruel despots: many of them enjoyed strong popular support. The old hereditary monarchies had long since given way to the rule of aristocrats. A tyrant typically came from outside (or from the fringes of) this privileged group: he seized power for himself, promising benefits to the ordinary people. Although this might seem a backward step in the long-term process of spreading political power more widely, tyranny in fact usually functioned as a stimulus to further change. Few tyrannies lasted beyond a second generation: charismatic, often insecure, rule could not easily be passed on. The fact that the tyrant had been able to seize power inspired larger groups to do so, and tyrannies were typically followed at least by *oligarchies* (= rule of the few) more broadly-based than the earlier aristocracies, and in some cases (notably Athens) by *democracy* (= rule of the people: though in practice this meant adult male citizens).

The colourful figures of the tyrants (often very wealthy, attracting artists to their courts and spending lavishly to adorn their cities) provide Herodotus with many stories to illustrate his moral and theological beliefs: in particular that human prosperity does not abide long in one place, and that pride frequently comes before a fall.

Exercise 10.10

Psammetichus

The king of Egypt conducts an experiment, based on an analogy between the development of an individual and the development of human society.

οἱ δ' <u>Αἰγύπτιοι</u>, <u>πρὸ</u> τῆς τοῦ <u>Ψαμμητίχου</u> ἀρχῆς, ἐνόμιζον πρῶτοι γενέσθαι πάντων ἀνθρώπων. νῦν δὲ νομίζουσι τὸ τῶν <u>Φρυγῶν</u> ἔθνος ἀρχαιότερον εἶναι τοῦ τῶν Αἰγυπτίων. ὁ γὰρ Ψαμμήτιχος, ἐπεὶ βασιλεὺς τῶν Αἰγυπτίων ἐγένετο, ἐβούλετο τὸ ἀληθὲς εὑρεῖν. ἐζήτει οὖν πύθεσθαι τίνες οἱ πρῶτοι
5 ἄνθρωποι ἐγένοντο, ἀλλ' οὐχ οἷός τ' ἦν τοῦτο μαθεῖν. λαβὼν οὖν δύο παῖδας <u>νεογνοὺς</u> ἐνοίκων τινῶν τῆς ἑαυτοῦ χώρας, τούτους <u>ποιμένι</u> τινὶ <u>ἔδωκεν</u>. ἔπειτα δὲ ὁ βασιλεὺς ἐκέλευσε τὸν ποιμένα τοῖς παῖσι μηδὲν λέγειν ἀλλ' ἐν <u>καλύβῃ</u> <u>ἐρήμῃ</u> φυλάσσειν αὐτοὺς καὶ <u>καθ' ἡμέραν</u> <u>αἶγας</u> ἐναγαγόντα γάλακτι αὐτοὺς <u>τρέφειν</u>. ταῦτα ἐποίησε καὶ ἐκέλευσεν ὁ
10 Ψαμμήτιχος διότι ἐβούλετο ἀκοῦσαι τίνα λόγον οἱ παῖδες πρῶτον λέξουσι, παυσάμενοι τῶν <u>κνυζημάτων</u>. μετὰ δὲ δύο ἔτη, τῷ ποιμένι εἰς τὴν καλύβην ποτὲ εἰσελθόντι προσέδραμον οἱ παῖδες "βέκος" <u>ἅμα</u> λέγοντες καὶ τὰς χεῖρας <u>προτείνοντες</u>. ὁ δὲ ποιμὴν τοῦτο ἄκουσας πρῶτον μὲν οὐδὲν ἐποίησεν. ἐπεὶ δὲ οἱ παῖδες πολλάκις τὸν αὐτὸν λόγον ἔλεγον,
15 ὁ ποιμὴν τὰ γενόμενα τῷ βασιλεῖ ἤγγειλεν. ὁ οὖν Ψαμμήτιχος τοὺς παῖδας εὐθὺς <u>μεταπεμψάμενος</u> καὶ αὐτὸς ἄκουσας, ἀγγέλους πρὸς πᾶσαν χώραν ἔπεμψεν ὡς πευσομένους τίνες ἀνθρώπων "βέκος" τι καλοῦσιν. καὶ διὰ τούτους ἔγνω τοὺς Φρυγὰς τὸν <u>ἄρτον</u> οὕτω καλοῦντας. οἱ οὖν Αἰγύπτιοι ἀπὸ τούτου τοῦ χρόνου νομίζουσι τοὺς μὲν Φρυγὰς πρώτους
20 γενέσθαι πάντων ἀνθρώπων, αὐτοὶ δὲ δεύτεροι.

	Αἰγύπτιοι -ων οἱ	Egyptians
	πρό	before (+ *gen*)
	Ψαμμήτιχος -ου ὁ	Psammetichus
	Φρυγές -ῶν οἱ	Phrygians (*from Phrygia, in modern northern Turkey*)
5	νεογνός -όν	new-born
	ποιμήν -ένος ὁ	shepherd
	ἔδωκα	(*irreg aor*) I gave
	καλύβη -ης ἡ	hut
	ἐρῆμος -η -ον	lonely, deserted
	καθ' ἡμέραν	every day
	αἴξ αἰγός ὁ	goat
	γάλα γάλακτος τό	milk
	τρέφω	feed
10	κνυζήματα -ων τά	baby-talk
	ἅμα	at the same time
	προτείνω	I stretch out
15	μεταπέμπομαι μετεπεμψάμην	I send for
	ἄρτος -ου ὁ	bread

143

Exercise 10.11

Polycrates and the Ring

Herodotus has many stories illustrating the dangers of excessive prosperity and complacency.
Tyrants often provide telling illustrations. The gods are shown as jealous, and prone to upset human
calculations. This story (set in the sixth century BC) resembles many of the myths from an older
Greek world in stressing that men cannot avoid what is fated.

ὁ δὲ <u>Πολυκράτης</u> <u>Σάμου</u> <u>τύραννος</u> ἐγένετο ὧδε· ὀλίγους ἄνδρας ἔχων ἐν
<u>στάσει</u> τῆς νήσου ἐκράτησε, καὶ πρῶτον μὲν μετὰ τῶν δυοῖν ἀδελφῶν
<u>ἐτυράννευεν</u> (ἕκαστος γὰρ τρίτην <u>μοῖραν</u> εἶχεν). ἔπειτα δὲ ὁ Πολυκράτης,
τὸν μὲν τῶν ἀδελφῶν ἀπόκτεινας, τὸν δὲ <u>ἐξέλασας</u>, τύραννος πάσης τῆς
5   Σάμου ἐγένετο. <u>δυνατώτατος</u> οὖν ἤδη ὤν, <u>φιλίαν</u> ἐποιήσατο <u>πρὸς</u> Ἄμασιν
τὸν τῆς <u>Αἰγύπτου</u> βασιλέα, πέμπων τε δῶρα καὶ δεχόμενος ἄλλα <u>παρ'</u>
αὐτοῦ.

ὁ οὖν Πολυκράτης ἔτι δυνατώτερός τε καὶ πλουσιώτερος ἐγίγνετο. ἦσαν
αὐτῷ νῆες <u>ἑκατόν</u>, <u>τοξόται</u> <u>χίλιοι</u>. πολλῶν νήσων καὶ πόλεων ἐκράτησε,
10 καὶ πολλοὺς ἀνθρώπους δούλους ἐποίησεν. τὸ ὄνομα αὐτοῦ μέγα ἐγένετο
<u>κατὰ</u> τὴν Ἑλλάδα. ἐπεὶ τοὺς <u>Λεσβίους</u> ναυμαχίᾳ ἐκράτησε, τοὺς
αἰχμαλώτους ἠνάγκασε <u>τάφρον</u> περὶ τὴν ἑαυτοῦ πόλιν <u>ὀρύσσειν</u>. ὁ μέντοι
Ἄμασις ἀκούσας περὶ τῶν τοῦ Πολυκράτους πραγμάτων ἐφοβεῖτο διότι
εὐτυχέστερος ἦν ὁ τύραννος ἢ ἀνθρώπῳ ἀγαθόν ἐστιν.

	Πολυκράτης -ους ὁ	Polycrates
	Σάμος -ου ἡ	Samos (*Greek island off modern Turkey*)
	τύραννος -ου ὁ	tyrant
	στάσις -εως ἡ	rebellion, civil war
	τυραννεύω	I am tyrant
	μοῖρα -ας ἡ	share, part
	ἐξελαύνω ἐξήλασα	I drive out
5	δυνατός -ή -όν	powerful
	φιλία -ας ἡ	friendship
	πρός	(+ *acc*) (*here*) with
	Ἄμασις -εως ὁ	Amasis
	Αἴγυπτος -ου ἡ	Egypt
	παρ' (= παρά)	(+ *gen*) from
	ἑκατόν	100
	τοξότης -ου ὁ	archer
	χίλιοι -αι -α	1000
10	κατά	(+ *acc*) throughout
	Λέσβιοι -ων οἱ	Lesbians, men of Lesbos (*Greek island north of Samos*)
	τάφρος -ου ἡ	moat
	ὀρύσσω	I dig

15 ἐπιστολὴν οὖν γράψας πρὸς τὴν Σάμον ἔπεμψεν. "Ἄμασις Πολυκράτει
ὧδε λέγει· ἀγαθὸν μέν ἐστιν ἀκούειν ἄνδρα φίλον εὖ πράσσοντα. ἐμοὶ δ᾽
οὐ πάνυ ἀρέσκει ἡ σὴ μεγάλη εὐτυχία. εἰ γάρ τις εὐτυχὴς ἀεί ἐστιν, οἱ
θεοὶ φθονοῦσιν. ἄμεινόν ἐστι καὶ ἀγαθὸν καὶ κακὸν ἐν τῷ βίῳ ἔχειν. δεῖ
οὖν σὲ πειθόμενόν μοι ὧδε πράσσειν· τῶν σῶν κτημάτων ἀποβαλὲ τὸ
20 πλείστου ἄξιον. οὕτως παύσεις τὸν τῶν θεῶν φθόνον."

τῷ δὲ Πολυκράτει τὴν ἐπιστολὴν δεξαμένῳ ἔδοξε τῷ βασιλεῖ πίθεσθαι.
ἦν δ᾽ αὐτῷ σφραγίς τις χρυσοῦ, πλείστου ἄξια· καὶ ἐβουλεύσατο ταύτην
ἀποβάλλειν. κελεύσας οὖν τοὺς ἑαυτοῦ ναῦν παρασκευάσαι, αὐτὸς τὴν
σφραγίδα φέρων ἀπὸ γῆς ἑκὰς ἀπέπλευσεν. ἔπειτα δὲ τὴν σφραγίδα εἰς
25 τὴν θάλασσαν εἰσέβαλεν· καὶ πάντες οἱ ναῦται εἶδον τὸ γενόμενον.

μετὰ δὲ ταῦτα τῇ πέμπτῃ ἢ ἕκτῃ ἡμέρᾳ ἁλιεύς τις ἰχθὺν μέγιστόν τε καὶ
κάλλιστον ἔλαβεν. καὶ οὐκ ἤθελε πρὸς τὴν ἀγορὰν φέρειν τὸν ἰχθύν·
δῶρον γὰρ ἔδοξεν ἄξιον τοῦ τυράννου εἶναι. εἰς δὲ τὴν τοῦ Πολυκράτους
οἰκίαν ἀφικόμενος ὁ ἁλιεὺς εἶπε, "τοῦτον τὸν ἰχθὺν τὸν μέγιστόν τε καὶ
30 κάλλιστον λαβών, καίπερ πένης ὢν οὐκ ἐθέλω πρὸς τὴν ἀγορὰν φέρειν. ὁ
γὰρ ἰχθὺς φαίνεται σοῦ ἄξιος εἶναι καὶ τῆς σῆς ἀρχῆς. αἰτῶ σε τὸ δῶρον
δέχεσθαι."

ὁ οὖν Πολυκράτης, τῷ τε δώρῳ καὶ τοῖς λόγοις ἡδόμενος, ἀπεκρίνατο,
"ἀγαθόν ἐστι καὶ τὸ σὸν δῶρον δέχεσθαι καὶ τοὺς σοὺς λόγους ἀκούειν.
35 καλοῦμέν σε ἐπὶ δεῖπνον." οἱ δὲ τοῦ Πολυκράτους δοῦλοι, τὸν ἰχθὺν
διατέμνοντες, ἐν τῇ γαστρὶ τὴν σφραγίδα εὗρον. διὰ ταῦτα πολὺ ἡδόμενοι
παρὰ τὸν Πολυκράτη ἔφερον τὴν σφραγίδα καὶ εἶπον ὅπως εὗρον. ὁ δὲ
τύραννος νῦν ἐφοβεῖτο. ἐπύθετο γὰρ τὸ ἔργον τῶν θεῶν ὄν. ἐπιστολὴν
ἔγραψε περὶ τῶν γενομένων· γράψας δὲ πρὸς τὴν Αἴγυπτον ἔπεμψεν.

15	πάνυ	entirely
	ἀρέσκω	I please, I am pleasing to (+ dat)
	εὐτυχία -ας ἡ	good fortune
	φθονέω	I am jealous
	ἄμεινον	better
20	πλεῖστος -η -ον	most
	φθόνος -ου ὁ	envy, jealousy
	σφραγίς -ῖδος ἡ	ring
	βουλεύομαι ἐβουλευσάμην	I plan
	ἑκάς	far
25	ἁλιεύς -έως ὁ	fisherman
	τύραννος -ου ὁ	tyrant
30	πένης -ητος ὁ	poor man
	ἥδομαι	I am pleased (by, + dat)
35	διατέμνω	I cut open
	γαστήρ -τρός ἡ	stomach
	παρά	(+ acc) here to, into the presence of
	ὅπως	how

145

40 ὁ οὖν Ἄμασις οὕτω περὶ τῶν τοῦ Πολυκράτους πραγμάτων ἀκούσας
ἠθύμησε, διότι οὐχ οἷός τ' ἦν σῶσαι τὸν φίλον ἀπὸ τοῦ τῶν θεῶν
<u>φθόνου</u>. ἄγγελον οὖν πέμψας <u>διέλυσε</u> τὴν <u>φιλίαν</u>. οὐκέτι γὰρ ἤθελε φίλος
εἶναι τοῦ Πολυκράτους, εἰ τὰ πράγματα αὐτοῦ ἀεί ἐστιν εὐτυχῆ. καὶ
ὕστερον οὐ πολλῷ οἱ <u>Πέρσαι</u> τῆς Σάμου ἐκράτησαν καὶ τὸν <u>τύραννον</u>
45 ἀπέκτειναν. τῆς οὖν μεγάλης τοῦ Πολυκράτους <u>εὐτυχίας</u> τοῦτο τὸ τέλος
ἦν.

40	φθόνος -ου ὁ	jealousy
	διαλύω διέλυσα	I break off
	φιλία -ας ἡ	friendship
	Πέρσαι -ων οἱ	Persians
	τύραννος -ου ὁ	tyrant
45	εὐτυχία -ας ἡ	good fortune

Result clauses with infinitive

In Chapter 7 we saw that result clauses with ὥστε (e.g. *He is so clever that he always learns everything*) commonly have their verb in the indicative if the result is one which actually occurs.

Result clauses can however also have their verb in the infinitive. This version *must* be used if the result is only a *likely* or *expected* one, rather than one that actually occurs (but it *can* be used anyway, even if the result does actually occur). In the infinitive version (as will now be familiar from other infinitive constructions), a new subject in the result clause is *accusative*.

• With the infinitive version, a translation such as *so X as to* ... is often appropriate (avoiding the issue of whether the result does actually happen):

οὕτω σοφῶς λέγει ὥστε πείθειν πάντας τοὺς πολίτας.
He speaks so wisely as to (*or* wisely enough to) persuade all the citizens.

• As with other infinitive constructions, you must distinguish (by context) an accusative which is a new subject for the infinitive from one which (understanding again the same subject) is its object:

οὕτως ἀνδρεῖοί εἰσιν ὥστε τοὺς πολεμίους φοβεῖσθαι.
They are so brave that the enemy (*accusative as new subject*) are afraid.

οὕτως ἀνδρεῖοί εἰσιν ὥστε τοὺς πολεμίους ἀποκτείνειν.
They are so brave that they (*or* as to) kill the enemy (*accusative as object*).

• The negatives used in the two constructions mirror the distinction in meaning. In the indicative version (dealing with *facts*) the negative is οὐ. In the infinitive version (with its *potential* flavour) the negative is μή. This is of course in line with the normal distinction between οὐ and μή.

Exercise 10.12

Translate into English:

1 ἐκεῖνοι οἱ στρατιῶται οὕτως ἀνδρεῖοί εἰσιν ὥστε ἀεὶ εὖ μάχεσθαι.
2 ὁ γέρων οὕτω σοφός ἐστιν ὥστε πάντας θαυμάζειν αὐτόν.
3 τοσαύτη ἐστὶν ἡ βοὴ ὥστε τοὺς ἐν τῇ κώμῃ ἀκούειν.
4 τὸ τείχισμα οὕτω ταχέως ἐλήφθη ὥστε οὐδεὶς ἔφυγεν.
5 ὁ ποταμός ἐστιν οὕτω βαθὺς ὥστε μηδένα διαβαίνειν.
6 ὁ ῥήτωρ οὕτω σοφῶς λέγει ὥστε ἀεὶ πείθειν τοὺς πολίτας.
7 ἡ ἐν τῇ νήσῳ ὕλη τοιαύτη ἐστὶν ὥστε μηδὲν ἐκεῖ εὑρίσκεσθαι.
8 οἱ πολέμιοι τέλος ἔφυγον· ὥστε ἡ μάχη ἐπαύσατο.
9 ἡ ναῦς οὕτω ταχέως ἔπλευσεν ὥστε οὐχ οἷοί τ' ἦμεν λαβεῖν.
10 τοσοῦτός τε καὶ τοιοῦτος ἦν ὁ ἡμέτερος στρατὸς ὥστε τοὺς
   βαρβάρους φοβεῖσθαι.

Exercise 10.13

Translate into Greek:

1 Few slaves are so foolish as to run away.
2 The sea was so dangerous that it was not possible to sail.
3 He teaches so wisely that those present learn everything.
4 The city was so big that we could not find the judge's house.
5 There were enough* soldiers to capture the city

   * enough = so many (as to)

147

Exercise 10.14

Amasis and the Statue

The canny prudence Amasis revealed in his dealings with Polycrates had also been shown at the beginning of his own reign.

ἐπεὶ ὁ Ἄμασις βασιλεὺς τῆς Αἰγύπτου ἐγένετο, πρῶτον μὲν οἱ Αἰγύπτιοι ὠλιγώρουν αὐτοῦ ὡς δημότου πρότερον ὄντος καὶ γένους οὐκ ἐπιφανοῦς, μετὰ δ᾽ ὀλίγον χρόνον ὁ Ἄμασις οὕτω σοφῶς αὐτοὺς προσηγάγετο ὥστε ὑπὸ πάντων θαυμάζεσθαι. πολλὰ γὰρ κτήματα εἶχε καὶ θαυμάσια, ἐν δ᾽
5 αὐτοῖς ποδανιπτῆρα χρυσοῦ ἐν ᾧ αὐτὸς ὁ Ἄμασις καὶ πάντες οἱ ξένοι τοὺς πόδας ἀπενίζοντο. τοῦτον οὖν κατακόψας ἄγαλμα θεοῦ τινος ἐξ αὐτοῦ ἐποιήσατο, καὶ τοῦτο ἐν τῇ ἀγορᾷ ἵδρυσεν. οἱ δ᾽ Αἰγύπτιοι δι᾽ ὀλίγου τὸ ἄγαλμα ἐσέβοντο πολύ. ὁ δ᾽ Ἄμασις, ἐπεὶ ἔμαθε ταῦτα, συγκαλέσας τοὺς Αἰγυπτίους εἶπε τάδε· "τὸ ἄγαλμα ἐκ τοῦ ποδανιπτῆρος
10 ἐποιήθη· πρότερον μὲν πάντες ἐν τούτῳ τοὺς πόδας ἀπενίζεσθε, νῦν δὲ μάλιστα σέβεσθε. καὶ ἐγὼ ὁμοίως τῷ ποδανιπτῆρι ἔπαθον· πρότερον γὰρ δημότης ὤν, νῦν βασιλεύς εἰμι. οὕτως οὖν ἄξιός εἰμι τῆς τιμῆς." καὶ τοιούτῳ τρόπῳ ὁ Ἄμασις προσηγάγετο τοὺς Αἰγυπτίους.

	Ἄμασις -εως ὁ	Amasis
	Αἴγυπτος -ου ἡ	Egypt
	Αἰγύπτιοι -ων οἱ	Egyptians
	ὀλιγωρέω	I despise (+ gen)
	δημότης -ου ὁ	commoner
	ἐπιφανής -ές	distinguished
	προσάγομαι προσηγαγόμην	I win over
	θαυμάσιος -α -ον	wonderful
5	ποδανιπτήρ -ῆρος ὁ	bowl for washing feet
	ξένος -ου ὁ	(*here*) guest
	ἀπονίζομαι	I wash
	κατακόπτω κατέκοψα	(*here*) I melt (something) down
	ἄγαλμα -ατος τό	statue
	ἱδρύω ἵδρυσα	I set up
	δι᾽ (=δια) ὀλίγου	soon, after a short time
	σέβομαι	I revere, I worship
	πολύ	(*neuter as adv*) greatly
	συγκαλέω συνεκάλεσα	I call together
10	μάλιστα	especially
	ὁμοίως	in the same way
	τρόπος -ου ὁ	way, method

Verbs with alpha contraction

We saw in Chapter 9 the principle of epsilon contraction, and its application to verbs, adjectives and nouns. Contraction with alpha works in a broadly similar way, but is less common. In practice it affects only verbs, and there are relatively few of those. Again it is most economical of effort simply to learn the rules of contraction and apply them. For contraction with alpha the rules are:

        α followed by an e sound (ε or η) becomes long α
        α followed by an o sound (o or ω) becomes ω
        ι becomes subscript, and υ disappears

Hence:

τιμάω = I honour

		present active		*present middle/passive:*	
sg	1	τιμῶ	[τιμα-ω]	τιμῶμαι	[τιμα-ομαι]
	2	τιμᾷς	[τιμα-εις]	τιμᾷ	[τιμα-η (or -ει)]
	3	τιμᾷ	[τιμα-ει]	τιμᾶται	[τιμα-εται]
pl	1	τιμῶμεν	[τιμα-ομεν]	τιμώμεθα	[τιμα-ομεθα]
	2	τιμᾶτε	[τιμα-ετε]	τιμᾶσθε	[τιμα-εσθε]
	3	τιμῶσι(ν)	[τιμα-ουσι(ν)]	τιμῶνται	[τιμα-ονται]

participle:
τιμῶν -ῶσα -ῶν (stem τιμωντ-)
[τιμα-ων -ουσα -ον (τιμα-οντ-)]

participle:
τιμώμενος -η -ον
[τιμα-ομενος -η -ον]

infinitive:
τιμᾶν
[τιμα-ειν: iota disappears here]

infinitive:
τιμᾶσθαι
[τιμα-εσθαι]

imperative:
sg τιμᾶ pl τιμᾶτε
[τιμα-ε, -ετε]

imperative:
sg τιμῶ pl τιμᾶσθε
[τιμα-ου, -εσθε]

		imperfect active		*imperfect middle/passive*	
sg	1	ἐτίμων	[ἐτιμα-ον]	ἐτιμώμην	[ἐτιμα-ομην]
	2	ἐτίμας	[ἐτιμα-ες]	ἐτιμῶ	[ἐτιμα-ου]
	3	ἐτίμα	[ἐτιμα-ε]	ἐτιμᾶτο	[ἐτιμα-ετο]
pl	1	ἐτιμῶμεν	[ἐτιμα-ομεν]	ἐτιμώμεθα	[ἐτιμα-ομεθα]
	2	ἐτιμᾶτε	[ἐτιμα-ετε]	ἐτιμᾶσθε	[ἐτιμα-εσθε]
	3	ἐτίμων	[ἐτιμα-ον]	ἐτιμῶντο	[ἐτιμα-οντο]

For the regular pattern of alpha verbs, the first (weak) aorist and future are formed exactly as with epsilon verbs: the alpha (like the epsilon) is lengthened to eta before adding the sigma, but the endings after the sigma are normal. Hence:

aorist active   ἐτίμησα
aorist middle   ἐτιμησάμην
aorist passive ἐτιμήθην

future active   τιμήσω
future middle   τιμήσομαι
future passive τιμηθήσομαι

• Again it is conventional to quote these verbs in uncontracted form in a wordlist or dictionary (to make the formation clear), but to write them with the contraction in a sentence or passage.

Regular verbs with alpha contraction:

		aorist
βοάω	I shout	ἐβόησα
ἐρωτάω	I ask (a question)	ἠρώτησα *or* ἠρόμην
νικάω	I conquer, I win	ἐνίκησα

Regular deponent:

κτάομαι	I acquire	ἐκτησάμην

The following verbs use alpha rather than eta before the sigma for the future and aorist:

γελάω	I laugh	ἐγέλασα
ἐάω	I allow	εἴασα*

> * note that adding the augment to the epsilon of the stem here (as for example with ἔχω)
> produces the diphthong εἰ (rather than the more usual eta)

And a deponent:

πειράομαι	I try, I attempt	ἐπειρασάμην

In the case of ἐρωτάω (above), the second (strong) aorist form ἠρόμην is an alternative. The following verb however has only a second (strong) aorist (from a different stem), with which you are already familiar:

ὁράω	I see	εἶδον

Note that this verb changes the stem slightly in the imperfect: ἑώρων (α-ον)

Finally the following deponent verb contracts in a slightly different way: instead of alpha plus an *e* sound making long alpha (the normal rule), alpha plus an *e* sound here makes eta:

χράομαι	I use (+ *dat*)	ἐχρησάμην

hence e.g. present tense third person singular χρῆται (rather than χρᾶται)

• We saw in Chapter 9 that some (otherwise normal) verbs form their future like the present of an epsilon contraction verb. There is just one common corresponding example of a verb with an alpha contraction future: ἐλαύνω = *I drive*, future ἐλάω contracted as ἐλῶ.

• Again, you should not worry too much about the minor irregularities. The common forms quickly become familiar, and the less common ones can be easily be checked in the Reference Grammar.

Exercise 10.15

Translate into English:
1   ὁ Σωκράτης ὑπὸ τῶν Ἀθηναίων ἐτιμᾶτο.
2   τῶν τὴν πόλιν πολιορκούντων τέλος ἐκρατήσαμεν.
3   τοὺς τοῦ ἀγγέλου λόγους ἀκούσαντες πάντες ἐγέλασαν.
4   οἱ ἐκεῖ πολέμιοι ἅρμασί τε καὶ λίθοις ἐχρήσαντο.
5   τοὺς ἱππέας πολλὰ περὶ τῆς μάχης ἠρώτησα.
6   οἱ πολῖται καίπερ πολὺν χρόνον βοήσαντες οὐκ ἔπεισαν τὸν ῥήτορα.
7   οἱ τοῦ βασιλέως στρατιῶται ἀφίκοντο ὡς τὸν χρυσὸν κτησόμενοι.
8   ὁ διδάσκαλος οὐκ εἴασε τοὺς παῖδας ἐγγὺς τοῦ ποταμοῦ τρέχειν.
9   αἱ γυναῖκες ἐπειρῶντο τοὺς παῖδας τοὺς φεύγοντας διώκειν.
10   ἆρα ὁ διδάσκαλος ταύταις ταῖς βίβλοις χρῆται;

Exercise 10.16

Translate into Greek:
1   Why are all the boys now shouting?
2   The girl was laughing on account of the strange old man.
3   After the war, the citizens acquired many islands.
4   Did you (*pl*) finally conquer those who were helping the enemy?
5   We often used to see the men who were trying to capture the ships.

Exercise 10.17

Arion and the Dolphin

Many tyrants attracted artists and musicians to their courts, which became important cultural centres. This story about a famous musician also illustrates how the colony cities of Italy and Sicily had become a major element in the wider Greek world.

ἦν δέ ποτε ἐν Κορίνθῳ κιθαρῳδός τις, Ἀρίων ὀνόματι. καὶ οὗτος ἄριστος
ἦν, ὡς λέγουσι, τῶν τότε κιθαρῳδῶν. πολὺν χρόνον ἔμενε παρὰ τῷ
Περιάνδρῳ, τῷ τῆς Κορίνθου τυράννῳ. ὕστερον δ' ἐβούλετο εἰς Ἰταλίαν
τε καὶ Σικελίαν πλεῦσαι. πολλὰ δὲ χρήματα ἐκεῖ δεξάμενος διὰ τὴν τῆς
5 κιθάρας τέχνην, ἐβούλετο πρὸς Κόρινθον ἐπανελθεῖν. εὗρεν οὖν ναῦν
Κορινθίων τινῶν ἐν τῇ Ἰταλίᾳ ὄντων, πιστεύων οὐδενὶ μᾶλλον ἢ τοῖς
Κορινθίοις. καὶ ἀπέπλευσαν ἐκ Τάραντος.

οἱ δὲ ναῦται, ἀπὸ τῆς γῆς ἤδη ἑκὰς ὄντες, ἐβουλεύσαντο τὸν Ἀρίονα
ἐκβαλόντες τὰ χρήματα κλέψαι. ὁ δέ, τοῦτο μαθών, ᾔτησεν αὐτοὺς τὰ
10 μὲν χρήματα λαβεῖν, ἑαυτὸν δὲ σῶσαι. οἱ μέντοι ναῦται οὐδαμῶς
ἐπείσθησαν, ἀλλ' ἐκέλευσαν αὐτὸν ἢ ἑαυτὸν ἀποκτεῖναι ἢ εἰς τὴν
θάλασσαν ἐκπηδῆσαι. ὁ δ' Ἀρίων, "πρῶτον," ἔφη, "ἐάσατε με κιθαρίζειν".
καὶ ὑπέσχετο τοῦτο ποιήσας εἰς τὴν θάλασσαν ἐκπηδήσειν. οἱ δὲ ναῦται,
ἡδόμενοι διότι τοῦ ἀρίστου κιθαρῳδοῦ ἀκούσεσθαι ἔμελλον, ἐδέξαντο
15 τοὺς λόγους· καὶ εἰς μέσην τὴν ναῦν εἰσῆλθον ὡς ἀκουσόμενοι.

ἔπειτα δὲ ὁ Ἀρίων, φορῶν πᾶσαν τὴν σκευὴν καὶ τὴν κιθάραν λαβών,

	ποτε	once
	Κόρινθος -ου ἡ	Corinth (*important city in south-central Greece*)
	κιθαρῳδός -οῦ ὁ	lyre-player
	Ἀρίων -ονος ὁ	Arion
	παρά	(+ *dat*) (*here*) at the court of
	Περίανδρος -ου ὁ	Periander
	τύραννος -ου ὁ	tyrant
	Ἰταλία -ας ἡ	Italy
	Σικελία -ας ἡ	Sicily
5	κιθάρα -ας ἡ	lyre
	ἐπανέρχομαι ἐπανῆλθον	I return, I go back
	Κορίνθιοι -ων οἱ	Corinthians
	Τάρας -αντος ὁ	Tarentum (*Greek city at southern tip of Italy*)
	ἑκάς	far
	βουλεύομαι ἐβουλευσάμην	I plot, I conspire
10	ἐκπηδάω ἐξεπήδησα	I jump out
	κιθαρίζω	I play the lyre
	ἥδομαι	I am delighted
15	μέσος -η -ον	middle (part of)
	φορέω	I wear
	σκευή -ῆς ἡ	gear

διεξῆλθε τὸν ὄρθιον νόμον. καὶ τοῦτο ποιήσας εἰς τὴν θάλασσαν ἐξεπήδησε σὺν πάσῃ τῇ σκευῇ. οἱ δὲ ναῦται πρὸς τὴν Κόρινθον ἀπέπλευσαν.

20 τὸν δ' Ἀρίονα δελφίς τις, ὡς λέγουσιν, ὑπολαβὼν εἰς τὴν Ταίναρον ἤνεγκεν. ἔπειτα δὲ ὁ κιθαρῳδός, πᾶσαν τὴν σκευὴν ἔτι ἔχων, πρὸς τὴν Κόρινθον κατὰ γῆν ἐπορεύετο· καὶ ἀφικόμενος εἶπε τῷ Περιάνδρῳ πάντα τὰ γενόμενα. ὁ δὲ τύραννος, τοῖς λόγοις οὐ πιστεύων, ἐκέλευσε τὸν Ἀρίονα φυλάσσεσθαι, καὶ τοὺς ναύτας ἔμενεν. ἐπεὶ δὲ παρῆσαν ὁ
25 Περίανδρος ἠρώτησεν αὐτοὺς περὶ τοῦ Ἀρίονος. οἱ δὲ ἀπεκρίναντο ὅτι ἔλιπον αὐτὸν εὖ πράσσοντα ἐν Ἰταλίᾳ. τῶν δὲ ναύτων ἔτι λεγόντων, ὁ Ἀρίων, πᾶσαν τὴν σκευὴν ἔτι καὶ νῦν ἔχων, ἐπιφαίνεται* αὐτοῖς. οἱ οὖν ναῦται ὡμολόγησαν τὸ πρᾶγμα.

	διεξέρχομαι διεξῆλθον	I go through, I perform
	ὄρθιος νόμος ὁ	the 'orthian [lit upright] chant' (a traditional stirring tune of very high pitch)
	ἐκπηδάω ἐξεπήδησα	I jump out
	σύν	with (+ dat)
	σκευή -ῆς ἡ	gear
20	δελφίς -ῖνος ὁ	dolphin
	ὑπολαμβάνω ὑπέλαβον	I scoop up
	Ταίναρος -ου ἡ	Taenarus (city at southern tip of Greece)
	κιθαρῳδός -οῦ ὁ	lyre-player
	κατά	(+ acc) (here) by
	τύραννος -ου ὁ	tyrant
25	ἐπιφαίνομαι	I appear (commonly used of gods, giving here a sense of the uncanny)
	ὁμολογέω ὡμολόγησα	(here) I confess

* this is a 'historic present': a present tense used for vividness and immediacy in a narrative taking place in the past

Irregular comparatives and superlatives

In Chapter 7 we met the regular comparative and superlative of 2-1-2 adjectives:

positive		comparative	superlative
σοφός	wise	σοφώτερος	σοφώτατος
δεινός	strange	δεινότερος	δεινότατος

In Chapter 9 we met the comparative of third-declension (3-1-3 and 3-3) adjectives, which represent minor variations on the same pattern:

βαθύς	deep	βαθύτερος	βαθύτατος
ἀληθής	true	ἀληθέστερος	ἀληθέστατος

A further small variation is:

ἴσος	equal	ἰσαίτερος	ἰσαίτατος
φίλος	dear	φιλαίτερος	φιλαίτατος

We have also however met some superlatives formed in a different way: ἄριστος (*best/very good*), κάκιστος (*worst/very bad*), κάλλιστος (*most beautiful/very beautiful*), μέγιστος (*greatest/very great*). Associated with these is a different way of forming the comparative:

μείζων = greater, bigger

		masculine/feminine	*neuter*
sg	nom	μείζων	μεῖζον
	acc	μείζον-α (*or* μείζω)	μεῖζον
	gen	μείζον-ος	μείζον-ος
	dat	μείζον-ι	μείζον-ι
pl	nom	μείζον-ες (*or* μείζους)	μείζον-α (*or* μείζω)
	acc	μείζον-ας (*or* μείζους)	μείζον-α (*or* μείζω)
	gen	μειζόν-ων	μειζόν-ων
	dat	μείζοσι(ν)	μείζοσι(ν)

This is similar in declension to an active participle (e.g. παύων) but:
   (a) there is no separate feminine (it is 3-3, not 3-1-3)
   (b) the stem ends in -ον, not -οντ
The dative plural undergoes the telescoping which we have seen in many third declension words. With these comparatives however this principle can operate in other parts too: the alternative forms shown in brackets represent the effect of the nu dropping out, and the remaining vowels contracting:
   -ονα becomes -οα becomes -ω
   -ονες becomes -οες becomes -ους
(the accusative plural simply follows the nominative rather than creating its own contracted form). These contracted forms need particular care (μείζω might be mistaken for a verb; μείζους might be mistaken for accusative plural of second declension).

A number of very common adjectives (in most cases you have already met the positive) form their comparative like this, along with the associated superlative:

positive		*comparative*	*superlative*
ἀγαθός	good	ἀμείνων	ἄριστος
	or	βελτίων	βέλτιστος*
αἰσχρός	shameful	αἰσχίων	αἴσχιστος
ἐχθρός	hostile	ἐχθίων	ἔχθιστος
ἡδύς	sweet	ἡδίων	ἥδιστος
κακός	bad	κακίων	κάκιστος
	or	χείρων	χείριστος*
καλός	fine, beautiful	καλλίων	κάλλιστος
μέγας	great	μείζων	μέγιστος
ὀλίγος	small amount	ἐλάσσων	ἐλάχιστος
πολύς	much	πλείων †	πλεῖστος
ῥάδιος	easy	ῥάων	ῥᾷστος
ταχύς	quick	θάσσων	τάχιστος

* the alternative forms have particular shades of meaning: βελτίων βέλτιστος is used of moral virtue (rather than efficiency or excellence); χείρων χείριστος implies *inferior*

† a shorter form πλέων is also found

The following are more common in the plural:

ὀλίγοι	few	ἐλάσσονες	ἐλάχιστοι
πολλοί	many	πλείονες	πλεῖστοι

As we have seen repeatedly, the commonest words are often the most irregular. This means they quickly become familiar. There is however a full list in the Reference Grammar, where forms can be checked.

• Comparatives are (as we saw in Chapter 7) normally followed by ἤ = *than* and another noun (the things being compared both in the same grammatical case), or (without ἤ) by a genitive of comparison. Sometimes however comparatives are used without a comparison actually expressed. In such cases (where a comparison is merely implied), alternative translations of the comparative are often appropriate: e.g.

> rather easy   (*implying* easier than average)
> too easy   (*implying* easier than required in the situation)

• The rules about the formation of adverbs which we met in Chapter 3 (positive ending in -ως) and Chapter 7 (comparative = neuter singular, and superlative = neuter plural, of corresponding adjective) apply here too:

e.g.	ῥᾳδίως	ῥᾷον	ῥᾷστα
	easily	more easily	most easily

• Note the following adverbs:

μάλα	μᾶλλον	μάλιστα
very	more, rather	especially, very much

ἥκιστα
least, not at all

• A very important idiom is the use of ὡς with a superlative (though this can be done with the adjective, it is normally found with the adverb):

> ὡς τάχιστα   as quickly as possible

• Note that the familiar adverbs ὕστερον = *later* and πρότερον = *earlier, previously* are in origin comparatives.

• The adjective ἴσος = *equal* (mentioned above for its slightly irregular comparative ἰσαίτερος) has an associated adverb ἴσως whose use involves an important idiom: ἴσως *can* be used simply to mean *equally*, but it very commonly means *perhaps* or *probably* (the thought behind this being that it is *equally* likely that something is or is not the case).

Exercise 10.18

Translate into English:

1   ὅδε ὁ ἵππος ἴσως ἐστὶ θάσσων ἐκείνου.
2   ἆρα οἱ πολέμιοι ἐν τῷ πολέμῳ αἴσχιον ἔπραξαν ἢ οἱ ἡμέτεροι
     σύμμαχοι;
3   οἶδα τὴν τῆς κόρης φωνὴν ἡδίστην οὖσαν.
4   τὸ τοῦ δούλου ἔργον φαίνεται ῥᾷον εἶναι.
5   πλείονες στρατιῶται ἡμῖν εἰσιν ἢ τοῖς Ἀθηναίοις.
6   ὁ γέρων σῖτον ἐλάχιστον εἶχεν.
7   ἡ νέα οἰκία μείζων ἐστὶ τῆς ἀρχαίας.
8   ὁ διδάσκαλος καλῶς μὲν λέγει, κάλλιστα δὲ γράφει.
9   τὸ τοῦ βασιλέως ναυτικὸν χεῖρόν ἐστι τοῦ ὑμετέρου.
10   τίς τῶν ῥητόρων βέλτιστός ἐστιν;

Exercise 10.19

Translate into Greek:
1   The temple of the god is very beautiful.
2   This book is bigger than all the others.
3   The boys ran away as quickly as possible.
4   Those women will probably hear the shouts more easily than the old man (will).
5   I know that you have the finest of the prizes, young man.

156

Exercise 10.20

Periander and Thrasybulus

Tyrants in different Greek cities had a network of connections for mutual benefit. The son of a tyrant often had a hard time when he succeeded his father: the original tyrant may have won and held power by personal qualities the son did not share, and to pass on power to him made the regime look uncomfortably like an old-fashioned hereditary monarchy. Many tyrannies therefore did not last beyond a second generation. Here Periander (whom we have already met as host to Arion) early in his reign receives some advice from the established tyrant of Miletus.

ὁ δὲ <u>Κύψελος</u> ὁ τῆς <u>Κορίνθου</u> <u>τύραννος</u> ἀπέθανεν ἄρξας πολλὰ ἔτη. ὁ δὲ
υἱὸς αὐτοῦ, <u>Περίανδρος</u> ὀνόματι, πρῶτον μὲν τοῦ πατρὸς <u>ἠπιώτερος</u>
ἐφαίνετο εἶναι, ἔπειτα δὲ πολλῷ κακίων ἐγένετο. ἄγγελον γὰρ <u>ὡς</u>
<u>Θρασύβουλον</u> τὸν τῆς <u>Μιλήτου</u> τύραννον πέμψας ἐπυνθάνετο <u>ὅπως</u>
5   ἄριστα τύραννός τις οἷός τ' ἐστὶ τὰ τῆς πόλεως πράσσειν. ὁ οὖν
Θρασύβουλος τὸν παρὰ τοῦ Περιάνδρου ἐλθόντα ἐκ τῆς πόλεως ἐξήγαγεν
εἰς ἀγρόν τινα <u>ἐσπαρμένον</u>. καὶ διὰ τοῦ ἀγροῦ <u>βαδίζων</u>, ὁ Θρασύβουλος
<u>ἔκοπτε</u> τοὺς <u>ὑπερέχοντας</u> τῶν <u>σταχύων</u>, ὥστε πάντες διεφθάρησαν. οὐδὲν
μέντοι λόγοις ἀπεκρίνατο.

10   ὁ οὖν ἄγγελος μάλιστα θαυμάζων εἰς τὴν Κόρινθον <u>ἐπανῆλθεν</u>. καὶ ὁ
Περίανδρος αὐτῷ ἀφικομένῳ "ἆρ' οὐκ, ὦ ἄνθρωπε," ἔφη, "ἀγαθὰ ἀγγελεῖς
μοι;" ὁ δὲ εἶπεν ὅτι νομίζει τὸν Θρασύβουλον, ὡς τούς τε ἑαυτοῦ
στάχυας διαφθείραντα καὶ οὐδὲν ἀποκριναμένον, σαφῶς <u>μαίνεσθαι</u>. ὁ
μέντοι Περίανδρος, ἀκούσας τὸν Θρασύβουλον ταῦτα τὰ δεινὰ πράξαντα,
15   καίπερ τοῦ ἀγγέλου ἀποροῦντος, εὐθὺς αὐτὸς ᾔσθετο τί χρὴ ποιεῖν. ὁ γὰρ
Θρασύβουλος, ὡς σαφέστατα ἐπύθετο, παρῄνει αὐτῷ ἀποκτεῖναι τοὺς
ὑπερέχοντας τῶν πολιτῶν, ὡς παύσοντι αὐτοὺς ὕστερον ἐχθροὺς γένεσθαι.
μετὰ δὲ ταῦτα ὁ Περίανδρος, τοῖς τοῦ Θρασυβούλου λόγοις πειθόμενος,
ἐκείνους τοὺς πολίτας ὡς τάχιστα ἀπέκτεινεν.

	Κύψελος -ου ὁ	Cypselus
	Κόρινθος -ου ἡ	Corinth
	τύραννος -ου ὁ	tyrant
	Περίανδρος -ου ὁ	Periander
	ἤπιος -α -ον	mild
	ὡς	(*as prep + acc*) to (a person)
	Θρασύβουλος -ου ὁ	Thrasybulus
	Μίλητος -ου ὁ	Miletus (*Greek city in modern Turkey*)
	ὅπως	how
5	ἐσπαρμένος -η -ον	with a standing crop
	βαδίζω	I walk
	κόπτω	I cut, I knock off
	ὑπερέχω	I stick up, I stand out
	στάχυς -υος ὁ	ear of corn
10	ἐπανέρχομαι ἐπανῆλθον	I return, I go back
	μαίνομαι	I am mad

157

Prepositions

We have met a considerable number of prepositions since Chapter 1. The following points should be familiar:

(a) prepositions take the accusative, genitive, or dative case (and some can take more than one of these)

(b) prepositions make more specific a meaning or flavour which the case has already:

with the accusative - motion towards or through
with the genitive - separation, going away from
with the dative - rest, staying put

(not every example fits this pattern neatly or obviously, but it is a good general guide)

(c) many prepositions are also found as prefixes in compound verbs

A good illustration of all this is provided by παρά, the basic meaning of which is *beside*:

παρά + acc	- literally *to beside*, i.e. *into the presence of* (or *before* in the sense *he was brought before the king*); but also *to a position beside* (rather than hitting the target itself), hence *contrary to*
παρά + gen	- literally *from beside*, used particularly for *from* a person
παρά + dat	- literally *(resting) beside*, used for *position*
παραβαίνω	- literally *I go beside*, i.e. I pass, go beyond, hence *transgress*

• Some words can be either adverbs (with a verb, and telling you for example where or when something happened) or prepositions (with a noun). In this category are ἐγγύς = *near* (which you met in Chapter 5) and ἅμα = *at the same time (as)*.

The following table shows the common meanings with the different cases of all the common prepositions (you have seen one or more usages of most of them already):

preposition	+ acc	+ gen	+ dat
ἅμα			at the same time as
ἀνά	up		
ἄνευ		without	
ἀντί		instead of, opposite	
ἀπό		from, away from	
διά	on account of, because of	through	
ἐγγύς		near	
εἰς, ἐς	into, onto, to		
ἐκ, ἐξ	out of		
ἐν			in, on, among
ἐπί	against, to, onto, for the purpose of	in the time of	on
κατά	down, throughout, according to	down from	
μετά	after	with	
παρά	to the presence of, alongside, contrary to	from (a person)	beside

158

περί	around	about, concerning	
πλήν		except	
πρό		before, in front of	
πρός	towards, to, against	at the hands of	in addition to
ὑπέρ	beyond, to beyond	above, on behalf of	
ὑπό	under, to under	by (a person)	under
ὡς	to (a person)		

The following special prepositional phrases are worth noting:

ἅμ' ἡμέρᾳ	at daybreak, at first light
δι' ὀλίγου	after a short time
διὰ πολλοῦ	after a long time
διὰ πέντε ἐτῶν	every five years
εἰς καιρόν*	at the right time
ἐκ τούτου	after this, as a result
ἐξ ἴσου	equally
ἐν τούτῳ	meanwhile
ἐπὶ τούτοις	on these terms
καθ' ἡμέραν	daily
κατὰ γῆν	by land
κατὰ θάλασσαν	by sea
κατὰ τοὺς νόμους	according to the laws
μετὰ ταῦτα	after this (lit after these things)
περὶ πολλοῦ ποιεῖσθαι	to regard as important
ὑπὸ νύκτα	just before nightfall

*καιρός -οῦ ὁ   right time, opportunity, occasion

Compound verbs

We have met many compound verbs since Chapter 4. You are expected to be able to work out the meaning of compound verbs using common prefixes (which equate to some of these prepositions). It is not necessary to learn them all individually, nor is it usual to list them all separately: they are in effect formed and used as needed (so for example παρατρέχω is not common enough for it normally to feature separately in vocabulary lists, but if you meet it you should be able to work out easily enough that it means *run beside, run past* hence *outrun, escape* etc).

As well as the obvious meanings (mostly to do with motion or position), there are a few idiomatic usages worth noting: both δια- and ἐκ- are often intensifiers, implying *through* or *out* to a successful conclusion (compare English *wet through, work out*); μετα- as well as meaning *with* (hence μετέχω = *I share*) often implies *change* (compare *metamorphosis*).

Remember that the augment in compound verbs comes after the prefix. It usually displaces a vowel on the prefix (hence ἀπέβαλον), but προ- contracts (hence προὔβην, often written προὒβην), and περί keeps the iota (hence περιέδραμον). Sometimes the Greeks seem to have forgotten that a word was a compound (hence both ἐκάθευδον and καθηῦδον are found as the imperfect of καθεύδω = *I sleep*).

As in other contexts, small adjustments are made in the interest of pronunciation: hence ἐν + βάλλω becomes ἐμβάλλω (but ἐνέβαλον in the aorist, where the change is not needed).

Exercise 10.21

Translate into English:
1   ἐπὶ ἐκείνου τοῦ βασιλέως, εἰρήνη ἦν κατὰ πᾶσαν τὴν χώραν.
2   ὁ γέρων, ὑπὸ δένδρῳ καθίζων, δι' ὀλίγου ἐκάθευδεν.
3   αὗται αἱ παῖδες ἀεὶ εἰς καιρὸν ἀφικνοῦνται.
4   ὁ στρατηγὸς εἶπεν ὅτι ἐπὶ τούτοις ὁ πόλεμος παύσεται.
5   οἱ στρατιῶται ἄνευ ὕδατος ἀνὰ τὸ ὄρος ἀνέβησαν.
6   ὁ τῶν βαρβάρων ἄγγελος παρὰ τὸν δῆμον ὡς τάχιστα ἤχθη.
7   τούτῳ τῷ ἔθνει ἡ βία ἀντὶ τῶν νόμων ἐστίν.
8   οἱ τῶν πολεμίων ἱππεῖς πρὸ τῶν τῆς πόλεως πυλῶν μένουσιν.
9   πολλὰ κακὰ πρὸς τῶν φυλάκων ἐπάθομεν.
10   ἆρ' ἐλπίζετε κατὰ θάλασσαν νικήσειν;

Exercise 10.22

Translate into Greek:
1   These girls ran down from the mountain just before nightfall.
2   New laws are written every five years.
3   The prisoners meanwhile were sent into the prison.
4   The man who fights well and the man who speaks well are honoured equally.
5   After this we always regarded it as important to guard the walls.

Exercise 10.23

Hippocleides dances away his marriage

This story deals with another tyrant, typical in his lavish lifestyle, prestigious victories in the Olympic Games, and concern with marrying his daughter advantageously. But the intended son-in-law proves a rebel. His final words here became proverbial for a devil-may-care attitude.

ὁ <u>Κλεισθένης</u> τοῦ <u>Σικυῶνος</u> <u>ἐτυράννευεν</u>. ἦν δ' αὐτῷ θυγάτηρ καλλίστη, Ἀγαρίστη ὀνόματι. ὁ οὖν πατὴρ ἐβούλετο τὸν ἄριστον πάντων τῶν <u>Ἑλλήνων</u> εὑρεῖν ὡς <u>κηδεστήν</u>. τῶν δ' <u>Ὀλυμπίων</u> τότε γενομένων, ὁ Κλεισθένης ἐνίκησε τῷ ἅρματι τῷ <u>τεθρίππῳ</u>. τὸ οὖν ὄνομα αὐτοῦ ἔτι
5 μεῖζον <u>κατὰ</u> τὴν <u>Ἑλλάδα</u> ἐγένετο. καὶ ἤγγειλε τῷ πλήθει τῷ ἐν τοῖς Ὀλυμπίοις παρόντι, "εἴ τις βούλεται κηδεστής μοι γένεσθαι, δεῖ αὐτὸν εἰς τὸν Σικυῶνα ἀφικόμενον <u>ἀγωνίζεσθαι</u>". πολλοὶ οὖν νεανίαι ἀπὸ τῶν τῆς Ἑλλάδος πόλεων πρὸς τὸν Σικυῶνα προσῆλθον. καὶ ὁ Κλεισθένης <u>δρόμον</u> τε καὶ <u>παλαίστραν</u> τοῖς ἀγωνιζομένοις παρεσκεύασεν.

10 οἱ δὲ νεανίαι ἐν τῷ Σικυῶνι πολὺν χρόνον ἔμενον. καὶ <u>ἥδοντο</u> τοῦτο ποιοῦντες διότι ὁ Κλεισθένης τήν τε θυγατέρα καὶ πολλὰ χρήματα τῷ νικήσαντι ὑπέσχετο. ὁ δὲ <u>τύραννος</u> τοὺς νεανίας περὶ τοῦ γένους, τῆς <u>παιδείας</u>, τῶν <u>τρόπων</u> πολλὰ ἠρώτα, καὶ ἐσκόπει αὐτοὺς ἐν τοῖς ἀγῶσιν. ἐκ δὲ πάντων τῶν παρόντων Ἀθηναῖός τις <u>Ἱπποκλείδης</u> ὀνόματι τῷ
15 Κλεισθένει μάλιστα <u>ἤρεσκεν</u>. τέλος οὖν ὁ τύραννος ἔμελλεν ἀγγελεῖν τὸν νικήσαντα.

	Κλεισθένης -ους ὁ	Cleisthenes
	Σικυών -ῶνος ὁ	Sicyon (*city in north Peloponnese*)
	τυραννεύω	I am tyrant
	Ἀγαρίστη -ης ἡ	Agariste
	Ἕλλην -ηνος ὁ	Greek, Greek man
	κηδεστής -οῦ ὁ	son-in-law
	Ὀλύμπια -ων τά	Olympic games
	τέθριππος -ον	four-horse
5	κατά	(+ *acc*) (*here*) throughout
	Ἑλλάς -άδος ἡ	Greece
	ἀγωνίζομαι	I take part in contests
	δρόμος -ου ὁ	running track
	παλαίστρα -ας ἡ	wrestling ground
10	ἥδομαι	I enjoy (+ *participle*)
	τύραννος -ου ὁ	tyrant
	παιδεία -ας ἡ	education
	τρόπος -ου ὁ	*lit* way, (*pl here*) lifestyle
	Ἱπποκλείδης -ου ὁ	Hippocleides
15	ἀρέσκω	I please, I am pleasing to (+ *dat*)

καὶ βοῦς ἑκατὸν θύσας δεῖπνον μέγιστον τοῖς νεανίαις παρέσχεν. μετὰ δὲ
τὸ δεῖπνον πάντες οἱ παρόντες περὶ τῆς μουσικῆς διελέγοντο. τότε δὴ ὁ
Ἱπποκλείδης, πολὺν οἶνον ἤδη πιών, ἐκέλευσε τὸν αὐλητὴν αὐλῆσαι. τοῦ
20 δ᾿ αὐλητοῦ πειθομένου, ὁ Ἱπποκλείδης ὠρχήσατο.

καὶ ἐδόκει μὲν ἑαυτῷ καλῶς ὀρχεῖσθαι· τῷ δὲ Κλεισθένει οὐδαμῶς
ἤρεσκε ταῦτα πράσσων. καὶ δι᾿ ὀλίγου ὁ Ἱπποκλείδης ἐκέλευσε τοὺς
δούλους τράπεζαν εἰσενεγκεῖν. εἰσελθούσης δὲ τῆς τραπέζης πολλὰ
σχήματα ὠρχήσατο. τέλος δέ, τὴν κεφαλὴν ἐπὶ τὴν τράπεζαν ἐρείσας,
25 τοῖς σκέλεσιν ἐχειρονόμησεν. ὁ δὲ Κλεισθένης, καίπερ οὐδαμῶς τῇ
ὀρχήσει ἡδόμενος ἀλλὰ μάλιστα ὀργιζόμενος, πρῶτον μὲν οὐδὲν εἶπεν.
ἐπεὶ δ᾿ εἶδε τὸν Ἱπποκλείδη τοῖς σκέλεσιν χειρονομοῦντα, οὐκέτι ἑαυτὸν
κατέχειν οἷός τ᾿ ὤν, εἶπεν, "ἀπωρχήσω τὸν γάμον". ὁ δὲ Ἱπποκλείδης
ἀπεκρίνατο, "οὐ φροντὶς Ἱπποκλείδῃ".

	βοῦς βοός ὁ	ox
	ἑκατόν	100
	θύω ἔθυσα	I sacrifice
	μουσική -ῆς ἡ	music
	διαλέγομαι	I have a discussion
	δή	indeed
	αὐλητής -οῦ ὁ	flute-player
	αὐλέω ηὔλησα	I play the flute
20	ὀρχέομαι ὠρχησάμην	I dance
	ἀρέσκω	I please, I am pleasing to (+ dat)
	τράπεζα -ης ἡ	table
	εἰσφέρω εἰσήνεγκον	I bring in
	σχῆμα -ατος τό	dance-figure
	ἐρείδω ἤρεισα	I lean (something), I rest (something)
25	σκέλος -ους τό	leg
	χειρονομέω ἐχειρονόμησα	I gesticulate
	ὄρχησις -εως ἡ	dancing
	ἥδομαι	I enjoy (+ dat)
	κατέχω	I restrain
	ἀπορχέομαι ἀπωρχησάμην	I dance away
	γάμος -ου ὁ	marriage
	φροντίς -ίδος ἡ	concern

Vocabulary checklist for Chapter 10

αἰσχρός -ά -όν	shameful
αἴτιος -α -ον	to blame (for), responsible (for) (+ *gen*)
ἅμα	at the same time (as) (+ *dat, or as adv*)
ἅμ᾽ ἡμέρᾳ	at daybreak, at first light
ἀμείνων -ον (ἀμεινον-)	better (more excellent/more able)
ἀνά	up (+ *acc*)
ἄνευ	without (+ *gen*)
ἀντί	instead of, opposite (+ *gen*)
βέλτιστος -η -ον	best, very good (most virtuous, very virtuous)
βελτίων -ον (βελτιον-)	better (more virtuous)
βοάω ἐβόησα	I shout
γελάω ἐγέλασα	I laugh
δεῖ *imperfect* ἔδει	it is necessary (+ *acc* + *inf*)
δι᾽ ὀλίγου	after a short time, soon
δοκεῖ ἔδοξε(ν)	*lit* it seems good (to X *dat*), i.e. X decides
ἐάω εἴασα	I allow
ἐλάσσονες -α (ἐλασσον-)	fewer
ἐλάσσων -ον (ἐλασσον-)	less, weaker, inferior
Ἑλλάς -άδος ἡ	Greece
Ἕλλην -ηνος ὁ	Greek, Greek man
ἐλπίζω ἤλπισα	I hope (+ *fut inf*)
ἐν τούτῳ	meanwhile
ἐξέστι(ν) *imperfect* ἐξῆν	it is possible (+ *dat and/or* + *inf*)
ἐπί	(+ *acc*) against, to, onto, for the purpose of
	(+ *gen*) in the time of
	(+ *dat*) on
ἐρωτάω ἠρώτησα *or* ἠρόμην	I ask (a question)
ἥκιστα	least (*adv*), very little, not at all
θάσσων -ον (θασσον-)	quicker, swifter
ἱκανός -ή -όν	enough, sufficient
ἴσος -η -ον	equal
ἴσως	perhaps, probably
καθεύδω *imperfect* ἐκαθεῦδον *or* καθηῦδον	I sleep
καιρός -οῦ ὁ	right time, opportunity, occasion
κακίων -ον (κακιον-)	worse
κατά	(+ *acc*) down, throughout, according to
	(+ *gen*) down from
κατὰ γῆν	by land
καθ᾽ ἡμέραν	daily
κοινός -ή -όν	common
κτάομαι ἐκτησάμην	I obtain, I acquire
λοιπός -ή -όν	left, remaining
μάλα	very, very much (*adv*)

μάλιστα	especially, most of all (*adv*)
μείζων -ον (μειζον-)	greater, bigger
μέχρι	as far as (+ *gen*)
νικάω ἐνίκησα	I conquer, I win
νομίζω ἐνόμισα	I think, I consider
οἶδα ᾔδη	I know
ὁράω εἶδον	I see
παρά	(+ *acc*) to the presence of, alongside, contrary to
	(+ *gen*) from (a person)
	(+ *dat*) beside
πειράομαι ἐπειρασάμην	I try
πένης -ητος ὁ	poor man (*or as adj*)
περί	(+ *acc*) around
πλείονες -α	more (*pl*)
πλεῖστοι -αι -α	most, very many
πλεῖστος -η -ον	very much (of), very great
πλείων -ον (πλειον-)	more (*sg*)
πλήν	except (+ *gen*)
πολέμιος -α -ον	hostile
πρό	before, in front of (+ *gen*)
πρός	(+ *gen*) at the hands of
	(+ *dat*) in addition to
ῥᾳδιος -α -ον	easy
ῥᾳστος -η -ον	easiest, very easy
ῥᾳων -ον (ῥᾳον-)	easier
τάχιστος -η -ον	quickest, swiftest, very quick, very swift
τιμάω ἐτίμησα	I honour
ὑπέρ	(+ *acc*) beyond, to beyond
	(+ *gen*) above, on behalf of
ὑπό	(+ *acc*) under, to under
φημί *imperfect* ἔφην	
aorist (less common) ἔφησα	I say
φίλος -η -ον	dear
χείριστος -η -ον	worst
χείρων -ον (χειρον-)	worse, inferior
χράομαι ἐχρησάμην	I use (+ *dat*)
χρή (ἐ)χρῆν	it is necessary
ὡς	(*introducing indirect statement*) that
	(+ *acc*) to (a person)
ὡς τάχιστα	as quickly as possible; as soon as
(75 words)	

164

Chapter 11

Direct and indirect questions: Correlatives

We first met direct questions in Chapter 3. Any sentence can be made into a question simply by adding a question mark, but we saw that open questions (asking whether a statement is true, so that the answer will be *yes* or *no*) are commonly signalled by ἆρα the beginning of the sentence:

> ἆρα ὁ παῖς μῶρός ἐστιν;
> Is the boy stupid?

As we saw in Chapter 8, by adding οὐ after ἆρα (elided to ἆρ' οὐ, and with οὐ changing to οὐκ or οὐχ according to the usual rule) the question is *loaded* to expect or invite the answer *yes*:

> ἆρ' οὐχ ὁ παῖς μῶρός ἐστιν;
> Isn't the boy stupid?
>
> or   Surely the boy is stupid?

With the alternative negative μή, the question is loaded in the other direction, to expect or invite *no*:

> ἆρα μὴ ὁ παῖς μῶρός ἐστιν;
> The boy isn't stupid, is he?
>
> or   Surely the boy isn't stupid?

• The easiest way to remember these is to think of ἆρ' οὐ as *surely* and of ἆρα μή as *surely not*. They correpond respectively to Latin *nonne* (expecting *yes*) and *num* (expecting *no*).

We also in Chapter 3 met direct questions asking for specific information, introduced by one of a number of question words (mostly beginning with π-, where the equivalent Latin words often have *qu-* and the English ones *wh-*, all of which are historically related), for example:

πότε;	when?
ποῦ;	where?
πῶς;	how?

As well as these adverbs, we met in Chapter 5 the question (or *interrogative*) pronoun/ adjective τίς; τί; = *who? which? what?*

Indirect (or *reported*) questions operate in a very similar way to indirect statements using a 'that' clause: the tense of the original direct speech is retained (with adjustment of the English if the introductory verb is past tense). They are most commonly introduced by the verb ἐρωτάω = *I ask* (which we met in Chapter 10), with its alternative aorists: the first (weak) aorist ἠρώτησα and the rather commoner second (strong) aorist ἠρόμην.

• Note the distinction between ἐρωτάω = *I ask (a question)* and αἰτέω = *I ask (for something), I beg*.

Open questions (asking whether a statement is true) are normally introduced by εἰ:

ἠρωτήσω τὸν γέροντα εἰ ὁ παῖς μῶρός ἐστιν.
I shall ask the old man if (or whether) the boy is stupid.

(εἰ is of course the normal Greek word for *if*, used in other contexts too; *if* is perfectly possible in English to represent an indirect question, but *whether* often sounds better).

• Note that the 'loading' of the direct question to expect *yes* or *no* cannot be reproduced in the indirect form: ἆρα, ἆρ' οὐ, and ἆρα μή have all to be represented by εἰ.

• 'Whether' in the question above implies '... (or not)'. If an alternative is actually expressed in an indirect question, Greek uses paired introductory words, either

        εἴτε ... εἴτε   whether ... or
or   πότερον ... ἤ   whether ... or (rather)

(both pairs have similar meaning, except that πότερον ... ἤ tends to imply that the second alternative is more important or likely: *whether X or rather Y*)

ἡ παῖς ἠρώτησεν εἴτε ὁ ἀδελφὸς εἴτε ὁ δοῦλος τὸν ἵππον ἔλυσεν.
The girl asked whether her brother or the slave had released the horse.

ὁ κριτὴς ἐπύθετο πότερον ὁ ἄγγελος αἴτιός ἐστιν ἤ οἱ πέμψαντες.
The judge enquired whether the messenger was guilty or (rather) those who had sent him.

πότερον ... ἤ can in fact be used in a direct question too, but this cannot easily be represented in English: πότερον here just signals that an alternative question is coming
    πότερον οἱ σύμμαχοι πρῶτον ἀφίκοντο ἤ οἱ πολέμιοι;
    Did the allies or the enemy arrive first?

• Most of the question words asking for specific information can (but do not have to) add ὁ-onto the beginning in an indirect question. Hence:

direct question   ποῦ ἐστιν ὁ ἵππος;
                    Where is the horse?

indirect question   ὁ ξένος ἤρετο ὅπου ὁ ἵππος ἐστίν.
                    The stranger asked where the horse was.

• As with indirect statements using a 'that' clause, if the introductory verb in an indirect question is past tense the verb in the indirect question can be put in a form called the *optative* - see Chapter 12. But here too the indicative is often kept, to give a sense of the vividness or immediacy of the original words. It is for a similar reason that the normal π- form of the question word is often preferred to the ὁπ- form which is strictly appropriate for indirect questions.

• Although verbs such as ἐρωτάω and πυνθάνομαι commonly introduce indirect questions, many other verbs can do so. The question need not have been actually spoken, but may be

166

only implied:

βούλομαι γνῶναι ὅπως ἡ τριήρης ἐποιήθη.
I want to know how the trireme was made.

οὔποτε ἠγγέλθη πότερον ὁ αἰχμάλωτος ἔφυγεν ἢ ἀπέθανεν.
It was never reported whether the prisoner ran away or died.

This means that indirect questions are slightly less easy to spot than some constructions, but the presence of an interrogative word usually gives a clue.

Exercise 11.1

Translate into English:
1   ἆρα μὴ πάντα τὸν σῖτον ἐφάγετε, ὦ παῖδες;
2   οὗτος ὁ ἄγγελος ἐρώτα εἰ ἴσμεν περὶ τῶν ἐκεῖ γενομένων.
3   πότερον τόδε τὸ πλοῖον ἄμεινον ἐστιν ἢ ἐκεῖνο, ὦ ναῦτα;
4   ἆρ᾽ ἐπύθου ὁπότε οἱ νέοι στρατιῶται ἀφίξονται;
5   χαλεπόν ἐστι γνῶναι εἰ χειμῶνός ἐστιν ἀσφαλὴς ἡ ὁδός.
6   αἱ ἐν τῇ πόλει ἤροντο ὁπόθεν οἱ σύμμαχοι πέμπονται.
7   αἰτήσω τὸν ῥήτορα εἰπεῖν ὅπως τὴν ἐκκλησίαν ἔπεισεν.
8   πολλοὶ πυνθάνονται εἴτε νομίζω τὸν δοῦλον αὐτὸν εἴτε τὸν δεσπότην
    αἴτιον εἶναι.
9   βούλομαι μαθεῖν πότερον ἱκανά ἐστι τὰ χρήματα ἢ οὐκ, ὦ δοῦλε.
10 ἆρ᾽ οὐ φιλεῖς τὴν λόγοις οὕτω χρωμένην, ὦ νεανία;

* χειμών -ῶνος ὁ = winter (*also, according to context,* storm, bad weather)

NB: third declension nouns with nominative singular ending in -ων can form their genitive in one of several different ways:
(1) -ων -οντος like γέρων and active participles (this is commonest)
(2) -ων -ονος like ἡγεμών
(3) -ων -ωνος like χειμών

Exercise 11.2

Translate into Greek:
1   This woman asked whether I had seen the slave running away.
2   Surely the citizens do not trust that politician?
3   Do you know who wrote the best letter, teacher?
4   The stranger is asking where it is possible for him to find food.
5   I want to find out whether the enemy damaged the fields or the houses.

• As we already saw with the use of τίς/τις, the *question* (or *interrogative*) form *who?/which?* has an equivalent *indefinite* form *someone/a certain*, and they are distinguished by accent). The interrogative adverbs similarly have indefinite forms:

interrogative		*indefinite*	
πότε;	when?	ποτέ	sometime, once, ever
ποῦ;	where?	που	somewhere
πῶς;	how?	πως	somehow, in some way

In fact it is possible to build up whole sets of words.

Hence with a pronoun:

direct interrogative	*Who* escaped?
indirect interrogative	He asked *who* had escaped
indefinite	*Someone* escaped
relative	The man *who* escaped is my brother
demonstrative	*This* man escaped

And with an adverb:

direct interrogative	*When* did the ship arrive?
indirect interrogative	He asked *when* the ship had arrived
indefinite	The ship arrived *sometime*
relative	At the time *when* the ship arrived I was away
demonstrative	The ship arrived *at that time*

These are called *correlatives*. They are formed (apart from a few irregular exceptions) according to a distinct pattern. The words in each set typically begin:

direct interrogative	π-
indirect interrogative	ὀπ-
indefinite	(like the direct interrogative, but with different or no accent)
relative	(drops the π-/ὀπ- of the interrogatives)
demonstrative	τ-

• We have met some of the demonstratives already: τότε, τοιοῦτος, τοσοῦτος, and of course οὗτος (where the τ- is seen after the nominative). Again there is a parallel with Latin (*tum, talis, tantus* etc).

The following table shows the correlatives in common use.

Table of correlatives:
(note how accents affect the meaning)

direct	*indirect*	*indefinite*	*relative*	*demonstrative*
Pronouns/adjectives:				
τίς; who?	ὅστις	τις a certain	ὅς (the one) who	οὗτος (ὅδε, ἐκεῖνος) this (this here, that)
πότερος; which (of two)?	ὁπότερος			ἕτερος one (of two)/the other
πόσος; how big? *plural* how many?	ὁπόσος		ὅσος the size which all those who	τοσοῦτος* so big so many
ποῖος; what sort of?	ὁποῖος		οἷος the sort which	τοιοῦτος* this sort of
Adverbs:				
ποῦ; where?	ὅπου	που somewhere, anywhere	οὗ (the place) where	ἐνθάδε (ἐκεῖ) here (there)
ποῖ; where to?	ὅποι	ποι to somewhere	οἷ to (the place) where	δεῦρο to here
πόθεν; where from?	ὁπόθεν	ποθέν † from somewhere	ὅθεν from (the place) where	
πότε; when?	ὁπότε	ποτέ † sometime, ever, once	ὅτε (at the time) when	τότε then, at that time
πῶς; how?	ὅπως	πως somehow	ὡς how, as, in the way in which	οὕτω(ς) so, in this way

* the more predictable forms τόσος and τοῖος also exist, and are commonly found in early Greek
† because indefinites are *enclitic* (attached closely to the preceding word), the two-syllable indefinites frequently lose their accent in a sentence

• Note especially the use of ὅσοι = *all those who* (equivalent to πάντες οἵ).

• It is important to distinguish τότε = *then (at that time)* from ἔπειτα = *then (next)*.
They correspond respectively to Latin *tum* and *deinde*.

• Exclamations introduced by ὡς = *how ... !* are extremely common; οἷος and ὅσος can also used in exclamations: *What a ... ! What a great ... !*

• ὅστις (the indirect question form of τίς) at first sight resembles the indirect version of other interrogative words by beginning with omicron. But in fact it is the relative pronoun ὅς stuck onto the front of τις, and although it is normally written as one word, both bits of it decline separately. Hence:

		masculine	*feminine*	*neuter*
sg	nom	ὅστις	ἥτις	ὅ τι
	acc	ὅντινα	ἥντινα	ὅ τι
	gen	οὗτινος	ἧστινος	οὗτινος
	dat	ᾧτινι	ᾗτινι	ᾧτινι
pl	nom	οἵτινες	αἵτινες	ἅτινα
	acc	οὕστινας	ἅστινας	ἅτινα
	gen	ὧντινων	ὧντινων	ὧντινων
	dat	οἷστισι(ν)	αἷστισι(ν)	οἷστισι(ν)

The neuter nominative and accusative singular are usually written as two words to avoid confusion with ὅτι = *that/because.*

• Alternative forms for the masculine and neuter genitive and dative singular and plural (ὅτου, ὅτῳ, ὅτων, ὅτοις) are formed as if from a nominative singular ὅτος (the ὁτ- bit staying the same).

• As noted above, indirect questions can be difficult to spot because the question may be only implied, in which case there is no verb of asking. *I will ask who the stranger is* is obviously an indirect question; but so too is *I know who the stranger is* (because it means *I know* [the answer to the implied question in my own or someone else's mind as to] *who the stranger is*).

• The sentence *I know who the stranger is* could be translated into Greek literally as:
    οἶδα ὅστις ὁ ξένος ἐστίν.
But note the common idiom whereby the subject of the indirect question is extracted and put before the question in the accusative, as direct object of the introductory verb:
    οἶδα τὸν ξένον ὅστις ἐστίν.
Literally *I know the stranger* (as to the question) *who he is*: the sentence was grammatically complete and could have stopped after *the stranger*, but then an indirect question is tagged on specifying in what regard he is known. This cannot be reproduced in modern English, but Shakespeare (in an identical idiom) often writes *I know you who you are.*

• In addition to its use as the indirect question form of τίς (e.g. *She asked who had done this*), ὅστις is very common as *indefinite* or *generalised* version of the *relative* pronoun ὅς. This is translated *whoever* or *anyone who* (neuter *whatever* or *anything which*). It is used like the ordinary relative pronoun, but when reference is not to a specific person. Contrast:
(i) ὁ δοῦλος ὃς ἐκεῖνον τὸν ἵππον διώκει μῶρός ἐστιν.
    The slave who is chasing that horse is stupid.   (*normal relative*)

(ii) μῶρός ἐστιν ὅστις ἐκεῖνον τὸν ἵππον διώκει.
    Anyone who chases that horse is stupid.   (*indefinite relative*)

170

• Indirect questions and relative clauses can in some contexts seem very similar, and it is significant that in Greek ὅστις can occur in either (the other indirect question pronouns and adverbs can in fact be used in an indefinite relative way too: e.g. ὅπου as *wherever*). Nonetheless they are distinct. Consider the following colloquial saying (characterising, and usually mocking, a stick-in-the-mud attitude):

We know what we like, and we like what we know.

The two halves of this seem parallel, but in fact the first is an indirect question (*we know [the answer to the implied question] what it is that we like*), whereas the second is a relative clause (*we like those things which we do in fact know*).

Exercise 11.3

Translate into English:

1   οὐκ οἶδα ὅστις τὴν ἐπιστολὴν ἔπεμψεν.
2   ὁ διδάσκαλος ἐβούλετο γνῶναι ὁπόσοι τῶν παίδων πάρεισιν.
3   ἆρ' οὐχ οἱ νεανίαι τοσαῦτα ἆθλα ἐκτήσαντο ὥστε ὑπὸ πάντων
       θαυμάζεσθαι;
4   χαλεπόν ἐστι πυθέσθαι ὁπόθεν ἡ νόσος ἤρξατο καὶ ὅπως.
5   ποῖ φεύγεις, ὦ δοῦλε, καὶ διὰ τί;
6   ἆρα μὴ ἡ παῖς τοιαύτη ἐστὶν ὥστε ταῦτα πράσσειν;
7   τοσοῦτοι τότε ἀφίκοντο ὥστ' οὐχ οἷοι τ' ἦμεν μαθεῖν ὁπόθεν
       ἦλθον.
8   ἆρ' ὅδε ἐστὶν ὁ τόπος οὗ ἡ συμφορὰ ἐγένετο;
9   ὁ στρατιώτης ξίφος ἔχει οἷον οὔποτε πρότερον εἶδον.
10 καίπερ εἰδὼς οὔτε ὅπως οὔτε ὁπότε ταῦτα τὰ τείχη ἐποιήθη, νομίζω
       αὐτὰ ὑπ' ἀνθρώπων πως ποιηθῆναι.

Exercise 11.4

Translate into Greek:

1   What sort of food do you like, children?
2   The old man asked the stranger where the temple was.
3   Who are those slaves, and where are they running to?
4   Does the judge know how many of the women helped the man guarding the gate?
5   From where did these slaves whom I saw in the marketplace come?

Present and aorist subjunctive

As well as the indicative, used to express *facts*, verbs in Greek (like Latin and other languages) have a *subjunctive* form (or *mood*). This has a number of jobs, but essentially it expresses a *proposition* or *possibility*, often represented in English by a translation such as *may*.

The forms of the subjunctive are extremely simple. Only present and aorist forms are in common use (differentiated by *aspect*: present for a general proposition, aorist if the reference is to one occasion). There are just two sets of endings for all subjunctives. These are simply versions of the normal primary active and middle/passive endings with lengthened vowel (if the vowel is long already, it just stays the same). Hence:

		active		middle/passive (except aorist passive*)	
		indicative	subjunctive	indicative	subjunctive
sg	1	-ω	-ω	-ομαι	-ωμαι
	2	-εις	-ῃς	-ῃ**	-ῃ
	3	-ει	-ῃ	-εται	-ηται
pl	1	-ομεν	-ωμεν	-ομεθα	-ωμεθα
	2	-ετε	-ητε	-εσθε	-ησθε
	3	-ουσι(ν)	-ωσι(ν)	-ονται	-ωνται

** the indicative has the alternative ending -ει, but the subjunctive must always be -ῃ

* The aorist passive uses the *active* subjunctive endings on its distinctive stem.

• Note that (as also happens for example in alpha contraction) iota becomes subscript, and upsilon simply disappears.

• Ambiguous forms have to be determined from context.

• The various subjunctive forms are made up using these endings on the appropriate stem (by the familiar building-block method) in a predictable way. As indicated above, the aorist passive uses the active endings: this is of course consistent with its indicative (ἐπαύσθην, like a root aorist active such as ἔβην) and its participle (παυσθείς, 3-1-3 in declension like an active participle such as παύων). Hence:

present subjunctive

		active	middle/passive
sg	1	παύ-ω	παύ-ωμαι
	2	παύ-ῃς	παύ-ῃ
	3	παύ-ῃ	παύ-ηται
pl	1	παύ-ωμεν	παυ-ώμεθα
	2	παύ-ητε	παύ-ησθε
	3	παύ-ωσι(ν)	παύ-ωνται

aorist subjunctive

		active	middle	passive
sg	1	παύσ-ω	παύσ-ωμαι	παυσθ-ῶ
	2	παύσ-ῃς	παύσ-ῃ	παυσθ-ῇς
	3	παύσ-ῃ	παύσ-ηται	παυσθ-ῇ
pl	1	παύσ-ωμεν	παυσ-ώμεθα	παυσθ-ῶμεν
	2	παύσ-ητε	παύσ-ησθε	παυσθ-ῆτε
	3	παύσ-ωσι(ν)	παύσ-ωνται	παυσθ-ῶσι(ν)

Exercise 11.7 (Revision)

Translate into English:

1 τούτῳ τῷ ῥήτορι μηδαμῶς πιστεύσητε, ὦ πολῖται.
2 πόσας ναῦς ἔπεμψαν οἱ Ἀθηναῖοι;
3 ὑπὲρ τῆς πατρίδος ἀεὶ ἀνδρειότατα μαχώμεθα, ὦ φίλοι.
4 ἠρώτησα τὸν στρατηγὸν ὁπόσους στρατιώτας ἄγει καὶ ὁποῖα ἔπαθον.
5 μὴ κρύψῃς τὸν χρυσόν, ὦ δοῦλε.
6 σοφός ἐστι πᾶς ὅστις τοῖς νόμοις πείθεται.
7 ἆρ᾽ οἶσθα ἐκεῖνον τὸν ξένον ὅστις ἐστίν;
8 λυσώμεθα τοὺς ὑπὸ τῶν πολεμίων ληφθέντας.
9 ἆρα μὴ ἀληθῆ ἐστι τὰ ὑπὸ τοῦ ἀγγέλου λεχθέντα;
10 οἶδα σὲ ὅπως ἀνδρεῖος εἶ.

Use of the subjunctive (2): Purpose clauses

We saw in Chapter 6 that the future participle (particularly when preceded by ὡς) can be used to express purpose: *they arrived (as) being about to do X = they arrived in order to do X*.

Purpose can also be expressed (and this in fact is the commoner, standard method) by a clause introduced by ἵνα = *in order to* (less often ὅπως, with the same meaning). The verb in this clause is commonly subjunctive.

e.g.   οἱ ξένοι πάρεισιν ἵνα τὴν πόλιν ἴδωσιν.
     The foreigners are here in order to (*literally* in order that they may) see the city.
(notice again *aorist* subjunctive because the reference is to one occasion)

A negative purpose clause has ἵνα μή = *in order not to*:
     οἱ ναῦται φεύγουσιν ἵνα μὴ ὑπὸ τοῦ γίγαντος ληφθῶσιν.
     The sailors are running away in order not to (*literally* in order that they may not)
     be captured by the giant.
The use of μή (rather than οὐ) here is in line with its general application to possibilities rather than facts.

• Note that Latin likewise uses the 'non-factual' negative *ne* rather than *non* in purpose clauses, but uses it instead of *ut* (= in order to). Greek uses μή <u>as well as</u> ἵνα.

If the main verb of the sentence is in the present or future, the verb in the ἵνα clause will *always* be subjunctive. If the main verb is in the past, the verb in the ἵνα clause can instead be in a form called the *optative* (see Chapter 12), but in fact is commonly subjunctive here too, on the principle (which we have seen in other contexts) of *vividness*, of retaining the immediacy of the intention the people had at the time. Remember that the subjunctive is formed from the *primary* endings, i.e. those normally used for present and future tenses. This *primary* flavour is part of its meaning (regardless of whether the subjunctive is present or aorist: the aorist, used by aspect, has of course no reference to the past here).

• A purpose clause may have the same subject as the main clause, or a new one (normally put in, and of course in the nominative; but sometimes indicated simply by a change of person ending).

• The use of ὅπως with the subjunctive in a purpose clause (= *in order to*) must be carefully distinguished from its use in an indirect question (= *how*).

There is not a great distinction of meaning between the two constructions for expressing purpose (ὡς + future participle, and ἵνα + subjunctive), but the participle version tends to be used for an assumed purpose, rather than one known for a fact:

> ἤκουον ὡς χρήσιμόν τι μαθησόμενοι.
> They were listening in order to learn someting useful.
> (*implying* at least I presume that is why they were doing it)

• Note that (contrary to what might be assumed from English) the infinitive is not normally used in Greek (or in Latin) to express purpose.

Exercise 11.8

Translate into English:
1   οἱ πολῖται μένουσιν ἵνα τοῦ ῥήτορος ἀκούσωσιν.
2   οἱ δοῦλοι ἐπέμφθησαν ἵνα τὰ δένδρα κόψωσιν.
3   τὸν ποταμὸν διέβημεν ἵνα ἐκ τοῦ κινδύνου φύγωμεν.
4   ἆρ' ἀεὶ τρέχετε ἵνα ἆθλα φέρησθε, ὦ νεανίαι;
5   βοηθήσατε ἡμῖν, ὦ σύμμαχοι, ἵνα μὴ ὑπὸ τῶν πολεμίων ληφθῶμεν.
6   οὗτος ὁ δοῦλος πάρεστιν ὅπως κολάσθη.
7   πάντες οἱ στρατιῶται μάχονται ὡς τὴν πατρίδα σώσοντες.
8   ἀεὶ τὸ ἀληθὲς λέγε, ἵνα πάντες πιστεύωσί σοι.
9   τοὺς τοῦ διδασκάλου λόγους ἀκούωμεν ἵνα σοφοὶ γιγνώμεθα.
10   δεῖ ἡμᾶς ἡγεμόνα ἔχειν, ἵνα φαίνῃ ἡμῖν τὴν ὁδόν.

Exercise 11.9

Translate into Greek:
1   I am sending these gifts in order to honour the god.
2   The allies are here in order to help us.
3   Let us march to the city to attack the enemy.
4   We sent a messenger in order to ransom the prisoners.
5   We are guarding the women so that they may be safe.

Exercise 11.10

Rhampsinitus and the Thieves (1)

This is one of the best and most famous stories in Herodotus. It forms part of his long account of Egypt (introduced at the point when the Persians invade it). Herodotus is recounting what he says he heard from Egyptian priests about the history of their country: the story of Rhampsinitus comes immediately after the account of Helen never really going to Troy. Despite its ostensible source, the story shows an entirely Greek admiration for cunning intelligence (μῆτις), much in the spirit of the Odyssey.

ὁ Ῥαμψίνιτος βασιλεὺς τῶν Αἰγυπτίων ποτὲ ἐγένετο. ἦν δὲ τούτῳ
τοσοῦτος πλοῦτος ὅσος οὐδενὶ τῶν μετ᾽ αὐτὸν βασιλέων. βουλόμενος δ᾽
ἀσφαλῶς φυλάσσειν τὰ χρήματα, ἐκέλευσεν οἰκοδόμον τινὰ θησαυρὸν
παρασκευάσαι. ὁ οὖν οἰκοδόμος τῷ βασιλει ἐπίθετο. καὶ ὁ θησαυρὸς
5   μέγιστός τε καὶ κάλλιστος ποιηθεὶς τῷ βασιλεῖ μάλιστα ἤρεσκεν. ἔπειτα
δὲ ὁ Ῥαμψίνιτος τὰ χρήματα ἐν αὐτῷ ἔθηκεν. ἀλλὰ ὁ οἰκόδομος ἕνα
λίθον ἐξαιρετὸν ἐν τῷ τοῦ θησαυροῦ τείχει ἐποίησεν.

καὶ μετὰ πολὺν χρόνον ὁ οἰκοδόμος ᾔσθετο ἀποθανούμενος. ἐκάλεσεν
οὖν τοὺς παῖδας, οὓς δύο εἶχε, καὶ εἶπεν αὐτοῖς, "βουλόμενος μὲν ὑμᾶς
10   βίον ἀγαθὸν καὶ πλούσιον ἔχειν, αὐτὸς δὲ οὐ πολλὰ χρήματα ἔχων, ἐγὼ
ἐβουλευσάμην τάδε". καὶ σαφῶς ἐξηγήσατο αὐτοῖς ὅπως ὁ θησαυρὸς
ἐποιήθη, καὶ ὅπου ἐστὶν ὁ λίθος ὁ ἐξαιρετός· τὰ μέτρα ταῦτα
διαφυλάσσοντες, ταμίαι τῶν τοῦ βασιλέως χρημάτων ἔσονται. ἔπειτα δὲ ὁ
οἰκόδομος ἀπέθανεν.

15   οἱ δὲ παῖδες οὐ πολὺν χρόνον μείναντες πρὸς τὸν θησαυρὸν νυκτὸς
προσῆλθον. καὶ τὸν λίθον τὸν ἐξαιρετὸν ῥᾳδίως ηὗρον. ῥᾳδίως καὶ εἰς
τὸν θησαυρὸν εἰσελθόντες πολλὰ χρήματα ἐξέφερον. μετὰ δὲ τοῦτο ὁ
βασιλεύς, εἰς τὸν θησαυρὸν εἰσελθών, ἐθαύμασεν ἰδὼν τὰ μὲν ἀγγεῖα

	Ῥαμψίνιτος -ου ὁ	Rhampsinitus
	Αἰγύπτιοι -ων οἱ	Egyptians
	πλοῦτος -ου ὁ	wealth
	οἰκοδόμος -ου ὁ	builder
	θησαυρός -οῦ ὁ	treasure house
5	ἀρέσκω *imperfect* ἤρεσκον	I please, I am pleasing to (+ *dat*)
	ἔθηκα	(*irreg aor*) I placed, I put
	ἐξαιρετός -όν	removable
10	βουλεύομαι ἐβουλευσάμην	I plan, I contrive
	ἐξηγέομαι ἐξηγησάμην	I explain
	μέτρον -ου τό	measurement
	διαφυλάσσω	I preserve, I keep in mind
	ταμίας -ου ὁ	steward
15	ἀγγεῖον -ου τό	vessel, jar

177

χρημάτων <u>κατεδεῆ</u> ὄντα, τὰ δὲ τῶν θύρων <u>σήμαντρα</u> οὐδαμῶς
20 διαφθαρέντα.

ἐπεὶ δ' αὐτῷ καὶ <u>δὶς</u> καὶ <u>τρὶς</u> εἰσελθόντι ἀεὶ ἐλάσσω ἐφαίνετο τὰ <u>ἀγγεῖα</u>
(οἱ γὰρ <u>κλέπται</u> πολλάκις ἀφῇρουν), τότε <u>δὴ</u> ἐποίησε τάδε· <u>πάγας</u> τινὰς
<u>ἔθηκε</u> περὶ τὰ ἀγγεῖα ἐν οἷς τὰ χρήματα ἐνῆν. οἱ δὲ κλέπται ἦλθον
ὥσπερ καὶ πρότερον. καὶ ὁ μὲν αὐτῶν, εἰς τὸν <u>θησαυρὸν</u> εἰσελθών, ἐπεὶ
25 πρὸς τὸ πρῶτον ἀγγεῖον προσέβαινεν, εὐθὺς τῇ πάγῃ <u>ἐνείχετο</u>. ὡς δ' ἔγνω
τὸ κακὸν ὁποῖόν ἐστι, τὸν ἀδελφὸν ἐκάλεσε καί, τὰ παρόντα φαίνων,
ἐκέλευσεν αὐτὸν ὡς τάχιστα τὴν κεφαλὴν <u>ἀποτεμεῖν</u>, ὅπως μὴ <u>γνωρισθεὶς</u>
διαφθείρῃ καὶ ἐκεῖνον. ὁ οὖν <u>ἕτερος</u> εὖ τε λέγειν αὐτὸν ἐνόμισε καὶ
πεισθεὶς ταῦτα ἐποίησεν. ἔπειτα δὲ <u>καθαρμόσας</u> τὸν λίθον <u>οἴκαδε</u> ἀπῆλθε,
30 φέρων τὴν τοῦ ἀδελφοῦ κεφαλήν.

	καταδεής -ές	not full, with some missing
	σήμαντρον -ου τό	seal
20	δίς	twice
	τρίς	three times
	ἀγγεῖον -ου τό	vessel, jar
	κλέπτης -ου ὁ	thief
	δή	indeed
	πάγη -ης ἡ	trap
	ἔθηκα	(*irreg aor*) I placed, I put
	θησαυρός -οῦ ὁ	treasure house
25	ἐνέχω	I catch, I hold
	ἀποτέμνω ἀπέτεμον	I cut off
	γνωρίζω *aor pass* ἐγνωρίσθην	I recognise
	ἕτερος -α -ον	the other (of two)
	καθαρμόζω καθήρμοσα	I fit in place
	οἴκαδε	home, homewards

Conditional sentences (1)

The basic pattern for any conditional sentence is: *If X happens, (then) Y happens*. We have
seen several already, using εἰ (the normal word for *if*).

'Open' conditions carry no implication about whether the condition is fulfilled or not. They
can be any tense, and are normally indicative and straightforward to translate:

present:
εἰ ταῦτα λέγει, σοφῶς λέγει.
If he says these things, he speaks wisely.

past:
εἰ ταῦτα εἶπε, σοφῶς εἶπεν.
If he said these things, he spoke wisely.

Similarly it is possible to find
future:
εἰ ταῦτα λέξει, σοφῶς λέξει.
If he says these things (*i.e. in the future*), he will speak wisely.

Notice however that in this example, English has a 'hidden future' in the first half.
In a rather similar way, Greek very commonly expresses the first half of a future condition
with a distinctive idiom, using (instead of the future indicative, as above) a subjunctive
(determined as usual by aspect, not tense), and a special word for *if* - ἐάν:

ἐάν ταῦτα λέξῃ, σοφῶς λέξει.
If he says these things (*i.e. in the future*), he will speak wisely.

This use of the subjunctive is in line with other constructions where the subjunctive
expresses something *indefinite* or a *possibility*: this construction emphasises that the future is
by its nature indefinite.

In contrast, the type of open future condition using εἰ and the future indicative stresses the
unavoidable nature of the consequence, so it tends to be found in threats and warnings:
εἰ ταῦτα λέξει, ἀποθανεῖται.
If he says these things (*i.e. in the future*), he will die.

All these conditions are *open* (as distinct from the type where fulfilment is implied to be
unlikely, or already ruled out: *If X had happened, Y would have happened*, implying *but in
fact ...* : these, signalled by the appearance of *would* in English, are dealt with in Chapter 12).
However the sense in which they are open varies with the tense. A *future* open condition is
fully and genuinely open: *X may or may not happen, but if and when it does, Y will follow.*
Clearly a *past* condition cannot be open in this sense. We cannot go back and change the
events; what is *open* or unresolved is just the speaker's knowledge: *I don't know whether you
did X or not, but if you did (it necessarily follows that) you did something stupid.* This type
of condition could therefore also be called past *unknown*. A *present* open condition can also
be *unknown* in this way, especially if it refers to something habitual (*If you are working for
five hours every evening, you are doing too much*); or it can simply state an axiom, a self-
evident truth (*If a number is divisible only by itself or one, it is a prime number*).

• The 'if' clause is technically called the *protasis* (literally *put forward* as a premise), and the
main clause the *apodosis* (literally *giving back*, i.e. providing an answer).

• The protasis usually comes before the apodosis, but (in both Greek and English) can come
after:
σοφώτατός ἐστιν ὁ γέρων εἰ τοιαῦτα λέγει.
The old man is very wise if he says such things.

• It is also possible to mix tenses:
εἰ ἐκείνην τὴν βίβλον διέφθειρας, μῶρος εἶ.
If you destroyed that book (*at some point in the past*), you are stupid (*now/generally*).

179

• It is also possible to replace the apodosis by e.g. an imperative:

εἰ τοιαύτας ἐπιστολὰς πέμπεις, παῦσαι.

If you are sending such letters, stop (doing so)!

• In any type of conditional sentence, the negative in the protasis is μή and in the apodosis is οὐ.

Exercise 11.11

Translate into English:

1   εἰ ὁ ῥήτωρ ταῦτα λέγει, καλῶς λέγει.
2   εἰ πάντες οἱ αἰχμάλωτοι ἐκ τοῦ τειχίσματος ἔφυγον, εὐτυχεῖς ἦσαν.
3   εἰ τὸν ἵππον ἔτι ἔχετε, λύσατε αὐτόν.
4   ἐὰν τὴν παῖδα ἐπαινέσῃς, ἑκοῦσα βοηθήσει σοι.
5   εἰ ὁ στρατηγὸς μὴ σοφός ἐστιν, οὐχ οἷός τ' ἐστὶν σοφῶς βουλεύεσθαι.
6   εἰ πᾶν τὸ ἔργον τῇ πρώτῃ ἡμέρᾳ ἔπραξας, εὐτυχὴς εἶ.
7   μῶροί ἐστε εἰ ταύτην τὴν βουλὴν φιλεῖτε, ὦ πολῖται.
8   εἰ τιμᾷς ἐκείνην τὴν γυναῖκα, τί λέξεις περὶ ταύτης;
9   ἐὰν τὰ αὐτὰ αὖθις λέξῃ, μὴ πιστεύσῃς τῷ ῥήτορι.
10   εἰ ἡ πόλις τοιαῦτα τείχη ἔχει, οὐδαμῶς φοβοῦμαι.

Exercise 11.12

Translate into Greek:

1   If the old man says this, he is foolish.
2   If the citizens waited all night, they were very brave.
3   If that slave is in the house, send him to the marketplace, mother!
4   If you stop the battle, general, we shall never conquer the enemy.
5   If you learned all the words, you are very wise.

Exercise 11.13

Rhampsinitus and the Thieves (2)

ἡμέρας δὲ γενομένης, ὁ βασιλεὺς εἰς τὸν <u>θησαυρὸν</u> εἰσελθὼν μάλιστα
ἠπόρει ὁρῶν τὸ μὲν τοῦ <u>κλέπτου</u> σῶμα ἐν τῇ <u>πάγῃ</u> ἄνευ τῆς κεφαλῆς
λειφθέν, τὸν δὲ θησαυρὸν οὔτ᾽ <u>εἴσοδον</u> οὔτ᾽ <u>ἔξοδον</u> ἔχοντα. πολὺν δὲ
χρόνον ἀπορῶν τί χρὴ ποιεῖν, τέλος <u>κατεκρέμασε</u> τὸν τοῦ κλέπτου νεκρὸν
5 <u>ἔξω</u> τοῦ τῶν <u>βασιλείων</u> τείχους. ἔπειτα δὲ φύλακας ἐκεῖ τάξας ἐκέλευσεν,
ἐὰν ἴδωσί τινα δακρύοντα, <u>συλλαβόντας</u> ἄγειν πρὸς ἑαυτόν. ἡ δὲ τῶν
κλεπτῶν μήτηρ, ἰδοῦσα τὸν νεκρὸν οὕτως φαινόμενον, ἐκέλευσε τὸν
<u>περιόντα</u> παῖδα κτησάμενον <u>οἴκαδε</u> <u>κομίσαι</u> τὸ τοῦ ἀδελφοῦ σῶμα. "ἐὰν
μὴ τοῦτο ποιήσῃς," ἔφη, "ἐγὼ παρὰ τὸν βασιλέα ἐλθοῦσα πάντα λέξω."

10 ἐπεὶ δὲ ὁ υἱὸς καίπερ πολλὰ λέγων οὐκ ἔπεισεν αὐτήν, τέλος
παρεσκεύασεν <u>ὄνους</u> καὶ <u>ἀσκοὺς</u> οἴνου <u>πληρεῖς</u>. ἔπειτα δὲ τοὺς ἀσκοὺς
ἐπὶ τοὺς ὄνους <u>ἔθηκε</u> καὶ ἤλασεν αὐτοὺς πρὸς τὴν πόλιν. ἰδὼν δὲ τοὺς
τὸν νεκρὸν φυλάσσοντας, λάθρᾳ ἔλυσε τοὺς <u>ποδεῶνας</u> δυοῖν ἢ τριῶν
ἀσκῶν. <u>ἐκρέοντος</u> δὲ τοῦ οἴνου, ἐβόα καὶ τὴν κεφαλὴν <u>ἔκοπτεν</u>, ὥσπερ
15 ἀπορῶν τί χρὴ ποιεῖν. οἱ δὲ φύλακες, ἰδόντες πολὺν οἶνον <u>ῥέοντα</u>,
<u>συνέτρεχον</u> εἰς τὴν ὁδὸν <u>ἀγγεῖα</u> ἔχοντες, καὶ ἐπειρῶντο ὡς πλεῖστον
συλλέγειν.

	θησαυρός -οῦ ὁ	treasure house
	κλέπτης -ου ὁ	thief
	πάγη -ης ἡ	trap
	εἴσοδος -ου ἡ	entrance
	ἔξοδος -ου ἡ	exit
	κατεκρέμασα	(irreg aor) I hung up
5	ἔξω	outside (+ gen)
	βασίλεια -ων τά	palace
	συλλαμβάνω συνέλαβον	I seize, I arrest
	περίειμι	I survive
	οἴκαδε	home, homewards
	κομίζω ἐκόμισα	I fetch
10	ὄνος -ου ὁ	donkey
	ἀσκός -οῦ ὁ	wine-skin
	πλήρης -ές	full
	ἔθηκα	(irreg aor) I placed, I put
	ποδεών -ῶνος ὁ	neck
	ἐκρέω	I flow out
	κόπτω	I hit, I strike
15	ῥέω	I flow
	συντρέχω	I run together
	ἀγγεῖον -ου τό	vessel, jar

ὁ δὲ κλέπτης πρῶτον μὲν ὀργὴν προσποιούμενος ἐλοιδόρει τοὺς φύλακας.
ἔπειτα δέ, τῶν φυλάκων γελώντων καὶ κελευόντων αὐτὸν μὴ φροντίζειν,
20 προσεποιήσατο καὶ παύσασθαι τῆς ὀργῆς. τοὺς οὖν ὄνους ἐκ τῆς ὁδοῦ
ἐξελάσας ἀσκὸν ἕνα τοῖς φύλαξιν ἔδωκε, καὶ ὕστερον ἄλλον. πολὺν δ᾽
οἶνον πιόντες οἱ φύλακες ἐμεθύσθησαν· καὶ τέλος ὕπνῳ ἐκρατήθησαν.
ὁ οὖν κλέπτης, νυκτὸς ἤδη γενομένης, οὐ μόνον τὸ τοῦ ἀδελφοῦ σῶμα
κατέλυσεν, ἀλλὰ καὶ ἐξύρησεν ἐπὶ λύμῃ τὰς τῶν φυλάκων παρειὰς τὰς
25 δεξιάς. καὶ οὕτως τὸν νεκρὸν ἐπί τινα τῶν ὄνων ἔθηκε καὶ οἴκαδε
ἤλασε, τὰ ὑπὸ τῆς μητρὸς κελευσθέντα ποιήσας.

ὁ δὲ βασιλεὺς ὁ Ῥαμψίνιτος, ὡς ἤκουσε τὸν νεκρὸν λάθρᾳ κλεφθέντα,
μάλιστα ὠργίσθη. καὶ ἔτι μᾶλλον ἐβούλετο εἰδέναι ὅστις ἐστὶν ὁ τοιαῦτα
μηχανησάμενος. λέγεται δὲ καὶ τόδε, εἰ δὴ πιστόν ἐστιν, ὅτι ὁ βασιλεὺς
30 τὴν ἑαυτοῦ θυγατέρα εἰς πορνεῖον ἔπεμψεν. καὶ ἐκέλευσεν αὐτὴν πάντας
ἄνδρας ὁμοίως δέχεσθαι, ἀλλ᾽ ἑκάστῳ πρῶτον εἰπεῖν τάδε· "ἐγώ σε
φιλήσω ἐὰν λέγῃς μοι τὸ σοφώτατόν τε καὶ ἀνοσιώτατον τῶν σῶν ἔργων".
ὁ δὲ βασιλεὺς εἶπε τῇ θυγατρί ὅτι, εἴ τις τὰ περὶ τοῦ κλέπτου λέξει, χρὴ
συλλαβεῖν αὐτόν.

35 ἡ μὲν οὖν θυγάτηρ ἐποίησε τὰ ὑπὸ τοῦ πατρὸς κελευσθέντα. ὁ δὲ
κλέπτης (ἤκουσε γὰρ διὰ τί ὁ Ῥαμψίνιτος ταῦτα ποιεῖ) ἐβούλετο καὶ

	κλέπτης -ου ὁ	thief
	προσποιέομαι	
	προσεποιησάμην	I pretend
	λοιδορέω	I curse, I insult
	φροντίζω	I worry
20	ὄνος -ου ὁ	donkey
	ἀσκός -οῦ ὁ	wine-skin
	ἔδωκα	(irreg aor) I gave
	μεθύω aor pass ἐμεθύσθην	I make drunk pass I get drunk
	οὐ μόνον ... ἀλλὰ καί	not only ... but also
	καταλύω κατέλυσα	I cut down
	ξυράω ἐξύρησα	I shave
	ἐπί	(+ dat) (here) for
	λύμη -ης ἡ	insult
	παρειά -ᾶς ἡ	cheek
25	ἔθηκα	(irreg aor) I placed, I put
	οἴκαδε	home, homewards
	μηχανάομαι ἐμηχανησάμην	I contrive
	δή	indeed
	πιστός -ή -όν	(here) believable
30	πορνεῖον -ου τό	brothel
	ὁμοίως	alike, in the same way
	ἀνόσιος -ον	wicked
	συλλαμβάνω συνέλαβον	I seize

182

αὖθις τέχναις <u>περιγενέσθαι</u> τοῦ βασιλέως. <u>ἀποτεμὼν</u> οὖν χεῖρα νεκροῦ
τινος <u>προσφάτου</u> εἰς τὸ <u>πορνεῖον</u> εἰσῆλθε ταύτην ἔχων ὑπὸ τῷ <u>ἱματίῳ</u>
κρυφθεῖσαν. καὶ ἡ τοῦ βασιλέως θυγάτηρ τὰ αὐτὰ ἠρώτησεν. ὁ δὲ
40 <u>κλέπτης</u> εἶπεν ὅτι τὸ μὲν <u>ἀνοσιώτατον</u> ἔργον ἐποίησε τὴν τοῦ ἀδελφοῦ
κεφαλὴν ἐν τῷ <u>θησαυρῷ</u> ἀποτεμών, τὸ δὲ σοφώτατον τούς τε φύλακας
<u>μεθύσας</u> καὶ τὸ τοῦ ἀδελφοῦ σῶμα λάθρᾳ <u>καταλύσας</u>. ἡ δὲ τοῦ
Ῥαμψινίτου θυγάτηρ ταῦτα ἀκούσασα ἐπειράσατο <u>συλλαβεῖν</u> τὸν
κλέπτην. ὁ δὲ <u>προύτεινε</u> τὴν τοῦ νεκροῦ χεῖρα. ἡ δὲ παῖς, διὰ τόν τε
45 σκότον καὶ τὴν <u>σπουδὴν</u> οὐ σαφῶς ἰδοῦσα, ταύτην συλλαβοῦσα
ἐνόμισεν ἔχειν τὸν ἄνδρα. ὁ μέντοι κλέπτης αὖθις ἐξέφυγεν.

ὁ οὖν βασιλεύς, ἐπεὶ περὶ τούτων ἤκουσεν, ἐπαύσατο τῆς ὀργῆς. οὕτως
γὰρ ἐθαύμασε τήν τε σοφίαν καὶ τὴν <u>τόλμαν</u> τοῦ ἀνθρώπου. τέλος δὲ
ἀγγέλους πρὸς πάσας τὰς πόλεις πέμψας ὑπέσχετο μεγάλα δῶρα παρέξειν
50 τῷ ταῦτα τὰ <u>θαυμαστὰ</u> ποιήσαντι· οὐκέτι γὰρ ἔδει τοῦτον κολάζεσθαι.
ὁ οὖν κλέπτης, ταῦτα ἀκούσας, ἐπίστευσε καὶ παρὰ τὸν Ῥαμψίνιτον
ἦλθεν. καὶ οὕτως ἐθαύμασε τὸν ἄνδρα ὁ βασιλεὺς ὥστ' <u>ἔδωκεν</u> αὐτῷ τὴν
θυγατέρα.

	περιγίγνομαι περιεγενόμην	I get the better of (+ *gen*)
	ἀποτέμνω ἀπέτεμον	I cut off
	πρόσφατος -ον	recently dead, recently killed
	πορνεῖον -ου τό	brothel
	ἱμάτιον -ου τό	cloak
40	κλέπτης -ου ὁ	thief
	ἀνόσιος -ον	wicked
	θησαυρός -οῦ ὁ	treasure house
	μεθύω ἐμέθυσα	I make (someone) drunk
	καταλύω κατέλυσα	I cut down
	συλλαμβάνω συνέλαβον	I seize
	προτείνω προύτεινα	I hold out
45	σπουδή -ῆς ἡ	haste
	τόλμα -ης ἡ	daring
50	θαυμαστός -ή -όν	wonderful
	ἔδωκα	(*irreg aor*) I gave

Perfect tense

As we saw in Chapter 4 (and in constant use since), the aorist is the normal tense in Greek
for a single action in the past. There is however also a *perfect* tense, used only as a 'true'
perfect, i.e. to stress that *the effects of a past event still continue*. It is virtually equivalent to
a present tense. The distinction is shown by comparing:

    aorist   The allies arrived on the third day (*saying nothing about whether or not they
                 stayed*).
and *perfect*   The allies have arrived (*implying* and are still here).
The second sentence is in effect the same as *The allies are present*. The perfect predictably
therefore counts as a *primary* tense. This means it is categorised with the present and future,

rather than with other past tenses (categorised as *historic*). Thus for example the perfect is always followed by the subjunctive in a ἵνα clause: more will be said about this principle of primary or historic *sequence* in Chapter 12.)

• As was pointed out in Chapter 4, this is different from Latin, where the so-called perfect tense has to do the job of a simple past tense (regarded as historic) as well as the less common job of a true perfect (regarded as primary).

In form however the perfect active tense uses endings similar to those of the first (weak) aorist. These are put onto a distinctive stem: kappa (rather than the sigma of the first aorist) is added just before the ending, and (for verbs beginning with a consonant) the first consonant is *reduplicated* (i.e. repeated, after inserting epsilon). Latin has a few reduplicated perfects (e.g. *cecidi* from *cado* = I fall, *tetigi* from *tango* = I touch).

perfect active

sg	1	πέπαυκ-α		I have stopped
	2	πέπαυκ-ας		you (*sg*) have stopped
	3	πέπαυκ-ε(ν)		he/she/it has stopped
pl	1	πεπαύκ-αμεν		we have stopped
	2	πεπαύκ-ατε		you (*pl*) have stopped
	3	πεπαύκ-ασι(ν)		they have stopped

Note that the endings after the kappa are like those of the first (weak) aorist except in the third-person plural.

The perfect middle/passive (as in the present and imperfect, they have the same form) goes as follows:

perfect middle/passive

sg	1	πέπαυ-μαι		I have ceased *or* been stopped
	2	πέπαυ-σαι		you (*sg*) have ceased *or* been stopped
	3	πέπαυ-ται		he/she/it has ceased *or* been stopped
pl	1	πεπαύ-μεθα		we have ceased *or* been stopped
	2	πέπαυ-σθε		you (*pl*) have ceased *or* been stopped
	3	πέπαυ-νται		they have ceased *or* been stopped

Note that the endings here (apart from the second person singular) are like the normal primary middle/passive ones (-ομαι etc) without the initial vowel of the ending.

• A few of the verbs which (as we saw in Chapter 8) insert a sigma before the aorist passive endings insert it also in the perfect middle/passive (e.g. κεκέλευσμαι).

Perfect participles are predictable: the perfect active (like other active participles) is 3-1-3 in declension (with the neuter as usual a variant of the masculine, and the feminine adding

184

another syllable, in this case -υι-). The middle/passive is (like for example the present middle/passive participle) 2-1-2 in declension, and completely predictable. Note that the reduplication (unlike the augment in the aorist) is retained by the participle.

perfect active participle: πεπαυκώς -υῖα -ός (stem for masculine/neuter πεπαυκοτ-)

		masculine	feminine	neuter	
sg	nom	πεπαυκώς	πεπαυκυῖα-α	πεπαυκός	having stopped
	acc	πεπαυκότ-α	πεπαυκυῖ-αν	πεπαυκός	
	gen	πεπαυκότ-ος	πεπαυκυί-ας	πεπαυκότ-ος	
	dat	πεπαυκότ-ι	πεπαυκυί-ᾳ	πεπαυκότ-ι	
pl	nom	πεπαυκότ-ες	πεπαυκυῖ-αι	πεπαυκότ-α	
	acc	πεπαυκότ-ας	πεπαυκυί-ας	πεπαυκότ-α	
	gen	πεπαυκότ-ων	πεπαυκυι-ῶν	πεπαυκότ-ων	
	dat	πεπαυκόσι(ν)	πεπαυκυί-αις	πεπαυκόσι(ν)	

perfect middle/passive participle: πεπαυμένος -η -ον (normal 2-1-2)

perfect active infinitive:	πεπαυκέναι
perfect passive infinitive:	πεπαύσθαι

• Because, as we saw above, the perfect middle/passive endings begin with a consonant, adjustments to ease pronunciation need to be made when they are added to a verb stem ending in a consonant. Study of two typical examples illustrates what happens. (Because the changes are predictable, and because perfect passives are relatively uncommon anyway, there is no need to learn every example: there is a list in the Reference Grammar where details can be checked.)

perfect middle/passives of λείπω *and* διώκω:

sg	1	λέλειμμαι	δεδίωγμαι
	2	λέλειψαι	δεδίωξαι
	3	λέλειπται	δεδίωκται
pl	1	λελείμμεθα	δεδιώγμεθα
	2	λέλειφθε	δεδίωχθε
	3	λελειμμένοι εἰσί(ν)	δεδιωγμένοι εἰσί(ν)

Notice that the third-person plural circumvents the problem of adding an unpronounceable -νται to a consonant stem by using the participle (which must of course agree with the subject) with an auxiliary verb. This corresponds to the Latin form of *all* perfect passives (e.g. *portatus sum* = I have been carried [*literally* I am in a state of having been carried]).

• Verbs that begin with an *aspirated* consonant (e.g. theta, phi) reduplicate with the unaspirated equivalent (tau, pi). Hence:

θύω	I sacrifice	*perfect* τέθυκα
φεύγω	I run away	*perfect* πέφευκα

Also in this category but with the peculiarity of dropping the prefix used in other tenses is:

| ἀποθνήσκω | I die | *perfect* τέθνηκα |

• Verbs that begin with the vowel cannot reduplicate (i.e. double the opening sound) in the obvious way those with consonants can. The reduplication of verbs beginning with a vowel is exactly like adding the augment (essentially lengthening the vowel, as we saw in Chapter 9), except that because with a perfect tense the process is technically reduplication (rather than augmentation), the reduplicated form is retained in the participle and infinitive. This can be seen by comparing:

	indicative	*participle*	*infinitive*
aorist (with augment)	ἠρώτησα	ἐρωτήσας	ἐρωτῆσαι
perfect (with reduplication)	ἠρώτηκα	ἠρωτηκώς	ἠρωτηκέναι

• This reduplication with epsilon is also used for verbs beginning with two consonants or a consonant that counts as double, e.g. ζητέω, perfect ἐζήτηκα.

• Any kind of reduplication in compounds comes (like the augment) after the prefix:

ἀποπέπομφα I have sent away

There are two middle/deponent verbs whose present tense is like a perfect middle/passive:

		I am able	I know (how to)
sg	*1*	δύναμαι	ἐπίσταμαι
	2	δύνασαι	ἐπίστασαι
	3	δύναται	ἐπίσταται
pl	*1*	δυνάμεθα	ἐπιστάμεθα
	2	δύνασθε	ἐπίστασθε
	3	δύνανται	ἐπίστανται

participle:	δυνάμενος	ἐπιστάμενος
infinitive:	δύνασθαι	ἐπίστασθαι

• Both these have similar meanings to other verbs we have met already, but δύναμαι (rather than οἷός τ' εἰμί) is particularly used for *have the physical strength to*, and ἐπίσταμαι (rather than οἶδα) is particularly used for *know how to* (hence both are often found with the infinitive).

• Irregular perfect tenses can easily be checked in the Reference Grammar, but here are fourteen common ones which will quickly become familiar:

ἀγγέλλω	I announce	*perfect*	ἤγγελκα
αἱρέω	I take		ᾕρηκα
ἀκούω	I hear		ἀκήκοα
ἀποθνῄσκω	I die		τέθνηκα
γίγνομαι	I become, I happen		γέγονα
γιγνώσκω	I get to know		ἔγνωκα
ἔρχομαι	I come, I go		ἐλήλυθα
λαμβάνω	I take		εἴληφα
λέγω	I say, I speak		εἴρηκα
λείπω	I leave		λέλοιπα
ὁράω	I see		ἑόρακα *or* ἑώρακα
πάσχω	I suffer		πέπονθα

πέμπω	I send	πέπομφα
πίπτω	I fall	πέπτωκα

• Because the present and perfect tenses are so close in meaning, it is not surprising that there is some overlap in form. The irregular verb οἶδα (= *I know*) is, as we noted in Chapter 10, in origin a perfect tense (= *I have seen*): Latin verbs such as *coepi* (= *I begin*) and *odi* (= *I hate*), are roughly comparable (with the form of a perfect tense but the meaning of a present). In Greek there is also one important example the other way round: ἥκω = *I have come* is present tense in form but perfect in meaning, often used instead of ἐλήλυθα as the perfect of ἔρχομαι.

Exercise 11.14

Translate into English:
1   αἱ παῖδες τοὺς νέους λόγους μεμαθήκασιν.
2   ἆρα ὁ στρατηγὸς ἤδη πέπαυκε τὴν μάχην;
3   ὁ ἄγγελος ὁ παρὼν τὰ περὶ τῆς συμφορᾶς ἡμῖν ἤγγελκεν.
4   ἀρ' οὐ περὶ τῆς ἡμετέρας νίκης ἀκηκόατε, ὦ σύμμαχοι;
5   χρήματα πεπόμφαμεν τοῖς πρὸς τῶν βαρβάρων πεπόνθοσιν.*
6   τοὺς αἰχμαλώτους ἐπὶ τούτοις τέλος λελύμεθα.
7   ἀρ' ἐπίστασαι τὴν ὁδὸν ἐν σκότῳ εὑρίσκειν;
8   διὰ τὴν ἀρετὴν τοὺς πολίτας σεσώκατε, ὦ στρατιῶται.
9   δικαίως τετίμηκας τὸν ταῦτα πράξαντα.
10   καίπερ πολλάκις ἠδικηκότες, τὸ ἀληθὲς ἔτι ζητοῦμεν.

* note that, because the perfect is virtually a present tense, a perfect or aorist participle in a sentence with a perfect main verb does not 'move back a tense' in translation (as it would with an aorist main verb)

Exercise 11.15

Translate into Greek:
1   The old man released all the animals.
2   Have you already seen the messenger, citizens?
3   The boys have been chased by the giant.
4   The woman who has asked these things is very wise.
5   Do you know how to escape secretly, soldiers?

Exercise 11.16

Read the following passage and answer the questions below:

Libyans and Pygmies

In the course of his description of Egypt and North Africa, Herodotus tells a story he has heard about some young Libyans who crossed the Sahara and discovered the pygmies who lived around a river which he and his informants presume to be part of the Nile but was probably in fact the Niger.

187

ὁ δ' Ἐτέαρχος, ὁ τῶν Νασαμώνων βασιλεύς, ἄνδρας Λιβυκούς ποτε
ἠρώτησε περὶ τῶν τῆς Λιβύης ἐρήμων. ἤθελε γὰρ γνῶναι πότερον
ἄνθρωποι ἐκεῖ οἰκοῦσιν ἢ οὔ. ἐκεῖνοι οὕτως ἀπεκρίναντο· "νεανίαι τινὲς
τῶν Λιβύων, πολίτων πλουσίων υἱοὶ ὄντες, ὑβριστικῶς ἔπρασσον. διὰ δὲ
5   τοῦτο τοῖς πατράσιν ἔδοξεν ἀποπέμψαι αὐτοὺς ἵνα οἱ μὲν ἄλλοι πολῖται
ἡσυχάζωσιν, οἱ δὲ νεανίαι αὐτοὶ δύνωνται χρήσιμόν τι ποιεῖν. πρῶτον
μὲν οὖν διὰ τῆς οἰκουμένης χώρας ἐπορεύοντο. ταύτην δὲ διεξελθόντες,
ἀφίκοντο εἰς χωρίον ἐν ᾧ ἄνθρωποι οὐκέτι ἦσαν, θῆρες δὲ πολλοί.
ἀσφαλῶς ὅμως διαβάντες, πέντε ἡμέρας τὴν ὁδὸν ἐποιοῦντο διὰ τῶν
10 ἐρήμων· τέλος δὲ δένδρα εἶδον. πρὸς δὲ ταῦτα ὡς τάχιστα προσελθόντες,
ἐλήφθησαν ὑπ' ἀνδρῶν μικρῶν. οὗτοι δὲ πολλῷ μικρότεροι ἦσαν ἢ
πάντα ἄλλα ἔθνη. καὶ δὴ μέλανες ἦσαν. καὶ οὔθ' οἱ Λίβυες οἷοί τ' ἦσαν
μαθεῖν τοὺς λόγους ἐκείνων, οὔτ' ἐκεῖνοι τοὺς τῶν Λιβύων. ἀγαγόντες δὲ
τοὺς νεανίας πρὸς τὴν ἑαυτῶν πόλιν, οἱ μικροὶ αὐτοῖς ἔφηναν τὸν
15 ποταμὸν διὰ τῆς πόλεως διαρρέοντα. καὶ οἱ νεανίαι ᾔσθοντο οὐ μόνον
τοῦτον τὸν ποταμὸν μέγιστον ὄντα, ἀλλὰ καὶ ἐν αὐτῷ νέοντας
κροκοδείλους."

	Ἐτέαρχος -ου ὁ	Etearchus
	Νασαμῶνες -ων οἱ	Nasamonians (*a North African tribe*)
	Λιβυκός -ή -όν	Libyan (*adj*)
	Λιβύη -ης ἡ	Libya
	ἔρημα -ων τά	desert
	Λίβυς -υος ὁ	Libyan, Libyan man
	ὑβριστικῶς	arrogantly
5	ἡσυχάζω	I am quiet, I live in peace
	διεξέρχομαι διεξῆλθον	I go right through
	χωρίον -ου τό	place
	θήρ θηρός ὁ	wild beast
	ὅμως	nonetheless
10	δή	indeed
	μέλας -αινα -αν (μελαν-)	black
15	διαρρέω	I flow through
	νέω	I swim
	κροκόδειλος -ου ὁ	crocodile

(1) What did the king of the Nasamoneans ask the Libyans about
    (lines 1-2)?   (2)
(2) What did he want to find out (lines 2-3)?   (3)
(3) What are we told about the background of the young men, and
    about their behaviour (lines 3-4)?   (3)
(4) For what two purposes did their fathers send them away (lines 4-6)? (4)
(5) What sort of place did they reach after passing through the
    inhabited areas (lines 7-8)?   (2)
(6) How long did they travel through the desert (lines 9-10)?   (1)
(7) What did they then see (line 10)?   (1)
(8) Describe the men who seized them (lines 11-13).   (5)
(9) What happened next (lines 13-15)?   (1)
(10) What did the young men find out about the river (lines 15-17)? (3)
                                                                     (25 marks)

Exercise 11.17
Crocodiles

The confusion between the Niger and the Nile in the story about the Pygmies may have arisen beacuse the Nile was famous for its crocodiles. Herodotus describes the crocodile for Greek readers who had never seen one. He also shows his usual interest in the cultural and religious significance of what he describes, and the different customs in different places.

ἡ τῶν <u>κροκοδείλων</u> <u>φύσις</u> τοιαύτη ἐστίν· τοὺς τοῦ <u>χειμῶνος</u> <u>μῆνας</u>
τέσσαρας ὁ κροκόδειλος ἐσθίει οὐδέν. τέσσαρας δὲ πόδας ἔχων, καὶ ἐν
τῷ ποταμῷ καὶ ἐν τῇ γῇ οἰκεῖ. ἡ δὲ <u>θήλεια</u> <u>τίκτει</u> μὲν <u>ᾠὰ</u> καὶ <u>ἐκλέπει</u> ἐν
τῇ γῇ καὶ ἐκεῖ <u>διατρίβει</u> τὴν ἡμέραν, τὴν δὲ νύκτα πᾶσαν ἐν τῷ ποταμῷ·
5 <u>θερμότερον</u> γάρ ἐστι τὸ ὕδωρ τῆς <u>δρόσου</u>. πάντων δὲ ζῴων περὶ ὧν ἡμεῖς
ἴσμεν ὁ κροκόδειλος ἐξ ἐλαχίστου μέγιστον γίγνεται· τὰ μὲν γὰρ ᾠὰ οὐ
πολλῷ μείζονα τίκτει τῶν τοῦ <u>χηνός</u>· <u>αὐξανόμενος</u> δὲ ὁ κροκόδειλος
γίγνεται καὶ εἰς <u>ἑπτακαίδεκα</u> <u>πήχεις</u> καὶ μείζων ἔτι. καὶ ἔχει ὀφθαλμοὺς
μὲν <u>ὑός</u>, <u>ὀδόντας</u> δὲ μεγάλους· γλῶσσαν δὲ μόνον <u>θηρίων</u> οὐκ ἔχει, οὐδὲ
10 τὴν <u>κάτω</u> <u>γνάθον</u> <u>κινεῖ</u>, ἀλλὰ τὴν <u>ἄνω</u> γνάθον προσάγει τῇ κάτω.

τοῖς μὲν δὴ τῶν <u>Αἰγυπτίων</u> ἱεροί εἰσιν οἱ κροκόδειλοι, τοῖς δὲ οὔχ· οὗτοι

	κροκόδειλος -ου ὁ	crocodile
	φύσις -εως ἡ	nature
	χειμών -ῶνος ὁ	winter
	μήν μηνός ὁ	month
	θῆλυς -εια -υ	female
	τίκτω	(*here*) I lay
	ᾠόν -οῦ τό	egg
	ἐκλέπω	I hatch (something)
	διατρίβω	I spend (time)
5	θερμός -ή -όν	warm
	δρόσος -ου ἡ	dew
	χήν χηνός ὁ	goose
	αὐξάνομαι	I grow bigger
	ἑπτακαίδεκα	seventeen
	πῆχυς -εως ὁ	cubit (*literally* forearm: *unit of measurement*, = *about eighteen inches*)
	ὑς ὑός ὁ	pig
	ὀδούς -όντος ὁ	tooth
	θηρίον -ου τό	wild animal, beast
10	κάτω	(*here*) lower
	γνάθος -ου ἡ	jaw
	κινέω	I move (something)
	ἄνω	(*here*) upper
	Αἰγύπτιοι -ων οἱ	Egyptians

γὰρ ὡς πολεμίοις χρῶνται. οἱ δὲ περὶ τὰς Θήβας οἰκοῦντες τοὺς
κροκοδείλους μάλιστα τιμῶσιν. ἐν γὰρ ἑκάστῃ κώμῃ ἕνα κροκόδειλον
τρέφουσι σίτῳ καὶ τά τ᾽ ὦτα καὶ τοὺς πόδας κοσμοῦσι χρυσῷ. οἱ μέντοι
15 περὶ τὴν Ἐλεφαντίνην οἰκοῦντες καὶ ἐσθίουσι τοὺς κροκοδείλους,
οὐδαμῶς νομίζοντες αὐτοὺς ἱεροὺς εἶναι. ὁ δὲ βουλόμενος κροκόδειλον
αἱρεῖν δελεάζει νῶτον ὑὸς περὶ ἄγκιστρον καὶ εἰσβάλλει εἰς μέσον τὸν
ποταμόν· αὐτὸς δ᾽ ἐπὶ τῆς τοῦ ποταμοῦ ὄχθης ἔχων ὗν ζωόν, τύπτει
τοῦτον. ἀκούσας δὲ τὴν φωνὴν ὁ κροκόδειλος σπεύδει πρὸς τὴν φωνὴν
20 καὶ τὸ νῶτον καταπίνει· οἱ δ᾽ ἐν τῇ ὄχθῃ ἕλκουσιν. πρῶτον δὲ πάντων ὁ
θηρευτὴς πηλῷ καλύπτει τοὺς ὀφθαλμοὺς αὐτοῦ· τοῦτο δὲ ποιήσας ῥᾷστα
ἀποκτείνει τὸν κροκόδειλον.

	χράομαι	(here) I treat
	Θῆβαι -ων αἱ	Thebes (i.e. Egyptian Thebes, not the Thebes in central Greece; = modern Luxor)
	τρέφω	I nourish, I support
	ὦτα -ων τά	ears
	κοσμέω	I decorate, I adorn
15	Ἐλεφαντίνη -ης ἡ	Elephantine (city about 120 miles further up the Nile than Thebes)
	δελεάζω	I put (something) as bait
	νῶτον -ου τό	back
	ὗς ὑός ὁ	pig
	ἄγκιστρον -ου τό	hook
	μέσος -η -ον	middle, middle (part) of
	ὄχθη -ης ἡ	bank
	ζωός -ή -όν	living
	σπεύδω	I rush
20	καταπίνω	I swallow down
	ἕλκω	I pull, I drag
	θηρευτής -οῦ ὁ	hunter
	πηλός -οῦ ὁ	mud, clay
	καλύπτω	I cover

Revision checkpoint

Make sure you know:
• direct and indirect questions, with use of interrogative words and table of correlatives
• present and aorist subjunctive, and use of subjunctive as jussive and in prohibitions
• use of subjunctive in purpose clauses
• open (or unknown) conditions referring to past, present, or future
• perfect tense

Background: Herodotus (2)

At the very beginning of his work, Herodotus traces the origin of the quarrel between East and West (in effect, Asia and Europe) to a series of tit-for-tat snatchings of women (of which Helen is the most famous) by one side then the other. Though 'Persian learned men' are cited as the source for some of these stories, they are in fact typically Greek myths. Herodotus tells them in a tongue-in-cheek way: here as often, he does not commit himself to the truth of everything he records. As we noticed in Chapter 10, he has a clear sense of the difference between traditional tales of this kind and real historical events. In the following short passage 'the first man I myself *know* wronged the Greeks' (as distinct from some hazy figure in a myth) is Croesus, king of Lydia (in modern Turkey) in the mid-sixth century BC.

Croesus was proverbial for his wealth. He clearly fascinated the Greeks. His treatment of them and their attitude to him were both ambiguous. Herodotus introduces him initially as the first eastern aggressor against the Greeks, and thus the forerunner of the Persians (above all their king Xerxes, who led the great expedition against Greece soon after Herodotus was born). It is true that Croesus subdued a number of the Greek cities on the Asia Minor (Turkish) coast. But in many respects he showed favour to the Greeks, and made rich offerings at Greek shrines (especially Delphi). And Croesus was himself eventually the victim of Persian aggression, as we shall see in Chapter 12.

Herodotus was strongly influenced by tragic drama (as well as by Homeric epic). Croesus is seen as a real-life equivalent of the main character in a tragedy, who at the beginning of the story is happy and successful (though often in a dangerously self-satisfied, fate-tempting way), then is brought low (sometimes by his own faults or mistakes or unwitting actions, sometimes by the jealous intervention of a god, sometimes by apparently arbitrary happenings - or by any combination of these things). Herodotus, like many Greek writers, has a strong sense of the instability of human prosperity: things may seem to be going well now, but you can never be sure what is round the corner. Alongside this sense of almost random unpredictability however he also seeks to show that the gods punish wrongdoing sooner or later.

Exercise 11.18

Human Prosperity

οἱ μὲν οὖν μῦθοι οἱ τῶν <u>Περσῶν</u> καὶ τῶν ἄλλων ἀνθρώπων πολλοὶ καὶ
<u>παντοῖοί</u> εἰσιν· ἐγὼ δὲ περὶ τούτων οὐκετι λέξω ὅτι οὕτως ἢ <u>ἄλλως</u> πως
ἐγένετο τὰ λεγόμενα. τὸν μέντοι ἄνθρωπον <u>σημήνας</u> ὃν αὐτὸς οἶδα
πρῶτον τοὺς Ἕλληνας ἀδικήσαντα, <u>προβήσομαι ἐς τὸ πρόσω</u> τοῦ λόγου,
5   καὶ μεγάλα καὶ μικρὰ ἄστη ἀνθρώπων <u>ἐξηγούμενος</u>. τῶν γὰρ ἄστεων ἃ
πάλαι μεγάλα ἦν, τὰ πολλὰ μικρὰ γέγονε· τὰ δὲ ἄστη ἐπ᾽ ἐμοῦ μεγάλα
ὄντα πρότερον ἦν μικρά. τὴν οὖν τῶν ἀνθρώπων <u>εὐδαιμονίαν</u> εἰδὼς
οὐδέποτε ἐν τῷ αὐτῷ τόπῳ μένουσαν, περὶ <u>ἀμφοτέρων</u> ὁμοίως λέξω.

Πέρσαι -ῶν οἱ	Persians
παντοῖος -α -ον	of all kinds
ἄλλως	otherwise, in some other way
σημαίνω ἐσήμηνα	I indicate, I point out
προβαίνω *fut* προβήσομαι	I proceed, I go on
ἐς* τὸ πρόσω	forwards
5 ἐξηγέομαι	I describe
εὐδαιμονία -ας ἡ	prosperity, happiness
ἀμφότεροι -αι -α	both

* note that ἐς is an alternative form of εἰς

Exercise 11.19

Gyges and Candaules

After introducing Croesus, king of Lydia from about 560 until 546 BC, Herodotus plunges further back five generations to Croesus' ancestor Gyges, telling how he seized the throne from Candaules, last of the previous dynasty. Croesus will in due course pay the penalty for the actions of Gyges.

Κροῖσος ἦν Λυδὸς μὲν γένος*, τύραννος δὲ πάντων τῶν ἐθνῶν ἐντὸς τοῦ
Ἅλυος ποταμοῦ, ὃς ῥέων ἀπὸ μεσημβρίας ἐκρεῖ εἰς τὸν Εὔξεινον πόντον.
οὗτος ὁ Κροῖσος πρῶτος τῶν βαρβάρων περὶ ὧν ἡμεῖς ἴσμεν τοὺς μὲν
τῶν Ἑλλήνων κατεστρέψατο εἰς φόρου ἀπαγωγήν, τοὺς δὲ ἐποιήσατο
5   φίλους. πρὸ δὲ τῆς τοῦ Κροίσου ἀρχῆς πάντες οἱ Ἕλληνες ἐλεύθεροι
ἦσαν.

ἡ τῶν Λυδῶν ἀρχή, ὑπ᾽ ἄλλων πρότερον ἐχομένη, εἰς τὸ τοῦ Κροίσου
γένος ὧδε ἦλθεν. οἱ Ἡρακλεῖδαι, τοῦ Ἡρακλέους ἔκγονοι ὄντες,
πεντακόσια ἔτη τῆς Λυδίας ἐβασίλευον, μέχρι τοῦ Κανδαύλου. οὗτος γὰρ
10   ὁ Κανδαύλης τὴν ἑαυτοῦ γυναῖκα μάλιστα φιλῶν ἐνόμιζε πολλῷ
καλλίστην πασῶν εἶναι. ἦν δὲ τῷ Κανδαύλῃ αἰχμοφόρος τις, Γύγης

* 'accusative of respect': *literally* with respect to his race/birth *i.e.* by ~

	Κροῖσος -ου ὁ	Croesus
	Λυδός -οῦ ὁ	Lydian (man of Lydia)
	τύραννος -ου ὁ	ruler (*the Greek word was originally borrowed from Lydian, to describe a distinctive type of ruler*)
	ἐντός	*lit* within (+ gen) *here* on this (*i.e. the western*) side of
	Ἅλυς -υος ὁ	Halys
	ῥέω	I flow
	μεσημβρία -ας ἡ	south
	ἐκρέω	I flow out
	Εὔξεινος	Euxine (*literally* hospitable, *probably as 'apotropaic euphemism' for a wild and hostile place in fact feared;* = *modern Black Sea*)
	πόντος -ου ὁ	sea (*word used for particular named seas*)
	Ἕλλην -ηνος ὁ	Greek
	καταστρέφω κατεστρεψάμην	I subdue
	φόρος -ου ὁ	tribute, tax
	ἀπαγωγή -ῆς ἡ	bringing, payment
5	ὧδε	in this way, in the following way (*adverb from* ὅδε)
	Ἡρακλεῖδαι -ων οἱ	Heraclidae (*lit* children of Heracles)
	Ἡρακλῆς -έους ὁ	Heracles
	ἔκγονος -ου ὁ	descendant
	πεντακόσιοι -αι -α	500
	Λυδία -ας ἡ	Lydia
	βασιλεύω	I am king
	μέχρι	until (+ gen)
	Κανδαύλης -ου ὁ	Candaules
10	αἰχμοφόρος -ου ὁ	spear-carrier, bodyguard
	Γύγης -ου ὁ	Gyges

ὀνόματι. τούτῳ δὲ ὁ βασιλεὺς <u>ἐπέτρεπε</u> τὰ <u>σπουδαιότατα</u> τῶν πραγμάτων, καὶ τὸ τῆς γυναικὸς <u>κάλλος</u> ποτὲ ἐπήνεσεν. οὐ δὲ πολλῷ ὕστερον (χρῆν γὰρ τῷ Κανδαύλῃ γενέσθαι κακῶς) ἔλεξε πρὸς τὸν Γύγην τάδε· "ὦ
15 Γύγη, οὐ δοκεῖς πιστεύειν μοι περὶ τοῦ τῆς γυναικὸς κάλλους λέγοντι. τὰ γὰρ <u>ὦτα</u> τοῖς ἀνθρώποις <u>ἀπιστότερά</u> ἐστι τῶν ὀφθαλμῶν. δεῖ οὖν σε ἰδεῖν αὐτὴν <u>γυμνήν</u>". ὁ δὲ Γύγης ἐβόησεν, "ὦ δέσποτα, τίνα λόγον λέγεις, κελεύων με τὴν <u>δέσποιναν</u> ἰδεῖν γυμνήν; ἅμα γὰρ τῷ <u>χιτῶνι</u> καὶ ἡ <u>αἰδὼς</u> <u>ἐκδύεται</u>. ἐγὼ πιστεύω σοι περὶ τῆς γυναικὸς λέγοντι. μηδαμῶς κελεύσῃς
20 με ἄδικα πράσσειν".

ὁ μὲν οὖν Γύγης ταῦτα εἶπε, μάλιστα φοβούμενος. ὁ δὲ Κανδαύλης ἀπεκρίνατο τάδε· "<u>θάρσει</u>, ὦ Γύγη· μήτ' ἐμὲ μήτε τὴν γυναῖκα φοβοῦ. οὐ γὰρ λέγω ὡς πειρασόμενός σου. πάντα <u>μηχανήσομαι</u> ἵνα ἡ γόνη μὴ μάθῃ ὑπὸ σοῦ ὁρωμένη. δεῖ δέ σε ἐν τῷ ἡμετέρῳ <u>δωματίῳ</u> <u>ὄπισθε</u> τῆς
25 <u>ἀνοίκτου</u> θύρας μένειν. μετὰ δ' ἐμὲ εἰσελθόντα πάρεσται καὶ ἡ γόνη. ἔστι δ' ἐγγὺς τῆς θύρας <u>θρόνος</u> τις. ἐπὶ δὲ τοῦτον τὰ <u>ἱμάτια</u> <u>καθ' ἓν</u> <u>ἕκαστον</u> <u>ἐκδύνουσα</u> <u>θήσει</u>. καὶ ἐξέσται σοι <u>καθ' ἡσυχίαν</u> <u>θεᾶσθαι</u>. τῆς δὲ γυναικὸς <u>ἀποτρεπομένης</u> καὶ ἐπὶ τὴν <u>εὐνὴν</u> ἰούσης, δεῖ σε λάθρα ἐξελθεῖν." ἐπεὶ οὖν ὁ Γύγης οὐχ οἷός τ' ἦν <u>διαφυγεῖν</u>, ἕτοιμος ἦν ταῦτα
30 πρᾶξαι. ὁ δὲ Κανδαύλης, ἐπεὶ ἔδοξε καιρὸς εἶναι, ἤγαγε τὸν Γύγην εἰς τὸ δωμάτιον. καὶ δι' ὀλίγου <u>ἐπανῆλθεν</u> ὁ βασιλεύς, καὶ μετ' αὐτὸν ἡ γυνή.

	ἐπιτρέπω	I entrust something (*acc*) to someone (*dat*)
	σπουδαῖος -α -ον	serious
	κάλλος -ους τό	beauty
15	ὦτα -ων τα	ears
	ἄπιστος -ον	untrustworthy
	γυμνός -ή -όν	naked
	δέσποινα -ης ἡ	mistress
	χιτών -ῶνος ὁ	dress
	αἰδώς -οῦς ἡ	shame, modesty
	ἐκδύω	I take off
20	θαρσέω	I take heart, I cheer up
	μηχανάομαι	I arrange, I contrive
	δωμάτιον -ου τό	bedroom
	ὄπισθε	behind (+ *gen*)
25	ἄνοικτος -ον	open
	θρόνος -ου ὁ	chair
	ἱμάτιον -ου τό	garment
	καθ' ἓν ἕκαστον	one by one
	ἐκδύνω	I take off
	θήσω	(*irreg fut*) I shall place
	καθ' ἡσυχίαν	at leisure
	θεάομαι	I watch
	ἀποτρέπομαι	I turn away
	εὐνή -ῆς ἡ	bed
	διαφεύγω διέφυγον	I escape
30	ἐπανέρχομαι ἐπανῆλθον	I return

καὶ ὁ Γύγης <u>ἐθεᾶτο</u> αὐτὴν εἰσελθοῦσαν καὶ <u>ἐκδύνουσαν</u>. ἐπεὶ δὲ <u>κατὰ</u>
<u>νώτου</u> ἦν τῆς γυναικὸς ἐπὶ τὴν <u>εὐνὴν</u> ἰούσης, εὐθὺς ἐξῆλθεν· ἡ δὲ εἶδεν
αὐτὸν ἐξιόντα.

35 πρῶτον μὲν οὖν ἡ γυνὴ οὐδὲν εἶπε, καίπερ γνοῦσα τὸν Κανδαύλην τοῦ
ἔργου αἴτιον ὄντα. ἐπεὶ δὲ ἡμέρα ἐγένετο, τοὺς πιστοτάτους τῶν δούλων
<u>μεταπεμψαμένη</u>, ἐκάλεσε τὸν Γύγην. ὁ δὲ εὐθὺς ἦλθε κληθείς, οὐδὲν
κακὸν <u>ὑποπτεύων</u>. ἐπειδὴ μέντοι ἀφίκετο, ἡ γυνὴ ἔλεξε τάδε· "νῦν δυοῖν
ὁδῶν παρουσῶν παρέχω σοι <u>αἴρεσιν</u>. ἢ γὰρ τὸν Κανδαύλην ἀποκτείνας
40 ἐμέ τε καὶ τὴν τῆς Λυδίας ἀρχὴν ἔχε, ἢ δεῖ σε ἀποθανεῖν. οὕτως γὰρ
οὐδέποτε αὖθις ὄψῃ τὰ <u>ἀπόρρητα</u>, τῷ Κανδαύλῃ ἄγαν πειθόμενος. δεῖ οὖν
ἕνα ἀποθανεῖν, ἢ ἐκεῖνον τὸν ταῦτα <u>μηχανησάμενον</u> ἤ σε τὸν ἐμὲ
<u>γυμνὴν</u> ἰδόντα καὶ παρὰ νόμον ποιήσαντα." ὁ δὲ Γύγης πρῶτον μὲν
ἐθαύμασε τὰ λεγόμενα, ἔπειτα δ᾽ ᾔτησε τὴν γυναῖκα μὴ ἀναγκάσαι
45 τοιαύτην αἴρεσιν. οὐδαμῶς μέντοι πείσας αὐτὴν ἔγνω ἢ τὸν Κανδαύλην
ἀποθανούμενον ἢ αὐτός· καὶ εἵλετο <u>περιεῖναι</u>. τὴν οὖν γυναῖκα ἠρώτησε
τάδε· "ἐπεὶ ἀναγκάζεις με τὸν δεσπότην ἀποκτεῖναι, εἰπέ μοι ᾧτινι <u>τρόπῳ</u>
τοῦτο ποιήσω". ἡ δὲ ἀπεκρίνατο, "ἐν τῷ αὐτῷ τόπῳ ἔσται καὶ τοῦτο τὸ
ἔργον· δεῖ γάρ σε ἀποκτεῖναι αὐτὸν καθεύδοντα".

50 ἐπεὶ οὖν ταύτην τὴν βουλὴν παρεσκεύασαν, νυκτὸς γενομένης ὁ Γύγης
(οὐ γὰρ ἐξῆν αὐτῷ ἀποφυγεῖν) τῇ γυναικὶ εἰς τὸ <u>δωμάτιον</u> ἕσπετο. καὶ
ἐκείνη, <u>ἐγχειρίδιον</u> παρέχουσα, ἔκρυψεν αὐτὸν <u>ὄπισθε</u> τῆς αὐτῆς θύρας.
καὶ μετὰ ταῦτα τὸν Κανδαύλην καθεύδοντα ἀποκτείνας ἔσχε καὶ τὴν
γυναῖκα καὶ τὴν τῆς Λυδίας ἀρχήν.

55 πολλοὶ μὲν οὖν τῶν Λυδῶν, ὀργισθέντες διὰ τὸν τοῦ Κανδαύλου θάνατον,
ἐν ὅπλοις ἦσαν· ἄλλοι δὲ τὸν Γύγην ἐτίμων. τέλος δ᾽ ἐπὶ τούτοις

	θεάομαι	I watch
	ἐκδύνω	I undress
	κατά	(+ gen) (here) behind
	νῶτον -ου τό	back
	εὐνή -ῆς ἡ	bed
35	μεταπέμπομαι μετεπεμψάμην	I send for
	ὑποπτεύω	I suspect
	αἵρεσις -εως ἡ	choice
40	ἀπόρρητος -ον	forbidden
	μηχανάομαι ἐμηχανησάμην	I arrange, I contrive
	γυμνός -ή -όν	naked
45	περίειμι	I survive
	τρόπος -ου ὁ	way, method
50	δωμάτιον -ου τό	bedroom
	ἐγχειρίδιον -ου τό	dagger
	ὄπισθε	behind (+ gen)

194

ὡμολόγησαν· τῷ ἐν <u>Δελφοῖς χρηστηρίῳ χρήσασθαι</u>, καὶ τοῖς τοῦ θεοῦ
λόγοις πείθεσθαι. καὶ ὁ θεὸς τόν Γύγην εἵλετο· οὕτως οὖν τῆς Λυδίας
<u>ἐβασίλευσεν</u> ὁ Γύγης. πρὸς δὲ τούτοις εἶπεν ἡ <u>Πυθία</u> ὅτι <u>τίσις</u> ἔσται τοῖς
60 Ἡρακλείδαις μετὰ πέντε <u>γενεάς</u>. τούτου μέντοι τοῦ λόγου οἵ τε Λυδοὶ καὶ
οἱ βασιλῆς <u>ὠλιγώρουν</u>, <u>πρὶν</u> <u>δὴ</u> <u>ἐτελέσθη</u>.

	Δελφοί -ῶν οἱ	Delphi
	χρηστήριον -ου τό	oracle
	χράομαι ἐχρησάμην	(*of an oracle*) I consult (+ *dat*)
	βασιλεύω ἐβασίλευσα	(*in aorist here*) I become king
	Πυθία -ας ἡ	the Pythia (*priestess of Apollo at Delphi*)
	τίσις -εως ἡ	vengeance, retribution
60	γενεά -ᾶς ἡ	generation
	ὀλιγωρέω	I ignore, I take no notice of (+ *gen*)
	πρίν	until
	δή	indeed
	τελέω *aor pass* ἐτελέσθην	I fulfil

Exercise 11.20

Solon and Croesus

*This passage sums up many of Herodotus' leading themes: the contrast between the Athenian wise
man and legislator Solon (about 640-560 BC) and the wealthy eastern despot Croesus; the
unpredictability of fortune. The choice of ways of life is also a traditional Greek theme: we saw it in
Plato's* Myth of Er *in Chapter 7 (written fifty years or so after Herodotus), but it was already
important in Homer: the Athenian Tellus (whose life Solon considers enviable) represents a resolution
of the stark choice offered to Achilles (hero of the* Iliad*) between a short glorious life and a long
inglorious one. But although the story of the meeting of Solon and Croesus is rich in symbolic
meaning, it is unlikely to be historical: Solon probably did live just into the reign of Croesus, but other
evidence puts his travels earlier in his career. Solon perhaps acts in this story as the voice of
Herodotus.*

ὁ δὲ <u>Κροῖσος</u>, βασιλεὺς ὢν τῶν <u>Λυδῶν</u>, πόλεων πλείστων ἐκράτησεν, ὧν
αἱ μὲν τῶν <u>Ἑλλήνων</u>, αἱ δὲ τῶν βαρβάρων ἦσαν. πλουσιώτατος οὖν
ἐγένετο ὁ Κροῖσος. καὶ πολλοὶ πρὸς τὰς <u>Σάρδεις</u>, τὴν πόλιν αὐτοῦ,
ἀφίκοντο. ἐν δὲ τούτοις ἦσαν <u>σοφισταὶ</u> ἄλλοι τε καὶ ἐκ τῆς Ἑλλάδος καὶ
5 <u>δὴ</u> ὁ <u>Σόλων</u>. οὗτος δὲ <u>νομοθέτης</u> τῶν Ἀθηναίων ἦν. βουλόμενοι γὰρ οἱ
Ἀθηναῖοι νόμους νέους ἔχειν, ἐκέλευσαν τὸν Σόλωνα νόμους ἑαυτοῖς
ποιῆσαι. τοῦτο οὖν πράξας ὁ Σόλων <u>ἀπεδήμησε</u> δέκα ἔτη, ἵνα οἵ τε

	Κροῖσος -ου ὁ	Croesus
	Λυδοί -ῶν οἱ	Lydians (*in modern western Turkey*)
	Ἕλληνες -ων οἱ	Greeks
	Σάρδεις -εων αἱ	Sardis (*capital of Lydia*)
	σοφιστής -οῦ ὁ	(*here*) wise man
5	δή	indeed
	Σόλων -ωνος ὁ	Solon
	νομοθέτης -ου ὁ	lawgiver
	ἀποδημέω ἀπεδήμησα	I go abroad, I am abroad

Ἀθηναῖοι χρῶνται τῇ <u>πολιτείᾳ</u> τῇ νέᾳ, καὶ μὴ αὐτὸς ἀναγκάσθῃ
λῦσαί τινα τῶν νόμων οὓς <u>ἔθηκεν</u>. οἱ γὰρ Ἀθηναῖοι ὑπέσχοντο τούτους
10 τοὺς νόμους δέκα ἔτη φυλάσσειν τοῦ Σόλωνος ἀπόντος. ὁ οὖν Σόλων,
<u>πρόφασιν</u> ἔχων τὴν <u>θεωρίαν</u>, ἐξέπλευσε καὶ εἴς τε τὴν <u>Αἴγυπτον</u> ὡς
τὸν βασιλέα τὸν <u>Ἄμασιν</u> <u>καὶ δὴ καὶ</u> εἰς τὴν <u>Λυδίαν</u> ὡς τὸν Κροῖσον
ἀφίκετο.

ἀφικόμενος δὲ ὁ Σόλων εἰς τὰς Σάρδεις <u>ἐξενίζετο</u> ἐν τοῖς <u>βασιλείοις</u> ὑπὸ
15 τοῦ Κροίσου. τῇ οὖν τρίτῃ ἢ τετάρτῃ ἡμέρᾳ οἱ δοῦλοι ὑπὸ τοῦ βασιλέως
κελευσθέντες περιήγαγον τὸν Σόλωνα περὶ τὸν τοῦ βασιλέως <u>θησαυρὸν</u>
καὶ ἔφηναν πάντα <u>ὄλβια</u> ὄντα.

ἔπειτα δὲ τὸν Σόλωνα πάντα ἰδόντα ἠρώτησεν ὁ Κροῖσος τάδε· "ὦ ξένε
Ἀθηναῖε, πολλὰ ἀκήκοα περὶ τῆς τε σοφίας τῆς σῆς καὶ τῆς θεωρίας.
20 νῦν οὖν βούλομαι ἐρωτῆσαι εἴ τινα εἶδες πάντων ὀλβιώτατον." ὁ γὰρ
βασιλεὺς ἐνόμιζεν ὀλβιώτατος εἶναι, καὶ διὰ ταῦτα ἠρώτησεν. ὁ μέντοι
Σόλων οὐδαμῶς <u>ἐθώπευσε</u> τὸν Κροῖσον ἀλλὰ τὸ ἀληθὲς ἔλεξεν· "ὦ
βασιλεῦ, Ἀθηναῖόν τινα <u>Τέλλον</u> ὀνόματι ὀλβιώτατον <u>κρίνω</u>".

ὁ δὲ Κροῖσος θαυμάσας τοὺς λόγους, "διὰ τί," ἔφη, "κρίνεις τὸν Τέλλον
25 ὀλβιώτατον εἶναι;" ὁ δὲ Σόλων ἀπεκρίνατο, "διότι ἡ πόλις αὐτοῦ καλῶς
<u>εἶχεν</u>. ἦσαν δ' αὐτῷ υἱοὶ καλοὶ καὶ ἀγαθοί, καὶ υἱοὶ τοῖς υἱοῖς αὐτοῖς·
καὶ πάντες <u>περιεγένοντο</u>. <u>πλοῦτον</u> δὲ ἱκανὸν εἶχε, ὥς <u>γε</u> ἡμεῖς κρίνομεν.
καὶ τὸ τοῦ βίου τέλος <u>λαμπρότατον</u> ἦν. μάχης γὰρ τοῖς Ἀθηναίοις
γενομένης πρὸς τοὺς <u>Μεγαρέας</u>, ὁ Τέλλος πολλοὺς τῶν πολεμίων <u>τρέψας</u>

	πολιτεία -ας ἡ	constitution
	ἔθηκα	(*irreg aor*) (*here*) I put in place
10	πρόφασις -εως ἡ	pretext, excuse
	θεωρία -ας ἡ	sight-seeing
	Αἴγυπτος -ου ἡ	Egypt
	Ἄμασις -εως ὁ	Amasis
	καὶ δὴ καί	and what is more
	Λυδία -ας ἡ	Lydia
	ξενίζω	I entertain
	βασίλεια -ων τά	palace
15	θησαυρός -οῦ ὁ	treasury
	ὄλβιος -α -ον	prosperous/happy
20	θωπεύω ἐθώπευσα	I flatter
	Τέλλος -ου ὁ	Tellus
	κρίνω	I judge
25	ἔχω	(+ *adv*) I am
	περιγίγνομαι περιεγενόμην	I survive
	πλοῦτος -ου ὁ	wealth
	γε	at least
	λαμπρός -ά -όν	distinguished
	Μεγαρεῖς -έων οἱ	Megarians (*Megara borders Attica to the west*)
	τρέπω ἔτρεψα	(*here*) I rout

30 κάλλιστα ἀπέθανεν. καὶ οἱ Ἀθηναῖοι <u>δημοσίᾳ</u> ἔθαψαν αὐτὸν ἐν τῷ τόπῳ
οὗ ἔπεσεν, καὶ ἐτίμησαν μεγάλως."

ἐπεὶ δὲ ὁ Σόλων τὰ περὶ τοῦ Τέλλου εἶπεν, ὁ Κροῖσος ἠρώτησε τίνα
δεύτερον μετὰ τοῦτον <u>κρίνει·</u> ἤλπιζε γὰρ ἀθλόν <u>γε</u> δεύτερον δέξεσθαι.
ὁ μέντοι Σόλων εἶπεν, "ὦ βασιλεῦ, ὅ τε <u>Κλέοβις</u> καὶ ὁ <u>Βίτων</u> δεύτεροι ἐν
35 <u>ὄλβῳ</u> εἰσίν, ὡς <u>ἔγωγε</u> κρίνω. οὗτοι γὰρ <u>Ἀργεῖοι</u> ὄντες <u>βίον</u> ἱκανὸν εἶχον
καὶ μεγάλην <u>ῥώμην</u> σώματος, περὶ οὗ ὅδε ὁ λόγος λέγεται. <u>ἑορτή</u> ποτε
τῆς <u>Ἥρας</u> ἦν τοῖς Ἀργείοις, καὶ ἔδει τὴν τῶν παίδων μητέρα πρὸς τὸ
ἱερὸν ἐν <u>ἁμάξῃ</u> <u>κομίζεσθαι·</u> <u>ἱέρεια</u> γὰρ ἦν. οἱ μέντοι <u>βόες</u> ἐν τοῖς ἀγροῖς
ἀπόντες οὐκ εἰς καιρὸν παρῆσαν. οἱ οὖν παῖδες αὐτοὶ ὑπὸ τὸ <u>ζυγὸν</u>
40 <u>εἵλκυσαν</u> τὴν ἅμαξαν. καὶ ἐν τῇ ἁμάξῃ ἦν ἡ μήτηρ.

"<u>στάδια</u> δὲ πέντε καὶ <u>τεσσαράκοντα</u> τὴν ἅμαξαν ἑλκύσαντες εἰς τὸ
ἱερὸν ἀφίκοντο. καὶ τοῖς παισὶ τοῦτο ποιήσασιν καὶ ὑπὸ πάντων
ὀφθεῖσι, τὸ τοῦ βίου τέλος ἄριστον ἐγένετο. καὶ οὕτως ἔφηναν οἱ θεοὶ
ὅτι ὁ θάνατος ἀμείνων ἐστὶν ἀνθρώπῳ ἢ ὁ βίος. οἱ γὰρ Ἀργεῖοι οἱ
45 παρόντες ἐπήνεσαν τὴν τῶν νεανιῶν ῥώμην, καὶ αἱ Ἀργεῖαι αἱ παροῦσαι
τὴν μητέρα αὐτῶν διότι τοιούτους υἱοὺς ἔχει. ἡ δὲ μήτηρ, <u>ἡδομένη</u> τῷ τε
ἔργῳ καὶ τοῖς λόγοις, πρὸς τὸ τῆς Ἥρας <u>ἄγαλμα</u> προσελθοῦσα ᾔτησε τὴν
θεὰν τοῖς παισὶ παρέχειν τὸ κάλλιστον δῶρον. ὁ οὖν Κλέοβις καὶ ὁ
Βίτων, <u>θύσαντές</u> τε καὶ φαγόντες, ἐν τῷ ἱερῷ <u>κατεκοίμησαν</u> καὶ οὐκέτι
50 <u>ἀνέστησαν,</u> ἀλλὰ τοῦτο τὸ τοῦ βίου τέλος εἶχον. καὶ οἱ Ἀργεῖοι

30	δημοσίᾳ	publicly
	κρίνω	I judge
	γε	at least
	Κλέοβις ὁ	Cleobis
	Βίτων ὁ	Biton
35	ὄλβος -ου ὁ	prosperity/happiness
	ἔγωγε	I at least, I for my part
	Ἀργεῖοι -ων οἱ	Argives
	βίος -ου ὁ	(here) livelihood
	ῥώμη -ης ἡ	strength
	ἑορτή -ῆς ἡ	festival
	Ἥρα -ας ἡ	Hera (goddess, wife of Zeus)
	ἅμαξα -ης ἡ	wagon
	κομίζω	I bring, I transport
	ἱέρεια -ας ἡ	priestess
	βόες -ῶν οἱ	oxen
	ζυγόν -οῦ τό	yoke
40	ἕλκω εἵλκυσα	I drag
	στάδιον -ου τό	stade (about 200 metres)
	τεσσαράκοντα	forty
45	ἥδομαι	I am pleased (by, + dat)
	ἄγαλμα -ατος τό	statue
	θύω ἔθυσα	I sacrifice
	κατακοιμάω κατεκοίμησα	I lie down to sleep
50	ἀνέστην	(irreg aor) I stood up, I got up

197

ἀγάλματα αὐτῶν ποιησάμενοι ἵδρυσαν ἐν τοῖς Δελφοῖς ὡς ἀνδρῶν
ἀγαθῶν γενομένων."

ὁ οὖν Σόλων τὸ δεύτερον τῆς εὐτυχίας ἆθλον τούτοις ἔνειμεν. ὁ δὲ
Κροῖσος μάλιστα ὀργιζόμενος εἶπεν, "ὦ ξένε Ἀθηναῖε, οὕτως καταφρονεῖς
55 τοῦ ἐμοῦ ὄλβου ὥστε κρίνεις με οὐδαμῶς ἀμείνονα τούτων τῶν ἰδιωτῶν
καὶ οὐτιδανῶν;" ὁ δὲ Σόλων εἶπεν, "ὦ Κροῖσε, οἶδα τοὺς θεοὺς φθονερούς
τε καὶ ταραχώδεις ὄντας, καὶ ἐρωτᾷς με περὶ τῶν ἀνθρωπίνων
πραγμάτων. ἐν γὰρ τῷ μακρῷ τοῦ βίου χρόνῳ δεῖ ἰδεῖν τε καὶ παθεῖν
πολλὰ κακά. τὸν δὲ τοῦ βίου ὅρον ἑβδομήκοντα ἔτη νομίζω εἶναι. καὶ ἐν
60 τούτοις τοῖς ἔτεσιν ἔνεισιν ἡμέραι πλείονες ἢ δισμύριοι καὶ
πεντακισχίλιοι. καὶ πασῶν τούτων τῶν ἡμερῶν, ἡ μὲν οὐδὲν ὅμοιον τῇ
δὲ προσάγει. οὕτως οὖν, ὦ Κροῖσε, ὁ ἄνθρωπος συμφορά ἐστιν.

"σὺ δὲ φαίνῃ μοι πλουσιώτατος εἶναι καὶ βασιλεὺς πολλῶν ἀνθρώπων.
τοῦτο μέντοι ὃ ἐρωτᾷς οὔπω οἷός τ᾽ εἰμὶ λέγειν. οὔπω γὰρ ἀκήκοά σε
65 καλῶς τελευτῆσαι τὸν βίον. ὁ γὰρ πλούσιος οὐκ ἔστιν εὐτυχέστερος τοῦ
ἱκανὸν ἔχοντος εἰ μὴ τὴν τύχην ἔχει καὶ καλῶς τελευτᾷ τὸν βίον. δεῖ
γὰρ παντὸς πράγματος τὸ τέλος σκοπεῖν, ὅπως ἀποβήσεται. πολλοῖς γὰρ
ἀνθρώποις ὁ θεὸς πρῶτον μὲν ὄλβον ἔφηνεν, ἔπειτα δὲ παντελῶς
διέφθειρεν."

	ἄγαλμα -ατος τό	statue
	ἱδρύω ἵδρυσα	I set up, I dedicate
	Δελφοί -ῶν οἱ	Delphi
	εὐτυχία -ας ἡ	good fortune
	νέμω ἔνειμα	I allocate
	καταφρονέω	I despise (+ gen)
55	ὄλβος -ου ὁ	prosperity/happiness
	κρίνω	I judge
	ἰδιώτης -ου ὁ	private citizen
	οὐτιδανός -οῦ ὁ	nonentity, insignificant person
	φθονερός -ά -όν	jealous
	ταραχώδης -ες	trouble-causing
	ἀνθρώπινος -η -ον	human
	πρᾶγμα -ατος τό	affair
	ὅρος -ου ὁ	limit, boundary
	ἑβδομήκοντα	seventy
60	δισμύριοι -αι -α	20,000
	πεντακισχίλιοι -αι -α	5,000
	ὅμοιος -α -ον	similar, of the same sort
	συμφορά -ᾶς ἡ	(here) chance
	οὔπω	not yet
65	τελευτάω ἐτελεύτησα	I end, I complete
	τύχη -ης ἡ	(good) luck
	σκοπέω	I look at
	ἀποβαίνω future ἀποβήσομαι	I turn out
	παντελῶς	entirely

70 ὁ δὲ Κροῖσος <u>οὔπω</u> <u>ἥδετο</u> τοῖς τοῦ Σόλωνος λόγοις. ἐνόμιζε γὰρ αὐτὸν
μῶρον εἶναι, περὶ τοῦ τέλους παντὸς πράγματος ἀεὶ λέγοντα, καὶ τῶν
παρόντων ἀγαθῶν <u>ἀμελοῦντα</u>. καὶ ἀπέπεμψεν ὁ βασιλεὺς τὸν Σόλωνα.

70	οὔπω	not yet
	ἥδομαι	I am pleased (by, + *dat*)
	ἀμελέω	I do not care about (+ *gen*)

Exercise 11.21

Croesus and Adrastus

*The downfall of Croesus now begins. Many motifs echo myth, and tragic drama: the ominous dream,
and the way (as we saw in the story of Acrisius and Perseus in Chapter 9) the steps taken to avert a
prophesied disaster are the very things that bring it about. The ominously named Adrastus (meaning
'that cannot be run away from') is a figure familiar in a world before legal systems and extradition
procedures: a killer who goes into voluntary exile, then throws himself on the mercy of a powerful
man in another country as a suppliant (someone who seeks protection and sanctuary). The grim scene
at the end echoes the close of many plays, where a procession comes on stage bringing a body home.*

τοῦ δὲ Σόλωνος ἀπελθόντος, οὐ πολλῷ ὕστερον <u>νέμεσις</u> μεγάλη ἐκ τῶν
θεῶν ἔλαβε τὸν Κροῖσον διότι (ὡς φαίνεται) ἐνόμιζεν <u>ὀλβιώτατος</u> εἶναι
πάντων ἀνθρώπων. τῷ γὰρ Κροίσῳ καθεύδοντι ἦλθεν <u>ὄνειρος</u> ὃς ἔφηνε
τὸ ἀληθὲς τῶν κακῶν τῶν μελλόντων γενήσεσθαι περὶ τοῦ υἱοῦ. ἦσαν δὲ
5 τῷ Κροίσῳ δύο παῖδες ὧν ὁ μὲν <u>κωφὸς</u> ἦν, ὁ δὲ <u>μακρῷ</u> πρῶτος τῶν τότε.
τὸ δ' ὄνομα τούτῳ Ἄτυς. περὶ δὲ τοῦ Ἄτυος τούτου <u>ἐσήμαινεν</u> ὁ ὄνειρος
τῷ Κροίσῳ, ὅτι ἀποθανεῖται <u>αἰχμῇ</u> <u>σιδήρου</u> βληθείς. ὁ οὖν Κροῖσος ἐπεὶ
ἡμέρα ἐγένετο μάλιστα ἐφοβεῖτο διὰ τὸν ὄνειρον καὶ <u>ἐφρόντιζεν</u> ὅπως
ἄριστα φεύξεται τὴν συμφοράν. ηὗρε δὲ γυναῖκα τῷ νεανίᾳ καὶ ἐπεὶ
10 <u>ἔγημε</u> ταύτην οὐκέτι εἴασεν αὐτὸν τοῦ τῶν <u>Λυδῶν</u> στρατοῦ <u>στρατηγεῖν</u>.
πρότερον γὰρ ὁ Ἄτυς στρατηγὸς ἀεὶ ἦν καὶ καλὰ ἔργα ἔπρασσεν.
ἔπειτα δὲ ὁ Κροῖσος <u>ἐξεκόμισε</u> πάντα τὰ <u>δοράτια</u> καὶ ἄλλα ὅπλα, ἃ ἐν

	νέμεσις -εως ἡ	retribution
	ὄλβιος -α -ον	happy/prosperous
	ὄνειρος -ου ὁ	dream
5	κωφός -ή -όν	deaf and dumb
	μακρῷ	by far
	Ἄτυς -υος ὁ	Atys
	σημαίνω ἐσήμηνα	I indicate, I signal
	αἰχμή -ῆς ἡ	spear-point
	σίδηρος -ου ὁ	iron
	φροντίζω	I consider
10	γαμέω ἔγημα	I marry
	Λυδοί -ῶν οἱ	Lydians
	στρατηγέω	I am general, I am commander (of, + *gen*)
	ἐκκομίζω ἐξεκόμισα	I take out
	δοράτιον -ου τό	spear

τοῖς τῶν βασιλείων τείχεσι κρεμαστὰ ἦν, καὶ ἐν θαλάμῳ τινὶ ἔθηκε, μή τι τῶν κρεμαστῶν τῷ παιδὶ ἐμπέσῃ.

15　μετὰ δὲ τὸν τοῦ παιδὸς γάμον ἀφίκετο εἰς τὰς Σάρδεις ἀνήρ τις συμφορᾷ ἐχόμενος καὶ οὐ καθαρὸς τὰς χεῖρας. οὗτος δὲ Φρὺξ ἦν, καὶ τοῦ βασιλικοῦ γένους. εἰσελθὼν δ᾽ εἰς τὴν τοῦ Κροίσου οἰκίαν ᾔτησε τὸν βασιλέα καθαίρειν αὐτὸν κατὰ τὸν νόμον. καὶ ὁ Κροῖσος ἐκάθηρεν αὐτόν. ἐπεὶ δὲ ταῦτα ἔπραξεν, ἠρώτησεν ὁ Κροῖσος τάδε· "ὦ ξένε, τίς ὢν
20　καὶ πόθεν ἐλθὼν ἱκέτης μοι ἐγένου; τίνα ἀπέκτεινας;" ὁ δ᾽ ἀνὴρ ἀπεκρίνατο, "ὦ βασιλεῦ, τοῦ Γορδίου τοῦ Μίδου παῖς ὢν ὀνομάζομαι Ἄδραστος, καὶ τὸν ἀδελφὸν ἄκων ἀποκτείνας ἐνθάδε πάρειμι, ὑπὸ τοῦ πατρὸς ἐκβληθεὶς καὶ οὐδὲν ἔχων". ὁ δὲ Κροῖσος ἀπεκρίνατο τάδε· "τὸ σὸν γένος οἶδα, καὶ ὡς φίλους ἐλήλυθας. οὐδαμῶς οὖν ἀπορήσεις ἐν τῇ
25　ἐμῇ οἰκίᾳ μένων· πάντα γὰρ παρέξω σοι. συμφορὰν δὲ δεινὴν πέπονθας, ἀλλὰ χρὴ φέρειν ὡς κουφότατα." καὶ ὁ Ἄδραστος ἐν τῇ τοῦ Κροίσου οἰκίᾳ ἔμενεν.

περὶ δὲ τοῦ αὐτοῦ χρόνου ἐν τῷ Ὀλύμπῳ ὄρει τῷ τῆς Μυσίας ἐγένετο μέγα χρῆμα ὑός. οὗτος δὲ πολλάκις κατὰ τοῦ ὄρους καταβαίνων τοὺς
30　τῶν Μυσῶν ἀγροὺς διέφθειρεν. πολλάκις καὶ δὴ οἱ Μυσοὶ ἐπὶ τὸν ὗν ἐξῆλθον· ἀλλ᾽ ἐποίουν μὲν οὐδὲν κακόν, ἔπασχον δὲ πρὸς αὐτοῦ. τέλος δ᾽ ἄγγελοι τῶν Μυσῶν παρὰ τὸν Κροῖσον ἀφικόμενοι εἶπον τάδε· "ὦ βασιλεῦ, ὗς χρῆμα μέγιστον ἐν τῇ ἡμετέρᾳ χώρᾳ ἀναφηνάμενον τὰ

βασίλεια -ων τά	palace
κρεμαστός -ή -όν	hung up
θάλαμος -ου ὁ	store-room
ἔθηκα	(irreg aor) I placed, I put
μή	(here) in case, for fear that
ἐμπίπτω ἐνέπεσον	I fall on (+ dat)
15　γάμος -ου ὁ	marriage
Σάρδεις -εων αἱ	Sardis (capital of Lydia)
καθαρός -ά -όν	clean (here followed by 'accusative of respect' or of 'part affected')
Φρύξ Φρυγός ὁ	Phrygian (Phrygia is north-east of Lydia)
βασιλικός -ή -όν	royal
καθαίρω ἐκάθηρα	I purify
20　ἱκέτης -ου ὁ	suppliant
Γορδίας -ου ὁ	Gordias
Μίδας -ου ὁ	Midas
ὀνομάζω	I call, I name
Ἄδραστος -ου ὁ	Adrastus
ἄκων -ουσα -ον (ἀκοντ-)	unwillingly
25　κοῦφος -η -ον	light
Ὄλυμπος -ου ὁ	Olympus
Μυσία -ας ἡ	Mysia (north-west of Lydia, west of Phrygia)
χρῆμα -ατος τό	thing
ὗς ὑός ὁ	boar (idiom a big thing of a boar = a very big boar)
30　Μυσοί -ῶν οἱ	Mysians
ἀναφαίνομαι ἀνεφηνάμην	I appear

τῶν ἀνθρώπων ἔργα διαφθείρει. τοῦτο δὲ βουλόμενοι ἑλεῖν οὐδαμῶς
35 δυνάμεθα. νῦν οὖν αἰτοῦμέν σε τόν τε υἱὸν καὶ νεανίας <u>ἐξαιρέτους</u>
<u>συμπέμψαι</u> ἡμῖν, ἵνα ἐξέλωμεν τὸν <u>ὗν</u> ἐκ τῆς χώρας." οἱ μὲν οὖν
ἄγγελοι ταῦτα εἶπον, ὁ δὲ Κροῖσος τοὺς τοῦ <u>ὀνείρου</u> λόγους
<u>μνημονεύων</u> ἀπεκρίνατο τάδε· "περὶ τοῦ παιδὸς τοῦ ἐμοῦ μήκετι
λέγετε. οὐ γὰρ ἐθέλω συμπέμψαι αὐτὸν ὑμῖν. <u>νεόγαμος</u> γάρ ἐστι καὶ
40 ταῦτα νῦν <u>μέλει</u> αὐτῷ. ἄνδρας μέντοι ἐξαιρέτους τῶν Λυδῶν καὶ πᾶν τὸ
<u>κυνηγέσιον</u> συμπέμψω, καὶ κελεύσω τοὺς ἰόντας ὡς <u>προθυμότατα</u>
<u>συνεξελεῖν</u> ὑμῖν τὸ <u>θηρίον</u> ἐκ τῆς χώρας."

ταῦτα ἀπεκρίνατο ὁ Κροῖσος, καὶ οἱ Λυδοὶ <u>ἠρέσκοντο</u> τοῖς λόγοις. ὁ δὲ
τοῦ Κροίσου υἱὸς νῦν εἰσῆλθεν, ἀκούσας τοὺς τῶν Λυδῶν λόγους. ἐπεὶ
45 οὖν ὁ Κροῖσος οὐκ ἤθελε πέμψαι αὐτὸν ὡς τοῖς Λυδοῖς βοηθήσοντα,
ὁ Ἄτυς εἶπε τάδε· "ὦ πάτερ, πρότερον μὲν κάλλιστόν τε καὶ
<u>γενναιότατον</u> ἦν μοι εἰς πόλεμον καὶ εἰς <u>ἄγραν</u> ἰόντα <u>δόξαν</u> φέρεσθαι.
νῦν δὲ κωλύεις με πάντων τούτων, καίπερ ἰδών με οὔτε φοβούμενον οὔτ'
ἀθυμοῦντα. ποῖος μέν τις τοῖς πολίταις δόξω εἶναι, ποῖος δέ τις τῇ
50 γυναικὶ τῇ νεογάμῳ; ἐμὲ οὖν ἢ ἔασον εἰς τὴν ἄγραν ἰέναι, ἢ πεῖσον ὅπως
ἄμεινόν ἐστι τοῦτο οὕτω ποιούμενον."

ὁ δὲ Κροῖσος ἀπεκρίνατο τάδε· "ὦ παῖ, οὔτε <u>δειλίαν</u> σοι οὔτ' ἄλλο τι
κακὸν ἰδὼν τοῦτο ποιῶ, ἀλλ' ὄνειρος ἐν τῷ ὕπνῳ ἔφη σε <u>ὀλιγοχρόνιον</u>
ἔσεσθαι· <u>αἰχμῇ</u> γὰρ <u>σιδήρου</u> σε ἀποθανεῖσθαι. κατὰ οὖν ταῦτα τὰ
55 ἀγγελθέντα ηὗρόν τε γυναῖκά σοι καὶ οὐκέτι εἰς κίνδυνόν σε πέμπω,
ἀλλὰ φυλάσσω σε, ἐλπίζων ἐπί <u>γε</u> τοῦ ἐμοῦ βίου ἀπὸ θανάτου σε
ἀποκλέψειν. εἷς μόνος υἱός μοι εἶ· τὸν γὰρ <u>ἕτερον</u> <u>κωφὸν</u> ὄντα οὐκ εἶναί

35	ἐξαίρετος -ον	chosen
	συμπέμπω συνέπεμψα	I send X (acc) with Y (dat)
	ὗς ὑός ὁ	boar
	ὄνειρος -ου ὁ	dream
	μνημονεύω	I remember
	νεόγαμος -ον	newly married
40	μέλω	I am a concern
	κυνηγέσιον -ου τό	hunting pack
	πρόθυμος -ον	eager
	συνεξαιρέω συνεξεῖλον	I join in removing
	θηρίον -ου τό	beast
	ἀρέσκομαι	I am satisfied (with, + dat)
45	γενναῖος -α -ον	noble
	ἄγρα -ας ἡ	hunt
	δόξα -ης ἡ	glory
50	δειλία -ας ἡ	cowardice
	ὀλιγοχρόνιος -ον	short-lived
	αἰχμή -ῆς ἡ	spear-point
	σίδηρος -ου ὁ	iron
55	γε	at least
	ἕτερος -α -ον	the other
	κωφός -ή -όν	deaf and dumb

μοι νομίζω." ὁ δὲ νεανίας ἀπεκρίνατο, "<u>συγγνώμη</u> μὲν ὦ πάτερ ἐστί σοι, τοιοῦτον <u>ὄνειρον</u> ἰδόντι, φυλάσσειν με. τόδε γὰρ περὶ τοῦ ὀνείρου οὐ
60 μανθάνεις· δεῖ με <u>αἰχμῇ</u> <u>σιδήρου</u> ἀποθανεῖν, ὡς ὁ ὄνειρος λέγει· ἀλλὰ ποῖαι χεῖρες, ποῖα αἰχμὴ σιδήρου (ἣν συ φοβῇ) ἐστιν <u>ὑΐ</u>; οὐ γὰρ <u>ὀδόντι</u> λέγει με ἀποθανεῖν ἢ τοιούτῳ τινί, ὥστε σε δικαίως ταῦτα πράσσειν, ἀλλ᾽ αἰχμῇ σιδήρου. ἐπεὶ οὖν οὐκ ἐπ᾽ ἄνδρας ἡ μάχη ἔσται, ἔασόν με ἰέναι."

65 ἔπειτα δὲ ὁ Κροῖσος, "ὦ παῖ," ἔφη, "τὴν περὶ τοῦ ὀνείρου <u>γνώμην</u> <u>ἀποφαίνων</u> νικᾷς με. ἔξεστί σοι εἰς τὴν <u>ἄγραν</u> ἰέναι." λέξας δὲ ταῦτα <u>μετεπέμψατο</u> τὸν Ἄδραστον. ἀφικομένῳ δ᾽ αὐτῷ εἶπεν, "Ἄδραστε, ἐγώ σε συφορὰν δεινὴν παθόντα <u>ἐκάθηρα</u>, καὶ εἰς τὴν ἐμὴν οἰκίαν ἐδεξάμην, καὶ σῖτον καὶ πάντα παρέχω. νῦν δὲ δεῖ σε, ἀγαθὰ δεξάμενον, ἀγαθὰ καὶ
70 πράσσειν. βούλομαί σε φύλακα τοῦ ἐμοῦ υἱοῦ γενέσθαι εἰς ἄγραν ἰόντος, <u>μὴ</u> <u>κλέπται</u> τινὲς ἐν τῇ ὁδῷ κακὸν ποιήσωσιν. πρὸς δὲ τούτοις ἐξέσται σοι καλὰ ἔργα πράσσοντι <u>δόξαν</u> φέρεσθαι. τοῦτο γὰρ <u>πατρῷόν</u> ἐστί σοι, καὶ ἡ <u>ῥώμη</u> πάρεστιν."

ὁ δ᾽ Ἄδραστος ἀπεκρίνατο, "ὦ βασιλεῦ, καίπερ <u>ἄλλως</u> οὐκ ἐθέλων τοῦτο
75 ποιῆσαι (οὐ γὰρ <u>πρέπει</u> ἀνδρὶ συμφορὰν παθόντι μετὰ τῶν εὖ πρασσόντων ἰέναι), ἐπεὶ σὺ βούλῃ καὶ δεῖ με <u>χαρίζεσθαί</u> σοι, ἕτοιμος εἰμί. καὶ ἔλπισον τὸν παῖδα ὃν κελεύεις με φυλάξαι <u>ἀπήμονα</u> διὰ τὸν φυλάσσοντα <u>ἐπανελθεῖν</u>."

ἐπεὶ οὖν ὁ Ἄδραστος ταῦτα τῷ Κροίσῳ ἀπεκρίνατο, ἐξῆλθον μετὰ

	συγγνώμη -ης ἡ	pardon
	ὄνειρος -ου ὁ	dream
60	αἰχμή -ῆς ἡ	spear-point
	σίδηρος -ου ὁ	iron
	ὗς ὑός ὁ	boar
	ὀδούς -όντος ὁ	(*here*) tusk
65	γνώμη -ης ἡ	message, meaning
	ἀποφαίνω	I reveal
	ἄγρα -ας ἡ	hunt
	μεταπέμπομαι μετεπεμψάμην	I send for
	καθαίρω ἐκάθηρα	I purify
70	μή	(*here*) in case, for fear that (+ *subjunctive*)
	κλέπτης -ου ὁ	robber
	δόξα -ης ἡ	glory
	πατρῷος -α -ον	ancestral, in accordance with family tradition
	ῥώμη -ης ἡ	strength
	ἄλλως	otherwise
75	πρέπει	it is appropriate (for, + *dat*)
	χαρίζομαι	I gratify (+ *dat*)
	ἀπήμων -ον (-ονος)	unharmed
	ἐπανέρχομαι ἐπανῆλθον	I return

80 νεανιῶν <u>ἐξαιρέτων</u> καὶ <u>κυνῶν</u>. ἀφικόμενοι δ' εἰς τὸ Ὄλυμπον ὄρος
ἐζήτουν τὸ <u>θηρίον</u>, εὑρόντες δὲ καὶ <u>κύκλῳ</u> <u>περιστάντες</u> <u>εἰσηκόντιζον</u>.

τότε <u>δὴ</u> ὁ ξένος, οὗτος ὁ <u>καθαρθεὶς</u> τον <u>φόνον</u>, καλούμενος δ' Ἄδραστος,
<u>ἀκοντίζων</u> τὸν <u>ὗν</u> τοῦ μὲν <u>ἁμαρτάνει</u>, <u>τυγχάνει</u> δὲ τοῦ Κροίσου παιδός.
ἐκεῖνος μὲν δὴ <u>βληθεὶς</u> τῇ <u>αἰχμῇ</u> <u>ἐξέπλησε</u> τοὺς τοῦ <u>ὀνείρου</u> λόγους. καὶ
85 ἔδραμέ τις ἀγγελῶν τῷ Κροίσῳ τὰ γεγενήμενα· ἀφικόμενος δ' εἰς τὰς
Σάρδεις τήν τε μάχην καὶ τὸν τοῦ υἱοῦ θάνατον ἔλεξεν αὐτῷ.

ὁ δὲ Κροῖσος τῷ τοῦ παιδὸς θανάτῳ <u>ταραχθεὶς</u> ἔτι μᾶλλον ἠθύμει διότι
ἀπέκτεινεν αὐτὸν ὁ ὑφ' ἑαυτοῦ <u>καθαρθείς</u>. καὶ χαλεπῶς φέρων τὴν
συμφορὰν <u>τρὶς</u> ἐκάλει τὸν Δία, τὸν τοῦ τε <u>καθαρμοῦ</u> καὶ τῆς <u>ξενίας</u> καὶ
90 τῆς <u>ἑταιρείας</u> θεόν. ὁ γὰρ ξένος ὁ καθαρθεὶς καὶ φιλίως δεχθεὶς μάλιστα
ἠδίκησεν αὐτόν, καὶ λάθρα <u>ἐξένιζεν</u> ὁ Κροῖσος τὸν τοῦ υἱοῦ <u>φονέα</u>.

παρῆσαν δὲ μετὰ ταῦτα οἱ Λυδοὶ φέροντες τὸν νεκρόν. εἵπετο δ' αὐτοῖς
ὁ φονεύς. οὗτος δὲ πρὸ τοῦ νεκροῦ παρὼν ἐκέλευσε τὸν Κροῖσον
ἀποκτεῖναι, λέγων ὅτι ὁ βίος οὐκέτι <u>ἀνασχετός</u> ἐστιν αὐτῷ, πρὸς τῇ
95 <u>προτέρᾳ</u> συφορᾷ τὸν καθήραντα νῦν διαφθείραντι. ὁ δὲ Κροῖσος ταῦτα
ἀκούσας, "ὦ ξένε," ἔφη, "πᾶσαν δίκην παρά σου ἔχω, ἐπεὶ θάνατον

80	ἐξαίρετος -ον	chosen
	κύων κυνός ὁ/ἡ	dog
	θηρίον -ου τό	wild animal, beast
	κύκλος -ου ὁ	circle
	περιστάντες	(*irreg aor participle*) standing around
	εἰσακοντίζω	I throw a spear at
	δή	indeed
	καθαρθείς	(*aor pass participle of* καθαίρω = I purify, *here followed by 'accusative of respect'*)
	φόνος -ου ὁ	murder, homicide
	ἀκοντίζω	I throw a spear
	ὗς ὑός ὁ	boar
	ἁμαρτάνω	I miss (+ *gen*)
	τυγχάνω	I hit (+ *gen*)
	βληθείς	(*aor pass participle of* βάλλω)
	αἰχμή -ῆς ἡ	spear-point
	ἐξέπλησα	(*irreg aor*) I fulfilled
	ὄνειρος -ου ὁ	dream
85	ταράσσω *aor pass* ἐταράχθην	I disturb, I trouble
	καθαίρω *aor pass* ἐκαθάρθην	I purify
	τρίς	three times
	καθαρμός -οῦ ὁ	purification
	ξενία -ας ἡ	hospitality
90	ἑταιρεία -ας ἡ	companionship
	ξενίζω	I entertain
	φονεύς -έως ὁ	murderer
	ἀνασχετός -όν	bearable, tolerable
95	πρότερος -α -ον	previous, former

σεαυτοῦ <u>καταδικάζεις</u>. οὐ γὰρ σύ μοι τοῦδε τοῦ κακοῦ αἴτιος ἀλλὰ θεός τις ὃς πάλαι ἔφη ταῦτα γενήσεσθαι." ὁ μὲν οὖν Κροῖσος ἔθαψε τὸν ἑαυτοῦ παῖδα. ὁ δ' Ἄδραστος ὁ τοῦ Γορδίου τοῦ Μίδου, ὃς ἀπέκτεινε

100 τόν τε ἑαυτοῦ ἀδελφὸν καὶ τὸν τοῦ <u>καθήραντος</u> υἱόν, ἐπεὶ πάντες ἀπὸ τοῦ <u>τάφου</u> ἀπῆλθον, <u>συγγιγνωσκόμενος</u> ἀνθρώπων οὓς ᾔδει <u>βαρυσυμφορώτατος</u> ἀπέκτεινεν ἑαυτὸν παρὰ τῷ τάφῳ.

	καταδικάζω	I condemn X (*gen*) to Y (*acc*)
100	καθαίρω ἐκάθηρα	I purify
	τάφος -ου ὁ	tomb
	συγγιγνώσκομαι	I acknowledge
	βαρυσύμφορος -ον	heavily oppressed by misfortune

Vocabulary checklist for Chapter 11

ἆρα μή;	surely ... not?
βουλεύομαι ἐβουλευσάμην	I deliberate, I consider, I plan
γε	at least, at any rate
δή	indeed, certainly, surely
δύναμαι	I am able, I have power (to)
ἔαν	if (+ *subj, in fut open conditional*)
εἴτε ... εἴτε	whether ... or
ἐπίσταμαι	I know (how to)
ἕτερος -α -ον	one/the other (of two)
ἥδομαι ἥσθην	I enjoy, I take pleasure (in) (+ *dat*)
ἥκω	I have come
θύω ἔθυσα	I sacrifice
ἵνα	in order to (+ *subj*)
ὅθεν	from (the place) where
οἷ	to (the place) where
οἷος -α -ον	(of) the sort which; what a ... !
ὁπόθεν	from where (*indirect question*)
ὅποι	where, where to (*indirect question*)
ὁποῖος -α -ον	what sort of (*indirect question*)
ὁπόσοι -αι -α	how many (*indirect question*)
ὁπόσος -η -ον	how big (*indirect question*)
ὁπότερος -α -ον	which (of two) (*indirect question*)
ὅπου	where (at) (*indirect question*)
ὅπως	how (*indirect question*)
	(+ *subj*) in order to, so that
ὅσοι -αι -α	as many as, all those who; how many ... !
ὅσος -η -ον	(of) the size which, as great/much as; what a great ... !
ὅστις, ἥτις, ὅ τι	who, which (*indirect question*); whoever, whichever
ὅτε	(at the time) when
οὗ	(the place) where
Πέρσης -ου ὁ	Persian, Persian man
ποθέν	from somewhere
ποῖ;	where (to)?
ποι	to somewhere
ποῖος; -α; -ον;	what sort of?
πόσοι; -αι; -α;	how many?
πόσος; -η; -ον;	how big?
ποτέ	once, sometime, ever
πότερον ... ἤ	whether ... or
πότερος; -α; -ον;	which (of two)?
που	somewhere, anywhere
πως	somehow, in some way

τέμνω ἔτεμον   I cut, I cut down, I ravage
χειμών -ῶνος ὁ   winter; storm, bad weather
χείρ, χειρός ἡ   hand
χωρίον -ου τό   place; estate, farm
ὧδε   in this way, in the following way
ὡς   (*introducing exclamation*) how ... !
(47 words)

Chapter 12

Present, aorist and future optative

As well as the subjunctive, Greek verbs have a mood called the *optative*. It is in effect like the subjunctive but more so: remoter in likelihood or time. Where the indicative states a fact (*we are doing X*), the subjunctive indicates an immediate possibility (*we may do X, let's do X*) and the optative indicates a more remote possibility (*we might do X, if only we could do X*). The optative has a very distinctive form. Where the subjunctive always has a long vowel in the ending, the optative always has a *diphthong* (οι, αι or less commonly ει). The form of the endings is slightly different from others you have met (but compare εἰμί, εἶμι, φημί, and the other -μι verbs later in this chapter).

		present optative	
		active	*middle/passive*
sg	1	παύ-οιμι	παυ-οίμην
	2	παύ-οις	παύ-οιο
	3	παύ-οι	παύ-οιτο
pl	1	παύ-οιμεν	παυ-οίμεθα
	2	παύ-οιτε	παύ-οισθε
	3	παύ-οιεν	παύ-οιντο

Notice that the middle/passive endings resemble the normal *historic* middle/passive ones (-ομην, -ου, -ετο, -ομεθα, -εσθε, -οντο), where in contrast both sets of subjunctive endings were variants of the normal *primary* ones.

The verb *to be* has its own distinctive optative form:

sg	1	εἴην
	2	εἴης
	3	εἴη
pl	1	εἶμεν
	2	εἶτε
	3	εἶεν

(Slightly different alternative forms of the plural are shown in the Reference Grammar.)

Aorist optatives of ordinary verbs are to a large extent predictable. The second (strong) aorist form uses the same endings for the active and middle as the equivalent present optative, but added to the aorist stem. As in the indicative, middle and passive are differentiated in the aorist, and (as with all aorist passives) endings normally active are used to form the aorist passive - not however those of the present tense, but the optative of the verb *to be* used as a set of endings:

second (strong) aorist optative

		active	middle	passive
sg	1	λάβ-οιμι	λαβ-οίμην	ληφθ-είην
	2	λάβ-οις	λάβ-οιο	ληφθ-είης
	3	λάβ-οι	λάβ-οιτο	ληφθ-είη
pl	1	λάβ-οιμεν	λαβ-οίμεθα	ληφθ-εῖμεν
	2	λάβ-οιτε	λάβ-οισθε	ληφθ-εῖτε
	3	λάβ-οιεν	λάβ-οιντο	ληφθ-εῖεν

• For the use of a tense of the verb *to be* as a building-block to form another tense of an ordinary verb, compare how Latin *eram* etc (imperfect of *to be*) is used to form the pluperfect e.g. *portaveram*.

The first (weak) aorist changes οι in the active and middle endings to αι (this is of course consistent with its use of alpha in the indicative, participle, and elsewhere):

first (weak) aorist optative

		active	middle	passive
sg	1	παύσ-αιμι	παυσ-αίμην	παυσθ-είην
	2	παύσ-αις *or* -ειας*	παύσ-αιο	παυσθ-είης
	3	παύσ-αι *or* -ειε(ν)*	παύσ-αιτο	παυσθ-είη
pl	1	παύσ-αιμεν	παυσ-αίμεθα	παυσθ-εῖμεν
	2	παύσ-αιτε	παύσ-αισθε	παυσ-θεῖτε
	3	παύσ-αιεν *or* -ειαν*	παύσ-αιντο	παυσθ-εῖεν

* the alternative forms (i.e. not exactly as would be deduced from converting οι to αι) are commonly found

There is a future optative (though it is less common than the present and aorist), of entirely predictable form:

future optative

active	middle	passive
παύσ-οιμι	παυσ-οίμην	παυσθησ-οίμην
etc	etc	etc

The optative forms of contracted verbs are largely predictable, but in the singular of the active use the endings:

sg	1	-οιην
	2	-οιης
	3	-οιη

(these seem like a cross between the -οιμι -οις -οι ones of a normal present optative, and the -ειην -ειης -ειη of the verb *to be* and the aorist passive). Applying the rules of contraction we therefore get:

present optative

		active	middle/passive	active	middle/passive
sg	1	φιλ-οίην	φιλ-οίμην	τιμ-ῴην	τιμ-ῴμην
	2	φιλ-οίης	φιλ-οῖο	τιμ-ῴης	τιμ-ῷο
	3	φιλ-οίη	φιλ-οῖτο	τιμ-ῴη	τιμ-ῷτο
pl	1	φιλ-οῖμεν	φιλ-οίμεθα	τιμ-ῷμεν	τιμ-ῴμεθα
	2	φιλ-οῖτε	φιλ-οῖσθε	τιμ-ῷτε	τιμ-ῷσθε
	3	φιλ-οῖεν	φιλ-οῖντο	τιμ-ῷεν	τιμ-ῷντο

As usual, the aorist and future are completely regular as contraction is not involved, hence:

aorist optatives

active	middle	passive
φιλήσ-αιμι	φιληοσ-αίμην	φιληθ-είην
τιμήσ-αιμι	τιμησ-αίμην	τιμηθ-είην

future optatives

φιλήσ-οιμι	φιλησ-οίμην	φιληθησ-οίμην
τιμήσ-οιμι	τιμησ-οίμην	τιμηθησ-οίμην

Use of the optative (1): Wishes

When the optative is the only or main verb of a sentence, it usually expresses a wish for the future, often introduced by εἴθε (literally *if only* ... ! or, in old-fashioned English, *would that* ... ! - compare εἰ, the normal word for *if*). In this and most of its uses, the optative operates by *aspect* (i.e. present for a generalised wish, optative for a wish for one specific occasion). The negative in a wish is μή. Hence:

> εἴθε οἱ ἡμέτεροι στρατιῶται ἀεὶ ἀνδρείως μάχοιντο.
> If only our soldiers would always fight bravely.

Instead of *If only* ... it would often be justifiable to translate (according to context) e.g. *I wish* ... (even though there is no first-person verb), or *May* ... (the effect differing only slightly from the subjunctive, which would imply something more immediate):

> εἴθε οἱ Ἀθηναῖοι μηδέποτε πολέμιοι ἡμῖν γένοιντο.
> May the Athenians never become enemies to us (*or* our enemies).

Exercise 12.1

Translate into English:

1   εἴθε αἱ τῶν συμμάχων νῆες ἀφίκοιντο.
2   εἴθε οἱ ῥήτορες ἀεὶ δικαίως λέγοιεν.
3   εἴθε μὴ νικήσαιεν οἱ πολέμιοι.
4   εἴθε ὑπὸ τῶν πολιτῶν ἀεὶ τιμῷο, ὦ γύναι.
5   μὴ τοιαῦτα γένοιτο.

Exercise 12.2

Translate into Greek:

1   If only those women would send us money!
2   If only the allies would always fight bravely!
3   May wars of this sort never happen!
4   If only you would learn these words, boys!
5   Would that the king might always honour the citizens!

Use of the optative (2): Sequence of tenses and moods in purpose clauses

We have seen that tenses are divided into *primary* (present, future, and perfect) and *historic* (imperfect and aorist). *Sequence* (literally *following on*) refers to the process whereby the form of the verb in a clause that *follows on* from the main clause is determined by whether the main or introductory verb is *primary* (when we say the sentence is in *primary sequence*) or *historic* (so the sentence is in *historic sequence*). This principle is seen in very formal and old-fashioned English:

> I am going to London in order that I *may* see the Queen. (*primary sequence*)
> I went to London in order that I *might* see the Queen. (*historic sequence*)

In a sentence involving a purpose clause, if the rule of sequence is followed strictly, a *primary* main verb is followed by a *subjunctive* in the purpose clause, and an *historic* main verb by an *optative* in the purpose clause. Notice that this corresponds to the *formation* of these moods: the subjunctive is based on the primary endings throughout, and some parts at least of the optative (its present middle/passive) are based on the historic ones. Hence:

> πάρεσμεν ἵνα μανθάνωμεν.
> We are here in order to learn. (*primary sequence, with subjunctive*)

> ἐμάχοντο ἵνα τιμῷντο.
> They used to fight in order to be honoured. (*historic sequence, with optative*)

However as we saw in Chapter 11, it is possible to use the subjunctive in *any* purpose clause, i.e. to regard it as if it were in primary sequence even after a past tense main verb: the justification of this is the now-familiar principle of vividness. If we wrote

> ἀφίκοντο ἵνα μάχωνται.
> They arrived in order to fight. ('*vivid*' *construction using subjunctive, rather than following strict rule of sequence*)

we would as it were be entering the minds of the people at the time.

In Latin, the principle of sequence differentiates between *different tenses of the subjunctive* (present subjunctive in primary sequence, imperfect subjunctive in historic sequence; and the rule has to be followed strictly). In Greek, the principle of sequence differentiates between *moods*: the *subjunctive* (by nature primary) in primary sequence, and the *optative* (by nature historic) in historic sequence. Sequence determines whether the subjunctive or the optative is used; whether the present or the aorist *of that subjunctive or optative* is then used is determined entirely by *aspect* (general or one occasion, without reference to tense).

Hence (showing examples following the strict rule of sequence):

ἐσθίομεν ἵνα ἰσχυροὶ ὦμεν.
We eat in order to be strong.
(*primary sequence and general, with present subjunctive*)

μένομεν ἵνα τοῦ ἀγγέλου ἀκούσωμεν.
We are waiting in order to hear the messenger.
(*primary sequence and particular, with aorist subjunctive*)

ὁ παῖς ἔτρεχεν ἵνα ἆθλα φέροιτο.
The boy used to run in order to win prizes.
(*historic sequence and general, with present optative*)

οἱ σύμμαχοι τότε ἀφίκοντο ἵνα μαχέσαιντο.
The allies arrived at that time in order to fight.
(*historic sequence and particular, with aorist optative*)

Use of the optative (3): Indirect statement and question

As we briefly noted in Chapter 10, there is another important context where the optative can (and according to strict rules should) be used in historic sequence, but often is not because of the 'vividness' principle: indirect statement using a 'that' clause, and the equivalent contruction for indirect question, in both cases when the introductory verb is historic. Hence:

ὁ Σωκράτης εἶπεν ὅτι ὁ γέρων σοφώτατος εἴη.
Socrates said that the old man was very wise.
(*optative because historic sequence, but ἐστίν could be used for vividness*)

ὁ ἄγγελος ἠρώτησεν ὅστις λύσειε τὸν ἵππον.
The messenger asked who had released the horse.
(*optative because historic sequence, but ἔλυσε could be used for vividness*)

As we saw in Chapter 10, indirect speech constructions keep the tense of the original direct speech: *The old man is very wise* (present), *Who released the horse?* (aorist), but English adjusts the tense after a past introductory verb. All this *remains true if the verb is optative*: in this construction the optative operates *not* (as it usually does elsewhere) by *aspect*, but by *tense*, i.e. the aorist here refers to the *past* (not simply to a single act regardless of time). Note also that the optative here (unlike most of its other uses) has no sense of (for example)

211

might, could, or *were to.*

The explanation for all this is the principle of *behaving like what it is replacing* in the original direct speech: the original was an aorist indicative operating by tense (*Who released?*), so the optative does likewise.

• We saw this same principle in Chapter 9 with the aorist infinitive: in an indirect *command* it operates by aspect because it replaces an original imperative (*Do this immediately!* becomes *He ordered him to do this immediately*), but in an indirect *statement* it operates by tense because it replaces an original indicative (*They won a victory* becomes - literally - *I believe them to have won* a victory, or in better English *I believe that they ...*).

The use of the optative by tense in indirect statement and question explains why there is a future optative (whereas there is no future subjunctive, because the subjunctive always operates by aspect):

ἡ γυνὴ εἶπεν ὅτι οἱ σύμμαχοι δι' ὀλίγου νικήσοιεν.

The woman said that the allies would (*or* were going to) soon win.

She said at the time *The allies will soon win*: the future tense of that original is retained, and so in strict historic sequence the future optative is used (but the future indicative νικήσουσιν could be used for vividness).

Exercise 12.3

Translate into English:
1   οἱ νεανίαι ἐπέμφθησαν ἵνα τὰ ἐν τῇ νήσῳ δένδρα κόψαιεν.
2   ἡ γυνὴ εἶπεν ὅτι ἡ τῶν συμμάχων ναῦς προσπλέοι.*
3   οἱ πολῖται ἐν τῇ ἀγορᾷ ἔμενον ἵνα τὸν στρατὸν τον νενικηκότα ἴδοιεν.
4   οἱ τὰ τείχη φυλάσσοντες ἔλεξαν ὅτι οὐδὲν ἴδοιεν.
5   ἐκεῖνοι οἱ δοῦλοι ἔφυγον ἵνα μὴ αὖθις ληφθεῖεν.
6   ἡ μήτηρ ἠρώτησε τὸν παῖδα ὁπόθεν ἔλθοι.
7   οἱ γέροντες ἀπεπέμφθησαν ἵνα ἀσφαλεῖς εἶεν.
8   ἆρα μὴ ἐλήλυθας ὅπως τοῦ ῥήτορος ἀκούσῃς;
9   ὁ στρατηγὸς ἤγαγε τοὺς στρατιώτας εἰς τὸ τείχισμα ἵνα τοὺς ἐκεῖ λάβοιεν.
10   ἔπεισα τὸν ἄγγελον εἰπεῖν ὁπότε ἡ ναυμαχία γένοιτο.

* as we saw in Chapter 9, verbs with epsilon stem whose stem is a single syllable behave in many respects like ordinary uncontracted verbs: hence the optative is -οιμι etc, not -οιην etc

Exercise 12.4

Translate into Greek (using optatives according to the strict rule of sequence):
1   The messenger said that the allies were already approaching.
2   The Athenians marched quickly in order to attack the enemies' city.
3   The slave said that he had heard no shout during the night.
4   The old man asked when the messenger had arrived.
5   All the women ran into the street to see what had happened.

Tense and aspect in the aorist: a summary

Indicative *always by tense*
οἱ Ἀθηναῖοι ἐνίκησαν.
The Athenians won a victory.

Imperative *always by aspect*
λαβὲ τοῦτον τὸν ἵππον.
Take this horse!

Participle *almost always by tense*
ἀφικόμενοι ἐστρατοπεδεύσαντο.
Having arrived they set up camp.
but: γελάσας ἔφη
He said with a laugh (*not necessarily before he started speaking*)
This applies only to a few idiomatic usages. *

Infinitive *usually by aspect, but by tense in indirect statement (replacing indicative)*
οἱ πολῖται ἐπείσθησαν φυγεῖν.
The citizens were persuaded to run away.
but: ὁ ἄγγελος ἐνόμιζε τοὺς πολίτας φυγεῖν.
The messenger believed the citizens to have run away.

Subjunctive *always by aspect*
διώξωμεν ἐκεῖνον τὸν δοῦλον.
Let's chase that slave!

Optative *usually by aspect, but by tense in indirect statement/question in historic sequence (replacing indicative)*
εἴθε ὁ πόλεμος παύσαιτο.
If only the war would cease!
but: ὁ ἄγγελος εἶπεν ὅτι ὁ πόλεμος παύσαιτο.
The messenger said that the war had ceased.

---

* However, note also:
(a) Greek quite often uses an aorist participle when a present one would also have been acceptable (and the aorist is translated like a present):
νομίσαντες τὸν ποταμὸν χαλεπὸν εἶναι, ἄλλην ὁδὸν εἱλόμεθα.
Believing the river to be dangerous, we chose another road.
Here choice of the aorist (better explained as by aspect rather than by tense) stresses the moment of coming to the belief, or the moment when it becomes relevant.
(b) Even where the aorist participle clearly is used (as it normally is) by tense, English idiom can represent it by a present:
ἀκούσας τοὺς τοῦ βασιλέως λόγους, ὁ ἄγγελος μάλιστα ἐφοβεῖτο.
Hearing the king's words, the messenger was very frightened.
In this case *hearing* means *on/after hearing* (not *whilst hearing*, which would translate a present participle).

Exercise 12.5

Croesus and Cyrus

This is the conclusion of the story of Croesus. The Delphic oracle plays a prominent role, though despite the lavish gifts Croesus had earlier made to it, he is here given a famously ambiguous response. In the battle over the city of Sardis, Croesus' deaf and dumb second son comes into his own (earlier in the story he had been dismissed with a callousness shocking to modern readers: ancient attitudes to disability were not enlightened). As often with stories in Herodotus, basically historical events have been overlaid with elements that recall myth: this is particularly true in the account of Croesus on the pyre. But underlying the whole story is the historical fact of the conquest of Lydia by the expansionist power of Persia in the middle of the sixth century BC.

μετὰ δὲ τὸν τοῦ Ἄτυος θάνατον ὁ Κροῖσος δύο ἔτη ἐν πένθει δεινῷ ἦν. ἔπειτα δ᾽ ἐλέχθη αὐτῷ περὶ Κύρου τοῦ Πέρσου ὅτι αὐξάνοιτο ἤδη τὰ βασιλέως πράγματα. ἤλπιζεν οὖν τὴν δύναμιν αὐτοῦ καθαιρήσειν οὔπω μεγάλην γενομένην. μέλλων δ᾽ ἐπὶ τοὺς Πέρσας στρατεύσειν, δῶρά τε
5 πολλὰ πρὸς τοὺς Δελφοὺς ἔπεμψε, καὶ τὸν θεὸν ἠρώτησεν εἰ εὐτυχὴς γενήσοιτο ἡ στρατεία. μαντεῖον δὲ ὁ Κροῖσος ἐδέξατο τόδε· "ἐὰν ὁ Κροῖσος ἐπὶ τοὺς Πέρσας στρατεύσῃ, μεγάλην ἀρχὴν καταλύσει".

τούτοις οὖν τοῖς λόγοις πεισθεὶς ὁ Κροῖσος τὸν ποταμον τὸν Ἄλυν διέβη (οὗτος γὰρ τὴν τῶν Περσῶν χώραν ὁρίζει), καὶ μάχη ἐγένετο δεινή τε καὶ
10 καρτερά. ὡς δὲ πολλῶν πεσόντων οὐδέτεροι ἐνίκησαν, ὁ μὲν Κροῖσος οἴκαδε ἐπανῆλθεν, μέλλων συμμάχων πολὺ πλῆθος συλλέξειν, ἵνα αὖθις ἐπὶ τοὺς Πέρσας στρατεύσειεν. ὁ δὲ Κῦρος ἐπεὶ ᾔσθετο τὸν

	Ἄτυς -υος ὁ	Atys
	Κροῖσος -ου ὁ	Croesus
	πένθος -ους τό	grief
	Κῦρος -ου ὁ	Cyrus (*king of Persia 559-529 BC*)
	αὐξάνομαι	I increase, I get bigger
	δύναμις -εως ἡ	power
	καθαιρέω	I destroy
	οὔπω	not yet
5	Δελφοί -ῶν οἱ	Delphi
	στρατεία -ας ἡ	expedition
	μαντεῖον -ου τό	oracular response
	καταλύω	I destroy
	Ἄλυς -υος ὁ	Halys
	ὁρίζω	I border, I form the boundary of
10	καρτερός -ά -όν	strong, violent
	οὐδέτεροι	neither side
	οἴκαδε	home, homewards
	ἐπανέρχομαι ἐπανῆλθον	I return, I go back

214

Κροῖσον ἀπελθόντα, ἐπορεύθη ὡς τάχιστα πρὸς τὰς Σάρδεις, οὗ ἦν τὰ
τοῦ Κροίσου βασίλεια· εὑρὼν δ' αὐτὸν ἀπαράσκευον (διελύθη γὰρ ἤδη
15 τὸ τῆς στρατιᾶς πλεῖστον μέρος) μάχῃ τ' ἐνίκησε καὶ εἰς τὴν πόλιν
καθεῖρξεν.

ἦν δὲ τῷ Κροίσῳ (ὡς καὶ πρότερον ἐλέχθη) ἄλλος υἱός, τὰ μὲν ἄλλα
ἐπιεικής, ἄφωνος δέ. πρὸ τοῦ ἐπὶ τοὺς Πέρσας πολέμου ὁ Κροῖσος
πολλάκις ἔλεγεν, "εἴθε λέγοι ὁ ἐμὸς παῖς". καὶ διότι περὶ πολλοῦ ἐποιεῖτο
20 τοῦτον ἀκεῖσθαι, ἀγγέλους πρὸς τοὺς Δελφοὺς αὖθις ἔπεμψεν. μαντεῖον δ'
ἐδέξατο τόδε· "ἀμεῖνόν ἐστι τὸν παῖδα ἄφωνον εἶναι. πρῶτον γὰρ λέξει
ἡμέρα ἀνόλβῳ." καὶ δὴ αἱρουμένης τῆς τοῦ Κροίσου πόλεως Πέρσης τις
τὸν Κροῖσον οὐκ ἐπιγιγνώσκων προσέδραμεν ὡς ἀποκτενῶν αὐτόν. ὁ μὲν
οὖν Κροῖσος τοῦτον ἰδὼν ἠμέλει, διὰ τὴν παροῦσαν συμφορὰν τὸν βίον
25 οὐκέτι βιωτὸν νομίζων· ὁ δὲ παῖς ὁ ἄφωνος ἐπεὶ εἶδε τὸν Πέρσην ἐπιόντα
μάλιστα φοβούμενος μεγάλη φωνῇ εἶπεν, "ὦ ἄνθρωπε, μὴ ἀποκτείνῃς τὸν
Κροῖσον". οὗτος μὲν δὴ τοῦτο πρῶτον ἔλεξε, μετὰ δὲ τοῦτο ἔλεγε πάντα
τὸν τοῦ βίου χρόνον. οἱ δὲ Πέρσαι τάς τε Σάρδεις ἔλαβον καὶ τὸν
Κροῖσον αὐτὸν ἐζώγρησαν, ἄρξαντά τε τέσσαρα καὶ δέκα ἔτη, καὶ
30 ἡμέρας τέσσαρας καὶ δέκα πολιορκηθέντα, καὶ κατὰ τὸ μαντεῖον ἀρχὴν
μεγάλην καταλύσαντα, τὴν ἑαυτοῦ.

ὁ δὲ Κῦρος πυρὰν μεγάλην συννήσας τὸν Κροῖσον ἀνεβίβασε, μέλλων
ζῶντα κατακαύσειν. τῷ δὲ Κροίσῳ ἐπὶ τῆς πυρᾶς ἤδη ὄντι λέγεται
εἰσελθεῖν τὸν τοῦ Σόλωνος λόγον, ὅτι οὐδεὶς τῶν ἔτι ζώντων ὄλβιός

	Σάρδεις -εων αἱ	Sardis
	βασίλεια -ων τά	palace
	ἀπαράσκευος -ον	unprepared
	διαλύω aor pass διελύθην	I disband, I dismiss
15	μέρος -ους τό	part
	καθείργω καθεῖρξα	I confine, I shut in
	ἐπιεικής -ές	capable
	ἄφωνος -ον	dumb, unable to speak
20	ἀκέω	I cure
	μαντεῖον -ου τό	oracular response
	ἄνολβος -ον	unlucky, unfortunate
	ἐπιγιγνώσκω	I recognise
	ἀμελέω	I do not care
25	βιωτός -όν	worth living
	ζωγρέω ἐζώγρησα	I take prisoner
30	καταλύω κατέλυσα	I destroy
	πυρά -ᾶς ἡ	pyre
	συννέω συνένησα	I heap up
	ἀναβιβάζω ἀνεβίβασα	I make (someone) go up, I put (someone) up
	ζάω	I live, I am alive
	κατακαίω fut κατακαύσω	I burn
	Σόλων -ωνος ὁ	Solon
	ὄλβιος -α -ον	happy

215

35 ἐστιν. καὶ τούτου τοῦ λόγου μνήμων ὁ Κροῖσος "Σόλων" τρὶς ἐβόησεν.
ὁ δὲ Κῦρος ἀκούσας ἐκέλευσε τοὺς ἑρμηνέας τὸν Κροῖσον ἐρωτῆσαι
ὅστις εἴη ὁ Σόλων. ὁ δὲ Κροῖσος πρῶτον μὲν ἐσίγησεν. ἔπειτα δέ,
τοῦ Κύρου πολλάκις ἐρωτήσαντος, εἶπεν ὅτι δέοι πάντα τύραννον τῷ
Σόλωνι διαλέγεσθαι, τῷ νομίζοντι πάντα τὸν ἑαυτοῦ ὄλβον οὐδὲν εἶναι.

40 ὁ δὲ Κῦρος νῦν μετέγνω, ἐννοήσας ὅτι αὐτὸς ἄνθρωπος ὢν μέλλει ἄλλον
ἄνθρωπον, ὄλβῳ οὐκ ἐλάσσονα ἑαυτοῦ γενόμενον, ζῶντα κατακαύσειν.
τοὺς οὖν δούλους ἐκέλευσε τό τε πῦρ σβέσαι καὶ τὸν Λυδὸν εὐθὺς
καταβιβάσαι. τὰ μέντοι τῆς πυρᾶς ἔσχατα ἤδη ἔκαιεν, ὥσθ' οἱ δοῦλοι
(καίπερ τοῦ Κύρου προθύμως κελεύοντος) οὐχ οἷοί τ' ἦσαν τοῦ πυρὸς
45 ἐπικρατῆσαι. ἐν ταύτῃ δὴ τῇ ἀπορίᾳ οἱ Λυδοὶ τὸν Κροῖσόν φασιν
Ἀπόλλωνα ἐπικαλέσασθαι, εἴ τι ἀγαθὸν παρ' αὐτοῦ ὁ θεὸς ἐδέξατο,
σῶσαι ἀπὸ τοῦ παρόντος κινδύνου· ἐξαίφνης δ' ἐξ αἰθρίας γενέσθαι
ὑετὸν πολύν, καὶ τὸ πῦρ παντελῶς σβέσαι.

ἐκ δὲ τούτου ὁ Κῦρος ἔμαθε τὸν Κροῖσον ἄνδρα ἀγαθόν τε καὶ θεοφιλῆ
50 ὄντα. ἠρώτησεν οὖν αὐτὸν διὰ τί ἐπὶ τὴν τῶν Περσῶν γῆν ἐστράτευσεν.
ὁ δὲ ἀπεκρίνατο, "ὦ βασιλεῦ, οὐδεὶς οὕτως ἀνόητός ἐστιν ὥστε τὸν
πόλεμον ἀντὶ τῆς εἰρήνης αἱρεῖσθαι. ἐν μὲν γὰρ ταύτῃ, οἱ παῖδες τοὺς
πατέρας θάπτουσιν· ἐν δ' ἐκείνῳ, οἱ πατέρες τοὺς παῖδας. ἀλλὰ
ἐπείσθην στρατεῦσαι ὑπὸ τοῦ τῶν Ἑλλήνων θεοῦ· τοῖς γὰρ θεοῖς φίλον
55 ἦν σε μὲν εὖ πράσσειν, ἐμὲ δὲ κακῶς".

35	μνήμων -ον (μνημον-)	mindful (of), remembering (+ *gen*)
	τρίς	three times
	ἑρμηνεύς -έως ὁ	interpreter
	σιγάω ἐσίγησα	I am silent
	τύραννος -ου ὁ	ruler
	διαλέγομαι	I have a conversation (with, + *dat*)
	ὄλβος -ου ὁ	prosperity/happiness
40	μεταγιγνώσκω μετέγνων	I repent, I change my mind
	ἐννοέω ἐνενόησα	I consider, I bear in mind
	ζάω	I live, I am alive
	κατακαίω κατεκαύσω	I burn
	σβέσαι	(*irreg aor inf*) to extinguish
	καταβιβάζω κατεβίβασα	I bring down
	πυρά -ᾶς ἡ	pyre
	ἔσχατος -η -ον	*lit* furthest, *n pl here* edges
	προθύμως	eagerly
45	ἐπικρατέω ἐπεκράτησα	I gain control of (+ *gen*)
	ἀπορία -ας ἡ	difficulty, crisis
	Ἀπόλλων -ωνος ὁ	Apollo
	ἐπικαλέομαι ἀπεκαλεσάμην	I call upon
	ἐξαίφνης	suddenly
	αἰθρία -ας ἡ	clear sky
	ὑετός -οῦ ὁ	rain
	παντελῶς	entirely, completely
	θεοφιλής -ές	loved by the gods
50	ἀνόητος -ον	foolish, senseless

216

Conditional sentences (2)

We saw in Chapter 11 that *open* conditions (where nothing is implied about fulfilment) in general use the indicative (in the same tense as English) in both the *protasis* (the 'if' clause) and the *apodosis* (the main clause). We also saw however that in a *future* open condition the protasis very often uses ἐάν with the subjunctive (present or aorist by aspect), instead of εἰ with the indicative, to give an *indefinite* flavour appropriate to the future. Past conditions, we saw in contrast, cannot be 'open' in the full sense (we cannot go back and change the events), but merely indicate that the outcome is *unknown* (the speaker has an open mind on the subject).

A second broad category of consists of *unfulfilled* conditions, and those which the speaker implies are unlikely to be fulfilled. For the past and present we can call these *closed* (the possibility of fulfillment is already closed off). Corresponding however to the way the past cannot be truly 'open', the future cannot ever be 'closed': possible future events can only be described as unlikely or *remote*. A *remote future condition* uses the optative (present or aorist by aspect) in both protasis and apodosis, εἰ for *if* in the protasis, and the indefinite particle ἄν in the apodosis (ἄν generally gives a flavour of *would* or *might*: here it reinforces a sense which the optative already has).

> *future remote condition:*
> εἰ ταῦτα λέγοι, σοφῶς ἂν λέγοι.
> If he were to say these things (*but the speaker implies this is unlikely*), he would speak wisely.

Closed or unfulfilled conditions in the present and past envisage situations which are already known not to be true. They do not involve any subjunctive or optative (this may seem surprising, especially given the use of the subjunctive for the equivalent construction in Latin), but rely instead on the indefinite particle ἄν with tenses of the indicative to give the flavour of *would*. A *present closed* condition uses the imperfect indicative in both protasis and apodosis, εἰ for *if* in the protasis, and the indefinite particle ἄν in the apodosis.

> *present closed condition:*
> εἰ ταῦτα ἔλεγε, σοφῶς ἂν ἔλεγεν.
> If he were saying these things (now) (*but in fact he is not*), he would be speaking wisely.

A *past closed* condition normally uses the aorist indicative in both protasis and apodosis, εἰ for *if* in the protasis, and the indefinite particle ἄν in the apodosis.

> *past closed condition:*
> εἰ ταῦτα εἶπε, σοφῶς ἂν εἶπεν.
> If he had said these things (*but in fact he did not*), he would have spoken wisely.

• Notice in these examples that the indefinite particle ἄν does not just put a *would* into the apodosis but affects how you translate the whole sentence. The protasis
> εἰ ταῦτα εἶπε ...
could (if there were no ἄν in the apodosis) be the first part of a past open/unknown condition (*If he said this, he spoke wisely*). You cannot translate the protasis until you have

looked carefully at the whole sentence and decided (from whether ἄν is present or not) what kind of condition is involved.

• Note that because the verb *to be* has no aorist, its imperfect form has to be used where an aorist would strictly be required. Again you need to look at the whole sentence before trying to translate the apodosis:

εἰ σοφὸς ἦν, σοφῶς ἄν ἔλεγεν.
If he were wise, he would be speaking wisely (now).
(*present closed: imperfect*)

εἰ σοφὸς ἦν, σοφῶς ἄν εἶπεν.
If he had been wise (at the time), he would have spoken wisely.
(*past closed: imperfect acting as aorist*)

• As with open conditions, it is possible to have mixed tenses (protasis and apodosis different), but it is not possible to mix types of condition (closed/remote with open/ unknown).

εἰ οἱ στρατιῶται τοὺς πολεμίους ἐνίκησαν, οἱ πολῖται ἄν ἐτίμων αὐτούς.
If the soldiers had conquered the enemy, the citizens would be honouring them (now).
(*protasis past closed, apodosis present closed*)

On this principle, the sentence above:
εἰ σοφὸς ἦν, σοφῶς ἄν εἶπεν *could be read as*
If he were (*permanently/still*) wise, he would (*on that occasion too*) have spoken wisely.
(*protasis present closed, apodosis past closed*), but the difference in practice is so small it hardly matters.

Summary table of conditionals

	Open (or unknown)	Unfulfilled (closed or remote)
Future		
protasis	ἐάν + subjunctive*	εἰ + optative
apodosis	future indicative	optative + ἄν
Present		
protasis	εἰ + present indicative	εἰ + imperfect indicative
apodosis	present indicative	imperfect indicative + ἄν
Past		
protasis	εἰ + any past indicative	εἰ + aorist indicative
apodosis	any past indicative	aorist indicative + ἄν

*or εἰ + future indicative

Note:
(1) Only in future conditionals is a subjunctive or optative involved.
(2) All unfulfilled/closed/remote conditions have ἄν in the apodosis.
(3) In any type of conditional, the negative in the protasis is μή and the negative in the apodosis is οὐ.

Exercise 12.6 (Remote/closed conditionals)

Translate into English:
1   εἰ μὴ ἐζήτησα τὴν διὰ τῶν ὀρῶν ὁδόν, οὔποτε ἂν ηὗρον.
2   εἰ εἰρήνη γένοιτο, πάντες ἂν ἐπαινέσειαν τοὺς ῥήτορας.
3   εἰ ὁ Σωκράτης νῦν παρῆν, τί ἐδίδασκεν ἄν;
4   εἰ οἱ πολῖται μὴ ἐφύλαξαν τὰς πύλας, ἐλήφθη ἂν ἡ πόλις.
5   εἰ τὸν τῶν συμμάχων ἄγγελον ἀπεπέμψατε, τὰ περὶ τῆς μάχης οὐκ ἂν
    ἠκούσατε.
6   δεινότατα ἂν ἔπαθες εἰ τὸν ἄρχοντα ἠδίκησας.
7   εἰ τοὺς πολεμίους οὕτως ἀνδρείως ἀεὶ <u>ἀμυνοίμεθα</u>, οὐδαμῶς δέοι ἂν
    φοβεῖσθαι αὐτούς.
8   εἰ περὶ τῆς ἡμετέρας βουλῆς ἤκουσας, ἐν τῇ ἐκκλησίᾳ νῦν ἂν
    παρῆσθα.
9   εἰ αἱ γυναῖκες ὑπὸ νύκτα ἀφίκοντο, εἴδομεν ἂν αὐτάς.
10 εἰ ἐν τῇ Περσικῇ ἀπέθανον οἱ στρατιῶται, οὐκ ἂν ἐξῆν θάψαι
    αὐτούς.

    ἀμύνομαι   I resist, I defend myself (against)

Exercise 12.7

Translate into Greek:
1   If the Athenians were to send an army, they would defeat the Spartans.
2   If you had not obeyed the king, slave, you would have been punished.
3   If our allies were fighting now, we should not be running away.
4   If the poet had not died, he would be winning many prizes.
5   If I had been present myself, these things would not have happened.

Exercise 12.8 (Assorted conditionals)

Translate into English:
1   εἰ λέξειας, ἀκούσαιμι ἄν.
2   εἰ οἱ ἄγγελοι εἰς καιρὸν ἀφίκοντο, αὕτη ἡ συμφορὰ οὐκ ἂν ἐγένετο.
3   εἰ τοὺς λόγους καθ᾽ ἡμέραν ἐμανθάνετε, ἐνομίζετε ἂν τὸ ἔργον ῥᾷον
    εἶναι.
4   λύσομέν σε ἐὰν πολλὰ χρήματα παράσχῃς.
5   εἰ Λακεδαιμόνιός τις τοιοῦτο πράξειε, δεινότατα ἂν κολασθείη.
6   εἰ οἱ Πέρσαι τὰς Ἀθήνας ἔλαβον, ἆρ᾽ οὐχ οἷοί τ᾽ εἰσὶ καὶ τὴν
    Σπάρτην λαβεῖν;
7   εἰ τὸν αἰχμάλωτον ἔτι ἔχεις, λῦσον αὐτόν.
8   εἰ ὁ μῦθος ἀληθής ἐστιν, ὁ γίγας δεινὰ ἔπρασσεν.
9   ἐὰν οἱ πολῖται μὴ ἔλθωσιν, ἀποπέμψωμεν τὸν ῥήτορα.
10 εἰ τούτῳ τῷ γέροντι βοηθήσαις, ὑπὸ τῶν φίλων ἀεὶ ἂν τιμῷο.

Revision checkpoint

Make sure you know:
• present, aorist and future optative
• use of the optative in wishes
• sequence of tenses and moods
• use of the subjunctive/optative in purpose clauses
• use of the optative in indirect statements and questions
• unfulfilled conditionals (future remote, present and past closed)

Exercise 12.9

The Infancy of Cyrus (1)

Cyrus the Great (who conquered Croesus' kingdom of Lydia) was the founder of the Persian empire, and king of Persia 559-529 BC. This story takes us back to the beginning of his life. His father was a Persian noble, but his mother was daughter of Astyages king of the Medes. The Medes were for a century or so the leading power in the Middle East (after their rebellion from the previously dominant empire of the Assyrians, and before the rise of Persia). Cyrus was to shift power decisively from the Medes to the Persians. As often in ancient literature, stories akin to myth are told about the childhood of an historical figure in order to demonstrate his significance. The prophecy given at the beginning to his grandfather Astyages is strikingly similar to the one Acrisius receives in the Perseus story (Chapter 9). The 'exposure' of unwanted babies (leaving them in a lonely place to die, rather than incurring religious pollution by actually killing them) was undoubtedly practised in the ancient world, though it is unclear on what scale; in stories, it is often the context for an unexpected rescue or miraculous deliverance.

οἱ δὲ τῶν <u>Μάγων</u> <u>ὀνειροπόλοι</u> εἶπον τῷ ᾿Αστυάγει τῷ τῶν <u>Μήδων</u> βασιλεῖ
ἐξ <u>ὄψεώς</u> τινος ὅτι ὁ τῆς θυγατρὸς υἱὸς <u>βασιλεύσει</u> ἀντὶ ἐκείνου. ταῦτα
οὖν μαθὼν ὁ ᾿Αστυάγης, ἐπεὶ ἡ θυγάτηρ <u>Μανδάνη</u> ὀνόματι παῖδα <u>ἔτεκεν</u>,
ἐκάλεσε τὸν ῞Αρπαγον ἄνδρα <u>συγγενῆ</u> τε καὶ <u>πιστὸν</u> ᾧ πάντα τὰ ἑαυτοῦ
5 <u>ἐπέτρεπεν</u>. τῷ δὲ ῾Αρπάγῳ παρόντι ὁ ᾿Αστυάγης εἶπε τάδε· "ὦ ῞Αρπαγε,
πρᾶγμα μέγιστον βούλομαί σε πρᾶξαι, ὃ μὴ <u>ἀποκνήσῃς</u>· λαβὲ τὸν τῆς
Μανδάνης παῖδα, καὶ εἰς τὴν σὴν οἰκίαν ἐνεγκὼν ἀπόκτεινον. μετὰ δὲ
ταῦτα θάψον αὐτὸν ὥσπερ βούλῃ." ὁ δὲ ἀπεκρίνατο· "ὦ βασιλεῦ, εἰ

	Μάγοι -ων οἱ	Magi (*caste of wise/holy men*)
	ὀνειροπόλος -ου ὁ	dream-interpreter
	᾿Αστυάγης -ους ὁ	Astyages
	Μῆδοι -ων οἱ	Medes
	ὄψις -εως ἡ	vision
	βασιλεύω	I am king
	Μανδάνη -ης ἡ	Mandane
	τίκτω ἔτεκον	I give birth to
	῞Αρπαγος -ου ὁ	Harpagus
	συγγενής -ές	related
	πιστός -ή -όν	loyal, reliable
5	ἐπιτρέπω	I entrust (X *acc* to Y *dat*)
	ἀποκνέω ἀπέκνησα	I shrink from

φίλον ἐστί σοι τοῦτο οὕτως γίγνεσθαι, χρὴ τὸ ἐμὸν <u>ἐπιτηδείως</u> ποιῆσαι".

10 ταῦτα δ' ἀποκρινάμενος ὁ Ἅρπαγος, ἐπεὶ τὸ <u>παιδίον</u> ἐδέξατο, ἀπῆλθε
δακρύων πρὸς τὴν οἰκίαν. καὶ ἀφικόμενος εἶπε τῇ γυναικὶ πάντα τὸν
λόγον τὸν ὑπ' Ἀστυάγους λεχθέντα. ἡ δὲ εἶπε, "τί οὖν μέλλεις νῦν
ποιήσειν;" ὁ δὲ ἀπεκρίνατο, "οὐχ ὡς ὁ Ἀστυάγης ἐκέλευσεν. οὐδὲ γὰρ
ἐὰν <u>μαίνηται</u> κάκιον ἢ νῦν μαίνεται τοῦτο ποιήσω. διὰ δὲ πολλὰ οὐκ
15 ἀποκτενῶ τὸ παιδίον. πρῶτον μὲν <u>συγγενές</u> ἐστί μοι, ὁ δὲ Ἀστυάγης
γέρων ἐστὶ καὶ <u>ἄπαις</u> <u>ἄρσενος</u> <u>τέκνου</u>. ἐὰν δὲ τὴν ἀρχήν, ἐκείνου
ἀποθανόντος, κτήσηται ἡ παῖς, ἧς τὸν υἱὸν ὁ Ἀστυάγης νῦν βούλεται
ἀποκτεῖναι δι' ἐμοῦ, λειφθήσεταί μοι μετὰ ταῦτα κινδύνων ὁ μέγιστος.
ἀλλὰ δεῖ φυλάσσειν τὴν ἐμὴν <u>σωτηρίαν</u>· δεῖ οὖν τὸν παῖδα ἀποθανεῖν.
20 ἄμεινον μέντοι ἐστὶν εἰ ἀποθανεῖται πρός τινος τῶν τοῦ Ἀστυάγους, καὶ
μὴ πρὸς ἐμοῦ."

ταῦτα εἶπε καὶ εὐθὺς <u>μετεπέμψατο</u> <u>βουκόλον</u> τινὰ τῶν τοῦ Ἀστυάγους,
ὃν ᾔδει ὄρη <u>ἔρημα</u> <u>νέμοντα</u>. καὶ τὸ ὄνομα τούτῳ ἦν <u>Μιτραδάτης</u>. ἐπεὶ
οὖν ὁ βουκόλος τάχιστα ἀφίκετο κληθείς, εἶπεν ὁ Ἅρπαγος τάδε· "κελεύει
25 σε ὁ Ἀστυάγης τοῦτο τὸ παιδίον πρὸς τὸ ἐρημότατον τῶν ὀρῶν φέρειν,
ἵνα ἐκεῖ ταχέως ἀποθάνῃ. λέγει δὲ καὶ τόδε ὁ βασιλεύς, ὅτι ἐὰν <u>ὀκνήσῃς</u>
καὶ μὴ ποιήσῃς τὸ κελευσθέν, ἔσται σοι θάνατος κάκιστος."

ὁ οὖν βουκόλος ταῦτα ἀκούσας καὶ τὸ παιδίον <u>ἀναλαβὼν</u> <u>ἐπανῆλθε</u> τὴν
αὐτὴν ὁδόν. καὶ ἐκείνῃ τῇ ἡμέρᾳ ἡ τοῦ βουκόλου γυνὴ παιδίον <u>ἔτεκεν</u>.
30 τὸν δ' ἄνδρα ἀφικόμενον ἡ γυνὴ εὐθὺς ᾔρετο διὰ τί οὕτω <u>προθύμως</u>
μετεπέμψατο αὐτὸν ὁ Ἅρπαγος. ὁ δὲ εἶπεν, "ὦ γύναι, εἶδόν τε εἰς τὴν
πόλιν ἐλθὼν καὶ ἤκουσα ὃ ἤλπιζον μηδέποτε ὄψεσθαι. πᾶσα γὰρ ἡ τοῦ
Ἁρπάγου οἰκία <u>κλαυθμῷ</u> <u>κατείχετο</u>. ἐγὼ εἰσῆλθον φοβούμενος, καὶ εἶδον

	ἐπιτηδείως	suitably, properly
10	παιδίον -ου τό	baby
	μαίνομαι	I am mad
15	συγγενής -ές	related
	ἄπαις -αιδος	childless, without offspring
	ἄρσην -ενος	male
	τέκνον -ου τό	child
	σωτηρία -ας ἡ	safety
20	μεταπέμπομαι	I send for
	βουκόλος -ου ὁ	herdsman
	ἔρημος -η -ον	lonely, deserted
	νέμω	pasture (animals in)
	Μιτραδάτης -ου ὁ	Mitradates
25	ὀκνέω ὤκνησα	I hesitate
	ἀναλαμβάνω ἀνέλαβον	I pick up
	ἐπανέρχομαι ἐπανῆλθον	I return, I go back
	τίκτω ἔτεκον	I give birth to
30	προθύμως	eagerly
	κλαυθμός -οῦ ὁ	weeping, mourning
	κατέχω	I occupy

221

<u>παιδίον</u> χρυσῷ τε καὶ <u>ἐσθῆτι</u> καλλίστη <u>κεκοσμημένον</u>. καὶ ἐδάκρυε τὸ
35 παιδίον."

παιδίον -ου τό	baby
ἐσθής -ῆτος ἡ	clothing
κοσμέω *perfect passive*	
κεκόσμημαι	I adorn, I dress (someone) elaborately

Verbs with omicron contraction

Very much rarer than verbs contracted with epsilon (e.g. φιλέω, Chapter 9) or alpha (e.g.
τιμάω, Chapter 10) are those with omicron. Here the rules of contraction are:
          o followed by a long vowel becomes ω
          o followed by a short vowel becomes ου
          any combination with ι becomes οι
Hence:
δηλόω = I show

		present active		*present middle/passive:*	
sg	1	δηλῶ	[δηλο-ω]	δηλοῦμαι	[δηλο-ομαι]
	2	δηλοῖς	[δηλο-εις]	δηλοῖ	[δηλο-η]
	3	δηλοῖ	[δηλο-ει]	δηλοῦται	[δηλο-εται]
pl	1	δηλοῦμεν	[δηλο-ομεν]	δηλούμεθα	[δηλο-ομεθα]
	2	δηλοῦτε	[δηλο-ετε]	δηλοῦσθε	[δηλο-εσθε]
	3	δηλοῦσι(ν)	[δηλο-ουσι(ν)]	δηλοῦνται	[δηλο-ονται]

participle:
δηλῶν -οῦσα -οῦν (stem δηλουντ-)
[δηλο-ων -ουσα -ον (δηλο-οντ-)]

participle:
δηλούμενος -η -ον
[δηλο-ομενος]

infinitive:
δηλοῦν
[δηλο-ειν: iota disappears here]

infinitive:
δηλοῦσθαι
[δηλο-εσθαι]

imperative:
sg δήλου pl δηλοῦτε
[δηλο-ε, -ετε]

imperative:
sg δηλοῦ pl δηλοῦσθε
[δηλο-ου, -εσθε]

		imperfect active:		*imperfect middle/passive:*	
sg	1	ἐδήλουν	[ἐδηλο-ον]	ἐδηλούμην	[ἐδηλο-ομην]
	2	ἐδήλους	[ἐδηλο-ες]	ἐδηλοῦ	[ἐδηλο-ου]
	3	ἐδήλου	[ἐδηλο-ε]	ἐδηλοῦτο	[ἐδηλο-ετο]
pl	1	ἐδηλοῦμεν	[ἐδηλο-ομεν]	ἐδηλούμεθα	[ἐδηλο-ομεθα]
	2	ἐδηλοῦτε	[ἐδηλο-ετε]	ἐδηλοῦσθε	[ἐδηλο-εσθε]
	3	ἐδήλουν	[ἐδηλο-ον]	ἐδηλοῦντο	[ἐδηλο-οντο]

For the first (weak) aorist and future, the omicron is lengthened to omega before adding the sigma, but the endings after the sigma are normal. Hence:

aorist active	ἐδήλωσα
aorist middle	ἐδηλωσάμην
aorist passive	ἐδηλώθην

future active	δηλώσω
future middle	δηλώσομαι
future passive	δηλωθήσομαι

Other forms should be deducible, but note that (as with epsilon and alpha verbs) there is a distinctive form of the singular of the present active optative:

1   δηλοίην
2   δηλοίης
3   δηλοίη

A few indicative forms of omicron verbs look at first sight (because of the diphthong οι) like the optative of an ordinary verb, but because there are so few omicron verbs there is little risk of confusion.

• Omicron verbs like δηλόω:

δουλόω	I enslave
ἐλευθερόω	I set free

Exercise 12.10

Translate into English:
1   ἔδοξε τῇ ἐκκλησίᾳ τοὺς μὲν δούλους ἐλευθερῶσαι, τοὺς δὲ αἰχμαλώτους δουλῶσαι.
2   ὁ τῶν συμμάχων ἄγγελος τὴν βουλὴν ἡμῖν νῦν δηλοῖ.
3   οὗτος οὐδέποτε δουλωθήσεται.
4   ἀεὶ ἐλευθέρου τοὺς ἀδίκως δουλωθέντας, ὦ νεανία.
5   τίνες εἰσὶν οἱ τὰς βίβλους πᾶσι δηλοῦντες;

Exercise 12.11

Translate into Greek:
1   Enslave this boy now, master!
2   If the teacher were to show us the letter, we should learn many strange things.
3   It is easy to set such women free.
4   The horse now being shown to the general is excellent.
5   Surely that magistrate was not freeing all the slaves?

Pluperfect tense

The pluperfect (literally *more than* the *completed* perfect) refers, as in other languages, to something two stages back in the past (e.g. *they had done X*). But it is much rarer in Greek even than the perfect. As so often, the explanation for this is the amount of work done both by participles, and by the aorist. The normal Greek for a sentence involving an English pluperfect uses an aorist participle:

οἱ σύμμαχοι ἀφικόμενοι εὐθὺς ἐστρατοπεδεύσαντο.
When the allies had arrived, they immediately set up camp.

Even if a *when* clause is used, the verb in it is still normally aorist:

ἐπεὶ οἱ σύμμαχοι ἀφίκοντο, εὐθὺς ἐστρατοπεδεύσαντο.

Here the two aorist verbs naturally imply one single action followed by another. The pluperfect tense is not normally used in subordinate clauses such as this (where Latin *does* use a pluperfect). The Greek pluperfect is more likely to be met in a main clause, indicating that *at a given point in the past the effect of a previous action was still continuing*. It is not a high priority for learning, but you need to be able to recognise it. This is easy, because it has *both* the augment *and* reduplication (and the same stem as the perfect):

		pluperfect *active*	*middle/passive*
sg	*1*	ἐπεπαύκ-η	ἐπεπαύ-μην
	2	ἐπεπαύκ-ης	ἐπέπαυ-σο
	3	ἐπεπαύκ-ει(ν)	ἐπέπαυ-το
pl	*1*	ἐπεπαύκ-εμεν	ἐπεπαύ-μεθα
	2	ἐπεπαύκ-ετε	ἐπέπαυ-σθε
	3	ἐπεπαύκ-εσαν	ἐπέπαυ-ντο

Note the similarity of middle/passive endings to the normal historic middle/passive ones.

• The two middle/deponent verbs we met in Chapter 11 whose present tense is like a perfect middle/passive (δύναμαι = *I am able* and ἐπίσταμαι = *I know [how to]*) have corresponding imperfect tenses which conjugate like a pluperfect middle/passive: ἐδυνάμην (though this is rare) and ἠπιστάμην respectively.

Exercise 12.12

Translate into English:
1   ἐπεπαιδεύκεμεν τοὺς νέους δούλους πρὸ τοῦ πολέμου.
2   ὁ διδάσκαλος πρότερον μὲν ἐπεπαύκει τὸν ἀγῶνα, ὕστερον δὲ εἴασεν.
3   ἐπεὶ εἰς τὸν ἀγρὸν ἀφικόμην, οἱ δοῦλοι ἤδη ἐλελύκεσαν τοὺς ἵππους.
4   πρὸ τῆς νυκτὸς ἡ μάχη ὑπο τοῦ στρατηγοῦ ἐπέπαυτο.
5   ἆρα τὴν βουλὴν ἤδη ἐκεκωλύκης, καίπερ τὴν ἐμὴν ἐπιστολὴν οὐ
        δεξάμενος;

Exercise 12.13

Translate into Greek (using the pluperfect tense where appropriate):
1   The allies had been hindered by the storm.
2   You had released some of the prisoners, friends, but others were still waiting.
3   The women had trained their daughters well.
4   Many soldiers had been pursued into the sea.
5   When we saw the city, the battle had already been stopped.

225

Exercise 12.14

The Infancy of Cyrus (2)

ὁ οὖν βουκόλος τῇ γυναικὶ διετέλει λέγων, "ὁ δὲ Ἅρπαγος, δηλώσας τὸ
παιδίον ἐκέλευσέ με ὡς τάχιστα ἀναλαβόντα φέρειν πρὸς τὸ ἐρημότατον
τῶν ὀρῶν, ἵνα ἐκεῖ ἀποθάνῃ. καὶ κακὰ πολλὰ ἠπείλησεν εἰ μὴ ταῦτα
ποιήσαιμι. ἐγὼ δ' ἀναλαβὼν ἔφερον, καὶ κατὰ τὴν ὁδὸν πάντα τὸν λόγον
5 ἐπυθόμην παρὰ δούλου τινός, ὅτι τῆς Μανδάνης ἐστὶ τὸ παιδίον καὶ τοῦ
Καμβύσου, καὶ ὁ Ἀστυάγης κελεύει ἀποκτεῖναι αὐτόν. καὶ νῦν ὅδε
ἐστίν." ἅμα δὲ ταῦτα ἔλεγεν ὁ βουκόλος καὶ ἐκκαλύψας ἐδήλωσεν.

ἡ δὲ γυνή, ἐπεὶ εἶδε τὸ παιδίον μέγα τε καὶ καλὸν ὄν, δακρύσασα καὶ
τῶν τοῦ ἀνδρὸς γονάτων λαβομένη, ᾔτησε μηδαμῶς ἐν τοῖς ὀρεσιν λιπεῖν
10 αὐτό. ὁ δὲ οὐκ ἔφη οἷός τ' εἶναι ἄλλως ποιεῖν· ἀφίξεσθαι γὰρ
κατασκόπους τοῦ Ἀστυάγους ὡς ἐποψομένους· καὶ ἑαυτῷ μετὰ ταῦτα
θάνατον κάκιστον ἔσεσθαι. ἡ δὲ γυνή, ἐπεὶ οὐκ ἔπεισε τὸν ἄνδρα, εἶπε
τάδε· "ἐπεὶ οὖν οὐχ οἷά τ' εἰμὶ πεῖσαί σε, ὧδε ποίησον, εἰ χρὴ παιδίον τι
ἐν τῷ ὄρει ὀφθῆναι. ἐγὼ γὰρ σήμερον τέτοκα, τὸ δὲ παιδίον τέθνηκεν.
15 τοῦτο δὲ φέρων ἐν τῷ ὄρει λίπε, τὸν δὲ παῖδα τὸν τῆς τοῦ Ἀστυάγους
θυγατρὸς ὡς τὸν ἡμέτερον τρέφωμεν. καὶ οὕτως οὔθ' εὑρεθήσῃ ἀδικῶν τὸν
δεσπότην οὔτε κίνδυνος ἡμῖν ἔσται. πρὸς δὲ τούτοις, ὅ τε παῖς ὁ
τεθνηκὼς τάφον βασιλικὸν ἕξει, ὁ δὲ περιὼν οὐκ ἀποθανεῖται."

	βουκόλος -ου ὁ	herdsman
	διατελέω	I continue, I carry on
	Ἅρπαγος -ου ὁ	Harpagus
	παιδίον -ου τό	baby
	ἀναλαμβάνω ἀνέλαβον	I pick up
	ἔρημος -η -ον	lonely, deserted
	ἀπειλέω ἠπείλησα	I threaten
	κατά	(+ acc) on, along
5	Μανδάνη -ης ἡ	Mandane
	Καμβύσης -ου ὁ	Cambyses
	Ἀστυάγης -ους ὁ	Astyages
	ἐκκαλύπτω ἐξεκάλυψα	I uncover
	γόνυ -ατος τό	knee
10	κατάσκοπος -ου ὁ	spy, scout
	ἐφοράω *future* ἐπόψομαι	I oversee, I inspect
	σήμερον	today
	τίκτω *perfect* τέτοκα	I give birth
15	τρέφω	I bring up
	τάφος -ου ὁ	burial, tomb
	βασιλικός -ή -όν	royal
	περίειμι	I survive

226

ἔδοξε δὲ τῷ <u>βουκόλῳ</u> εὖ εἰπεῖν ἡ γυνή, καὶ εὐθὺς ἐποίησε ταῦτα· μετὰ
20 οὖν τῆς γυναικὸς ἔλιπε τὸν παῖδα ὃν ἔφερεν ὡς ἀποκτενῶν· τὸν δὲ
ἑαυτοῦ, νέκρον ὄντα, ἐπεὶ τῷ τε χρυσῷ καὶ τῇ <u>ἐσθῆτι</u> τοῦ ἑτέρου παιδὸς
<u>ἐκόσμησεν</u>, ἐν τῷ <u>ἀγγείῳ</u> (ἐν ᾧ πρότερον ἔφερε τὸν ἕτερον) πρὸς τὸ
<u>ἐρημότατον</u> τῶν ὀρῶν ἐνέγκας ἐκεῖ ἔλιπεν.

τῇ δὲ τρίτῃ ἡμέρᾳ μετὰ ταῦτα, ὁ βουκόλος παρὰ τὸν Ἅρπαγον ἐλθὼν
25 ἔφη ἕτοιμος εἶναι δηλῶσαι τὸν τοῦ <u>παιδίου</u> νέκρον. πέμψας δὲ ὁ
Ἅρπαγος τῶν ἑαυτοῦ <u>δορυφόρων</u> τοὺς <u>πιστοτάτους</u>, εἶδε διὰ τούτων καὶ
ἔθαψε τὸ τοῦ βουκόλου παιδίον. τὸν δὲ Κῦρον <u>ἔτρεφεν</u> ἡ τοῦ βουκόλου
γυνή.

	βουκόλος -ου ὁ	herdsman
20	ἐσθής -ῆτος ἡ	clothing
	κοσμέω	I dress (someone) up
	ἀγγεῖον -ου τό	container
	ἔρημος -η -ον	lonely, deserted
25	παιδίον -ου τό	baby
	δορυφόρος -ου ὁ	bodyguard
	πιστός -ή -όν	faithful, reliable
	τρέφω	I bring up

Verbs ending in -μι

We have already met the irregular verbs εἰμί (*I am*), εἶμι (*I shall go*) and φημί (*I say*). As
well as these there are a few verbs whose first-person present indicative active ends -μι, but
which follow more regular patterns. These represent an older stratum of the language than
the ordinary verbs ending in -ω. Though the various verbs use different vowels, they follow
a common pattern, so it is convenient to show them together:

present active

		I give	I place*	I show
sg	1	δίδωμι	τίθημι	δείκνυμι
	2	δίδως	τίθης	δείκνυς
	3	δίδωσι(ν)	τίθησι(ν)	δείκνυσι(ν)
pl	1	δίδομεν	τίθεμεν	δείκνυμεν
	2	δίδοτε	τίθετε	δείκνυτε
	3	διδόασι(ν)	τιθέασι(ν)	δεικνύασι(ν)

* *also* I set up, I establish

Many of the endings recall familiar patterns of ordinary verbs: thus -ς in the second person singular, -μεν
and -τε in the first and second person plural, whilst -ασι(ν) in the third-person plural recalls the perfect
tense. Note that the characteristic vowel in the endings of each verb shortens in the plural (this is seen more
obviously with δίδωμι and τίθημι, but applies to δείκνυμι as well).

227

The imperfects are also broadly similar, and also have the vowel shortening in the plural (but here sometimes with a diphthong rather than a long vowel in the singular):

imperfect active

sg				
	1	ἐδίδουν	ἐτίθην	ἐδείκνυν
	2	ἐδίδους	ἐτίθης	ἐδείκνυς
	3	ἐδίδου	ἐτίθει	ἐδείκνυ

pl				
	1	ἐδίδομεν	ἐτίθεμεν	ἐδείκνυμεν
	2	ἐδίδοτε	ἐτίθετε	ἐδείκνυτε
	3	ἐδίδοσαν	ἐτίθεσαν	ἐδείκνυσαν

In the aorist, δίδωμι and τίθημι follow a pattern similar to each other, and yet again with the vowel-shortening, but δείκνυμι has a regular first (weak) aorist form:

aorist active

sg				
	1	ἔδωκα	ἔθηκα	ἔδειξα
	2	ἔδωκας	ἔθηκας	etc (regular first [weak] aorist)
	3	ἔδωκε(ν)	ἔθηκε(ν)	

pl			
	1	ἔδομεν	ἔθεμεν
	2	ἔδοτε	ἔθετε
	3	ἔδοσαν	ἔθεσαν

Alternative third-person plurals ἔδωκαν, ἔθηκαν (on the model of the singular) are also found. Note how the ordinary plurals of these two verbs are shortened forms of the imperfect (their present and imperfect involving a form of reduplication).

Many other parts of these verbs are more predictable, with endings like the equivalent tenses of ordinary verbs:

future indicative active

δώσω	θήσω	δείξω

perfect indicative active

δέδωκα	τέθηκα	δέδειχα

• Less common parts of these verbs are set out in the Reference Grammar, pages 305-7.

• Note that the aorist stem of δείκνυμι is δειξ-. Care needs to be taken to avoid confusing parts of this verb with parts of δέχομαι (= *I receive*), whose aorist stem is δεξ-.

• Another common example of a verb ending in -μι is ὄμνυμι = *I swear*. In the present and imperfect it goes like δείκνυμι, and it has a first (weak) aorist ὤμοσα (stem ὀμοσ-). Its normal construction is with a future infinitive, which simply reinforces the meaning of the verb: hence *swear to do X* (rather than *swear to be going to do X*: this is exactly the same as the construction with ἐλπίζω, μέλλω and ὑπισχνέομαι).

Exercise 12.15 (See pages 305-7)

Translate into English:

1   ὁ οἶνος ὁ τῷ γίγαντι δοθεὶς ἄριστος ἦν.
2   ἐὰν τοσαῦτα χρήματα τῇ γυναικὶ δίδως, ταχέως πλουσία γενήσεται.
3   οἱ παῖδες ὤμοσαν μηδέποτε τοὺς ἵππους λύσειν.
4   ἆρα σῖτον τῷ γέροντι πολλάκις ἐδίδους;
5   ὁ φύλαξ τὸ ξίφος ἐγγὺς τῆς θύρας ἔθηκεν.
6   ἐκέλευσα τὸν δοῦλον τὴν ὁδὸν ὑμῖν δεῖξαι.
7   δός μοι ἐκείνην τὴν βίβλον, ὦ δοῦλε.
8   εἰ ἡ ἐπιστολὴ δειχθείη μοι, οἷός τ' εἴην ἂν τὴν τῶν πολεμίων βουλὴν
       μαθεῖν.
9   μὴ δῶτε δῶρον τούτῳ, ὦ κριταί.
10   ἐὰν τὴν χεῖρα εἰς τὸ πῦρ θῇς, δεινότατα πείσῃ.

Exercise 12.16 (See pages 305-7)

Translate into Greek:
1   The gods gave many gifts to the Athenians.
2   Let us always establish good laws.
3   To whom were you showing the road towards the sea, slave?
4   The gold was placed near the temple of the goddess.
5   If the teacher were to give us prizes, we should learn more quickly.

Exercise 12.17

The Boyhood of Cyrus

Ancient authors often told stories about the childhood of great men which in some way indicated their character or foreshadowed their later achievements. This is seen here, along with the assumption that kingliness is an inborn characteristic which will inevitably reveal itself. The stage is thus set for the recognition of Cyrus and his true identity.

ὁ δὲ Κῦρος ὅτε <u>δεκαέτης</u> ἦν καὶ ἔτι ἐνομίζετο υἱὸς τοῦ <u>βουκόλου</u> εἶναι,
<u>ἔπαιζεν</u> ἐν τῇ κώμῃ μετ᾽ ἄλλων τινῶν παίδων. καὶ οἱ παῖδες παίζοντες
εἴλοντο τοῦτον ἑαυτῶν βασιλέα εἶναι. ὁ δὲ τοὺς μὲν ἐκέλευσεν οἰκίας
<u>οἰκοδομεῖν</u>, τοὺς δὲ <u>δορυφόρους</u> εἶναι, τοὺς δὲ ἄλλα ἔργα ποιεῖν. εἰς
5   μέντοι τούτων τῶν παίδων <u>συμπαιζόντων</u>, υἱὸς ὢν τοῦ <u>Ἀρτεμβάρους</u>
ἀνδρὸς <u>δοκίμου</u> ἐν τοῖς <u>Μήδοις</u>, οὐκ ἐποίησε τὸ ὑπὸ τοῦ Κύρου
<u>προσταχθέν</u>. ὁ οὖν Κῦρος ἐκέλευσε τοὺς ἄλλους παῖδας λαβεῖν αὐτόν.
πιθομένων δὲ τῶν παίδων ὁ Κῦρος τὸν παῖδα <u>ἐμαστίγωσεν</u>. ὁ δέ, ἐπεὶ
<u>τάχιστα</u> ἐλύθη, ὡς οὐκ ἄξια παθὼν μάλιστα ὀργιζόμενος ἤγγειλε τῷ πατρὶ
10 τὰ γενόμενα. ὁ δ᾽ Ἀρτεμβάρης, ἐλθὼν παρὰ τὸν <u>Ἀστυάγη</u> καὶ ἅμα τὸν
παῖδα ἄγων εἶπεν, "ὦ βασιλεῦ, ὑπὸ τοῦ σοῦ δούλου, ὃς βουκόλου τινὸς
υἱός ἐστιν, ὧδε ἐπάθομεν". καὶ ἔδειξε τοὺς τοῦ παιδὸς <u>ὤμους</u>.

ἀκούσας δὲ καὶ ἰδών, ὁ Ἀστυάγης <u>μετεπέμψατο</u> τόν τε βουκόλον καὶ τὸν
παῖδα. ἐπεὶ δὲ παρῆσαν <u>ἀμφότεροι</u>, <u>βλέψας</u> πρὸς τὸν Κῦρον ἔφη, "ἆρα δὴ
15 σύ, βουκόλου παῖς ὤν, <u>ἐτόλμησας</u> τὸν παῖδα τοῦδε, ὄντος ἀνδρὸς
<u>εὐγενοῦς</u> τε καὶ δοκίμου, ὧδε <u>ὑβρίζειν</u>;"

	δεκαέτης -ες	ten years old
	βουκόλος -ου ὁ	herdsman
	παίζω	I play
	οἰκοδομέω	I build
	δορύφορος -ου ὁ	bodyguard (*literally* spear-carrier)
5	συμπαίζω	I play together
	Ἀρτεμβάρης -ους ὁ	Artembares
	δόκιμος -ον	distinguished
	Μῆδοι -ων οἱ	Medes
	προστάσσω	
	aor pass προσετάχθην	I assign, I instruct
	μαστιγόω ἐμαστίγωσα	I whip
	ἐπεὶ τάχιστα	as soon as
10	Ἀστυάγης -ους ὁ	Astyages
	ὦμος -ου ὁ	shoulder
	μεταπέμπομαι μετεπεμψάμην	I send for
	ἀμφότεροι -αι -α	both
	βλέπω ἔβλεψα	I look
15	τολμάω ἐτόλμησα	I dare
	εὐγενής -ές	noble
	ὑβρίζω	I treat (someone) violently

ὁ δὲ Κῦρος ἀπεκρίνατο, "ὦ δέσποτα, ἐγὼ ταῦτα δικαιότατα ἐποίησα. οἱ γὰρ τῆς κώμης παῖδες, ὧν καὶ ὅδε ἦν, <u>παίζοντες</u> ἐμὲ εἵλοντο βασιλέα ἑαυτῶν· ἐδόκουν γὰρ αὐτοῖς εἶναι εἰς τοῦτο <u>ἐπιτηδειότατος</u>. οἱ μέν νυν
20 ἄλλοι παῖδες τὰ κελευσθέντα ἔπρασσον· οὗτος δ' <u>ἀνηκούστει</u> τε καὶ οὐδένα λόγον εἶχεν. τούτων οὖν ἔδει αὐτὸν <u>δίκην δοῦναι</u>. εἰ δὲ διὰ ταῦτα ἄξιός εἰμι κολάζεσθαι, ὧδέ σοι πάρειμι."

τοῦ δὲ παιδὸς ταῦτα λέγοντος, <u>ἀναγνώρισις</u> ἔλαβε τὸν Ἀστυάγη. ὅ τε γὰρ τοῦ <u>προσώπου χαρακτὴρ</u> ἐδόκει <u>προσφέρεσθαι</u> τῷ ἑαυτοῦ, καὶ ὁ παῖς
25 ἐλευθερώτατα ἀπεκρίνατο. πρὸς δὲ τούτοις, ὁ τῆς <u>ἐκθέσεως</u> χρόνος ἐδόκει <u>συμβαίνειν</u> τῇ τοῦ παιδὸς <u>ἡλικίᾳ</u>. ταῦτα οὖν θαυμάζων, πολὺν χρόνον <u>ἄφθογγος</u> ἦν.

ἔπειτα δέ, βουλόμενος ἐκπέμψαι τὸν Ἀρτεμβάρη, ἵνα τὸν <u>βουκόλον</u> μόνον λαβὼν <u>βασανίσῃ</u>, "Ἀρτέμβαρες," ἔφη, "πάντα ποιήσω ἵνα σύ τε καὶ ὁ
30 υἱὸς μὴ <u>ἐπιμέμψησθε</u>". καὶ ἀπέπεμψε τόν τε Ἀρτεμβάρη καὶ τὸν παῖδα. καὶ οἱ δοῦλοι τὸν Κῦρον εἰς ἄλλο <u>δωμάτιον</u> ἤγαγον. ἐπεὶ δὲ ὁ βουκόλος ἐλείφθη μόνος, ὁ Ἀστυάγης ἤρετο αὐτὸν ὁπόθεν λάβοι τὸν παῖδα, καὶ τίς εἴη ὁ <u>παραδούς</u>. ὁ δὲ βουκόλος ἔφη τὸν παῖδα ἑαυτοῦ εἶναι, καὶ τὴν γυναῖκα <u>τεκεῖν</u> αὐτόν. ὁ δ' Ἀστυάγης ὀργιζόμενος ἐκέλευσε τοὺς
35 <u>δορυφόρους</u> λαβεῖν αὐτόν. ἀπορῶν οὖν ὁ βουκόλος ἀληθῶς πάντα <u>ἐξηγήσατο</u>, καὶ ᾔτησε τὸν βασιλέα ἑαυτῷ <u>συγγιγνώσκειν</u>.

ὁ δ' Ἀστυάγης τὸν μὲν βουκόλον ὡς τὸ ἀληθὲς λέξαντα οὐκέτι <u>ᾐτιᾶτο</u>· τὸν δὲ Ἅρπαγον μάλιστα ὀργιζόμενος <u>μετεπέμψατο</u>. καὶ τοῦτον

	παίζω	I play
	ἐπιτήδειος -α -ον	suitable
20	ἀνηκουστέω	I disobey
	δίκην δίδωμι	I pay the penalty (for, + gen)
	ἀναγνώρισις -εως ἡ	recognition
	πρόσωπον -ου τό	face
	χαρακτήρ -ῆρος ὁ	character, appearance
	προσφέρομαι	I resemble (+ dat)
25	ἔκθεσις -εως ἡ	exposure
	συμβαίνω	(here) I am consistent with, I match (+ dat)
	ἡλικία -ας ἡ	age
	ἄφθογγος -ον	silent
	βουκολος -ου ὁ	herdsman
	βασανίζω ἐβασάνισα	I test, I examine
30	ἐπιμέμφομαι ἐπεμεμψάμην	I have cause to complain
	δωμάτιον -ου τό	room
	παραδίδωμι *aor pple* παραδούς	I hand over
	τίκτω ἔτεκον	I give birth to
35	δορυφορος -ου ὁ	bodyguard
	ἐξηγέομαι ἐξηγησάμην	I explain
	συγγιγνώσκω	I forgive (+ dat)
	αἰτιάομαι	I blame
	μεταπέμπομαι μετεπεμψάμην	I send for

ἀφικόμενον ἠρώτησεν, "Ἅρπαγε, τίνι <u>τρόπῳ</u> ἀπέκτεινας τὸν παῖδα ὃν
40 ἔδωκά σοι, τὸν τῆς ἐμῆς θυγατρὸς υἱόν;" ὁ δὲ Ἅρπαγος, ὡς εἶδε τὸν
βουκόλον παρόντα, οὐκ <u>ἐψεύσατο</u> ἀλλ᾽ εὐθὺς <u>ἐξηγήσατο</u> τὰ ἐξ ἀρχῆς
γενόμενα.

ὁ δ᾽ Ἀστυάγης, κρύπτων τὴν ὀργήν, εἶπε, "<u>περίεστί</u> τε ὁ παῖς, καὶ τὸ
πρᾶγμα <u>ἔχει</u> καλῶς· ἐπεὶ γὰρ ἐκέλευσά σε τὸν παῖδα ἀποκτεῖναι,
45 οὐδαμῶς <u>ἡδόμην</u>, καὶ περὶ πολλοῦ ἐποιούμην τὴν τῆς θυγατρὸς ὀργήν.
νῦν δὲ πάντα εὐτυχῶς <u>ἀπέβη</u>. πέμψον οὖν τὸν σὸν παῖδα ὡς φίλον τῷ
παιδὶ τῷ περιόντι. ἔπειτα δὲ (<u>σῶστρα</u> γὰρ τοῦ παιδὸς τοῖς θεοῖς μέλλω
θύσειν) πάρισθί μοι <u>ἐπὶ</u> δεῖπνον."

ὁ δὲ Ἅρπαγος ταῦτα ἀκούσας <u>προσεκύνησεν</u>. ἔπειτα δὲ <u>οἴκαδε</u> ἀπελθὼν
50 τὸν παῖδα τὸν <u>μονογενῆ</u> ἔτη τρία καὶ δέκα γεγονότα ὡς τὸν Ἀστυάγη
ἔπεμψεν. καὶ ὁ Ἀστυάγης, <u>ἐπειδὴ</u> ἀφίκετο ὁ τοῦ Ἁρπάγου παῖς, <u>σφάξας</u>
αὐτὸν καὶ <u>κατὰ μέλη διελών</u>, τὰ μὲν τῶν <u>κρεῶν</u> <u>ὤπτησε</u>, τὰ δὲ <u>ἥψησεν</u>.
ἐπεὶ δὲ ἡ τοῦ δείπνου ὥρα ἐγένετο, <u>παρέθηκε</u> ταῦτα τῷ Ἁρπάγῳ, πλὴν
τῆς τε κεφαλῆς καὶ τῶν χειρῶν καὶ τῶν ποδῶν· ταῦτα δὲ <u>χωρὶς</u> ἦν ἐν
55 <u>ἀγγείῳ</u> <u>κατακαλυμμένα</u>. ὡς δὲ ὁ Ἅρπαγος ἐδόκει <u>ἅλις</u> ἔχειν τοῦ δείπνου,
ὁ Ἀστυάγης ἤρετο αὐτὸν εἰ ἥδοιτο τῇ <u>θοίνῃ</u>. τοῦ δὲ Ἁρπάγου εἰπόντος
μάλιστα ἥδεσθαι, δοῦλοί τινες ἐνέφερον τὴν τοῦ παιδὸς κεφαλὴν

	τρόπος -ου ὁ	way
40	ψεύδομαι ἐψευσάμην	I lie
	ἐξηγέομαι ἐξηγησάμην	I explain
	περίειμι	I survive
	ἔχω	(+ adv) I am
45	ἥδομαι	I am pleased
	ἀποβαίνω ἀπέβην	I turn out
	σῶστρα -ων τά	thank-offerings
	ἐπί	(+ acc) (here) for
	προσκυνέω προσεκύνησα	I bow
	οἴκαδε	home, homewards
50	μονογενής -ές	only (child)
	ἐπειδή	when, since
	σφάζω ἔσφαξα	slaughter
	κατά	(+ acc) (here) into separate ...
	μέλος -ους τό	limb
	διαιρέω διεῖλον	I cut up
	κρέα -ων τά	flesh
	ὀπτάω ὤπτησα	I roast
	ἕψω ἥψησα	I boil
	παρατίθημι παρέθηκα	I place X (acc) in front of Y (dat)
	χωρίς	apart, separate
55	ἀγγεῖον -ου τό	vessel, pot
	κατακαλύπτω perfect passive participle κατακελυμμένος	I cover over
	ἅλις	enough
	θοίνη -ης ἡ	feast

232

<u>κατακαλυμμένην</u> καὶ τὰς χεῖρας καὶ τοὺς πόδας. τὸν δὲ Ἅρπαγον
ἐκέλευσεν ὁ βασιλεὺς <u>ἀποκαλύψαι</u> τε καὶ λαβεῖν ὃ βούλεται. πιθόμενος
60 δὲ ὁ Ἅρπαγος καὶ ἀποκαλύψας, εἶδε τὰ τοῦ παιδὸς λοιπά. ἰδὼν δὲ οὐκ
<u>ἀνεβόησεν</u> ἀλλ' ἐν ἑαυτῷ ἐγένετο. ἤρετο δὲ αὐτὸν ὁ Ἀστυάγης εἰ
γιγνώσκει οὗτινος <u>θηρίου</u> <u>κρέα</u> ἔφαγεν. ὁ δὲ καὶ γιγνώσκειν ἔφη καὶ
ἥδεσθαι πᾶσι τοῖς ὑπὸ τοῦ βασιλέως πεπραγμένοις. οὕτω δ'
ἀποκρινάμενος καὶ <u>ἀναλαβὼν</u> τὰ λοιπὰ τῶν κρεῶν οἴκαδε ἀπῆλθεν. ἐκεῖ
65 γὰρ ἔμελλε θάψειν πάντα.

ὁ οὖν Ἀστυάγης τὸν Ἅρπαγον οὕτως ἐκόλασεν. περὶ δὲ τοῦ Κύρου
βουλευόμενος αὖθις ἐκάλεσε τοὺς τῶν <u>Μάγων</u> <u>ὀνειροπόλους</u>. καὶ αὖθις
εἶπον ὅτι χρὴ τὸν παῖδα <u>βασιλεύειν</u> εἰ μὴ ἤδη ἀπέθανεν. ὁ δὲ
Ἀστυάγης ἔφη, "<u>περίεστιν</u> ὁ παῖς. καὶ οἰκοῦντα αὐτὸν ἐν τοῖς ἀγροῖς οἱ
70 τῆς κώμης παῖδες εἵλοντο βασιλέα. καὶ ἐποίησε πάντα ὅσα οἱ ἀληθεῖς
βασιλῆς· καὶ γὰρ <u>δορυφόρους</u> εἶχε, καὶ <u>κατὰ πάντα</u> <u>εὐκόσμως</u>
ἐβασίλευεν. πῶς οὖν ταῦτα <u>κρίνετε</u>;" οἱ δὲ Μάγοι εἶπον, "εἰ περίεστιν ὁ
παῖς καὶ ἤδη ἐβασίλευσεν ἄνευ <u>προνοίας</u>, <u>θυμὸν</u> ἔχε ἀγαθόν· οὐ γὰρ ἔτι
δεύτερον ἄρξει". ὁ οὖν Ἀστυάγης, τοῖς λόγοις <u>ἡσθείς</u>, τὸν Κῦρον πρὸς
75 τὴν <u>Περσικὴν</u> ἀπέπεμψεν. καὶ <u>νοστήσαντα</u> αὐτὸν ὅ τε πατὴρ καὶ ἡ μήτηρ
μάλιστα <u>χαίροντες</u> ἐδέξαντο.

	κατακαλύπτω *perfect passive*	
	participle κατακελυμμένος	I cover over
	ἀποκαλύπτω ἀπεκάλυψα	I uncover
60	ἀναβοάω ἀνεβόησα	I shout out
	θηρίον -ου τό	animal
	κρεα -ων τά	flesh
	ἀναλαμβάνω ἀνέλαβον	I pick up
65	Μάγοι -ων οἱ	Magi (*caste of wise/holy men*)
	ὀνειροπόλος -ου ὁ	dream-interpreter
	βασιλεύω ἐβασίλευσα	I am king, I rule
	περίειμι	I survive
70	δορυφόρος -ου ὁ	bodyguard
	κατὰ πάντα	in all respects
	εὐκόσμως	in a well-ordered way
	κρίνω	I judge
	πρόνοια -ας ἡ	forethought, deliberate planning
	θυμός -οῦ ὁ	heart, spirit
	ἥδομαι ἥσθην	I am pleased (by, + *dat*)
75	Περσική -ῆς ἡ	Persia
	νοστέω	I return home
	χαίρω	I rejoice, I am happy

The Magi were however proved wrong: Cyrus, as we have seen, grew up to be the founder of the
Persian empire. He ousted Astyages from his throne and by 547 BC had extended Persian rule as far
west as the river Halys. This was the point at which he overthrew and captured Croesus. Cyrus
administered a vast empire with wisdom and tolerance: to Xenophon (writing in the fourth
century BC) he was an example of the ideal ruler, despite the intervening history of conflict between
Greece and Persia (traced in the Practice Passages in the next section of this book).

Subordination and the complex sentence

You have seen since the early chapters of this book that Greek depends heavily on the principle of *subordination*. In continuous narrative most sentences (except the very simplest) consist of a main, finite verb and one or more subordinate elements:

- participles and participle phrases (with or without an introductory word such as ὡς or καίπερ, signalling how the participle is to be taken), including genitive absolute
- temporal and causal clauses (introduced by ἐπεί, ὅτε, ὡς, ὅτι, διότι)
- relative clauses (introduced by ὅς, or one of the more specialised relative pronouns from the table of correlatives, such as οἷος)
- purpose clauses (introduced by ὡς, ἵνα, ὅπως)
- result clauses (introduced by ὥστε)
- conditional clauses (introduced by εἰ, ἐάν; the apodosis counts as the main clause)
- indirect statement (with ὅτι clause, or infinitive, or participle)
- indirect command (with infinitive)
- indirect question (introduced by εἰ or by one of the interrogative words from the table of correlatives, often in the form beginning ὁ-)

Greek builds up sentences not by just piling up the various elements (saying *X happened; Y happened; Z happened*) but by expressing their relation to each other, saying for example *Because X had happened, Y happened, with the result that Z then happened.*

Central to this is the use of participles, perhaps the single most important element in Greek sentence construction (and certainly one of the distinguishing features of the language, being far more central than in Latin). We saw at an early stage that Greek does not like to pile up main verbs. On the same principle, it avoids piling up infinitives in indirect speech (which themselves stand for main verbs in the original direct speech). Hence

> The king ordered us to leave our homes and (then) run away.

would be translated

> ὁ βασιλεὺς ἐκέλευσεν ἡμᾶς τὰς οἰκίας λιπόντας φυγεῖν.

(rather than ... λιπεῖν καὶ φυγεῖν). The participle here would naturally be read as part of the command: *He ordered us having done X to do Y* naturally means *He ordered us, after doing X (which we have not done yet), to do Y* rather than *He ordered us, as we had (already) done X, to do Y*. The aorist participle in this idiom expresses something (that will be) past in relation to the time the command expressed by the infinitive (φυγεῖν) is carried out, rather than something past in relation to the main verb of the sentence (ἐκέλευσεν).

Exercise 12.18

Translate into English:

1. ὁ διδάσκαλος ἐκέλευσε τοὺς παῖδας τὰς βίβλους καταθέντας ἐξελθεῖν.
2. ἕως* ὁ τῶν συμμάχων ἄγγελος ἔλεγεν, οἱ Πέρσαι σιγῇ ἐκάθιζον ὡς μάλιστα θαυμάζοντες.
3. αἱ θεαί, καίπερ οὐδαμῶς ὁμολογοῦσαι, ὑπὸ τοῦ ποιητοῦ ἐτιμῶντο.
4. τῶν ἐν τῇ νήσῳ ὑπὸ τῶν στρατιωτῶν ἐλευθερωθέντων, οἱ ἐκεῖ φύλακες ἠποροῦν ἕως* ἄλλοι τινὲς προσήχθησαν.
5. ἆρα οἷαί τ᾽ ἐστὲ δεῖξαι ἡμῖν ὅπου ὁ βασιλεὺς ἀπέθανεν, ὦ γυναῖκες;
6. μωρότατοί εἰσιν ὅσοι ταῦτα τὰ ἔργα ἐπαινοῦσιν.
7. τῆς μάχης τοιαύτης οὔσης, οὐδεὶς οὕτως ἰσχυρός ἐστιν ὥστε αὖθις μάχεσθαι.
8. ἡ τοῦ νεανίου μήτηρ ἔφη τοὺς φίλους δύο ὥρας μείναντας ἀπελθεῖν.
9. ἐκεῖνος ὁ γέρων περὶ τοῦ πολέμου οὔποτε λέγει διότι δεινότατα ἔπαθεν.
10. ἡμέρας γενομένης, αἰτήσω τοὺς πολίτας τὸν χρυσὸν κρύψαντας πρὸς τὰ ὄρη φυγεῖν.

> * ἕως (referring to the past) means *while* (of two actions happening simultaneously) or *until* (of one action following another): word order and context should make clear which sense is appropriate

Revision checkpoint

Make sure you know:
- verbs with omicron contraction
- pluperfect tense
- the commoner parts of verbs ending in -μι
- the principle of subordination in complex sentences

Idiom and flexibility in translation

Inevitably you tend to learn a single meaning for a Greek word, but it is important to be flexible in translation and aim at good, natural English. Because languages conceptualise (that is, think about the world) differently, there is frequently not a simple one-to-one correspondence of meaning between words in different languages. This may initially make things difficult for the learner, but in fact it is a major source of fascination in learning any language, and thus learning about the culture that produced it. This is particularly true with Greek. Both the language and the culture are immensely rich. They belong to a world distant in time, which is simultaneously very alien to us in some respects and uncannily familiar in others.

If you look up a Greek word that appears to have a list of meanings, at first sight unrelated, this is not (of course) because the Greeks just put up with an unavoidable inconvenience, but because to them the meanings were importantly related. Thus for example ξένος may according to context need to be translated as *stranger, foreigner, host* or *guest*: various facets or stages of a person interacting outside his immediate community, and forming a relationship of reciprocal obligation.

Conversely several Greek words may be conventionally translated by the same English word. Sometimes they are synonyms in Greek too, with no particular significance attached (thus either στρατός or στρατιά for *army*). More often there is some difference of meaning or emphasis. We noted in Chapter 9 the distinction between λαμβάνω and the rather more assertive αἱρέω. You have met three different words translated as *I show*: φαίνω (with the flavour *I reveal*), δηλόω (with the flavour *I make clear*), δείκνυμι (with the flavour *I point out*). Words that are virtually synonymous most of the time can acquire idiomatic distinctions in a particular context: we noticed in Chapter 7 the difference between εἶπε ταῦτα = *he said this (already quoted)* and εἶπε τάδε = *he said this (just about to be quoted)*. Although ποιέω often means *I make*, it is in many contexts interchangeable with πράσσω as *I do*. Yet if these verbs are used with an adverb, there is an important distinction: εὖ ποιέω means *I treat (someone) well*, whereas εὖ πράσσω means *I fare well (i.e. come off well myself)*.

Often the meaning required for a word in a sentence or passage will be an intelligible extension of the basic meaning. Thus νέος = *new* can when required also mean *young*. The same applies to phrases. The idiom ὡς τάχιστα normally means *as quickly as possible*. But if it introduces a subordinate clause at the start of a sentence (ὡς τάχιστα *X happened, Y happened*), it is easy to see it needs to be translated *as soon as*.

Often words can be built into sentences in ways that in English require different translations. Thus some adjectives can be active or passive in flavour: δυνατός can mean *capable* (able to do) or *possible* (able to be done). In a rather similar way some verbs can have sentences constructed around them in more than one way. The classic example here is βάλλω:

> ὁ παῖς λίθους εἰς τὸν ποταμὸν ἔβαλλεν.
> The boy was throwing stones into the river.

But:

> ὁ παῖς τὸν λέοντα λίθοις ἔβαλλεν.
> The boy was pelting the lion with stones.

(Note also the distinction between βάλλω = *I pelt [typically from a distance]* and τύπτω = *I hit, I strike [successfully/at close quarters]*.)

However βάλλω is an extremely common, versatile and flexible word: often neither *I throw* nor *I pelt* is appropriate, and the meaning is no stronger than *I put*. This flexibility in the meaning of very common verbs is particularly evident in compounds. A compound of βάλλω frequently met is προσβάλλω = *I attack*. This (like other Greek verbs with similar meaning) takes the dative. But εἰσβάλλω (also = *I attack*, but more particularly *I invade*) normally (as might be predicted) takes εἰς + accusative. There are two issues involved: the prefixes of compounds tend to behave like the prepositions which they can also function as;

and with εἰσβάλλω there is also an understood object (*I hurl myself/an army into ...*). We looked in Chapter 3 at cases taken by verbs: the point here is that, though not all can be predicted, all have some explanation. The middle λαμβάνομαι = *I take hold of* takes the genitive, as do other verbs (such as ἅπτομαι = *I grasp*, or just *I touch*) implying getting *part* of something (this is the *partitive* genitive, as in phrases like *some of*).

Finally there are idioms with obvious cultural or historical resonance. The singular βασιλεύς (no article, no following phrase 'of X', yet not a proper name needing a capital letter) in classical authors invariably means 'the king of Persia', because the power of Persia was a major fact of political life, and the Persian king was the only one that people in the republican city-states of Greece would normally have occasion to talk about. 'The Persian' could be a collective singular ('when we fought the Persian'), as could (anybody's) cavalry: the feminine ἡ ἵππος usually means that, rather than an individual mare (as in English 'a regiment of horse').

Exercise 12.19

Translate into English:
1   εἴθε οἱ ξένοι ἡμᾶς ἀεὶ οὕτω ποίοιεν.
2   ὡς τάχιστα φωνήν τινα ἤκουσαν, οἱ παῖδες τῶν χρημάτων
     ἁψάμενοι ἔφυγον.
3   βούλομαι γνῶναι ὅ τι εἶπεν ὁ ἄγγελος ὁ ὑπὸ βασιλέως πεμφθείς.
4   αἱ ἐγγὺς τοῦ ὄρους οἰκοῦσαι ἔδειξαν ἡμῖν τὴν ὁδόν.
5   ἆρ' οὐ οἱ τοιούτους νόμους ἐπαινοῦντες ἀσθενεῖς εἰσιν;
6   πάντες ἐν τῷ τειχίσματι τὸν Πέρσην ἠμυνόμεθα ἕως ἡ ἵππος
     ἀφίκετο.
7   οἱ δοῦλοι οὕτω σοφῶς τότε ἔπραξαν ὥστε πάντες ὕστερον
     ἐλευθερώθησαν.
8   εἰ ἡ γυνὴ ἴδοι με κακῶς πράσσοντα, εὐθὺς βοηθήσειεν.
9   οἱ ἡμέτεροι σύμμαχοι εἰς τὴν Περσικὴν εἰσέβαλον.
10   πάντα πέπρακται ἵνα ῥᾳδίως μανθάνητε.

Exercise 12.20

Read the following passage and answer the questions below:

The Power of Custom

This story sums up much in Herodotus. Darius was king of Persia 521-486 BC. He reorganized and strengthened the empire: he seems to have been impressed by its great size, and conscious of the difficulties of ruling the diverse peoples it contained. As told by Herodotus, this account of cultural relativism is perhaps influenced by the ideas of thinkers like Protagoras (whom we met in Chapter 7) in his own day.

ἕκαστοι νομίζουσι τοὺς ἑαυτῶν <u>νόμους</u> πολλῷ καλλίστους εἶναι. τοῦτο δὲ
πολλοῖς τε ἄλλοις <u>τεκμηρίοις</u> ἔξεστι γνῶναι καὶ δὴ τῷδε. ὁ γὰρ <u>Δαρεῖος</u>
ἐπὶ τῆς ἑαυτοῦ ἀρχῆς καλέσας Ἕλληνάς τινας ἤρετο <u>ἐφ'</u> ὁπόσῳ <u>ἂν</u>
χρυσῷ <u>ἐθέλοιεν</u> τοὺς πατέρας ἀποθανόντας φαγεῖν· οἱ δὲ ἐπ' οὐδενὶ
5 ἔφασαν τοῦτο ποιήσειν. μετὰ δὲ ταῦτα ὁ Δαρεῖος ἐκάλεσεν Ἰνδούς τινας
οἳ τοὺς ἀποθανόντας ἐσθίουσιν· καὶ οὗτοι οἱ ἄνθρωποι <u>Καλλατίαι</u>
<u>ὀνομάζονται</u>. ἔπειτα δὲ βασιλεὺς τοὺς Καλλατίας ἤρετο (τῶν Ἑλλήνων
παρόντων καὶ διὰ <u>ἑρμηνέως</u> τὰ λεγόμενα μανθανόντων) ἐφ' ὁπόσῳ ἂν
χρυσῷ ἐθέλοιεν τοὺς πατέρας ἀποθανόντας <u>κατακαῦσαι</u>. οἱ δέ,
10 <u>ἀναβοήσαντες</u> μέγα, <u>σιγῆσαι</u> αὐτὸν ἐκέλευσαν. οὕτως οὖν <u>ὀρθῶς</u> δοκεῖ
μοι ὁ <u>Πίνδαρος</u> ἐν τῷ <u>μέλει</u> λέγειν ὅτι νόμος πάντων βασιλεύς.

	νόμος -ου ὁ	(here) custom
	τεκμήριον -ου τό	piece of evidence, proof
	Δαρεῖος -ου ὁ	Darius (King of Persia 521-486 BC)
	ἐφ' (= ἐπί)	(+ dat) here for
	ἂν ἐθέλοιεν	they would be willing
5	Ἰνδοί -ῶν οἱ	Indians
	Καλλατίαι -ων οἱ	Callatiae (an Indian tribe)
	ὀνομάζω	I name, I call
	ἑρμηνεύς -έως ὁ	interpreter
	κατακαίω κατέκαυσα	I burn
10	ἀναβοάω ἀνεβόησα	I cry out
	σιγάω ἐσίγησα	I am silent
	ὀρθῶς	rightly
	Πίνδαρος -ου ὁ	Pindar (lyric poet, about 518-446 BC)
	μέλος -ους τό	poem

(1) What are we told that all men believe (line 1)? (3)

(2) What did Darius ask some Greeks (lines 2-4)? (4)

(3) What was their reply (lines 4-5)? (2)

(4) Whom did Darius summon next, and what custom do they have
(lines 5-7)? (3)

(5) What did Darius ask them (lines 7-9)? (3)

(6) How could the Greeks who were present understand this
conversation (line 8)? (1)

(7) What was the reaction to Darius' question (lines 9-10)? (3)

(8) What was said in Pindar's poem (line 11)? (2)

(9) Does this story in fact illustrate complete relativism, or was
there any underlying agreement between the two sides? (4)

---

25 marks

Vocabulary checklist for Chapter 12

ἀμύνομαι ἠμυνάμην	I resist, I defend myself (against) (+ *acc*)
ἄν	(*makes indefinite; often associated with translation such as* would ...)
ἅπτομαι ἡψάμην	I touch (+ *gen*)
δείκνυμι ἔδειξα	I show, I point out
δηλόω ἐδήλωσα	I show, I make clear
δίδωμι ἔδωκα	I give
δουλόω ἐδούλωσα	I enslave
δυνατός -ή -όν	able, capable; possible
εἴθε	if only ... , would that ... (+ *opt, expressing wish*)
εἰσβάλλω εἰσέβαλον	I invade (+ εἰς + *acc*)
ἐλευθερόω ἠλευθέρωσα	I set free (*especially* from slavery)
ἐπειδή	when, since
ἕως	while; until
ἵππος -ου ἡ	cavalry (*collective singular*)
ὄμνυμι ὤμοσα	I swear
Περσική -ῆς ἡ	Persia
τίθημι ἔθηκα	I place, I put
(17 words)	

Practice passages

These passages continue to follow the main narrative of Herodotus, to its climax in his description of the wars between Greece and Persia in 490-479 BC.

Exercise PP.1

Darius and Intaphrenes' Wife

As we saw in Chapter 12, Darius was king of Persia 521-486 BC. The devotion of the woman in this story to her brother is expressed in very similar terms to that of Antigone (whom we met in Chapter 9) in Sophocles' play about her: one may have influenced the other, or they may have a common source.

ὁ δὲ <u>Δαρεῖος</u> <u>συνέλαβε</u> τόν τε Ἰνταφρένη καὶ τοὺς παῖδας αὐτοῦ καὶ τοὺς <u>συγγενεῖς</u>· ἐνόμιζε γὰρ τὸν Ἰνταφρένη <u>ἐπιβουλεύειν</u> ἑαυτῷ. καὶ διὰ τοῦτο πάντας <u>δήσας</u>, ὀλίγων ἡμερῶν ἂν ἀπέκτεινεν, εἰ μὴ ἐγένετο τόδε δεινόν. ἡ γὰρ τοῦ Ἰνταφρένους γυνὴ ἐπὶ τὰς τῶν <u>βασιλείων</u> θύρας
5 ἐλθοῦσα τοσοῦτον χρόνον ἐδάκρυεν ὥστε τέλος βασιλεὺς <u>ᾤκτειρεν</u> αὐτήν. ἄγγελον οὖν πέμψας εἶπε τάδε· "ὦ γύναι, βασιλεὺς Δαρεῖος <u>δίδωσί</u> σοι ἕνα τῶν δεδεμένων σῶσαι ὃν βούλη ἐκ πάντων". ἡ δὲ βουλευσαμένη εἶπεν ὅτι βούλοιτο βασιλέα λύειν τὸν ἑαυτῆς ἀδελφόν. ὁ δὲ Δαρεῖος ταῦτα ἀκούσας ἐθαύμασεν· καὶ ἄλλον ἄγγελον πέμψας ἠρώτησεν, "ὦ
10 γύναι, διὰ τί τόν τε ἄνδρα καὶ τοὺς παῖδας <u>παραλιποῦσα</u> αἱρῇ τὸν ἀδελφὸν σῶσαι;" ἡ δ' ἀπεκρίνατο, "εἴθε πάντας τοὺς συγγενεῖς σώσαιμι, ὦ βασιλεῦ. ἐπεὶ μέντοι τοῦτο οὐδαμῶς ἔξεστί μοι, τὸν ἀδελφὸν αἱροῦμαι, ὧδε <u>λογιζομένη</u>· ἀνὴρ μὲν γὰρ ἄλλος ἂν γένοιτο, εἰ ἐθέλοιεν οἱ θεοί, καὶ παῖδες ἄλλοι εἰ οὗτοι πάθοιέν τι· πατρὸς μέντοι καὶ μητρὸς οὐκέτι μοι
15 <u>ζώντων</u>, ἀδελφὸς ἂν ἄλλος οὐδενὶ <u>τρόπῳ</u> γένοιτο".

	Δαρεῖος -ου ὁ	Darius
	συλλαμβάνω συνέλαβον	I arrest, I seize
	Ἰνταφρένης -ους ὁ	Intaphrenes (*a Persian nobleman*)
	συγγενεῖς -ῶν οἱ	relatives
	ἐπιβουλεύω	I plot against (+ *dat*)
	δέω ἔδησα	I bind, I tie up
	βασίλεια -ων τά	palace
5	οἰκτείρω *imperfect* ᾤκτειρον	I pity
	δίδωμι	(*here*) I grant permission
10	παραλείπω παρέλιπον	I leave aside
	λογίζομαι	I reason, I calculate
15	ζάω	I live, I am alive
	τρόπος -ου ὁ	way

Exercise PP.2

Darius and Democedes

Democedes was a Greek doctor from southern Italy who fell on hard times and became a slave in the Persian empire.

καὶ οὐ πολλῷ ὕστερον <u>Δαρεῖος</u>, ἐν τοῖς ἀγροῖς <u>θηρεύων</u>, ἀπὸ τοῦ ἵππου ἀπέπεσεν. τὸν δὲ πόδα <u>στρέψας</u> <u>Αἰγυπτίους</u> τινὰς <u>μετεπέμψατο</u>, ὧν τῇ τέχνῃ πρότερον ἐχρήσατο, νομίζων αὐτοὺς ἰατροὺς βελτίστους ἐν τῇ τῶν Περσῶν ἀρχῇ εἶναι. οὗτοι οὖν τὸν βασιλέως πόδα <u>στρεβλοῦντες</u>
5 ἵνα <u>ὀρθὸς</u> γένηται, <u>τῷ ὄντι</u> πολλῷ κακίονα ἐποίησαν. διὰ δὲ ταῦτα ὁ Δαρεῖος ἕπτα μὲν ἡμέρας οὐχ οἷός τ᾽ ἦν καθεύδειν· τῇ δὲ ὀγδόῃ, ἤγγειλέ τις ὅτι <u>Δημοκήδης</u> ἄριστος εἴη περὶ τῆς <u>ἰατρικῆς</u> ἐν πάσῃ τῇ ἀρχῇ. καὶ βασιλεῖ <u>προθύμως</u> ἐρωτῶντι ὅπου τοῦτον τὸν ἄνδρα εὑρήσει, οἱ φίλοι ἀπεκρίναντο τάδε· "εὑρήσεις αὐτόν, ὦ βασιλεῦ, ἐν τοῖς δούλοις."

	Δαρεῖος -ου ὁ	Darius
	θηρεύω	I hunt
	στρέφω ἔστρεψα	(*here*) I twist
	Αἰγύπτιοι -ων οἱ	Egyptians
	μεταπέμπομαι	I send for
	στρεβλόω	I wrench
5	ὀρθός -ή -όν	straight
	τῷ ὄντι	really, in fact
	Δημοκήδης -ους ὁ	Democedes
	ἰατρική -ῆς ἡ	medicine, medical skill
	προθύμως	eagerly

Read the rest of this passage on the next page and answer the questions below.

10　ἐκέλευσεν οὖν ὁ Δαρεῖος τὸν δοῦλον πρὸς τὰ <u>βασίλεια</u> ἄγεσθαι. καὶ ὁ
Δημοκήδης ἀφίκετο μάλιστα φοβούμενος. ἐπεὶ δὲ ὑπὸ βασιλέως ἐρωτήθη
εἰ πολλὰ οἶδε περὶ τῆς <u>ἰατρικῆς</u>, πρῶτον μὲν οὐκ ἔφη τοῦτο ἀληθὲς
εἶναι· ἔπειτα δὲ (αὖθις ἐρωτηθείς, καὶ ἀνδρειότερος γενόμενος) ὡμολόγησε
τὴν τέχνην ποτὲ μαθεῖν. ταῦτα οὖν ἀκούσας βασιλεὺς <u>ἐπέτρεψεν</u> ἑαυτὸν
15　τῷ δούλῳ. ὁ οὖν Δημοκήδης, τέχνῃ τε Ἑλληνικῇ καὶ <u>ἰάμασιν ἠπίοις</u>
χρώμενος, δι' ὀλίγου βασιλέα <u>ὑγιῆ</u> ἐποίησεν. ὁ οὖν Δαρεῖος, πρότερον
οὐκ ἐλπίσας αὖθις οἷός τ' ἔσεσθαι <u>βαδίζειν</u>, μάλιστα <u>ἥσθη</u>. καὶ ἀπέπεμψε
τὸν Δημοκήδη πρὸς τὰς ἑαυτοῦ γυναῖκας, ὧν ἑκάστη πολὺν χρυσὸν αὐτῷ
ἔδωκεν.

10	βασίλεια -ων τά	palace
	ἰατρική -ῆς ἡ	medicine, medical skill
	ἐπιτρέπω ἐπέτρεψα	I entrust X (*acc*) to Y (*dat*)
15	ἴαμα -ατος τό	cure, treatment
	ἤπιος -α -ον	gentle
	ὑγιής -ές	healthy
	βαδίζω	I walk
	ἥσθην	*aorist of* ἥδομαι

(1)　What order did Darius give (line 10)?　　　　　　　　　　　　　(2)
(2)　How did Democedes feel (line 11)?　　　　　　　　　　　　　　(2)
(3)　What was he asked by the king, and what was his initial reply
　　　(lines 11-13)?　　　　　　　　　　　　　　　　　　　　　(4)
(4)　Why and to what did he change his reply (lines 13-14)?　　　　　(4)
(5)　What did Darius do as a result (lines 14-15)?　　　　　　　　　(2)
(6)　What methods did Democedes use, and with what result
　　　(lines 15-16)?　　　　　　　　　　　　　　　　　　　　　(3)
(7)　What was Darius' reaction, and why (lines 16-17)?　　　　　　　(4)
(8)　What happened to Democedes as a result (lines 17-19)?　　　　　(4)

25 marks

Exercise PP.3

Miltiades becomes ruler of the Dolonci

This story describes a time (the sixth century BC) when Athens was just beginning to expand her interests overseas. The Dolonci were a tribe in the Thracian Chersonese, a peninsula (separated from Asia by the Hellespont) important for its natural resources and because it lay on the route to the Black Sea. The response of the Delphic oracle follows a typical folktale pattern (the first person to do X will be the one destined or prophesied).

οἱ δὲ <u>Δόλογκοι</u>, τῶν πολεμίων ἀεὶ προσβαλλόντων, ἀγγέλους ἔπεμψαν
εἰς <u>Δελφοὺς</u> ἐρωτήσοντας τὸν θεὸν περὶ τοῦ πολέμου. ἡ δὲ <u>Πυθία</u>
ἐκέλευσεν αὐτοὺς αἰτεῖν τὸν ἄνδρα ὃς πρῶτος αὐτοὺς εἰς τὴν ἑαυτοῦ
οἰκίαν καλέσει, <u>τύραννον</u> γενέσθαι. οἱ δὲ Δόλογκοι, ἐκ Δελφῶν ἐξελθόντες
5 ἐπορεύοντο διὰ τῆς <u>Βοιωτίας</u>· ἐπεὶ δ᾿ οὐδεὶς εἰς τὴν οἰκίαν ἐκέλευεν
εἰσιέναι, ἔδοξεν αὐτοῖς πρὸς ᾿Αθήνας προσιέναι. ἦν τότε ἐν τῇ πόλει
ἀνὴρ πλούσιος, <u>Μιλτιάδης</u> ὀνόματι, ὃς καθίζων ἐν τοῖς <u>προθύροις</u> καὶ
ὁρῶν τοὺς Δολόγκους παριόντας, <u>σκευὴν</u> ἔχοντας οὐχ ῾Ελληνικήν, εἰς τὴν
οἰκίαν ἐκάλεσεν. οἱ δὲ εἰσελθόντες <u>ἐξηγήσαντο</u> πάντα τὰ ὑπὸ τῆς Πυθίας
10 κελευσθέντα. τέλος δ᾿ αἰσθόμενοι τὸν Μιλτιάδην πλούσιον καὶ <u>δυνατὸν</u>
ὄντα ᾔτησαν αὐτὸν τύραννον τῶν Δολόγκων γενέσθαι. ὁ δὲ Μιλτιάδης ὃς
<u>ἐχαλέπαινε</u> τῇ τοῦ <u>Πεισιστράτου</u> <u>τυραννίδι</u> καὶ ἐβούλετο ἐκ τῶν ᾿Αθηνῶν
ἀπελθεῖν, λαβὼν τῶν ᾿Αθηναίων πάντας τοὺς βουλομένους ἑαυτῷ ἕπεσθαι,
ἔπλει μετὰ τῶν Δολόγκων καὶ τύραννος τῆς χώρας ἐκείνοις ἐγένετο.

	Δόλογκοι -ων οἱ	Dolonci
	Δελφοί -ῶν οἱ	Delphi
	Πυθία -ας ἡ	Pythia (*priestess of Apollo at Delphi*)
	τύραννος -ου ὁ	ruler
5	Βοιωτία -ας ἡ	Boeotia (*region of central Greece*)
	Μιλτιάδης -ου ὁ	Miltiades
	πρόθυρα -ων τά	porch
	σκευή -ῆς ἡ	clothes
	῾Ελληνικός -ή -όν	Greek
	ἐξηγέομαι ἐξηγησάμην	I explain
10	δυνατός -ή -όν	powerful
	χαλεπαίνω	I am discontented (with, + *dat*)
	Πεισίστρατος -ου ὁ	Peisistratus (*ruler of Athens in the mid-sixth century*)
	τυραννίς -ίδος ἡ	tyranny, rule

Exercise PP.4

Athens appeals for help

In 490 BC the Persians attacked Athenian territory (landing at Marathon), in revenge for help Athens had earlier given to the Greeks of the Ionian (now Turkish) coast in their attempt to rebel from the Persian empire to which they were subject. The distance between Athens and Sparta covered by Pheidippides is about 125 miles. (The 26 miles of the modern Marathon race is the distance between Athens and Marathon: an unreliable story says that, after returning from Sparta, Pheidippides ran from Athens to Marathon to join in the battle; afterwards ran back with news of the victory; then dropped dead from his exertions.) The influence of superstition on Spartan policy was notorious, and may at least sometimes have been a cover for the fact that Sparta did not want to get involved in campaigns outside the Peloponnese.

Read the passage and answer the questions below.

οἱ δὲ Πέρσαι ἔπλευσαν πρὸς κώμην τινὰ τῆς Ἀττικῆς Μαραθῶνα
ὀνόματι. οἱ δ' Ἀθηναῖοι, ὡς ἐπύθοντο, ἐστράτευον εἰς τὸν Μαραθῶνα. οἱ
δὲ στρατηγοί, ἔτι ὄντες ἐν τῇ πόλει, ἀπέπεμψαν εἰς Σπάρτην κήρυκα
Φειδιππίδην (τάχιστα γὰρ τρέχειν ἐδύνατο). οὗτος, πεμφθεὶς ὑπὸ τῶν
5   στρατηγῶν, τῇ ὑστεραίᾳ ἀφίκετο εἰς Σπάρτην. ἀφικόμενος δὲ τοῖς
ἄρχουσιν ἔλεγε τάδε· "ὦ Λακεδαιμόνιοι, οἱ Ἀθηναῖοι ὑμᾶς αἰτοῦσι
βοηθῆσαι. μὴ ἐάσητε τὴν πόλιν τὴν ἀρχαιοτάτην ἐν τοῖς Ἕλλησι
διαφθείρεσθαι ὑπ' ἀνδρῶν βαρβάρων." ὁ μὲν δὴ ἤγγειλεν αὐτοῖς τὰ
κελευσθέντα. καὶ τοῖς Λακεδαιμονίοις ἐδόκει μὲν βοηθεῖν τοῖς Ἀθηναίοις,
10   ἀδύνατον δ' ἐνόμιζον εἶναι τοῦτο παραυτίκα πράσσειν. δεισιδαιμονίᾳ
γὰρ ἐκωλύοντο, οὐκ ἐθέλοντες λύειν τὸν νόμον καθ' ὃν ἔδει τὴν
πανσέληνον μένειν.

	Ἀττική -ῆς ἡ	Attica (*territory of Athens*)
	Μαραθών -ῶνος ὁ	Marathon
	κῆρυξ -υκος ὁ	herald
	Φειδιππίδης -ου ὁ	Pheidippides
5	τῇ ὑστεραίᾳ	on the next day
10	ἀδύνατος -ον	impossible
	παραυτίκα	straightaway
	δεισιδαιμονία -ας ἡ	superstition
	πανσέληνος -ου ἡ	full moon

(1)   Where did the Persians sail to (lines 1-2)?   (2)
(2)   How did the Athenians react when they found out (line 2)?   (2)
(3)   What did the generals do while still in Athens, and why (lines 3-4)?   (3)
(4)   When did Pheipippides reach Sparta (line 5)?   (1)
(5)   Summarise the message he delivered to the Spartan authorities
         (lines 6-8).   (6)
(6)   What was the Spartans' initial reaction (line 9)?   (2)
(7)   What prevented them from acting immediately (lines 10-12)?   (4)

_____

20 marks

Athenian generals at Marathon divided

Callimachus as polemarch (a high-ranking magistrate) was in overall command of the Athenian army, but Miltiades (one of the ten annually elected generals) was responsible for the plan of the campaign. Some of the other generals were unwilling to rush into action, because the Athenians (helped only by a detachment from Plataea: see passage PP.7) were vastly outnumbered. Here Miltiades persuades Callimachus to give his casting vote in favour of fighting.

τοῖς δὲ τῶν Ἀθηναίων στρατηγοῖς ἐγίγνοντο <u>δίχα</u> αἱ γνῶμαι· οἱ μὲν γὰρ οὐκ εἶων μάχεσθαι, ὡς εἰδότες αὐτοὶ μὲν ὀλίγοι ὄντες, τοὺς δὲ Πέρσας πολλῷ πλείονας, οἱ δὲ ἐκέλευον ὡς τάχιστα προσβαλεῖν τοῖς πολεμίοις. καὶ ἐν τούτοις ἦν ὁ <u>Μιλτιάδης</u>. τότε δὲ <u>πολέμαρχος</u> ἦν ὁ <u>Καλλίμαχος</u>,
5 <u>ἰσόψηφος</u> ὢν τοῖς στρατηγοῖς. τούτῳ οὖν εἶπεν ὁ Μιλτιάδης, "σὺ νῦν, ὦ Καλλίμαχε, δύνασαι ἢ δουλῶσαι τοὺς Ἀθηναίους ἢ ἐλευθέρους ποιῆσαι. νῦν γὰρ δὴ εἰς κίνδυνον ἥκουσι μέγιστον· ἐὰν γὰρ <u>ἐνδίδωσι</u> τοῖς Πέρσαις, πολλὰ πείσονται <u>τυράννῳ</u> <u>παραδεδομένοι</u>, ἐὰν δὲ <u>περιγένηται</u> αὕτη ἡ πόλις, δύναται πρώτη τῶν ἐν τῇ Ἑλλάδι πόλεων γενέσθαι. ὅπως
10 οὖν τοῦτο δύναται γενέσθαι νῦν σοι λέξω· ἡμῶν τῶν στρατηγῶν ὄντων δέκα δίχα γίγνονται αἱ γνῶμαι, τῶν μὲν κελευόντων μάχεσθαι, τῶν δὲ οὔ. ἐὰν μὲν μὴ εὐθὺς <u>συμβάλωμεν</u>, εἰς <u>στάσιν</u> πεσοῦνται οἱ ἡμέτεροι πολῖται· ἐὰν δὲ πρὸ τούτου συμβάλωμεν, ἔτι δυνάμεθα νικῆσαι. ταῦτα οὖν πάντα ἐν σοί ἐστιν." ταῦτα οὖν λέγων ὁ Μιλτιάδης ἔπεισε τὸν
15 Καλλίμαχον· <u>προσγενομένης</u> δὲ τῆς τοῦ πολεμάρχου γνώμης, ἔδοξε μάχεσθαι.

	δίχα	at odds, inclining different ways
	Μιλτιάδης -ου ὁ	Miltiades (*nephew of the Miltiades who became ruler of the Dolonci in passage PP.3*)
	πολέμαρχος -ου ὁ	polemarch
	Καλλίμαχος -ου ὁ	Callimachus
5	ἰσόψηφος -ον	having an equal vote
	ἐνδίδωμι	I give in, I surrender
	τύραννος -ου ὁ	(*here*) tyrant, despot
	παραδίδωμι *perfect passive*	
	παραδέδομαι	I hand over
	περιγίγνομαι περιεγενόμην	I survive
10	συμβάλλω συνέβαλον	I join battle
	στάσις -εως ἡ	civil unrest
15	προσγίγνομαι προσεγενόμην	I am added on

The Athenian Charge

Although Herodotus is by no means expert in military matters (his accounts of battles leave many questions unanswered), he conveys how unusual and innovative the Athenian tactics at Marathon were. He also has a strong sense of Marathon as a watershed, when the Persians lost their mystique and something of their power to inspire terror.

Read the first part of the passage and answer the questions below.

οἱ δὲ Ἀθηναῖοι ἐν <u>Μαραθῶνι</u> ὑπὸ τοῦ <u>Μιλτιάδου</u> ὧδε ἐτάχθησαν· τὸ μὲν <u>μέσον</u> τοῦ στρατοῦ <u>ἐπ</u>᾽ ἀσπίδων ὀλίγων μόνον ἦν, καὶ διὰ τοῦτο ἀσθενέστατον, τὸ δὲ <u>κέρας</u> <u>ἑκάτερον</u> ἰσχυρὸν ἦν πλήθει. ἐπεὶ δὲ τὰ <u>σφάγια</u> ἐγίγνετο καλά, εὐθὺς ἐπὶ τοὺς βαρβάρους <u>δρόμῳ</u> <u>ὡρμήσαντο</u>· ἦν
5 δὲ <u>μεταξὺ</u> <u>στάδια</u> οὐκ ἐλάσσονα ἢ ὄκτω. οἱ δὲ Πέρσαι, ὁρῶντες αὐτοὺς δρόμῳ προσιόντας, παρεσκευάζοντο ὡς δεξόμενοι. ἐνόμιζον δὲ <u>μαίνεσθαι</u> τοὺς Ἀθηναίους, καὶ πρὸς <u>ὄλεθρον</u> φέρεσθαι· ἠσθάνοντο γὰρ αὐτοὺς ὀλίγους ὄντας καὶ δρόμῳ προσελθεῖν κελευσθέντας, καίπερ οὔθ᾽ ἱππέας οὔτε <u>τοξότας</u> ἔχοντας. ταῦτα μὲν οἱ βάρβαροι <u>ἐλογίζοντο</u>·

Μαραθών -ῶνος ὁ	Marathon
Μιλτιάδης -ου ὁ	Miltiades
μέσον -ου τό	middle
ἐπί	(+ *gen*) (*here*) to a depth of
κέρας -ατος τό	wing (of an army; *literally* horn, *from its shape*)
ἑκάτερος -α -ον	each (of two)
σφαγια -ων τά	sacrificial victims (*sacrifices always preceded battle*)
δρόμος -ου ὁ	run, act of running
ὁρμάομαι ὡρμησάμην	I set out
5 μεταξύ	in between
στάδιον -ου τό	stade (*unit of length, about 200 metres*)
μαίνομαι	I am mad
ὄλεθρος -ου ὁ	destruction
τοξότης -ου ὁ	archer
λογίζομαι	I reckon, I calculate

(1) Describe how the Athenians were drawn up by Miltiades (lines 1-3). (6)
(2) What good omen for the battle was there (lines 3-4)? (2)
(3) How did they set out against the enemy (line 4)? (1)
(4) How far were the two armies apart (line 5)? (2)
(5) What did the Persians do when they saw the Athenians approaching (lines 5-6)? (2)
(6) What did the Persians think about the Athenians (lines 6-7)? (3)
(7) What observations prompted this view (lines 7-9)? (4)

---

20 marks

Translate the rest of the passage which follows on the next page.

10 Ἀθηναῖοι δέ, ἐπεὶ πάντες <u>προσέμιξαν</u> τοῖς βαρβάροις, ἐμάχοντο ἀξίως
λόγου. πρῶτοι μὲν γὰρ Ἑλλήνων πάντων <u>δρόμῳ</u> ἐπὶ πολεμίους ἐχρήσαντο,
πρῶτοι δ' οὐκ ἐφοβοῦντο <u>ἐσθῆτά</u> τε <u>Περσικὴν</u> ὁρῶντες καὶ τοὺς ἄνδρας
ταύτην <u>φοροῦντας</u>· πρότερον δ' ἦν τοῖς Ἕλλησι καὶ τὸ ὄνομα τῶν
Περσῶν <u>φοβερόν</u>.

10	προσμίγνυμι προσέμιξα	I engage in close combat (with, + *dat*)
	δρόμος -ου ὁ	run, act of running
	ἐσθής -ῆτος ἡ	clothing, gear
	Περσικός -ή -όν	Persian
	φορέω	I wear
	φοβερός -ά -όν	formidable, terrifying

Exercise PP.7

The Athenian Victory

Miltiades' battle plan is vindicated. The Persians, encouraged by Athenian traitors, sail round the coast of Attica in an unsuccessful attempt to take the city by surprise.

μάχης δ' ἐν <u>Μαραθῶνι</u> πολὺν χρόνον ἤδη γιγνομένης, τὸ μὲν <u>μέσον</u> τοῦ
στρατοῦ ἐνίκων οἱ βάρβαροι (ἐν μέσῳ γὰρ ἐτάχθησαν οἱ τῶν Περσῶν
στρατιῶται οἱ ἄριστοι), καὶ <u>ῥήξαντες</u> ἐδίωκον εἰς τὴν <u>μεσογείαν</u>· τὸ δὲ
<u>κέρας</u> <u>ἑκάτερον</u> ἐνίκων οἵ τ' Ἀθηναῖοι καὶ οἱ ἐκ τῆς <u>Πλαταίας</u>
5 σύμμαχοι. νικῶντες δέ, τοὺς μὲν <u>τετραμμένους</u> τῶν βαρβάρων φεύγειν
εἶων, τοῖς δὲ τὸ μέσον ῥήξασιν ἐμάχοντο, συναγαγόντες τὰ κέρατα
<u>ἀμφότερα</u>· οὕτως οὖν ἐνίκησαν οἱ Ἀθηναῖοι. φεύγουσι δὲ τοῖς Πέρσαις
εἵποντο τύπτοντες ἕως, ἐπὶ τὴν θάλασσαν ἀφικόμενοι, πῦρ τ' ἤτουν καὶ
<u>ἐπελαμβάνοντο</u> τῶν νεῶν. καὶ ἐν ταύτῃ τῇ μάχῃ ὁ <u>πολέμαρχος</u>
10 <u>Καλλίμαχος</u> ἀπέθανεν, ἀνὴρ γενόμενος ἀγαθός.

	Μαραθών -ῶνος ὁ	Marathon
	μέσον -ου τό	middle
	ῥήγνυμι ἔρρηξα	I break
	μεσογεία -ας ἡ	inland region
	κέρας -ατος τό	wing (of an army; *literally* horn, *from its shape*)
	ἑκάτερος -α -ον	each (of two)
	Πλάταια -ας ἡ	Plataea (*small town in central Greece; longstanding ally of Athens*)
5	τρέπω *perfect passive* τέτραμμαι	(*here*) I rout
	ἀμφότεροι -αι -α	both
	ἐπιλαμβάνομαι ἐπελαβόμην	I seize hold of (+ *gen*)
	πολέμαρχος -ου ὁ	polemarch (*high-ranking magistrate in overall command of the Athenian army*)
10	Καλλίμαχος -ου ὁ	Callimachus

ἑπτὰ μὲν τῶν νεῶν ἐπεκράτησαν τρόπῳ τοιούτῳ οἱ Ἀθηναῖοι, ταῖς δὲ
λοιπαῖς οἱ βάρβαροι ἀνακρουσάμενοι περιέπλεον Σούνιον, βουλόμενοι
πρὸ τῶν Ἀθηναίων εἰς τὴν πόλιν ἀφικέσθαι. τῶν γὰρ ἐν Ἀθήναις
προδόται τινὲς ἔδειξαν αὐτοῖς ἐκ τῶν ὅρων ἀσπίδα λαμπράν, ἵνα τοῦτο
15 τὸ σημεῖον ἰδόντες ἀπροσδοκήτως προσβάλοιεν τῇ πόλει. οἱ μέντοι
Ἀθηναῖοι ταχέως στρατεύοντες ἀφίκοντο πρὸ τῶν βαρβάρων. οὗτοι οὖν,
ὡς ἐπύθοντο τοὺς ἀπὸ Μαραθῶνος ἥκοντας, ἀπέπλεον εἰς τὴν Ἀσίαν. ἐν
δὲ ταύτῃ τῇ ἐν Μαραθῶνι μάχῃ ἀπέθανον τῶν βαρβάρων ἑξακισχίλιοι
καὶ τετρακόσιοι ἄνδρες· Ἀθηναίων δὲ ἑκατὸν ἐνενήκοντα καὶ δύο.

ἐπικρατέω ἐπεκράτησα	I take possession of (+ gen)
τρόπος -ου ὁ	way
ἀνακρούομαι ἀνεκρουσάμην	I back into the sea
περιπλέω	I sail round
Σούνιον -ου τό	Sunium (cape at southern tip of Attica)
προδότης -ου ὁ	traitor
λαμπρός -ά -όν	bright, shining
15 σημεῖον -ου τό	sign, signal
ἀπροσδοκήτως	unexpectedly
ἀποπλέω	I sail away
Ἀσία -ας ἡ	Asia
ἑξακισχίλιοι -αι -α	6,000
τετρακόσιοι -αι -α	400
ἑκατόν	100
ἐνενήκοντα	90

Exercise PP.8

The advice of Mardonius to Xerxes

*After the Persian defeat at Marathon, Darius started to make plans for a new invasion. But a revolt
against Persian rule broke out in Egypt, and before this was subdued Darius died (485 BC). His son
Xerxes succeeded him and devoted several years to diplomatic and military preparations. He received
conflicting advice from other members of the Persian royal family about whether the expedition
should go ahead. Here his cousin Mardonius persuades him that it should. Xerxes then tells the
Persian nobles that he is going to continue the enterprise begun by his father, and take vengeance on
the Greeks.*

τὸ μὲν πρῶτον ὁ Ξέρξης οὐδαμῶς ἐβούλετο ἐπὶ τὴν Ἑλλάδα στρατεύειν·
ὕστερον δ' ἔπεισεν αὐτὸν ὁ Μαρδόνιος, υἱὸς ὢν τῆς τοῦ πατρὸς ἀδελφῆς,
ὃς εἶπε τάδε· "ὦ δέσποτα, δεῖ τοὺς Ἀθηναίους πολλὰ κακῶς ποιήσαντας
τοὺς Πέρσας δίκην δοῦναι. ταῖς οὖν Ἀθήναις πρόσβαλε, ἵνα μηδεὶς
5 ὕστερον ἐπὶ τὴν σὴν χώραν στρατεύῃ. τῶν δὲ Ἑλλήνων οὔτ' ἀνδρῶν

τὸ πρῶτον	at first (*literally* with respect to the first thing)
Ξέρξης -ου ὁ	Xerxes
Μαρδόνιος -ου ὁ	Mardonius
ἀδελφή -ῆς ἡ	sister
δίκην δίδωμι	I pay the penalty

πλῆθος οὔτε χρημάτων <u>δύναμιν</u> δεῖ φοβεῖσθαι· ἀσθενεῖς γὰρ ὄντες, πρὸς ἀλλήλους μάχονται <u>ἀβουλότατα</u>· οὓς ἐχρῆν, ἐπεὶ <u>ὁμόγλωσσοί</u> εἰσι, διὰ <u>κηρύκων</u> τε καὶ ἀγγέλων παῦσαι τὰς <u>διαφοράς</u>. πρὸς δὲ τούτοις ἡ <u>Εὐρώπη</u>, χώρα καλλίστη οὖσα, <u>παντοῖα</u> φέρει βασιλέως μόνου ἄξια."
10 οὕτως οὖν ἐπείσθη ὁ Ξέρξης.

δύναμις -εως ἡ	power
ἀβουλότατα	senselessly
ὁμόγλωσσος -ον	speaking the same language
κῆρυξ -υκος ὁ	herald
διαφορά -ᾶς ἡ	difference, dispute
Εὐρώπη -ης ἡ	Europe
παντοῖος -α -ον	of all kinds

Read the rest of the passage and answer the questions below.

11 μετὰ δὲ ταῦτα τοῖς τῶν Περσῶν ἀρίστοις ἔλεξε τάδε· "ἄνδρες Πέρσαι, νέον μὲν νόμον ἐν ὑμῖν τιθέναι οὐδαμῶς ἐθέλω· τῶν δὲ <u>Περσικῶν</u> βασιλέων οὐδεὶς <u>ῥάθυμος</u> γέγονεν. καὶ ἐγὼ ἐπεὶ τοῦτον τὸν <u>θρόνον</u> <u>παρέλαβον</u> πάντα πεποίηκα ἵνα μὴ ἐλάσσων γένηται ἡ τῶν Περσῶν
15 δύναμις. μέλλω οὖν τὸν <u>Ἑλλήσποντον</u> <u>ζεύξας</u> στρατιὰν διὰ τῆς <u>Εὐρώπης</u> ἐπὶ τὴν Ἑλλάδα ἄξειν, ἵνα τοὺς Ἀθηναίους κολάσω ὅσα* πεποιήκασι τούς τε Πέρσας καὶ τὸν ἐμὸν πατέρα. τὸν δὲ <u>Δαρεῖον</u> ἤδη ἑοράκατε στρατὸν ἐπὶ τούτους τοὺς ἄνδρας παρασκευάζοντα. οὗτος μέντοι ἀποτέθνηκεν· ἐγὼ δὲ ὑπὲρ τοῦ πατρὸς καὶ τῶν ἄλλων Περσῶν αἱρήσω τε
20 καὶ <u>κατακαύσω</u> τὰς Ἀθήνας."
* 'accusative of respect': translate *for all the things which*

	Περσικός -ή -όν	Persian
	ῥάθυμος -ον	lazy, inactive
	θρόνος -ου ὁ	throne
	παραλαμβάνω παρέλαβον	I take over, I succeed to
15	Ἑλλήσποντος -ου ὁ	Hellespont (*the Dardanelles, dividing Europe from Asia*)
	ζεύγνυμι ἔζευξα	I yoke
	Εὐρώπη -ης ἡ	Europe
	Δαρεῖος -ου ὁ	Darius
20	κατακαίω *fut* κατακαύσω	I burn down

(1) What did Xerxes assure the Persian nobles he did not want to do (lines 11-12)? (2)

(2) How did he characterise Persian kings (lines 12-13?) (2)

(3) What did he say he had done since taking over the throne (lines 13-15)? (3)

(4) What did he say he intended to do, and by what means (lines 15-16)? (4)

(5) Why did he want to punish the Athenians (lines 16-17)? (3)

(6) What did he say about Darius (lines 17-19)? (3)

(7) What did he say he would do, and on whose behalf (lines 19-20)? (3)

20 marks

Exercise PP.9

An Ingenious Message

The exiled Spartan king Demaratus informs his fellow Spartans about the planned expedition of Xerxes. Herodotus speculates about his motive for doing so.

ἐπύθοντο οἱ Λακεδαιμόνιοι πρῶτοι βασιλέα ἐπὶ τὴν Ἑλλάδα
στρατεύοντα, ἐπύθοντο δὲ <u>τρόπῳ θαυμασίῳ</u>. ὁ γὰρ <u>Δημάρητος</u>, ὥς γε
δοκεῖ, οὐκέτι φίλος ἦν τοῖς ἄλλοις Λακεδαιμονίοις· ἔξεστιν οὖν <u>εἰκάζειν</u>
εἴτ' <u>εὐνοίᾳ</u> ταῦτα ἐποίησεν εἴτε καὶ <u>χαίρων</u>. ἐπειδὴ μέντοι τῷ <u>Ξέρξῃ</u>
5 ἔδοξεν ἐπὶ τὴν Ἑλλάδα στρατεύειν, ὁ Δημάρητος ἐν <u>Σούσοις</u> ὢν καὶ
ταῦτα πυθόμενος, ἠθέλησε τοῖς Λακεδαιμονίοις ἀγγεῖλαι. τάδε οὖν
<u>ἐμηχανήσατο· δελτίον δίπτυχον</u> λαβὼν τὸν <u>κηρὸν</u> αὐτοῦ <u>ἐξέκνησεν</u>.
ἔπειτα δ' ἔγραψεν ἐν τῷ τοῦ δελτίου <u>ξύλῳ</u> τὴν βασιλέως <u>γνώμην</u>, ποιήσας
δὲ ταῦτα αὖθις <u>ἐπέτηξε</u> τὸν κηρὸν ἐπὶ τὰ <u>γράμματα</u>, ἵνα οἱ ἐν τῇ ὁδῷ
10 φύλακες μηδεμίαν <u>ὑποψίαν</u> τοῦ δελτίου φερομένου λάβοιντο. ἐπεὶ δ'
ἐδέξαντο τὸ δελτίον οἱ Λακεδαιμόνιοι, πρῶτον μὲν οὐχ οἷοί τ' ἦσαν
<u>συμβαλέσθαι</u>. τέλος δὲ (ὡς ἐγὼ πυνθάνομαι) ἡ <u>Γοργώ</u>, τοῦ μὲν
<u>Κλεομένους</u> θυγάτηρ, τοῦ δὲ <u>Λεωνίδου</u> γυνή, ἐκέλευσεν αὐτοὺς τὸν
κηρὸν ἐκκνᾶν. ἐνόμισε γὰρ αὐτοὺς γράμματα ἐν τῷ ξύλῳ εὑρήσειν.

τρόπος -ου ὁ	way
θαυμάσιος -α -ον	wonderful, marvellous
Δημάρητος -ου ὁ	Demaratus (*exiled Spartan king, who had gone over to Persia*)
εἰκάζω	I guess
εὔνοια -ας ἡ	kindness, goodwill
χαίρω	I rejoice, I am happy
Ξέρξης -ου ὁ	Xerxes
5 Σοῦσα -ων τά	Susa (*important Persian city and royal residence*)
μηχανάομαι ἐμηχανησάμην	I contrive
δελτίον -ου τό	tablet
δίπτυχος -ον	folded, double (*two writing surfaces protected by raised edges were hinged like a book*)
κηρός -οῦ ὁ	wax
ἐκκνάω ἐξέκνησα	I scrape (something) off
ξύλον -ου τό	wood
γνώμη -ης ἡ	plan
ἐπιτήκω ἐπέτηξα	I melt (something) onto
γράμματα -ων τά	letters (of the alphabet)
10 ὑποψία -ας ἡ	suspicion
συμβάλλομαι συνεβαλόμην	I understand, I interpret
Γοργώ ἡ	Gorgo
Κλεομένης -ους ὁ	Cleomenes (*Spartan king of the other royal line to Demaratus, and responsible for his exile*)
Λεωνίδας -ου ὁ	Leonidas (*half-brother and successor of Cleomenes; hero of Thermopylae - see passages PP.13-17*)

15 οὗτοι οὖν πειθόμενοι ηὗρον καὶ <u>ἀνέγνωσαν</u>. ἔπειτα δὲ τοῖς ἄλλοις
    Ἕλλησιν πάντα ἤγγειλαν.

15 ἀναγιγνώσκω ἀνέγνων   I read

Exercise PP.10

Xerxes whips the sea

Xerxes is presented by Herodotus as the archetypal oriental despot. His excessive pride is summed up by his determination to allow no natural obstacle to obstruct him, and by his expectation that even the elements should obey him. Greek readers, with their wide experience of tragic drama, would sense strongly that he is riding for a fall.

Read the passage and answer the questions below.

ἐπεὶ οὖν ἔδοξεν ἐπὶ τοὺς Ἀθηναίους ἰέναι, ὁ Ξέρξης, στρατὸν συλλέξας
θαυμάσιον <u>ὅσον</u>, αὐτὸς εἰς <u>Σάρδεις</u> κατήγαγεν. τρία δ' ἔτη ἤδη
<u>διώρυσσεν</u> τὸν ὑπὸ τῷ <u>Ἄθῳ ἰσθμὸν παντοδαπῶν</u> ἀνθρώπων πλῆθος, ἵνα
μὴ περὶ τὸ ὄρος πλεοῦσαι διαφθείρωνται αἱ νῆες. ἄλλοι δὲ <u>γέφυραν</u>
5 ἐποίησαν ἐν τῷ <u>Ἑλλησπόντῳ</u>, ὃς τὴν <u>Εὐρώπην</u> ἀπὸ τῆς <u>Ἀσίας ἀπέχει</u>, ὧν
ἑπτὰ <u>σταδίων</u> τὸ <u>εὖρος</u>. πεποιημένην δὲ ταύτην χειμὼν μέγας <u>διέλυσεν</u>. ὡς
δ' ἐπύθετο ταῦτα ὁ Ξέρξης, κελεῦσαι λέγεται <u>μαστιγοῦν</u> τε τὴν θάλασσαν
καὶ βάλλειν εἰς αὐτὴν <u>πέδας</u>. καὶ ἠναγκάσθησαν οἱ μαστιγοῦντες τάδε
τὰ βάρβαρά τε καὶ <u>ἀτάσθαλα</u> λέγειν· "<u>ὦ πικρὸν</u> ὕδωρ, ὁ δεσπότης ὧδε

Ξέρξης -ου ὁ	Xerxes
θαυμάσιος -α -ον	wonderful, marvellous
ὅσος -η -ον	(*here*) in size, as to its size
Σάρδεις -εων αἱ	Sardis (*the old Lydian capital, incorporated into the Persian empire*)
διορύσσω	I dig through
Ἄθως -ω ὁ	Athos (*mountain and peninsula in Thrace, to the north of Greece*)
ἰσθμός -οῦ ὁ	isthmus, narrow neck of land
παντοδαπός -ή -όν	of all kinds
γέφυρα -ας ἡ	bridge
5 Ἑλλήσποντος -ου ὁ	Hellespont (*the Dardanelles*)
Εὐρώπη -ης ἡ	Europe
Ἀσία -ας ἡ	Asia
ἀπέχω	I separate
στάδιον -ου τό	stade (*unit of length, about 200 metres*)
εὖρος -ους τό	width (*here accusative of respect, literally* as to the width *i.e.* in width)
διαλύω διέλυσα	I destroy
μαστιγόω	I whip
πέδη -ης ἡ	fetter, shackle
ἀτάσθαλος -ον	presumptuous, reckless
πικρός -ά -όν	bitter

251

10 κολάζει, διότι ἠδίκησας αὐτὸν καίπερ οὐδὲν πρὸς αὐτοῦ ἄδικον παθόν.
καὶ βασιλεὺς Ξέρξης διαβήσεταί σε, ἐάν τε σὺ βούλῃ ἐάν τε μή.
δικαίως οὖν οὐδεὶς ἀνθρώπων θύει σοι ὡς ὄντι θολερῷ καὶ ἁλμυρῷ
ποταμῷ." οὕτως οὖν ὁ Ξέρξης ἐκέλευσεν αὐτοὺς κολάζειν τὴν θάλασσαν·
καὶ ἀπέτεμε τὰς κεφαλὰς τῶν τὴν γέφυραν ποιησάντων.

15 ἔπειτα δ' ἐκέλευσε τοὺς ἑαυτοῦ τὸν πορθμὸν ἄλλῃ γεφύρᾳ ζεῦξαι. οἱ οὖν
ἀρχιτέκτονες δυοῖν γεφύραις ἔζευξαν, ὧν ἑκάστη ναυσὶ τριακοσίαις
ἐποιήθη. σχοινίοις δ' ἰσχυροῖς τὰς ναῦς συνέδησαν, καὶ ἐξ ἑκάστης
ἄγκυρα εἰς τὴν θάλασσαν κατεβλήθη. καὶ ἐπὶ μὲν τὰς ναῦς ἐπέθηκαν
ξύλα, ἐπὶ δὲ τὰ ξύλα ὕλην· φραγμοὺς δ' ἐποίησαν ἀμφοτέρωθεν, ἵνα μὴ
20 οἱ ἵπποι τὴν θάλασσαν ὁρῶντες φοβῶνται.

10	θολερός -ά -όν	muddy
	ἁλμυρός -ά -όν	salty
	ἀποτέμνω ἀπέτεμον	I cut off
	γέφυρα -ας ἡ	bridge
15	πορθμός -οῦ ὁ	channel
	ζεύγνυμι ἔζευξα	I yoke
	ἀρχιτέκτων -ονος ὁ	engineer
	τριακόσιοι -αι -α	three hundred
	σχοινίον -ου τό	cable
	συνδέω συνέδησα	I bind (something) together
	ἄγκυρα -ας ἡ	anchor
	ξύλον -ου τό	log, piece of wood
	ὕλη -ης ἡ	(here) brushwood
	φραγμός -οῦ ὁ	barricade
	ἀμφοτέρωθεν	on both sides

(1) What did Xerxes do after deciding to attack the Athenians
(lines 1-2)? (5)
(2) What task occupied three years, and why was it done (lines 2-4)? (6)
(3) What facts are we told about the Hellespont, which Xerxes bridged
(lines 5-6)? (3)
(4) What happened to the bridge (line 6)? (2)
(5) What actions is Xerxes said to have commanded in response to this
(lines 7-8)? (4)
(6) What description is given of the words the men carrying out Xerxes'
order were commanded to utter (lines 8-9)? (2)
(7) Summarise what the men said on Xerxes' behalf (lines 9-13). (6)
(8) What did Xerxes do to the men who had built the bridge (line 14)? (1)
(9) Describe the second solution to bridging the Hellespont (lines 15-18). (6)
(10) How was the surface of the new bridges made, and why were
barricades put along the sides (lines 18-20)? (5)

40 marks

Exercise PP.11

The Sons of Pythius

This story, like the previous one, contributes importantly to the characterisation of Xerxes. It is not simply that he is wicked, but rather that his gestures both of generosity and of vindictiveness are on a grand scale - and it is unpredictable how the despot will behave in any situation. Herodotus intends a lesson about types of government: Greek readers would be thankful that the republican constitutions of their small city-states were usually free from the corrupting effects of absolute power.

ἦν δὲ <u>Λυδός</u> τις, <u>Πύθιος</u> ὀνόματι, ὃς πρότερον τὸν <u>Ξέρξην</u> <u>ἐξένισε</u>, καὶ χρήματα πολλὰ τῇ στρατιᾷ παρέσχεν. καὶ νῦν παρὰ βασιλέα ἐλθὼν ἔλεξε τάδε· "ὦ δέσποτα, ἀγαθά σε ποιήσας βούλομαι τι παρά σου αἰτεῖν, σοὶ μὲν μικρόν, ἐμοὶ δὲ μέγα". ὁ δὲ Ξέρξης, οὐκ εἰδὼς ὅ τι ὁ Πύθιος
5 λέξει, ἔφη ποιήσειν τοῦτο. ὁ οὖν Πύθιος εἶπεν, "ὦ δέσποτα, εἰσί μοι παῖδες πέντε, καὶ πάντες μετά σου ἐπὶ τὴν Ἑλλάδα στρατεύουσιν. ἕνα οὖν τὸν <u>πρεσβύτατον</u> <u>παράλυσον</u>, ἐμὲ τὸν γέροντα <u>οἰκτείρων</u>, ἵνα ἐνθάδε μένῃ τὸν πατέρα ὠφελήσων. τοὺς δὲ τέσσαρας ἄγε, καὶ εὖ γένοιτο τὸ σὸν ἔργον." ὁ δὲ Ξέρξης μάλιστα ὀργισθεὶς ἀπεκρίνατο, "ὦ κακὲ ἄνθρωπε, σὺ
10 <u>ἐτόλμησας</u> περὶ τοῦ παιδὸς λέγειν, ἐμοῦ βασιλέως ἐπὶ τὴν Ἑλλάδα στρατεύοντος καὶ τοὺς ἐμοὺς παῖδας ἄγοντος; δεῖ σε μαθεῖν δοῦλον ὄντα. σὲ μέντοι καὶ τοὺς τέσσαρας σῴζει ἡ πρότερον <u>ξενία</u>. τὸν δὲ πρεσβύτατον, ὃν μάλιστα φιλεῖς, <u>δίκην δοῦναι</u> δεῖ." ἔπειτα δ' ἐκέλευσε στρατιώτας τινὰς τὸν πρεσβύτατον παῖδα εὑρόντας <u>μέσον</u> <u>διατεμεῖν</u>·
15 διατεμόντας δὲ τὰ <u>ἡμίτομα</u> <u>διαθεῖναι</u> τὸ μὲν <u>ἐπὶ δεξιὰ</u> τῆς ὁδοῦ, τὸ δὲ <u>ἐπ' ἀριστερά</u>. ἔπειτα δὲ ὁ Ξέρξης πάντα τὸν στρατὸν <u>διεξήγαγεν</u>.

	Λυδός -οῦ ὁ	Lydian
	Πύθιος -ου ὁ	Pythius
	Ξέρξης -ου ὁ	Xerxes
	ξενίζω ἐξένισα	I entertain
5	πρεσβύτατος -η -ον	eldest
	παραλύω παρέλυσα	I release
	οἰκτείρω	I pity
10	τολμάω	I dare
	ξενία -ας ἡ	hospitality
	δίκην δίδωμι	I pay the penalty
	μέσος -η -ον	in the middle
	διατέμνω διέτεμον	I cut apart
15	ἡμίτομος -ον	cut in half
	διατίθημι	
	aorist infinitive διαθεῖναι	I arrange
	ἐπὶ δεξιά	on the right
	ἐπ' ἀριστερά	on the left
	διεξάγω διεξήγαγον	I lead right through

Xerxes weeps

Part of the genius of Herodotus is the way in which his portrayal of Xerxes, alongside the uncontrolled temper and arbitrary cruelty, allows glimpses too of a more sympathetic side. In this story Xerxes has a moment of insight into a universal human truth. The story is also rich in dramatic irony: many of the men will, we realise, be dead long before Xerxes imagines. Here again Xerxes resembles the main character of a tragic drama: we can pity him even as we condemn his behaviour. The two sides of Xerxes also echo Herodotus' portrayal of Croesus (which we looked at in Chapters 11 and 12): Xerxes dominates the last part of the historian's work as Croesus dominated the first part. But with Croesus (who was himself a victim of Persian aggression) the positive side was much more strongly emphasised.

ἐπεὶ δ' ἐγένοντο ἐν Ἀβύδῳ (αὕτη δὲ ἡ πόλις ἐστὶ τῶν ἐν Ἀσίᾳ ἐσχάτη), μέλλων διαβήσειν τὸν Ἑλλήσποντον, ὁ Ξέρξης ἐπὶ κολωνοῦ ἐν ἕδρᾳ λιθίνῃ καθίζων πάντα τὸν στρατὸν ἐθεᾶτο. ὡς δὲ ἑώρα τόν τε Ἑλλήσποντον ταῖς ναυσὶν ἀποκεκρυμμένον, τά τε πεδία ἀνθρώπων πλήρη,
5 πρῶτον μὲν ἑαυτὸν ἐμακάρισεν· μετὰ δὲ τοῦτο ἐδάκρυσεν. ἰδόντος δὲ τοῦ Ἀρταβάνου τοῦ πατρὸς ἀδελφοῦ, ὃς πρότερον συνεβούλευσε τῷ Ξέρξῃ μὴ στρατεύεσθαι, καὶ τὴν τῶν δακρύων αἰτίαν ἐρομένου, ἀπεκρίνατο βασιλεὺς τάδε· "εἰσῆλθέ με κατοικτείρειν τούτους, λογισάμενον ὡς βραχύς ἐστιν ὁ πᾶς ἀνθρώπινος βίος· ἐπεὶ τούτων τοσούτων ὄντων οὐδεὶς εἰς
10 ἑκατοστὸν ἔτος περιέσται".

Ἄβυδος -ου ἡ	Abydus
Ἀσία -ας ἡ	Asia
ἔσχατος -η -ον	last, furthest
Ἑλλήσποντος -ου ὁ	Hellespont (*the Dardanelles, dividing Europe from Asia*)
κολωνός -οῦ ὁ	hill
ἕδρα -ας ἡ	seat
λίθινος -η -ον	stone, made of stone
θεάομαι	I watch
ἀποκρύπτω *perfect passive*	
ἀποκέκρυμμαι	I hide, I cover completely
πλήρης -ες	full
5 μακαρίζω ἐμακάρισα	I congratulate, I bless
Ἀρτάβανος -ου ὁ	Artabanus
συμβουλεύω συνεβούλευσα	I advise (+ *dat*)
αἰτία -ας ἡ	cause, reason
κατοικτείρω	I pity
λογίζομαι ἐλογισάμην	I reason
βραχύς -εῖα -ύ	brief, short
ἀνθρώπινος -η -ον	human
10 ἑκατοστός -ή -όν	hundredth
περίειμι	I survive

Exercise PP.13

Spartan behaviour at Thermopylae

Thermopylae was a narrow pass (between mountains and sea) linking Greece with the north. It gave access to central and southern Greece. As the Persians approach (in the summer of 480 BC), most of the Peloponnesians among the combined Greek forces favour retreating, putting up resistance much further south and defending only the Peloponnese. The Spartan king Leonidas stands firm. The Spartans were famous not only for military prowess but for a cool and apparently unconcerned attitude which constantly disconcerted their enemies. The long hair of Spartan warriors may have been linked to a vow (they would not cut it until victorious).

Read the first part of the passage and answer the questions below.

οἱ δὲ ἐν Θερμοπύλαις Ἕλληνες, ἐπειδὴ οἱ Πέρσαι ἀφικνοῦντο, μάλιστα
φοβούμενοι ἐβουλεύοντο περὶ φυγῆς. τοῖς μὲν γὰρ ἄλλοις Πελοποννησίοις
ἐδόκει ἀπελθοῦσιν τὸν Ἰσθμὸν φυλάσσειν, τῷ δὲ Λεωνίδᾳ ἐκεῖ μένειν.
ταῦτα δὲ βουλευομένων αὐτῶν, ἔπεμψεν ὁ Ξέρξης ἱππέα τινὰ ὡς
5 ἀγγελοῦντα ὁπόσοι εἰσὶν οἱ Ἕλληνες καὶ ὅ τι ποιοῦσιν. ἐπεὶ δὲ
προσήλασεν ὁ ἱππεὺς πρὸς τὸ τῶν Πελοποννησίων στρατόπεδον, τοὺς μὲν
ἔσω τοῦ τείχους τεταγμένους οὐκ ἐδύνατο ἰδεῖν, τοὺς δ' ἔξω ἐθεᾶτο.

Θερμοπύλαι -ῶν αἱ		Thermopylae
φυγή -ῆς ἡ		flight, escape
Πελοποννήσιοι -ων οἱ		Peloponnesians
Ἰσθμός -οῦ ὁ		the Isthmus (of Corinth, *dividing the Peloponnese from the rest of Greece*)
Λεωνίδας -ου ὁ		Leonidas
Ξέρξης -ου ὁ		Xerxes
	5	προσελαύνω προσήλασα	I ride up to
ἔσω		inside (+ *gen*)
ἔξω		outside
θεάομαι		I watch

(1) What was the initial reaction of the Greeks at Thermopylae as the
    Persians were approaching (lines 1-2)?   (4)
(2) What did most of the Peloponnesians favour doing (lines 2-3)?   (4)
(3) What did Leonidas decide to do (line 3)?   (2)
(4) Which is the correct translation of ταῦτα δὲ βουλευομένων
    αὐτῶν (line 4)?   (1)
    [a] *But when they had decided these things*
    [b] *And as they themselves wanted these things*
    [c] *But as they were discussing these things*
(5) Why did Xerxes send a horseman (line 4-5)?   (4)
(6) What was the horseman find when he rode up to the Peloponnesian
    camp (lines 5-7)?   (5)

                                                                        ———
                                                                    20 marks

Translate the rest of the passage which follows on the next page.

καὶ τοὺς μὲν τῶν ἀνδρῶν ἑώρα <u>γυμναζομένους</u>, τοὺς δὲ τὰς <u>κόμας</u>
<u>κτενιζομένους</u>. πάντα οὖν ταῦτα <u>θεώμενος</u> καὶ θαυμάζων <u>καθ᾽ ἡσυχίαν</u>
10 <u>ἀπήλασεν</u>, οὐδενὸς διώκοντος. εἰς δὲ τὸ τῶν Περσῶν στρατόπεδον
ἀφικόμενος ἤγγειλε τῷ Ξέρξῃ πάντα ἃ ἑώρακεν. ἀκούσας μέντοι ὁ Ξέρξης
οὐκ ἔγνω τοὺς Λακεδαιμονίους παρασκευαζομένους ὡς ἰσχυρότατα
μαχεσομένους· ἐφαίνοντο γὰρ αὐτῷ <u>γελοῖα</u> ποιεῖν.

	γυμνάζομαι	I exercise
	κόμαι -ῶν αἱ	hair
	κτενίζομαι	I comb
	θεάομαι	I watch
	καθ᾽ ἡσυχίαν	at leisure
10	ἀπελαύνω ἀπήλασα	I ride away
	γελοῖος -α -ον	laughable

Exercise PP.14

Xerxes loses patience

Xerxes is unnerved by the Spartan resistance and by the heavy losses they inflict on his army. He threatens his officers, but there is no breakthrough.

ὁ οὖν <u>Ξέρξης</u> πρὸ τῆς <u>εἰσβολῆς</u> τέσσαρας ἡμέρας ἔμενεν. τῇ δὲ πέμπτῃ
ἡμέρᾳ, τῶν Λακεδαιμονίων οὐκ ἀπελθόντων, βασιλεὺς ἤδη μάλιστα
ὀργιζόμενος τοὺς ἑαυτοῦ στρατιώτας ἐπ᾽ αὐτοὺς ἔπεμψεν ἵνα τὴν
εἰσβολὴν λάβοι. τῶν δὲ Περσῶν, οἳ ὑπὸ βασιλέως τοὺς Λακεδαιμονίους
5 <u>ζωγρῆσαι</u> ἐκελεύσθησαν, πλεῖστοι μὲν ἐν τῇ μάχῃ ἔπιπτον, τοσοῦτοι δὲ
προὐχώρησαν ὥστε τὴν μάχην μὴ παύσασθαι. Λακεδαιμόνιοι δέ τινες
καὶ ἀπέθανον, ἀλλ᾽ ἐλάσσονες ἢ οἱ Πέρσαι. <u>τῇ δὲ ὑστεραίᾳ</u> ὁ Ξέρξης,
ἐλπίσας τοὺς Λακεδαιμονίους (καίπερ ἀνδρείως μαχεσαμένους) ῥᾷον νῦν
νικηθήσεσθαι, τοῖς μεθ᾽ ἑαυτοῦ ὧδε εἶπεν· "ὦ Πέρσαι, ἐὰν μὴ τοὺς
10 πολεμίους τοὺς τὴν εἰσβολὴν φυλάσσοντας εἰς τὴν θάλασσαν <u>σήμερον</u>
διώξητε, ἐγὼ αὐτὸς ὑμᾶς δεινότατα κολάσω". οἱ μὲν οὖν Πέρσαι, <u>πάντως</u>
φοβούμενοι, αὖθις τοῖς Λακεδαιμονίοις προσέβαλον ὡς τὴν εἰσβολὴν
αἱρήσοντες, οἱ δὲ Λακεδαιμόνιοι αὐτοὺς ταχέως <u>ἔτρεψαν</u>.

	Ξέρξης -ου ὁ	Xerxes
	εἰσβολή -ῆς ἡ	pass
5	ζωγρέω ἐζώγρησα	I take prisoner, I capture alive
	τῇ ὑστεραίᾳ	on the next day
10	σήμερον	today
	πάντως	utterly
	τρέπω ἔτρεψα	I rout, I make (someone) turn and run

Exercise PP.15

The Mountain Path

The weakness of Thermopylae as a defensive position was the alternative route along the ridge of the mountains above. This was relatively easy for those who could find the way. Here a local man shows it to the Persians.

τῇ δὲ ὑστεραίᾳ, ὡς ἐν ἀπορίᾳ ἦν βασιλεὺς (οὐ γὰρ ἄμεινον ἔπρασσον οἱ
Πέρσαι) ἦλθεν αὐτῷ εἰς λόγους ἀνήρ τις τῶν ἐπιχωρίων, ὃς ἡγεμὼν
γενόμενος τοῖς Πέρσαις ἀτραπὸν ἔδειξε διὰ τοῦ ὄρους εἰς Θερμοπύλας
φέρουσαν. ὁ δὲ Ξέρξης εὐθὺς περιχαρὴς γενόμενος πέμπει ταύτῃ τοὺς
5 ἀθανάτους, ὧν ἐστρατηγεῖ ὁ Ὑδάρνης. οἱ δέ, πᾶσαν τὴν νύκτα
πορευόμενοι, ἅμ' ἡμέρᾳ ἐπ' ἄκρῳ ἐγένοντο τῷ ὄρει, ἐν ᾧ φύλακες ἔμενον
ἄνδρες τῆς Φωκίδος χίλιοι. οὗτοι δὲ φύλλων ψόφον ἀκούοντες τῶν ὑπὸ
τοῖς ποσὶν ὑποκεχυμένων (δρυῶν γὰρ πλῆρες ἦν τὸ ὄρος) ἔγνωσάν τε
ἀναβεβηκότας τοὺς πολεμίους καὶ εἰς μάχην ὡπλίζοντο. ὡς δὲ πολλοῖς
10 ἐβάλλοντο τοῖς οἰστοῖς, ἐπ' ἄλλο ὄρος ἔφευγον, ὡς ἐντεῦθεν μέχρι
θανάτου ἀμυνούμενοι, οἱ δὲ Πέρσαι, οὐδένα λόγον αὐτῶν ποιούμενοι,
κατὰ τάχος κατέβαινον εἰς τὰς Θερμοπύλας.

	τῇ ὑστεραίᾳ	on the the next day
	ἀπορία -ας ἡ	perplexity
	ἐπιχώριοι -ων οἱ	local inhabitants
	ἡγεμών -όνος ὁ	(*here*) guide
	ἀτραπός -οῦ ἡ	path
	Θερμοπύλαι -ῶν αἱ	Thermopylae
	φέρω	(*here*) I lead
	περιχαρής -ές	delighted
5	ἀθάνατος -ον	immortal (*in pl as proper name* The Immortals, *crack division of Persian troops*)
	στρατηγέω	I am general, I command
	Ὑδάρνης -ους ὁ	Hydarnes
	ἄκρος -α -ον	top (part of)
	Φωκίς -ίδος ἡ	Phocis (*region of central Greece*)
	χίλιοι -αι -α	one thousand
	φύλλον -ου τό	leaf
	ψόφος -ου ὁ	noise, sound
	ὑποχέω	
	perfect passive ὑποκέχυμαι	*literally* I pour under; *perfect passive* I am spread under
	δρῦς δρυός ἡ	oak tree
	πλήρης -ες	full
	ὁπλίζομαι	I arm (myself), I put on armour
10	οἰστός -οῦ ὁ	arrow
	ἐντεῦθεν	from there
	κατὰ τάχος	with haste, speedily

Exercise PP.16

The Last Stand

Realising that the Persians have found the mountain path and so outflanked the Greek defenders of the pass, Leonidas remains with his 300 Spartans to die heroically in an impossible last stand. Although Thermopylae was a defeat for the Greeks, it is always listed with the great victories in the war, both because of the self-sacrificing heroism of the Spartans, and because their resistance delayed the Persians and allowed Greek forces further south to improve their state of preparedness.

ὡς δ' ἔμαθον οἱ ἐν Θερμοπύλαις τὴν τῶν Περσῶν περίοδον, ἐβουλεύοντο
τί χρὴ ποιεῖν. βουλευσάμενοι δὲ οἱ μὲν πλεῖστοι οἴκαδε ἀπῆλθον, οἱ δὲ
μετὰ τοῦ Λεωνίδου καὶ τῶν τριακοσίων μένοντες διεκινδύνευον. ἐκεῖνος
γὰρ οὐκ ἤθελεν ἀπιέναι διὰ τὸ μαντεῖον ὃ τοῖς Λακεδαιμονίοις ἐν
5   Δελφοῖς ἐδόθη, ὡς δεῖ δυοῖν ἓν γενέσθαι· ἢ ὑπὸ Περσῶν αἱρεθῆναι τὴν
Σπάρτην, ἢ ἀποθανεῖν τὸν βασιλέα.

	Θερμοπύλαι -ῶν αἱ	Thermopylae
	περίοδος -ου ἡ	way round
	οἴκαδε	home, homewards
	τριακόσιοι -αι -α	three hundred
	διακινδυνεύω	I endure danger to the end
	μαντεῖον -ου τό	oracle
5	Δελφοί -ῶν οἱ	Delphi

Read the rest of the passage on the next page and answer the questions below.

7 ὁ δὲ Ξέρξης, νομίζων ἤδη ἐκ τοῦ ὄρους καταβεβηκέναι τοὺς ἑαυτοῦ, τὸν
στρατὸν αὖθις ἐκέλευσε προσιέναι· προσιόντων δ᾽ αὐτῶν πολὺ πλῆθος
ἔπιπτεν. ὄπισθε γὰρ οἱ ἡγεμόνες μάστιξιν αὐτοὺς ἔτυπτον, ἀεὶ εἰς τὸ
10 πρόσω ἐποτρύνοντες· καὶ πολλοὶ μὲν δὴ εἰς τὴν θάλασσαν εἰσέπιπτον,
πλείονες δ᾽ ἔτι ὑπ᾽ ἀλλήλων κατεπατοῦντο. ἦν δὲ λόγος οὐδεὶς τῶν
ἀποθανόντων. ἐπιστάμενοι γὰρ οἱ Ἕλληνες τὸν μέλλοντα ἑαυτοῖς ἔσεσθαι
θάνατον ἐκ τῶν τὸ ὄρος περιιόντων, ἀπέδειξαν ῥώμης ὅσον εἶχον
μέγιστον εἰς τοὺς πολεμίους.

	ὄπισθε	behind
	μάστιξ -ιγος ἡ	whip, lash
	εἰς τὸ πρόσω	forwards, to the front
10	ἐποτρύνω	I urge on
	καταπατέω	I trample down
	λόγος -ου ὁ	(here) count, reckoning
	ἀποδείκνυμι ἀπέδειξα	I show, I reveal
	ῥώμη -ης ἡ	strength

(1) What did Xerxes think had happened by now (line 7)?   (3)
(2) What order did he give as a result (lines 7-8)?   (2)
(3) How were the Persian troops urged on by their leaders (lines 9-10)?   (4)
(4) What two disastrous effects did this have (lines 10-11)?   (5)
(5) What did the Greeks know was in store for them, and at whose
     hands (lines 12-13)?   (3)
(6) What did they do in these circumstances (lines 13-14)?   (3)

                                                      20 marks

Exercise PP.17

Leonidas and Dieneces

This passage includes the two-line epigram written by the poet Simonides for the Spartans who died at Thermopylae, and the 'laconic' remark of Dieneces before the battle. Both became famous. The stone lion commemorating Leonidas paid tribute to the meaning of his name.

ἐν δὲ τούτῳ τῷ <u>πόνῳ</u> αὐτός τε πίπτει ὁ <u>Λεωνίδας</u> καὶ μετ' αὐτοῦ
Λακεδαιμονίων ἄνδρες ἄριστοι· πίπτουσι δὲ καὶ τῶν <u>Ξέρξου</u> ἀδελφῶν δύο,
ὑπὲρ τοῦ νεκροῦ τοῦ Λεωνίδου μαχόμενοι. ὡς δὲ τοὺς σὺν τῷ <u>Ὑδάρνῃ</u>
ἥκειν ἐπύθοντο, ἐπὶ <u>κολωνόν</u> τινα συνελέχθησαν οἱ Ἕλληνες, οὗ νῦν ὁ
5   <u>λίθινος</u> λέων ἐστὶν ὑπὲρ τῷ Λεωνίδᾳ. τούτους δ' ἀμυνομένους <u>μαχαίραις</u>
τε καὶ χερσὶ καὶ στόμασι τέλος <u>κατέχωσαν</u> οἱ πολέμιοι βάλλοντες.
ταφεῖσι δὲ οὗ καὶ ἔπεσον τοῖς Λακεδαιμονίοις <u>ἔπος</u> <u>ἐπιγέγραπται</u> τόδε·
    ὦ <u>ξεῖν'</u>, ἄγγειλον Λακεδαιμονίοις ὅτι <u>τῇδε</u>
      <u>κείμεθα</u> τοῖς <u>κείνων</u> <u>ῥήμασι</u> πειθόμενοι.
10 τῶν δὲ μετὰ τοῦ Λεωνίδου ἀποθανόντων ἄριστος λέγεται γενέσθαι
Λακεδαιμόνιός τις <u>Διηνέκης</u>, ὃν πρὸ τῆς μάχης εἰπεῖν φασὶ τόδε·
πυθόμενος γὰρ παρὰ <u>Τραχινίου</u> τινὸς ὅτι οἱ βάρβαροι τοξευόμενοι τὸν
ἥλιον τῷ τῶν <u>οἰστῶν</u> πλήθει <u>ἀποκρύπτουσιν</u>, "ἀγαθά γε," ἔφη, "ἡμῖν
πάντα ἀγγέλλεις· ἀποκρυπτόντων γὰρ τῶν Περσῶν τὸν ἥλιον, ὑπὸ <u>σκιᾷ</u>
ἔσται ἡ πρὸς αὐτοὺς μάχη".

	πόνος -ου ὁ	struggle, toil
	Λεωνίδας -ου ὁ	Leonidas
	Ξέρξης -ου ὁ	Xerxes
	Ὑδάρνης -ους ὁ	Hydarnes
	κολωνός -οῦ ὁ	hill
5	λίθινος -η -ον	(made of) stone
	μάχαιρα -ας ἡ	dagger, short sword
	καταχώννυμι κατέχωσα	I overwhelm
	ἔπος -ους τό	(*here*) inscription, text
	ἐπιγράφω	I inscribe
	ξεῖνος	= ξένος (*dialect form*)
	τῇδε	here
	κεῖμαι	I lie
	κεῖνος	= ἐκεῖνος (*dialect form*)
	ῥῆμα -ατος τό	word
10	Διηνέκης -ους ὁ	Dieneces
	Τραχίνιος -ου ὁ	Trachinian, man of Trachis (*region in central Greece*)
	οἰστός -οῦ ὁ	arrow
	ἀποκρύπτω	I conceal, I hide (something) from view
	σκία -ᾱς ἡ	shade, shadow

260

Exercise PP.18

Artemisia at Salamis

The Persians advanced southward, by land and sea simultaneously. Athens was evacuated after the Delphic oracle told the Athenians to 'put their trust in wooden walls': the great statesman and military leader Themistocles persuaded his fellow citizens that this referred to the fleet (rather than, as others claimed, the wooden stockade that then surrounded the Acropolis). His policy was vindicated when a major naval victory was won just off Salamis (an island close to Athens) in September of 480 BC. As in the land battle at Marathon ten years earlier, clever Greek tactics made up for numerical inferiority: Themistocles enticed the Persians to fight in a narrow channel where the smaller and faster Greek ships had the advantage, and sheer numbers were of little help to the enemy. As is usual with his descriptions of battles, Herodotus gives the broad picture but leaves many questions of detail unanswered. He prefers to focus instead on anecdotes of human interest: this story of the Carian queen Artemisia (an ally of Xerxes) is one of his best, illustrating the Greek admiration for cunning intelligence (in whatever context) such as we first saw in the Cyclops story in Chapter 5.

περὶ δὲ τῶν ἄλλων οὐκ ἔξεστιν ἀκριβῶς γνῶναι ὡς ἕκαστοι τῶν
βαρβάρων ἢ τῶν Ἑλλήνων ἠγωνίζοντο· περὶ δὲ τῆς Ἀρτεμισίας τάδε
ἐγένετο, ἀφ' ὧν ἐτιμᾶτο μᾶλλον ὑπὸ βασιλέως. ἐπειδὴ γὰρ εἰς θόρυβον
πολὺν ἀφίκετο τὰ βασιλέως πράγματα, ἡ τῆς Ἀρτεμισίας ναῦς ἐδιώκετο
5 νηὶ Ἀττικῇ. καὶ οὐ δυναμένη αὐτὴ διαφυγεῖν (ἔμπροσθε γὰρ αὐτῆς ἦσαν
ἄλλαι νῆες φίλιαι) ἔδοξε τάδε ποιῆσαι. διωκομένη γὰρ ἐνέβαλε νηὶ φιλίᾳ
ἀνδρῶν τῶν Καλυνδίων. ὡς δὲ τὴν ναῦν κατέδυσε, δύο ἀγαθὰ ἑαυτὴν
ἐποίησεν· ὁ γὰρ τῆς Ἀττικῆς νεὼς τριήραρχος, ὡς εἶδεν αὐτὴν
ἐμβάλλουσαν νηὶ πολεμίᾳ, νομίσας τὴν τῆς Ἀρτεμισίας ναῦν Ἑλληνικὴν
10 εἶναι, πρὸς ἄλλας ἀπέτρεψεν. τοῦτο μὲν οὖν ὠφέλησεν αὐτήν, ὅτι
διαφυγοῦσα περιεγένετο· ἐκεῖνο δὲ μάλιστα ὠφέλιμον ἐγένετο, ὅτι ἐκ
τῆς Καλυνδικῆς νεὼς οὐδεὶς ἐσώθη ὥστε κατηγορεῖν αὐτῆς. ὁ γὰρ Ξέρξης
ἐνόμισε τὴν ναῦν τὴν διαφθαρεῖσαν εἶναι πολεμίαν, καὶ εἶπεν, "οἱ μὲν
ἄνδρες γεγόνασί μοι γυναῖκες, αἱ δὲ γυναῖκες ἄνδρες."

	ἀκριβῶς	exactly, accurately
	ἀγωνίζομαι	I compete
	Ἀρτεμισία -ας ἡ	Artemisia (*queen of Carian kingdom including Halicarnassus, on the coast of modern Turkey*)
	θόρυβος -ου ὁ	confusion, disturbance
5	Ἀττικός -ή -όν	Attic, Athenian
	διαφεύγω διέφυγον	I escape
	ἔμπροσθε	in front of (+ *gen*)
	ἐμβάλλω ἐνέβαλον	I ram (+ *dat*)
	Καλύνδιοι -ων οἱ	Calyndians (*Calynda was a town in Caria near to Halicarnassus*)
	καταδύω κατέδυσα	I sink (something)
	τριήραρχος -ου ὁ	captain
	Ἑλληνικός -ή -όν	Greek
10	ἀποτρέπω ἀπέτρεψα	I turn aside
	Καλυνδικός -ή -όν	Calyndian
	κατηγορέω	I accuse (+ *gen*)

Exercise PP.19

A confused end to the battle

Just as in the battle itself, the Persians are hampered by their numbers in trying to get away afterwards.

Read the passage and answer the questions below.

ἐν δὲ τῇ μάχῃ ταύτῃ ἀπέθανε μὲν ὁ στρατηγὸς <u>Ἀραβίγνης</u> ὁ τοῦ <u>Δαρείου</u>
υἱός, τοῦ <u>Ξέρξου</u> ὢν ἀδελφός· ἀπέθανον δ' ἄλλοι πολλοί τε καὶ
<u>ὀνομαστοὶ</u> τῶν Περσῶν τε καὶ τῶν ἄλλων συμμάχων, ὀλίγοι δέ τινες τῶν
Ἑλλήνων. ὅτι γὰρ <u>νεῖν</u> ἐδύναντο εἰς τὴν <u>Σαλαμῖνα</u> <u>διένεόν</u> τινες ὧν αἱ
5 νῆες διεφθείροντο. τῶν δὲ βαρβάρων οἱ πολλοὶ ἐν τῇ θαλάσσῃ
διεφθάρησαν, νεῖν οὐ δυνάμενοι. ἐπεὶ δὲ αἱ πρῶται νῆες ἔφευγον, τότε
αἱ πλεῖσται διεφθείροντο. οἱ γὰρ <u>ὄπισθε</u> τεταγμένοι <u>εἰς τὸ πρόσθεν</u> ἰέναι
ταῖς ναυσὶ πειρώμενοι, ὡς δειξόμενοι ἔργον τι καὶ αὐτοὶ βασιλεῖ, ταῖς
ἄλλαις ναυσὶ φευγούσαις <u>περιέπιπτον</u>. οἱ δὲ βάρβαροι ὧν αἱ νῆες
10 <u>περιεγένοντο</u> φεύγοντες ἀφίκοντο εἰς τὸ <u>Φάληρον</u>.

	Ἀραβίγνης ὁ	Arabignes
	Δαρεῖος -ου ὁ	Darius
	Ξέρξης -ου ὁ	Xerxes
	ὀνομαστός -ή -όν	distinguished
	νέω	I swim
	Σαλαμίς -ῖνος ἡ	Salamis (*island close to Athens*)
	διανέω	I reach by swimming
5	ὄπισθε	behind
	εἰς τὸ πρόσθεν	forwards
	περιπίπτω	I fall foul of, I get dashed against (+ *dat*)
10	περιγίγνομαι περιεγενόμην	I survive
	Φάληρον -ου τό	Phalerum (*harbour of Athens*)

(1)	Who was Ariabignes, and what happened to him (lines 1-2)?	(4)
(2)	What is said about the casualties on the two sides (lines 2-4)?	(5)
(3)	What were some of the shipwrecked Greeks able to do (lines 4-5)?	(2)
(4)	Why were most of the enemy unable to do the same (lines 5-6)?	(1)
(5)	How and why did the Persian ships fall foul of each other (lines 7-9)?	(6)
(6)	Which men managed to reach Phalerum (lines 9-10)?	(2)

20 marks

Exercise PP.20

Persian and Spartan Banquets

Despite the messy and confused ending to the fighting at Salamis (passage PP.19), the message of the battle was clear. Xerxes at once returned to Persia with the remnant of his fleet, leaving his cousin and subordinate Mardonius with a picked force to stay in Greece over the winter and continue the campaign by land. Mardonius was duly defeated by the Greeks at Plataea in 479 BC under the command of the Spartan Pausanias. This final story takes place just after the Greek victory there. (It refers at the start to Xerxes' departure after the defeat at Salamis the previous autumn.) The contrast between the oriental wealth and luxury represented by the Persians, and the more frugal lifestyle of the Greeks (particularly the austere Spartans) runs all through Herodotus' work. He believes it goes with political differences: servile obedience to a despot, as against participation in a free and open society. Yet Herodotus also stresses that the Persians had themselves started as a poor but disciplined and energetic people, before their career of conquest: the change illustrates his belief about the instability of fortune, which we saw constantly illustrated in the stories in Chapters 11 and 12. And the reverse can happen too: Herodotus perhaps hints that Athens in his own day, emboldened by her victories in the Persian Wars to embark upon her own career of conquest and imperialism, risks falling prey to a quasi-oriental despotism and self-indulgence.

μετὰ δὲ τὴν ἐν <u>Σαλαμῖνι</u> μάχην λέγεται καὶ τάδε γενέσθαι, ὅτι ὁ <u>Ξέρξης</u>
φεύγων ἐκ τῆς Ἑλλάδος τῷ <u>Μαρδονίῳ</u> τὴν <u>κατασκευὴν</u> <u>καταλίποι</u> τὴν
ἑαυτοῦ· τὸν οὖν <u>Παυσανίαν</u>* ὁρῶντα τὴν τοῦ Μαρδονίου κατασκευὴν
χρυσῷ τε καὶ <u>ἀργύρῳ</u> <u>κατεσκευασμένην</u> κελεῦσαι* τοὺς <u>ὀψοποιοὺς</u> ὥσπερ
5 τῷ Μαρδονίῳ δεῖπνον παρασκευάζειν. ὡς δὲ κελευόμενοι οὗτοι ἐποίουν
ταῦτα, ἐνταῦθα τὸν Παυσανίαν ἰδόντα <u>κλίνας</u> τε καὶ <u>τραπέζας</u> χρυσοῦ
καὶ ἀργύρου, καὶ <u>παρασκευὴν</u> <u>μεγαλοπρεπῆ</u> τοῦ δείπνου, θαυμάζοντα τὰ
παρόντα ἀγαθὰ κελεῦσαι <u>ἐπὶ</u> <u>γέλωτι</u> τοὺς ἑαυτοῦ δούλους παρασκευάσαι

* note that, despite starting with a ὅτι clause, the construction (as often) switches to accusative and infinitive for an extended indirect statement (here occupying most of the passage)

Σαλαμίς -ῖνος ἡ	Salamis
Ξέρξης -ου ὁ	Xerxes
Μαρδόνιος -ου ὁ	Mardonius
κατασκευή -ῆς ἡ	(*here*) (royal) tent (*a large and elaborate tent, along with its furnishings*)
καταλείπω κατέλιπον	leave behind
Παυσανίας -ου ὁ	Pausanias (Spartan commander, nephew of Leonidas)
ἄργυρος -ου ὁ	silver
κατασκευάζω *perfect passive*	
κατεσκεύασμαι	I prepare, I furnish
ὀψοποιός -οῦ ὁ	cook
5 κλίνη -ης ἡ	couch
τράπεζα -ης ἡ	table
παρασκευή -ῆς ἡ	preparation
μεγαλοπρεπής -ές	magnificent
ἐπί	(+ *dat*) (*here*) for
γέλως -ωτος ὁ	laugh, joke

δεῖπνον Λακεδαιμόνιον. ὡς δὲ τῶν δείπνων ποιηθέντων ἦν πολὺ τὸ μέσον,
10 τὸν Παυσανίαν γελάσαντα μεταπέμψασθαι τοὺς τῶν Ἑλλήνων
στρατηγούς. συνελθόντων δὲ τούτων εἶπειν τὸν Παυσανίαν, δεικνύντα
ἑκατέρου δείπνου τὴν παρασκευήν, "ἄνδρες Ἕλληνες, τῶνδε ἕνεκα ἐγὼ
ὑμᾶς συνήγαγον, βουλόμενος ὑμῖν τὴν τοῦ Πέρσου ἀφροσύνην δεῖξαι, ὃς
τοιαύτην δίαιταν ἔχων ἦλθεν ὡς ἀφαιρησόμενος τὰ ἡμέτερα οὕτως
15 ὀϊζυρὰ ὄντα."

	μέσον -ου τό	*literally* middle, *here* distance between, difference
10	μεταπέμπομαι μετεπεμψάμην	I send for
	ἑκάτερος -α -ον	each (of two)
	ἕνεκα	for the sake of (*follows gen*)
	ἀφροσύνη -ης ἡ	foolishness
	δίαιτα -ης ἡ	lifestyle
15	ὀϊζυρός -ά -όν*	pitiful, miserable

* the *umlaut* (two dots over a letter) is often used to indicate (as the position of the breathing also
does) when a vowel does not, as it usually would, form a diphthong with the preceding vowel

Revision sentences

Exercise RS.1: Definite article

1 οἱ ἀνδρεῖοι φυλάσσουσι τοὺς ἀσθενεῖς.
2 οἱ τὸ δίκαιον πράσσοντες ὑπὸ τῶν σοφῶν τιμῶνται.
3 ἡ Ἑλλὰς ἐλευθέρα ἔσται.
4 οἱ τῶν τότε λόγοι χρήσιμοί εἰσι τοῖς νῦν.
5 αἱ ἐν τῇ πόλει ἀσφαλεῖς ἔσονται.
6 τὰ τῆς πόλεως κακῶς πράσσεται.
7 οἱ κριταὶ οἱ ἀγαθοὶ τὴν δικαιοσύνην φυλάσσουσιν.
8 ὁ βαθύτατος ποταμός ἐστι χαλεπώτατος.
9 ὁ μὲν φιλεῖ τὸν πόλεμον, ὁ δὲ τὴν εἰρήνην.
10 ἀγαθόν ἐστιν ἐλπίζειν.

Exercise RS.2: Agreement of nouns and adjectives

1 οἱ κριταὶ οἱ σοφοὶ λόγους ἀληθεῖς λέγουσιν.
2 ἐν τῇ νήσῳ ἐστὶ πολλὰ ὄρη.
3 ἡ εἰρήνη ἡδεῖα.
4 νομίζω τοῦτον τὸν νόμον σαφῆ εἶναι.
5 ποῖος καὶ πόσος ἐστὶν ὁ ἵππος;
6 ἐκεῖνοι οἱ στρατιῶται καλοί τε καὶ ἀγαθοί εἰσιν.
7 ὁ ἡμέτερος ἡγεμὼν ἄξιός ἐστι τῆς τιμῆς.
8 βουλὴν χρησίμην ἐποιησάμεθα.
9 ἡ τριήρης βαρυτάτη ἐστίν.
10 ὅ τε γέρων καὶ ὁ θεὸς σοφοὶ ἦσαν.

Exercise RS.3: Verb tenses

1 οἱ δοῦλοι ἐπὶ τούτοις ἐλευθερωθήσονται.
2 πολὺν χρόνον ἐμαχόμεθα· ἔπειτα δὲ ἐνικήσαμεν.
3 ὃ γέγραφα, γέγραφα.
4 οἱ στρατιῶται πρὸς τὴν νῆσον ἤχθησαν.
5 ηὕρηκα τὸ ἀληθές.
6 οἱ πολέμιοι πρὸς τὴν θάλασσαν ἐδιώχθησαν.
7 τὰ περὶ τῆς μάχης νῦν ἤγγελται.
8 ὁ φεύγων ὤφθη ὑπὸ τοῦ γέροντος.
9 σοφώτερος γέγονα τῷ χρόνῳ.
10 τὰ ὅπλα εἰς τὸ στρατόπεδον ἠνέχθη.

Exercise RS.4: Passives

1   οἱ λόγοι ὑπὸ τῶν παίδων μανθάνονται.
2   ἡ ναῦς ἐν τῷ λιμένι λείπεται.
3   τὸ τεῖχος τοῖς τῶν στρατιωτῶν ὅπλοις φυλάσσεται.
4   τὸ ὕδωρ ὑπὸ τοῦ δούλου φέρεται.
5   οἱ ἵπποι ἐλύθησαν ὑπὸ τοῦ ἡγεμόνος.
6   οἱ νόμοι ὑπὸ τῶν Ἑλλήνων τιμῶνται.
7   ἐπεὶ ὁ περὶ τῆς μάχης λόγος ἠγγέλλετο, ὁ ἄγγελος ὑπὸ τῶν
         στρατιωτῶν ἀπέθανεν.
8   μετὰ τρεῖς ἡμέρας ἡ πόλις ληφθήσεται.
9   οἱ παῖδες πολὺν χρόνον ἐδιδάσκοντο.
10   ὁ δῆμος ὑπὸ τοῦ ῥήτορος πείθεται.

Exercise RS.5: Middles and deponent verbs

1   ὁ τῶν συμμάχων ἄγγελος ἀφίκετο.
2   διδάσκομαι τοὺς παῖδας.
3   ὁ στρατὸς διὰ χώρας ἀσφαλοῦς ἐπορεύετο.
4   ἡ νόσος φαίνεται δεινοτάτη εἶναι.
5   ὁ γέρων λύεται τὸν δοῦλον.
6   ἡ μάχη ὑπὸ νύκτα παύεται.
7   βουλόμεθα παρὰ τῷ ποταμῷ στρατοπεδεύεσθαι.
8   ὁ νεανίας ἐφέρετο πολλὰ ἆθλα.
9   ὁ παῖς ἀνὴρ ἐγένετο.
10   οἱ πολῖται τοῖς τοῦ στρατηγοῦ λόγοις πείθονται.

Exercise RS.6: Prepositions

1   αἱ τριήρεις ἀπὸ τοῦ λιμένος πρὸς τὴν νῆσον προσῆλθον.
2   ἐπὶ ἐκείνου τοῦ βασιλέως, οἱ νόμοι κάκιστοι ἦσαν.
3   ἐδίωξα τοὺς δούλους κατὰ τὴν ὁδόν.
4   οἱ ἄδικοι παρὰ τοὺς νόμους καὶ παρὰ τοὺς θεοὺς πράσσουσιν.
5   οἱ στρατιῶται περὶ τῶν τοῦ ἄστεως τειχῶν ἐστρατοπεδεύσαντο.
6   ὁ ἄγγελος πολλὰ εἶπε περὶ τῆς μακρᾶς μάχης.
7   ἀνδρείως ἐμαχέσαντο ὑπὲρ τῆς πόλεως.
8   μετὰ δύο ἔτη οἱ πολέμιοι ἐνικήθησαν.
9   πρὸς τοῖς ἄλλοις δώροις τήνδε τὴν βίβλον ἐδεξάμην.
10   μετὰ τῶν φίλων πολὺν χρόνον ἐμένομεν.

Exercise RS.7: Prepositional set phrases

1   πολὺν χρόνον ἐμένομεν· ἐν δὲ τούτῳ ὁ ποταμὸς χαλεπὸς ἐγένετο.
2   ὁ τῶν συμμάχων στρατὸς εἰς καιρὸν ἀφίκετο.
3   τὸ τεῖχος καθ' ἡμέραν μεῖζον γίγνεται.
4   οἱ πολέμιοι ὑπέσχοντο ἀπιέναι· ἐπὶ τούτοις ἐπαύσαμεν τὸν πόλεμον.
5   τὰ δῶρα πᾶσι τοῖς παισὶν ἐξ ἴσου ἐδόθη.
6   ὑπὸ νύκτα τὰς ναῦς προσιούσας εἴδομεν.
7   ὁ τοῦ θεοῦ ἄγγελος διὰ πέντε ἐτῶν φαίνεται.
8   οἱ Ἕλληνες περὶ πολλοῦ ἐποιοῦντο ἐλεύθεροι εἶναι.
9   διὰ τριῶν ἡμερῶν ἔξεστι τοῖς δούλοις ἐξελθεῖν.
10 διδάσκω καὶ ἐν τούτῳ μανθάνω.

Exercise RS.8: Compound verbs

1   ἀναβησόμεθα ἀνὰ τὸ ὄρος.
2   ἐκ τῆς οἰκίας εἰς τὴν ὁδὸν ἐξέβην.
3   οἱ πολῖται εἰς τὴν ἀγορὰν ἐξῆλθον.
4   οὐκ ἔξεστι διαβαίνειν ἐκεῖνον τὸν ποταμόν.
5   βούλομαι ἀποβάλλειν πάντα ταῦτα.
6   ὁ ἡγεμὼν τὸν στρατὸν περὶ τὴν πόλιν περιήγαγεν.
7   οἱ φύλακες κατὰ τῶν τειχῶν κατέβησαν.
8   ὁ βασιλεὺς ἄγγελον πρὸς τὴν πόλιν προσέπεμψεν.
9   οἱ πολέμιοι ἐν τῷ στρατοπέδῳ ἔνεισιν.
10 οἱ σύμμαχοι ὑπὲρ τὸ ὄρος ὑπερέβαινον.

Exercise RS.9: Uses of αὐτός

1   ὁ βασιλεὺς αὐτὸς ἀφίκετο.
2   τῇ αὐτῇ ἡμέρᾳ ἐνικήσαμεν.
3   οἱ πολέμιοι τιμῶσι τὴν πόλιν καὶ τοὺς νόμους αὐτῆς.
4   αὕτη ἐστὶν ἡ θεὰ αὐτή.
5   αὐτὸς ἔγραψα τὴν βίβλον.
6   ὁ δοῦλος ἔφυγε, καὶ οὐδεὶς εἶδεν αὐτόν.
7   ὁ ἄγγελος καὶ ὁ παῖς λέγουσι τὰ αὐτά.
8   αὐτοὶ οἱ Ἕλληνες οὔποτε νικῶνται.
9   αὐτὸς ἀπέκτεινας αὐτόν.
10 αἱ γυναῖκες αὐταὶ ἐφύλασσον τὰ τείχη.

Exercise RS.10: Pronouns, possessives and demonstratives

1   ἡμεῖς μὲν Ἕλληνές ἐσμεν, ὑμεῖς δὲ βάρβαροι.
2   φοβοῦμαι οὐ τὸν ἐμὸν πατέρα ἀλλὰ τὸν σόν.
3   ὁ στρατιώτης φυλάσσει τὸν βασιλέα καὶ τὴν γυναῖκα αὐτοῦ.
4   οὗτός ἐστι σὸς δοῦλος.
5   ἐκείνη ἡ βίβλος οὐκ ἔστιν ἐμή.
6   ταῦτα ἀκούσας, ὁ στρατηγὸς ἀπῆλθεν.
7   ἐκεῖνος ὁ γέρων φίλιός ἐστιν.
8   ὁ ἡγεμὼν ἔδωκέ μοι τὸν ἑαυτοῦ ἵππον.
9   ἡ ἡμετέρα ἐκκλησία ἀεὶ δίκαια πράσσει.
10   οὐκ οἶδα τὸ ὄνομα τὸ σόν.

Exercise RS.11: Circumstantial use of participles

1   οἱ στρατιῶται, ὑπὸ τῶν πολεμίων διωκόμενοι, πρὸς τὴν πόλιν ἔφυγον.
2   τὸ ναυτικὸν ἰδόντες ἐθαυμάσαμεν.
3   ὁ στρατηγὸς τὰ γενόμενα πυθόμενος ἐξέπεμψε τὸν στρατόν.
4   οἱ βάρβαροι, ὀλίγους τῶν Ἑλλήνων ἀποκτείναντες, ἀπῆλθον.
5   δίκαιος ὤν, δίκαια πράσσει.
6   εἰς τὸ ὄρος ἀφικόμενοι, ὑπὸ νύκτα ἐστρατοπεδευσάμεθα.
7   ὁ ἵππος, ταχὺς ὤν, χρήσιμος ἔσται.
8   ὁ παῖς, τὰ ὅπλα εὑρών, ἐβούλετο μάχεσθαι.
9   αἱ γυναῖκες, ἀνδρεῖαι οὖσαι, ἐν τῇ πόλει ἔμενον.
10   φιλοῦμεν τὴν βουλὴν ὡς σοφήν τε καὶ χρησίμην οὖσαν.

Exercise RS.12: Attributive use of participles

1   ὁ ἄγγελος ὁ ἀφικόμενος δεινὰ λέγει.
2   ἆρα ὁρᾶτε τοὺς δούλους τοὺς φεύγοντας;
3   οἱ στρατιῶται οἱ τεθνηκότες ἀνδρειότατοι ἦσαν.
4   ὁ στρατὸς ὁ ἐκεῖ ταχθεὶς εὖ ἐμαχέσατο.
5   αἱ βοαὶ αἱ τότε ἀκουσθεῖσαι δειναὶ ἦσαν.
6   ἔξεστι τοῖς δούλοις τοῖς μαχεσαμένοις ἐλευθεροῦσθαι.
7   οὐχ οἷός τ' εἰμὶ εὑρεῖν τὸν στρατιώτην τὸν φυγόντα.
8   τὰ δῶρα τὰ ὑπὸ τοῦ βασιλέως δοθέντα ἦν κάλλιστα.
9   ἡ βίβλος ἡ σαφῶς γραφεῖσα χρησίμη ἐστίν.
10   τὰ ἔργα τὰ τότε πραχθέντα κάλλιστα ἦν.

Exercise RS.13: Relative clauses

1   εἴδομεν τοὺς δούλους οἳ ἔφυγον.
2   ἐφυλάσσομεν τοὺς πολεμίους οἳ ἐλήφθησαν.
3   αὕτη ἐστιν ἡ βίβλος ἣν ἔγραψα.
4   ἐγὼ ηὗρον τὸν στρατιώτην ὃς ἔφευγεν.
5   ἐκεῖνός ἐστιν ὁ παῖς ᾧ τὸ ἆθλον ἔδωκα.
6   ἔχομεν δοῦλον οὗ αἱ χεῖρές εἰσι μέγισται.
7   ταῦτα ἔλεξα τοῖς πολίταις οἳ ἤκουον.
8   ὁ ἀνὴρ ὃν ὁρᾷς βάρβαρός ἐστιν.
9   οὐκ οἶδα τὴν γυναῖκα ἣ πάρεστιν.
10 παύσω τοὺς στρατιώτας οἳ πορεύονται.

Exercise RS.14: Genitive absolute

1   τῶν λόγων λεχθέντων, ὁ δῆμος ἐπείσθη.
2   οἱ Ἕλληνες, τῶν βαρβάρων νικηθέντων, εἰρήνην εἶχον.
3   τοῦ ὕδατος δεινοῦ ὄντος, οὐκ ἐθέλομεν στρατοπεδεύσασθαι.
4   τοῦ ἀγγέλου ἀφικομένου, πάντες οἱ πολῖται συνελέγοντο.
5   τοῦ ποταμοῦ βαθοῦς ὄντος, ἔδει ἡμᾶς ἐκεῖ μένειν.
6   ἀσφαλεῖς νῦν ἐσμεν, τῶν πολεμίων ἀπελθόντων.
7   τοῦ κινδύνου μείζονος γενομένου, βουλὴν περὶ πολέμου ἐποιησάμεθα.
8   τῆς ὁδοῦ χαλεπῆς οὔσης, ταῖς ναυσὶ χρῆσθαι βουλόμεθα.
9   τῶν συμμάχων ὀλίγων ὄντων, πόλεμον φοβούμεθα.
10 τῶν στρατιωτῶν μαχομένων, οἱ σύμμαχοι ἀφίκοντο.

Exercise RS.15: Adverbs

1   ὁ θεὸς οὐ σαφῶς ἀλλὰ σοφῶς ἀποκρίνεται.
2   οἱ στρατιῶται, ἀνδρεῖοι ὄντες, ἀνδρείως καὶ μάχονται.
3   ὁ δοῦλος ἀεὶ εὖ ἀπεκρίνατο.
4   τοὺς βαρβάρους ῥᾳδίως νικήσομεν.
5   οὗτοι οἱ παῖδες βραδέως ἐπορεύοντο.
6   ὁ ἄγγελος ἀσφαλῶς ἀφίκετο.
7   ἐκεῖνος ἀξίως ἀπέθανεν.
8   οἱ ναῦται εὐθὺς ἐξεπέμφθησαν.
9   αὕτη ἡ βίβλος μάλιστα φιλεῖται.
10 τὰ ἄριστα ὅπλα πολλάκις ἐκεῖ εὑρίσκεται.

Exercise RS.16: Numerals and time expressions

1 τρεῖς μὲν ἡμέρας ἐπορευόμεθα, τῇ δὲ τετάρτῃ ἀφικόμεθα.
2 ἔχομεν μίαν χώραν καὶ ἕνα βασιλέα.
3 εἰσὶ τῷ κριτῇ δύο δοῦλοι.
4 τῷ δεκάτῳ ἔτει ὁ πόλεμος ἐπαύσατο.
5 ὁ δοῦλος ἔφυγε τῆς νυκτός.
6 πᾶσαν τὴν ἡμέραν ἐδιώκομεν τοὺς πολεμίους.
7 ἑπτὰ δῶρα αὐτῇ ἔδωκα, ἀλλὰ τὸ ὄγδοον ἔτι ἔχω.
8 ἐν τῇ νήσῳ ἐστὶν ἓν ὄρος.
9 τέσσαρας νύκτας ἐμένομεν τοὺς συμμάχους.
10 εἷς βίος ἑκάστῳ ἐστίν.

Exercise RS.17: Comparative and superlative adjectives

1 οἱ Ἕλληνες πολλῷ σοφώτεροί εἰσιν ἢ οἱ βάρβαροι.
2 τὰ τῆς πόλεως τείχη ἐστὶν ἀσθενέστατα.
3 ὁ λιμὴν μείζων ἐστὶ τῆς ἀγορᾶς.
4 ἡ θάλασσα βαθυτέρα ἐστὶν ἢ ὁ ποταμός.
5 οὗτός ἐστιν ἄριστος τῶν στρατιωτῶν.
6 ὁ δικαιότατος κριτὴς ἐπέμφθη.
7 ἡ νέα ὁδός ἐστι βραδυτέρα.
8 οἱ ἵπποι θάσσονές εἰσι τῶν ἀνθρώπων.
9 ὁ χρόνος ἐστὶν ἀληθέστατος κριτής.
10 ἥδε ἡ ὁδὸς μακροτέρα ἐστὶν ἢ ἐκείνη.

Exercise RS.18: Comparative and superlative adverbs

1 ὁ παῖς σαφέστατα ἀπεκρίνατο.
2 ὁ ῥήτωρ λέγει ῥᾷον ἢ ἀκούει.
3 ὁ δοῦλος ὡς τάχιστα ἔφυγεν.
4 οὗτος ὁ στρατὸς θᾶσσον πορεύεται ἢ ἐκεῖνος.
5 οἱ στρατιῶται ὡς ἀνδρειότατα ἐμαχέσαντο.
6 πότερος λόγος ἀληθέστερον ἐλέχθη;
7 οἱ σύμμαχοι βραδύτερον ἀφίκοντο ἢ ἠλπίσαμεν.
8 τοῦτο τὸ ἔργον αἴσχιστα ἐποιήθη.
9 οἱ πολῖται χρησιμώτερον ἔπραξαν ἢ οἱ ῥήτορες.
10 ἡ ναῦς ἄριστα ἐποιήθη.

Exercise RS.19: Irregular aorists

1   χειμῶνος γενομένου, οὐχ ηὕρομεν τὴν ὁδόν.
2   οἱ Ἕλληνες, ἑλόντες τὴν πόλιν, ἄλλους βαρβάρους προσβαίνοντας εἶδον.
3   οἱ στρατιῶται ἤνεγκαν τὰς τριήρεις πρὸς τὴν θάλασσαν.
4   ταῦτα εἰπών, ὁ διδάσκαλος ἔλαβε τὴν βίβλον.
5   τῇ τρίτῃ ἡμέρᾳ τὸ ὄνομα τὸ τῶν βαρβάρων ἔγνωμεν.
6   "ἄπελθε, ὦ ἄνθρωπε," ἔφη ὁ βασιλεύς, "καὶ ἀπόθανε".
7   τοὺς λόγους μαθόντες, οἱ νεανίαι σοφώτεροι ἐγένοντο.
8   ὁ στρατηγός, ἰδὼν τὰς ναῦς, προσήγαγε τοὺς στρατιώτας πρὸς τὸν λιμένα.
9   τὴν πόλιν λιπόντες, πολὺν χρόνον ἐν τοῖς ὄρεσιν ἐμένομεν.
10   οἱ ῥήτορες ἐν τῇ ἐκκλησίᾳ πολλὰ ὤμοσάν τε καὶ ὑπέσχοντο.

Exercise RS.20: Infinitives

1   βουλόμεθα εἰδέναι ὅ τι ἐγένετο.
2   καλόν ἐστιν ὑπὲρ τῆς πόλεως ἀποθνῄσκειν.
3   ἀεὶ κελεύω τοὺς στρατιώτας εὖ μάχεσθαι.
4   νῦν παραινέσω τοῖς Ἕλλησιν ἀνδρείως μαχέσασθαι.
5   ὁ ἄγγελός φησι τὸν ἡμέτερον στρατὸν νικῆσαι τοὺς βαρβάρους.
6   ὁ βασιλεὺς ἐνόμιζε τοὺς στρατηγοὺς εὖ ποιῆσαι.
7   ἄμεινόν ἐστι μάχεσθαι ἢ φεύγειν.
8   ἐπείσθημεν αἱρεῖσθαι ἄλλους στρατηγούς.
9   δεῖ ἀποκτεῖναι τούτους τοὺς πολεμίους.
10   ἔξεστί μοι πράσσειν ὡς βούλομαι.

Exercise RS.21: Indirect statements (1) with 'that' clause

1   ὁ ἄγγελος λέγει ὅτι αἱ νῆες προσέρχονται.
2   ὁ φύλαξ εἶπεν ὅτι ὁ δοῦλος φεύγει.
3   αἱ γυναῖκες λέγουσιν ὅτι βοὴν μεγάλην ἤκουσαν.
4   οἱ ἐν τῇ νήσῳ ἔλεξαν ὡς οὐδὲν εἶδον.
5   ὁ στρατηγὸς αὐτὸς λέγει ὅτι ἡ μάχη παύσεται.
6   ὁ ναύτης εἶπεν ὅτι οἱ πολέμιοι ἀπῆλθον.
7   ὁ βασιλεὺς ἔλεξεν ὅτι ἡ πόλις ληφθήσεται.
8   οὗτος ὁ παῖς λέγει ὅτι λέλυκε τὸν ἵππον.
9   πάντες οἱ παρόντες εἶπον ὅτι βούλοιντο μένειν.
10   ἡ τοῦ κριτοῦ θυγάτηρ ἔλεξεν ὅτι ἔμαθε πάντας τοὺς λόγους.

Exercise RS.22: Indirect statements (2) with infinitive

1   ὁ φύλαξ νῦν φησι τοὺς πολεμίους προσιέναι.
2   οἱ ἐν τῇ πόλει ἐνόμιζον τὸν ποταμὸν ἔτι χαλεπὸν εἶναι.
3   ἐνομίζομεν τὸν δοῦλον ἤδη φυγεῖν.
4   ὁ ἄγγελός φησι τοὺς φύλακας παρεῖναι.
5   μετὰ τὴν πρώτην μάχην οὐκέτι ἐνομίζομεν νικήσειν.
6   ἡ τοῦ παιδὸς μήτηρ ἔφη εὑρεῖν τὰς βίβλους.
7   ὁ παῖς οὔ φησιν αἴτιος εἶναι.
8   ὁ ξένος ἔφη ἀποκτεῖναι τὸν δοῦλον.
9   ἆρα νομίζεις τὸν ἄνδρα τὸ ἀληθὲς λέγειν;
10   ἡ γυνὴ οὐκ ἔφη τὸ δῶρον δέξασθαι.

Exercise RS.23: Indirect statements (3) with participle

1   οἶδα τὸν γέροντα σοφὸν ὄντα.
2   ἀκούομεν τὸν τῶν πολεμίων ἄγγελον παρόντα.
3   ἀρ' οἶσθα τὸν ποταμὸν βαθὺν ὄντα;
4   ὁ γέρων οἶδεν οὐχ οἷός τ' ὢν τοῦτο ποιεῖν.
5   ὁ διδάσκαλος ἐπύθετο τοὺς δούλους φεύγοντας.
6   ὁ βασιλεὺς ἤκουσε τοὺς στρατιώτας εὖ μαχεσαμένους.
7   οἱ Ἕλληνες ἔγνωσαν τὸν πόλεμον ἐσόμενον.
8   ὁ ξένος εἶδε τοὺς ἄνδρας δουλωθέντας.
9   ὁ παῖς ἔγνω τὰ ὄρη χαλεπώτατα ὄντα.
10   οἱ ἐν τῇ νήσῳ εὗρον τὴν ναῦν ἀπελθοῦσαν.

Exercise RS.24: Direct questions

1   τίς ἔχει πλεῖστα ἆθλα;
2   ἆρα ἀληθής ἐστιν ὁ τοῦ ἀγγέλου λόγος;
3   ποῖος βίος ἐστὶν ἄριστος;
4   διὰ τί οὐκ ἐφύλαξας τὰ τείχη;
5   πόσοι δοῦλοι ἐν τῷ ἄστει εἰσίν;
6   πόθεν ἦλθεν οὗτος ὁ γέρων;
7   ἀρ' οὐ φιλεῖς τὴν βίβλον;
8   πῶς ἐγένετο ἐκείνη ἡ μάχη;
9   ποῖ πορεύεσθε, ὦ στρατιῶται;
10   πότε παύσεται ὁ πόλεμος;

Exercise RS.25: Indirect questions

1 ἐρωτήσω αὐτὸν ὁπόσους τῶν πολεμίων ἀπέκτεινεν.
2 ὁ βασιλεὺς ἠρώτησε τὸν δοῦλον ὁπόθεν ἦλθεν.
3 χαλεπόν ἐστι γνῶναι ὁποία ἐστὶν ἡ χώρα.
4 βούλομαι εἰδέναι ὅστις ἔγραψε τούτους τοὺς λόγους.
5 τὸν πατέρα ἠρώτησα τί ἐν τῷ πολέμῳ ἔπραξεν.
6 ἐπείσαμεν τὸν ἄγγελον λέξαι ὁπότε ὁ χειμὼν γένοιτο.
7 οἱ πολῖται πολλάκις ἐρωτῶσιν ὁπότερος τῶν βασιλέων ἐστὶν ἀμείνων.
8 ὁ στρατηγὸς ἠρώτησε τοὺς φύλακας εἰ τοὺς πολεμίους ἴδοιεν.
9 ἡ βίβλος δηλώσει πότερον ἡ συμφορὰ ἐκείνη τῇ ἡμέρᾳ ἢ πρότερον ἐγένετο.
10 λέξω τῷ διδασκάλῳ ἅτινα ἤκουσα.

Exercise RS.26: Direct commands

1 ἀεὶ ἀνδρεῖος ἴσθι, ὦ παῖ.
2 φυλάξατε τούσδε τοὺς δούλους, ὦ στρατιῶται.
3 φύγετε, ὦ πολῖται, ἐκ τοῦ ἄστεως.
4 λῦσον τόνδε τὸν ἵππον, ὦ δοῦλε.
5 μὴ βαίνετε εἰς τὴν θάλασσαν.
6 μὴ λάβητε ταύτας τὰς ναῦς, ὦ σύμμαχοι.
7 γράφετε πάντα ἃ λέγω.
8 μήποτε φοβεῖσθε τοὺς πολεμίους, ὦ Ἕλληνες.
9 ἀγάγετε τοὺς ξένους εἰς τὴν πόλιν.
10 ἐλευθερώσατε τούσδε τοὺς ἀνθρώπους, ὦ φίλοι.

Exercise RS.27: Indirect commands

1 ἐκέλευσα τοὺς πολίτας μὴ φυγεῖν.
2 κελεύσομεν τοὺς συμμάχους ἀεὶ ἀνδρείως μάχεσθαι.
3 οἱ στρατιῶται ὑπὸ τοῦ στρατηγοῦ ἐκελεύσθησαν φυλάξαι τὸν λιμένα.
4 οἱ νεανίαι κελευσθήσονται ἐκεῖ μένειν.
5 ἐγὼ εἶπον τῷ ναύτῃ μὴ λιπεῖν τὴν ναῦν.
6 οἱ νόμοι κελεύουσιν ἡμᾶς ἀεὶ ὑπὲρ τῆς πόλεως πράσσειν.
7 παραινῶ τοῖς στρατιώταις ἀεὶ πείθεσθαι.
8 ὁ διδάσκαλος παρῄνεσε τοῖς παισὶ σαφῶς λέξαι.
9 ὁ ῥήτωρ πείθει τὴν ἐκκλησίαν πόλεμον ποιῆσαι.
10 ὁ δῆμος πείθεται ἐλευθερῶσαι τοὺς δούλους.

Exercise RS.28: Purpose clauses

1   οἱ στρατιῶται ἐτάχθησαν ἵνα εὖ μαχέσωνται.
2   ὁ δοῦλος ἐπέμφθη ὡς ἀγγελῶν τὰ γενόμενα.
3   πορεύομαι πρὸς τὴν πόλιν ἵνα τὸν πατέρα ἴδω.
4   οἱ πολῖται ἔφυγον ἵνα μὴ δουλωθεῖεν.
5   αἱ γυναῖκες παρὰ τῇ ὁδῷ μένουσιν ὡς τὸν βασιλέα ὀψόμεναι.
6   ἡμεῖς πάρεσμεν ὅπως τοὺς τοῦ ῥήτορος λόγους ἀκούωμεν.
7   ἀεὶ μαχόμεθα ἵνα νικῶμεν.
8   ὁ ἀνὴρ κατέβη ὡς τὴν γυναῖκα εὑρήσων.
9   διδάσκεσθε ἵνα μανθάνητε.
10 ὁ ἄγγελος ἀφίκετο ἵνα τὰ περὶ τοῦ πολέμου ἀγγεῖλαι.

Exercise RS.29: Result clauses

1   ὁ δοῦλος οὕτω σοφῶς ἀποκρίνεται ὥστε πάντες θαυμάζουσιν.
2   τοσοῦτός ἐστιν ὁ στρατὸς ὥστε τοὺς πολεμίους φοβεῖσθαι.
3   οὕτως ἀνδρείως μάχεται ὥστε πολλὴν τιμὴν δέχεται.
4   οἱ βάρβαροι ἐνικήθησαν· ὥστε ὁ πόλεμος ἐπαύσατο.
5   οὕτω διδάσκει ὥστε πάντες μανθάνουσιν.
6   οἱ πολῖται τοιοῦτοί εἰσιν ὥστε μὴ ῥαδίως πείθεσθαι.
7   τὰ ὄρη τοσαῦτά ἐστιν ὥστε μηδένα ὑπερβαίνειν.
8   οὕτως ἐφοβοῦντο οἱ πολῖται ὥστε εὐθὺς ἔφυγον.
9   τοιοῦτός ἐστιν ὁ ἄνθρωπος ὥστε ταῦτα ἑκὼν πράσσειν.
10 οὕτως εὐρύς ἐστιν ὁ ποταμὸς ὥστ᾽ οὐχ οἷοί τ᾽ ἐσμὲν διαβῆναι.

Exercise RS.30: Conditionals (1) open/unknown

1   εἰ ἡ γυνὴ ταῦτα λέγει, τὰ ἀληθῆ λέγει.
2   εἰ ἐποίησαν ἐκεῖνο, καλὸν ἔργον ἔπραξαν.
3   ἐὰν ἀνδρείως μαχώμεθα, ἀεὶ νικήσομεν.
4   εἰ ἡ θεὰ ταῦτα τὰ δῶρα ἔδωκε, δεῖ ἡμᾶς ἐπαινεῖν αὐτήν.
5   εἰ οὗτος ὁ ῥήτωρ τοιαῦτα λέγει, μωρότερός ἐστιν ἢ ὁ πατήρ.
6   εἰ τὸν ἵππον ἔτι ἔχεις, εὐθὺς δός μοι.
7   εἰ ὁ παῖς νῦν πάσχει διὰ τὰ τραύματα, ἔτι μᾶλλον ὕστερον πείσεται.
8   ἐὰν μὴ ἀκούσητε, οὐ μαθήσεσθε.
9   εἰ τὸν ἄγγελον ἀπεπέμψατε, ὦ νεανίαι, μωροί ἐστε.
10 τῷ χειμῶνι ἀποθνήσκουσιν εἰ παύονται πορευόμενοι.

Exercise RS.31: Conditionals (2) closed/remote

1 εἰ φύγοις, ἀποθάνοις ἄν.
2 εἰ ὁ βασιλεὺς νῦν παρῆν, οἱ πολῖται ἂν ἐτιμῶν αὐτόν.
3 εἰ σὺ ἐβόησας, ἐγὼ ἂν ἤκουσα.
4 εἰ σῖτον τῷ ἵππῳ δοίης, ῥᾷον ἂν εἴη κρατῆσαι αὐτοῦ.
5 εἰ μὴ ἐφύγετε, τότε ἂν ἀποθάνετε.
6 εἰ ἄλλος τις τούτους ἔτασσεν, οὐκ ἂν ἐπείθοντο.
7 καὶ εἰ ἐπιστολὴν τῷ ἀδελφῷ πέμψαιμι, οὐκ ἂν ἀποκρίναιτο.
8 εἰ πλείονας συμμάχους τότε ἐκτησάμεθα, νῦν ἂν ἦμεν ἰσχυρότεροι.
9 εἰ τὴν παῖδα αὖθις ἴδοιμι, ἐπαινέσαιμι ἂν αὐτὴν διὰ τόδε τὸ ἔργον.
10 εἰ εὐθὺς προσέβαλον οἱ Ἀθηναῖοι, τὴν πόλιν ταχέως ἂν ἔλαβον.

Exercise RS.32: Uses of the subjunctive and optative

1 ἐκ τοῦ κινδύνου φύγωμεν, ὦ φίλοι.
2 μὴ εἰσέλθητε εἰς τὴν πόλιν, ὦ στρατιῶται.
3 ἀνδρειότατα νῦν μαχεσώμεθα.
4 εἴθε οἱ σύμμαχοι ἀφίκοιντο.
5 πρὸς τὴν Ἑλλάδα πορεύομαι ἵνα τὰς πόλεις καὶ τὰ ὄρη ἴδω.
6 εἴθε ὁ πόλεμος παύσαιτο.
7 ὁ διδάσκαλος εἶπεν ὅτι τὸ ἔργον ῥᾴδιον εἴη.
8 εἰ ἴδοις τὴν ἡμετέραν πόλιν, θαυμάσαις ἄν.
9 εἴθε οἱ Ἕλληνες ἀεὶ ἐλεύθεροι εἶεν.
10 ἠρώτησα τὸν ἄγγελον ὁπόσους τῶν πολεμίων ἴδοι.

Exercise RS.33: Verbs with epsilon contraction

1 φίλει τὸ ἀληθές, ὦ παῖ.
2 ἔξεστιν ἡμῖν τοὺς συμμάχους ἀφικνουμένους δέχεσθαι.
3 οἱ πολῖται λίθους ἔβαλλον, ἀλλὰ οὐδὲν ἄλλο ἐποίουν.
4 ἆρ' οὐ φοβεῖσθε ἐν τῇ ἐκκλησίᾳ ἀδικεῖν, ὦ πολῖται;
5 ἐκ τοῦ λιμένος νῦν πλέομεν ὡς ἐπὶ τοὺς πολεμίους ναυμαχήσοντες.
6 αἱ τοῦτον τὸν ἰατρὸν ἐπαινέσασαι σοφώταταί εἰσιν.
7 εἰ ὁ γέρων ζητοίη τοὺς ἐκεῖ οἰκοῦντας, ῥᾳδίως ἂν εὕροι αὐτούς.
8 τῶν στρατιωτῶν τὴν πόλιν πολιορκούντων, χειμὼν μέγιστος ἐγένετο.
9 οὐδαμῶς ἀθυμοῦμεν καίπερ ἀποροῦντες.
10 τί καλεῖτε τὸν νέον ἵππον, ὦ φίλοι;

Exercise RS.34: Verbs with alpha contraction

1   φοβούμεθα χρῆσθαι τῷ τοῦ θεοῦ ὀνόματι.
2   τί βοᾷ ὁ ἀνήρ; ἆρ' ἐρωτᾷ τι περὶ τῆς μάχης;
3   οἱ ἐκείνης τῆς χώρας ἔνοικοι ἐτίμων τὸν βασιλέα.
4   οἱ βάρβαροι πολλάκις νικῶνται.
5   οἱ νεανίαι ἔτι φεύγουσι καίπερ ὁρώμενοι.
6   ἡ μήτηρ οὔποτε εἴασεν ἡμᾶς τοιαῦτα ἐρωτᾶν.
7   οἱ πολέμιοι οὐδέποτε νικήσουσι καίπερ πολλάκις πειρώμενοι.
8   οἱ τὸν χρυσὸν κτησάμενοι ἀπῆλθον γελῶντες.
9   χαλεπώτατόν ἐστιν ἡμῖν τὰς ναῦς ὁρᾶν.
10   ἆρα μὴ τιμᾷς τοὺς ὑπὸ τῶν πολλῶν τιμωμένους;

Exercise RS.35: Verbs with omicron contraction

1   διὰ τί ἐλευθεροῦτε τούτους τοὺς δούλους;
2   ἄδικόν ἐστι τοὺς Ἕλληνας δουλοῦν.
3   πότε δηλωθήσεται τοῖς πολίταις τὰ ζῷα τὰ ἀπὸ τῆς νήσου ληφθέντα;
4   εἰ δηλοίης μοι τὴν τῆς ὁδοῦ βουλήν, οἷός τ' ἂν εἴη βοηθεῖν σοι.
5   ἆρα χαλεπόν ἐστιν ἐλευθερῶσαι τοιούτους;
6   οἱ ὑπὲρ τῆς πατρίδος μαχεσάμενοι οὔποτε δουλοῦνται.
7   ἀεὶ ἐλευθέρου τοὺς οὕτω ληφθέντας, ὦ παῖ.
8   κελεύσομεν τὴν παῖδα τὰς βίβλους ὑμῖν δηλῶσαι.
9   ἆρα πάρεστε ὡς τοὺς ἡμετέρους δούλους ἐλευθερώσοντες;
10   οὐδὲν κωλύει με ταῦτά σοι δηλώσαντα ἀπελθεῖν.

Exercise RS.36: Verbs ending in -μι

1   ὁ βασιλεὺς δείκνυσι τὴν πόλιν τοῖς συμμάχοις.
2   ἡ παῖς δῶρον τῇ μητρὶ δίδωσιν.
3   οἱ πολῖται ὤμοσαν ἀεὶ τοῖς νόμοις πείσεσθαι.
4   βούλομαι τὰς βίβλους τῷ διδασκάλῳ διδόναι.
5   ὁ στρατηγὸς ἔθηκε τὰ ὅπλα εἰς τὴν οἰκίαν.
6   "οἱ πολέμιοι," ἔφη ὁ ἄγγελος, "νῦν προσέρχονται".
7   αἱ ἐν τῇ πόλει θήσουσι τὸν σῖτον εἰς τὰ πλοῖα.
8   οἱ σοφοὶ τοῖς δικαίοις τιμὴν διδόασιν.
9   οὐδαμῶς οἷός τ' εἰμὶ τοιαῦτα ὀμνύναι.
10   οἱ Ἕλληνες τοῖς τῶν βαρβάρων θεοῖς ὀνόματα ἔδοσαν.

Exercise RS.37: Miscellaneous constructions (1)

1   πέντε μὲν ἡμέρας ἐμαχόμεθα, τῇ δ' ἕκτῃ ὑπὸ νύκτα ἐνικήθημεν.
2   τοῦ ὕδατος καθ' ἡμέραν βαθυτέρου γιγνομένου, ἐν μεγίστῳ κινδύνῳ
     ἦμεν.
3   κάλλιστόν ἐστιν ὑπὲρ τῆς πόλεως ἀνδρείως μάχεσθαι.
4   οὗτοι ἀπέθανον ἵνα ἡμεῖς ἀσφαλεῖς εἶμεν.
5   νομίζομεν αὐτοὶ μὲν νικήσειν, τοὺς δὲ βαρβάρους νικηθήσεσθαι.
6   ὁ στρατηγὸς παρήνεσε τοῖς συμμάχοις μὴ ὀργισθῆναι.
7   εἴθε μὴ γένοιτο ὃ λέγεις, ὦ ἄγγελε.
8   ἡ ἀγορὰ τοσαύτη ἐστὶν ὥστε πάντας τοὺς στρατιώτας ἐκεῖ
     τάσσεσθαι.
9   μὴ δεχώμεθα τὰ δῶρα τὰ ὑπὸ τοῦ βασιλέως πεμφθέντα.
10   τῶν πολεμίων τέλος ἀπελθόντων, οἱ ἐν τῇ πόλει οὕτως ἀσθενεῖς ἦσαν
     ὥστ' οὐκέτι οἷοί τ' ἦσαν τὰ τείχη φυλάσσειν.

Exercise RS.38: Miscellaneous constructions (2)

1   μετὰ δύο ἔτη ηὕρομεν τὴν τῆς θεᾶς νῆσον.
2   αὐτὸς ὁ ἄγγελος τὰ αὐτὰ εἶπεν.
3   οἱ φεύγοντες οὐκ ἀεὶ τὸν ἑαυτῶν κίνδυνον ὁρῶσιν.
4   ὁ διδάσκαλος οὐχ οἷός τ' ἦν γνῶναι ὅστις ἀπέβαλε τὴν βίβλον.
5   εἰ ὁ δοῦλος νῦν παρῆν, πῶς ἂν τῷ κριτῇ ἀπεκρίνατο;
6   ἐκεῖνος ὁ παῖς φαίνεται τάχιστος τῶν νῦν εἶναι.
7   ἔστι τῷ βασιλεῖ θυγάτηρ καλλίστη, ἣν αὖθις ἰδεῖν βούλομαι.
8   οἱ τοιαῦτα λέγοντες οὔποτε πείθουσι τὸν δῆμον.
9   οἱ στρατιῶται, καίπερ πολλάκις νικήσαντες, ἔτι ἐφοβοῦντο τοὺς
     πολεμίους.
10   "μὴ φύγῃς τοῦτον τὸν κίνδυνον, ὦ παῖ," ἔφη ὁ στρατηγός, "ἀλλ' ἀεὶ
     μένων μάχου".

Exercise RS.39: Miscellaneous constructions (3)

1   τίνες εἰσὶν οἱ ἐκεῖ ἁρπασθέντες;
2   αἵδε αἱ γυναῖκες ὑπέσχοντο τὰ χρήματα φυλάξειν.
3   ὀλίγοι μὲν περὶ τοῦ πολέμου βουλεύονται, πᾶσι δὲ κοινός ἐστιν ὁ
     κίνδυνος.
4   εἴθε εὐτυχέστερος εἴης τοῦ πατρός, ὦ παῖ.
5   εἰ οἱ στρατηγοὶ μισοῦσιν ἀλλήλους, οὐδαμῶς ὠφελήσουσι τὴν πόλιν.
6   ὁ τῶν βαρβάρων ἡγεμὼν φαίνεται ἕτοιμος ὢν ταῦτα ὁμολογῆσαι.
7   ἡ κόρη εἶπεν ἡμῖν ὅτι τὸν δοῦλον σιγῇ φεύγοντα ἴδοι.
8   τοξεύσωμεν τοὺς τὸν ἵππον διώκοντας, ὦ νεανίαι.
9   οὐδεὶς εὑρηθήσεται ἀνδρειότερος τοῦ γέροντος τοῦ τεθνηκότος.
10   τοῦτον τὸν σῖτον ἥδιστον ἐν τῷ στόματι εἶναι νομίζω.

Exercise RS:40: Miscellaneous constructions (4)

1   εἰς τὴν πόλιν τέλος ἀφικόμεθα καίπερ βραδύτερον πορευόμενοι.
2   τὸ ἐν τῇ νήσῳ ὄρος ὑψηλότατόν ἐστιν.
3   τοῦ αὐτοῦ χειμῶνος ἡ ὕλη ἀνέμῳ δεινοτάτῳ διεφθάρη.
4   ἔπεμψα τὸν ἄγγελον ἵνα τὸ ἀληθὲς περὶ τῶν ἐνθάδε γενομένων εἴποι.
5   ἀρ᾽ οὐ αἰσθάνῃ τοὺς ἐν σκότῳ φεύγοντας;
6   αἱ ἡμέτεραι τριήρεις ταχέως εἰς τὸν λιμένα ἔπλευσαν.
7   χαλκὸν μὲν ἔδωκα, χρυσὸν δὲ ἐδεξάμην.
8   οὕτως ἰσχυρός ἐστιν ὁ γίγας ὥστε τὸ πλοῖον ῥᾷστα φέρει.
9   αἱ ἐν τῇ κώμῃ λειφθεῖσαι τέλος ἤκουσαν φωνήν τινα φιλίαν.
10   οἱ ταῦτα μανθάνοντες ἐλάσσονές εἰσιν ἢ πρότερον, ἀλλὰ δικαίως
      τιμῶνται.

Reference Grammar

The definite article

		masculine	feminine	neuter	
sg	nom	ὁ	ἡ	τό	the
	acc	τόν	τήν	τό	
	gen	τοῦ	τῆς	τοῦ	
	dat	τῷ	τῇ	τῷ	
pl	nom	οἱ	αἱ	τά	
	acc	τούς	τάς	τά	
	gen	τῶν	τῶν	τῶν	
	dat	τοῖς	ταῖς	τοῖς	

Nouns

First declension

Pattern of endings for singular:

nom	-η/-α	(adds -ς if masculine)
acc	-ην/-αν	
gen	-ης/-ας	(changes to -ου if masculine)
dat	-η/-α	

All plurals are -αι, -ας, -ων, -αις.

		feminine:			masculine:	
		honour	country	sea	judge	young man
sg	nom	τιμ-ή	χώρ-α	θάλασσ-α	κριτ-ής	νεανί-ας
	acc	τιμ-ήν	χώρ-αν	θάλασσ-αν	κριτ-ήν	νεανί-αν
	gen	τιμ-ῆς	χώρ-ας	θαλάσσ-ης	κριτ-οῦ	νεανί-ου
	dat	τιμ-ῇ	χώρ-ᾳ	θαλάσσ-η	κριτ-ῇ	νεανί-ᾳ
					(voc κριτ-ά)	(voc νεανί-α)
pl	nom	τιμ-αί	χῶρ-αι	θάλασσ-αι	κριτ-αί	νεανί-αι
	acc	τιμ-άς	χώρ-ας	θαλάσσ-ας	κριτ-άς	νεανί-ας
	gen	τιμ-ῶν	χωρ-ῶν	θαλασσ-ῶν	κριτ-ῶν	νεανι-ῶν
	dat	τιμ-αῖς	χώρ-αις	θαλάσσ-αις	κριτ-αῖς	νεανί-αις

Second declension

		masculine: * word	*neuter:* gift
sg	*nom*	λόγ-ος	δῶρ-ον
	acc	λόγ-ον	δῶρ-ον
	gen	λόγ-ου	δώρ-ου
	dat	λόγ-ῳ	δώρ-ῳ
		(*voc* λόγ-ε)	
pl	*nom*	λόγ-οι	δῶρ-α
	acc	λόγ-ους	δῶρ-α
	gen	λόγ-ων	δώρ-ων
	dat	λόγ-οις	δώρ-οις

* *feminine nouns such as* βίβλος = book *are identical in declension*

Third declension

Pattern of endings:

sg	*nom*	(wide range of possibilities)
	acc	stem + α for masc and fem; same as nom if neuter
	gen	stem + ος
	dat	stem + ι

pl	*nom*	stem + ες for masc and fem; stem + α if neuter
	acc	stem + ας for masc and fem; stem + α if neuter
	gen	stem + ων
	dat	stem + σι(ν)*

* the nu is added if the next word begins with a vowel, or at the end of a sentence

Examples:

		guard (stem φυλακ-)	old man (stem γεροντ-)
sg	*nom*	φύλαξ	γέρων
	acc	φύλακ-α	γέροντ-α
	gen	φύλακ-ος	γέροντ-ος
	dat	φύλακ-ι	γέροντ-ι
			(*voc* γέρον)
pl	*nom*	φύλακ-ες	γέροντ-ες
	acc	φύλακ-ας	γέροντ-ας
	gen	φυλάκ-ων	γερόντ-ων
	dat	φύλαξι(ν)	γέρουσι(ν)
		[*dat pl represents* φυλακ-σι(ν)]	[*dat pl represents* γεροντ-σι(ν)]

280

giant (stem γιγαντ-)

sg	nom	γίγας
	acc	γίγαντ-α
	gen	γίγαντ-ος
	dat	γίγαντ-ι

pl	nom	γίγαντ-ες
	acc	γίγαντ-ας
	gen	γιγάντ-ων
	dat	γίγασι(ν)
	[dat pl represents γιγαντ-σι(ν)]

These three examples are all masculine, but feminine nouns e.g. νύξ, νυκτός (stem νυκτ-) = *night* decline in the same way.

Neuter example:

body (stem σωματ-)

sg	nom	σῶμα
	acc	σῶμα
	gen	σώματ-ος
	dat	σώματ-ι

pl	nom	σώματ-α
	acc	σώματ-α
	gen	σωμάτ-ων
	dat	σώμασι(ν)
	[dat pl represents σωματ-σι(ν)]

Irregular third declension nouns

		fish *(m)*	father *(m)*	man *(m)*	woman *(f)*	Zeus *(m)*
sg	nom	ἰχθύς	πατήρ	ἀνήρ	γυνή	Ζεύς
	acc	ἰχθύ-ν	πατέρα	ἄνδρ-α	γυναῖκ-α	Δί-α
	gen	ἰχθύ-ος	πατρός	ἀνδρ-ός	γυναικ-ός	Δι-ός
	dat	ἰχθύ-ι	πατρί	ἀνδρ-ί	γυναικ-ί	Δι-ί
pl	nom	ἰχθύ-ες	πατέρες	ἄνδρ-ες	γυναῖκ-ες	
	acc	ἰχθύ-ας	πατέρας	ἄνδρ-ας	γυναῖκ-ας	
	gen	ἰχθύ-ων	πατέρων	ἀνδρ-ῶν	γυναικ-ῶν	
	dat	ἰχθύ-σι(ν)	πατράσι(ν)	ἀνδράσι(ν)	γυναιξί(ν)	

voc sg forms: ἰχθύ, πάτερ, ἄνερ, γύναι, Ζεῦ

		king *(m)*	city *(f)*	ship *(f)*	town *(n)*
sg	nom	βασιλεύς	πόλις	ναῦς	ἄστυ
	acc	βασιλέα	πόλιν	ναῦν	ἄστυ
	gen	βασιλέως	πόλεως	νε-ώς	ἄστεως
	dat	βασιλεῖ	πόλει	νη-ί	ἄστει
pl	nom	βασιλῆς (/-εῖς)	πόλεις	νῆ-ες	ἄστη
	acc	βασιλέας	πόλεις	ναῦς	ἄστη
	gen	βασιλέων	πόλεων	νε-ῶν	ἄστεων
	dat	βασιλεῦσι(ν)	πόλεσι(ν)	ναυσί(ν)	ἄστεσι(ν)

voc sg forms: βασιλεῦ, πόλι, ναῦ

		trireme *(f)*	race, family *(n)*
sg	nom	τριήρ-ης	γέν-ος
	acc	τριήρ-η	γέν-ος
	gen	τριήρ-ους	γέν-ους
	dat	τριήρ-ει	γέν-ει
pl	nom	τριήρ-εις	γέν-η
	acc	τριήρ-εις	γέν-η
	gen	τριήρ-ων	γεν-ῶν
	dat	τριήρ-εσι(ν)	γέν-εσι(ν)

Adjectives

2-1-2 declensions

		masculine	*feminine*	*neuter*	
sg	nom	σοφ-ός	σοφ-ή	σοφ-όν	wise
	acc	σοφ-όν	σοφ-ήν	σοφ-όν	
	gen	σοφ-οῦ	σοφ-ῆς	σοφ-οῦ	
	dat	σοφ-ῷ	σοφ-ῇ	σοφ-ῷ	
pl	nom	σοφ-οί	σοφ-αί	σοφ-ά	
	acc	σοφ-ούς	σοφ-άς	σοφ-ά	
	gen	σοφ-ῶν	σοφ-ῶν	σοφ-ῶν	
	dat	σοφ-οῖς	σοφ-αῖς	σοφ-οῖς	

Variant feminine singular if stem ends with a vowel or rho:

sg	nom	φιλί-α	friendly
	acc	φιλί-αν	
	gen	φιλί-ας	
	dat	φιλί-ᾳ	

Some adjectives (normally *compounds*: stem has a prefix, or more than one element) do not have separate feminine but use masculine form again (i.e. are 2-2 rather than 2-1-2), for example:

ἄδικος -ον = unjust

βάρβαρος -ον = barbarian, foreign

Irregular 2-1-2 (singular starts as if 3-1-3):

		masculine	feminine	neuter	
sg	nom	πολύς	πολλ-ή	πολύ	much, *pl* many
	acc	πολύν	πολλ-ήν	πολύ	
	gen	πολλ-οῦ	πολλ-ῆς	πολλ-οῦ	
	dat	πολλ-ῷ	πολλ-ῇ	πολλ-ῷ	
pl	nom	πολλ-οί	πολλ-αί	πολλ-ά	
	acc	πολλ-ούς	πολλ-άς	πολλ-ά	
	gen	πολλ-ῶν	πολλ-ῶν	πολλ-ῶν	
	dat	πολλ-οῖς	πολλ-αῖς	πολλ-οῖς	

		masculine	feminine	neuter	
sg	nom	μέγας	μεγάλ-η	μέγα	big, great
	acc	μέγαν	μεγάλ-ην	μέγα	
	gen	μεγάλ-ου	μεγάλ-ης	μεγάλ-ου	
	dat	μεγάλ-ῳ	μεγάλ-ῃ	μεγάλ-ῳ	
pl	nom	μεγάλ-οι	μεγάλ-αι	μεγάλ-α	
	acc	μεγάλ-ους	μεγάλ-ας	μεγάλ-α	
	gen	μεγάλ-ων	μεγάλ-ων	μεγάλ-ων	
	dat	μεγάλ-οις	μεγάλ-αις	μεγάλ-οις	

3-1-3 declensions

		masculine	feminine	neuter	
sg	nom	βαρ-ύς	βαρ-εῖα	βαρ-ύ	heavy
	acc	βαρ-ύν	βαρ-εῖαν	βαρ-ύ	
	gen	βαρ-έος	βαρ-είας	βαρ-έος	
	dat	βαρ-εῖ	βαρ-είᾳ	βαρ-εῖ	
pl	nom	βαρ-εῖς	βαρ-εῖαι	βαρ-έα	
	acc	βαρ-εῖς	βαρ-είας	βαρ-έα	
	gen	βαρ-έων	βαρ-ειῶν	βαρ-έων	
	dat	βαρε-έσι(ν)	βαρ-είαις	βαρ-έσι(ν)	

The 3-1-3 adjective πᾶς, πᾶσα, πᾶν (παντ-) = *all* declines like the first (weak) aorist participle

3-3 declensions (no separate feminine): (a) with epsilon contraction

		m/f	n	
sg	nom	ἀληθ-ής	ἀληθ-ές	true
	acc	ἀληθ-ῆ	ἀληθ-ές	
	gen	ἀληθ-οῦς	ἀληθ-οῦς	
	dat	ἀληθ-εῖ	ἀληθ-εῖ	

		m/f	n
pl	nom	ἀληθ-εῖς	ἀληθ-ῆ
	acc	ἀληθ-εῖς	ἀληθ-ῆ
	gen	ἀληθ-ῶν	ἀληθ-ῶν
	dat	ἀληθ-έσι(ν)	ἀληθ-έσι(ν)

3-3 declensions (no separate feminine): (b) irregular comparative

		m/f	n	
sg	nom	μείζων	μεῖζον	bigger, greater
	acc	μείζον-α	μεῖζον	
	gen	μείζον-ος	μείζον-ος	
	dat	μείζον-ι	μείζον-ι	

		m/f	n
pl	nom	μείζον-ες	μείζον-α
	acc	μείζον-ας	μείζον-α
	gen	μειζόν-ων	μειζόν-ων
	dat	μείζοσι(ν)	μείζοσι(ν)

Alternative contracted forms are:
m/f acc sg and n nom/acc pl   μείζω
m/f nom and acc pl   μείζους

Comparison of adjectives

'Positive' (=normal adjective)		Comparative	Superlative
Regular patterns:			
σοφός -ή -όν	wise	σοφώτερος -α -ον	σοφώτατος -η -ον
φίλιος -α -ον	friendly	φιλιώτερος -α -ον	φιλιώτατος -η -ον
δεινός -ή -όν	strange; terrible	δεινότερος -α -ον	δεινότατος -η -ον
βαθύς -εῖα -ύ	deep	βαθύτερος -α -ον	βαθύτατος -η -ον
ἀληθής -ές	true	ἀληθέστερος -α -ον	ἀληθέστατος -η -ον
Irregulars:			
ἀγαθός -ή -όν	good	ἀμείνων -ον	ἄριστος -η -ον
		βελτίων -ον*	βέλτιστος -η -ον
αἰσχρός -ά -όν	shameful	αἰσχίων -ον	αἴσχιστος -η -ον
ἐχθρός -ά -όν	hostile	ἐχθίων -ον	ἔχθιστος -η -ον
ἡδύς -εῖα -ύ	sweet	ἡδίων -ον	ἥδιστος -η -ον
ἴσος -η -ον	equal	ἰσαίτερος -α -ον	ἰσαίτατος -η -ον
κακός -ή -όν	bad	κακίων -ον	κάκιστος -η -ον
		χείρων -ον*	χείριστος -η -ον
καλός -ή -όν	fine	καλλίων -ον	κάλλιστος -η -ον
μέγας μεγάλη			
μέγα	big	μείζων -ον	μέγιστος -η -ον
μικρός -ά -όν	small	μικρότερος -α -ον	μικρότατος -η -ον
ὀλίγος -η -ον	small (amount of)	ἐλάσσων -ον	ἐλάχιστος -η -ον
ὀλίγοι -αι -α	few	ἐλάσσονες -α	ἐλαχίστοι -αι -α
πολύς πολλή			
πολύ	much	πλείων -ον	πλεῖστος -η -ον
		πλέων -ον*	
πολλοί -αί -ά	many	πλείονες -α	πλεῖστοι -αι -α
		πλέονες -α*	
ῥάδιος -α -ον	easy	ῥάων -ον	ῥᾷστος -η -ον
ταχύς -εῖα -ύ	swift	θάσσων -ον	τάχιστος -η -ον
φίλος -η -ον	dear	φιλαίτερος -α -ον	φιλαίτατος -η -ον

* alternative forms of the comparative

Comparatives ending in -τερος decline like φιλιος; comparatives ending in -ων decline like μειζων; all superlatives decline like σοφος.

Participles

Grammar detail and meanings:

present *active*   παύων -ουσα -ον (3-1-3 decl; m/n gen stem παυοντ-)
stopping
(*indicative:* παύω I stop)

middle/passive   παυόμενος -η -ον (2-1-2 decl)
ceasing, stopping oneself (*middle*); being stopped (*passive*)
(*indicative:* παύομαι I cease, I stop myself; I am stopped)

future *active*   παύσων -ουσα -ον (3-1-3 decl; m/n gen stem παυσοντ-)
about to stop
(*indicative:* παύσω I shall stop)

middle   παυσόμενος -η -ον (2-1-2 decl)
about to cease, about to stop oneself
(*indicative:* παύσομαι I shall cease, I shall stop myself)

passive   παυσθησόμενος -η -ον (2-1-2 decl)
about to be stopped
(*indicative:* παυσθήσομαι I shall be stopped)

aorist *first (weak) active*   παύσας -ασα -αν (3-1-3 decl; m/n gen stem παυσαντ-)
having stopped
(*indicative:* ἔπαυσα I stopped)

first (weak) middle   παυσάμενος -η -ον (2-1-2 decl)
having ceased, having stopped oneself
(*indicative:* ἐπαυσάμην I ceased, I stopped myself)

second (strong) active λαβών -ουσα, -όν (3-1-3 decl; m/n gen stem λαβοντ-)
having taken
(*indicative:* ἔλαβον I took)

second (strong) middle λαβόμενος -η -ον (2-1-2 decl)
having taken for oneself
(*indicative:* ἐλαβόμην I took for myself)

passive   παυσθείς -εῖσα -έν (3-1-3 decl; m/n gen stem παυσθεντ-)
having been stopped
(*indicative:* ἐπαύσθην I was stopped)

perfect *active*   πεπαυκώς -υῖα -ός (3-1-3 decl; m/n gen stem πεπαυκοτ-)
having stopped (effect continuing)
(*indicative:* πέπαυκα I have stopped)

middle/passive   πεπαυμένος -η -ον (2-1-2 decl)
having ceased, having stopped oneself; having been stopped (*all with effect continuing*)
(*indicative:* πέπαυμαι I have ceased, I have stopped myself; I have been stopped)

286

Participle declensions: (1) active

present active participle

		masculine	feminine	neuter	
sg	nom	παύ-ων	παύ-ουσ-α	παῦ-ον	stopping
	acc	παύ-οντα	παύ-ουσ-αν	παῦ-ον	
	gen	παύ-οντος	παυ-ούσ-ης	παύ-οντος	
	dat	παύ-οντι	παυ-ούσ-ῃ	παύ-οντι	
pl	nom	παύ-οντες	παύ-ουσ-αι	παύ-οντα	
	acc	παύ-οντας	παυ-ούσ-ας	παύ-οντα	
	gen	παυ-όντων	παυ-ουσ-ῶν	παυ-όντων	
	dat	παύ-ουσι(ν)	παυ-ούσ-αις	παύ-ουσι(ν)	

similarly:

future participle

	παύσων	παύσουσα	παῦσον	about to stop

stem *(for masc and neut):* παυσοντ-

second (strong) aorist participle

	λαβών	λαβοῦσα	λαβόν	having taken

stem *(for masc and neut):* λαβοντ-

first (weak) aorist participle

		masculine	femimine	neuter	
sg	nom	παύσ-ας	παύσ-ασ-α	παῦσ-αν	having stopped
	acc	παύσ-αντα	παύσ-ασ-αν	παῦσ-αν	
	gen	παύσ-αντος	παυσ-άσ-ης	παύσ-αντος	
	dat	παύσ-αντι	παυσ-άσ-ῃ	παύσ-αντι	
pl	nom	παύσ-αντες	παύσ-ασ-αι	παύσ-αντα	
	acc	παύσ-αντας	παυσ-άσ-ας	παύσ-αντα	
	gen	παυσ-άντων	παυσ-ασ-ῶν	παυσ-άντων	
	dat	παύσ-ασι(ν)	παυσ-άσ-αις	παύσ-ασι(ν)	

perfect active participle

(stem for masculine/neuter πεπαυκοτ-)

		masculine	feminine	neuter	
sg	nom	πεπαυκώς	πεπαυκυῖ-α	πεπαυκός	having stopped (*effect continuing*)
	acc	πεπαυκότ-α	πεπαυκυῖ-αν	πεπαυκός	
	gen	πεπαυκότ-ος	πεπαυκυί-ας	πεπαυκότ-ος	
	dat	πεπαυκότ-ι	πεπαυκυί-ᾳ	πεπαυκότ-ι	
pl	nom	πεπαυκότ-ες	πεπαυκυῖ-αι	πεπαυκότ-α	
	acc	πεπαυκότ-ας	πεπαυκυί-ας	πεπαυκότ-α	
	gen	πεπαυκότ-ων	πεπαυκυι-ῶν	πεπαυκότ-ων	
	dat	πεπαυκόσι(ν)	πεπαυκυί-αις	πεπαυκόσι(ν)	

Participle declensions: (2) middle and passive

present middle/passive participle

		masculine	feminine	neuter	
sg	nom	παυόμεν-ος	παυομέν-η	παυόμεν-ον	ceasing/being stopped
	acc	παυόμεν-ον	παυομέν-ην	παυόμεν-ον	
	gen	παυομέν-ου	παυομέν-ης	παυομέν-ου	
	dat	παυομέν-ῳ	παυομέν-ῃ	παυομέν-ῳ	
pl	nom	παυόμεν-οι	παυόμεν-αι	παυόμεν-α	
	acc	παυομέν-ους	παυομέν-ας	παυόμεν-α	
	gen	παυομέν-ων	παυομέν-ων	παυομέν-ων	
	dat	παυομέν-οις	παυομέν-αις	παυομέν-οις	

similarly:
future middle participle   παυσόμενος -η -ον
future passive participle   παυσθησόμενος -η -ον
second (strong) aorist middle participle   λαβόμενος -η -ον
perfect middle/passive participle   πεπαυμένος -η -ον
and (substituting alpha for omicron thoughout)
first (weak) aorist middle participle   παυσάμενος -η -ον

aorist passive participle: (basic aorist passive stem παυσθ- ; masculine/neuter genitive stem of participle παυσθεντ-)

		masculine	feminine	neuter	
sg	nom	παυσθείς	παυσθεῖσ-α	παυσθέν	having been stopped
	acc	παυσθέντ-α	παυσθεῖσ-αν	παυσθέν	
	gen	παυσθέντ-ος	παυσθείσ-ης	παυσθέντ-ος	
	dat	παυσθέντ-ι	παυσθείσ-ῃ	παυσθέντ-ι	
pl	nom	παυσθέντ-ες	παυσθεῖσ-αι	παυσθέντ-α	
	acc	παυσθέντ-ας	παυσθείσ-ας	παυσθέντ-α	
	gen	παυσθέντ-ων	παυσθεισ-ῶν	παυσθέντ-ων	
	dat	παυσθεῖσι(ν)	παυσθείσ-αις	παυσθεῖσι(ν)	

Pronouns

First and second person:

	I	you (*sg*)
nom	ἐγώ	σύ
acc	ἐμέ, με	σέ
gen	ἐμοῦ, μου	σοῦ
dat	ἐμοί, μοι	σοί

	we	you (*pl*)
nom	ἡμεῖς	ὑμεῖς
acc	ἡμᾶς	ὑμᾶς
gen	ἡμῶν	ὑμῶν
dat	ἡμῖν	ὑμῖν

αὐτός

Three meanings: (1) self; (2) (*with definite article*) the same; (3) (*not nominative*) him, her, it, *pl* them

		masculine	*feminine*	*neuter*
sg	*nom*	αὐτ-ός	αὐτ-ή	αὐτ-ό
	acc	αὐτ-όν	αὐτ-ήν	αὐτ-ό
	gen	αὐτ-οῦ	αὐτ-ῆς	αὐτ-οῦ
	dat	αὐτ-ῷ	αὐτ-ῇ	αὐτ-ῷ
pl	*nom*	αὐτ-οί	αὐτ-αί	αὐτ-ά
	acc	αὐτ-ούς	αὐτ-άς	αὐτ-ά
	gen	αὐτ-ῶν	αὐτ-ῶν	αὐτ-ῶν
	dat	αὐτ-οῖς	αὐτ-αῖς	αὐτ-οῖς

Reflexive pronouns (first and second persons):

		myself, *pl* ourselves		yourself, *pl* yourselves	
		masculine	*feminine*	*masculine*	*feminine*
sg	*acc*	ἐμαυτόν	ἐμαυτήν	σεαυτόν	σεαυτήν
	gen	ἐμαυτοῦ	ἐμουτῆς	σεαυτοῦ	σεαυτῆς
	dat	ἐμαυτῷ	ἐμαυτῇ	σεαυτῷ	σεαυτῇ
pl	*acc*	ἡμᾶς αὐτούς	ἡμᾶς αὐτάς	ὑμᾶς αὐτούς	ὑμᾶς αὐτάς
	gen	ἡμῶν αὐτῶν	ἡμῶν αὐτῶν	ὑμῶν αὐτῶν	ὑμῶν αὐτῶν
	dat	ἡμῖν αὐτοῖς	ἡμῖν αὐταῖς	ὑμῖν αὐτοῖς	ὑμῖν αὐταῖς

Reflexive pronouns (third person):

		himself, herself, itself, *pl* themselves		
		masculine	*feminine*	*neuter*
sg	*acc*	ἑαυτόν	ἑαυτήν	ἑαυτό
	gen	ἑαυτοῦ	ἑαυτῆς	ἑαυτοῦ
	dat	ἑαυτῷ	ἑαυτῇ	ἑαυτῷ

pl	acc	ἑαυτούς	ἑαυτάς	ἑαυτά
	gen	ἑαυτῶν	ἑαυτῶν	ἑαυτῶν
	dat	ἑαυτοῖς	ἑαυταῖς	ἑαυτοῖς

There are also alternative plural forms using σφᾶς = *them* (on the pattern of ἡμᾶς αὐτούς etc): hence accusative masculine σφᾶς αὐτούς, feminine σφᾶς αὐτάς; genitive σφῶν αὐτῶν; dative masculine σφίσιν αὐτοῖς, feminine σφίσιν αὐταῖς.

The reciprocal pronoun ἀλλήλους = *each other* (which like the relexives has no nominative) declines as normal 2-1-2 plural.

τις

Two meanings:

(1) In a question, and with an acute accent on the first syllable: *who? what? which?*

		masculine/feminine	*neuter*
sg	nom	τίς	τί
	acc	τίν-α	τί
	gen	τίν-ος	τίν-ος
	dat	τίν-ι	τίν-ι
pl	nom	τίν-ες	τίν-α
	acc	τίν-ας	τίν-α
	gen	τίν-ων	τίν-ων
	dat	τίσι(ν)	τίσι(ν) — *dat pl represents* τιν-σι(ν)

(2) As an indefinite adjective/pronoun, with no accent or with an accent on the second syllable, and never as first word in a sentence or clause: *a (certain), some (one/thing)*

		masculine/feminine	*neuter*
sg	nom	τις	τι
	acc	τιν-ά	τι
	gen	τιν-ός	τιν-ός
	dat	τιν-ί	τιν-ί
pl	nom	τιν-ές	τιν-ά
	acc	τιν-άς	τιν-ά
	gen	τιν-ῶν	τιν-ῶν
	dat	τισί(ν)	τισί(ν) — *dat pl represents* τιν-σι(ν)

Relative pronoun

who, which

		masculine	*feminine*	*neuter*
sg	nom	ὅς	ἥ	ὅ
	acc	ὅν	ἥν	ὅ
	gen	οὗ	ἧς	οὗ
	dat	ᾧ	ᾗ	ᾧ
pl	nom	οἵ	αἵ	ἅ
	acc	οὕς	ἅς	ἅ
	gen	ὧν	ὧν	ὧν
	dat	οἷς	αἷς	οἷς

Indefinite relative (*whoever, anyone who, whatever, anything which*) and indirect question form of *who, which*:

		masculine	feminine	neuter
sg	nom	ὅστις	ἥτις	ὅ τι
	acc	ὅντινα	ἥντινα	ὅ τι
	gen	οὗτινος	ἧστινος	οὗτινος
	dat	ᾧτινι	ᾗτινι	ᾧτινι
pl	nom	οἵτινες	αἵτινες	ἅτινα
	acc	οὕστινας	ἅστινας	ἅτινα
	gen	ὧντινων	ὧντινων	ὧντινων
	dat	οἷστισι(ν)	αἷστισι(ν)	οἷστισι(ν)

Alternative forms for m and n gen and dat sg and pl (ὅτου, ὅτῳ, ὅτων, ὅτοις) are formed as if from a m nom sg ὅτος.

Demonstrative pronouns

Two different words for *this*:

(1)		masculine	feminine	neuter
sg	nom	οὗτος	αὕτη	τοῦτο
	acc	τοῦτον	ταύτην	τοῦτο
	gen	τούτου	ταύτης	τούτου
	dat	τούτῳ	ταύτῃ	τούτῳ
pl	nom	οὗτοι	αὗται	ταῦτα
	acc	τούτους	ταύτας	ταῦτα
	gen	τούτων	τούτων	τούτων
	dat	τούτοις	ταύταις	τούτοις

(2)		masculine	feminine	neuter	
sg	nom	ὅδε	ἥδε	τόδε	*(often used for 'this here',*
	acc	τόνδε	τήνδε	τόδε	*or 'the following')*

etc: simply the article with δε attached

That (compare ἐκεῖ: literally *the one over there*)

		masculine	feminine	neuter
sg	nom	ἐκεῖνος	ἐκείνη	ἐκεῖνο
	acc	ἐκεῖνον	ἐκείνην	ἐκεῖνο

etc: declines like αὐτός (or like σοφός with -ο neuter)

Numeral declensions

	masculine	*feminine*	*neuter*	
nom	εἷς	μία	ἕν	one (3-1-3 declensions)
acc	ἕνα	μίαν	ἕν	
gen	ἑνός	μιᾶς	ἑνός	
dat	ἑνί	μιᾷ	ἑνί	

	all genders	
nom	δύο	two (dual forms)
acc	δύο	
gen	δυοῖν	
dat	δυοῖν	

	masc/fem	*neuter*	
nom	τρεῖς	τρία	three (3-3 declensions)
acc	τρεῖς	τρία	
gen	τριῶν	τριῶν	
dat	τρισί(ν)	τρισί(ν)	

	masc/fem	*neuter*	
nom	τέσσαρες	τέσσαρα	four (3-3 declensions)
acc	τέσσαρας	τέσσαρα	
gen	τεσσάρων	τεσσάρων	
dat	τέσσαρσι(ν)	τέσσαρσι(ν)	

no-one/nothing/no ~ (stem οὐδεν-)

	masculine	*feminine*	*neuter*
nom	οὐδείς	οὐδεμία	οὐδέν
acc	οὐδένα	οὐδεμίαν	οὐδέν
gen	οὐδενός	οὐδεμιᾶς	οὐδενός
dat	οὐδενί	οὐδεμιᾷ	οὐδενί

Correlatives

direct question	*indirect*	*indefinite*	*relative*	*demonstrative*
Pronouns/adjectives:				
τίς; who?	ὅστις	τις a certain	ὅς (the one) who	οὗτος (ὅδε, ἐκεῖνος) this (this here, that)
πότερος; which (of two)?	ὁπότερος			ἕτερος one (of two)/the other
πόσος; how big? *plural* how many?	ὁπόσος		ὅσος the size which all those who	τοσοῦτος* so big so many
ποῖος; what sort of?	ὁποῖος		οἷος the sort which	τοιοῦτος* this sort of
Adverbs:				
ποῦ; where?	ὅπου	που somewhere	οὗ (the place) where	ἐνθάδε (ἐκεῖ) here (there)
ποῖ; where to?	ὅποι	ποι to somewhere	οἷ to (the place) where	δεῦρο to here
πόθεν; where from?	ὁπόθεν	ποθέν from somewhere	ὅθεν from (the place) where	
πότε; when?	ὁπότε	ποτέ sometime, ever	ὅτε (at the time) when	τότε then, at that time
πῶς; how?	ὅπως	πως somehow	ὡς how, as, in the way in which	οὕτω(ς) (ὧδε) so, in this way (as follows)

* the more predictable forms τόσος and τοῖος also exist, and are commonly found in early Greek

Prepositions

preposition	+ acc	+ gen	+ dat
ἀνά	up		
ἄνευ		without	
ἀντί		instead of, opposite	
ἀπό		from, away from	
διά	on account of, because of	through	
εἰς, ἐς	into, onto, to		
ἐκ, ἐξ	out of		
ἐν			in, on, among
ἐπί	against, to, onto, for the purpose of	in the time of	on
κατά	down, throughout, according to	down from	
μετά	after	with	
παρά	to the presence of, alongside, contrary to	from (a person)	beside
περί	around	about, concerning	
πλήν		except	
πρό		before, in front of	
πρός	towards, to, against	at the hands of	in addition to
ὑπέρ	beyond, to beyond	above, on behalf of	
ὑπό	under, to under	by (a person)	under
ὡς	to (a person)		

Prepositional set phrases:

ἅμ' ἡμέρᾳ	at daybreak, at first light
δι' ὀλίγου	after a short time
διὰ πολλοῦ	after a long time
διὰ πέντε ἐτῶν	every five years
εἰς καιρόν	at the right time
ἐκ τούτου	after this, as a result
ἐξ ἴσου	equally
ἐν τούτῳ	meanwhile
ἐπὶ τούτοις	on these terms
καθ' ἡμέραν	daily
κατὰ γήν	by land
κατὰ θάλασσαν	by sea
κατὰ τοὺς νόμους	according to the laws
μετὰ ταῦτα	after this (lit after these things)
περὶ πολλοῦ ποιεῖσθαι	to regard as important
ὑπὸ νύκτα	just before nightfall

Verbs (1): ending in -ω

Indicative tenses

		active	middle	passive
			middle/passive	

present

		I stop	I cease/I am stopped	
sg	1	παύ-ω	παύ-ομαι	
	2	παύ-εις	παύ-η *or* -ει	
	3	παύ-ει	παύ-εται	
pl	1	παύ-ομεν	παυ-όμεθα	
	2	παύ-ετε	παύ-εσθε	
	3	παύ-ουσι(ν)	παύ-ονται	

future

		I shall stop	I shall cease	I shall be stopped
sg	1	παύσ-ω	παύσ-ομαι	παυσθήσ-ομαι
	2	παύσ-εις	παύσ-η *or* -ει	παυσθήσ-η *or* -ει
	3	παύσ-ει	παύσ-εται	παυσθήσ-εται
pl	1	παύσ-ομεν	παυσ-όμεθα	παυσθησ-όμεθα
	2	παύσ-ετε	παύσ-εσθε	παυσθήσ-εσθε
	3	παύσ-ουσι(ν)	παύσ-ονται	παυσθήσ-ονται

imperfect

		I was stopping	I was ceasing/I was being stopped	
sg	1	ἔ-παυ-ον	ἐ-παυ-όμην	
	2	ἔ-παυ-ες	ἐ-παύ-ου	
	3	ἔ-παυ-ε(ν)	ἐ-παύ-ετο	
pl	1	ἐ-παύομεν	ἐ-παυ-όμεθα	
	2	ἐ-παύετε	ἐ-παύ-εσθε	
	3	ἔ-παυον	ἐ-παύ-οντο	

1st (weak) aorist

		I stopped	I ceased	I was stopped
sg	1	ἔ-παυσ-α	ἐ-παυσ-άμην	ἐ-παύσ-θην
	2	ἔ-παυσ-ας	ἐ-παύσ-ω	ἐ-παύσ-θης
	3	ἔ-παυσ-ε(ν)	ἐ-παύσ-ατο	ἐ-παύσ-θη
pl	1	ἐ-παύσ-αμεν	ἐ-παυσ-άμεθα	ἐ-παύσ-θημεν
	2	ἐ-παύσ-ατε	ἐ-παύσ-ασθε	ἐ-παύσ-θητε
	3	ἔ-παυσ-αν	ἐ-παύσ-αντο	ἐ-παύσ-θησαν

2nd (strong) aorist

		I took	I took for myself	I was taken
sg	1	ἔ-λαβ-ον	ἐ-λαβ-όμην	ἐ-λήφ-θην
	2	ἔ-λαβ-ες	ἐ-λάβ-ου	ἐ-λήφ-θης
	3	ἔ-λαβ-ε(ν)	ἐ-λάβ-ετο	ἐ-λήφ-θη
pl	1	ἐ-λάβ-ομεν	ἐ-λαβ-όμεθα	ἐλήφ-θημεν
	2	ἐ-λάβ-ετε	ἐ-λάβ-εσθε	ἐ-λήφ-θητε
	3	ἔ-λαβ-ον	ἐ-λάβ-οντο	ἐ-λήφ-θησαν

perfect

		I have stopped	I have ceased/I have been stopped
sg	1	πέ-παυκ-α	πέ-παυ-μαι
	2	πέ-παυκ-ας	πέ-παυ-σαι
	3	πέ-παυκ-ε(ν)	πέ-παυ-ται
pl	1	πε-παύκ-αμεν	πε-παύ-μεθα
	2	πε-παύκ-ατε	πέ-παυ-σθε
	3	πε-παύκ-ασι(ν)	πέ-παυ-νται

pluperfect

		I had stopped	I had ceased/I had been stopped
sg	1	ἐ-πε-παύκ-η	ἐ-πε-παύ-μην
	2	ἐ-πε-παύκ-ης	ἐ-πέ-παυ-σο
	3	ἐ-πε-παύκ-ει(ν)	ἐ-πέ-παυ-το
pl	1	ἐ-πε-παύκ-εμεν	ἐ-πε-παύ-μεθα
	2	ἐ-πε-παύκ-ετε	ἐ-πέ-παυ-σθε
	3	ἐ-πε-παύκ-εσαν	ἐ-πέ-παυ-ντο

Note:

(1) Verbs with consonant stems make adjustments of spelling in the perfect and pluperfect middle/passive to ease pronunciation (hence e.g. δεδίωγμαι, δεδίωξαι *etc*), with a third person plural made from the perfect participle plus auxiliary verb (e.g. δεδιωγμένοι εἰσί): see chapters 11 and 12 for details.

(2) The irregular verbs δύναμαι = *I am able*, ἐπίσταμαι = *I know (how to)* are formed like the perfect middle/passive of an ordinary verb.

Imperatives

	active	*middle*
present		
	stop! (*generally*)	cease! (*generally*)
sg	παῦε	παύου
pl	παύετε	παύεσθε

	first (weak) aorist	
	stop! (*one occasion*)	cease! (*one occasion*)
sg	παῦσον	παῦσαι
pl	παύσατε	παύσασθε

second (strong) aorist

	take! (*one occasion*)	take for yourself! (*one occasion*)
sg	λαβέ	λαβοῦ
pl	λάβετε	λάβεσθε

Participles: summary table

masculine nominative singular shown here - for grammar details see pages 286-8 above

	active	*middle*	*passive*
present	παύων	παυόμενος	
future	παύσων	παυσόμενος	παυσθησόμενος
1st (weak) aor	παύσας	παυσάμενος	παυσθείς
2nd (strong) aor	λαβών	λαβόμενος	ληφθείς
perfect	πεπαυκώς	πεπαυμένος	

Infinitives

	active	*middle*	*passive*
		middle/passive	
present	παύειν	παύεσθαι	
	to stop	to cease	to be stopped
future	παύσειν	παύσεσθαι	παυσθήσεσθαι
	to be about	to be about	to be about
	to stop	to cease	to be stopped
first (weak) aorist	παῦσαι	παύσασθαι	παυσθῆναι
	to stop (*once*)/	to cease (*once*)/	to be stopped (*once*)/
	to have stopped	to have ceased	to have been stopped
second (strong) aorist	λαβεῖν	λαβέσθαι	ληφθῆναι
	to take (*once*)/	to take for	to be taken (*once*)/
	to have taken	onself (*once*)/	to have been taken
		to have taken	
		for onself	
perfect	πεπαυκέναι	πεπαύσθαι	
	to have stopped	to have ceased	to have been stopped
	(*effect	(*effect	(*effect
	continuing*)	continuing*)	continuing*)

Correlation of indicative/imperative/infinitive/participle:

		indicative (1 sg)	imperative (sg)	infinitive	participle (m nom sg)
present	active	παύω	παῦε	παύειν	παύων
	middle	παύομαι	παύου	παύεσθαι	παυόμενος
	passive	(all same as middle)			
future	active	παύσω	-	παύσειν	παύσων
	middle	παύσομαι	-	παύσεσθαι	παυσόμενος
	passive	παυσθήσομαι	-	παυσθήσεσθαι	παυσθησόμενος
imperfect	active	ἔπαυον	-	-	-
	middle	ἐπαυόμην	-	-	-
	passive	(same as middle)			
1st (weak) aor	active	ἔπαυσα	παῦσον	παῦσαι	παύσας
	middle	ἐπαυσάμην	παῦσαι	παύσασθαι	παυσάμενος
	passive	ἐπαύσθην	(παύσθητι)	παυσθῆναι	παυσθείς
2nd (strong) aor	active	ἔλαβον	λαβέ	λαβεῖν	λαβών
	middle	ἐλαβόμην	λαβοῦ	λαβέσθαι	λαβόμενος
	passive	ἐλήφθην	(λήφθητι)	ληφθῆναι	ληφθείς
perfect	active	πέπαυκα	-	πεπαυκέναι	πεπαυκώς
	middle	πέπαυμαι	-	πεπαύσθαι	πεπαυμένος
	passive	(same as middle)			

Subjunctive forms

		active	middle	passive
			middle/passive	
present				
sg	1	παύ-ω	παύ-ωμαι	
	2	παύ-ῃς	παύ-ῃ	
	3	παύ-ῃ	παύ-ηται	
pl	1	παύ-ωμεν	παυ-ώμεθα	
	2	παύ-ητε	παύ-ησθε	
	3	παύ-ωσι(ν)	παύ-ωνται	

1st (weak) aorist

sg	1	παύσ-ω	παύσ-ωμαι	παυσ-θῶ
	2	παύσ-ῃς	παύσ-ῃ	παυσ-θῇς
	3	παύσ-ῃ	παύσ-ηται	παυσ-θῇ
pl	1	παύσ-ωμεν	παυσ-ώμεθα	παυσ-θῶμεν
	2	παύσ-ητε	παύσ-ησθε	παυσ-θῆτε
	3	παύσ-ωσι(ν)	παύσ-ωνται	παυσ-θῶσι(ν)

	active	middle	passive

2nd (strong) aorist

sg	1	λάβ-ω	λάβ-ωμαι	ληφ-θῶ
	2	λάβ-ης	λάβ-η	ληφ-θῆς
	3	λάβ-η	λάβ-ηται	ληφ-ῇ

pl	1	λάβ-ωμεν	λαβ-ώμεθα	ληφ-θῶμεν
	2	λάβ-ητε	λάβ-ησθε	ληφ-θῆτε
	3	λάβ-ωσι(ν)	λάβ-ωνται	ληφ-θῶσι(ν)

Optative forms

			middle/passive

present

sg	1	παύ-οιμι	παυ-οίμην
	2	παύ-οις	παύ-οιο
	3	παύ-οι	παύ-οιτο

pl	1	παύ-οιμεν	παυ-οίμεθα
	2	παύ-οιτε	παύ-οισθε
	3	παύ-οιεν	παύ-οιντο

future

sg	1	παύσ-οιμι	παυσ-οίμην	παυσθησ-οίμην
		etc	etc	etc

1st (weak) aorist

sg	1	παύσ-αιμι	παυσ-αίμην	παυσ-θείην
	2	παύσ-ειας/-αις	παύσ-αιο	παυσ-θείης
	3	παύσ-ειε(ν)/-αι	παύσ-αιτο	παυσ-θείη

pl	1	παύσ-αιμεν	παυσ-αίμεθα	παυσ-θεῖμεν
	2	παύσ-αιτε	παύσ-αισθε	παυσ-θεῖτε
	3	παύσ-ειαν/-αιεν	παύσ-αιντο	παυσ-θεῖεν

2nd (strong) aorist

sg	1	λάβ-οιμι	λαβ-οίμην	ληφ-θείην
	2	λάβ-οις	λάβ-οιο	ληφ-θείης
	3	λάβ-οι	λά-β-οιτο	ληφ-θείη

pl	1	λάβ-οιμεν	λαβ-οίμεθα	ληφ-θεῖμεν
	2	λάβ-οιτε	λάβ-οισθε	ληφ-θεῖτε
	3	λάβ-οιεν	λάβ-οιντο	ληφ-θεῖεν

Verbs (2): contracted (ending in -αω, -εω, -οω)

(a) With alpha contraction

Rules of contraction:

α followed by an *e* sound (ε or η) becomes long α
α followed by an *o* sound (o or ω) becomes ω
ι becomes subscript, and υ disappears

		I honour	
		active	*middle/passive*
present			
sg	*1*	τιμ-ῶ	τιμ-ῶμαι
	2	τιμ-ᾷς	τιμ-ᾷ
	3	τιμ-ᾷ	τιμ-ᾶται
pl	*1*	τιμ-ῶμεν	τιμ-ώμεθα
	2	τιμ-ᾶτε	τιμ-ᾶσθε
	3	τιμ-ῶσι(ν)	τιμ-ῶνται
participle		τιμῶν -ῶσα -ῶν (stem τιμωντ-)	τιμώμενος -η -ον
infinitive		τιμᾶν	τιμᾶσθαι
imperative		sg τίμα pl τιμᾶτε	sg τιμῶ pl τιμᾶσθε
imperfect			
sg	*1*	ἐ-τίμ-ων	ἐ-τιμ-ώμην
	2	ἐ-τίμ-ας	ἐ-τιμ-ῶ
	3	ἐ-τίμ-α	ἐ-τιμ-ᾶτο
pl	*1*	ἐ-τιμ-ῶμεν	ἐ-τιμ-ώμεθα
	2	ἐ-τιμ-ᾶτε	ἐ-τιμ-ᾶσθε
	3	ἐ-τίμ-ων	ἐ-τιμ-ῶντο

		present subjunctive		*present optative*	
		active	*middle/passive*	*active*	*middle/passive*
sg	*1*	τιμ-ῶ	τιμ-ῶμαι	τιμ-ῴην	τιμ-ῴμην
	2	τιμ-ᾷς	τιμ-ᾷ	τιμ-ῴης	τιμ-ῷο
	3	etc: as indicative	etc: as indicative	τιμ-ῴη	τιμ-ῷτο
pl	*1*			τιμ-ῷμεν	τιμ-ῴμεθα
	2			τιμ-ῷτε	τιμ-ῷσθε
	3			τιμ-ῷεν	τιμ-ῷντο

Other tenses

	active	*middle*	*passive*
		middle/passive	
future	τιμήσω	τιμήσομαι	τιμηθήσομαι
1st (weak) aor	ἐτίμησα	ἐτιμησάμην	ἐτιμήθην
perfect	τετίμηκα	τετίμημαι	

(b) With epsilon contraction

Rules of contraction:

      ε followed by ε becomes ει
      ε followed by o becomes ου
      ε followed by a long vowel or diphthong disappears

I like, I love

present	*active*	*middle/passive*
sg 1	φιλ-ῶ	φιλ-οῦμαι
2	φιλ-εῖς	φιλ-ῇ *or* εῖ
3	φιλ-εῖ	φιλ-εῖται
pl 1	φιλ-οῦμεν	φιλ-ούμεθα
2	φιλ-εῖτε	φιλ-εῖσθε
3	φιλ-οῦσι(ν)	φιλ-οῦνται

participle	φιλῶν -οῦσα -οῦν	φιλούμενος -η -ον
	(*stem* φιλουντ-)	
infinitive	φιλεῖν	φιλεῖσθαι
imperative	*sg* φίλει *pl* φιλεῖτε	*sg* φιλοῦ *pl* φιλεῖσθε

imperfect		
sg 1	ἐ-φίλ-ουν	ἐ-φιλ-ούμην
2	ἐ-φίλ-εις	ἐ-φιλ-οῦ
3	ἐ-φίλ-ει	ἐ-φιλ-εῖτο
pl 1	ἐ-φιλ-οῦμεν	ἐ-φιλ-ούμεθα
2	ἐ-φιλ-εῖτε	ἐ-φιλ-εῖσθε
3	ἐ-φίλ-ουν	ἐ-φιλ-οῦντο

	present subjunctive		*present optative*	
	active	*middle/passive*	*active*	*middle/passive*
sg 1	φιλ-ῶ	φιλ-ῶμαι	φιλ-οίην	φιλ-οίμην
2	φιλ-ῇς	φιλ-ῇ	φιλ-οίης	φιλ-οῖο
3	φιλ-ῇ	φιλ-ῆται	φιλ-οίη	φιλ-οῖτο
pl 1	φιλ-ῶμεν	φιλ-ώμεθα	φιλ-οῖμεν	φιλ-οίμεθα
2	φιλ-ῆτε	φιλ-ῆσθε	φιλ-οῖτε	φιλ-οῖσθε
3	φιλ-ῶσι(ν)	φιλ-ῶνται	φιλ-οῖεν	φιλ-οῖντο

Other tenses

	active	*middle*	*passive*
		middle/passive	
future	φιλήσω	φιλήσομαι	φιληθήσομαι
1st (weak) aor	ἐφίλησα	ἐφιλησάμην	ἐφιλήθην
perfect	πεφίληκα	πεφίλημαι	

301

(c) With omicron contraction

Rules of contraction:
    o followed by a long vowel becomes ω
    o followed by a short vowel becomes ου
    any combination with ι becomes οι

I show

present	active	middle/passive
sg 1	δηλ-ῶ	δηλ-οῦμαι
2	δηλ-οῖς	δηλ-οῖ
3	δηλ-οῖ	δηλ-οῦται
pl 1	δηλ-οῦμεν	δηλ-ούμεθα
2	δηλ-οῦτε	δηλ-οῦσθε
3	δηλ-οῦσι(ν)	δηλ-οῦνται

	active	middle/passive
participle	δηλῶν -οῦσα -οῦν (stem δηλουντ-)	δηλούμενος -η -ον
infinitive	δηλοῦν	δηλοῦσθαι
imperative	sg δήλου pl δηλοῦτε	sg δηλοῦ pl δηλοῦσθε

imperfect

	active	middle/passive
sg 1	ἐ-δήλ-ουν	ἐ-δηλ-ούμην
2	ἐ-δήλ-ους	ἐ-δηλ-οῦ
3	ἐ-δήλ-ου	ἐ-δηλ-οῦτο
pl 1	ἐ-δηλ-οῦμεν	ἐ-δηλ-ούμεθα
2	ἐ-δηλ-οῦτε	ἐ-δηλ-οῦσθε
3	ἐ-δήλ-ουν	ἐ-δηλ-οῦντο

	present subjunctive		present optative	
	active	middle/passive	active	middle/passive
sg 1	δηλ-ῶ	δηλ-ῶμαι	δηλ-οίην	δηλ-οίμην
2	δηλ-οῖς	δηλ-οῖ	δηλ-οίης	δηλ-οῖο
3	δηλ-οῖ	δηλ-ῶται	δηλ-οίη	δηλ-οῖτο
pl 1	δηλ-ῶμεν	δηλ-ώμεθα	δηλ-οῖμεν	δηλ-οίμεθα
2	δηλ-ῶτε	δηλ-ῶσθε	δηλ-οῖτε	δηλ-οῖσθε
3	δηλ-ῶσι(ν)	δηλ-ῶνται	δηλ-οῖεν	δηλ-οῖντο

Other tenses

	active	middle	passive
			middle/passive
future	δηλώσω	δηλώσομαι	δηλωθήσομαι
1st aorist	ἐδήλωσα	ἐδηλωσάμην	ἐδηλώθην
perfect	δεδήλωκα	δεδήλωμαι	

Verbs (3): irregular

The verb *to be* - εἰμί = I am:

present	*indicative*	*subjunctive*	*optative*
sg 1	εἰμί	ὦ	εἴην
2	εἶ	ᾖς	εἴης
3	ἐστί(ν)	ᾖ	εἴη
pl 1	ἐσμέν	ὦμεν	εἶμεν (*or* εἴημεν)
2	ἐστέ	ἦτε	εἶτε (*or* εἴητε)
3	εἰσί(ν)	ὦσι(ν)	εἶεν (*or* εἴησαν)

participle	ὤν οὖσα ὄν (*stem* ὀντ-)
infinitive	εἶναι
imperative	*sg* ἴσθι *pl* ἔστε

	imperfect	*future*
sg 1	ἦ (*or* ἦν)	ἔσομαι
2	ἦσθα	ἔσῃ (*or* ἔσει)
3	ἦν	ἔσται
pl 1	ἦμεν	ἐσόμεθα
2	ἦτε	ἔσεσθε
3	ἦσαν	ἔσονται

future participle	ἐσόμενος -η -ον
future infinitive	ἔσεσθαι
future optative	ἐσοίμην *etc*

εἶμι = I shall go

	indicative	*subjunctive*	*optative*
sg 1	εἶμι	ἴω	ἴοιμι (*or* ἰοίην)
2	εἶ	ἴῃς	ἴοις
3	εἶσι(ν)	ἴῃ	ἴοι
pl 1	ἴμεν	ἴωμεν	ἴοιμεν
2	ἴτε	ἴητε	ἴοιτε
3	ἴασι(ν)	ἴωσι(ν)	ἴοιεν

participle	ἰών ἰοῦσα ἰόν (*stem* ἰοντ-)
infinitive	ἰέναι
imperative	*sg* ἴθι *pl* ἴτε

Note that in parts other than the indicative the meaning is usually present rather than future.

οἶδα = I know

present*	indicative	subjunctive	optative
sg 1	οἶδα	εἰδῶ	εἰδείην
2	οἶσθα	εἰδῇς	εἰδείης
3	οἶδε(ν)	εἰδῇ	εἰδείη
pl 1	ἴσμεν	εἰδῶμεν	εἰδεῖμεν (or εἰδείημεν)
2	ἴστε	εἰδῆτε	εἰδεῖτε (or εἰδείητε)
3	ἴσασι(ν)	εἰδῶσι(ν)	εἰδεῖεν (or εἰδείησαν)

participle	εἰδώς -υῖα -ός (stem εἰδοτ-)
infinitive	εἰδέναι
imperative	sg ἴσθι pl ἴστε

past*
sg 1	ἤδη
2	ἤδησθα
3	ἤδει(ν)
pl 1	ἦσμεν
2	ἦστε
3	ἦσαν (or ἤδεσαν)

* the present tense is strictly a perfect (= *I have come to see*, i.e. I do now know), the past a pluperfect

φημί = I say

present	indicative	subjunctive	optative
sg 1	φημί	φῶ	φαίην
2	φής	φῇς	φαίης
3	φησί(ν)	φῇ	φαίη
pl 1	φαμέν	φῶμεν	φαῖμεν
2	φατέ	φῆτε	φαῖτε (or φαίητε)
3	φασί(ν)	φῶσι(ν)	φαῖεν

participle	φάσκων -ουσα -ον (stem φασκοντ-)
infinitive	φάναι
imperative	sg φάθι pl φάτε

imperfect
sg 1	ἔφην
2	ἔφησθα
3	ἔφη
pl 1	ἔφαμεν
2	ἔφατε
3	ἔφασαν

Verbs (4): ending in -μι

(a) Active forms

present

		I give	I place	I show
sg	1	δίδωμι	τίθημι	δείκνυμι
	2	δίδως	τίθης	δείκνυς
	3	δίδωσι(ν)	τίθησι(ν)	δείκνυσι(ν)
pl	1	δίδομεν	τίθεμεν	δείκνυμεν
	2	δίδοτε	τίθετε	δείκνυτε
	3	διδόασι(ν)	τιθέασι(ν)	δεικνύασι(ν)

imperfect

sg	1	ἐδίδουν	ἐτίθην	ἐδείκνυν
	2	ἐδίδους	ἐτίθεις	ἐδείκνυς
	3	ἐδίδου	ἐτίθει	ἐδείκνυ
pl	1	ἐδίδομεν	ἐτίθεμεν	ἐδείκνυμεν
	2	ἐδίδοτε	ἐτίθετε	ἐδείκνυτε
	3	ἐδίδοσαν	ἐτίθεσαν	ἐδείκνυσαν

aorist

sg	1	ἔδωκα	ἔθηκα	ἔδειξα
	2	ἔδωκας	ἔθηκας	etc (regular first [weak] aorist)
	3	ἔδωκε(ν)	ἔθηκε(ν)	
pl	1	ἔδομεν	ἔθεμεν	
	2	ἔδοτε	ἔθετε	
	3	ἔδοσαν	ἔθεσαν	

Alternative third-person plurals ἔδωκαν, ἔθηκαν (on the model of the singular) are also found.

Many other parts of these verbs have endings like the equivalent tenses of ordinary verbs:

future	δώσω	θήσω	δείξω
perfect	δέδωκα	τέθηκα	δέδειχα

imperatives (singular then plural each time)

present	δίδου, δίδοτε	τίθει, τίθετε	δείκνυ, δείκνυτε
aorist	δός, δότε	θές, θέτε	δεῖξον, δείξατε

infinitives

present	διδόναι	τιθέναι	δεικνύναι
aorist	δοῦναι	θεῖναι	δεῖξαι

present participles

δώσω -οῦσα -όν (*stem* διδοντ-)
διδούς -οῦσα -όν (*stem* διδοντ-)
τιθείς -εῖσα -έν (*stem* τιθεντ-)
δεικνύς -ῦσα -ύν (*stem* δεικνυντ-)

aorist participles

        δούς, δοῦσα, δόν (*stem* δοντ-)
        θείς, θεῖσα, θέν (*stem* θεντ-)
        δείξας -ασα -αν (*stem* δειξαντ-)

(b) Middle and passive forms

present middle/passive

sg				
	1	δίδομαι	τίθεμαι	δείκνυμαι
	2	δίδοσαι	τίθεσαι	δείκνυσαι
	3	δίδοται	τίθεται	δείκνυται
pl	1	διδόμεθα	τιθέμεθα	δεικνύμεθα
	2	δίδοσθε	τίθεσθε	δείκνυσθε
	3	δίδονται	τίθενται	δείκνυνται

imperfect middle/passive

sg				
	1	ἐδιδόμην	ἐτιθέμην	ἐδεικνύμην
	2	ἐδίδοσο	ἐτίθεσο	ἐδείκνυσο
	3	ἐδίδοτο	ἐτίθετο	ἐδείκνυτο
pl	1	ἐδιδόμεθα	ἐτιθέμεθα	ἐδεικνύμεθα
	2	ἐδίδοσθε	ἐτίθεσθε	ἐδείκνυσθε
	3	ἐδίδοντο	ἐτίθεντο	ἐδείκνυντο

aorist middle

sg				
	1	ἐδόμην	ἐθέμην	ἐδειξάμην
	2	ἔδου	ἔθου	etc (regular first [weak] aorist middle)
	3	ἔδοτο	ἔθετο	
pl	1	ἐδόμεθα	ἐθέμεθα	
	2	ἔδοσθε	ἔθεσθε	
	3	ἔδοντο	ἔθεντο	

aorist passive

sg				
	1	ἐδόθην	ἐτέθην	ἐδείχθην
		etc	etc	etc	(all regular aorist passives)

infinitives:

    present middle/passive δίδοσθαι, τίθεσθαι, δείκνυσθαι
    aorist middle δόσθαι, θέσθαι, δείξασθαι
    aorist passive δοθῆναι, τεθῆναι, δειχθῆναι

participles:

    present middle/passive διδόμενος -η -ον, τιθέμενος -η -ον, δεικνύμενος -η -ον
    aorist middle δόμενος -η -ον, θέμενος -η -ον, δειξάμενος -η -ον
    aorist passive δοθείς -εῖσα -έν (δοθεντ-), τεθείς -εῖσα -έν (τεθεντ-), δειχθείς -εῖσα -έν
        (δειχθεντ-)

(c) Subjunctive and optative forms

δίδωμι			active	middle	passive
present subjunctive	sg	1	διδῶ	διδῶμαι	(as middle)
		2	διδῷς	διδῷ	
		3	διδῷ	διδῶται	
	pl	1	διδῶμεν	διδώμεθα	
		2	διδῶτε	διδῶσθε	
		3	διδῶσι(ν)	διδῶνται	
aorist subjunctive	pl	1	δῶ	δῶμαι	δοθῶ
		2	δῷς	δῷ	δοθῇς
			etc	etc	etc (all regular aorist subjunctive)

δίδωμι in the optative uses the -οιην/-οιμην endings like a contracted verb, with the aorist again shortening the stem.

	active	middle	passive
present optative	διδοίην	διδοίμην	(as middle)
aorist optative	δοίην	δοίμην	δοθείην (like -ω verb)

τίθημι (regular subjunctive endings)

	active	middle	passive
present subjunctive	τιθῶ	τιθῶμαι	(as middle)
aorist subjunctive	θῶ	θῶμαι	τέθω
present optative	τιθείην	τιθείμην	(as middle)
	τιθείης	τιθεῖο	
	τιθείη	τιθεῖτο	
	τιθεῖμεν	τιθείμεθα	
	τιθεῖτε	τιθεῖσθε	
	τιθεῖεν	τιθεῖντο	
aorist optative	θείην	θείμην	τεθείην

δείκνυμι (regular subjunctive and optative endings throughout)

	active	middle	passive
present subjunctive	δεικνύω	δεικνύωμαι	(as middle)
aorist subjunctive	δείξω	δείξωμαι	δείχθω
present optative	δεικνύοιμι	δεικνυοίμην	(as middle)
aorist optative	δείξαιμι	δειξαίμην	δειχθείην

Verbs (5): 30 important irregular aorists

present	meaning	aorist	aorist stem
ἄγω	I lead	ἤγαγον	ἀγαγ-
αἱρέω	I take	εἷλον	ἑλ-
αἰσθάνομαι	I perceive	ἠσθόμην	αἰσθ-
ἀποθνήσκω	I die	ἀπέθανον	ἀποθαν-
ἀφικνέομαι	I arrive	ἀφικόμην	ἀφικ-
βαίνω	I go	ἔβην	(*participle* βάς, *inf* βῆναι)
βάλλω	I throw	ἔβαλον	βαλ-
γίγνομαι	I become, I happen	ἐγενόμην	γεν-
γιγνώσκω	I get to know	ἔγνων	(*participle* γνούς, *inf* γνῶναι)
ἐλαύνω	I drive	ἤλασα	ἐλασ-
ἔρχομαι	I come, I go	ἦλθον	ἐλθ-
ἐρωτάω	I ask (a question)	ἠρώτησα *or* ἠρόμην	ἐρωτησ- ἐρ-
ἐσθίω	I eat	ἔφαγον	φαγ-
εὑρίσκω	I find	ηὗρον	εὑρ-
ἔχω	I have, I hold	ἔσχον	σχ-
λαμβάνω	I take	ἔλαβον	λαβ-
λέγω	I say, I speak	(ἔλεξα *or*) εἶπον	(λεξ-) εἰπ-
λείπω	I leave	ἔλιπον	λιπ-
μανθάνω	I learn	ἔμαθον	μαθ-
μάχομαι	I fight	ἐμαχέσαμην	μαχεσ-
ὄμνυμι	I swear	ὤμοσα	ὀμοσ-
ὁράω	I see	εἶδον	ἰδ-
πάσχω	I suffer	ἔπαθον	παθ-
πίπτω	I fall	ἔπεσον	πεσ-
πλέω	I sail	ἔπλευσα	πλευσ-
πράσσω	I do, I fare	ἔπραξα	πραξ-
τρέχω	I run	ἔδραμον	δραμ-
ὑπισχνέομαι	I follow	ὑπεσχόμην	ὑποσχ-
φέρω	I carry, I bear	ἤνεγκα *or* -ον	ἐνεγκ-
φεύγω	I run away, I flee	ἔφυγον	φυγ-

Verbs (6): reference list of tenses

present	meaning	future	aorist	aorist passive	perfect active, middle/passive (or perfect of deponent verbs)
ἀγγέλλω	I announce	ἀγγελῶ (εω)	ἤγγειλα	ἠγγέλθην	ἤγγελκα, ἤγγελμαι
ἄγω	I lead	ἄξω	ἤγαγον	ἤχθην	ἦχα, ἦγμαι
ἀδικέω	I act unjustly (to)	ἀδικήσω	ἠδίκησα	ἠδικήθην	ἠδίκηκα, ἠδίκημαι
ἀθυμέω	I am despondent	ἀθυμήσω	ἠθύμησα	–	–
αἱρέω	I take	αἱρήσω	εἷλον	ᾑρέθην	ᾕρηκα, ᾕρημαι
	middle I choose				
αἰσθάνομαι	I perceive	αἰσθήσομαι	ᾐσθόμην	–	ᾔσθημαι
αἰτέω	I ask for	αἰτήσω	ᾔτησα	ᾐτήθην	ᾔτηκα, ᾔτημαι
ἀκούω	I hear	ἀκούσομαι	ἤκουσα	ἠκούσθην	ἀκήκοα
ἀμύνομαι	I defend myself	ἀμυνοῦμαι (εο)	ἠμυνάμην	–	–
ἀναγκάζω	I force	ἀναγκάσω	ἠνάγκασα	ἠναγκάσθην	ἠνάγκακα, ἠνάγκασμαι
ἀναχωρέω	I retreat	ἀναχωρήσω	ἀνεχώρησα		ἀνακεχώρηκα
ἀποθνῄσκω	I die, I am killed	ἀποθανοῦμαι (εο)	ἀπέθανον		τέθνηκα
ἀποκρίνομαι	I answer	ἀποκρινοῦμαι (εο)	ἀπεκρινάμην		
ἀποκτείνω	I kill	ἀποκτενῶ (εω)	ἀπέκτεινα		ἀπέκτονα
ἀπορέω	I am at a loss	ἀπορήσω	ἠπόρησα		ἠπόρηκα
ἅπτομαι	I touch	ἅψομαι	ἡψάμην		ἧμμαι
ἁρπάζω	I seize	ἁρπάσομαι	ἥρπασα	ἡρπάσθην	ἥρπακα, ἥρπασμαι
ἄρχω	I rule	ἄρξω	ἦρξα	ἤρχθην	ἦρχα, ἦργμαι
	middle I begin				
ἀφικνέομαι	I arrive	ἀφίξομαι	ἀφικόμην	–	ἀφῖγμαι
βαίνω	I go	βήσομαι	ἔβην	–	βέβηκα
βάλλω	I throw, I pelt	βαλῶ (εω)	ἔβαλον	ἐβλήθην	βέβληκα, βέβλημαι
βλάπτω	I harm	βλάψω	ἔβλαψα	ἐβλάβην	βέβλαφα, βέβλαμμαι
βοάω	I shout	βοήσω	ἐβόησα	ἐβοήθην	βεβόηκα
βουλεύομαι	I plan	βουλεύσομαι	ἐβουλευσάμην	ἐβουλεύθην	βεβούλευκα, βεβούλευμαι
βούλομαι	I wish, I want	βουλήσομαι	(ἐβουλόμην)†	[ἐβουλήθην]*	βεβούλημαι*
γελάω	I laugh (at)	γελάσομαι	ἐγέλασα	ἐγελάσθην	–
γίγνομαι	I become, I happen	γενήσομαι	ἐγενόμην	–	γέγονα
γιγνώσκω	I get to know	γνώσομαι	ἔγνων	ἐγνώσθην	ἔγνωκα, ἔγνωσμαι
γράφω	I write	γράψω	ἔγραψα	ἐγράφην	γέγραφα, γέγραμμαι

Present	Meaning	Future	Aorist	Aorist passive	Perfect act., Perfect mid./pass.
δακρύω	I cry	δακρύσω	ἐδάκρυσα	—	—
δεῖ	it is necessary	δεήσει	ἐδέησε(ν)	—	—
δείκνυμι	I show	δείξω	ἔδειξα	ἐδείχθην	δέδειχα, δέδειγμαι
δέχομαι	I receive	δέξομαι	ἐδεξάμην	ἐδέχθην	—
δηλόω	I show	δηλώσω	ἐδήλωσα	ἐδηλώθην	δεδήλωκα, δεδήλωμαι
διαφθείρω	I destroy	διαφθερῶ (εω)	διέφθειρα	διεφθάρην	διέφθαρκα, διέφθαρμαι
διδάσκω	I teach	διδάξω	ἐδίδαξα	ἐδιδάχθην	δεδίδαχα, δεδίδαγμαι
δίδωμι	I give	δώσω	ἔδωκα	ἐδόθην	δέδωκα, δέδομαι
διώκω	I chase	διώξομαι	ἐδίωξα	ἐδιώχθην	δεδίωχα, δεδίωγμαι
δοκέω	I seem, I think	δόξω	ἔδοξα	—	-, δέδογμαι
δουλόω	I enslave	δουλώσω	ἐδούλωσα	ἐδουλώθην	δεδούλωκα, δεδούλωμαι
δύναμαι	I am able	δυνήσομαι	(ἐδυνάμην)†	ἐδυνήθην*	—
ἐάω	I allow	ἐάσω	εἴασα	εἱάθην	εἴακα, εἴαμαι
ἐθέλω	I am willing	ἐθελήσω	ἠθέλησα	—	ἠθέληκα
εἰμί	I am	ἔσομαι	(ἦ or ἦν)†	—	—
εἰσβάλλω	I invade	εἰσβαλῶ (εω)	εἰσέβαλον	—	—
ἐλαύνω	I drive	ἐλῶ (αω)	ἤλασα	ἠλάθην	ἐλήλακα, ἐλήλαμαι
ἐλευθερόω	I set free	ἐλευθερώσω	ἠλευθέρωσα	ἠλευθερώθην	—
ἐλπίζω	I hope	ἐλπιῶ (εω)	ἤλπισα	ἠλπίσθην	ἤλπικα
ἔξεστι(ν)	it is possible	ἐξέσται	ἐξῆν	—	—
ἐπαινέω	I praise	ἐπαινέσω	ἐπῄνεσα	ἐπῃνέθην	ἐπῄνεκα
ἐπίσταμαι	I know (how to)	ἐπιστήσομαι	(ἠπιστάμην)†	—	—
ἕπομαι	I follow	ἕψομαι	ἑσπόμην	—	—
ἔρχομαι	I go, I come	εἶμι	ἦλθον	—	ἐλήλυθα or ἥκω
ἐρωτάω	I ask (a question)	ἐρωτήσω	ἠρώτησα	ἠρωτήθην	ἠρώτηκα, ἠρώτημαι
	or	ἐρήσομαι	ἠρόμην		
ἐσθίω	I eat	ἔδομαι	ἔφαγον	ἠδέσθην	ἐδήδοκα
εὑρίσκω	I find	εὑρήσω	ηὗρον (or εὗρ-)	ηὑρέθην (or εὑρ-)	ηὕρηκα, ηὕρημαι
ἔχω	I have	ἕξω or σχήσω	ἔσχον	—	ἔσχηκα
ζητέω	I seek	ζητήσω	ἐζήτησα	ἐζητήθην	ἐζήτηκα
ἥδομαι	I enjoy	—	—	ἤσθην*	—
θάπτω	I bury	θάψω	ἔθαψα	ἐτάφην	-, τεθάμμαι
θαυμάζω	I am amazed (at)	θαυμάσομαι	ἐθαύμασα	ἐθαυμάσθην	τεθαύμακα

Present	Meaning	Future	Aorist	Aorist Passive	Perfect
θύω	I sacrifice	θύσω	ἔθυσα	ἐτύθην	τέθυκα, τέθυμαι
καθαιρέω	I take down	καθαιρήσω	καθεῖλον	καθηρέθην	καθῄρηκα, καθῄρημαι
καθεύδω	I sleep	καθευδήσω	(ἐκάθευδον)† or (καθηῦδον)†	-	-
καθίζω	I sit	καθίσω	ἐκάθισα	ἐκαθίσθην	
καίω	I burn	καύσω	ἔκαυσα	ἐκαύθην	κέκαυκα, κέκαυμαι
καλέω	I call	καλῶ (εω)	ἐκάλεσα	ἐκλήθην	κέκληκα, κέκλημαι
κελεύω	I order	κελεύσω	ἐκέλευσα	ἐκελεύσθην	κεκέλευκα, κεκέλευσμαι
κλέπτω	I steal	κλέψω	ἔκλεψα	ἐκλάπην	κέκλοφα, κέκλεμμαι
κολάζω	I punish	κολάσω	ἐκόλασα	ἐκολάσθην	-
κόπτω	I cut, I knock	κόψω	ἔκοψα	ἐκόπην	κέκοφα, κέκομμαι
κρατέω	I rule, I control	κρατήσω	ἐκράτησα	ἐκρατήθην	κεκράτηκα
κρύπτω	I hide	κρύψω	ἔκρυψα	ἐκρύφθην	κέκρυφα, κέκρυμμαι
κτάομαι	I obtain	κτήσομαι	ἐκτησάμην	ἐκτήθην	κέκτημαι
κωλύω	I hinder	κωλύσω	ἐκώλυσα	ἐκωλύθην	κεκώλυκα, κεκώλυμαι
λαμβάνω	I take	λήψομαι	ἔλαβον	ἐλήφθην	εἴληφα, εἴλημμαι
λέγω	I say, I speak	λέξω	εἶπον	ἐλέχθην or ἐρρήθην	-, λέλεγμαι / εἴρηκα, εἴρημαι
λείπω	I leave	λείψω	ἔλιπον	ἐλείφθην	λέλοιπα, λέλειμμαι
λύω	I release	λύσω	ἔλυσα	ἐλύθην	λέλυκα, λέλυμαι
	middle I ransom				
μανθάνω	I learn	μαθήσομαι	ἔμαθον	-	μεμάθηκα
μάχομαι	I fight	μαχοῦμαι (εο)	ἐμαχεσάμην	-	μεμάχημαι
μέλλω	I am about to	μελλήσω	ἐμέλλησα	-	-
μένω	I stay	μενῶ (εω)	ἔμεινα	-	μεμένηκα
μισέω	I hate	μισήσω	ἐμίσησα	ἐμισήθην	μεμίσηκα
ναυμαχέω	I fight a sea-battle	ναυμαχήσω	ἐναυμάχησα	-	νεναυμάχηκα
νικάω	I conquer, I win	νικήσω	ἐνίκησα	ἐνικήθην	νενίκηκα, νενίκημαι
νομίζω	I think, I consider	νομιῶ (εω)	ἐνόμισα	ἐνομίσθην	νενόμικα, νενόμισμαι
οἶδα	I know	εἴσομαι	(ᾔδη)†	-	-
οἰκέω	I live	οἰκήσω	ᾤκησα	-	-
οἷός τ' εἰμί	I am able	οἷός τ' ἔσομαι	(οἷός τ' ἦν)†	-	-
ὄμνυμι	I swear	ὀμοῦμαι (εο)	ὤμοσα	ὠμόθην	ὀμώμοκα

Present	Meaning	Future	Aorist	Aorist passive	Perfect
ὁμολογέω	I agree	ὁμολογήσω	ὡμολόγησα	ὡμολογήθην	ὡμολόγηκα, ὡμολόγημαι
ὁράω	I see	ὄψομαι	εἶδον	ὤφθην	ἑόρακα, ἑόραμαι or ἑώρακα
ὀργίζομαι	I get angry	ὀργιοῦμαι (εο)	(ὀργισάμην)	ὠργίσθην*	-, ὤργισμαι*
παιδεύω	I train, I educate	παιδεύσω	ἐπαίδευσα	ἐπαιδεύθην	πεπαίδευκα, πεπαίδευμαι
παραινέω	I advise	παραινέσω	παρῄνεσα	-	-
παρασκευάζω	I prepare	παρασκευάσω	παρεσκεύασα	παρεσκευάσθην	παρεσκεύασμαι
πάρειμι	I am present	παρέσομαι	(παρῆν)†	-	-
παρέχω	I provide	παρέξω / παρασχήσω *or*	παρέσχον	-	-
πάσχω	I suffer	πείσομαι	ἔπαθον	-	πέπονθα
παύω	I stop	παύσω	ἔπαυσα	ἐπαύσθην	πέπαυκα, πέπαυμαι
πείθω	I persuade / *middle* I obey	πείσω	ἔπεισα / *middle* ἐπιθόμην	ἐπείσθην	πέπεικα, πέπεισμαι
πειράομαι	I try	πειράσομαι	ἐπειρασάμην	-	πεπείραμαι
πέμπω	I send	πέμψω	ἔπεμψα	ἐπέμφθην	πέπομφα, πέπεμμαι
πίνω	I drink	πίομαι	ἔπιον	ἐπόθην	πέπωκα
πίπτω	I fall	πεσοῦμαι (εο)	ἔπεσον	-	πέπτωκα
πιστεύω	I believe, I trust	πιστεύσω	ἐπίστευσα	ἐπιστεύθην	πεπίστευκα
πλέω	I sail	πλεύσομαι	ἔπλευσα	-	πέπλευκα
ποιέω	I make, I do	ποιήσω	ἐποίησα	ἐποιήθην	πεποίηκα
πορεύομαι	I march	πορεύσομαι	ἐπορευσάμην	ἐπορεύθην*	-
πράσσω	I do, I fare	πράξω	ἔπραξα	ἐπράχθην	πέπραχα (have done), πέπραγμαι, πέπραγα (have fared)
προσβάλλω	I attack	προσβαλῶ (εο)	προσέβαλον	-	-
προχωρέω	I advance	προχωρήσω	προὐχώρησα	-	προκεχώρηκα
πυνθάνομαι	I enquire, I find out	πεύσομαι	ἐπυθόμην	-	πέπυσμαι
σκοπέω	I look at	σκέψομαι	ἐσκεψάμην	-	-, ἔσκεμμαι
στρατεύω	I march	στρατεύσω	ἐστράτευσα	-	-
στρατοπεδεύομαι	I encamp	στρατοπεδεύσομαι	ἐστρατοπεδευσάμην	-	-
συλλέγω	I collect	συλλέξω	συνέλεξα	συνελέχθην	-
σῴζω	I save	σώσω	ἔσωσα	ἐσώθην	σέσωκα, σέσωσμαι
τάσσω	I draw up	τάξω	ἔταξα	ἐτάχθην	τέταχα, τέταγμαι

Present	Meaning	Future	Aorist	Aorist passive	Perfect
τέμνω	I cut	τεμῶ (εω)	ἔτεμον	ἐτμήθην	τέτμηκα, τέτμημαι
τίθημι	I place	θήσω	ἔθηκα	ἐτέθην	τέθηκα
τιμάω	I honour	τιμήσω	ἐτίμησα	ἐτιμήθην	τετίμηκα, τετίμημαι
τοξεύω	I shoot (arrows)	τοξεύσω	ἐτόξευσα	-	-
τρέπω	I turn	τρέψω	ἔτρεψα	ἐτρέφθην	τέτροφα, τέτραμμαι
τρέχω	I run	δραμοῦμαι (εο)	ἔδραμον	-	δεδράμηκα
τύπτω	I hit	τύψω	ἔτυψα	ἐτύφθην	-, τέτυμμαι
ὑπισχνέομαι	I promise	ὑποσχήσομαι	ὑπεσχόμην		ὑπέσχημαι
φαίνω	I show	φανῶ (εω)	ἔφηνα	ἐφάνθην	
φέρω	I carry	οἴσω	ἤνεγκα or -ον	ἠνέχθην	ἐνήνοχα, ἐνήνεγμαι
	middle I win (prizes)				
φεύγω	I run away, I flee	φεύξομαι	ἔφυγον		πέφευγα
φημί	I say	φήσω	[ἔφησα] (ἔφην)†		-
φιλέω	I love, I like	φιλήσω	ἐφίλησα	ἐφιλήθην	πεφίληκα, πεφίλημαι
φοβέομαι	I fear	φοβήσομαι		ἐφοβήθην*	πεφόβημαι
φυλάσσω	I guard	φυλάξω	ἐφύλαξα	ἐφυλάχθην	πεφύλαχα, πεφύλαγμαι
χράομαι	I use	χρήσομαι	ἐχρησάμην		κέχρημαι
χρή	it is necessary	-	([ἐ]χρῆν)†		-
ὠφελέω	I help	ὠφελήσω	ὠφέλησα	ὠφελήθην	ὠφέληκα, ὠφέλημαι

† imperfect (aorist not in common use)

* active/middle sense

Appendix 1 :
Words easily confused

αἰτέω	I ask for, I beg	εὐθύς	immediately
αἴτιος	responsible, to blame for (+ *gen*)	εὐρύς	broad
ἀληθής	true	ἤθελον	I was willing (*imperf of* ἐθέλω)
ἀσθενής	weak	ἦλθον	I came (*aor of* ἔρχομαι)
ἀσφαλής	safe		
		ἡμεῖς	we
ἀνδρεῖος	brave	ὑμεῖς	you (*pl*)
ἀνήρ -δρός	man		
		ἡμέτερος	our
ἀποθνήσκω	I die, I am killed	ὑμέτερος	your (of you *pl*)
ἀποκτείνω	I kill		
		ἴθι	go! (*sg*)
βαθύς	deep	ἴσθι	be! (*sg*)
βαρύς	heavy	ἴσθι	know! (*sg*)
βραδύς	slow		
		καλέω	I call
γίγνομαι	I become	κελεύω	I order
γιγνώσκω	I get to know		
		μακρός	long
δείκνυμι	I show (*aor stem* δειξ-)	μέγας	big
δέχομαι	I receive (*aor stem* δεξ-)		
		ναῦς	ship
δηλόω	I show	ναύτης	sailor
δουλόω	I enslave	ναυτικόν	fleet
εἰ	if	νόμος	law, custom
εἶ	you (*sg*) are	νόσος	disease
εἰμί	I am	οὐ	not
εἶμι	I shall go (*fut of* ἔρχομαι)	οὗ	(the place) where
εἰς	into (+ *acc*)	ποῖος;	what sort of?
εἷς	one (*m nom sg*)	πόσος;	how big? (*pl:* how many?)
εἰσί(ν)	they are	πολέμιοι	enemy
εἶσι(ν)	he/she/it will go	πόλεμος	war
ἐν	in (+ *dat*)	πόλις	city
ἕν	one (*n nom sg*)	πολύς	much
ἐξ	out of (+ *gen*)	πότερον	whether
ἕξ	six	πρότερον	previously
ἐπεί, ἐπειδή	when, since	ποῦ;	where (at)?
ἔπειτα	then, next	ποῖ;	where to?
		πόθεν;	where from?
Ἑλλάς -άδος	Greece	πότε;	when?
Ἕλλην -ηνος	Greek	πῶς;	how?

σαφής	clear	ταχύς	swift
σοφός	wise	τεῖχος	wall
στρατηγός	general	τοιοῦτος	of such a sort
στρατιώτης	soldier	τοσοῦτος	so big (*pl:* so many)
στρατόπεδον	camp		
στρατιά	army	ὥσπερ	just as, as if
στρατός	army	ὥστε	(with the result) that

Appendix 2: Greek and Latin constructions compared

	GREEK	*LATIN*
Use of cases:		
- prepositions: motion to	+ accusative	+ accusative
motion from	+ genitive	+ ablative
resting in	+ dative	+ ablative
- time (or distance):		
how long	accusative	accusative
within which	genitive	ablative
at a point	dative	ablative
- person after		
passive verb ('agent')	ὑπό + genitive	*a/ab* + ablative
- thing after		
passive verb ('instrument')	dative (no preposition)	ablative (no preposition)
- participle phrase		
separate from main clause	genitive absolute	ablative absolute
- comparison:		
use word for *than*	ἤ	*quam*
(with same case after as before)		
- or without word for *than*		
comparative adjective +	genitive of comparison	ablative of comparison

Indirect statement:	*(3 methods)*	*(just one method)*
	ὅτι clause (verbs of saying)	
	usu + indicative; can be	
	+ optative if introductory	
	verb is past	
or	participle construction (verbs of	
	perception)	
or	infinitive construction	infinitive construction ('acc + inf')
subject of inf (or in Gk participle)		
same as that of main vb:	nom (or nothing) + inf/participle	reflexive acc (never left out) + inf
	- any of these has tense of	infinitive has tense of
	original direct speech	original direct speech
	- Engl 'moves back a tense'	
	if introductory verb is past	likewise

Direct question:	indicative verb	indicative verb
- asking if a statement true:		
open	ἆρα	*-ne* (on end of first word)
expects *yes*	ἆρ᾽ οὐ	*nonne*
expects *no*	ἆρα μή	*num*
- requesting specific info:	question word usu begins with π	question word usu begins with q

Indirect question		
	indicative verb; can be optative	subjunctive verb
	if introductory verb is past	
	- has tense of original	
	direct speech (as ind statement)	tense by sense (like English)
- word for *if / whether*	εἰ	*num*
- alternative question	πότερον ... ἤ	*utrum...an*

316

	Greek	Latin
<u>Direct command:</u>	imperative (aorist imperative if referring to one occasion)	imperative
- negative	μή (with imperative, or with aorist subjunctive if one occasion)	*noli*, plural *nolite* + infinitive
<u>Indirect command:</u>	infinitive (aorist if one occasion)	infinitive only with *iubeo/veto* otherwise *ut* + subjunctive (tense by sequence)
- negative	μή + infinitive (whereas indirect statement has οὐ + infinitive)	*ne* + subjunctive (tense by sequence) (unless using *veto*)
<u>Purpose clause:</u>	ὡς + future participle (neg. οὐ) ἵνα/ὅπως + subjunctive or (historic sequence) optative - if negative, ἵνα + μή	*ut* + subjunctive (tense by sequence) if negative, *ne* <u>instead of</u> *ut*

<u>Result clause:</u>	usu a *so...* word οὕτω(ς) - or more specific ones, usu begin with τ (e.g.τοσοῦτος)	*tam, adeo* usu begin with *t* (e.g. *tantus*)
a word for *that*	ὥστε verb is indicative or infinitive - if negative, ὥστε + οὐ with indicative, ὥστε + μή with infinitive	*ut* verb is subjunctive (tense by sense) negative is *non* (<u>as well as</u> *ut*, i.e. *ut non*)

<u>Conditional clause:</u> *if*	εἰ / ἐάν	*si*
'open' type	usually indicative verbs (but fut often has ἐάν + subj in protasis)	indicative verbs
'closed' or 'remote' type	always has ἄν in apodosis	
future remote	optative in both halves	present subjunctive in both halves
present closed	imperfect indicative in both	imperfect subjunctive in both
past closed	past (usu aorist) indicative in both - negative for any type is μή in protasis (so e.g. εἰ μή), οὐ in apodosis	pluperfect subjunctive in both - negative for any type is *nisi* in protasis, *non* in apodosis

Vocabulary

English to Greek

Verbs are usually given with present and aorist.
Nouns are given with nominative and genitive, and article to show gender.
Adjectives are given with masculine, feminine, and neuter (if there are only two endings, there is no separate femimine: the feminine is the same as the masculine).
* = comes second word in sentence or clause.

able	(powerful, capable) δυνατός -ή -όν, (sufficient) ἱκανός -ή -όν
able, I am	οἷός τ' εἰμί, (*implying* have the power to) δύναμαι *imperf* ἐδυνάμην
about	περί (+ *gen*)
about to, I am	μέλλω (+ *fut inf*)
above	ὑπέρ (+ *gen*)
according to	κατά (+ *acc*)
account of, on	διά (+ *acc*)
acquire, I	κτάομαι ἐκτησάμην
act unjustly (to), I	ἀδικέω ἠδίκησα
addition to, in	πρός (+ *dat*)
admire, I	θαυμάζω ἐθαύμασα
admit, I	ὁμολογέω ὡμολόγησα
advance, I	προχωρέω προὐχώρησα
advise, I	παραινέω (+ *dat*)
affair	πρᾶγμα -ατος τό
afraid (of), I am	φοβέομαι ἐφοβήθην
after (*prep*)	μετά (+ *acc*)
after (*introducing a clause*)	(*use aor participle*)
after a short time	δι' ὀλίγου
again	αὖθις, πάλιν
against	ἐπί (+ *acc*)
agora	ἀγορά -ᾶς ἡ
agree (with), I	ὁμολογέω ὡμολόγησα (+ *dat*)
all	πᾶς πᾶσα πᾶν (παντ-)
all those who	ὅσοι -αι -α
allow, I	ἐάω εἴασα
ally	σύμμαχος -ου ὁ
almost	σχεδόν
alone	μόνος -η -ον
along, alongside	παρά (+ *acc*)
already	ἤδη
also	καί
although	καίπερ (+ *participle*)
always	ἀεί
am, I	εἰμί
amazed (at), I am	θαυμάζω ἐθαύμασα
among	ἐν (+ *dat*)
ancient	ἀρχαῖος -α -ον

318

and	καί, δέ*
anger	ὀργή -ῆς ἡ
angry, I get	ὀργίζομαι ὠργίσθην (with, + *dat*)
animal, creature	ζῷον -ου τό
announce, I	ἀγγέλλω ἤγγειλα
another	ἄλλος -η -ο
answer, I	ἀποκρίνομαι ἀπεκρινάμην
anywhere	που
appear, I	φαίνομαι ἐφάνην
approach, I	προσέρχομαι προσῆλθον, προσβαίνω προσέβην
arms, armour	ὅπλα -ων τά
army	στρατός -οῦ ὁ, στρατιά -ᾶς ἡ
around	περί (+ *acc*)
arrange, I	τάσσω ἔταξα
arrive, I	ἀφικνέομαι ἀφικόμην
as	ὡς
as far as	μέχρι (+ *gen*)
as great as	ὅσος -η -ον
as if	ὥσπερ
as many as	ὅσοι -αι -α
as quickly as possible	ὡς τάχιστα
as soon as	ὡς τάχιστα
ask (a question), I	ἐρωτάω ἠρώτησα *or* ἠρόμην
ask for, I	αἰτέω ᾔτησα
assemble (people/things), I	συλλέγω συνέλεξα
assembly	ἐκκλησία -ας ἡ
at a loss, I am	ἀπορέω ἠπόρησα
at first	πρῶτον
at least	γε*
at the hands of	πρός (+ *gen*)
at the same time (as)	ἅμα (+ *dat*)
Athene (goddess)	᾿Αθήνη -ης ἡ
Athenian	᾿Αθηναῖος -α -ον
Athenians	᾿Αθηναῖοι -ων οἱ
Athens	᾿Αθῆναι -ῶν αἱ
attack, I	προσβάλλω προσέβαλον (+ *dat*), εἰσβάλλω εἰσέβαλον (+ εἰς + *acc*)
away, I am	ἄπειμι *imperf* ἀπῆν
away from	ἀπό (+ *gen*)
back (again)	πάλιν
bad	κακός -ή -όν
badly, I take (something)	βαρέως φέρω
barbarian	βάρβαρος -ον
battle	μάχη -ης ἡ
be, to	εἶναι
beautiful	καλός -ή -όν
because	διότι, ὅτι (*or use participle*)
because of	διά (+ *acc*)

become, I	γίγνομαι ἐγενόμην
before (*adv* previously)	πρότερον
before (*prep* in front of *or* prior to)	πρό (+ *gen*)
before (*prep* into the presence of)	παρά (+ *acc*)
beg, I	αἰτέω ᾔτησα
begin, I	ἄρχομαι ἠρξάμην (+ *gen*)
beginning	ἀρχή -ῆς ἡ
behalf of, on	ὑπέρ (+ *gen*)
belief	γνώμη -ης ἡ
believe (trust, believe in), I	πιστεύω ἐπίστευσα (+ *dat*)
believe (think to be so), I	νομίζω ἐνόμισα
benefit (someone), I	ὠφελέω ὠφέλησα
beside	παρά (+ *dat*)
besiege, I	πολιορκέω ἐπολιόρκησα
best	ἄριστος -η -ον, (most virtuous) βέλτιστος -η -ον
better	ἀμείνων -ον (ἀμεινον-), (more virtuous) βελτίων -ον (βελτιον-)
beyond, to beyond	ὑπέρ (+ *acc*)
big	μέγας μεγάλη μέγα (μεγαλ-)
bigger	μείζων -ον (μειζον-)
biggest	μέγιστος -η -ον
bird	ὄρνις -ιθος ὁ/ἡ
bitter	ὀξύς -εῖα -ύ
blood	αἷμα -ατος τό
boat	πλοῖον -ου τό
body	σῶμα -ατος τό
body, dead	νεκρός -οῦ ὁ
book	βίβλος -ου ἡ
both ... and	τε* ... καί, καί ... καί
bow	τόξον -ου τό
boy	παῖς παιδός ὁ
brave	ἀνδρεῖος -α -ον
bring, I	φέρω ἤνεγκα *or* ἤνεγκον
broad	εὐρύς -εῖα -ύ
bronze	χαλκός -οῦ ὁ
brother	ἀδελφός -οῦ ὁ
burn, I	καίω ἔκαυσα
bury, I	θάπτω ἔθαψα
business	πρᾶγμα -ατος τό
but	ἀλλά, δέ*
by (a person *as agent*)	ὑπό (+ *gen*)
by land	κατὰ γῆν
by sea	κατὰ θάλασσαν
call, I	καλέω ἐκάλεσα
came, I	ἦλθον
camp	στρατόπεδον -ου τό
camp, I (set up)	στρατοπεδεύομαι ἐστρατοπεδευσάμην

campaign, I (go on)	στρατεύω ἐστράτευσα
can, I	οἷός τ᾽ εἰμί, (*implying* have the power to) δύναμαι *imperf* ἐδυνάμην
capable	δυνατός -ή -όν, ἱκανός -ή -όν
capture, I	αἱρέω εἷλον
carry, I	φέρω ἤνεγκα *or* ἤνεγκον
catch, I	λαμβάνω ἔλαβον, αἱρέω εἷλον
cavalry	ἱππεῖς -έων οἱ, (*collective sg*) ἵππος -ου ἡ
cavalryman	ἱππεύς -έως ὁ
cease, I	παύομαι ἐπαυσάμην
certain, a	τις τι (τιν-)
certainly	δή
chain	δεσμός -οῦ ὁ
chariot	ἅρμα -ατος τό
chase, I	διώκω ἐδίωξα
child	παῖς παιδός ὁ/ἡ
choose, I	αἱρέομαι εἱλόμην
circle	κύκλος -ου ὁ
citizen	πολίτης -ου ὁ
city (city-state)	πόλις -εως ἡ
city (town as opposed to countryside)	ἄστυ -εως τό
clear	δῆλος -η -ον, σαφής -ές
clear, I make	δηλόω ἐδήλωσα
clever	σοφός -ή -όν
collect (something), I	συλλέγω συνέλεξα
come, I	ἔρχομαι ἦλθον
come, I have	ἥκω (*pres with perf sense*)
commander	στρατηγός -οῦ ὁ
common	κοινός -ή -όν
community	δῆμος -ου ὁ
compel, I	ἀναγκάζω ἠνάγκασα
compulsion	ἀνάγκη -ης ἡ
concerning	περί (+ *gen*)
conquer, I	νικάω ἐνίκησα
consider (think to be so), I	νομίζω ἐνόμισα,
consider (deliberate), I	βουλεύομαι ἐβουλευσάμην
consider (examine), I	σκοπέω ἐσκεψάμην
contest	ἀγών -ῶνος ὁ
contrary to	παρά (+ *acc*)
control, I	κρατέω ἐκτράτησα (+ *gen*)
corpse	νεκρός -οῦ ὁ
corrupt, I	διαφθείρω διέφθειρα
council	βουλή -ῆς ἡ
country, land	χώρα -ας ἡ
countryside	ἀγροί -ῶν οἱ
courage	ἀρετή -ῆς ἡ
craft	τέχνη -ης ἡ
creature	ζῷον -ου τό

criminal (*adj*)	ἄδικος -ον
crowd	πλῆθος -ους τό
cry, I	δακρύω ἐδάκρυσα
custom	νόμος -ου ὁ
cut, I	τέμνω ἔτεμον, κόπτω ἔκοψα
daily	καθ᾽ ἡμέραν
damage, I	βλάπτω ἔβλαψα
danger	κίνδυνος -ου ὁ
dangerous	χαλεπός -ή -όν
darkness	σκότος -ου ὁ
daughter	θυγάτηρ -τρος ἡ, παῖς παιδός ἡ
day	ἡμέρα -ας ἡ
daybreak, at	ἅμ᾽ ἡμέρᾳ
day by day	καθ᾽ ἡμέραν
dead body	νεκρός -οῦ ὁ
dear	φίλος -η -ον
death	θάνατος -ου ὁ
decide, I	(= it seems good to me) δοκεῖ ἔδοξε (+ *dat, e.g.* μοι), βουλεύομαι ἐβουλευσάμην
deed	ἔργον -ου τό
deep	βαθύς -εῖα -ύ
defend myself (against), I	ἀμύνομαι ἠμυνάμην
deliberate, I	βουλεύομαι ἐβουλευσάμην
demolish, I	καθαιρέω καθεῖλον
descent (ancestry)	γένος -ους τό
deserving (of)	ἄξιος -α -ον (+ *gen*)
despite (being)	καίπερ (+ *participle*)
despondent, I am	ἀθυμέω ἠθύμησα
destroy, I	διαφθείρω διέφθειρα
die, I	ἀποθνήσκω ἀπέθανον
difficult	χαλεπός -ή -όν
difficulty, with	μόλις
dinner	δεῖπνον -ου τό
disaster	συμφορά -ᾶς ἡ
discuss, I	βουλεύομαι ἐβουλευσάμην
disease	νόσος -ου ἡ
disgraceful	αἰσχρός -ά -όν
disheartened, I am	ἀθυμέω ἠθύμησα
do, I	πράσσω ἔπραξα, ποιέω ἐποίησα
do wrong (to), I	ἀδικέω ἠδίκησα
doctor	ἰατρός -οῦ ὁ
door	θύρα -ας ἡ
doubt, I am in	ἀπορέω ἠπόρησα
down	κατά (+ *acc*)
down from	κατά (+ *gen*)
draw up, I	τάσσω ἔταξα
drink, I	πίνω ἔπιον
drive, I	ἐλαύνω ἤλασα

322

each	ἕκαστος -η -ον
each other	ἀλλήλους -ας
earth	γῆ γῆς ἡ
easier	ῥᾴων -ον (ῥᾷον-)
easiest	ῥᾷστος -η -ον
easy	ῥᾴδιος -α -ον
eat, I	ἐσθίω ἔφαγον
educate, I	παιδεύω ἐπαίδευσα
eight	ὀκτώ
eighth	ὄγδοος -η -ον
either ... or	ἤ ... ἤ
empire	ἀρχή -ῆς ἡ
encamp, I	στρατοπεδεύομαι ἐστρατοπεδευσάμην
end	τέλος -ους τό
enemy (personal)	ἐχθρός -οῦ ὁ
enemy (in war)	πολέμιοι -ων οἱ
enjoy, I	ἥδομαι ἥσθην (+ *dat*)
enough	ἱκανός -ή -όν
enquire, I	πυνθάνομαι ἐπυθόμην
enslave, I	δουλόω ἐδούλωσα
equal	ἴσος -η -ον
especially	μάλιστα
even	καί
evening	ἑσπέρα -ας ἡ
event	συμφορά -ᾶς ἡ
ever	ποτέ
every	πᾶς πᾶσα πᾶν (παντ-), ἕκαστος -η -ον
everywhere	πανταχοῦ
examine, I	σκοπέω ἐσκεψάμην
excellence	ἀρετή -ῆς ἡ
except	πλήν (+ *gen*)
excessively, too much	ἄγαν
expedition (military),	
I make/go on an	στρατεύω ἐστράτευσα
experience, I	πάσχω ἔπαθον
eye	ὀφθαλμός -οῦ ὁ
fair (with justice)	δίκαιος -α -ον
faithful	πιστός -ή -όν
fall, I	πίπτω ἔπεσον
fall into, I	εἰσπίπτω εἰσέπεσον
family	γένος -ους τό
far as, as	μέχρι (+ *gen*)
fare, I	πράσσω ἔπραξα (*foll adv*)
father	πατήρ -τρός ὁ
fatherland	πατρίς -ίδος ἡ
fear	φόβος -ου ὁ
fear, I	φοβέομαι ἐφοβήθην

few	ὀλίγοι -αι -α
fewer	ἐλάσσονες -α
fewest	ἐλάχιστοι -αι -α
field	ἀγρός -οῦ ὁ
fifth	πέμπτος -η -ον
fight, I	μάχομαι ἐμαχεσάμην
fight a sea-battle, I	ναυμαχέω ἐναυμάχησα
finally	τέλος
find, I	εὑρίσκω ηὗρον
find out, I	γιγνώσκω ἔγνων, (*implying* by enquiry) πυνθάνομαι ἐπυθόμην
fine	καλός -ή -όν
fire	πῦρ πυρός τό
fire at, I	βάλλω ἔβαλον, (*implying* with arrows) τοξεύω ἐτόξευσα
first (*adj*)	πρῶτος -η -ον
first (*adv*), at first	πρῶτον
first light, at	ἅμ' ἡμέρᾳ
fish	ἰχθύς -ύος ὁ
five	πέντε
flee, I	φεύγω ἔφυγον
fleet	ναυτικόν -οῦ τό
follow, I	ἕπομαι ἑσπόμην (+ *dat*)
following way, in the	ὧδε
food	σῖτος -ου ὁ
foolish	μῶρος -α -ον
foot	πούς ποδός ὁ
footsoldiers	πεζοί -ῶν οἱ
for	γάρ*
for the purpose of	ἐπί (+ *acc*)
force	βία -ας ἡ
force, I	ἀναγκάζω ἠνάγκασα
foreign	βάρβαρος -ον
foreigner	ξένος -ου ὁ
forest	ὕλη -ης ἡ
fort, fortification	τείχισμα -ατος τό
fortunate	εὐτυχής -ές
forward, I go	προχωρέω προὐχώρησα
four	τέσσαρες τέσσαρα
fourth	τέταρτος -η -ον
free	ἐλεύθερος -α -ον
friend	φίλος -ου ὁ
friendly	φίλιος -α -ον
from	ἀπό (+ *gen*), (from a person) παρά (+ *gen*)
from beside	παρά (+ *gen*)
from (the place) where	ὅθεν
from where?	πόθεν; (*indirect question*) ὁπόθεν
front of, in	πρό (+ *gen*)
gate	πύλη -ης ἡ

gather (something), I	σύλλεγω συνέλεξα
general	στρατηγός -οῦ ὁ
get, I	κτάομαι ἐκτησάμην
get angry, I	ὀργίζομαι ὠργίσθην (with, + *dat*)
get to know, I	γιγνώσκω ἔγνων
giant	γίγας -αντος ὁ
gift	δῶρον -ου τό
girl	κόρη -ης ἡ, παῖς παιδός ἡ
give, I	δίδωμι ἔδωκα
gladly	ἡδέως
go, I	ἔρχομαι ἦλθον, βαίνω ἔβην (*usu in compounds*)
go, I shall	εἶμι
go away, I	ἀποβαίνω ἀπέβην
go forward, I	προχωρέω προὐχώρησα
go out, I	ἐκβαίνω ἐξέβην
go to(wards), I	προσβαίνω προσέβην
god	θεός -οῦ ὁ
goddess	θεά -ᾶς ἡ
going to, I am	μέλλω (+ *fut inf*)
gold	χρυσός -οῦ ὁ
good	ἀγαθός -ή -όν
grasp hold of, I	λαμβάνομαι ἐλαβόμην (+ *gen*)
great	μέγας μεγάλη μέγα (μεγαλ-)
greater	μείζων -ον (μειζον-)
greatest, very great	μέγιστος -η -ον
Greece	Ἑλλάς -άδος ἡ
Greek, Greek man	Ἕλλην -ηνος ὁ
guard	φύλαξ -ακος ὁ
guard, I	φυλάσσω ἐφύλαξα
guest	ξένος -ου ὁ
guide	ἡγεμών -όνος ὁ
hand	χείρ χειρός ἡ
hands of, at the	πρός (+ *gen*)
happen, I	γίγνομαι ἐγενόμην
harbour	λιμήν -ένος ὁ
harm, I	βλάπτω ἔβλαψα
hate, I	μισέω ἐμίσησα
have, I	ἔχω ἔσχον
have come, I	ἥκω
have power over, I	κρατέω ἐκράτησα (+ *gen*)
head	κεφαλή -ῆς ἡ
hear, I	ἀκούω ἤκουσα (+ *acc of thing, gen of person*)
heaven	οὐρανός -οῦ ὁ
heavy	βαρύς -εῖα -ύ
help, I	(*often implying* run to help) βοηθέω ἐβοήθησα (+ *dat*), (*implying* benefit) ὠφελέω ὠφέλησα
her (*acc pronoun*)	αὐτήν
here	ἐνθάδε

here, I am	πάρειμι *imperf* παρῆν
here, to	δεῦρο
herself (*reflexive*)	ἑαυτήν
hesitate, I	μέλλω (+ *fut inf*)
hide (something), I	κρύπτω ἔκρυψα
high	ὑψηλός -ή -όν
hill	ὄρος -ους τό
him	αὐτόν
himself (*reflexive*)	ἑαυτόν
hinder, I	κωλύω ἐκώλυσα
hit (strike), I	τύπτω ἔτυψα
hit (pelt), I	βάλλω ἔβαλον
holy	ἱερός -ά -όν
honour	τιμή -ῆς ἡ
honour, I	τιμάω ἐτίμησα
hope, I	ἐλπίζω ἤλπισα (+ *fut inf*)
horse	ἵππος -ου ὁ
horseman	ἱππεύς -έως ὁ
host	ξένος -ου ὁ
hostile (as personal enemy)	ἐχθρός -ά -όν
hostile (as enemy in war)	πολέμιος -α -ον
hour	ὥρα -ας ἡ
house	οἰκία -ας ἡ
how?	πῶς;
how big?	πόσος; -η; -ον; (*indirect question*) ὁπόσος -η -ον
how many?	πόσοι; -αι; -α; (*indirect question*) ὁπόσοι -αι -α
however	μέντοι*
human being	ἄνθρωπος -ου ὁ/ἡ
husband	ἀνήρ -δρός ὁ
I	ἐγώ
if	εἰ (+ *indic or opt*), ἐάν (+ *subj*)
if only ... !	εἴθε (+ *opt*)
illness	νόσος -ου ἡ
immediately	εὐθύς
in	ἐν (+ *dat*)
in addition to	πρός (+ *dat*)
in front of	πρό (+ *gen*)
in no way	οὐδαμῶς
in order to	ἵνα (+ *subj/opt*)
	ὅπως (+ *subj/opt*)
	ὡς (+ *fut participle*)
in some way	πως
in the following way	ὧδε
in the time of	ἐπί (+ *gen*)
in this way	οὕτω(ς)
in vain	μάτην
indeed	δή
infantry	πεζοί -ῶν οἱ

inhabit, I	οἰκέω ᾤκησα
inhabitant	ἔνοικος -ου ὁ
instead of	ἀντί (+ *gen*)
intend, I	μέλλω (+ *fut inf*)
into	εἰς (+ *acc*)
invade, I	προσβάλλω προσέβαλον (+ *dat*), εἰσβάλλω εἰσέβαλον (+ εἰς + *acc*)
invite, I	καλέω ἐκάλεσα
island	νῆσος -ου ἡ
it (*acc pronoun*)	αὐτό
it is necessary (for X to ...)	δεῖ *imperf* ἔδει (+ *acc* + *inf*), (*implying moral obligation*) χρή *imperf* (ἐ)χρῆν (+ *acc* + *inf*)
it is possible	ἔξεστι(ν) *imperf* ἐξῆν (+ *dat*)
journey	ὁδός -οῦ ἡ
judge	κριτής -οῦ ὁ
judgement	γνώμη -ης ἡ
just (with justice)	δίκαιος -α -ον
just as, just like	ὥσπερ
justice	δικαιοσύνη -ης ἡ, δίκη -ης ἡ
kill, I	ἀποκτείνω ἀπέκτεινα
killed, I am	ἀποθνήσκω ἀπέθανον
kind (type)	γένος -ους τό
king	βασιλεύς -έως ὁ
know, I	οἶδα *imperf* ᾔδη, (*implying* know how to) ἐπίσταμαι *imperf* ἠπιστάμην (+ *inf*)
know, I get to	γιγνώσκω ἔγνων
know how (to), I	ἐπίσταμαι ἠπιστάμην
land (country)	χώρα -ας ἡ
land (earth)	γῆ γῆς ἡ
land, by	κατὰ γῆν
language	γλῶσσα -ης ἡ
later	ὕστερον
laugh, I	γελάω ἐγέλασα
law	νόμος -ου ὁ
lawsuit	δίκη -ης ἡ
lead, I	ἄγω ἤγαγον
leader	ἡγεμών -όνος ὁ
lead out, I	ἐξάγω ἐξήγαγον
lead to(wards), I	προσάγω προσήγαγον
learn, I	μανθάνω ἔμαθον
learn by enquiry, I	πυνθάνομαι ἐπυθόμην
least (*adj*)	ἐλάχιστος -η -ον
least (*adv*)	ἥκιστα
least, at	γε*
leave, I	λείπω ἔλιπον
left (over)	λοιπός -ή -όν

less	ἐλάσσων -ον (ἐλασσον-)
letter	ἐπιστολή -ῆς ἡ
life	βίος -ου ὁ
light, at first	ἅμ' ἡμέρᾳ
like, just as	ὥσπερ
like, I	φιλέω ἐφίλησα
lion	λέων -οντος ὁ
listen (to), I	ἀκούω ἤκουσα (+ *acc of thing, gen of person*)
little of, a	ὀλίγος -η -ον
live (in), I	οἰκέω ᾤκησα
livelihood	βίος -ου ὁ
long	μακρός -ά -όν
long ago	πάλαι
look at, I	σκοπέω ἐσκεψάμην
look for, I	ζητέω ἐζήτησα
loss, I am at a	ἀπορέω ἠπόρησα
love, I	φιλέω ἐφίλησα
love (sexual passion)	ἔρως -ωτος ὁ
lucky	εὐτυχής -ές
magistrate	ἄρχων -οντος ὁ
make, I	ποιέω ἐποίησα
make (something) clear, I	δηλόω ἐδήλωσα
man, human being	ἄνθρωπος -ου ὁ
man, male	ἀνήρ -δρός ὁ
manage, I	πράσσω ἔπραξα
many	πολλοί -αί -ά
march, I	πορεύομαι ἐπορεύθην, (*implying* go on military campaign or expedition) στρατεύω ἐστράτευσα
marketplace	ἀγορά -ᾶς ἡ
master	δεσπότης -ου ὁ
matter (affair, business)	πρᾶγμα -ατος τό
meanwhile	ἐν τούτῳ
messenger	ἄγγελος -ου ὁ
military matters	τὰ τοῦ πολέμου
miserable	ἄθλιος -α -ον
money	χρήματα -ων τά
more (of) (*sg*)	πλείων -ον (πλειον-)
more (*pl*)	πλείονες -α
more (*adv*)	μᾶλλον
most (of) (*sg*)	πλεῖστος -η -ον
most (*pl*)	πλεῖστοι -αι -α
mother	μήτηρ -τρος ἡ
mountain	ὄρος -ους τό
mouth	στόμα -ατος τό
much	πολύς πολλή πολύ (πολλ-)
Muse (*goddess of poetic inspiration*)	Μοῦσα -ης ἡ
my	ἐμός -ή -όν

myself (*reflexive*)	ἐμαυτόν -ήν
name	ὄνομα -ατος τό
native land	πατρίς -ίδος ἡ
near	ἐγγύς (+ *gen*)
nearly	σχεδόν
necessary (for X to ...), it is	δεῖ *imperf* ἔδει (+ *acc*), (*implying moral obligation*) χρή *imperf* (ἐ)χρῆν (+ *acc*)
necessity	ἀνάγκη -ης ἡ
neither ... nor	οὔτε ... οὔτε, μήτε ... μήτε
never	οὔποτε, οὐδέποτε, μήποτε, μηδέποτε
new	νέος -α -ον
next	ἔπειτα
night	νύξ νυκτός ἡ
nine	ἐννέα
ninth	ἔνατος -η -ον
no ... , not any	οὐδείς οὐδεμία οὐδέν (οὐδεν-), μηδείς μηδεμία μηδέν (μηδεν-)
no longer	οὐκέτι, μηκέτι
no way, in	οὐδαμῶς, μηδαμῶς
no-one	οὐδείς (οὐδεν-) οὐδεμία, μηδείς (μηδεν-) μηδεμία
non-Greek	βάρβαρος -ον
not	οὐ (οὐκ *before smooth breathing*, οὐχ *before rough breathing*), (*in contexts other than statements of fact*) μή
not at all	ἥκιστα, (in no way) οὐδαμῶς
not even	οὐδέ, μηδέ
not only ... but also	οὐ μόνον ... ἀλλὰ καί
nothing	οὐδέν, μηδέν
notice, I	αἰσθάνομαι ᾐσθόμην
now (at this time)	νῦν
now (already, by now)	ἤδη
number, large	πλῆθος -ους τό
obey, I	πείθομαι ἐπιθόμην (+ *dat*)
obtain, I	κτάομαι ἐκτησάμην
obvious	δῆλος -η -ον
occasion	καιρός -οῦ ὁ
official (*noun*)	ἄρχων -οντος ὁ
often	πολλάκις
old	ἀρχαῖος -α -ον
old man	γέρων -οντος ὁ
on	ἐπί (+ *dat*)
on account of	διά (+ *acc*)
on behalf of	ὑπέρ (+ *gen*)
on the one hand	
... on the other	μέν* ... δέ*
once (at some time)	ποτε
one	εἷς μία ἕν (ἑν-)
one/the other (of two)	ἕτερος -α -ον

only (*adj*)	μόνος -η -ον
only (*adv*)	μόνον
onto	εἰς (+ *acc*), ἐπί (+ *acc*)
opinion	γνώμη -ης ἡ
opportunity	καιρός -οῦ ὁ
opposite	ἀντί (+ *gen*)
or	ἤ
orator	ῥήτωρ -ορος ὁ
order, I	κελεύω ἐκέλευσα
other	ἄλλος -η -ο
our	ἡμέτερος -α -ον
ourselves (*reflexive*)	ἡμᾶς αὐτούς -άς
out of	ἐκ (ἐξ *before vowel*) (+ *gen*)
outcome	τέλος -ους τό
passion (sexual love)	ἔρως -ωτος ὁ
past, in the	πάλαι
payment	μισθός -οῦ ὁ
peace	εἰρήνη -ης ἡ
pelt, I	βάλλω ἔβαλον
penalty	δίκη -κς ἡ
people (population, community)	δῆμος -ου ὁ
perceive, I	αἰσθάνομαι ἠσθόμην
perhaps	ἴσως
Persia	Περσική -ῆς ἡ
Persian (man)	Πέρσης -ου ὁ
person	ἄνθρωπος -ου ὁ/ἡ
persuade, I	πείθω ἔπεισα
place	τόπος -ου ὁ, χωρίον -ου τό
place, I	τίθημι ἔθηκα
plain	πεδίον -ου τό
plan	βουλή -ῆς ἡ
plan, I	βουλεύομαι ἐβουλευσάμην
pleasant	ἡδύς -εῖα -ύ
pleased (with), I am	ἥδομαι (+ *dat*)
poet	ποιητής -οῦ ὁ
point out, I	δείκνυμι ἔδειξα
politician	ῥήτωρ -ορος ὁ
poor (man, *or as adj*)	πένης -ητος ὁ
possession	κτῆμα -ατος τό
possible	δυνατός -ή -όν
possible, as quickly as	ὡς τάχιστα
possible, it is	ἔξεστι(ν) *imperf* ἐξῆν (+ *dat*)
power over, I have	κρατέω ἐκράτησα (+ *gen*)
power to, I have the	δύναμαι ἐδυνάμην (+ *inf*)
praise, I	ἐπαινέω ἐπήνησα
prepare, I	παρασκευάζω παρεσκεύασα
presence of, into the	παρά (+ *acc*)

present, I am	πάρειμι *imperf* παρῆν
prevent, I	κωλύω ἐκώλυσα (from, + *gen or inf*)
previously	πρότερον
prison	δεσμωτήριον -ου τό
prisoner (of war)	αἰχμάλωτος -ου ὁ
prize	ἆθλον -ου τό
produce, I	παρέχω παρέσχον
probably	ἴσως
produce, I	παρέχω παρέσχον
promise, I	ὑπισχνέομαι ὑπεσχόμην (+ *fut inf*)
provide, I	παρέχω παρέσχον
prowess	ἀρετή -ῆς ἡ
public speaker	ῥήτωρ -ορος ὁ
public square	ἀγορά -ᾶς ἡ
pull down, I	καθαιρέω καθεῖλον
punish, I	κολάζω ἐκόλασα
purpose	γνώμη -ης ἡ
pursue, I	διώκω ἐδίωξα
put, I	τίθημι ἔθηκα
quick	ταχύς -εῖα -ύ
quicker	θάσσων -ον (θασσον-)
quickest	τάχιστος -η -ον
quickly	ταχέως
quickly as possible, as	ὡς τάχιστα
race (nation *etc*)	γένος -ους τό, ἔθνος -ους τό
ransom, I	λύομαι ἐλυσάμην
rather	μᾶλλον
ravage, I	τέμνω ἔτεμον
ready	ἕτοῖμος -η -ον
ready, I get (something)	παρασκευάζω παρεσκεύασα
realise, I	γιγνώσκω ἔγνων
reason	λόγος -ου ὁ
receive, I	δέχομαι ἐδεξάμην
recent	νέος -α -ον
release, I	λύω ἔλυσα
released, I get (someone)	λύομαι ἐλυσάμην
reliable	πίστος -η -ον
remain, I	μένω ἔμεινα
remaining, left	λοιπός -ή -όν
reply, I	ἀποκρίνομαι ἀπεκρινάμην
report, I	ἀγγέλλω ἤγγειλα
resist, I	ἀμύνομαι ἠμυνάμην
responsible	αἴτιος -α -ον
result, as a	ὥστε
retreat, I	ἀναχωρέω ἀνεχώρησα
reveal, I	φαίνω ἔφηνα
reward	ἆθλον -ου τό

331

rich	πλούσιος -α -ον
right (hand side) (*adj*)	δεξιός -ά -όν
right (just)	δίκαιος -α -ον
right time	καιρός -οῦ ὁ
river	ποταμός -οῦ ὁ
road	ὁδός -οῦ ἡ
rule	ἀρχή -ῆς ἡ
rule, I	ἄρχω ἦρξα (+ *gen*), κρατέω ἐκράτησα (+ *gen*)
ruler (chief, magistrate)	ἄρχων -οντος ὁ
ruler (king)	βασιλεύς -έως
run, I	τρέχω ἔδραμον
run away, I	φεύγω ἔφυγον, ἀποτρέχω ἀπέδραμον
run out, I	ἐκτρέχω ἐξέδραμον
run to help, I	βοηθέω ἐβοήθησα (+ *dat*)
run to(wards), I	προστρέχω προσέδραμον
sacred	ἱερός -ά -όν
sacrifice, I	θύω ἔθυσα
safe	ἀσφαλής -ές
said, he/she (*usu interrupting*	
direct quotation)	ἔφη
sail, I	πλέω ἔπλευσα
sailor	ναύτης -ου ὁ
same, the	ὁ αὐτός, ἡ αὐτή, τὸ αὐτό
same time, at the ... (as)	ἅμα (+ *dat, or as adv*)
save, I	σῴζω ἔσωσα
saw, I	εἶδον
say, I	λέγω εἶπον *or (less commonly)* ἔλεξα, φημί *imperf* ἔφην
scarcely	μόλις
sea	θάλασσα -ης ἡ
sea-battle	ναυμαχία -ας ἡ
sea-battle, I fight a	ναυμαχέω ἐναυμάχησα
search for, I	ζητέω ἐζήτησα
second	δεύτερος -α -ον
secretly	λάθρα
see, I	ὁράω ὄψομαι
seek, I	ζητέω ἐζήτησα
seem, I	δοκέω ἔδοξα
seems good to, it	δοκεῖ ἔδοξε (+ *dat*)
seize, I	ἁρπάζω ἥρπασα
self	αὐτός -ή -ό
send, I	πέμπω ἔπεμψα
send to(wards), I	προσπέμπω προσέπεμψα
set free, I	ἐλευθερόω ἠλευθέρωσα
seven	ἑπτά
seventh	ἕβδομος -η -ον
shameful	αἰσχρός -ά -όν
sharp	ὀξύς -εῖα -ύ

shield	ἀσπίς -ίδος ἡ
ship	ναῦς νεώς ἡ
shoot (fire an arrow), I	τοξεύω ἐτόξευσα
short time, after a	δι' ὀλίγου
shout	βοή -ῆς ἡ
shout, I	βοάω ἐβόησα
show, I	(make clear) δηλόω ἐδήλωσα, (point out) δείκνυμι ἔδειξα, (reveal) φαίνω ἔφηνα
silence	σιγή -ῆς ἡ
silence, in	σιγῇ
since (as, because)	ἐπεί, ἐπειδή (or use participle)
sit, I	καθίζω ἐκάθισα
six	ἕξ
sixth	ἕκτος -η -ον
skilful	δεξιός -ά -όν
skill	τέχνη -ης ἡ
sky, heaven	οὐρανός -οῦ ὁ
slave	δοῦλος -ου ὁ
sleep	ὕπνος -ου ὁ
sleep, I	καθεύδω imperf ἐκάθευδον or καθηῦδον
slow	βραδύς -εῖα -ύ
small	μικρός -ά -όν
small amount of	ὀλίγος -η -ον
snatch, I	ἁρπάζω ἥρπασα
so	οὕτω(ς)
so big, so great	τοσοῦτος -αύτη -οῦτο
so many	τοσοῦτοι -αῦται -αῦτα
soldier	στρατιώτης -ου ὁ
somehow, in some way	πως
someone	τις τινός
something	τι τινός
sometime	ποτέ
somewhere	που
somewhere, from	ποθέν
somewhere, to	ποι
son	υἱός -οῦ ὁ, παῖς παιδός ὁ
soon, after a short time	δι' ὀλίγου
sort, of such a	τοιοῦτος -αύτη -οῦτο
sort of, what?	ποῖος; -α; -ον; (indirect question) ὁποῖος -α -ον
sort which, of the	οἷος -α -ον
Sparta	Σπάρτη -ης ἡ
Spartans	Λακεδαιμόνιοι -ων οἱ
speak, I	λέγω εἶπον or (less commonly) ἔλεξα
speaker (public)	ῥήτωρ -ορος ὁ
stay, I	μένω ἔμεινα
steal, I	κλέπτω ἔκλεψα
still, even now	ἔτι
stone	λίθος -ου ὁ
stop (something), I	παύω ἔπαυσα

stop (myself), I	παύομαι ἐπαυσάμην
storm	χειμών -ῶνος ὁ
story (myth, fable)	μῦθος -ου ὁ
story (factual or historical)	λόγος -ου ὁ
strange	δεινός -ή -όν
stranger	ξένος -ου ὁ
strength	βία -ας ἡ
strike, I	τύπτω ἔτυψα
strong	ἰσχυρός -ά -όν
strongly	σφόδρα
stupid	μῶρος -α -ον
such, of such a kind	τοιοῦτος -αύτη -οῦτο
suffer, I	πάσχω ἔπαθον
sufficient	ἱκανός -ή -όν
sun	ἥλιος -ου ὁ
supper	δεῖπνον -ου τό
surely	δή
surely ...?	ἀρ᾽ (= ἀρα) οὐ;
surely ... not?	ἀρα μή;
swear, I	ὄμνυμι ὤμοσα (*usu* + *fut inf*)
sweet	ἡδύς -εῖα -ύ
swift	ταχύς -εῖα -ύ
swifter	θάσσων -ον (θασσον-)
swiftest	τάχιστος -η -ον
sword	ξίφος -ους τό
take, I	λαμβάνω ἔλαβον, (*often implying* capture) αἱρέω εἷλον
take down, I	καθαιρέω καθεῖλον
take hold of, I	λαμβάνομαι ἐλαβόμην (+ *gen*)
take (something) badly, I	βαρέως φέρω
task	ἔργον -ου τό
teach, I	διδάσκω ἐδίδαξα
teacher	διδάσκαλος -ου ὁ
tear, teardrop	δάκρυον -ου τό
tell, I (say, speak)	λέγω εἶπον *or* (*less commonly*) ἔλεξα
tell, I (order)	κελεύω ἐκέλευσα
temple	ἱερόν -οῦ τό
ten	δέκα
tenth	δέκατος -η -ον
terrible	δεινός -ή -όν
than	ἤ
that (*pronoun* that one there)	ἐκεῖνος -η -ο
that (*conjunction* the fact that)	ὅτι, ὡς
that (*conjunction* with the result that)	ὥστε
the	ὁ ἡ τό
them (*acc pronoun*)	αὐτούς -άς
themselves (*reflexive*)	ἑαυτούς -άς, σφᾶς αὐτούς -άς
then (next)	ἔπειτα

then (at that time)	τότε
there	ἐκεῖ
therefore	οὖν*
these	οὗτοι αὗται ταῦτα, (*implying* here present *or* the following) οἵδε αἵδε τάδε
thing (matter, business)	πρᾶγμα -ατος τό
think, I	νομίζω ἐνόμισα
third	τρίτος -η -ον
this	οὗτος αὕτη τοῦτο, (*implying* here present *or* the following) ὅδε ἥδε τόδε
this way, in	οὗτω(ς)
those	ἐκεῖνοι -αι -α
three	τρεῖς τρία
through	δία (+ *gen*) (+ *acc* = on account of)
throughout	κατά (+ *acc*)
throw, I	βάλλω ἔβαλον
throw away, I	ἀποβάλλω ἀπέβαλον
throw in, I	ἐμβάλλω ἐνέβαλον
throw out, I	ἐκβάλλω ἐξέβαλον
time	χρόνος -ου ὁ
time, at the same ... (as)	ἅμα (+ *dat*, *or as adv*)
time of, in the	ἐπί (+ *gen*)
time, right / appropriate	καιρός -οῦ ὁ
to (towards)	πρός (+ *acc*)
to (a person)	ὡς (+ *acc*)
to (into)	εἰς (+ *acc*)
to here	δεῦρο
to (the place) where	οἷ
to the presence of	παρά (+ *acc*)
tongue	γλῶσσα -ης ἡ
too much	ἄγαν
touch, I	ἅπτομαι ἡψάμην (+ *gen*)
towards	πρός (+ *acc*)
town	ἄστυ -εως τό
train, I	παιδεύω ἐπαίδευσα
travel, I	πορεύομαι ἐπορεύθην
treat (someone) (e.g. well), I	ποιέω ἐποίησα (*foll adv*, + *acc*)
tree	δένδρον -ου τό
tribe	ἔθνος -ους τό
trireme	τριήρης -ους ἡ
true	ἀληθής -ές
trust, I	πιστεύω ἐπίστευσα (+ *dat*)
trustworthy	πιστός -ή -όν
try, I	πειράομαι ἐπειρασάμην
turn, I	τρέπω ἔτρεψα
two	δύο
type	γενος -ους τό
ugly	αἰσχρός -ά -όν

under (to under)	ὑπό (+ acc)
under (resting under)	ὑπό (+ dat)
understand (learn), I	μανθάνω ἔμαθον
understand (have the skill), I	ἐπίσταμαι imperf ἠπιστάμην
unfasten	λύω ἔλυσα
unfortunate	δυστυχής -ές
unjust	ἄδικος -ον
unjustly (to), I act	ἀδικέω ἠδίκησα (+ acc)
unlucky	δυστυχής -ές
unsuccessfully	μάτην
until	μέχρι (+ gen), ἑώς
up	ἀνά (+ acc)
use, I	χράομαι ἐχρησάμην (+ dat)
useful	χρήσιμος -η -ον
vain, in	μάτην
very	μάλα
very bad	κάκιστος -η -ον
very fine, very beautiful	κάλλιστος -η -ον
very good	ἄριστος -η -ον, (implying very virtuous) βέλτιστος -η -ον
very great	μέγιστος -η -ον
very many	πλεῖστοι -αι -α
very much (adv)	μάλιστα, (implying strongly) σφόδρα
victory	νίκη -ης ἡ
village	κώμη -ης ἡ
violence	βία -ας ἡ
virtue	ἀρετή -ῆς ἡ
voice	φωνή -ῆς ἡ
wages	μισθός -οῦ ὁ
wait (for), I	μένω ἔμεινα
wall	τεῖχος -ους τό
want, I	βούλομαι imperf ἐβουλόμην
war	πόλεμος -ου ὁ
warfare	τὰ τοῦ πολέμου
warship	τριήρης -ους ἡ
water	ὕδωρ -ατος τό
way	ὁδός -οῦ ὁ
way, in no	οὐδαμῶς
way, in this	οὕτω(ς), (implying as follows) ὧδε
we	ἡμεῖς
weak	ἀσθενής -ές
wealthy	πλούσιος -α -ον
weapons	ὅπλα -ων τά
weather, bad	χειμών -ῶνος ὁ
weep, I	δακρύω ἐδάκρυσα
well	εὖ
went, I	ἦλθον
what?	τί; τίνος;

what sort of?	ποῖος; -α; -ον; (*indirect question*) ὁποῖος -α -ον
when?	πότε;
when (since)	ἐπεί, ἐπειδή (*or use participle*)
when (at the time when)	ὅτε (*or use participle*)
where (at)?	ποῦ; (*indirect question*) ὅπου
where (in the place in which)	οὗ
where from?	πόθεν; (*indirect question*) ὁπόθεν
where to?	ποῖ; (*indirect question*)ὅποι
whether ... or	εἴτε ... εἴτε, πότερον ... ἤ
which?	τίς; τί; (τίν-;)
which (of two)?	πότερος; -α; -ον; (*indirect question*) ὁπότερος -α -ον
which (*relative*)	ὅς ἥ ὅ
while	ἕως (*or use pres participle*)
who?	τίς; (τιν-;)
who, which (*relative*)	ὅς ἥ ὅ (*or use participle*)
whoever, whichever	ὅστις ἥτις ὅ τι
why?	διὰ τί;
wide	εὐρύς -εῖα -ύ
wife	γυνή γυναικός ἡ
willing, willingly	ἑκών -οῦσα -όν (ἑκοντ-)
willing, I am	ἐθέλω ἠθέλησα
win (conquer), I	νικάω ἐνίκησα
win (prizes), I	φέρομαι ἠνεγκάμην/-όμην
wind	ἄνεμος -ου ὁ
wine	οἶνος -ου ὁ
winter	χειμών -ῶνος ὁ
wisdom	σοφία -ας ἡ
wise	σοφός -ή -όν
wish, I	βούλομαι *imperf* ἐβουλόμην, ἐθέλω ἠθέλησα
with	μετά (+ *gen*)
with difficulty	μόλις
with the result that	ὥστε
withdraw, I	ἀναχωρέω ἀνεχώρησα
without	ἄνευ (+ *gen*)
woman	γυνή γυναικός ἡ
wood (forest)	ὕλη -ης ἡ
word	λόγος -ου ὁ
work	ἔργον -ου τό
worse	κακίων -ον (κακιον-), (*implying* inferior) χείρων -ον (χειρον-)
worst	κάκιστος -η -ον, (*implying* most inferior) χείριστος -η -ον
worthy (of)	ἄξιος -α -ον (+ *gen*)
wound	τραῦμα -ατος τό
wretched	ἄθλιος -α -ον, δυστυχής -ές
write, I	γράφω ἔγραψα
wrong, I do	ἀδικέω ἠδίκησα
year	ἔτος -ους τό
yet	ἔτι
you (*sg*)	σύ

you (*pl*)	ὑμεῖς
young	νέος -α -ον
young man	νεανίας -ου ὁ
your (of you *sg*)	σός σή σόν
your (of you *pl*)	ὑμέτερος -α -ον
yourself (*reflexive*)	σεαυτόν -ήν
yourselves (*reflexive*)	ὑμᾶς αὐτούς -άς
Zeus	Ζεύς Διός ὁ

Greek to English

Verbs are usually given with present and aorist (compound verbs whose meaning can easily be deduced are not usually given).
Nouns are given with nominative, genitive, and article to show gender.
Adjectives are given with masculine, feminine, and neuter.
* = comes second word in sentence or clause.

		chapter:
ἀγαγ-	(*aor stem of* ἄγω)	
ἀγαθός -ή -όν	good; brave	(3)
ἄγαν	(*adv*) too much, excessively	(9)
ἀγγέλλω ἤγγειλα	I report, I announce	(6)
ἄγγελος -ου ὁ	messenger	(1)
ἀγορά -ᾶς ἡ	agora, marketplace, public square	(2)
ἀγρός -οῦ ὁ	field; *pl* countryside	(5)
ἄγω ἤγαγον	I lead	(1)
ἀγών -ῶνος ὁ	contest	(5)
ἀδελφός -οῦ ὁ	brother	(7)
ἀδικέω ἠδίκησα	I do wrong to (someone), I act unjustly	(9)
ἄδικος -ον	unjust, criminal	(9)
ἀεί	always	(3)
Ἀθῆναι -ῶν αἱ	Athens	(7)
Ἀθηναῖος -α -ον	Athenian	(3)
Ἀθήνη -ης ἡ	Athene (goddess)	(7)
ἄθλιος -α -ον	miserable, wretched	(7)
ἄθλον -ου τό	prize, reward	(2)
ἀθυμέω ἠθύμησα	I am despondent, I am disheartened	(9)
αἷμα -ατος τό	blood	(8)
αἱρέω εἷλον	I take	(9)
αἱρέομαι εἱλόμην	I choose	(9)
αἰσθάνομαι ᾐσθόμην	I perceive, I notice	(8)
αἰσχρός -ά -όν	disgraceful, shameful; ugly	(10)
αἰτέω ᾔτησα	I ask for, I beg	(9)
αἴτιος -α -ον	responsible (for), to blame (for) (+ *gen*)	(10)
αἰχμάλωτος -ου ὁ	prisoner, prisoner of war	(7)
ἀκούω ἤκουσα	I hear, I listen (to) (+ *acc of thing/gen of person*)	(1)
ἀληθής -ές	true	(9)
ἀλλά	but	(2)
ἀλλήλους -ας	each other	(8)
ἄλλος -η -ο	other, another	(5)
ἅμα	at the same time (as + *dat*)	(10)
ἅμ᾽ ἡμέρᾳ	at daybreak, at first light	(10)
ἀμείνων -ον (ἄμεινον-)	better (*comparative of* ἀγαθός)	(10)
ἀμύνομαι ἠμυνάμην	I resist, I defend myself (against) (+ *acc*)	(12)
ἄν	(*makes indefinite/potential/conditional e.g.*	

	would, could)	(12)
ἀνά	(+ *acc*) up	(10)
ἀναγκάζω ἠνάγκασα	I force, I compel	(7)
ἀνάγκη -ης ἡ	necessity, compulsion	(7)
ἀναχωρέω ἀνεχώρησα	I retreat, I withdraw	(9)
ἀνδρεῖος -α -ον	brave	(3)
ἄνεμος -ου ὁ	wind	(5)
ἄνευ	without (+ *gen*)	(10)
ἀνήρ ἀνδρός ὁ	man, male, husband	(7)
ἄνθρωπος -ου ὁ (/ἡ)	man, human being, person; (*as f*) woman	(2)
ἀντί	instead of, opposite (+ *gen*)	(10)
ἄξιος -α -ον	worthy, deserving (of + *gen*)	(7)
ἄξω	(*fut of* ἄγω)	
ἄπειμι	I am away	(5)
ἀπό	from, away from (+ *gen*)	(3)
ἀποβάλλω ἀπέβαλον	I throw away	(4)
ἀποθνῄσκω ἀπέθανον	I die, I am killed	(3)
ἀποκρίνομαι		
ἀπεκρινάμην	I answer, I reply	(8)
ἀποκτείνω ἀπέκτεινα	I kill	(2)
ἀπορέω ἠπόρησα	I am at a loss, I am in doubt	(9)
ἅπτομαι ἡψάμην	I touch (+ *gen*)	(12)
ἆρα	(*introduces an open question e.g.* Is it?)	(3)
ἆρ' (= ἆρα) οὐ;	surely ... ? (*introduces a question expecting the answer* Yes)	(8)
ἆρα μή;	surely ... not? (*introduces a question expecting the answer* No)	(11)
ἀρετή -ῆς ἡ	excellence, prowess, courage, virtue	(7)
ἄριστος -η -ον	best, very good (*superlative of* ἀγαθός)	(8)
ἅρμα -ατος τό	chariot	(8)
ἁρπάζω ἥρπασα	I seize, I snatch	(7)
ἀρχαῖος -α -ον	old, ancient	(7)
ἀρχή -ῆς ἡ	rule, empire; beginning	(7)
ἄρχω ἦρξα	I rule (+ *gen*)	(8)
ἄρχομαι ἠρξάμην	I begin (+ *gen*)	(8)
ἄρχων -οντος ὁ	ruler, official, magistrate	(5)
ἀσθενής -ές	weak	(9)
ἀσπίς -ίδος ἡ	shield	(9)
ἄστυ -εως τό	city, town	(9)
ἀσφαλής -ές	safe	(9)
αὖθις	again	(6)
αὐτός -ή -ό	self; same; (*not nom*) him, her, it	(6)
ἀφικνέομαι ἀφικόμην	I arrive	(9)
βαθύς -εῖα -ύ	deep	(9)
βαίνω ἔβην	I go	(1)

βαλ-	(*aor stem of* βάλλω)	
βάλλω ἔβαλον	I throw; I pelt, I fire at	(4)
βάρβαρος -ον	non-Greek, foreign, strange, barbarian	(9)
βαρύς -εῖα -ύ	heavy	(9)
βαρέως φέρω	I take (something) badly	(9)
βασιλεύς -έως ὁ	king	(9)
βέλτιστος -η -ον	best, very good, most/very virtuous (*superlative of* ἀγαθός)	(10)
βελτίων -ον (βελτιον-)	better, more virtuous (*comparative of* ἀγαθός)	(10)
βία -ας ἡ	force, strength, violence	(8)
βίβλος -ου ἡ	book	(4)
βίος -ου ὁ	life, livelihood	(2)
βλάπτω ἔβλαψα	I harm, I damage	(5)
βοάω ἐβόησα	I shout	(10)
βοή -ῆς ἡ	shout	(1)
βοηθέω ἐβοήθησα	I help, I run to help (+ *dat*)	(9)
βουλεύομαι ἐβουλευσάμην	I discuss, I deliberate, I plan, I decide	(11)
βουλή -ῆς ἡ	plan; council	(1)
βούλομαι *imperf* ἐβουλόμην	I wish, I want	(8)
βραδύς -εῖα -ύ	slow	(9)
γάρ*	for	(3)
γε*	at least, at any rate, even	(11)
γελάω ἐγέλασα	I laugh	(10)
γεν-	(*aor stem of* γίγνομαι)	
γενήσομαι	(*fut of* γίγνομαι)	
γένος -ους τό	type, family, race, descent, birth	(9)
γέρων -οντος ὁ	old man	(5)
γῆ γῆς ἡ	earth, land	(1)
γίγας -αντος ὁ	giant	(5)
γίγνομαι ἐγενόμην	I become, I happen	(8)
γιγνώσκω ἔγνων	I get to know, I realise	(3)
γλῶσσα -ης ἡ	tongue, language	(8)
γνώμη -ης ἡ	opinion, belief, judgement, purpose	(8)
γνώσομαι	(*fut of* γιγνώσκω)	
γράφω ἔγραψα	I write, I draw	(1)
γυνή γυναικός ἡ	woman, wife	(7)
δάκρυον -ου τό	tear, teardrop	(8)
δακρύω ἐδάκρυσα	I cry, I weep	(7)
δέ*	and; but	(3)
δεῖ *imperf* ἔδει	it is necessary (for X to ..., + *acc* + *inf*)	(10)
δείκνυμι ἔδειξα	I show, I point out	(12)

341

δεινός -ή -όν	strange, terrible, formidably clever	(3)
δειξ-	(*aor stem of* δείκνυμι)	
δεῖπνον -ου τό	dinner	(4)
δέκα	ten	(2)
δέκατος -η -ον	tenth	(6)
δένδρον -ου τό	tree	(2)
δεξ-	(*aor stem of* δέχομαι)	
δεξιός -ά -όν	right (hand side); clever, skilful	(6)
δεσμός -οῦ ὁ	chain, binding, fetter	(7)
δεσμωτήριον -ου τό	prison	(2)
δεσπότης -ου ὁ	master	(7)
δεῦρο	here, to here	(8)
δεύτερος -α -ον	second	(6)
δέχομαι ἐδεξάμην	I receive	(8)
δή	indeed, certainly, surely	(11)
δῆλος -η -ον	clear, obvious	(7)
δηλόω ἐδήλωσα	I show, I reveal	(12)
δῆμος -ου ὁ	people, community	(2)
διά	(+ *acc*) on account of, because of	(5)
	(+ *gen*) through	(5)
δι' ὀλίγου	after a short time, soon	(10)
διὰ τί;	why?	(5)
διαφθείρω διέφθειρα	I destroy, I corrupt	(7)
διδάσκαλος -ου ὁ	teacher	(1)
διδάσκω ἐδίδαξα	I teach	(1)
δίδωμι ἔδωκα	I give	(12)
δίκαιος -α -ον	just, fair, upright, moral	(7)
δικαιοσύνη -ης ἡ	justice	(1)
δίκη -ης ἡ	justice; lawsuit; penalty	(7)
Διός	(*irreg gen of* Ζεύς)	
διότι	because	(3)
διώκω ἐδίωξα	I chase, I pursue	(1)
δοκέω ἔδοξα	I seem; I think	(9)
δοκεῖ ἔδοξε	(+ *dat*) it seems good to X, X decides	
	(to, + *inf*)	(10)
δοῦλος -ου ὁ	slave	(1)
δουλόω ἐδούλωσα	I enslave	(12)
δραμ-	(*aor stem of* τρέχω)	
δραμοῦμαι	(*fut of* τρέχω)	
δύναμαι		
imperf ἐδυνάμην	I can, I am able, I have the power (to, + *inf*)	(11)
δυνατός -ή -όν	capable, able; possible	(12)
δύο	two	(4)
δυστυχής -ές	unfortunate, unlucky	(9)
δῶρον -ου τό	gift	(2)
δώσω	(*fut of* δίδωμι)	

ἐάν	if (+ *subj, in fut open condition*)	(11)
ἑαυτόν -ήν -ό	himself, herself, itself	(8)
ἑαυτούς -άς -ά	themselves	(8)
ἐάω εἴασα	I allow	(10)
ἔβαλον	(*aor of* βάλλω)	
ἕβδομος -η -ον	seventh	(6)
ἔβην	(*aor of* βαίνω)	
ἐβλήθην	(*aor passive of* βάλλω)	
ἐγγύς	near (+ *gen*)	(5)
ἐγενόμην	(*aor of* γίγνομαι)	
ἔγνων	(*aor of* γιγνώσκω)	
ἐγνώσθην	(*aor passive of* γιγνώσκω)	
ἐγώ ἐμοῦ/μου	I, me	(5)
ἔδομαι	(*fut of* ἐσθίω)	
ἔδραμον	(*aor of* τρέχω)	
ἐθέλω ἠθέλησα	I wish, I am willing	(3)
ἔθνος -ους τό	tribe, race, nation	(9)
εἰ	if	(7)
εἴασα	(*aor of* ἐάω)	
εἶδον	I saw (*aor of* ὁράω)	(5)
εἴθε	if only ... ! would that! (+ *opt, introducing a wish*)	(12)
εἷλον	(*aor of* αἱρέω)	
εἰμί *imperf* ἦ (*or* ἦν)	I am	(2)
εἶμι	I shall go	(8)
εἶναι	(*inf of* εἰμί = to be)	(6)
εἶπον	I said (*used as aor of* λέγω)	(4)
εἰρήνη -ης ἡ	peace	(1)
εἰς (*or* ἐς)	into, onto, to (+ *acc*)	(1)
εἷς μία ἕν (ἑν-)	one	(6)
εἰσβάλλω εἰσέβαλον	I invade (+ εἰς + *acc*)	(12)
εἰσπίπτω εἰσέπεσον	I fall into	(4)
εἴτε ... εἴτε	whether ... or	(11)
ἐκ (ἐξ *before vowel*)	out of (+ *gen*)	(3)
ἕκαστος -η -ον	each	(5)
ἐκβαίνω ἐξέβην	I go out	(4)
ἐκεῖ	there	(3)
ἐκεῖνος -η -ο	that, *pl* those	(7)
ἐκκλησία -ας ἡ	assembly, meeting	(2)
ἕκτος -η -ον	sixth	(6)
ἐκτρέχω ἐξέδραμον	I run out	(4)
ἑκών -οῦσα -όν (ἑκοντ-)	willing, willingly	(7)
ἑλ-	(*aor stem of* αἱρέω)	
ἔλαβον	(*aor of* λαμβάνω)	
ἐλασ-	(*aor stem of* ἐλαύνω)	

343

ἐλάσσων -ον (ἔλασσον-)	less, smaller (amount of), weaker, inferior,	
	pl fewer (*comparative of* ὀλίγος)	(10)
ἐλαύνω ἤλασα	I drive	(3)
ἐλάχιστος -η -ον	least, smallest, *pl* fewest (*superlative of*	
	ὀλίγος)	(10)
ἐλεύθερος -α -ον	free	(3)
ἐλευθερόω ἠλευθέρωσα	I set free	(12)
ἐλήφθην	(*aor passive of* λαμβάνω)	
ἐλθ-	(*aor stem of* ἔρχομαι)	
ἔλιπον	(*aor of* λείπω)	
Ἑλλάς -άδος ἡ	Greece	(10)
Ἕλλην -ηνος ὁ	Greek, Greek man	(10)
ἐλπίζω ἤλπισα	I hope (+ *fut inf*)	(10)
ἔμαθον	(*aor of* μανθάνω)	
ἐμαυτόν -ήν	myself	(8)
ἐμβάλλω ἐνέβαλον	I throw in, I thrust in	(5)
ἔμεινα	(*aor of* μένω)	
ἐμός -ή -όν	my	(5)
ἐν	in, on, among (+ *dat*)	(3)
ἐν τούτῳ	meanwhile	(10)
ἕν	one (*n*)	(6)
ἔνατος -η -ον	ninth	(6)
ἐνεγκ-	(*aor stem of* φέρω)	
ἐνθάδε	here	(3)
ἐννέα	nine	(6)
ἔνοικος -ου ὁ	inhabitant	(7)
ἕξ	six	(6)
ἐξάγω ἐξήγαγον	I lead out	(4)
ἔξεστι(ν) *imperf* ἐξῆν	it is possible (for X to ... , + *dat* + *inf*)	(10)
ἐπαινέω ἐπήνεσα	I praise	(9)
ἔπαθον	(*aor of* πάσχω)	
ἐπεί	when, since	(4)
ἐπειδή	when, since	(12)
ἔπειτα	then, next	(4)
ἔπεσον	(*aor of* πίπτω)	
ἐπί	(+ *acc*) against, to, onto, for the purpose of	(10)
	(+ *gen*) in the time of	(10)
	(+ *dat*) on, on the condition of	(10)
ἔπιον	(*aor of* πίνω)	
ἐπίσταμαι		
imperf ἠπιστάμην	I understand, I know (how to, + *inf*)	(11)
ἐπιστολή -ῆς ἡ	letter	(1)
ἔπλευσα	(*aor of* πλέω)	
ἕπομαι ἑσπόμην	I follow (+ *dat*)	(8)
ἑπτά	seven	(6)
ἐπυθόμην	(*aor of* πυνθάνομαι)	

ἔργον -ου τό	work, task, deed, action	(2)
ἔρχομαι ἦλθον	I come, I go	(8)
ἔρως -ωτος ὁ	love, sexual passion	(9)
ἐρωτάω ἠρώτησα		
or ἠρόμην	I ask (a question)	(10)
ἐσθίω ἔφαγον	I eat	(4)
ἐσκεψάμην	(aor of σκοπέω)	
ἑσπέρα -ας ἡ	evening	(2)
ἑσπόμην	(aor of ἕπομαι)	
ἔσχον	(aor of ἔχω)	
ἔσωσα	(aor of σῴζω)	
ἔταξα	(aor of τάσσω)	
ἐτάφην	(aor passive of θάπτω)	
ἔτεμον	(aor of τέμνω)	
ἕτερος -α -ον	one/the other (of two); different	(11)
ἔτι	still	(5)
ἕτοῖμος -η -ον	ready	(5)
ἔτος -ους τό	year	(9)
εὖ	well	(7)
εὐθύς	immediately	(6)
εὑρ-	(aor stem of εὑρίσκω)	
εὑρήσω	(fut of εὑρίσκω)	
εὑρίσκω ηὗρον	I find	(2)
εὐρύς -εῖα -ύ	broad, wide	(9)
εὐτυχής -ές	fortunate, lucky	(9)
ἔφαγον	(aor of ἐσθίω)	
ἔφη	he/she said (often interrupting direct quotation; imperf of φημί)	(7)
ἔφυγον	(aor of φεύγω)	
ἐχθρός -οῦ ὁ	(personal) enemy	(6)
ἐχθρός -ά -όν	hostile	(3)
ἔχω ἔσχον	I have	(1)
ἑώς	while, until	(12)
Ζεύς Διός ὁ	Zeus	(6)
ζητέω ἐζήτησα	I seek, I look for	(9)
ζῷον -ου τό	animal, creature	(4)
ἤ	or; than	(7)
ἤ ...ἤ	either ... or	(8)
ἤγαγον	(aor of ἄγω)	
ἤγγειλα	(aor of ἀγγέλλω)	
ἡγεμών -όνος ὁ	leader, guide	(8)
ἤδη	now, by now, already	(8)
ἥδομαι ἥσθην	I enjoy, I am pleased with (+ dat)	(11)
ἡδύς -εῖα -ύ	sweet, pleasant	(9)

345

ἡδέως	(adv) sweetly, gladly	(9)
ἠθέλησα	(aor of ἐθέλω)	
ἥκιστα	least (adv), very little; not at all	(10)
ἥκω	I have come (perf with pres sense)	(11)
ἠλάθην	(aor passive of ἐλαύνω)	
ἤλασα	(aor of ἐλαύνω)	
ἦλθον	(aor of ἔρχομαι)	(6)
ἥλιος -ου ὁ	sun	(7)
ἡμᾶς αὐτούς -άς	ourselves	(8)
ἡμεῖς -ῶν	we	(6)
ἡμέρα -ας ἡ	day	(2)
ἡμέτερος -α -ον	our	(6)
ἤνεγκα or ἤνεγκον	(aor of φέρω)	
ἠνέχθην	(aor passive of φέρω)	
ἡρέθην	(aor passive of αἱρέω)	
ἠρόμην	(aor of ἐρωτάω)	
ἥσθην	(aor passive, with active sense, of ἥδομαι)	
ηὑρέθην	(aor passive of εὑρίσκω)	
ηὗρον	(aor of εὑρίσκω)	
ἤχθην	(aor passive of ἄγω)	
θάλασσα -ης ἡ	sea	(4)
θάνατος -ου ὁ	death	(2)
θάπτω ἔθαψα	I bury	(6)
θάσσων -ον (θασσον-)	quicker, swifter (comparative of ταχύς)	(10)
θαυμάζω ἐθαύμασα	I am amazed (at), I admire	(3)
θεά -ᾶς ἡ	goddess	(2)
θεός -οῦ ὁ	god	(1)
θήσω	(fut of τίθημι)	
θυγάτηρ -τρος ἡ	daughter	(7)
θύρα -ας ἡ	door	(2)
θύω ἔθυσα	I sacrifice	(11)
ἰατρός -οῦ ὁ	doctor	(7)
ἰδ-	(aor stem of ὁράω)	
ἰέναι	(inf of εἶμι, = to go)	
ἱερόν -οῦ τό	temple	(2)
ἱερός -ά -όν	holy, sacred	(7)
ἱκανός -ή -όν	sufficient, enough; capable, able to (+ inf)	(10)
ἵνα	in order to, so that (+ subj/opt)	(11)
ἱππεύς -έως ὁ	horseman, pl cavalry	(9)
ἵππος -ου ὁ	horse	(1)
ἵππος -ου ἡ	(collective sg) cavalry	(12)
ἴσος -η -ον	equal	(10)
ἰσχυρός -ά -όν	strong	(7)
ἴσως	perhaps; probably	(10)

346

ἰχθύς -ύος ὁ	fish	(9)
καθαιρέω καθεῖλον	I take down, I demolish	(9)
καθεύδω *imperf*		
ἐκάθευδον		
or καθηῦδον	I sleep	(10)
καθίζω ἐκάθισα	I sit	(7)
καί	and; also, even	(2)
καίπερ	although, despite (+ *participle*)	(6)
καιρός -οῦ ὁ	right time, opportunity, occasion	(10)
καίω ἔκαυσα	I burn, I set on fire	(7)
κάκιστος -η -ον	worst, very bad (*superlative of* κακός)	(8)
κακίων -ον (κακιον-)	worse (*comparative of* κακός)	(10)
κακός -ή -όν	bad, wicked	(3)
καλέω ἐκάλεσα	I call	(9)
κάλλιστος -η -ον	very fine, very beautiful	(5)
καλός -ή -όν	fine, beautiful, handsome	(3)
κατά	(+ *acc*) down, throughout, according to	(10)
	(+ *gen*) down from	(10)
κατὰ γῆν	by land	(10)
καθ᾽ ἡμέραν	daily, day by day	(10)
κελεύω ἐκέλευσα	I order	(3)
κεφαλή -ῆς ἡ	head	(7)
κίνδυνος -ου ὁ	danger	(2)
κλέπτω ἔκλεψα	I steal	(5)
κοινός -ή -όν	common, shared	(10)
κολάζω ἐκόλασα	I punish	(7)
κόπτω ἔκοψα	I cut, I cut down; I knock	(8)
κόρη -ης ἡ	girl	(4)
κρατέω ἐκράτησα	I control, I have power over (+ *gen*)	(9)
κριτής -οῦ ὁ	judge	(4)
κρύπτω ἔκρυψα	I hide (something)	(7)
κτάομαι ἐκτησάμην	I obtain, I get, I acquire	(10)
κτῆμα -ατος τό	possession	(8)
κύκλος -ου ὁ	circle	(5)
κωλύω ἐκώλυσα	I prevent, I hinder (someone from doing)	
	(+ *acc* + *inf*)	(5)
κώμη -ης ἡ	village	(1)
λαβ-	(*aor stem of* λαμβάνω)	
λάθρᾳ	secretly, in secret	(8)
Λακεδαιμόνιοι -ων οἱ	Spartans	(7)
λαμβάνω ἔλαβον	I take, I capture	(2)
λαμβάνομαι		
ἐλαβόμην	I take for myself, I grasp hold of (+ *gen*)	(8)

λέγω ἔλεξα *or* εἶπον	I say, I speak, I tell	(1)
λείπω ἔλιπον	I leave	(2)
λέων -οντος ὁ	lion	(5)
ληφθ-	(*aor passive stem of* λαμβάνω)	
λήψομαι	(*fut of* λαμβάνω)	
λίθος -ου ὁ	stone	(5)
λιμήν -ένος ὁ	harbour	(5)
λιπ-	(*aor stem of* λείπω)	
λόγος -ου ὁ	word, reason; story	(1)
λοιπός -ή -όν	left, remaining	(10)
λύω ἔλυσα	I release, I unfasten	(2)
λύομαι ἐλυσάμην	I ransom, I get (someone) released	(8)
μαθ-	(*aor stem of* μανθάνω)	
μακρός -ά -όν	long	(4)
μάλα	very, very much	(10)
μάλιστα	especially, very much (*superlative of* μάλα)	(10)
μᾶλλον	more (*adv*), rather (*comparative of* μάλα)	(7)
μανθάνω ἔμαθον	I learn	(2)
μάτην	in vain, unsuccessfully	(8)
μάχη -ης ἡ	battle	(6)
μάχομαι ἐμαχεσάμην	I fight	(8)
μέγας μεγάλη μέγα		
(μεγαλ-)	great, big	(9)
μέγιστος -η -ον	very great (*superlative of* μέγας)	(4)
μείζων -ον (μειζον-)	greater, bigger (*comparative of* μέγας)	(10)
μειν-	(*aor stem of* μένω)	
μέλλω	I intend, I am going to (+ *fut inf*); I hesitate	(8)
μέν* ... δέ*	on the one hand ... on the other	(3)
μέντοι*	however	(3)
μένω ἔμεινα	I stay, I remain; I wait for	(2)
μετά	(+ *acc*) after	(4)
	(+ *gen*) with	(5)
μέχρι	(+ *gen*) as far as, until	(10)
μή	not (*in contexts other than statements of fact*)	(9)
μηδαμῶς	in no way, not at all	(9)
μηδέ	and not, nor, not even	(9)
μηδείς μηδεμία μηδέν		
(μηδεν-)	no-one, nothing, no (not any)	(9)
μηδέποτε	never	(9)
μηκέτι	no longer	(9)
μήποτε	never	(9)
μήτε ... μήτε	neither ... nor	(9)
μήτηρ -τρός ἡ	mother	(7)
μία	one (*f*)	(6)

348

μικρός -ά -όν	small	(3)
μισέω ἐμίσησα	I hate	(9)
μισθός -οῦ ὁ	payment, wages	(6)
μόλις	scarcely, with difficulty	(8)
μόνος -η -ον	only, alone	(5)
μόνον	only (*adv*)	(5)
οὐ μόνον ...		
ἀλλὰ καί	not only ... but also	(8)
μοῦσα -ης ἡ	Muse (goddess of poetic inspiration)	(4)
μῦθος -ου ὁ	story (myth, fable)	(4)
μῶρος -α -ον	stupid, foolish	(5)
ναυμαχέω ἐναυμάχησα	I fight a sea-battle	(9)
ναυμαχία -ας ἡ	sea-battle	(2)
ναῦς νεώς ἡ	ship	(9)
ναύτης -ου ὁ	sailor	(4)
ναυτικόν -οῦ τό	fleet	(2)
νεανίας -ου ὁ	young man	(4)
νεκρός -οῦ ὁ	corpse, dead body	(6)
νέος -α -ον	new, young, recent	(3)
νῆσος -ου ἡ	island	(4)
νικάω ἐνίκησα	I conquer, I win	(10)
νίκη -ης ἡ	victory	(1)
νομίζω ἐνόμισα	I think, I consider, I believe	(10)
νόμος -ου ὁ	law; custom	(2)
νόσος -ου ἡ	disease, illness	(4)
νῦν	now	(3)
νύξ νυκτός ἡ	night	(5)
ξένος -ου ὁ	stranger, foreigner; host, guest	(1)
ξίφος -ους τό	sword	(9)
ὁ ἡ τό	the	(1)
ὄγδοος -η -ον	eighth	(6)
ὅδε ἥδε τόδε	this, *pl* these (*implying* here present, near me), the following,	(7)
ὁδός -οῦ ἡ	road, path, way; journey	(4)
ὅθεν	from (the place) where	(11)
οἷ	to (the place) where	(11)
οἶδα *imperf* ᾔδη	I know	(10)
οἰκέω ᾤκησα	I live (in), I inhabit	(9)
οἰκία -ας ἡ	house	(2)
οἶνος -ου ὁ	wine	(5)
οἷος -α -ον	(of) the sort which	(11)
οἷός τ' εἰμί	I am able (to, + *inf*)	(5)
οἴσω	(*fut of* φέρω)	

ὀκτώ	eight	(6)
ὀλίγος -η -ον	small (amount of)	(6)
ὀλίγοι -αι -α	few	(5)
ὄμνυμι ὤμοσα	I swear	(12)
ὁμολογέω ὡμολόγησα	I agree (with, + *dat*), I admit	(9)
ὀμοσ-	(*aor stem of* ὄμνυμι)	
ὄνομα -ατος τό	name	(5)
ὀξύς -εῖα -ύ	sharp, bitter	(9)
ὅπλα -ων τά	arms, weapons, gear, tackle	(2)
ὁπόθεν	from where (*usu in indirect question*)	(11)
ὅποι	where to (*usu in indirect question*)	(11)
ὁποῖος -α -ον	what sort of (*usu in indirect question*)	(11)
ὁπόσοι -αι -α	how many (*usu in indirect question*)	(11)
ὁπόσος -η -ον	how big (*usu in indirect question*)	(11)
ὁπότερος -α -ον	which (of two) (*usu in indirect question*)	(11)
ὅπου	where (at) (*usu in indirect question*)	(11)
ὅπως	how (*usu in indirect question*)	(11)
	in order to, so that (+ *subj/opt*)	(11)
ὁράω εἶδον	I see	(10)
ὀργή -ῆς ἡ	anger	(6)
ὀργίζομαι ὠργίσθην	I get angry, I am angry (with, + *dat*)	(8)
ὄρνις -ιθος ὁ/ἡ	bird	(5)
ὄρος -ους τό	hill, mountain	(9)
ὅς ἥ ὅ	who, which (*relative*)	(7)
ὅσος -η -ον	of the size which, as great/much as; how great!	(11)
ὅσοι -αι -α	as many as, all the ones who/which; how many!	(11)
ὅστις ἥτις ὅ τι (οὗτιν-)	who(ever), which(ever), what(ever)	(11)
ὅτε	(at the time) when	(11)
ὅτι	that, the fact that; because	(8)
οὐ (οὐκ *before smooth breathing,* οὐχ *before rough*)	not	(1)
οὐ μόνον ... ἀλλὰ καί	not only ... but also	(8)
οὗ	(the place) where	(11)
οὐδαμῶς	in no way, not at all	(8)
οὐδέ	and not, but not, not even	(8)
οὐδείς οὐδεμία οὐδέν (οὐδεν-)	no-one, nothing, no (*i.e.* not any)	(6)
οὐδέποτε	never	(8)
οὐκέτι	no longer	(6)
οὖν*	therefore	(3)
οὔποτε	never	(8)
οὐρανός -οῦ ὁ	sky, heaven	(6)

οὔτε ... οὔτε	neither ... nor	(8)
οὗτος αὕτη τοῦτο	this, *pl* these; the preceding	(7)
οὕτω(ς)	in this way, so	(7)
ὀφθ-	(*aor passive stem of* ὁράω)	
ὀφθαλμός -οῦ ὁ	eye	(3)
ὄψομαι	(*fut of* ὁράω)	
παθ-	(*aor stem of* πάσχω)	
παιδεύω ἐπαίδευσα	I train, I educate	(6)
παῖς παιδός ὁ/ἡ	boy, son; girl, daughter; child	(5)
πάλαι	long ago, formerly, in the past	(6)
πάλιν	again, back again	(8)
πανταχοῦ	everywhere	(8)
παρά	(+ *acc*) to the presence of; alongside;	
	contrary to	(10)
	(+ *gen*) from (a person)	(10)
	(+ *dat*) beside	(10)
παραινέω παρῄνεσα	I advise (+ *dat*)	(9)
παρασκευάζω		
παρεσκεύασα	I prepare	(6)
πάρειμι *imperf* παρῆν	I am here, I am present	(5)
παρέχω παρέσχον	I provide, I produce	(3)
πᾶς πᾶσα πᾶν (παντ-)	all, every	(6)
πάσχω ἔπαθον	I suffer, I experience	(4)
πατήρ -τρός ὁ	father	(7)
πατρίς -ίδος ἡ	fatherland, homeland	(8)
παύω ἔπαυσα	I stop	(1)
παύομαι ἐπαυσάμην	I cease, I stop myself (from doing	
	something) (*often* + *participle*)	(8)
πεδίον -ου τό	plain, level piece of ground, open country	(8)
πεζοί -ῶν οἱ	infantry, footsoldiers	(8)
πείθω ἔπεισα	I persuade	(3)
πείθομαι ἐπιθόμην	I obey (+ *dat*)	(8)
πειράομαι ἐπειρασάμην	I try	(10)
πείσομαι [1]	(*fut of* πάσχω)	
πείσομαι [2]	(*fut of* πείθομαι)	
πέμπτος -η -ον	fifth	(6)
πέμπω ἔπεμψα	I send	(2)
πένης -ητος ὁ	poor person, (*as adj*) poor	(10)
πέντε	five	(2)
περί	(+ *acc*) around	(10)
	(+ *gen*) about, concerning	(6)
Πέρσης -ου ὁ	Persian	(11)
Περσική -ῆς ἡ	Persia	(12)
πεσ-	(*aor stem of* πίπτω)	
πεύσομαι	(*fut of* πυνθάνομαι)	

πίνω ἔπιον	I drink	(5)
πίπτω ἔπεσον	I fall	(4)
πιστεύω ἐπίστευσα	I trust, I believe (+ *dat*)	(3)
πιστός -ή -όν	faithful, reliable	(7)
πλείονες -α	more (*pl*) (*comparative of* πολλοί)	(10)
πλεῖστος -η -ον	very much (of), very great (*superlative of* πολύς)	(10)
πλεῖστοι -αι -α	most, very many (*superlative of* πολλοί)	(10)
πλείων -ον (πλειον-)	more (of) (*sg*) (*comparative of* πολύς)	(10)
πλευσ-	(*aor stem of* πλέω)	
πλέω ἔπλευσα	I sail	(9)
πλῆθος -ους τό	crowd, large number	(9)
πλήν	except (+ *gen*)	(10)
πλοῖον -ου τό	boat	(2)
πλούσιος -α -ον	rich, wealthy	(7)
πόθεν;	where from?	(5)
ποθέν	from somewhere	(11)
ποῖ;	where to?	(11)
ποι	to somewhere	(11)
ποιέω ἐποίησα	I make, I do; I treat (+ *adv* + *acc*)	(9)
ποιητής -οῦ ὁ	poet	(4)
ποῖος; -α; -ον;	what sort of?	(11)
πολέμιοι -ων οἱ	enemy (in war)	(6)
πολέμιος -α -ον	hostile	(10)
πόλεμος -ου ὁ	war	(2)
τὰ τοῦ πολέμου	the affairs of war, warfare, military matters	(6)
πολιορκέω ἐπολιόρκησα	I besiege	(9)
πόλις -εως ἡ	city, city-state	(9)
πολίτης -ου ὁ	citizen	(4)
πολλάκις	often	(3)
πολύς πολλή πολύ (πολλ-)	much	(9)
πολλοί -αί -ά	many	(5)
πορεύομαι ἐπορεύθην	I march, I travel	(8)
πόσος; -η; -ον;	how great?	(11)
πόσοι; -αι; -α;	how many?	(11)
ποταμός -οῦ ὁ	river	(1)
πότε;	when?	(3)
ποτέ	once, sometime, ever	(11)
πότερον ... ἤ	whether ... or	(11)
πότερος -α -ον	which (of two)?	(11)
ποῦ;	where?	(3)
που	somewhere, anywhere	(11)
πούς ποδός ὁ	foot	(5)
πρᾶγμα -ατος τό	thing, matter, business	(8)
πράσσω ἔπραξα	I do, I fare (well/badly etc); I manage	(7)

πρό	in front of, before (+ *gen*)	(10)
πρός	(+ *acc*) towards, to, against	(1)
	(+ *gen*) at the hands of	(10)
	(+ *dat*) in addition to	(10)
προσάγω προσήγαγον	I lead to(wards)	(4)
προσβαίνω προσέβην	I go to(wards)	(4)
προσβάλλω προσέβαλον	I attack (+ *dat*)	(8)
προσπέμπω προσέπεμψα	I send to(wards)	(4)
προστρέχω προσέδραμον	I run to(wards)	(4)
πρότερον	previously, before	(3)
προχωρέω προὐχώρησα	I advance, I go forward	(9)
πρῶτον	first (*adv*), at first	(4)
πρῶτος -η -ον	first	(6)
πυθ-	(*aor stem of* πυνθάνομαι)	
πύλη -ης ἡ	gate	(1)
πυνθάνομαι ἐπυθόμην	I enquire; I learn by enquiry, I find out	(8)
πῦρ πυρός τό	fire	(5)
πῶς;	how?	(3)
πως	somehow, in some way	(11)
ῥᾴδιος -α -ον	easy	(10)
ῥᾷστος -η -ον	easiest, very easy (*superlative of* ῥᾴδιος)	(10)
ῥᾴων -ον (ῥαον-)	easier (*comparative of* ῥᾴδιος)	(10)
ῥήτωρ -ορος ὁ	public speaker, politician	(7)
σαφής -ές	clear	(9)
σεαυτόν -ήν	yourself	(8)
σιγή -ῆς ἡ	silence	(7)
σῖτος -ου ὁ	food, corn	(7)
σκοπέω ἐσκεψάμην	I look (at), I examine, I consider	(9)
σκότος -ου ὁ	darkness	(7)
σός σή σόν	your (of you *sg*)	(5)
σοφία -ας ἡ	wisdom	(2)
σοφός -ή -όν	wise, clever	(3)
Σπάρτη -ης ἡ	(the city of) Sparta	(7)
στόμα -ατος τό	mouth, entrance	(8)
στρατεύω ἐστράτευσα	I march, I go on an expedition, I campaign	(6)
στρατηγός -οῦ ὁ	general, commander	(1)
στρατιά -ᾶς ἡ	army	(8)
στρατιώτης -ου ὁ	soldier	(4)
στρατοπεδεύομαι		
ἐστρατοπεδευσάμην	I encamp	(8)
στρατόπεδον -ου τό	(army) camp	(2)
στρατός -οῦ ὁ	army	(1)
σύ σοῦ	you (*sg*)	(5)
συλλέγω συνέλεξα	I collect, I assemble	(6)

σύμμαχος -ου ὁ	ally	(1)
συμφορά -ᾶς ἡ	event; misfortune, disaster	(8)
σφᾶς *gen* σφῶν	them	(8)
σφᾶς αὐτούς -άς	themselves	(8)
σφόδρα	very much, strongly	(8)
σχ-	(*aor stem of* ἔχω)	
σχεδόν	nearly, almost	(8)
σῴζω ἔσωσα	I save	(7)
σῶμα -ατος τό	body	(5)
τάσσω ἔταξα	I draw up, I arrange	(2)
ταφ-	(*aor passive stem of* θάπτω)	
τάχιστος -η -ον	quickest, swiftest, very quick, very swift	
	(*superlative of* ταχύς)	(10)
ταχύς -εῖα -ύ	quick, swift	(9)
τε* ... καί	both ... and	(2)
τέθνηκα	(*perfect of* [ἀπο]θνῄσκω)	
τείχισμα -ατος τό	fort, fortification	(8)
τεῖχος -ους τό	wall	(9)
τέλος -ους τό	end, outcome; purpose	(9)
τέλος (*adv*)	in the end, finally	(6)
τέμνω ἔτεμον	I cut, I cut down, I ravage	(11)
τέσσαρες τέσσαρα	four	(6)
τέταρτος -η -ον	fourth	(6)
τέχνη -ης ἡ	skill, craft	(7)
τίθημι ἔθηκα	I place, I put	(12)
τιμάω ἐτίμησα	I honour, I respect	(10)
τιμή -ῆς ἡ	honour, respect	(1)
τίς; τί; (τίν-)	who? which? what?	(5)
τις τι (τιν-)	a, a certain, some(one/thing)	(5)
τοιοῦτος τοιαύτη		
τοιοῦτο	such, of such a kind	(7)
τοξεύω ἐτόξευσα	I shoot (fire an arrow)	(9)
τόξον -ου τό	bow	(2)
τόπος -ου ὁ	place	(6)
τοσοῦτος τοσαύτη		
τοσοῦτο	so great	(7)
τοσοῦτοι -αῦται		
-αῦτα	so many	(7)
τότε	then, at that time	(7)
τραῦμα -ατος τό	wound	(8)
τρεῖς τρία	three	(6)
τρέπω ἔτρεψα	I turn	(7)
τρέχω ἔδραμον	I run	(1)
τριήρης -ους ἡ	trireme, warship (with three banks of oars)	(9)
τρίτος -η -ον	third	(6)

τύπτω ἔτυψα	I hit, I strike	(7)
ὕδωρ -ατος τό	water	(6)
υἱός -οῦ ὁ	son	(8)
ὕλη -ης ἡ	wood, forest	(7)
ὑμεῖς -ῶν	you (*pl*)	(6)
ὑμᾶς αὐτούς -άς	yourselves	(8)
ὑμέτερος -α -ον	your (of you *pl*)	(6)
ὑπέρ	(+ *acc*) beyond, to beyond	(10)
	(+ *gen*) above, on behalf of	(10)
ὑπισχνέομαι ὑπεσχόμην	I promise	(9)
ὕπνος -ου ὁ	sleep	(5)
ὑπό	(+ *acc*) under, to under	(10)
	(+ *gen*) by (a person)	(7)
	(+ *dat*) under	(6)
ὑπὸ νύκτα	just before nightfall	(10)
ὕστερον	later	(8)
ὑψηλός -ή -όν	high	(7)
φαγ-	(*aor stem of* ἐσθίω)	
φαίνω ἔφηνα	I show, I make clear	(3)
φαίνομαι		
imperf ἐφαινόμην	I appear	(8)
φέρω ἤνεγκα *or* ἤνεγκον	I carry, I bring	(1)
φέρομαι ἠνεγκάμην	I win (prizes etc)	(8)
φεύγω ἔφυγον	I run away	(2)
φημί *imperf* ἔφην	I say	(10)
φιλέω ἐφίλησα	I like, I love	(9)
φίλιος -α -ον	friendly	(3)
φίλος -ου ὁ	friend	(2)
φίλος -η -ον	dear	(10)
φοβέομαι ἐφοβήθην	I fear	(9)
φόβος -ου ὁ	fear	(2)
φυγ-	(*aor stem of* φεύγω)	
φύλαξ -ακος ὁ	guard	(5)
φυλάσσω ἐφύλαξα	I guard	(1)
φωνή -ῆς ἡ	voice	(1)
χαλεπός -ή -όν	difficult; dangerous	(3)
χαλκός -οῦ ὁ	bronze	(8)
χειμών -ῶνος ὁ	winter; storm, bad weather	(11)
χείρ χειρός ἡ	hand	(11)
χείριστος -η -ον	worst, very bad (*superlative of* κακός)	(10)
χείρων -ον (χειρον-)	worse, inferior (*comparative of* κακός)	(10)
χράομαι ἐχρησάμην	I use (+ *dat*)	(10)
χρή *imperf* (ἐ)χρῆν	it is necessary	(10)

χρήματα -ων τά	money	(6)
χρήσιμος -η -ον	useful	(4)
χρόνος -ου ὁ	time	(2)
χρυσός -οῦ ὁ	gold	(7)
χώρα -ας ἡ	country	(2)
χωρίον -ου τό	place, estate, farm	(11)
ὦ	O ... (*addressing someone; often better omitted in English*)	(3)
ὧδε	in this way, so, as follows	(11)
ὤμοσα	(*aor of* ὄμνυμι)	
ὥρα -ας ἡ	hour	(2)
ὡς	as	(4)
	(*introducing indirect statement*) that	(10)
	(*introducing an exclamation*) how ... !	(11)
	(*prep + acc*) to (a person)	(10)
	(+ *present or past participle*) as, since, because, on the grounds that	(6)
	(+ *fut participle*) in order to	(6)
ὡς τάχιστα	as quickly as possible; as soon as	(10)
ὥσπερ	like, as; as if	(7)
ὥστε	(with the result) that, so that	(7)
ὠφελέω ὠφέλησα	I help, I benefit	(9)
ὤφθην	(*aor passive of* ὁράω)	

(625 words Greek-English)